The Mexican Frontier, 1821–1846

Military plaza of San Antonio. The open and unadorned military plaza of San Antonio, located behind the parish church of San Fernando. The church fronted on the town's main or civil plaza. Steel engraving from a drawing by Arthur Schott, 1853 (William H. Emory, *Report on the United States and Mexican Boundary Survey* [2 Vols.; Washington, D.C., 1857], I, frontispiece).

The Mexican Frontier, 1821–1846

The American Southwest Under Mexico

David J. Weber
Southern Methodist University

HISTORIES OF THE AMERICAN FRONTIER

Ray Allen Billington, General Editor
Howard R. Lamar, Coeditor

UNIVERSITY OF NEW MEXICO PRESS
Albuquerque

Chapter 4 appeared originally as "Failure of a Frontier
Institution: The Secular Church in the Borderlands Under
Independent Mexico, 1821–1846," *Western Historical
Quarterly*, XII (April 1981), pp. 125–43. © The Western
History Association. Reprinted by permission.

Chapter 5 appeared in an earlier version as "American
Westward Expansion and the Breakdown of Relations
Between Pobladores and 'Indios Bárbaros' on Mexico's
Far Northern Frontier, 1821–1846," *New Mexico Historical
Review*, LVI (July 1981), pp. 221–38. Reprinted with
permission of the Regents of the University of New Mexico
and the editor.

Library of Congress Cataloging in Publication Data
Weber, David J.
  The Mexican frontier, 1821–1846

  (Histories of the American frontier)
  Bibliography: p.
  Includes index.
  1. Southwest, New—History—To 1848. 2. Mexico—
History—1821–1861. I. Title. II. Series.
F800.W4   979′.02   82-2800
ISBN 0-8263-0602-0   AACR2
ISBN 0-8263-0603-9 (pbk.)

Designed by Emmy Ezzell
Cartography by Whitehead & Whitehead

For Scott and Amy
who have grown up with this book,
and sometimes in spite of it

Contents

Illustrations

Figures

Maps

Foreword

Ever since the publication of Herbert Eugene Bolton's seminal volume on *The Spanish Borderlands* in 1921, scores of historians have heeded his warning that the history of a broad "borderland" stretching across the southern United States from Florida to Alta California could be told only in terms of the cultural conflicts and adaptations that occurred as westward-thrusting Anglo-American pioneers and northern-advancing Spanish frontiersmen met and clashed there. Their efforts have produced a whole library full of learned books and articles exploring in detail almost every aspect of that story from the days when those two frontiers first conflicted during the sixteenth century down to modern times.

The term *almost* in the sentence above is used advisedly, for one of the most important and relevant areas involved in that centuries-long conflict has been largely—and surprisingly—neglected. This is the Mexican-American borderland during the years between 1821, when Mexico won its independence from Spain, and 1846, when its northern provinces were usurped by the United States during the Mexican War.

That this gap in the record exists is remarkable, for those years in the history of the American Southwest are vital to an understanding of the story of the westward expansion of the United States and the southward retreat of the Mexican Republic. They have been studied, of course. American historians have written hundreds of books and articles dealing with their own Southwest during that period, as the extensive documentation on the pages that follow convincingly illustrates. Yet those works have dealt with a succession of episodes, each treated in isolation from the others. They have explored in depth events in Texas and New Mexico and Arizona and California, but have made no attempt to link those events into the broader pattern that would give meaning to the entire period. Similarly, Mexican scholars have been reluctant to portray their nation's humiliation during its darkest hours. One eminent historian, Josefina Vásquez, has regretted that she and her fellow students have "forgotten all of the period from 1821 to 1854 in an almost systematic manner." Professor Weber himself characterizes this period as "the dark age in the historiography of the Southwest," and with good reason.

It is this gap in the history of Mexico, and of Mexican-American relations, that is admirably filled in this path-breaking study. Its author, Professor David J. Weber of Southern Methodist University, brings to his task a distinguished record as a borderlands historian. Trained at the University of New Mexico, and with teaching experience in Southern California and Texas, he has had ample opportunity to appreciate the distinctive environment of the Southwest of which he writes. And, despite his relative youth (he is still in his thirties at this writing), he has proven himself as a superb scholar, worthy of a rank among the most distinguished historians of the borderlands. He has written or edited some nine books, including such highly respected volumes as *The Taos Trappers, Foreigners in their Native Land, El México Perdido, Northern Mexico on the Eve of the United States Invasion,* and *New Spain's Far Northern Frontier* as well as more than two dozen scholarly articles. His merits have been recognized by awards from such prestigious organizations as the National Endowment for the Humanities and the American Council of Learned Societies. These grants have made possible study in the archives of Mexico and Spain, as well as in every major depository in the United States.

The results are abundantly apparent in this book. Professor Weber has for the first time assembled information from the hundreds of monographic studies by American scholars dealing with the Mexican borderlands, in itself a major contribution to scholarship. He himself calls his work "an effort at synthesis . . . built largely on the work of other scholars." This is far too modest an estimate. Others have told only half the story; the vast gaps between their findings he has filled with his own extensive archival research, as his documentation clearly shows. This is an original book, rich in fresh material and interpretation.

It is also a book that sheds new light on the history of the American Southwest, as well as on the history of northern Mexico. By viewing events from south, not north, of the border, Professor Weber casts a series of well-known episodes in new light, and clothes them in deeper meaning. The result is a valuable lesson in the dangers of ethnocentricity, as well as an enlightening reinterpretation of a period of our past. Viewed from this perspective, the peopling of Texas and California, the Santa Fe trade, the secularization of the missions, the Texan Revolution, the political turbulence in New Mexico and California, the Mexican War, and the whole borderlands story are more easily understood and more accurately portrayed. Seen as Mexican history they take on shades of meaning that they lacked when viewed as United States history. He has also made a distinct contribution by viewing the Southwest as a unit, rather than the usual practice of dealing separately with Texas, New Mexico, Arizona, and California. His interpretation reveals basic forces that helped shape the history of the entire region, as well as the demographic and environmental differences that account for the peculiar behavior of each province.

Professor Weber has wisely used a thematic approach to bring home his interpretation. After setting the stage with a revealing pen-portrait of each province on the eve of Mexican independence, he deals successively with the internal dynamics of Mexican politics, economics, society, the military establishment, and the church as they related to the frontier and as the frontier related to them. He surveys the impact of the Mexican Revolution on traditional frontier institutions, and tells us how those institutions either collapsed or were forced to adjust to the new circumstances: republican politics replaced monarchical despotism, the Jesuit and Franciscan orders were replaced by secular priests, local militia assumed the burdens of border defense as central authority lessened, private land ownership multiplied as ranches and towns grew in numbers and influence, new routes of trade and communication were opened as royal controls slackened, an invigorating laissez-faire spirit revitalized commerce, and entrepreneurs from other lands—particularly the United States—began the economic and social transformation that was to lead the northern provinces closer to a new allegiance.

Professor Weber shows us, too, how the struggle between centralism and federalism within Mexico weakened the sinews that held the northern provinces to the mother country and paved the way for their conquest by the United States in 1846. This is a stirring story, abounding in fresh viewpoints, and sprinkled with information unfamiliar to most historians of the United States. Certainly no one in the future can write about the American Southwest without listening to the lessons taught in this book. Nor should any historian fail to harken to its basic message: that nationalistic history, written from one perspective only, is both misleading and dangerous. Professor Weber's final chapter is a brilliant application of the theory of comparative frontier to the region that he surveys.

This volume is one of a multivolume series, "The Histories of the American Frontier," being published by the University of New Mexico Press. The series has a dual role: first, to describe in some fifteen volumes the advance of the frontier across that portion of the North American continent that we know today as the United States; second, to explore aspects of the pioneering experience that make the story of expansion meaningful to today's society. Within this second category, books are being prepared on the frontier family, women in the West, the lumber frontier, the expansion of western culture over the Pacific Basin, and law on the frontier.

Whatever its category, each volume in the series is written by a recognized authority who brings to his task an intimate knowledge of the subject that he covers and a demonstrated skill in narration and interpretation. Each will offer the general reader a sound but readable account of one phase of the frontiering experience, and the specialized student a documented study built on fresh information and integrated into the broader story of the nation's growth. It is the hope of the authors, editors, and publishers that this full account of the most American part of the American past will expand our understanding of an important portion of our national heritage and better enable the American people to understand themselves as they grapple with the global problems of the twentieth century.

Ray Allen Billington
The Huntington Library
Howard R. Lamar
Yale University

Preface

Through annexation, conquest, and purchase, the United States acquired half of Mexico between 1845 and 1854. Within a few moments in history, Mexico's far northern frontier thus became a portion of the American West. The heart of the region that Mexico lost lies within today's American Southwest—the four border states of California, Arizona, New Mexico, and Texas, where small, isolated pockets of Hispano frontiersmen, or *pobladores*, made their homes. In addition to these settled areas, Mexico also lost a vast unsettled swath of North America to her expansionist neighbor: all of today's states of Nevada and Utah, much of Colorado, and small parts of Oklahoma, Kansas, and Wyoming. These areas contained no Mexican settlement and remained, in effect, under the control of indigenous peoples, but in theory Mexico had held title to the entire area through international agreements.

The flag of independent Mexico had flown over the Far North only briefly. It rose in 1821 when Mexico won independence from Spain, and began its fall a decade and a half later in Texas when that province successfully revolted in 1836. During the war with the United States in 1846–48, Mexican flags were lowered for the last time over California and New Mexico. A few years later, in 1854, when the United States Senate ratified James Gadsden's purchase of a great strip of land below the Gila River, Mexico's flag ceased to fly in what we know today as Arizona.

The brevity of the Mexican period stands in marked contrast to the long years when what is today the American Southwest constituted an isolated corner of Spain's New World empire. Hispanic influence in western North America had its roots in the sixteenth-century explorations by men in armor, such as Francisco Vázquez de Coronado and Juan Rodríguez Cabrillo, who reconnoitered the region by land and sea in a futile search for wealthy kingdoms to match those of the Aztecs and

Incas. Beginning in 1598 in New Mexico, 1700 in Arizona, 1716 in Texas, and 1769 in Alta California, Spain planted permanent missions, military posts, towns, and ranchos in the Far North.

Some three centuries of Spanish activity in this region has tended to overshadow the brief period of Mexican rule. So too has a century and a quarter of American sovereignty, which some writers have stretched back into the Mexican era to include the explorers, trappers, and settlers—the Zebulon Pikes, Kit Carsons, Stephen Austins, and the lesser-known women who served as the vanguard of America's westward thrust into northern Mexico. Lost between the Spanish and American periods, the Mexican interlude has become something of a dark age in the historiography of the Southwest, even though it represented a turning point for both the United States and Mexico.[1]

In general, neither Mexican nor American historians have sharply illuminated the era. Mexican historians have slighted the history of their nation as a whole during the first decades after independence, in part because these were chaotic years, bitter to remember. In particular, Mexican historians have ignored almost entirely internal developments in the Far North between 1821 and 1846, perhaps because the region no longer belongs to Mexico. This has left United States historians with an open field and they have occupied it with alacrity. United States historians, in general, however, have ethnocentrically shoved their own countrymen to the front of the stage in the events of 1821 to 1846, leaving Mexico and Mexicans, to whom the stage still belonged, to serve as the backdrop.[2]

When American historians have dealt with Mexicans during these years, they have too often reduced them to stereotypes. The *californios,* especially, have been characterized as happy-go-lucky and childlike. Hubert Howe Bancroft, the encyclopedic nineteenth-century San Francisco-based historian, as well as his modern successors, described the Californians in terms such as "simple-minded," "carefree," and "indolent," living in a "golden age" where "life was a long happy holiday," "halfway between savagism and civilization."[3]

As a corollary to this notion of a Mexican frontier Arcadia, American writers have depicted the Mexican period as static—except for the activities of Anglo-Americans. Historians of Texas of this period, as one perceptive writer has noted, "have limited their work as it relates to Mexicans and Mexico to the 'official' or 'nuisance' levels."[4] In the case of New Mexico, historian Charles Coan wrote of "the absence of important internal developments in the Mexican period. . . ."[5] Charles Chapman described the period similarly in California: "strictly speaking there was no Mexican period. . . . The actual intervention of Mexico in the affairs of its distant province consisted in little more than the sending of governors and a few score of degraded soldiery."[6] Chapman entitled a chapter on the Mexican period, "Waiting for Old Glory," as if to suggest that the *californios* frittered those years away, waiting for deliverance by their conquerors.

Life on Mexico's far northern frontier between 1821 and 1846 was neither a romantic holiday nor simply static. To be sure, westward-moving Americans and their blatantly expansionist government threatened Mexican sovereignty over the area, although the Americans represented both a threat and an opportunity to Mexico's frontiersmen. The story of Mexico's Far North cannot be told in isolation from that of America's westward movement, for the two frontiers began to intersect dramatically in the years following Mexican independence. The United States, however, was not the only external power to concern Mexican officials. Russians seemed a threat to Mexico's hold on the Pacific slope; the British seemed eager to extend their influence in California and in Texas; and a variety of indigenous peoples, some armed and mounted on horseback, challenged Mexican frontiersmen for control of the region and hindered efforts at expansion.

In her infancy as a nation, Mexico remained too weak to deal effectively with these challenges, but her posture toward the northern frontier was not static. Profound changes in Mexico's political, economic, religious, and social institutions had begun just prior to independence, and the process was far from complete. As the nation struggled to overcome the effects of a ruinous decade of civil war that had given it life, it continued to stagger under repeated economic crises, quarrels between Church and State, the machinations of predatory and often illiterate army officers, the defiance of local leaders whose regional interests ran deeper than their allegiance to the nation, and the threats of foreign invasion. The magnitude of these problems overwhelmed Mexico's inexperienced and sometimes doctrinaire civilian leaders, who could neither bring order out of chaos nor maintain themselves in power. As governments came and went, frontier policies often disappeared in the shuffle and continuity was lost. Key officials understood the urgency of problems on the northern frontier, but they also saw that region's problems as only one of a series of urgencies.

Although Mexico's internal difficulties diverted resources and attention from the frontier, the frontier provinces continued to respond to, and sometimes mirror, changes in Mexico. Representative but inadequate political institutions began to replace the authoritarian monarchical structure; missions and military posts decayed for lack of support; modified laissez-faire economics replaced the closed mercantile system that had existed under Spain; new routes of commerce and communication developed; population grew, in large part through the influx of foreigners; private ranchos and land grants increased; the frontier economy underwent a realignment, moving away from Mexico and toward the United States; and frontier resentment against Mexico's acts of commission and omission erupted in the mid-1830s into open revolts.

In short, turbulence and change characterized the quarter century of Mexican sovereignty over what is today the American Southwest. Buffeted by powerful winds of change emanating from Mexico City, and subjected for the first time to significant exposure to foreign commerce and foreign ideas, the Far North represented one of the most dynamic regions of independent Mexico.

The complex events of this little understood era are examined in this volume in a way that has not been done before. First, it places today's American Southwest squarely within its Mexican context, without minimizing the significant activities of Anglo-Americans and other aliens. Second, the region is examined as a whole, whereas most scholars have confined their studies to individual states.[7] Discrete local studies are essential. No overview could be written without them, and they provide understanding and richness of detail that a synthesis cannot achieve. Indeed, most of the themes considered in this volume would profit from more detailed examinations, for there is much that we do not understand. There is considerable advantage, however, in also taking a larger view that puts local events in perspective, that highlights similarities and differences, and that seeks patterns.

Out of necessity, I have sliced through time and space to limit the scope of this book. Years such as 1821 and 1846 make neat chronological divisions, but such benchmark years denote change only in a superficial sense. Historical processes work slowly as a rule, although events may accelerate or retard them. Similarly, a line on the map dividing the region that is today the American Southwest from the rest of Mexico, and a projection of that line back in time, represents a somewhat arbitrary convenience that makes this study more manageable. In the case of Alta California, New Mexico, and Texas, the imposition of the present boundary on the past makes sense because Mexican settlements in those three areas all lie completely above the present border. Arizona poses a special problem, however, for it did not exist as a separate political jurisdiction during these years.

Present-day Arizona below the Gila River formed the northern part of the state of Sonora prior to the Gadsden Purchase. Jurisdiction over the portion above the Gila, which contained no Mexican settlement, remained murky, and it might have fallen within California, Sonora, or New Mexico if any had cared to claim or occupy it. Although Arizona did not exist as a separate political entity, any consideration of the American Southwest under Mexico would be remiss if it overlooked the activities of Mexicans in that area. Few in number, and out of the mainstream of events, the residents of Arizona occupied a small but interesting part of the larger picture. For convenience, I have followed the lead of Arizona historians and refer to the portion of Sonora which now lies north of the United States-Mexican border as Arizona, even though contemporaries did not know it by that name.[8]

Boundaries in the vast unsettled areas between California and New Mexico and New Mexico and Texas remained ill-defined during these years and generally represented little more than a sweep of the hand across the map. Until 1836, Texas extended no farther south than the Nueces River, which enters the Gulf of Mexico at present Corpus Christi. The region between the Nueces and the Rio Grande was nearly devoid of Mexican settlement except for a few isolated ranches and communities such as Laredo, perched on the north bank of the Rio Grande. Residents of this region, however, lived in Tamaulipas, the Mexican state which embraced the lower Rio Grande during those years and, as one historian has explained, "probably thought of themselves as 'Mexicanos' rather than as 'Texans'."[9] Their story, then, remains peripheral to events in Texas.

It might be argued that the portions of Mexico now occupied by the United States had no unity or regional identity between 1821 and 1846, except one imposed by hindsight, and that California, Arizona, New Mexico, and Texas cannot be understood apart from their neighboring states to the south. A complete study of Mexico's northern frontier, according to this line of reasoning, ought to embrace a larger region, corresponding roughly to the relatively autonomous governmental unit created late in the colonial period when Spain formed the Comandancia General de las Provincias Internas.[10] These Internal Provinces, headed by officers who operated with varying degrees of independence from the viceroy, at one time or another included the northern Mexican states of Baja California, Sonora, Sinaloa, Chihuahua, Durango, Coahuila, Nuevo León, and Tamaulipas, as well as California, New Mexico, and Texas. The argument that all of this area deserves consideration as a unit has considerable merit. All of these provinces went through similar frontier processes and the Provincias Internas endured well into the

Mexican period as an administrative unit for the military, even though it underwent a number of structural changes.[11]

It seems clear, however, that by the end of the colonial period Alta California, Arizona, New Mexico, and Texas stood apart from the rest of the Internal Provinces. Poised on the northern edge of New Spain, as Mexico was then known, Hispanic settlements faced dual dangers from potentially hostile indigenous peoples and avaricious foreign powers. The vast distances separating the frontier from the metropolis exacerbated both threats. When Spanish officials designed a cordon of military posts, or *presidios,* to stretch across the northern frontier in the 1760s, Alta California, New Mexico, and Texas stood alone, well to the north of the presidial line, as isolated outposts of the Spanish empire. During the wars of independence, rebels who formulated the Plan of Apatzingán in 1814 saw the present Southwest as an area that lay outside of what they termed *"America mexicana."* The rebels' call for an independent Mexican republic included all of central Mexico and went no farther north than Sonora, Durango, Coahuila, and Nuevo León.[12]

Under independent Mexico, those statesmen who understood the frontier regarded its northern edge, from the Pacific to the Gulf of Mexico, as a unified region with a common set of problems. Alta California, New Mexico, and Texas lacked significant population and adequate defense, but served as a bulwark against foreigners and hostile Indians for the rest of the nation. The widely traveled and well-informed liberal thinker, Tadeo Ortiz, for example, argued in 1830 that "Upper California is the fortress and the key of the Republic on the west, New Mexico and the Province of Texas are equally so on the north and northeast. . . ."[13] When the Mexican Congress passed a law in 1830 to prevent the growth of a potentially seditious community of Anglo-American aliens in Texas, Ortiz criticized the narrowness of the legislation because it "forgets the vast regions of New Mexico and Alta California whose position is identical and whose security is also in danger."[14]

By some definitions, such as a lack of amenities common to Western civilization, it is possible to define all of newly independent Mexico as "one vast frontier," as did one historian.[15] However, the more classical definition of a frontier as the part of a country bordering on another (which coincides with the early nineteenth-century usage of the word *frontier* in English and with the traditional meaning of *frontera* in Spanish), suggests that Mexico's northern frontier zone stood squarely within Alta California, New Mexico, and Texas during decades prior to their acquisition by the United States. A succession of Mexican governments singled out those provinces for special treatment precisely because they constituted the frontier, and in 1844 when members of the lower house of Congress debated the definition of a frontier province, they whittled the list down to Chiapas in the south, and Alta California, New Mexico, and Texas to the north (Mexico still did not recognize Texas's independence in 1844).[16]

Thus, in examining as a separate unit the region that is today the American Southwest, or what was then Mexico's far northern frontier, I am not imposing an entirely artificial or presentist arrangement on the past. As isolated as California, Arizona, New Mexico, and Texas were from one another, those provinces faced a common set of problems with unique local variations. Events in one province often made an impact on its neighbors, and this occurred more frequently in the Mexican years as the isolation of these provinces, one from the other as well as from the outside world, broke down with a speed that must have seemed dizzying to contemporaries.

In examining the broad contours of regional history, I have tried not to lose sight of the uniqueness of particular locales. Hispanic culture and institutions in the region were not homogeneous. The fashions of the historical epoch in which Hispanic settlers first entered an area, the customs of the region or regions from which those settlers and their families came, and the settlers' responses to the local environments and the cultures of the indigenous peoples who became their neighbors, all combined to create variations of Hispanic culture. Although aridity is the dominant geographical feature of Mexico's Far North, land forms and climate vary dramatically, from the temperate Pacific slope to the sun-parched Sonora desert, and from Alpine life zones in the mountains of northern New Mexico to woodlands of East Texas. Hence, some frontiersmen lived in adobes and others in log houses; red tile roofs became popular in California, but were unknown in New Mexico; cozy corner fireplaces were the heart of home life in New Mexico winters, but fireplaces of any shape or form were rare in California. Regional variations, as we shall see, embraced everything from subtle differences in institutions, such as the relative power of provincial legislatures, to obvious folk customs, such as the fact that women in Texas and New Mexico astounded foreigners by smoking small, hand-rolled cigars in public while California women apparently had not adopted that habit.

For the convenience of the reader I have minimized use of Spanish terms and employed present-day place names to avoid confusion. Although purists or pedants may disapprove, I consistently refer to the Villa de San Fernando de Béxar in Texas as San Antonio, even though contemporaries commonly knew it as San Fernando or as Béxar. Similarly, I avoid referring to present-day Goliad as La Bahía, even though La Bahía was its proper name until February 1829 when it was renamed Goliad as an anagram for one of the heroes of the Mexican Wars of Independence, Miguel Hidalgo.[17] Although California was properly Alta California in the Mexican era, as distinct from Baja California, Alta California and California appear as synonyms in this volume.

Spanish place names such as Mexico, Rio Grande, San Jose, and Santa Fe, which have become thoroughly incorporated into modern American usage, appear without diacritical markings. Spanish words appear in italics on the first occasion of their use, except for *californios, nuevo-mexicanos,* and *tejanos.* I have retained these terms in italics throughout the book partly to avoid confusion between California and Californio, but chiefly to identify the Spanish-speaking peoples of each frontier province. Both Mexicans and naturalized Anglo-Americans, for example, might be Mexican citizens and Texans during these years, but I have reserved the term *tejano* for Texans who are ethnically Mexicans.

As an effort at synthesis, this study is built mainly on the work of other scholars. I have made forays into the voluminous archival sources of the era in order to fill gaps in the literature, and I have reread primary materials to take a fresh look at events—including those as well-studied as the Texas Revolt. In the main, however, this overview depends heavily on the research of other historians. My intellectual debts to them should be apparent in the notes to each chapter. Only they know how this book, which students may regard as lengthy and exhaustive (if not exhausting), actually skims the surface of questions that have been explained elsewhere in greater depth. Readers who want to probe subjects in more detail will be rewarded by examining sources mentioned in the bibliographical essay at the end of this study.

Without funds for research, travel, and time to write, a book does not happen. It is with a deep sense of gratitude that I acknowledge a Younger Humanist Fellowship from the National Endowment for the Humanities, which enabled me to launch this project in 1974, grants from the American Philosophical Society and the Huntington Library, which facilitated research travel, and a fellowship from the American Council of Learned Societies in 1980, which provided time to complete the writing.

It has been my pleasure and privilege to work at all the great libraries and archival collections in the Southwest and Mexico where staff, too numerous to mention, graciously offered knowledge as well as research materials. None, however, exceeded the hospitality of Father Kieran McCarty of Tucson, who gave me a key to the library at Mission San Xavier del Bac, copies of his own transcripts from the Sonora archives, and access to the mission kitchen to nourish body as well as mind. Thanks to Father Kieran, I had the memorable experience of working in a seemingly timeless setting where Pimas still worship at dawn before tilling the irrigated fields that surround the massive white-walled mission.

At my own university, I am grateful to my friend and colleague R. Hal Williams, and to other administrators who have supported in tangible ways the notion that a university should produce new knowledge as well as disseminate the old—a principle that many universities espouse but fail to support in the allegedly unprofitable liberal arts. The fabulous DeGolyer Collection, presided over by the late Everett Lee DeGolyer, Jr., who never refused my request for even the most esoteric item, and now by the efficient and helpful Clifton Jones and encyclopedic Jim Phillips, has enabled me to do much of my research on my own campus. I am also indebted to my colleague, the incomparably gifted Jeremy Adams, and the ebullient and efficient Peggy Lynn Smith, who kept the History Department moving forward in my absence. Finally, but perhaps most important, Kathleen Triplett prepared the manuscript for publication with uncommon good sense and efficiency, and Fred and Barbara Whitehead, of the Austin-based graphic design firm of Whitehead and Whitehead, spared no pains to draw accurate and clear maps.

With the extraordinary generosity that characterizes our field, historians Ramón Gutiérrez of Pomona College, Elizabeth John of Austin, John Kessell of Albuquerque, Malcolm McLean of the University of Texas at Arlington, Daniel Orlovsky of Southern Methodist University, and Dan Tyler of Colorado State University read portions of the manuscript. Dennis Berge of San Diego State University, C. Alan Hutchinson of the University of Virginia, Janet Lecompte of Colorado Springs, and Marc Simmons of Cerrillos, New Mexico, critiqued the entire manuscript. All flagged errors, pruned out imprecise words and clumsy phrases, and offered sensitive and informed criticism. My brother, Dan, provided a learned layman's point of view. My most intimate critic for the last two decades, Carol Bryant Weber, offered a fine sense of language and style that is reflected on every page of this book.

As coeditors of the *Histories of the American Frontier Series*, Ray Allen Billington and Howard Lamar also read the entire manuscript. In addition to their good advice, they allowed the study to take shape according to the demands of the topic, rather than insisting that it be squeezed into the rigid format of a series. David Holtby of the University of New Mexico Press did the final editing with sensitivity, intelligence, and discrimination. One could not hope to work with better editors.

At the time I first proposed the idea for this book, some eight years ago, Ray Billington was sole editor of the *Histories of the American Frontier Series*. From the first, he gave the project his confidence, support, and guidance. In many respects this is his book, but he did not live to see it in print. Ray's death in March 1981 represented an incalculable loss for the profession and a personal loss for many of us who admired him not only for his wide-ranging intellect and vivid, well-organized prose, but also for his generosity, graciousness, decency, and good humor.

David J. Weber
Southern Methodist University
Dallas, Texas
Spring 1981

1

¡Viva la Independencia!

We expected to enter a new era of happiness.—Donaciano
Vigil, *New Mexico*

May God grant that all may be for the best.—Fray Vicente
Francisco de Sarría, *Alta California*

In the early nineteenth century, news usually travelled slowly along the
rutted, dusty, and dangerous highways that began in Mexico City and
ran north to the edge of New Spain. All roads led to and from Mexico
City, for no well-established routes connected the isolated frontier provinces of Alta California, Sonora, New Mexico, and Texas with one another.

In the spring of 1821, a stunning piece of news moved quickly north.
A Spanish officer, Agustín de Iturbide, had declared Mexico's independence from Spain. Reports of the rebellion first reached Texas, the frontier
province closest to Mexico City. The news had probably travelled to
Texas by way of San Luis Potosí, Saltillo, and Monterrey, then across the
Rio Grande at Laredo and the uninhabited sandy plains beyond to the
well-watered prairies around San Antonio and Goliad, altogether some
1,000 miles over twisting roads. San Antonio, founded in 1718, was a
modest community of perhaps 1,500 persons in 1821, notwithstanding
its position as provincial capital. One-storied, flat-roofed stone houses, a
church, a former mission, military barracks and government buildings
clustered around two unimposing plazas in the center of town. On the
edges of town, poorer folk lived in *jacales*—thatch-roofed houses made
of upright wooden poles chinked with adobe and sometimes plastered.
Except in times of drought, the San Antonio River, with its wooded
bottom lands, flowed into the canals that irrigated gardens and corn-

1

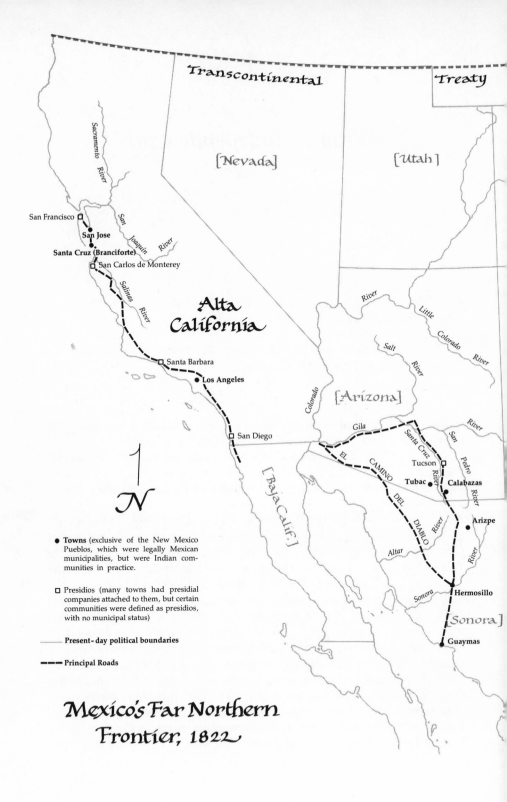

Transcontinental Treaty

[Nevada]

[Utah]

Sacramento River

San Francisco □
San Jose ●
Santa Cruz (Branciforte) ●
San Carlos de Monterey □

San Joaquín River

Salinas River

Alta California

□ Santa Barbara
● Los Angeles

□ San Diego

River

Little Colorado River

Salt River

Colorado

[Arizona]

Gila

Santa Cruz

San Pedro River

Tucson □
Tubac ● **Calabazas** □

EL CAMINO DEL DIABLO

River

● **Arizpe**

[Baja Calif.]

Altar

Sonora

River

● **Hermosillo**

[Sonora]

● **Guaymas**

N

● **Towns** (exclusive of the New Mexico Pueblos, which were legally Mexican municipalities, but were Indian communities in practice.

□ Presidios (many towns had presidial companies attached to them, but certain communities were defined as presidios, with no municipal status)

—— **Present-day political boundaries**

▬▬▬ **Principal Roads**

Mexico's Far Northern Frontier, 1822

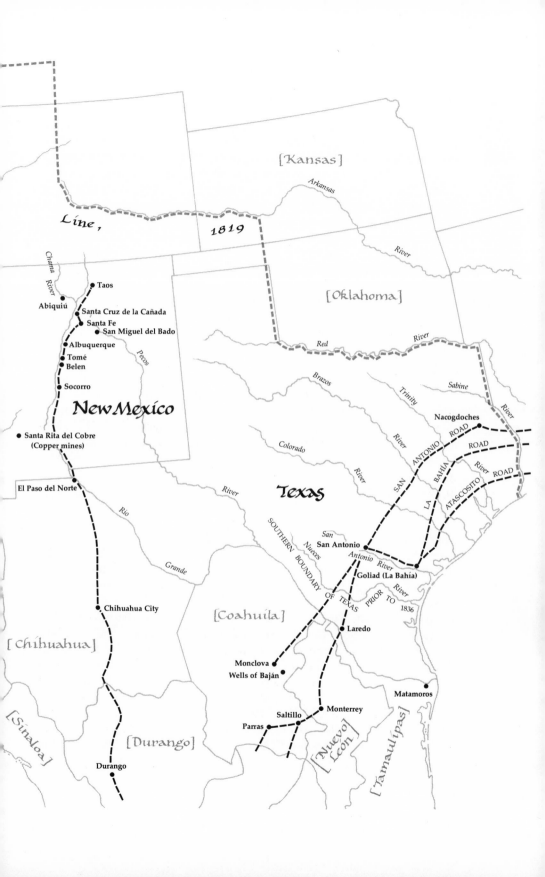

[Kansas]

Arkansas

Line, 1819

Chama River

● Taos
● Abiquiú
● Santa Cruz de la Cañada
● Santa Fe
● San Miguel del Bado
● Albuquerque
● Tomé
● Belen
● Socorro

Pecos

New Mexico

● Santa Rita del Cobre
(Copper mines)

● El Paso del Norte

Río

Grande

[Oklahoma]

River

Red *River*

Brazos

Trinity River

Sabine River

● Nacogdoches

SAN ANTONIO ROAD

LA BAHIA ROAD

ATASCOSITO ROAD

Colorado River

Texas

River

SOUTHERN BOUNDARY OF TEXAS PRIOR TO 1836

San Nueces River

San Antonio River

● San Antonio

● Goliad (La Bahía)

River

[Coahuila]

● Chihuahua City

[Chihuahua]

● Laredo

● Monclova
● Wells of Baján

● Matamoros

● Monterrey
● Saltillo
● Parras

[Nuevo León]

[Sinaloa]

[Durango]

● Durango

[Tamaulipas]

fields surrounding the settlement. The river also cut the city in two, but a log bridge linked the two parts.[1] On July 19, 1821, San Antonio severed its connection with the Spanish empire. Early that morning the *villa's* soldiers, clergy, politicians, and townspeople gathered in the plaza and swore before a raised crucifix to uphold Mexico's independence.

Four days later, residents of the crumbling town of Goliad, located some 100 miles downstream from San Antonio, and then called La Bahía del Espíritu Santo, also took an oath of allegiance to the new government. In 1821 San Antonio and Goliad were the only substantial Mexican settlements in Texas, a backwater province whose total non-Indian population hovered around 2,500. Nacogdoches, a once-flourishing village of wood frame houses in the rolling piney woods of East Texas, on the edge of Louisiana, had been nearly abandoned. Only a church, seven houses, and a scattering of residents remained in 1821.[2]

As autumn of 1821 approached, other areas in the far north also declared support of independence. On September 3, the *comandante* of the half-century-old adobe presidio of Tucson swore allegiance to the new government. Situated on the edge of a plateau where the mile-wide, green valley of the Río Santa Cruz met the parched, cactus-covered Sonoran desert, Tucson represented the northernmost point of Hispanic advance into what is today Arizona. Spain's explorers had probed farther north, but settlement had not followed their tracks. In 1821, nearly all of the non-Indian population of Arizona lived in the Santa Cruz Valley from Tucson south, although a handful of intrepid pioneers eked out a living along the Río San Pedro, the next major river to the east. All in all, in 1821 Hispanic Arizona probably held well over 1,000 *gente de razón*—literally "people of reason" of whatever race or combination of races whose way of life was essentially Hispanic rather than Indian. Tucson itself probably supported at least 400 gente de razón, not counting peaceful Apaches who had settled near the fort, and Pimas on the other side of the river who came under the care of a missionary, but were still considered *gente sin razón*—minors, or "people without reason."

Upstream from Tucson stood Arizona's two other large centers of Hispanic population: about 400 lived around the abandoned military post of Tubac and some 75 gente de razón lived near the mission of Tumacácori. A lull in hostilities with Apaches had given new life to these communities in the years prior to independence—population had grown, farming and ranching had expanded, and mines had reopened.[3]

On September 8, a few days after Tucson acted, residents of El Paso del Norte also took the oath of allegiance. Since 1680 El Paso had occupied the strategic spot some 1200 miles north of Mexico City where the

Rio Grande sliced its way through two mountains. The small center of the town stood on the site of today's Ciudad Juárez, on what is now the Mexican side of the river, but in 1821 the jurisdiction of New Mexico extended farther south and embraced the town. El Paso and outlying communities supported over 8,000 people. Nearly all lived in a narrow band along the river where a dam and irrigation canals watered fields of wheat and corn as well as orchards and vineyards. Compared to other frontier communities, the *paseños* seemed prosperous. When compared to cities in the interior of Mexico, on the other hand, El Paso and all of the communities on the northern frontier seemed poor indeed. Nowhere is this contrast better illustrated than in the architecture and furnishings of churches, which stood as the most prominent public manifestations of the wealth and values of communities throughout Mexico. A bishop's representative, who visited the church at El Paso on the eve of Mexican independence, described it as "the best kept" in New Mexico, but then condemned it as "worse than a warehouse for liquor in [central] Mexico . . . infested with bats, so full of birds' nests that one finds those filthy animals under the mantels of the altar and their excrement in the baptismal font."[4]

From El Paso, the contagion of independence spread northward late that summer of 1821 across a long waterless trail, the *Jornada del Muerto*, to the heart of New Mexico—a ribbon of settlements on the middle Rio Grande between Socorro in the south and Taos in the north. Some 30,000 gente de razón and perhaps 10,000 partly acculturated Pueblo Indian agriculturalists lived in this area, making it the largest nucleus of Hispanic settlement on Mexico's far northern frontier. Over 300 miles beyond El Paso and 1500 miles from Mexico City, New Mexico's capital, Santa Fe, stood at an altitude of 7,000 feet amidst piñón and juniper at the foot of the Sangre de Cristo Mountains overlooking the Rio Grande Valley. Since 1610, for over two centuries, Santa Fe had occupied the place where the little Río de Santa Fe emerged from the mountains on its way to the great river. In an arid land, the Río de Santa Fe made the town possible. Its waters filled irrigation ditches and nourished the unfenced fields that surrounded adobe homes scattered along the length of its banks. Perhaps 5,000 people, including a military garrison, lived in Santa Fe and its outskirts on the eve of independence. On September 11, 1821, in the ill-kept "palace" of the governors that fronted the town's dusty and treeless main square, officials administered the oath of allegiance. Within a few days, citizens in numerous smaller agricultural and ranching centers, such as Albuquerque, and some of the town-dwelling Indians the Spaniards called Pueblos, also swore dutifully to uphold the new regime.[5]

Isolated Alta California was the last of the northernmost provinces to swear loyalty to the new order. Ever since 1781, when Yuma Indians ousted Spanish intruders and regained control of the Colorado River crossing, the overland connection between Sonora and Alta California had ceased to exist. In a sense, California had become an island, dependent upon the sea for communication with the outside world. Nearly all of California's 3,200 gente de razón lived near streams on the edge of the sea on the temperate, 500-mile stretch of coastal plain between San Diego in the south and San Francisco in the north. Most *californios* lived in or near one of the province's three duly constituted municipalities, the pueblos of Los Angeles, San Jose, or Santa Cruz (then called Branciforte), or near the decaying military posts of San Diego, Santa Barbara, Monterey, or San Francisco. All of these urban centers were small. Monterey, for example, which had served as the provincial capital since its founding, consisted of a presidio and mission and, according to a French visitor who first saw it from the sea in 1827: "some forty scattered houses of quite a pretty appearance, also covered with tiles and whitewashed. This, with a few straw huts, is what constitutes the capital city of Alta California."[6] The presidial district of Monterey, which extended well beyond the urban center itself, consisted of perhaps 700 gente de razón in 1821.

By January 1822, if not before, the news of the insurgents' success had reached Monterey. A few months later, a junta consisting of the comandantes of the four presidios, along with two priests and other important figures, met at the governor's house in Monterey. On April 11, members of the junta, the troops, and the citizenry in general gathered in the plaza, and publically took an oath of allegiance to the new government. Within a matter of days that ceremony was repeated at each presidio, pueblo, and mission along the coast.[7]

News of the break with Spain had come to the frontier by mail, and the *pobladores* had acceded to it peacefully. The attitudes of the frontiersmen toward the independence movement have, in general, not found their way into historical records. Much must be inferred. Clearly, however, the three frontier governors, who were all military officers, had not endorsed independence with enthusiasm. Instead, they had cautiously watched the direction of the prevailing political winds.

The immediate force which set those winds in motion was the Plan of Iguala, issued on February 24, 1821 by the former Spanish officer, Agustín de Iturbide. This Plan, a declaration of independence from Spain, called for a constitutional monarchy and ingeniously if temporarily united all classes and political persuasions under a formula known as the "Three

Monterey, California, 1827. "The Presidio and Pueblo of Monterey" consisted of
houses scattered around a main square, formed by the buildings of the presidio,
as painted by a British mariner, William Smyth, in 1827 (courtesy, The Bancroft
Library).

Guarantees": independence from Spain; recognition of Catholicism as
Mexico's only religion; and equality of all Mexicans.[8]

At first, frontier governors opposed Iturbide's Plan. The Spanish-born
governors of Texas and New Mexico, Antonio Martínez and Facundo
Melgares, both staunch royalists, had known at least as early as April
1821 of Iturbide's pronouncement. Nonetheless, both remained loyal
until the Spanish regime collapsed in July and superior officers ordered
them to support the insurgents.[9] Similarly, California's Spanish-born

Governor Pablo Vicente de Sola at first ridiculed Iturbide's "absurd views" and termed independence "a dream."[10] A poor prophet but a good soldier, Sola also eventually responded to orders and supported Iturbide by April of 1822.

Governor Sola had been so slow to acknowledge independence, however, that the new government in Mexico City feared that California had remained loyal to Spain or that Russia had annexed it. Iturbide sent a cleric, Canon Agustín Fernández, to report on the local mood. Fernández, whose drinking and gambling raised eyebrows among many *californios*, found no evidence of disloyalty; neither did he discover enthusiasm for the new government. When Fernández ordered the Spanish flag lowered for the last time over the plaza at Monterey, the assemblage watched it descend in stony silence. The proud and polished Spanish-born governor, his hair and beard nearly white and his teeth nearly gone, stepped forward and swept the flag into his arms before it fell on the ground, then turned to Fernández and explained: "They do not cheer because they are unused to independence."[11]

Even local celebrations of independence on the frontier did not seem to arise out of spontaneous enthusiasm. In New Mexico, celebrations occurred only in response to government orders that all municipalities hold formal ceremonies to swear allegiance to the new government "in the form and with the magnificence that the oaths of allegiance to the Kings have previously been read."[12] In Santa Fe, New Mexicans followed instructions and celebrated independence on January 6, 1822, as a white banner imprinted with the Three Guarantees flew over the plaza. Dawn of that day arrived, according to Governor Melgares, with "bells ringing wildly," gunfire, and "a burst of music." A Mass and triumphal procession followed. Celebration and entertainment, including a "splendid dance" by Indians from the Pueblo of Tesuque, continued throughout the day and long into the night. A dance, where women stylishly sported sashes proclaiming "¡Viva la Independencia!" ended at 4:30 in the morning.[13]

Although the frontier governors were reluctant rebels, their willingness to accede peacefully to the new regime, and the willingness of the citizenry and the troops to follow them, spared the frontier a destructive civil war in 1821. Perhaps the only casualties to grow out of the Iturbide revolt on the frontier were the pigtails of California soldiers. According to Juana Machado, a young girl at the time, men "were accustomed to wear their hair long and braided with a knot of ribbon or silk at the end; on some it came below the waist." With the change of flags in California in 1822, Juana Machado remembered "an order was given to cut off the braids of the soldiers. . . . When papa came home with his braid in his hand and gave it to mama his face was very sad and . . . she looked at the braid and cried."[14]

The peaceful transition from Spanish to Mexican rule in 1821 came on the heels of a decade of destructive revolt and counterrevolt that affected the frontier in varying degrees. Those ten violent years had begun on September 16, 1810, when Padre Miguel Hidalgo called for independence in the town of Dolores, near Guanajuato, setting off a war between the exploited masses and the privileged few, many of whom happened to be Spanish-born.

Of the northernmost provinces, Texas was swept up most directly in the Hidalgo whirlwind. Proximity to the United States and to American arms, munitions, and mercenaries made Texas a strategic province for rebels and royalists alike. In January 1811, following his resounding defeat at the Bridge of Calderón near Guadalajara, Hidalgo retreated toward Texas and sent agents ahead to seek help in the United States.[15]

Meanwhile, in San Antonio on January 22, 1811, a former militia captain, thirty-six-year-old Juan Bautista de las Casas, led a successful coup against the royalist government. Las Casas won the support of poor soldiers and civilians who resented the Spanish-born upper class and the Mexican-born *criollos* who held most of the wealth. When Las Casas seized the property of local Spaniards, for example, he could not auction it off because, as he wrote, "they were the only ones able to buy."[16]

Las Casas opened correspondence with Hidalgo and other revolutionary leaders, but his short-lived revolt never merged into the larger struggle. On March 1, 1811, a few clergy and army officers staged a successful counter-coup in San Antonio. Sent to Monclova for trial and found guilty, Las Casas was shot in the back as a traitor and his head shipped back to San Antonio to be placed on public display as a reminder to other would-be insurgents. Among the five officers who voted to condemn Las Casas to death was Captain Facundo Melgares, who a decade later as Governor of New Mexico would reluctantly embrace independence.[17] Meanwhile, Hidalgo fared no better. On route north from Saltillo to San Antonio, he rode into a trap at the Wells of Baján on March 21, 1811. By summer's end, his rotting head stood on display in Guanajuato.

The most destructive impact of Hildalgo's revolt had not yet been felt in Texas. One of Hidalgo's agents, a criollo merchant named Bernardo Gutiérrez de Lara, had made it to the United States to seek aid for the cause of independence. With both tacit support and modest monetary aid from United States officials, Gutiérrez de Lara raised a small force and invaded Texas in 1812. By spring of 1813 he had captured San Antonio and proclaimed Texas an independent state in which "all legitimate authority shall emanate from the People."[18] Gutiérrez de Lara made some foolish mistakes, however, and members of his mercenary army began to quarrel among themselves. The rebels' disarray enabled a royalist force, led by José Joaquín Arredondo, to recapture the province easily. The merciless Arredondo executed *tejanos* suspected of republican tendencies, shooting 327 persons in San Antonio alone, and sent one of his lieutenants on a bloody purge of the Nacogdoches area in East Texas. Many *tejanos* took refuge in Louisiana. Winter of 1813 found Texas devastated, its population diminished, herds destroyed, and food in short supply as Arredondo's troops continued to pillage the countryside.[19]

Texas did not recover from these events prior to the Iturbide revolt. Instead it became the scene of two more invasions, in 1819 and 1821, by self-styled armies of liberation that included American mercenaries who coveted Texas. Both invasions failed, but not until they had devastated the province still further. Meanwhile, ill-provisioned royalist troops, assigned to protect Texas from insurgents, also became predators. By 1821 it must have been difficult to tell whether royalists or rebels had done the most harm. The "naked and starving" royalist troops, wrote Governor Antonio Martínez in 1821, "have drained the resources of the country, and laid their hand on everything that could sustain human life." Texas, he lamented, "has advanced at an amazing rate toward ruin and destruction."[20] By the end of the Spanish era, the population of Texas had dwindled to perhaps a third of what it had been in 1809, and the town of Nacogdoches had nearly expired.[21]

With Texas ravaged by a decade of warfare, the *tejano* oligarchy displayed an understandable reluctance to embrace the Plan of Iguala, lest it develop into still another chimera. Nonetheless, the situation in Texas was so dismal that the lowering of the Spanish flag for the last time was probably "painless to the inhabitanta," as one historian has suggested.[22] Could Texas be worse off under independent Mexico than it had been under Spain?

In other provinces on the far northern frontier, rumors of local insurrections proved false, and the effects of Mexico's decade-long struggle for independence were not felt as acutely as in Texas; however, Alta California was the scene of some violence. In 1818 Hippolyte de Bouchard, a French privateer who purported to represent the insurgent cause, sacked Monterey, set fire to the presidio, and despoiled other points along the coast. Alarmed Spanish officials sent unpaid troops to protect California but, as in Texas, the plundering done by poor soldiers apparently added to the burdens of the *californios* rather than relieving them.[23]

For most of the northern frontier the worst effects of the independence struggle were indirect. Paralyzed by the Napoleonic invasion of the Iberian peninsula in 1808 and distracted by rebellions in Mexico and throughout the New World, Spain could no longer effectively administer her empire. This crisis disrupted everyday life in areas as remote as Mexico's Far North. In the decade following the Hidalgo revolt, trade on the frontier was disrupted, supplies were cut off for the military and the missions, and the salaries of officials went unpaid. "For a good many years," wrote one California Franciscan, "the blows have succeeded one another with such violence as to render us almost insensible."[24]

In some areas, treaty relationships between Hispanic frontiersmen and Apaches, Comanches, and other autonomous and potentially hostile Indians began to unravel because the frontiersmen could no longer deliver gifts or command sufficient military respect. *Tejanos* labored under a special handicap. Punished for their disloyalty during the Hidalgo revolt by a ban on the ownership of firearms, *tejanos* claimed to be at the mercy of hostile tribes.[25] In New Mexico, a long period of peace with Navajos had ended in 1818 and on October 3, 1821, less than a month after swearing loyalty to the new government, Governor Melgares invaded the Navajo country with a contingent of militia and Pueblo Indian allies. New Mexicans feared a general Indian attack from all directions, and danger from potentially hostile Indians probably weighed more heavily on the minds of frontiersmen in 1821 than did the political uncertainties accompanying independence.[26]

In addition to the impact of turmoil in Spain and Mexico, the frontier faced other extraordinary problems in 1821. Two expanding nations, Russia and the United States, seemed poised to seize portions of the region. Long before independence, officials in New Spain had worried about foreign encroachment on the underpopulated Far North.[27] Without Spain's protection, the threat must have seemed even more immediate to officials of newly independent Mexico.

In December 1821, within months after Iturbide had established a new government, a special Committee on Foreign Relations reported to him that Russia and the United States threatened to dismember Mexico.[28] Russia, which had established Fort Ross just north of San Francisco Bay in 1812, had designs on California according to the Committee. In fact, a report that Russians already controlled that province had prompted Iturbide to send Agustín Fernández on his tour of inspection.[29] The Committee also warned of danger to the northeastern frontier from the United States, whose interest in expansion was well known in Mexico at the time of independence. In words that seem nearly prophetic in later years, Tadeo Ortiz, a former revolutionary who had visited the United

States in 1811, described the dangers of an Anglo-American invasion of Mexico by way of Texas and New Mexico. Individual Americans, Ortiz accurately reported in 1821, had already reached New Mexico. He predicted that they would soon penetrate Pimería Alta and cross the Rockies to California.[30] Similarly, Mexico's first minister to the United States warned from Washington in 1822 that "the haughtiness of these Republicans does not permit them to look upon us as equals but as inferiors; their conceit extends itself in my opinion to believe that their capital will be that of all the Americas."[31]

Mexican fears of United States aggression were firmly based. Within the memory of some Mexican leaders, Americans had pushed across the Appalachians to the Mississippi Valley, acquiring the Floridas and Louisiana, and insisting that the western boundary of Louisiana included Texas. Over the vigorous protests of American frontiersmen, the United States officially abandoned its inflated claims to Texas in 1819 and agreed to resolve the indefinite boundary between Louisiana and Spanish North America. This Adams-Onís Treaty, also known as the Transcontinental Treaty, placed one end of the international boundary in east Texas at the mouth of the Sabine River on the Gulf of Mexico. From there the boundary followed a broken northwesterly line along the Sabine, Red, and Arkansas rivers, before moving due west across the 42d parallel to the Pacific. Whatever hopes Spain had of regaining portions of Louisiana, which she had held between 1762 and 1800, or of maintaining a grip on the Pacific Northwest, which she claimed by right of prior exploration, all ended in 1819.[32]

Like Spain, Mexico quickly discovered that it had to struggle with the United States to preserve its inheritance. Because of delays in Madrid, the United States and Spain did not exchange ratifications of the Treaty of 1819 until February 22, 1821. Two days later Iturbide declared Mexico independent and the United States seized the opportunity to push the line farther west. Joel Roberts Poinsett, who would become the first United States minister to Mexico in 1825, visited Mexico City unofficially in 1822 and apparently suggested a new boundary that would place much of northern Mexico, including Texas, New Mexico, Sonora, and both Californias, in the United States. Mexican diplomats pressed to maintain the boundary at the line agreed upon in 1819, but the United States continued to urge renegotiation through a series of ingenious arguments. As secretary of state, Henry Clay in 1825 carried Yankee ingenuity to its extreme by suggesting that United States acquisition of Mexico's entire northern frontier would benefit Mexico by placing her capital in a more central location. Notwithstanding continuous American pressure, the Transcontinental Treaty line remained the de facto boundary until it became the official border with the ratification of a new treaty between the United States and Mexico in 1832. Although danger from Russia seemed to disappear in the early 1820s, the spector of American expansion hung steadily over the frontier in the years following independence until it became a reality in 1846.[33]

Although some officials in high places worried about Russian and American aggression in 1821, many frontiersmen looked toward the foreigners to deliver them from economic stagnation. Spain's policies had generally prohibited trade with foreigners and discouraged them from settling in Spanish territory. Signs of change began to appear on the frontier almost simultaneously with independence.

Summer of 1821 found young Virginia-born Stephen Austin riding toward San Antonio where he hoped to negotiate with the governor for permission to settle American colonists in Texas. At daybreak on Sunday, August 12, several *tejanos* rode into Austin's camp, just a few hours' ride out of San Antonio. These men, Austin wrote, "brought the glorious news of the Independence of Mexico" and "hailed this news with acclamations of 'viva independencia'. . . . "[34] Austin continued on to San Antonio where he concluded successful negotiations with Governor Antonio Martínez, and laid the groundwork to become the "founder" of the century-old province of Texas in the eyes of some of his ethnocentric countrymen.[35]

A few months after Austin reached San Antonio, in November 1821, William Becknell of Missouri and a small group of traders encountered troops from New Mexico on the high plains east of Santa Fe. The two groups could not communicate, Becknell said, but "their reception of us, fully convinced us of their hospitable feelings."[36] Becknell and his companions rode with the *nuevomexicanos* to the village of San Miguel on the edge of the plains, then over the Sangre de Cristo range by way of Glorieta Pass and into Santa Fe where the "well informed and gentlemanly" Governor Melgares received them. Melgares told Becknell that he welcomed trade with the Americans and that they might also settle in his province. Had Becknell arrived a year earlier, Melgares probably would have arrested him. Instead, just two months after Melgares swore allegiance to Mexican independence, Becknell, who might have known of the success of the Iturbide revolt and headed to New Mexico by design, had the good fortune to be permitted to sell trade goods from Missouri in Santa Fe and became the so-called father of the Santa Fe trade.[37]

The *californios,* too, seemed eager to trade with foreigners. Russians and Englishmen as well as Americans found themselves welcome in California ports. Indeed, the *californios'* enthusiasm for new trading arrangements with foreigners seemed so great that it, too, became cause for alarm in Mexico City.[38]

Thus, however great their loyalty to Spain or their reluctance to step into a new and uncertain era, some Mexican frontiersmen seem to have viewed the path of independence as leading to fresh opportunities. Those opportunities went beyond the chance for economic gain to the heart of politics and society, for the independence era promised greater local control over government and the end of racial and class distinctions. Even on the frontier, some young men, such as Donaciano Vigil of New Mexico, found themselves

> swept up by agreeable theories and by patriotic discourses that then circulated among us. We expected to enter a new era of happiness and this word, and the word "liberty," were those that were most used and most repeated in those days. We saw everything, then, through rose-colored glasses.[39]

The optimism that Vigil sensed in New Mexico permeated all of Mexico in the wake of Iturbide's triumph. Within months, however, pessimism replaced optimism as it became clear that raised expectations, some tending toward the utopian, would not be realized immediately, and that Mexico's leaders did not agree on an agenda for the future.[40] Mexicans agreed on independence from Spain in 1821, but little else. The Plan of Iguala produced only a momentary consensus. As one historian has recently suggested, the Plan was "a massive compromise of such proportions that it satisfied no one beyond the immediate moment."[41] After the shouts of "¡Viva la Independencia!" died down, Mexico faced decades of turmoil while her leaders sought a new consensus. Efforts to create a new order would affect the frontier profoundly and the frontier, in turn, would affect the rest of the nation.

In 1821, however, no one could have predicted with certainty the troubles that lay ahead. Many, however, would have agreed with the sentiments of one California Franciscan who took the oath of independence and then prayed: "may God grant that all may be for the best."[42]

2

The New Politics

It is unquestionable that the lack of a government which can respond directly to the needs of Texas . . . has been, is, and will continue to be the chief source of our sufferings.—Ayuntamiento of San Antonio, *December 1832*

The old monastic order is destroyed and nothing seems to have replaced it, except anarchy. The official power is weak and flutters irresolutely in the hands of its holders. Doubtless a new political order will arise out of this chaos but while waiting for it the country is badly administered, society is without ties, without guarantees, and the people are wretched.—A French visitor to California, Abel du Petit-Thouars, *1837*

Throughout the eighteenth century, pobladores on Mexico's far northern frontier had little voice in governing themselves. Like Spain's subjects everywhere, they had lived under the enlightened and paternalistic despotism of the Bourbon monarchs, who did not encumber themselves with constitutions or popular participation in government. No representative parliament met regularly in Spain; no legislatures met in her colonies. Local government had decayed and appointed officials held offices that had once been filled by elections. Outsiders, rather than local people, occupied key posts even in such remote areas as the northern frontier of New Spain.

Independence from Spain ushered in a new political order for Mexico. Like other Mexicans, frontiersmen gained a voice in national affairs for the first time; representative government began to function on the provincial level and enjoyed a new vitality at the municipal level; and the

15

frontier upper class gained access to offices that had previously been closed to them or had not existed. In short, the new politics provided opportunities for local autonomy and home rule such as frontiersmen had never known. At the same time, the new politics raised expectations—ones that a succession of volatile and perennially bankrupt governments in Mexico City could not fulfill.

The old political order died a decade before Mexico won independence in 1821. An extraordinary crisis in Spain provided impetus for profound political change in 1808, when French forces overran much of Iberia and Napoleon virtually kidnapped the legitimate monarchs, Charles IV and his ambitious son, Ferdinand VII. Resistance to the French invaders centered in the Spanish *Cortes*, a parliament that had languished under the Bourbon dynasty. Dominated by a group of young liberals, the revitalized Cortes not only led the resistance against the French, but also boldly restructured Spanish government at all levels in the absence of the legitimate king. The Cortes abolished feudal institutions, such as the Inquisition, and turned absolutist Spain into what one historian has termed "one of the most radical constitutional monarchies in Europe."[1]

Meeting between 1810 and 1814 at the port city of Cádiz in southern Spain, the Cortes passed a series of acts that reached into the most remote corners of the empire and would affect Mexico long after independence. The heart of this liberal legislation took the form of the 1812 Constitution of Cádiz, a blending of the Spanish Catholic tradition of natural rights and contractual law with secular rights doctrines that arose out of the Enlightenment.[2] Based on the premise that sovereignty resided with the nation and not solely with the monarch, the 1812 Constitution made the king more responsible to the Cortes and provided for greater representative government at all levels. At the municipal level it established guidelines for *ayuntamientos,* or town councils. The new regulations transformed ayuntamientos from closed corporations to popularly elected bodies and extended their jurisdictions to include nearby communities. Members were to be chosen through regular elections and lifetime positions on town councils were abolished.[3] At the provincial level the Constitution endorsed a relatively new institution, a legislature of elected representatives termed the *diputación.* At the national level, provinces throughout the empire were to send an elected delegate to represent them in the Cortes itself. The 1812 Constitution also increased the number of persons eligible to participate in political life by conferring citizenship upon all Spanish subjects, including Indians, and excluding only such types as domestic servants, the unemployed, debtors, criminals, certain blacks, and women.

The changes mandated by the liberal Cortes had just begun to be implemented in Mexico when the repressive and absolutist Ferdinand VII regained the throne in 1814, suspended the Constitution, disbanded the Cortes, and annulled its acts. Ferdinand proved both inept and unpopular, however, and in 1820 a segment of the Spanish military, in concert with liberal politicians, revolted and forced him to restore the Constitution of 1812 and the Cortes for both Spain and her American provinces.[4] Prior to independence, a new political order based on the Constitution of 1812 began to emerge in Mexico. In a variety of ways its effects reached the remote northern frontier and continued to be felt long after independence.

Municipal governments began to appear in towns where they had not existed before, and previously established town councils were revitalized. In New Mexico, where ayuntamientos had ceased to function by 1811, at least six full-fledged ayuntamientos had been formed by 1814 in compliance with the new regulations. Following Ferdinand's orders, the New Mexicans dismantled those councils in 1815, but convoked them again in 1820 when the Constitution of Cádiz was restored. By the time of independence, most New Mexico towns, including Pueblo Indian communities, had elected ayuntamientos. To conform with acts of the Cortes, Governor Facundo Melgares had ordered that Pueblo Indians be regarded "as Spaniards in all things, exercising especially their rights to vote and to stand as candidates for office."[5] Meanwhile, strife-torn Texas did not restructure its municipal governments in the mid-1810s, but in 1820 both San Antonio and Goliad held elections to reform their ayuntamientos under the new regulations.[6] California followed suit in 1822, expanding the membership of the ayuntamientos of San Jose and Los Angeles. Other sizeable non-Indian communities in California, such as Santa Barbara and Monterey, were not subject to civil government because they were essentially military posts.[7]

Provincial assemblies, or diputaciones, formed more slowly on the frontier than did ayuntamientos. The Constitution of 1812 authorized only six assemblies for all of Mexico. These were to correspond to six large autonomous provinces, including both the *Provincias Internas del Occidente* and *Oriente,* which embraced Sonora, New Mexico, and Texas, as well as much of the rest of the north. New Mexico and Texas elected a representative to the diputación of the Western Internal Provinces in 1814, but the return of Ferdinand made the election meaningless. Not until after independence did each frontier province form its own diputación.[8]

Following decades of exclusion from the decision-making process, the extraordinary idea of electing a representative to a provincial assembly must have seemed revolutionary to some frontiersmen. Even more remarkable, perhaps, was the call that the Cortes issued to the New World provinces to send delegates to Cádiz to participate in the Cortes. The Cortes went so far as to specify that delegates be natives of the province they represent. Neither California nor Texas could take advantage of the opportunity. The viceroy ruled that the Californias were not entitled to representation, and Texas could neither afford to send a delegate, nor did a suitable candidate emerge. According to one Spanish officer, the *tejanos* could not find a native son who met the necessary qualifications of "integrity, talent, and education."[9] To some extent, though, Texans were represented by Miguel Ramos Arizpe, a remarkable liberal from the neighboring province of Coahuila whose views not only influenced the Cortes, but won him a six year prison term upon the return of the repressive Ferdinand.[10]

Of the northernmost provinces, only New Mexico succeeded in sending a native son, Pedro Bautista Pino, to represent it in Cádiz. One of fifteen delegates from Mexico to serve in the Cortes between 1810 and 1813, Pino had the greatest distance to travel and was not seated until August 1812, after the Constitution had been published. The most enduring result of his journey was the publication of a small book in which he provided the Cortes and posterity with a succinct if somewhat polemical description of New Mexico and its problems. In 1820, *nuevomexicanos* elected Pino again to serve as delegate to the Cortes, but he got only as far as Vera Cruz. Expected funds did not materialize and he had to retrace a journey of over 1500 miles. Perhaps that explains why New Mexicans came to regard Pino's missions as fruitless and immortalize them in a schoolchildren's verse: *"Don Pedro Pino Fué; Don Pedro Pino vino* [Don Pedro Pino went away; Don Pedro Pino came back]."[11]

Although they were often halting and erratic, as in Pino's case, the first steps toward local autonomy and representative government on the frontier had been taken in the last decade of Spanish rule. The break with Spain and the coming to power of Agustín de Iturbide brought no sharp change in direction. Instead, the pace accelerated.

In an effort to maintain liberal support and avoid political chaos, Iturbide declared that those portions of the 1812 Constitution that did not run counter to the interests of independent Mexico would remain in force until a new constitution could be adopted. To provide continuity, Iturbide permitted those officials who had served under Spain to continue to exercise their usual functions.[12] Since a new constitution did not appear during Iturbide's year and a half in power, independent Mexico continued to be governed by the liberal legislation of the Cortes of Cádiz, including laws regulating ayuntamientos and provincial assemblies.

In 1820, just prior to independence, the Cortes had permitted more diputaciones to be formed in Mexico and the Iturbide government endorsed that idea in late 1821. As a result, assemblies proliferated. Throughout Mexico, local *políticos* sought greater home rule for their provinces. The Constitution of 1812 had authorized six diputaciones for all of Mexico; by November 1822 the number had tripled and a year later it rose to twenty-three.[13]

The frontier provinces joined this rush toward greater local autonomy with New Mexico leading the way. In January 1822, electors from fourteen municipal districts (*alcaldías*), including El Paso, met in Santa Fe and chose seven representatives, or *vocales*, to serve in the diputación. In a characteristic display of frontier independence, Governor Facundo Melgares had apparently called for this election even though he lacked authorization from Mexico City. The Iturbide administration regarded the newly formed New Mexico diputación as illegal, but the New Mexico vocales continued to meet for a year and a half, apparently unaware that their diputación lacked legitimacy until Congress formally sanctioned its existence. This seems to be the only case in all of Mexico of a province forming an assembly on its own initiative and subsequently gaining congressional approval.[14] Californians elected members of an assembly later that year, in November. They might have done so earlier, but Governor Pablo Vicente de Sola delayed in calling elections because he viewed the *californios* as unfit for self-government.[15] In October 1823, nearly a year after California acted, a diputación was installed in Texas, too late for it to have an impact on that province as subsequent events would reveal.[16]

Even as regional leaders on the frontier and elsewhere sought greater political autonomy for their provinces, the autocratic Iturbide began to centralize power in Mexico City. In May 1822, when it became clear that no member of a European royal family would accept the throne of Mexico, Iturbide arranged to have himself proclaimed emperor. In October 1822, in his new incarnation as Agustín I, the former Spanish army officer dissolved the nation's infant Congress. Among the delegates to that Congress was Francisco Pérez Serrano y Aguirre of New Mexico, who must have found representative government disillusioning. It had taken don Francisco six months to travel to Mexico City from the time of his election, longer than the time that he served in the short-lived Congress. He had better fortune, however, than the delegate from Alta California, former Governor Sola, who reached Mexico City well after Iturbide had abolished Congress.[17]

Provinces throughout Mexico reacted swiftly to Iturbide's seizure of power. During the first months of 1823 most provinces swore to uphold the Plan of Casa Mata, which called for an end to Iturbide's empire and demanded the establishment of a new congress composed of liberal delegates. Most provinces also severed relations with the central government and conducted their affairs as if they were autonomous states.[18] Left in control of little more than Mexico City, Iturbide abdicated on March 19, 1823, and went into exile. The following year, unaware of a decree that threatened him with execution if he returned to Mexico, Iturbide returned and was promptly executed.

Leadership in these efforts to topple Iturbide had come from provincial diputaciones, but frontier residents played no active role in the tumultuous events of 1823. Distance alone probably relegated frontier politicians to a minor role on the national stage, and probably also contributed to their cautious attitude toward matters about which they knew very little. In New Mexico, for example, Governor José Antonio Vizcarra, an Iturbide appointee, called the New Mexico assembly into session on March 26, 1823 to discuss an invitation to support the Plan of Casa Mata. Unaware that Iturbide had abdicated a week earlier, the New Mexico assembly resolved to support the emperor and not to "soil its hands with the vile stain of infidelity." Two months went by before officials in the isolated province learned that the Plan of Casa Mata had triumphed. Then they could do little more than offer an awkward explanation and swear allegiance to the new government.[19] Meanwhile, *tejanos* had taken a similar cautious stance. A provincial diputación had not yet been formed in Texas, but political, military, and religious leaders remained loyal to Iturbide until mid-April 1823, long after the rest of the Provincias Internas del Oriente had abandoned his government.[20]

Having toppled Iturbide, the provinces turned to reorganizing the government along federalist-liberal lines—permitting considerable regional autonomy and leaving the central government relatively weak (Mexican federalists should not be confused with those *American federalists* who advocated a strong central government following United States independence). Delegates from throughout Mexico met in the autumn of 1823 and on January 31, 1824 approved a national charter, the *Acta Constitutiva*. Nine months later, that document became a part of Mexico's first constitution, the Federal Constitution of the United States of Mexico, endorsed on October 4, 1824. Among the signatories were José Rafael Alarid of New Mexico and the widely read, patriotic, and progressive forty-two-year-old Erasmo Seguín of Texas. (California's delegate, former governor Sola, was apparently denied a seat.)[21]

The Constitution of 1824 remained in force until 1835 with no amendments—a period in Mexican history sometimes known as the federalist era, or the First Federal Republic. In many ways Mexico's 1824 Constitution emulated the United States Constitution, but it also contained

Mexican federalism. The theoretical autonomy and equality of Mexico's states and territories, united under the protective wings of the Mexican eagle and the Constitution of 1824, is illustrated graphically in this 1828 engraving (Vito Alessio Robles, *Coahuila y Texas desde la consumación de la independencia . . .* [2 vols.; Mexico, 1945–46] II, frontispiece).

important and sometimes contradictory ingredients from the Spanish Constitution of 1812, which continued to influence Mexican political structures on the state as well as the federal level.[22] The Constitution of 1824 made possible greater regional autonomy and participation in national affairs, breaking the extraodinary power that Mexico City had enjoyed in the colonial period. Politically it gave new opportunities to all Mexicans by eliminating in theory distinctions between all races and classes. But at the same time that it eliminated class distinctions, the 1824 Constitution maintained special privileges or *fueros* for members of the clergy and the military, and even as it guaranteed freedom of speech it recognized only one religion, Roman Catholicism. Notwithstanding these contradictions, a renewal of optimism accompanied the adoption of the Constitution of 1824.[23]

In a dozen years, then, between 1812 and 1824, Mexico had undergone a transformation from a political appendage of an absolutist monarchy to an independent federal republic. In accordance with reforms begun at Cádiz, frontiersmen became citizens instead of subjects; government by appointment of outsiders from the privileged class began to give way to a system of limited elections; representative institutions appeared at the provincial level; municipal government was revitalized; and for the first time the voices of frontiersmen could be heard on the national level through their elected delegates.

Under the 1824 Constitution, most Mexican provinces became states. They drew up their own constitutions, converted their diputaciones to legislatures, and became sovereign political entities with control over their internal affairs. Federalism did not bring those benefits to Alta California, Sonora, New Mexico, or Texas. Indeed, at first it appeared as though those frontier provinces would not exist as separate political entities.

The architects of the federalist system tried to link California, Sonora, New Mexico, and Texas with other large provinces, following the model of the colonial Provincias Internas. Large states in the underpopulated north, it was hoped, would maintain a demographic balance with the smaller, more populous states in the interior of the Republic.[24] Hence, the original draft of the Acta Constitutiva in 1823 had divided the Far North into three oversized states: the *Estado Interno del Occidente*, composed of Sonora, Sinaloa, and both Californias; the *Estado Interno del Norte*, which combined New Mexico with Chihuahua and Durango; and the *Estado Interno del Oriente*, which joined Texas to Coahuila, Nuevo León, and Tamaulipas (then called Nuevo Santander).[25]

Even before the Acta Constitutiva was approved on January 31, 1824 fragmentation had begun. Although some wished to maintain the four

Transcontinental

Territory of Alta California

Treaty

Territory of Nuevo México

Sonora y Sinaloa

Line

[Louisiana]

Pacific

Coahuila y Texas

Chihuahua

Gulf of California

Territory of
Baja California

Gulf of Mexico

Durango

Nuevo
León

Zacatecas

Tamaulipas

San
Luís
Potosí

Guanajuato

Querétaro

Jalisco

Mexico City

Yucatán

Ocean

Territory
of Colima

Michoacán

Tlaxcala

Veracruz

Puebla

México

Tabasco

Oaxaca

Chiapas

Soconusco

The United States
of Mexico,
1824

Under the 1824 Constitution, the provinces in the Far North either entered the
union as territories (the Californias and New Mexico) or as portions of larger
states (Sonora y Sinaloa and Coahuila y Texas).

large states, and even to enlarge them, regional forces prevailed on the frontier as they did throughout Mexico.[26] First, Congress put the Californias directly under its control as territories, rather than states, and reduced the Estado del Occidente to the provinces of Sonora and Sinaloa. Second, Congress permitted Tamaulipas to separate from the Estado del Oriente.

On May 7, 1824, following the adoption of the Acta, Congress permitted Nuevo León to break away from the Estado del Oriente, leaving Texas and Coahuila joined together as a single state. Texas, Congress decreed, would remain united with Coahuila until it could qualify for statehood on its own.[27]

The Texas representative in Congress, Erasmo Seguín, made some effort to separate Texas from Coahuila, a move that he might not have favored privately. Seguín recognized that by itself Texas lacked sufficient resources and population to support a state government, much less fight off hostile Indians, or control westward-moving Anglo-Americans. Indeed, even in combination, Texas and Coahuila constituted Mexico's poorest state according to a congressional study. Despite the vulnerable position of Texas, Seguín publicly opposed union with more populous Coahuila, which he predicted would dominate his province, and he argued that Texas would benefit most from territorial status because the federal government had an obligation to aid the territories. But Seguín could not or would not outmaneuver the influential and more experienced delegate from Coahuila, Miguel Ramos Arizpe, who wanted his underpopulated province linked to Texas lest Coahuila itself be reduced to territorial status. Ramos Arizpe, who had ably represented his province in the Cortes a decade earlier, had considered the alternative of Coahuila joining with a neighboring state other than Texas, but feared that his province would then be the weaker partner. He preferred instead to have Coahuila as the dominant partner in a relationship with Texas. In an effort to dissuade the Texans from choosing territorial status, Ramos Arizpe wrote to the ayuntamiento of San Antonio, warning that if Texas became a territory it would lose control of its public lands to the federal government. His argument worked. The San Antonio ayuntamiento approved the tie with Coahuila and Seguín stopped pressing the matter. The decision stood despite strenuous objections of some Texas leaders who nearly came to blows over the issue.[28]

Like the states of Occidente and Oriente, the immense Estado Interno del Norte also split apart in a matter of months. At the outset, the three provinces of New Mexico, Chihuahua, and Durango could not agree on the location for a capital. Congress had assigned the honor to the centrally located city of Chihuahua, but Durango objected. New Mexicans in turn protested the pretensions of Durango, pointing out not only its considerable distance from Santa Fe, but also noting the "short distance" between New Mexico and its menacing neighbor, the United States.[29] This was neither the first nor the last time that New Mexico políticos tried to use their exposed position on the frontier to their advantage. The problem was resolved when Durango's representative in Congress gained separate statehood for his province on May 22, 1824.[30] That left only Chihuahua and New Mexico in the Estado Interno del Norte. At that point New Mexico's representative, José Rafael Alarid, asked that New Mexico be separated from Chihuahua. Congress granted his request in a decree of July 6, 1824, making New Mexico a territory and Chihuahua a state. In the process, El Paso, historically part of New Mexico, was transferred to Chihuahua.[31]

Alarid's action incensed some members of the New Mexico diputación, for he had not consulted them, but he correctly explained that distance militated against consultation. A simple territorial government, he argued, would cost less than an elaborate state government, and New Mexico needed all of its limited revenue to pay for schools, to protect itself against the United States, and "to tame and settle the multitude of barbarous nations that surround it." Chihuahua, he said, lacked sufficient resources to alleviate New Mexico's poverty. Salvation, he optimistically believed, lay with the "infinite resources" of the central government. To substantiate his argument, Alarid reported that Texas, too, was seeking territorial status and that California had already achieved it.[32]

The political maneuvering ended, then, with the provinces on the northern edge of Mexico entering the United States of Mexico without full statehood. Texas entered the republic linked to Coahuila, to form the Estado de Coahuila y Texas; Sonora remained tied to Sinaloa as the Estado de Occidente. The two provinces most distant from Mexico City, Alta California and New Mexico, entered the union as territories. Only three other regions of Mexico held that status in 1824: Baja California, Colima, and Tlascala.[33]

These new arrangements were inherently unstable. Pressures from local interests began to build almost immediately to separate Texas from Coahuila and Sonora from Sinaloa, while in New Mexico and Alta California groups began to demand greater political autonomy. But so long as the 1824 Constitution was in force, only Sonora gained autonomy. In 1830 Congress permitted the Estado de Occidente to dissolve, making Sonora and Sinaloa separate states. Today's southern Arizona, from the present border up to the Gila River, constituted the northern edge of the new state. The lands beyond the Gila, as contemporaries recognized, remained in control of the "wild tribes."[34]

From the very beginning, when the state legislature infuriated them by abolishing their diputación, *tejanos* entered into an adversary relationship with Coahuila. When General Manuel Mier y Terán inspected Texas in 1828, he reported that "between the Mexicans and the foreigners there is a most evident unity of opinion on one point, namely the separation of Texas from Coahuila."[35] Texans deplored the failure of the state government to address the unusual needs of the frontier and the great distance that isolated them from the state capital in Saltillo, described by one visitor as "ridiculously placed. . . . The distance from Saltillo to Nacogdoches in the north is about three hundred leagues, whereas lands lying fifteen leagues to the south of Saltillo no longer belong to Coahuila y Texas."[36] Mier y Terán termed the arrangement a "monstrosity," and the ayuntamiento of San Antonio, in a memorial of 1832, blamed the lack of a responsive state government for the "paralysis" of Texas.[37] An official inspector who visited Texas in 1832, Tadeo Ortiz, concluded: "I am certain that all of the ills of Texas date from its annexation to the State of Coahuila."[38]

Those who knew Texas well agreed that it should be separated from Coahuila, but no consensus existed as to the form separation should take. Many advocated statehood, especially by the 1830s, but the population of Texas still seemed too small to support a state government. Others advocated territorial status, which would shift the burden of supporting local government to Mexico City and keep taxes down, but the federal government had done a poor job of administering the other territories. In the end, local opinion did not matter. Congress failed to approve a bill in 1828 to make Texas a state, or bills in 1833–34 to make it a territory.[39]

During its first years under the 1824 Constitution, all of Texas from the Nueces to the Sabine constituted a single "Department of Béxar" of the State of Coahuila y Texas, with a political chief, or *jefe político* in San Antonio responsible to the governor in Saltillo.[40] The need for more effective administration of the rapidly growing population of East Texas prompted the state to create the District of Nacogdoches in 1831, and then to divide all of Texas into three departments in 1834: Béxar, Brazos, and Nacogdoches, with their respective capitals at San Antonio, San Felipe de Austin, and Nacogdoches. These divisions increased local autonomy to some extent because each department was governed by its own jefe político.[41] The most important decisions, however, remained the prerogative of officials in Saltillo and discontent generated by that arrangement became one of the many burrs under the saddle that led Texas to throw off Mexican rule in 1836.[42]

Politicians in the territories of Alta California and New Mexico also sought greater autonomy. Under the 1824 Constitution, territorial government fell under the direct control of Congress. Whatever advantages that might have offered, it also ran contrary to the basic federalist ideal of regional autonomy. In the preamble to the Constitution, for example, Lorenzo de Zavala, the liberal from Yucatán, and others had recognized the "enormous differences of climate, temperature, and their consequent influence" on Mexico's many regions. The preamble contrasted "the baked soil of Veracruz and the frozen mountains of New Mexico" and asked, "can you demand that the inhabitants of California and Sonora have the same institutions as Yucatán and Tamaulipas?"[43] Under the 1824 Constitution, the answer for the territories of Alta California and New Mexico was "yes."

The territories not only came directly under congressional supervision, but remarkably they also lacked regulations for internal government. The 1824 Constitution left the details of internal administration, such as regulations for municipal government, to individual states.[44] In the case of the territories, however, Congress itself had responsibility for drawing up a plan for internal government. Congress came close. A committee of the lower house approved one plan in 1828, but no plan won approval of the entire Congress throughout the dozen years the Constitution of 1824 remained in effect.[45]

As a result, the internal governments of Alta California and New Mexico continued to operate under the laws of the Spanish Cortes, sprinkled with regulations of the Mexican republic. The diputaciones and the ayuntamientos, for example, functioned well into the 1830s under regulations of 1812 and 1813.[46] Instead of calling itself the "diputación provincial," the assembly became the "diputación territorial." Instead of sending a delegate to the Cortes in Spain, the territories regularly sent representatives to the Congress in Mexico City.

This arrangement worked poorly. Local institutions, especially the diputaciones, lacked sufficient authority to function effectively, in the view of frontiersmen, and were reduced to advisory bodies. Moreover, frontier officials could never be certain which Spanish regulations were still in force or if they conflicted with the new laws of the Republic. Each side in a controversy could usually find a law to support its position. New Mexico officials, for example, began in the mid-1820s to reapportion uncultivated lands of Pueblo Indians in compliance with a law of November 9, 1812. When Pueblos from Pecos challenged them, officials had to ask the central government for clarification of the law and several years went by before the question was resolved (in favor of the Indians).[47]

From the local level to Mexico City, officials deplored the ambiguities of the laws and the failure of Congress to clarify the situation. Melquiades Antonio Ortega of New Mexico, for example, lamented in 1831 that "the old Spanish laws are seen [still] in force, many of them incompatible with our present federal system."[48] He urged Congress to attend to the matter. His sentiments were echoed by *californios*, such as Juan Bandini and Carlos Carrillo who represented California in Congress,[49] and by a series of cabinet ministers who regularly issued warnings that the matter was "more urgent by the day," and that a solution was "absolutely indispensable." As the Secretary of Internal and Foreign Affairs explained to Congress in 1829, "the laws of the Spanish Cortes . . . present many difficulties, doubts, and perhaps errors in their application, because they were made for other countries, for another kind of government, and for other circumstances very different from ours."[50] Overlapping and contradictory laws caused problems throughout the young republic,[51] but they led to an unusual degree of confusion in the two isolated frontier territories where the government could not arbitrate disputes effectively.

By the 1830s, the frustrated frontiersmen tired of waiting for Congress. Some New Mexicans drew up a plan for statehood in 1831, proposing to name the territory the State of Hidalgo. Although the plan won the endorsement of many municipalities, the territorial assembly tabled it. The *californios* never went quite that far, although they too considered a name change when Juan Bandini proposed that California be known as the Territory of Montezuma.[52] In 1834, the independent-minded California diputación drew up regulations for its own operation and submitted them to Congress for approval. This document, the first pamphlet printed in California, fell short of serving as an organic law for territorial government and apparently never won congressional approval.[53]

Thus, the federalist promise of increased local autonomy was never fully kept in the Far North, where Texas remained tied to Coahuila, and New Mexico and Alta California retained a confusing territorial status.

The frontier provinces not only failed to enjoy the same degree of home rule as the states of central Mexico, but autonomy varied from one frontier province to another, depending upon local conditions. Considerable differences in local government existed even between Alta California and New Mexico, although both came under the territorial system.

The more populous and mature Territory of New Mexico proved more fertile for representative government than did California, which had been dominated by a military regime under Spain. Liberal legislation, originating in the Spanish Cortes, prohibited a single official from serving simultaneously as *jefe militar* and *jefe político* under ordinary circumstances.[54] New Mexico, which had established the precedent of civilians serving as governors in the Spanish period, moved quickly toward separating the two offices in the 1820s, although the exigencies of frontier life required that governors hold both positions from time to time, as New Mexico leaders recognized.[55] In California, on the other hand, it remained the norm for officers to hold both military and civil commands during the federalist era.[56] Some of these officers showed scant respect for civilian rule and used their power to thwart the development of representative institutions.[57] Bautista Alvarado, one of two civilians to serve as governor in Mexican California (1836–42), later recalled that "with military authority the governors of California might carry the entire legal code about in their own mouths."[58] Two of California's representatives to Congress, Carlos Carrillo and Juan Bandini, sought unsuccessfully to divide the two commands and end what one padre termed California's "military despotism." The issue was of such importance that it contributed to insurrection in California in 1831 and in 1836.[59]

In contrast to New Mexico, where the diputación met regularly, California's diputación was nearly defunct. The California legislators met only two years out of the six between 1825 and 1831.[60] In addition to difficulties imposed by the absence of clear laws regarding the administration of the territories and the great distances that representatives had to travel along the extended coastline to attend meetings, the failure of the California diputación to meet regularly resulted from active opposition by military officers. Lt. Col. Nicolás Gutiérrez, who occupied the governor's office from 1835 to 1836, reportedly articulated the military viewpoint by remarking that he "had no need of diputados of pen and voice while he had plenty of diputados of sword and gun."[61]

New Mexico had ayuntamientos functioning in its major towns and many of its Indian Pueblos by the early 1820s, but California was much slower to embrace municipal government by civilians. Town councils had existed at Los Angeles, San Jose, and Santa Cruz in the Spanish period, but remained powerless and immature because military officers, called *comisionados*, supervised all details of town government. These officers yielded power to civilians with reluctance in the 1820s and hindered the development of municipal government. The hostility of some officers to civilian control at the local level was unmistakable, as when Lt. Col. Manuel Victoria, who served as governor in 1831, urged the abolition of all ayuntamientos in California in favor of military rule.[62]

As a result of military recalcitrance and the slow growth of the civilian population, town councils formed more slowly in Alta California than in New Mexico. By 1830 ayuntamientos existed in only four communities:

Los Angeles and San Jose (both restructured in 1822) and Santa Barbara and Monterey (both formed in 1826). Yerba Buena, which eventually grew into the city of San Francisco, did not become a pueblo until 1834.[63] The decaying presidial community of San Diego was not granted the status of a town until 1835, when the government responded to a petition from local residents who complained about the "oppression" of military government and asked for the same rights enjoyed by other citizens of the republic.[64] Also, in contrast to New Mexico, communities of Hispanicized Indians in California did not enjoy self-government because they came under the nearly complete domination of the Franciscan mission system until the mid-1830s.

A substantial difference also existed in the kind of representation that New Mexico and Alta California had in Congress. The 1824 Constitution did not allow territories a voice in the Senate, but it did permit one elected representative to serve in the chamber of deputies (*cámara de diputados*), the lower house of Congress. Representatives from territories with fewer than 40,000 residents, however, could not vote.[65] Under this rule, New Mexico could send a voting representative to the chamber of deputies, but the diputado sent from less populous California was limited to speaking on issues.

This restriction on their deputy might have contributed to the doubts that many *californios* had about the wisdom of spending territorial revenue to send a representative to Congress, and *californios* did not regularly elect a delegate in the 1820s.[66] The two who did represent them in that decade did so poorly. Through no fault of his own, Spanish-born Capt. José de la Guerra y Noriega of Santa Barbara fell victim to fierce anti-Spanish sentiment in 1828. Although he had not set foot in Spain since age thirteen, he was denied his seat in the Chamber and had to flee central Mexico incognito. Congress accepted the credentials of his Mexican-born successor, José Joaquín Maitorena, but overdoses of alcohol limited Lieutenant Maitorena's effectiveness. Not until the 1830s did California regularly send effective representatives to Congress.[67]

New Mexicans, on the other hand, sent elected deputies to Congress at regular two-year intervals during all of these years. This constituted a major expense for the territory and frequently for the diputado when the territorial treasury could not afford to pay his salary or bills.[68] Having a voting representative in Congress, however, seems to have paid back dividends for the territory as well as for the diputado. For example, *nuevomexicanos* had better luck than the *californios* at having one of their own appointed to the governorship and the influence of their diputados on these choices seems clear. Santiago Abreú, who served as diputado in 1825–26, went on to become governor in 1832–33. José Antonio Chaves, diputado for the 1827–28 term, returned home with the governorship from 1829 to 1832. Rafael Sarracino, diputado in 1831–32, may have had something to do with the appointment of his brother, Francisco, to the governorship in 1833.

If variations existed between the internal governments of California and New Mexico, both of which were territories, the differences in government were even greater between the territories and Sonora and Texas, both of which were governed by state laws. It is difficult to generalize about the particulars of government throughout the frontier in the federalist era, but the overall pattern seems clear. The federalists retained and refined the philosophy and institutions of representative regional government of the Cortes of Cádiz. As a result, frontiersmen enjoyed more autonomy than ever before. They did not have the same degree of autonomy, however, as most other Mexican states, nor as much as they might reasonably have expected under a federalist regime.

The federalist system, with the liberal-leaning 1824 Constitution as its cornerstone, crumbled and fell apart in the mid-1830s. After the dust had cleared, a conservative, centralist regime emerged that was destined to last to 1846.[69]

The liberals had faced extraordinary problems that would have destabilized any regime. With little prior experience at self-government, they sought to restructure economic, political, and social institutions in the face of disruption: recurring international crises with Spain; interference in internal political and economic affairs by England and the United States; an economy in shambles; and an intransigent political opposition that did not want to see the traditional order altered. To bolster their positions, both the liberals and their conservative opponents had turned to military strongmen for help and the military responded with a vengeance. The orderly transfer of power from one elected official to another was dealt a death blow in 1828 when the legally elected administration of Manuel Gómez Pedraza was overthrown by the supporters of Vicente Guerrero, who in turn was ousted by his own vice-president Anastasio Bustamante. A pattern of military intervention and coup and counter coup, which would endure for a half century, had been established and Mexican politics quickly won a reputation for volatility. "The political character of this country," Stephen Austin wrote in 1835, "seems to partake of its geological features—all is volcanic."[70]

With a literate population of perhaps no more than five percent, few understood why the volcanoes smoked or knew the difference between liberals and conservatives. But most did understand, as one historian has suggested, that day-to-day life had worsened "with the disappearance of the strong and well-organized colonial administrative system."[71] Little wonder, then, that conservatives who sought to restore the highly centralized Spanish system of the late colonial period would have their day.

The conservative ascendency in national politics got underway in 1834 when President Antonio López de Santa Anna ousted leading liberals from his government largely because they had proposed reforms that threatened the privileged position of two powerful and conservative institutions, the Church and the military. Fearful that the conservatives would overthrow his government, Santa Anna switched sides and joined them. With his newfound allies, he formed a congress which met in 1835 and began to restructure the government on centralist principles. In October 1835 Congress dissolved the state legislatures, placed the state governors under the direct control of the central government by making them presidential appointees, and adopted the "bases for the new constitution." Over the next year Congress hotly debated seven new constitutional measures which finally went into effect on December 30, 1836, officially replacing the 1824 Constitution.[72]

The 1836 Constitution, also known as the "Seven Laws" or the "Seven Plagues" depending on one's side of the political spectrum, remained in force only briefly. Mexican politics deteriorated further, entering an era in which the nation "constantly teetered between simple chaos and unmitigated anarchy. . . . Between May 1833 and August 1855 the presidency changed hands thirty-six times, the average term being about seven and a half months."[73] Growing opposition to the Constitution of 1836 finally coalesced around a new national charter, the Bases of Tacubaya, adopted on September 28, 1841. The Tacubaya plan abrogated the 1836 Constitution and paved the way for still another constitution, popularly known as the Bases Orgánicas, published on June 14, 1843. Even more conservative and centralized than its predecessors, the Bases Orgánicas endured through the three chaotic years preceding war with the United States—characterized as "the most turbulent period of Mexican history."[74]

On August 22, 1846, shortly after the outbreak of war, troubled politicians in Mexico City abolished the Bases and temporarily restored the Constitution of 1824.[75] That return to federalism had no effect on the northern frontier. American naval forces had already seized Monterey in Alta California in July, and on August 18, just four days before the restoration of the 1824 Constitution, the American Army of the West had marched into Santa Fe. The centralist era lasted just over a decade, from 1835 to 1846, but it would have profound repercussions on the frontier.

The centralists reorganized the frontier in important ways. The 1836 Constitution and its successors converted all states and territories of the republic into "departments." This included both Alta and Baja California, which were combined as the single Department of the Californias, and the Department of New Mexico. The conservatives also granted Texas its long-sought autonomy, elevating it in 1836 to the status of a single department, separate from Coahuila. For *tejanos,* who had successfully seceded earlier in the year from the republic and carved a new nation out of the northeastern edge of the frontier, the gesture came too late. Although the central government refused to recognize Texas's independence as an accomplished fact and looked toward the "reestablishment of order" in that rebellious area, Texas remained independent from 1836 until its annexation by the United States in 1845.[76] Thus, the centralist era saw the settled area of Mexico's Far North reduced to Alta California, New Mexico, and southern Arizona.

The centralists proceeded to restructure departmental governments throughout the nation in an effort to provide a clear chain of command from the national to the local levels. Centralization of power, they hoped, would avoid some of the centrifugal excesses of federalism and forge a more unified nation. Therefore, regulations for the internal government of the new departments called for authority to reside in the office of the governor—now called a *gobernador* instead of a jefe político—named by and responsible to the president. Each department was divided into districts (*distritos*) headed by a prefect (*prefecto*) directly responsible to the governor. Districts, in turn, were to be divided into *partidos* headed by subprefects responsible to the prefects. Finally, below partidos came urban centers and town government. By 1836, any frontier community of importance had formed an ayuntamiento. The centralists abolished most of these institutions of representative government, permitting ayuntamientos to function only in the capitals of departments, in inland towns over 8,000 and coastal towns over 4,000, or in places where an ayuntamiento had existed prior to 1808.[77]

No town on the frontier was large enough to qualify for an ayuntamiento on the basis of population, but San Antonio, Santa Fe, and Monterey met the requirements as departmental capitals. Los Angeles, San Jose, and Santa Cruz qualified because they apparently had ayuntamientos prior to 1808.[78] Towns that did not qualify for an ayuntamiento under the centralist regulations were to be governed by an appointed *juez de paz,* or justice of the peace, responsible to the subprefect.

The centralists also abolished the once-independent and popularly elected state legislatures and replaced them with smaller, less powerful bodies. The legislative branches of departmental governments were usually

seven-member juntas, chosen through indirect elections and with cir-
cumscribed powers.[79] Congress, for example, retained the right to review
their enactments and budgets. These departmental legislatures were
called *juntas departamentales* under the 1836 Constitution, and *asambleas
departamentales* under the 1843 charter, but their responsibilities and
powers remained essentially the same.[80]

The conservatives not only sought to centralize government, but to
put it in the hands of the propertied classes—the group that they perceived as most able to manage the affairs of state. Both the 1836 and 1843
constitutions limited the right to vote and to hold office to adult males of
means. The 1836 Constitution, for example, conferred full citizenship
only on those Mexicans who had an income of at least 100 pesos a year.
All Mexican citizens or noncitizens possessed certain rights and protec-
tions under the law, but only those who met minimum income requirements could vote or hold office. The prerequisites for serving on an
ayuntamiento, for example, included an annual income of at least 500
pesos per year; a deputy to Congress or member of a departmental
assembly had to make 1500 pesos annually; minimum for a governor
was 2,000 pesos. The 1843 Constitution set similar standards, but raised
the annual income requirement for the privilege of citizenship to 200
pesos a year.[81] These restrictions, coupled with the continuation of a
system of indirect elections, effectively excluded all but frontier oligarchs
from positions of political power—and even excluded some of them.

The most immediate and stunning impact of the shift from liberalism
to conservatism and from federalism to centralism was a series of revolts.
Not only Texas, but Alta California, New Mexico, and several other
departments as well, declared against the central government between
1836 and 1838. Although some frontier leaders, such as Mariano Guadalupe Vallejo of California, sympathized with the point of view that the
central government needed to exert greater control over the beleaguered
frontier provinces, prevailing opinion among the frontier políticos ran in
favor of greater home rule.[82] Many would have agreed with California's
last Mexican governor, Pío Pico, who declared that he "would die of
hunger . . . rather than abandon my [federalist] principles."[83] The revolts
of 1836–38 are of such significance and their causes so profound, that
they form the subject of a single chapter later in this study.

All of the frontier provinces except Texas eventually returned to the
fold and began to restructure their governments, following the centralist
directives. In 1837 New Mexico was divided into two districts, each
district having two partidos. In 1839, following a period of revolt and
civil wars, the Californias were divided into three districts, one embrac-
ing all of Baja California and the more populous Alta California compris-

ing two districts.[84] At the same time, ayuntamientos stopped functioning nearly everywhere except in Santa Fe and justices of the peace took their place. Here and there a few *alcaldes,* officials who had held some executive and legislative as well as judicial powers under Spain, continued to hold court. The centralist system was not set in concrete. Further restructuring occurred in the 1840s. New Mexico, for example, was divided into three districts instead of two in 1844 and the number of alcaldes began to increase in both New Mexico and California.[85] Experiments with the system continued even as war loomed with the United States.

For Alta California and New Mexico, perhaps the most important effect of the departmental system was that it perpetuated the major weakness of the territorial system: it did not provide frontier departments with sufficient autonomy. Under the conservatives, however, this happened by design and not through oversight as it had under the federalists.

California and New Mexico received less autonomy under the conservatives than did other departments, just as they had played a subordinate role to the states when they were territories. The 1843 Constitution singled out the Californias and New Mexico as needing special management because of their vulnerable situation on the frontier and granted Congress the right to intervene in their internal affairs when necessary.[86] Similarly, both the constitutions of 1836 and 1843 set up special procedures for appointing governors for frontier departments. Ordinarily a departmental assembly was to furnish a short list of candidates from which the central government would make a choice. Under the centralist constitutions, however, the central government had no obligation to appoint a governor from the lists provided by frontier departments.[87] This, of course, gave Mexico City a greater degree of control over the frontier departments and may have represented a lack of faith in the locals to govern themselves as well as a recognition that the frontier required special treatment. Authorities had learned from General José de Figueroa, when he served as governor of California in 1833, that none of the *californios* were "even tolerably qualified for the office" of governor; similar reports probably reached Mexico City from other frontier provinces.[88]

Under these circumstances, military men who were not native to the frontier continued to be appointed to governorships and to win opprobrium for their lack of knowledge and scant sympathy for local conditions. In 1846, on the eve of war with the United States, Donaciano Vigil of New Mexico penned a vigorous protest against the policy of naming outsiders to positions of civil or military leadership and reviewed the terms of two governors sent by the centralists, Colonel Albino Pérez and

General Mariano Martínez. Vigil credited Pérez (1835–37) with "good intentions," but condemned "his lack of practical knowledge of the character, interests and traditional customs of New Mexicans, causing him to make mistakes which brought us days so bitter. . . ." Vigil dismissed Martínez as distinguishing himself "for his great ignorance of our situation and relations with neighboring heathen tribes."[89] In California the centralist appointees who served as governor in these years, Col. Mariano Chico (1836), Lt. Col. Nicolás Gutiérrez (1836), and Gen. Manuel Micheltorena (1842–45), failed to win the hearts of the *californios* and, like Pérez of New Mexico, were overthrown.[90]

Resentment toward the central government mounted as frontiersmen saw key decisions, which affected every part of their lives, being made by outsiders or by *políticos* in a faraway capital. Did the central government know enough about local conditions to meet the special needs of the frontier? It appeared not. The requirements that set a minimum income for office holders, for example, showed little understanding of economic conditions on the frontier. New Mexicans found it difficult to find qualified people to fill all the positions in the departmental assembly, and one visitor to the Californias, Capt. Andrés Castillero, noted that no one "has the capital indicated by law, in order to become governor, senator or deputy" under the 1836 Constitution and that "some allowances should be made."[91]

The central government also displayed insensitivity to frontier economic realities when it increased the number of salaried officials under the departmental system. The new laws put prefects, subprefects, and even members of the assembly on departmental payrolls and the always impecunious local treasuries fell deeper into debt. At times the New Mexico assembly did not meet for lack of funds and some of New Mexico's leading citizens went so far as to urge that the department be converted back to territorial status because it could not afford departmental government.[92] The *californios* simply dismantled the expensive system. In 1843, with the departmental treasury containing all of four *reales*— about fifty cents—Governor Manuel Micheltorena convoked the departmental junta, which effected a savings by temporarily abolishing the offices of the prefect and subprefect, eliminating several judgeships, and reducing salaries of other officials.[93]

In fact if not in theory, the departmental system designed by the centralists resembled the territorial structure of the federalists. Even the departmental assemblies, although they showed occasional sparks of independence, resembled the territorial *diputaciones* in that they remained small (seven members) and weak. Manuel Castañares, who represented the Californias in Congress in 1844, described the powers of these assemblies as "so slight and restricted that these bodies can do little good to benefit their localities."[94]

Thus, like federalism before it, centralism served the frontier poorly. Neither centralists nor federalists granted frontiersmen sufficient autonomy to deal effectively with local problems. Both the federalists and the centralists sought to maintain control over the frontier and reserved for the central government the right to make key decisions, but failed to implement them. Nowhere was that failure clearer than in the case of the judicial system, which some contemporaries regarded as the foundation of good government.[95]

Under Spain, the judiciary had functioned poorly on the frontier, with no level of justice higher than local courts, presided over by alcaldes empowered to treat only minor civil and criminal cases. Cases involving large sums of money, important issues, or the appeal of an alcalde's decision required a journey of extraordinary length to a higher court in Guadalajara or Mexico City. The high cost of travel—both in time and money—put appellate courts out of the reach of most pobladores, and the cost of justice often exceeded its rewards even for the well-to-do. The poor quality of local courts aggravated the situation. Local alcaldes often knew little of the law and some were corrupt. In California and Texas military officers often rendered legal decisions and earned a reputation as capricious and "absolutely ignorant of the simplest ideas of law."[96] Under independent Mexico, change began, but more in theory than in practice.

In the federalist era a series of new laws addressed the judicial problems that afflicted the frontier. An 1812 act of the Cortes of Cádiz, reenacted in 1833, required that judges learned in the law (*jueces letrados*) be available for residents of even the most remote communities.[97] The 1824 Constitution and subsequent acts provided that in New Mexico and Alta California district courts be established to hear cases involving large sums of money or serious crimes, or to take appeals beyond the local alcalde.[98] Beyond the district courts, appeals could be taken to circuit courts located near the edge of the frontier—New Mexico, for example, became part of a circuit which included Durango and Chihuahua under an 1826 law.[99] Thus, only the most serious case would need to be appealed all the way to Mexico City. Moreover, federalist legislation profoundly altered the legal system by creating an independent judiciary, separate from other branches of government. Whereas the Spanish system had blended the three traditional branches of government—executive, legislative, and judicial—the federalists specifically separated them and prohibited one person or one body from holding more than one of these powers.[100] Following the liberal model of the Cortes of Cádiz, federalist laws also prohibited military officers from hearing civil cases, as had commonly occurred on the frontier. The 1824 Constitution also maintained one of the contradictions endorsed by the Cádiz liberals. While maintaining the equality of all citizens before the law, the Constitution preserved the privilege, or *fuero,* of the military and the clergy to be exempt from civil courts and to be tried by their own tribunals. This fuero remained intact through most of the Mexican period.[101]

Despite its good intentions, the central government simply lacked the means to implement the new judicial system throughout the republic. Significant reforms reached as far north as the State of Chihuahua, but did not make serious inroads in the territories of Alta California and New Mexico.[102] Instead, a litany of complaints drifted back to Mexico City from the territories in the 1820s and early 1830s: the district courts required by law had not been established; the frontier still lacked trained lawyers (those who came stayed too briefly to have an effect); and marginally literate alcaldes with no training in the law continued to preside over the courts.[103] As Pablo Montoya of New Mexico modestly explained, all of the alcaldes "with the exception of myself and one other . . . lack the necesary knowledge of the method of holding a trial."[104] Chihuahua-born attorney Antonio Barreiro thought that the scarcity of literate and trained judges was so serious that it threatened the very ability of "free institutions" to function on the frontier.[105]

Thus, the independent and efficient judiciary that the federalists sought to establish never became a reality on the northern frontier. Alcaldes continued to exercise executive and legislative as well as judicial power. One visitor to California described the alcalde as a combination of "a mayor and a justice of the peace,"[106] and he might have added a city councilman as well because alcaldes also served on the town councils. For lack of higher courts in the territories, the governors continued to serve as "a sort of court of appeals," according to Barreiro, and military officials continued to hear cases in California.[107] In short, although Mexican legislation created a new judiciary on paper, a modified Spanish system remained in force in practice in the territories of Alta California and New Mexico throughout the federalist era.[108]

Texas shared many of the problems that plagued the frontier territories, even though it was part of the State of Coahuila: lack of trained judges and legal advisors, and extraordinary distance to the nearest appellate court in Saltillo, the state capital. The ayuntamiento of San Antonio explained the problem plainly in 1832: "the judicial branch [of government] has never been properly organized, and it can be said with good reason that in regard to this branch that there is not, nor has there

been government in Texas."[109] A judicial reform act approved by the
state legislature on April 17, 1834, established an appellate circuit court
in Texas, increased the number of local courts, and provided for trial by
jury in both civil and criminal cases. Although many liberals had favored
a jury system for Mexico, only a few states adopted the idea, Coahuila-
Texas being one of them.[110] The 1834 reform act might have improved
the administration of justice substantially in Texas, had it not become
lost in the events leading to the Texas revolt.

From Texas to California, then, the federalists failed to establish a
satisfactory judicial system. The centralists recognized the problem and
addressed it with sweeping legislation, but the results were modest.
Under the 1836 Constitution and subsequent acts, the centralists sought:
to extend the number of justices at the local level and increase their
efficiency; to create appellate courts in New Mexico and Alta California—
courts of the first instance (*juzgados de primera instancia*) and superior
courts (*tribunales superiores*); and to grant judicial functions to governors
and prefects.[111] These reforms brought some improvements, but a considerable gap remained between the good intentions expressed by legislation and its implementation on the frontier. By the mid-1840s, after a
decade of sometimes vacillating centralist policies, appellate courts had
begun to operate on the frontier, but on an irregular basis. The frontier
still lacked a sufficient number of *jueces de letras* to fill judicial positions,
and in California military officers continued to administer justice when
civil courts failed to function.[112]

The centralists' failure to revamp the judicial system probably strengthened the authority of local alcaldes.[113] Whatever their limitations, alcaldes often represented the only justice on the frontier. Indeed, for lack of
learned judges, the senior alcalde in a district might also double as the
Judge of the Court of First Instance. Until the end of the Mexican period,
then, minor civil and criminal cases continued to be heard by alcaldes
who had no formal training in the law and who largely followed traditional procedures dating back to the Spanish era. Under the centralist
regulations, for example, alcaldes treated disputes either through a process of nonbinding arbitration or through a process of binding verbal
decisions. With either method, the alcalde could receive advice from two
hombres buenos, arbitrators chosen by each party to the dispute. One
contemporary described the use of hombres buenos as "the nearest
approximation that is made to trial by jury," but no jury system such as
Anglo-Americans knew operated on the frontier.[114]

Whatever improvements occurred in the administration of justice under
independent Mexico, they remained insufficient to please either the
frontiersmen or the growing number of foreigners who came to the

region to do business. Josiah Gregg, an American merchant who traded in Santa Fe in the 1830s and early 1840s, echoed the sentiments of many of his countrymen when he wrote that "little or rather no attention is paid to any code of laws; in fact, there is scarcely one alcalde in a dozen who knows what a law is, or who ever saw a lawbook."[115] The Englishman, Sir George Simpson, who was in California in 1842, succinctly expressed the sentiments of many foreigners: "the judicial system is rotten to the core."[116]

Throughout Mexico, as contemporaries agreed, the administration of justice remained chaotic in the decades following independence. Lack of a "clear and precise legal code," one Mexican liberal complained, made the judicial process "long and costly" and confirmed the adage that "a bad agreement is worth more than a good lawsuit."[117] But it seems fair to conclude that if guarantees of life and property were weak in central Mexico, they were all the weaker on the northern frontier with its distance from appellate courts, shortage of attorneys and judges trained in the law, and welter of confusing and contradictory laws.

The judicial system provides just one example of the failure of the new politics, whether under liberal or conservative administrations, to deal effectively with frontier problems. One result of that failure was a growing discontent among frontier políticos who condemned the central government for neglecting them. "Hopes and promises are only what it [New Mexico] has received . . . from its mother country," Mariano Chávez, President of the New Mexico Assembly, wrote in 1844.[118] Mariano Guadalupe Vallejo of California deplored not only government neglect but, he added, "when the paternal government of the Mexican Republic remembered us, it did so in such a way as to fill us with dismay."[119]

The neglect and insensitivity that Chávez and other frontier leaders experienced seemed a result of the failure of the central government to put its own political house in order. From California to Texas, frontiersmen recognized that political turmoil in Mexico City since independence had prevented the central government from addressing problems on the frontier. As one New Mexican bitterly complained, "Mexico has never been able to protect us because, unfortunately, of continuous revolts . . . opportunism has smashed the union to pieces."[120]

Although frontier politicians continued to request help from the central government, they also continued to seek greater local autonomy until the end of the Mexican era. In mid-1845, for example, the California assembly asked for a return to the federalist system and the 1824 Constitution.[121] Failing to achieve autonomy through legal means, frontier políticos often accomplished it extralegally by simply ignoring or disobeying federal regulations. They neglected to send in annual reports required by law, or to seek congressional approval for local rules and regulations, or to pay assessments, or to enforce national tariff regulations.[122] The gap between law and practice probably widened during the Mexican era as pobladores grew more disaffected with the central government and implicitly questioned the legitimacy of laws, institutions, and politicians who upheld them.

The tendency of frontier officials to bend or break unpopular national laws, coupled with the kaleidoscopic changes of laws and governments in Mexico City, confirmed the prejudices of many foreigners that Mexicans lacked the capacity to govern themselves. "The government of California," wrote one American visitor in the 1840s, "has been, like all Mexican governments, very lax and inefficient . . . and infinitely worse than none."[123] Mexico's political turmoil convinced many foreigners, and frontiersmen as well, that "nothing more is wanted but just equal laws & a good government; yes any government that can be permanent & combine the confindence [sic] & goodwill of those who think."[124] If Mexico could not effectively govern her Far North, it became very clear by the 1840s that some other government would.

After a quarter-century of Mexican rule, then, the new politics had brought profound change to the frontier in the form of more representative institutions and greater political autonomy than had existed under Spain, but instability and unresponsiveness also characterized the new politics. Results had not kept pace with heightened expectations. As a result, the specter of separatism, which had first worried Spanish officials in the late colonial period, grew more menacing under independent Mexico as frontiersmen questioned the legitimacy of political leaders and institutions and wondered if political ties to Mexico benefited them. The message reached politicians in Mexico City from a variety of sources in unequivocal language. Manuel Castañares, for example, urged the government to reorganize the judicial system in the Californias because "without a doubt that would contribute to the growth of a spirit of nationality that would keep California united to the republic, in opposition to the ideas that have been ingeniously introduced to separate from the nation this interesting and rich portion of the territory."[125]

By 1846 the northern frontier was woven less firmly into the political fabric of the young nation than ever before. Texas had revolted a decade before and its annexation by the United States in 1845 would contribute to an international war. In Alta California and New Mexico disaffection with Mexico had grown to serious proportions, noticeable even to the casual visitor. But the forces that fed frontier separatism during these years were not just political. Thoughtful frontiersmen had also witnessed a weakening of economic, military, cultural, and religious ties to Mexico following independence from Spain. The military and the Church in particular, those twin bastions of Spanish institutional strength in the Far North during the Spanish era, became caught up in the new politics and lost much of their effectiveness on the frontier in the decades following Mexican independence, as we shall see.

3

The Collapse of the Missions

The [government] wants the Indians to be private owners of
lands and of other property; this is just. The Indians, however, want the freedom of vagabonds. The [non-Indians] want
the absolute liberation and emancipation of the neophytes
. . . in order that they may avail themselves of their lands and
other property as well as of their persons. I do not see how
these opposing interests can be harmonized. —Fray Narciso
Durán, *Alta California, 1833*

"It seems likely," one California Franciscan wrote in 1822, "that these
missions will fall to pieces within a few years."[1] His words were prophetic. Within a decade and a half, the last missions of Arizona, New
Mexico, and Texas, as well as those of California, had slipped from
Franciscan control. Indians deserted the missions, buildings began to
decay, fields lay fallow, orchards went untended, and the once common
sight of the robed and sandaled Franciscans became little more than a
memory in many frontier communities.

Although missions had been the key institution for expansion of the
frontier under Spain, they began to decline in the late eighteenth century and their complete collapse occurred under independent Mexico.
Much has been written about the establishment and operation of the
missions and their vital role in pushing the frontier north, but little has
been said about their disintegration. An examination of their demise
sheds considerable light on social, economic, political, and ideological
forces in Mexico and especially on its northern frontier where most
missions were located in 1821.[2] The long-term effects of divesting the
missionaries of control over mission lands were profound, especially in

California where the missions were most vigorous and where efforts to dismantle them were most strenuous and complex.

At the dawn of Mexican independence, the future of the frontier missions seemed bleak. Most immediately, the ten-year struggle for Mexican independence had disrupted the mission economies. Government aid to the distant northern missions had all but stopped by the mid-1810s as Spanish officials diverted resources to crushing rebel forces and stopped sending the padres' annual stipends (*sínodos*) and monies for supplies. Following independence, the economic situation remained dismal. The national treasury was often empty and traditional sources of funds, such as income from estates, mortgages, and contributions from wealthy and pious individuals, had become undependable.[3]

Loss of income was not the only cross the padres bore as a result of the turbulent struggle for independence. Government aid no longer reached the frontier military garrisons, so troops appropriated supplies and food from the missions and depleted still further the Franciscans' dwindling resources. At the already impoverished Texas missions, the few remaining friars claimed to be near starvation by 1822; most of their neophytes had left. In Alta California, where relatively young missions prospered more than anywhere else on the northern frontier, troops drained the mission economies but did not destroy them. By 1820, according to their own reckoning, Franciscans in Alta California had furnished nearly one half million pesos in supplies to the military and to government officials.[4] "Words are hardly adequate to describe the sacrifices and hardships of the missions since the year 1810," Fray José Señán wrote in 1819. The missions, he said, "have been the support and pillar of the province."[5]

The war for independence also hindered the Franciscans' ability to enlist new recruits. Instead of training Mexicans for the priesthood, the Order had depended almost entirely on Spain as a source of new priests. By 1820, however, few Spaniards wanted to go to the rebellious colony. That year the Franciscan College of Querétaro sent a representative to Spain in search of thirty new priests, but found only four willing to return to Mexico with him.[6]

Strained relations between Spain and Mexico in the 1820s probably made recruiting difficult. The shortage of priests in Mexico grew critical in the late 1820s, as aftershocks of the independence struggle heightened Mexican xenophobia against Spaniards. In 1827 and again in 1829 the government ordered Spanish residents of the republic, with few exceptions, to leave.[7] On the frontier, the expulsion of the Spaniards hit hardest at the Pimería Alta missions of present Arizona, leaving it practically without priests. Yet, the expulsion had no effect on Texas, which was served by only two Mexican-born Franciscans. In California and New Mexico the orders did not strike with full force because local officials balked at enforcing them. To expel the Spanish-born Franciscans would have been easy, but who would replace them? Three of New Mexico's five Spanish-born friars left the province voluntarily. Some of Alta California's twenty-five Spanish-born friars would have left, too, but Governor José María de Echeandía refused to issue them passports.[8]

The departure of most Spanish-born Franciscans during the revolt and its aftermath made its greatest impact on Mexico's five Franciscan colleges. The College of San Fernando in Mexico City, which had furnished all of the padres for Alta California's twenty-one coastal missions up to that time, and the College of Santa Cruz de Querétaro, which staffed the Pimería Alta missions, were both nearly closed by the end of the 1820s for lack of priests. Those colleges could no longer send replacements to the frontier for friars who grew aged, infirm, or died. Only the College of Guadalupe at Zacatecas, the largest of the five, seems to have recruited enough Mexican-born priests to continue operations in Texas and take up some of the slack in California.[9]

The impact of the struggle for independence on funds and priests constituted a serious threat to the continuance of missions on the frontier of independent Mexico. More profoundly threatening, however, were ideological pressures, which had been building up for decades.

A humanistic tradition that argued against the natural inferiority of Indians and in favor of the equality of Indians with other men had powerfully influenced Spanish thought since the sixteenth century. In the glow of the Enlightenment, eighteenth-century Spanish liberals rekindled the spark of humanism and combined it with an anticlericism that spelled trouble for the frontier missions.[10] The most dramatic manifestation of this new spirit had been the Crown's 1767 order to expel the Jesuits throughout Spain and her empire—an action inspired more by politics, however, than by ideology. As a result, officials removed Jesuits from their missions in Pimería Alta and replaced them with Franciscans, who inadvertently acquired a monopoly of the entire mission field from California to Texas.

In the late eighteenth century the Franciscans came under increasing pressure to secularize their missions. Secularization had always been the eventual goal of missionization, although the law specified no precise time for that to occur.[11] Secularization meant the replacement of state-supported missionaries from religious orders (regular clergy), whose task had been to propagate the faith, with parish-supported priests or *curas* (secular clergy), who would be responsible for the preservation of the faith. As missions became parishes, Indians would cease being wards and become parishioners and taxpayers—no small matter for the royal exchequer. Moreover, parishioners would assume support of the priest through the payment of *diezmos* or tithes, and other fees, thereby ending the government's responsibility to send annual sínodos to the missionaries. Secularization also implied that Indian communal property, held in trust by missionaries, would be returned to the Indians and the surplus would enter the public domain.

In theory, secularization seemed compatible with the goals of the Franciscans who saw their purpose, as one put it, in "denaturalizing" the Indians and transforming "a savage race . . . into a society that is human, Christian, civil, and industrious."[12] Having "civilized" the Indians, the Franciscans would turn them over to parish priests and move on to work among a new group of "savages."

In practice this seldom occurred. Franciscans consistently pronounced neophytes unfit and unready to take their place in Hispanic society. Indians, the padres reported, did not place sufficient value on private property, thrift, or hard work and would either "eagerly return to their former unrestricted habits" or become victimized by rapacious settlers.[13]

Whether the Franciscans' goal of Hispanizing Indians could have succeeded is another matter. Some contemporaries argued that acculturation would not take place because the missions kept Indians apart from other members of society.[14] Certainly the fact that the padres represented a minority trying to "denaturalize" a majority made the padres' task of directing cultural change more difficult. When they failed to alter Indian culture, some Franciscans blamed Indian obstinacy rather than questioning the goal. After forty years of experience with California Indians, Fray Narciso Durán wrote in 1845: "The Indians, in my opinion, do not deserve to be directed by a missionary. A slavedriver is what they ought to have."[15] The padres commonly compared Indians with "children" and termed them inferior and incapable of change. Fray Vicente Francisco de Sarría, for example, described the California Indians as possessing "congenital idleness" and a "natural repugnance . . . for work."[16] Such negative attitudes by persons who today we would identify as role models and teachers for Indians might have constituted what educators now term a "self-fulfilling prophecy." That is to say that regardless of a student's ability, his achievements seldom exceed his teacher's expectations.

In practice, then, many of the Indians who accepted the faith had to be forcibly held in missions through corporal punishment and few seemed ready to live as equals among non-Indians.[17] Franciscans gave up missions only in areas where the lack of cooperation by Indians or the decimation of their numbers by European diseases—a commonplace occurrence—made mission communities unworkable.

Notwithstanding objections from Franciscans, the process of secularization began in fits and starts in late eighteenth-century Texas, New Mexico, and Pimería Alta. That process nearly came to an abrupt end on September 13, 1813 when the liberal Spanish Cortes ordered the immediate conversion of all missions, ten years old or older, into parishes. Mission lands were to be distributed to Indians who would manage them for themselves. When Ferdinand VII regained control of the government in 1814, however, the 1813 decree was among the acts of the Cortes that he nullified.[18]

The 1813 secularization order continued to haunt the Franciscans, nonetheless. The last Spanish viceroy in Mexico restored the order in 1821, and when Mexico's liberator, Agustín de Iturbide, proclaimed independence he retained in force all acts of the liberal Cortes that did not affect Mexican sovereignty. Thus, in the years following independence, officials continued to regard the September 13, 1813 decree as still applicable, and it threatened the very existence of the frontier missions.[19]

For many thinkers, both in Spain and in Mexico, the idea of the equality of men had made the missions outmoded. The Spanish Cortes had declared "the social and civil equality of Spaniards, Indians and mestizos," and Iturbide echoed those sentiments in his Plan of Iguala in 1821, proclaiming that all Mexicans, "without any distinction of European, African, or Indian, are citizens." The following year, 1822, the Mexican government prohibited the identification of persons according to race in public and private documents. Soon after, the Constitution of 1824 affirmed the equality of *all* Mexicans, without mentioning Indians specifically.[20] In practice, of course, these strokes of the pen did not eliminate racial distinctions, which continued to appear in public documents, nor did they eliminate discrimination or exploitation. Nonetheless, such statements of the ideal of equality could be held up as evidence that the missions had fallen from fashion and, indeed, implicitly violated the nation's constitution.[21] In 1830, for example, the liberal philosopher Tadeo Ortiz condemned the missions as a "monstrous regime suited to the era of fanaticism of the Spanish people [which] cannot fit in with modern politics and much less with our social institutions."[22]

In the view of some liberals, missions not only represented antiquated institutions that oppressed Indians, but missions also aided the Church in amassing immense wealth and property and maintaining its influence in secular affairs. Undercutting the Church's economic power, those liberals reasoned, would also lessen its political influence, free capital for investment, and bring vast tracts of Church-controlled lands back into

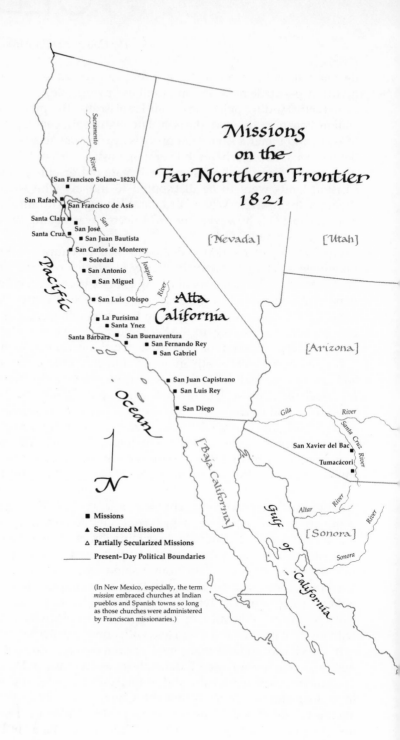

Missions
on the
Far Northern Frontier
1821

[Nevada]   [Utah]

Sacramento River

[San Francisco Solano–1823]
■
San Rafael ■
San Francisco de Asís
Santa Clara ■
San José ■
Santa Cruz ■   San
San Juan Bautista ■
San Carlos de Monterey ■
■ Soledad
■ San Antonio
■ San Miguel

Joaquín River

Alta
California

[Arizona]

Pacific

■ San Luis Obispo
■ La Purísima
■ Santa Ynez
Santa Bárbara ■   San Buenaventura
■   ■ San Fernando Rey
■ San Gabriel

■ San Juan Capistrano
■ San Luis Rey
■ San Diego

Ocean

Gila   River

Santa Cruz River

San Xavier del Bac ■
Tumacácori ■

N

[Baja California]

Altar   River

Gulf

of

Sonora   [Sonora]

California

■ Missions
▲ Secularized Missions
△ Partially Secularized Missions
____ Present-Day Political Boundaries

(In New Mexico, especially, the term
mission embraced churches at Indian
pueblos and Spanish towns so long
as those churches were administered
by Franciscan missionaries.)

Inset (top):

Chama River

Abiquiú
Las Trampas ■ ■ Picuris
San Juan ■ ■ Chimayó
Santa Clara ■ Santa Cruz
de la Cañada
San Ildefonso ■ Pojoaque ■
■ Nambé
■ Tesuque

[Colorado]

Rio Grande

[Kansas]

▲ SANTA FE
Cochití ■ Pecos
(abandoned) ■
■ Santo Domingo
San Miguel del Bado ■
■ San Felipe

[Oklahoma]

Main map (left):

Chama River

Taos Pueblo ■
■ Taos
▲ Santa Cruz
Jémez ■
Zia ■
Santa Ana ■ ■ Sandia
Laguna ■ ▲ Albuquerque
Zuñi ■ ■ Isleta
Ácoma ■ ■ Tomé
■ Belén

▲ SANTA FE

New Mexico

Pecos

Rio

▲ EL PASO DEL NORTE

Grande River

[Chihuahua]

[Coahuila]

Inset (right):

● ■▲ San Antonio de Valero
(Alamo)
SAN ANTONIO

△ Concepción

San

SAN ANTONIO
MISSIONS

San José △

Antonio

1 mile

San Juan △

River

San Francisco de la Espada △

Texas

Sabine
River

Lower right:

San
San Antonio de Valero (Alamo)
▲
Antonio
Espíritu Santo
SAN ANTONIO
River ■
Rosario (abandoned) ■
Refugio ■

the public domain.[23] Liberal antipathy to the frontier missions did not translate into consistent policy, however, because the liberals held power tentatively and sporadically, and conservatives generally favored retention of the missions.

To the consternation of some Franciscans, the government vacillated wildly in its efforts to enforce the law of September 13, 1813.[24] The liberal administration of Valentín Gómez Farías, for example, ordered an immediate end to all missions in the republic in a decree of April 16, 1834.[25] Gómez Farías soon fell from power, however, and his instructions had little effect on the frontier except in California. On the other hand, a decade later when the missions were largely dismantled, a conservative government with Antonio López de Santa Anna at the helm, took the opposite approach. Santa Anna called for the Jesuits, expelled in 1767, to return and establish missions throughout the northern frontier. "Force and conquest," he argued, "have not been sufficient in over 300 years to introduce civilized ways to the barbarous tribes that still inhabit some of our border Departments." Santa Anna wanted to use Jesuit missions as an instrument for Indian control and "in this way better assure the integrity of our territory."[26] Nothing came of Santa Anna's initiative, but his argument, so reminiscent of earlier Spanish policy, suggests the ideological distance between liberals and conservatives on this issue and the depth of confusion on the federal level.

The policies of the federal government, the effect of the war of independence on the mission economies, the shortage of priests, and ideological opposition all contributed mightily to the rapid deterioration of the frontier missions under independent Mexico. Of great importance, too, were local conditions: the vitality of individual missions and the size of their neophyte population; the demands of non-Indians for mission property; and attitudes of local officials toward the continuation of the missions as a form of Indian control. These varied from one locale to another and determined the uneven tempo of secularization processes.

An understanding of the disintegration of the frontier missions, then, requires a consideration of circumstances peculiar to each frontier province. Compared to California, for example, secularization of the missions in Arizona, New Mexico, and Texas in the 1820s moved along swiftly and without major disruptions of local economies. In those areas, the missions had already declined substantially prior to independence. Nonetheless, the scenario varied from place to place revealing substantial differences in local circumstances.

At the time of Mexican independence, the Santa Cruz Valley of today's Arizona represented the northern edge of Pimería Alta—a mission prov-

ince that covered both sides of the present United States-Mexican border. Six of the eight Pimería Alta missions were situated south of today's
border, in Sonora. Two missions, San Xavier del Bac and San José de
Tumacácori, lay in today's Arizona, nestled along the Santa Cruz River
between Tucson and Nogales, and separated by some thirty miles. Never
prosperous, these former Jesuit missions had been threatened sporadically by secularization ever since the Franciscans assumed their management in 1768.[27] The struggle for independence further weakened
them, as had the dramatic decline of the local Pima population, due
largely to European disease.[28] By recruiting Pápago neophytes, however, the padres kept the missions functioning. In 1820 the padres reckoned the number of neophytes attached to all eight Pimería Alta missions
at 1,127. Meanwhile, however, the number of non-Indians in the region
had more than doubled since 1800, climbing to 2,291 in 1820.[29] The
encroachment of non-Indians on mission lands had caused the padres
constant concern.

Until the 1820s, periodic efforts to secularize the Pimería Alta missions
had crashed on hard realities. Many frontier officials recognized that the
Franciscans helped control Indians and that missions produced grain,
livestock, and other goods. Moreover, experimentation had not revealed
an alternative to the traditional mission system. Nor were curas available to replace the Franciscans. Thus, while the temper of the times
suggested that missions were a thing of the past, the Franciscans had
withstood efforts to divest them of their Indian wards and properties.
Indeed, some Franciscans clung to the century-old hope of expanding
missions farther north in Arizona to the Gila River and west to the
Colorado. It was not a pipe dream. The idea still had the support of
important officials in the 1820s, including the state governor, who saw
missions as a tool to advance the frontier, control Indians, and aid in
opening a road to California.[30]

Thus, expansion rather than contraction still seemed possible in the
1820s for Franciscans in Arizona, and officials recognized that missions
filled a special need. Perhaps for those reasons, officials under independent Mexico did not try to apply the secularization order of September 13, 1813 to Pimería Alta, and when the liberal Gómez-Farías
government ordered all missions in the Republic secularized in 1834,
local officials waived the order. The missions crumbled nonetheless in
the area of today's Arizona, but their decline did not come about as a
result of deliberate policy. Instead, in one historian's vivid phrase, secularization occurred "by default."[31]

When the federal government ordered the expulsion of Spaniards
from Mexico on December 20, 1827, the Pimería Alta missions suffered a

blow from which they never recovered. Many Spanish-born Franciscans serving on the frontier might have been exempted from this decree on the basis of their age, health, or utility to the nation. Indeed, civil officials in the Estado de Occidente, of which today's Arizona was a part, made no effort to enforce the decree, but military officers did. *Comandante de armas* Mariano Paredes Arrillaga had heard rumors that the padres at Tumacácori and Bac were inciting mission Indians to revolt. During Holy Week of 1828 Paredes ordered a small force to remove all Spanish-born priests from Pimería Alta. At Tumacácori, troops seized Fray Ramón Liberós and escorted him away, leaving behind an unfinished church. At Bac, young Fray Rafael Díaz met the same fate.

Never again while Arizona belonged to Mexico would these two missions have resident priests. As the two grayrobes, Liberós and Díaz, rode southward, they paused along the way to marry anxious couples who feared they might not see a priest again soon. Although some settlers coveted mission lands, most apparently regretted the departure of the Franciscans.[32]

Only two Franciscans remained to serve all of Pimería Alta. Surprisingly, one was Spanish-born Rafael Díaz, who had become a naturalized Mexican citizen. In the summer of 1828, following his expulsion from Bac that spring, Díaz managed to return to the frontier to wait out the wave of anti-Spanish feeling that had crested in Mexico. Fray Rafael made his headquarters at Tucson, where he served as presidio chaplain, and rode the circuit up and down the Santa Cruz Valley. He dispensed the sacraments both north and south of the present-day border at places such as the presidio at Tubac and the disabled missions of Bac and Tumacácori, where a few Indians hung on. In the early 1830s Fray Rafael moved his headquarters south of the present border and Arizona lost its only resident priest. Thereafter, locals received only occasional visits from Díaz and others. The last Spanish Franciscan to serve in Pimería Alta, Rafael Díaz, died in 1841 at age forty-six. He had tried, but failed, to win a transfer to New Mexico; if he had sought the move because he thought conditions were better in New Mexico, he was mistaken.[33]

In addition to losing a resident priest during these years, the Arizona missions also saw their worldly wealth disappear. Immediately after the expulsion of the Spanish-born Franciscans from Pimería Alta in 1828, the state government had placed mission properties under the care of lay overseers, or *mayordomos.* Their alleged corruption, combined with intensified raids by Apaches, left the mission properties irreparably damaged. By 1830 herds had diminished, fields lay neglected, property had disappeared or been destroyed, and Indians had drifted away. Displeased with the turn of events, officials of the newly created state of Sonora ordered in 1830 that mission properties be transferred back to the Franciscans. These officials apparently believed that only the missions could control Indians and furnish supplies for the presidios and settlers.[34]

But the clock could not be turned back. The Franciscan College of Querétaro was short of manpower and in no position to take charge again. In 1839 the Father President of the Pimería Alta missions, Faustino González, reported to the governor that the mission properties remained "in hopeless disorder . . . up for grabs to all." González asked the governor to secularize all the missions except San Xavier del Bac; however, neither the governor nor the bishop wanted the responsibility. Finally, in 1842 the College of Querétaro withdrew its remaining Franciscans without official permission, to the annoyance of the bishop. After 1843 no Franciscan remained in all of Pimería Alta and the spiritual care of the residents of the Santa Cruz Valley was neglected except for occasional visits by secular priests.[35] Secularization of the Pimería Alta missions, then, did not occur by design. Indeed, during most of these years frontier officials generally sought to maintain the missions.

In contrast to Arizona, secularization of the Texas missions came about as a result of specific orders from the federal government. As weak as the Arizona missions were, missions in Texas were weaker. Few Indians remained at Texas missions in the 1820s and the Franciscans, who came from the College of Zacatecas, could not make a good case for holding on to the nearly abandoned mission lands.

By the time of Mexican independence many Texas missions had been completely abandoned. Although they once extended east to Louisiana and north to San Sabá, the only active missions by the 1820s were in the area of San Antonio and Goliad. Those missions clung so precariously to life that when pressures to secularize them grew in the 1820s, they succumbed easily.

The five stone missions located in and around San Antonio once had been the most prosperous in Spanish Texas. By the time of independence, they had been partially secularized, nearly abandoned by neophytes, and served by just one Franciscan. Closest to the town and just across the river stood the Mission San Antonio de Valero, better known today as the Alamo. It had been completely secularized in 1793 and its communicants absorbed into the town parish. From 1801 to 1825 the old buildings of this former mission served as an encampment for soldiers and their families attached to a cavalry unit, the Flying Company of San José y Santiago del Alamo de Parras, and from this the structure acquired its new name. After the cavalry abandoned the Alamo in 1825, it continued to deteriorate to such an extent that the *tejanos* and Americans who died defending it in 1836 apparently did not know they had taken refuge inside the walls of a former mission.[36]

Four more missions lie along the river to the south of San Antonio: Concepción, San José, San Juan Capistrano, and San Francisco de la Espada. In 1794 all had been partially secularized and some of their property alloted to the few remaining neophytes. The Franciscans had offered no opposition to partial secularization of the four missions. To the contrary, the father president of the Texas missions urged their secularization because the Coahuiltecan groups whom they served had received full instruction and the missions stood little chance of attracting new converts.[37] Following this partial secularization in the 1790s, non-Indians moved onto the mission lands and the remaining Indians apparently assimilated into the Mexican population. One visitor in 1819, for example, remarked that no Indians remained at missions San José and Concepción: "if there are any, they are but few in number and changed into castes [mixed bloods] by mixture with the settlers of Béxar."[38]

At the time of secularization, Texas missions fell under the jurisdiction of the Diocese of Nuevo León, whose bishop permitted Franciscans to remain in charge because he could find no secular priests to replace them. During their last years, 1820 to 1825, a lone Franciscan, Fray José Antonio Díaz de León, described by one contemporary as "an industrious, disinterested man, adored by the indigenes," served the four San Antonio missions from his headquarters at Mission San José.[39] The Mexican-born Fray José, destined to become the last Franciscan in Hispanic Texas, also served as president of the Texas missions, supervising the activities of one other missionary, Fray Miguel Muro, who oversaw the Goliad missions.

In 1822 Díaz de León added the care of the townsfolk at San Antonio to his duties when the one secular priest in the area, the Reverend Refugio de la Garza, abandoned his parishioners to represent Texas in Congress in Mexico City. Ironically, it was Cura Garza who brought about the full secularization of the remaining Texas missions.

In Mexico City Garza petitioned the federal government to apply the secularization law of September 13, 1813 to Texas. His request apparently reflected the desires of some of his constituents, who had been squatting on mission property, and of the townsfolk who coveted the rich bottom lands and an Indian-built irrigation system. The partial secularization of 1794 had left undisturbed most of the lands of the San Antonio missions. Garza's efforts resulted in an order in 1823 to secularize all Texas missions over ten years old. As a result, the four San Antonio missions were fully secularized in 1823–24, and the ayuntamiento distributed their lands to a host of eager petitioners. The chapels

San José Mission, near San Antonio. On the eve of its secularization, Mission San José, the largest of the San Antonio missions, served as headquarters for Father Díaz de León, 1820–1825. Like most missions, the church at San José deteriorated in the late 19th century until its roof collapsed. Today it is splendidly restored (William H. Emory, *Report on the United States and Mexican Boundary Survey* [2 vols.; Washington, D.C., 1857], I, 69).

themselves remained Church property, but priests no longer used them for religious services.[40]

Fray José Antonio Díaz de León seems to have acceded to the secularization of the San Antonio missions in light of local pressures for more cultivable lands and the lack of mission Indians to work those lands. Fray José did struggle, however, to stave off secularization of two of the three missions near Goliad (still called La Bahía)—Espíritu Santo, Rosario, and Refugio—which also fell under the 1823 orders. The government had exempted these three missions from secularization in the 1790s because it did not judge the local Indians sufficiently "civilized." By the time of Mexican independence, the Goliad missions were "almost abandoned," according to the ayuntamiento of Béxar, due in part to repeated Comanche attacks.[41] Indeed, the Franciscans had abandoned Rosario completely in 1806. They used Refugio only occasionally although it was the newest of the missions, built in 1793. Only a few Indian families remained at Espíritu Santo.

Díaz de León made no effort to save the abandoned Rosario mission, but he argued against secularization of Refugio on grounds that local Karankawas still needed religious instruction. At Mission Espíritu Santo, which he made his headquarters in 1825 after secularization forced him to leave the San Antonio area, Fray José took a different tack. He sought to have the mission lands divided among the twelve remaining families of Aranamas—a small group of Hispanized Coahuiltecans soon to become extinct. The idea of giving valuable fields and pastures to Indians incensed the ayuntamiento of Goliad, which in 1822 had formally petitioned the government for the mission's properties. If Fray José's plan were adopted, the ayuntamiento protested, Mexicans would have to rent land from "lazy and shiftless" Indians, or else work for them. Through numerous petitions, Díaz de León kept the bureaucracy off balance and delayed secularization at Espíritu Santo and Refugio until 1830. He might have succeeded even longer had not a resident of Goliad, Rafael Antonio Manchola, won election to the state legislature and obtained an order from the governor to implement the 1823 instructions to secularize the remaining Texas missions.[42]

By 1830, then, all Texas missions had been secularized; however, two Franciscans continued to serve in Texas. The highly respected, Mexican-born Fray Miguel Muro, who had administered Mission Refugio since 1820, remained in Texas as presidio chaplain at Goliad and parish priest to the townspeople. He returned to the College of Zacatecas in 1833. Then in 1841, at age fifty-one, he again journeyed north to the frontier, serving at the missions of San José and San Francisco, in California, until 1845. Meanwhile, Fray José Antonio Díaz de León had left the Indians of the Gulf Coast to become pastor at Nacogdoches in East Texas and work among a population consisting largely of recent immigrants from the United States. In 1834, the forty-eight-year-old missionary met a violent death when he either committed suicide or was murdered by an Anglo-American.[43]

Circumstances surrounding the demise of the Texas missions, where local politicians provided the impetus for secularization, differed from events in Arizona, where the missions disintegrated by default. In both areas, however, secularization took place without a major struggle because neither the Franciscans nor their neophyte communities had sufficient vigor or numbers to resist a process that had been underway since the late eighteenth century. This was true of New Mexico as well.

The last decades of the Spanish era saw a decline in the number of Franciscans and Pueblo Indians in New Mexico. Thirty Franciscans served the province in 1760, but only twenty-three remained in 1821.[44] At the same time, the Pueblo population dropped by 20 percent, according to some estimates, from over 12,000 in 1750 to under 10,000 in 1800. The non-Indian population, on the other hand, had nearly trebled during those decades, and the Franciscans came under increasing pressure to serve better the spiritual needs of the colonists who formed a majority in some communities.[45]

But the short-handed and demoralized Franciscans could not serve the Pueblos adequately in the late colonial period, much less minister to the colonists. Visitors to New Mexico agreed that the Franciscans had failed to convert the Pueblos fully.[46] A representative of the Bishop of Durango, who inspected the New Mexico missions in 1817–18, concluded that the Pueblos "know little more about God than do the pagans." The Pueblos' practice of their own religion in public dances and ceremonies shocked the sensibilities of the bishop's agent, who blamed the friars: "Not a single Franciscan knows the language of the Indians." Moreover, he charged that the Franciscans lived scandalous lives, "satisfying their passions" while their churches and their communicants suffered neglect.[47]

As the numbers of mission Indians and friars declined, successive bishops of Durango sought to extend their authority over New Mexico and create parishes in non-Indian communities. In 1767 the bishop recommended secularization of four of New Mexico's twenty-eight missions: the villas of Santa Fe, Santa Cruz de la Cañada, Albuquerque, and El Paso. The change took decades to effect, but by 1820 five secular priests served these four parishes. The next year, in the waning months of the Spanish era, a secular priest took over the community of Tomé as well. Thus, although the Franciscans objected strenuously and questioned the bishop's authority, secularization got underway in New Mexico prior to Mexican independence, as it had in Texas and Arizona.[48]

In one important respect, however, New Mexico differed from other frontier provinces. In New Mexico, Franciscans never had to entice Indians from scattered villages into artificial mission communities, or *congregaciones* as they did in California, Arizona, and Texas. The Pueblos already lived in tightly organized towns surrounded by communal lands.

El Paso del Norte. Today's Ciudad Juárez and its secularized parish church with an interior so filthy that one visitor in 1817 compared it to a warehouse (Emory, *Report*, I, facing p. 92).

The Franciscans established missions on the edge of those communities but never controlled the fields and pastures, which continued to be worked by Pueblos who gave up only modest amounts of land and labor to support a resident priest. At Cochití, for example, land set aside for the priest's maintenance amounted to about twenty acres.[49] Thus, in New Mexico the growing population of land-hungry pobladores had little to gain from secularizing the missions. The process did not become controversial, and was never actually completed. Nonetheless, the New Mexico missions declined rapidly in the 1820s and 1830s as a result of the weakening of the Franciscan community.

The only overt effort to secularize New Mexico missions following independence occurred in 1824 when the Reverend Antonio José Martínez of Taos, recently ordained as a priest after study in the seminary in Durango, asked the New Mexico diputación to secularize the mission at Taos and put him in charge of it. Cura Martínez's motives are not clear, but the diputación granted his request, then went beyond it. The legislators, one of whom viewed the matter as "one of the most important questions for the happiness of New Mexico," unanimously asked the bishop to secularize and furnish priests for Taos and four other missions as well: San Juan, Abiquiú, Belén, and San Miguel del Bado. These communities, like those previously secularized, contained substantial numbers of non-Indians. The principal motive for requesting their secularization might have been improvement of spiritual care of the gente de razón. If so, that was not the result. The bishop responded by sending a special representative to New Mexico, Agustín Fernández de San Vicente, the same fun-loving canon whom Iturbide had sent to Monterey in 1822 to report on the loyalty of the *californios*. In 1826 Fernández de San Vicente ordered the secularization of the five missions identified by the diputación. He reported that the Franciscans in New Mexico still questioned the bishop's authority, but that they offered no resistance.[50]

In practice, very little changed. The shortage of curas prevented secularization from being fully implemented. In 1826 the number of secular priests in New Mexico remained at five. Of necessity, Franciscans continued to serve as temporary pastors of most of the newly secularized parishes. That pleased some of the settlers. Residents of Belén, for example, balked at accepting Vicente Chávez as pastor and asked for permission to keep a Franciscan at their parish since the support of a friar cost half as much as maintaining a secular priest. Their request was refused.[51]

By 1826, however, the shortage of Franciscans had become as acute as the shortage of curas. In 1826 the number of Franciscans seems to have dropped to nine and by 1832 only five of New Mexico's missions had resident priests.[52]

New Mexico's remaining missions were not so much secularized as abandoned by the clergy. The April 16, 1834 federal decree, which secularized all missions in Mexico, seems to have gone unnoticed in New Mexico. By 1840 the province's few remaining Franciscans had died. Bishop José Antonio Laureano de Zubiría of Durango tried to revive the defunct order in New Mexico in 1845 by sending Fray Mariano de Jesús

López to serve the province. No other Franciscans accompanied him, however, leading one historian to term him "a Superior without subjects."[53] Fray Mariano, who made Isleta his headquarters but also served Laguna, Acoma, and Zuñi, died in February 1848, the same month in which Mexican and American representatives signed the treaty ending the Mexican War.

In New Mexico, Arizona, and Texas, the decline of the Franciscan missions under independent Mexico occurred quietly in comparison to their spectacular demise in Alta California. There, missions and missionaries remained a force to be reckoned with in the 1820s. In contrast to other provinces on the northern frontier, California's missions still possessed considerable vitality. The first of twenty-one Alta California missions had been built on San Diego Bay in 1769, just two years after the expulsion of the Jesuits from the Spanish Empire and at the same time that officials were pressuring Franciscans to secularize missions elsewhere. This contradiction arose out of necessity. The unoccupied California coast seemed menaced by the British and Russians, and some enlightened officials still regarded a modified form of missions as the most effective institution for extending the frontier. Not all officials shared that viewpoint. Just a decade after the founding of San Diego mission in 1769, some officials began to call for secularization of the Alta California missions. Such calls continued to be heard in the late colonial period, but they had little effect in California where the vigorous grayrobes from the College of San Fernando continued to plant missions along with citrus and olive trees in temperate valleys along the Pacific.[54]

By 1823, shortly after independence, the *fernandinos* (Franciscans from the College of San Fernando) had established their twenty-first and final mission in California, at Sonoma, north of San Francisco Bay. At about the same time, the number of Indians attached to those missions reached its zenith, over 21,000.[55] In the names of those neophytes, Franciscans held a near monopoly over the temperate coastal lands from San Diego to Sonoma. Mission orchards, fields, pastures, and shops, all operated by Indian labor, produced most of the food and manufactured goods for the isolated province.

The California Franciscans, despite their travails during the recent wars for independence, presided over the most prosperous missions on the frontier at the dawn of Mexican independence, and they fought to preserve them. In general, California Franciscans opposed the conversion of missions to parishes for the classic reasons: Indians were not yet prepared to assume the role of citizens and needed the protection of the padres, or pobladores would exploit them.[56] Some Franciscans appar-

Mission San Carlos Borromeo. On the Carmel River some four miles south of Monterey, the mission was founded in 1770 and was still thriving in 1827 when an English mariner painted this scene. A decade later the mission was in ruins. Lithograph from a painting by William Smyth (Alexander Forbes, *California: A History of Upper and Lower California* . . . [London, 1839], facing p. 199).

ently did not oppose secularization in itself. Those who were ill or "wearisome," such as the partially paralyzed Fray Felipe Arroyo de la Cuesta of Mission San Juan Bautista, would have happily relinquished responsibility for farming, ranching, and construction in order to tend to spiritual matters exclusively. Before surrendering control over their neophytes, however, most Franciscans wanted safeguards established so that Indians would not be exploited or return to their so-called pagan ways.[57]

One bold and ingenious plan came from Fray Narciso Durán. The genial, blue-eyed, Spanish-born padre, who had served at San José since 1806 and twice acted as father president of the California missions, suggested that construction of a new inland chain of missions accompany secularization of the coastal missions. In resurrecting this idea, which had been discussed in the first years of the century, Durán recognized the necessity of opening coastal lands to colonization if California was to attract immigrants and grow. At the same time, he argued, inland missions built to the east of the coastal ranges would block former mission Indians from fleeing into the interior: "They would either have to join the new missions or lead a rational life in the [coastal] pueblos."[58] Indians who seemed unsuited for life among the gente de razón could be relocated to the new missions as the old ones were abandoned. Too costly to implement (as Durán acknowledged), the idea of building an inland chain of missions continued to receive serious discussion as late as 1845, and one prelate even suggested that missions be extended north to Oregon.[59] The idea continued to receive attention because it represented the only way for the California missions to survive.

California's coastal missions met stiffer opposition than any other missions on the frontier, and the stakes were higher for all parties involved. Ideology aside, californios and federal officials alike saw missions as an obstacle to the economic development of the province. The missions' near monopoly over California's coastal strip and over the indigenous labor force hindered badly needed immigration and retarded growth of private ranches and farms. "The clamor for land is greater than ever," one foreign-born merchant reported in 1831. "Many soldiers . . . do not know how they are going to settle with their growing families."[60] Missions also retarded growth of new towns. Petaluma and Santa Rosa were needed to block the Russian advance from Fort Ross, but their sites occupied lands claimed by a mission.[61]

Thus, secularization seemed to represent the key to the prosperity of California and ultimately to its security. Thoughtful observers knew that if Mexico did not populate and develop the coast, another nation would seize it.[62] Because of the importance of these issues, and because California's territorial status brought it under federal jurisdiction, the government in Mexico City involved itself in secularization in California more than anywhere else on the northern frontier.

But the government faced a dilemma. Although long-range development of California seemed dependent upon secularization, the disruption of mission farms and ranches seemed certain to bring immediate ruin to the provincial economy. The military forces stationed in California and her public officials depended upon the missions as a source of food, supplies, "forced loans," and their very salaries, which the perennially impecunious federal treasury usually failed to provide.[63] California officials repeatedly acknowledged this dependence on the missions. Governor José María Echeandía, for example, declined to enforce laws requiring expulsion of the Spanish-born Franciscans, explaining to the federal government that twenty-five of California's twenty-eight padres would be required to leave under the law. This, he argued, would not only ruin the missions, but "the rest of the inhabitants and the troops would perish."[64]

Officials also feared that without Franciscan control, mission Indians might revolt. Mission Indians outnumbered the *californios* by at least six to one. The Chumash had revolted at Santa Barbara in 1824 and talk of secularization encouraged stirrings of revolt in other missions as well, giving prudent men pause about the wisdom of secularization.[65] California, it appeared, could not grow so long as the missions existed, but neither could it survive without them.

Under these circumstances, the government adopted a gradual approach toward secularization, hoping to weaken the power of the padres and make land and labor available for private development while avoiding economic ruin, Indian revolt, and maintaining the allegiance of the powerful Spanish-born Franciscans, whose loyalty was suspect. From 1825, when the prestigious Commission for the Development of the Californias recommended secularization of California's missions, until 1833, successive governments in Mexico City adopted remarkably similar strategies for implementing the secularization law of September 13, 1813 in California. The first three governors sent to California by independent Mexico—José María Echeandía, Manuel Victoria, and José Figueroa—carried instructions to proceed "slowly and prudently."[66]

The unpopular Manuel Victoria, who lasted in the governor's office for less than a year (1831) did nothing to promote secularization, but Echeandía (1825–31) and Figueroa (1832–35) both experimented with a cautious policy, which had been tried earlier by Pablo Sola, the last Spanish-appointed governor. Echeandía and Figueroa permitted select Indians to leave certain missions and granted them land and the full rights of citizens.[67]

Mission Indians did not clamor to be included in the new plan to make them property owners. Juan Bautista Alvarado recalled visiting the mission of San Miguel and making an impassioned speech on the rights of free men while standing in a cart in the middle of the courtyard. He concluded by saying, "those who prefer to be made proprietors and free men, step to my right." Overwhelmingly, the Indians ignored him and stayed with the priest. "It reminded me of the old Roman lady," Alvarado later wrote, "who began to weep when she learned about the death of Nero . . . [because] it was better to know one known bad person than a good one unknown."[68]

It is not surprising that the few Indians who were released from the restraints of institutional life did not turn into Mexicans overnight. Instead, as one historian has put it, many demonstrated "the kind of psychological disorientation that often accompanies decolonization."[69] Freed mission Indians, according to one British observer, were reduced to beggary and thieving after having "gambled away their clothes, implements, and even their land."[70] Fray Narciso Durán reported that liberated Indians became "slaves or servants of white men."[71] Nonetheless, Governor Echeandía thought the experiment had sufficient merit to extend it to still more missions in 1828, but he also built in more safeguards, one of which prohibited Indians from selling their property for five years. Political turmoil both in California and the nation, however, prevented full implementation of Echeandía's plans.

Governor Figueroa, who deplored the missions as a "monastic despotism," also adopted a gradual approach and his program began auspiciously. By 1834 he had established three Indian towns in southern California, at Las Flores, San Juan Capistrano, and San Dieguito. Ironically, it would be Figueroa, who had opposed secularization "at one blow" because "such a cure is worse than the disease," who would preside over the rapid dissolution of the Alta California missions.[72] A sudden shift in federal policy prompted Figueroa to act in a way that he otherwise would have viewed as unwise.

On August 17, 1833, almost a year before it ordered all missions in Mexico secularized, the liberal vice-president Gómez-Farías signed into law a bill specifically secularizing all missions in both Alta and Baja California and requiring the immediate replacement of Franciscans by secular clergy. The bill made no provision for the disposition of mission properties, but other legislation, not yet approved by Congress, contained a formula for distributing that property to various groups, including colonists from Mexico and from foreign countries.[73]

Due to faulty communication and poorly drafted legislation, the *californios* misunderstood these measures to mean that the Gómez-Farías administration intended to grant all of California's mission lands to a group of Mexican colonists led by José María Híjar and José María Padrés. The administration had recently appointed Híjar to replace Figueroa as *jefe político* and also to serve as commissioner of colonization for California. When the colonists led by Híjar and Padrés set out for California in 1834, they carried instructions to "occupy all the property belonging to the missions."[74]

Garbled reports of these matters reached California and alarmed settlers who had long coveted mission properties but now saw them slipping from their grasp. Meanwhile, however, Governor Figueroa had received no formal orders to implement the new secularization law; he expected Híjar, the new governor, to bring those instructions. In an

Diegueño couple and child. These Kumeyaay Indians in Southern California, whom the Spaniards called Diegueños after the mission of San Diego, had undergone changes in dress and mode of transportation as a result of mission influence. Lithograph from a sketch by Arthur Schott at Agua Caliente in 1854 (Emory, *Report*, I, facing p. 106).

effort to head off Híjar and make the best of a bad situation, Figueroa accepted a secularization program drawn up by the California diputación, and announced it on August 9, 1834, prior to Híjar's arrival. This plan called for the immediate secularization of ten missions and secularization of the remainder soon after. It permitted Franciscans to remain in order to tend to spiritual matters until secular priests arrived. Indians would receive private plots of land, which they could not sell, and would also get tools, seed, and livestock. As in Pimería Alta, a mayordomo, appointed by the governor, would take charge of surplus fields, orchards, and herds. Profits from this surplus property would be used for the expenses of "good government," such as the salary of the priests and the mayordomo, the support of schools, or supplies for the military garrisons. Lest mission ranches and farms cease operating and this income dry up, the plan permitted the governor to require Indians to labor on the surplus lands.[75]

The plan adopted by Figueroa and the diputación served the interests of upper class *californios*. It blocked the acquisition of mission lands by immigrants from Mexico, by foreigners, and by lower class *californios* who would have benefited from the Gómez Farías legislation. The Figueroa plan also kept the mission economy intact and maintained the flow of vital revenues by requiring the forced labor of Indians, even while freeing them in theory. The plan did not provide for *californios* to obtain mission lands directly, but it did the next best thing by opening the way for upper class *californios* to assume positions of mayordomos of mission property. Figueroa and the oligarchs in the legislature, then, seemed to have found an ingenious way to thwart the efforts of the liberal Gómez Farías to integrate the California Indians. The *californios* changed the legal status of mission Indians to conform to republicans ideals, without changing their actual status. Instead of remaining neophytes under the padres, Indians would become *peones* under a mayordomo.

Between 1834 and 1836 all twenty-one missions were secularized, but not in the manner Figueroa intended. He did not live long enough to supervise the process, dying in office in September 1835. Meanwhile, Híjar never had a chance to put the Gómez Farías plan into effect, either. In one of those quick shifts of power that increasingly characterized Mexican politics, Antonio López de Santa Anna ousted Gómez Farías and revoked Híjar's governorship. Santa Anna, now the champion of conservatives, hoped to reverse the process of secularization that his predecessor had set into motion, but the independent-minded California oligarchy ignored his instructions to delay and secularized the remaining missions.

Following the death of Figueroa, California government became more chaotic. During the turbulence, missions constituted the principle source of revenue for ambitious politicians. Mission overseers, who generally belonged to one faction or another, sold off cattle, grain, and lands that rightly belonged to former neophytes, and missions deteriorated under their stewardship. In 1839 Governor Juan Bautista Alvarado tried to check what nearly all writers have termed the "plunder" of the missions, but it was too late. The missions had "entirely gone to ruin," one of Alvarado's agents reported, and non-Indians had moved onto Indian lands.[76] "All is destruction, all is misery, humiliation and despair," wrote one padre in 1840.[77]

The destruction of California mission properties, however, did not come about solely because of the activities of unscrupulous mayordomos. Mission Indians themselves displayed contempt for the system that had kept them forcibly institutionalized and participated actively in destroying it. Under the padres, many Indians had resisted missionization in subtle ways, and one of every ten had attempted to run away. With the authority of the padres gone in the mid-1830s, most Indians refused to labor for the overseers and showed little interest in acquiring land near the missions; some fled civilization entirely to live among independent Indian societies; others drifted into white settlements where they became laborers or servants; and others went to work on the private ranchos that *californios* had begun carving out of former mission properties. The self-governing Indian towns, which Figueroa had begun to establish, disintegrated quickly and the number of Indians remaining on mission lands plummeted.[78]

The number of Franciscans in California also fell. Notwithstanding the arrival of reinforcements from the College of Guadalupe at Zacatecas, which sent eleven Mexican-born padres to California in 1833 to replace the depleted ranks of the Fernandinos, the number of Franciscans declined dramatically. Thirty-six grayrobes had served the province in 1820; twenty-one remained in 1836; and only eleven in 1846.[79] The last of the missionaries had no missions. In dire need of funds to run his government, Governor Pío Pico had put most of the remaining mission property—including the crumbling buildings and the chapels themselves—up for public auction in 1845. The central government and the Franciscans tried to prevent this sale, but the independent and desperate frontier governor proceeded nonetheless. The United States government would later judge Pico's action illegal, but at the outbreak of war between Mexico and the United States, California mission property had been secularized, nearly destroyed, and lost completely to the Church. Little wonder, then, that one Catholic historian has termed the Church in California "near extinction" in 1846.[80]

A consideration of local circumstances, from California to Texas, suggests that the frontier missions came to an end as a result of complex causes, both national and regional. If any one of these stand out, it may be that economic forces played the largest role in ending the mission era. For years pobladores had coveted the choice sites that the padres held in trust for the neophytes. Weakened by a loss of income, personnel, and influence following the struggle for independence, the padres could no longer hold out against the growing population of gente de razón. In this respect, events on the frontier followed a national pattern. "If there is one linear tendency which can be documented throughout Mexican history from 1527 to 1910," one historian has written, "it is the constant expansion of private property at the cost of communal property."[81] In their efforts to maintain the missions, the padres fought a holding action against a seemingly inexorable economic force.

National policies, however, did not determine how and when secularization took place on the frontier. On this issue, as on many others, frontiersmen modified or ignored national directives to suit what they perceived as their own interests.

Except in New Mexico, secularization enabled the pobladores to obtain title to former mission lands and Indian labor, thereby shifting the center of production to the private sector. But those gains came at a price. In areas such as Alta California and Pimería Alta, which had relied heavily on missions for Indian control, some officials doubted the wisdom of losing the missions and wished for their return. "To deny the utility of the missions in a country inhabited largely by barbarians, would be absurd," California's representative argued in Congress in 1844.[82] Secularization also cost the frontiersmen the spiritual services of Franciscans, whose stipends had been paid largely by the government and other external sources. With secularization, pobladores became parishioners with the additional obligation of supporting their own priests. Those frontiersmen who had expressed fears that it would be difficult to find curas to replace Franciscans soon learned their fears had been well-founded.

4

The Church in Jeopardy

How can a pastor bear to see his beloved children die without confession and the last sacraments? How can my pierced heart respond to the many souls who succumb without baptism . . . ?—Francisco García Diego y Moreno, Bishop of Both Californias, *Santa Barbara, July 4, 1845*

The dismantling of the missions and the rapid decrease of Franciscans on the frontier in the 1820s and 1830s left the way open for secular clergy to replace the padres, but the opportunity was lost. Beset by problems that arose out of the struggle for independence, the Church found itself weakened throughout Mexico and unable to move effectively onto the frontier.

In part, the Church failed to extend itself to the Far North because of weakened leadership. Under Spain, and on through the 1820s and 1830s, no bishop resided on the frontier. Closest to the northern edge of Mexico in theory was the Bishop of Sonora, whose diocese embraced Sinaloa, Sonora, and, until 1840, both Californias. Upon establishing the Diocese of Sonora in 1779, the papacy had designated the town of Arizpe, high on the Sonora River about seventy miles south of the present Arizona border, as the episcopal seat, but the first bishop chose a safer location in southern Sonora at the opulent silver mining community of Alamos. No bishop ever resided permanently in Arizpe and in 1799 the episcopal center moved still farther south to Culiacán in Sinaloa where it remained until 1883. Bishops also presided over Texas and New Mexico from distant cities. Texas formed part of the Diocese of Nuevo León with the episcopal See in Monterrey; New Mexico fell under the Diocese of Durango with its bishop in the city of the same name. It appeared as though the situation in New Mexico might improve in 1812 when the Spanish Cortes endorsed the idea of establishing a bishopric in Santa Fe—an idea first proposed in the early seventeenth century—but it failed to win papal approval.

For over a decade following Mexican independence, leadership on the frontier deteriorated rather than improved. Bishops throughout the young nation became casualties of the split with Spain and of a struggle between Mexico and the Vatican. The Church hierarchy, which had consisted largely of Spaniards at the time of independence, was decimated in the 1820s when the archbishop of Mexico loyally returned to Spain and some bishops followed his example. Others of that aged group died in office until by mid-1829 not a single bishop served Mexico. For over a decade the Vatican refused to make new appointments to fill those vacancies, in part because the papacy sought to restore Mexico to Spain and did not recognize Mexican independence until 1836. Following negotiations, however, the Vatican began to appoint new bishops in 1831, but filled those positions slowly; the Pope did not name a new archbishop for Mexico until 1838.[1]

This national crisis of leadership clearly affected the dioceses on Mexico's northern frontier. The See of Sonora lacked a bishop from the death of Fray Bernardo del Espíritu Santo in 1825 until 1838 when Lázaro de la Garza y Ballesteros assumed the office. The bishop's office in Monterrey remained empty from 1821 until 1832, when Fray José María de Jesús Belaunzarán was installed (although two years later he was forced to flee in disguise as a result of a quarrel with state officials). The See of Durango suffered the least interruption of leadership with a hiatus of only six years between the death of Bishop Juan Francisco Castañiza in 1825 and the appointment of José Antonio Laureano de Zubiría in 1831.[2]

Absence of a bishop did not mean complete lack of episcopal authority on the frontier. Ecclesiastical officials made special tours of inspection of the area, and a deputy of the bishop, a vicar forane, generally served in the capital of each frontier province. The vicar forane was usually a secular priest empowered by the bishop to perform special functions, such as granting certain dispensations and inspecting churches and parochial records. Where there were no secular priests, as in California, the Franciscan president of the missions served as vicar forane.[3]

In the view of many officials, however, the tottering Church on the frontier required stronger leadership than a vicar could provide. A bishop's deputy without a bishop seemed of limited utility. Officials in New Mexico and California, the most isolated areas in the north, urged the establishment of bishoprics in their provinces, since a bishop had authority to carry out tasks ranging from anointing sacramental oils to supervising a seminary for local boys and ordaining them as priests.[4] In 1836 Fray Francisco García Diego y Moreno, a Mexican-born Franciscan from the College of Zacatecas who had served for a few years as *presidente* of the Zacatecan missions in California, used this argument successfully with the Congress in Mexico City. His request to elevate both Californias to the status of a bishopric eventually received congressional approval and was sent to Rome where Pope Gregory XVI created the Diocese of the Californias in 1840, appointing Fray Francisco García Diego as its first bishop. In late 1841 the new bishop returned to California and chose Santa Barbara as the seat of his diocese instead of the declining town of San Diego, which the Pope had designated as the apostolic seat. The dark-skinned Bishop García Diego, despite his exalted position, lacked the respect of some of his flock who viewed Mexican mestizos from the mainland as inferior. Mariano Guadalupe Vallejo disparagingly termed the bishop "an Indian priest."[5]

By 1841, the *californios* had direct episcopal guidance, while residents of Texas and today's Arizona never saw a bishop set foot in their communities in the Mexican period. *Nuevomexicanos* received two visits from the bishop of Durango during the quarter-century of Mexican rule, and those visits must have seemed frequent in comparison to earlier neglect. In the eighteenth century, bishops had come to New Mexico on only three occasions, leading New Mexico's delegate to the Spanish Cortes, Pedro Pino, to lament, "I, an old man, did not know how bishops dressed."[6] More important, Pino deplored the spiritual consequences of those infrequent visits. Many people could not receive the sacrament of confirmation, which was ordinarily a bishop's prerogative, and others— according—to Pino could not receive special dispensations and so "live and rear their families in adultery." Little wonder that in 1833 when Bishop José Antonio de Zubiría became the first bishop to visit the province since 1760, New Mexicans welcomed him by repairing roads and bridges, sweeping streets, and decorating their homes. Zubiría responded by granting his vicar more powers, including the sacrament of confirmation, and by returning to the province twelve years later, in 1845.[7]

Although Church leaders began to play a more direct role in New Mexico and California, the problems they faced were beyond the power of an individual bishop to solve. In addition to a shortage of leaders, the Church in Mexico suffered from a sharp decline in the number of secular priests in the decade following independence. In 1830 Mexico had slightly over half as many curas as in 1810. This dramatic decline came about for several reasons, including the expulsion of Spanish-born clergy, the availability of other "honorable" careers for young men in the inde-

Main Cathedral, Mexico City. Opulent churches in central Mexico, such as the cathedral facing the main square (Zócalo) in Mexico City, generally proved more attractive to priests than did impoverished frontier parishes (Brantz Mayer, *Mexico: Aztec, Spanish and Republican . . .* [2 vols.; Hartford, 1851], I, facing p. 421).

pendence era, and the lack of Mexican bishops to ordain new priests.[8]

Meanwhile, the number of parishes in Mexico continued to grow. By 1828 nearly half lacked resident priests and a disproportionate share of empty parishes existed in rural and remote areas such as the frontier, because priests tended to avoid isolation, hardship, danger, and low salaries and to gravitate toward more comfortable urban parishes. At the beginning of the nineteenth century, for example, over 1,000 regular and secular priests served the single city of Puebla, while fewer than eighty ministered to the northernmost provinces of Texas, New Mexico,

Antonio José Martínez. Trained in a seminary in Durango, Antonio José Martínez (1793–1867) was probably the most educated and certainly the most influential New Mexico-born clergyman of his generation. He is shown here in the earliest known surviving New Mexico photograph (courtesy the New Mexico Hispanic Collection of Dr. and Mrs. Ward Alan Minge).

and California. In noting this discrepancy, one Mexican historian editorialized: "and then they ask why we lost these territories."[9]

Antonio Barreiro of New Mexico offered one solution. Priests ought to receive a reward for frontier duty. Those who served for ten years on the frontier, he suggested, should receive preference for a comfortable cathedral appointment in one of the nation's "civilized communities."[10] Some frontiersmen also saw as a solution the establishment of seminaries to train local boys for the priesthood.[11] That was accomplished only in California, where Bishop García Diego opened an impoverished seminary at Santa Inés in 1844—too late to add to the number of curas in California prior to war with the United States.[12] Without the advantages of a local seminary or good preparatory schools, sons of frontiersmen rarely entered the priesthood. One important exception was the able, energetic, and vain Antonio José Martínez, who received his training at the seminary in Durango and returned home to become a priest and politician at Taos, where he also operated a preparatory school. Martínez reportedly inspired and equipped thirty of his pupils to leave New Mexico to study for the priesthood, but the results of his work affected New Mexico chiefly following the United States invasion.[13]

Not only did the frontier lack institutions to train native sons to the clergy, it was also unable to attract sufficient priests from the faltering Church in Mexico or to afford to import them from Europe. As a result, the number of curas who served on the frontier at the end of the Mexican era remained pitifully small: New Mexico, which had five secular clergy at the outset of Mexican independence (the largest number on the frontier), saw that number increase to eight by 1829, and eleven by 1846. Five secular priests served Alta California in 1846 (there had been none as late as 1840); two served in Texas at the outbreak of the revolution in 1836; and none served the area of present-day Arizona before 1846.[14] Few as they were, the frontier clerics found themselves perpetually short of cash, unable to make ends meet.

The causes of the fiscal troubles that gripped the frontier parishes lay partly in Mexico, where the Church found itself struggling against the state to preserve its privileges and immense wealth and unable to divert resources to the frontier. The opulence of the Church stood in marked contrast to the empty coffers in the national treasury. Few administrations, even those friendly to the Church, could resist asking the Church for so-called voluntary loans, which at times amounted to outright confiscation, or placing special levies on Church property.[15]

In 1842, for example, President Santa Anna nationalized monies belonging to the Pious Fund, a private trust that had been established for the promotion of the faith in the Californias. Income from the Pious Fund had supported the labors of the Franciscans in Alta California and the fund's existence had helped persuade the Pope that California could support a bishop. The bishop had hardly set foot on California soil, however, before Santa Anna nationalized the fund, promising to pay 6 percent of its value annually to support the Church in the Californias. He did not keep the promise. As of 1845 Bishop García Diego had received only $603 from the government, and the Church in the Californias was reduced to "abject poverty."[16] Bishop García Diego of California was so pressed for funds that he could not construct his official residence, inspect his diocese, or operate an effective seminary. When the bishop sent a priest to serve Monterey, the priest had to leave for lack of financial support from parishioners in California's capital.[17] The case of the Pious Fund was unique, but no area of the frontier could hope to move ahead on funds from a Church that was fighting a rearguard action.

Under independent Mexico, Church leaders not only found themselves scurrying to protect their wealth, but they were also hindered from raising new income through tithing. Under Spain, and until 1833, most Mexicans had paid compulsory annual tithes (*diezmos*) on their agricultural produce and increases in their livestock. Following independence, a sharp decline in agriculture and ranching caused the amount of income from tithes to drop. In an effort to stimulate agricultural production, the government exempted certain products from the tithe, still further diminishing Church income. The final blow came when the Gómez-Farías administration, for ideological as well as economic reasons, ended the compulsory tithe entirely on October 27, 1833. With the abolition of the Inquisition prior to independence, the Church had lost power to force people to tithe. From 1833 on, the Church no longer had government support in making tithing compulsory. It became entirely a matter of conscience. Along with other Mexicans, many frontiersmen found that their consciences spoke very softly on this matter.[18]

Even before it became voluntary, tithing met considerable resistance in New Mexico. New Mexicans explained their reluctance to pay tithes on practical grounds that had little to do with the spiritual authority of the Church. Monies collected, they argued, did not all go to the Church, but instead a high percentage went to enrich a few collectors who worked on a commission.[19] Nor did all the income remain in the province. Much of the revenue, they claimed, trickled southward to Mexico's urban centers where the preponderance of clerics lived. This left frontier provinces short of cash that might have paid salaries for more priests, supported a seminary, or financed schools—all of which still depended on the tithe in the late 1820s. The system also removed hard cash from circulation on the frontier, further deepening resentments.[20] As the Reverend Manuel de Jesús Rada succinctly put it, tithes created "hatred between the ministers and the faithful."[21] Some New Mexicans, of course, continued to tithe even after it ceased to be obligatory.[22]

The practice of tithing seems to have fallen into disuse in Alta California and Texas by the time of Mexican independence, if, indeed, it had ever been a custom in those former mission provinces. In Texas, tithing was apparently not practiced in the Mexican era, and newly arrived colonists were specifically exempted from the tithe for the first six years, and then payments reduced by half for the next six years as an inducement to settle in Texas.[23] In California, Bishop García Diego attempted to resurrect tithes among the gente de razón on a voluntary basis. Having come to California in 1841 "without a single penny,"[24] but with ambitious plans for public schools and a seminary, the bishop viewed tithes as essential to the well being of his diocese. The results were disastrous.

The bishop concluded that many *californios* would not pay because they had grown accustomed to free services from the Franciscans. Others, he wrote, "do not pay what they should, some because of their immunity from being forced and others because of the anti-religious philosophies with which they are saturated."[25] Moreover, the cost of collecting tithes from a reluctant populace scattered over a great distance apparently exceeded the sum collected. By 1844 the beleaguered bishop had concluded that collecting tithes in California was "impossible." He angrily condemned the *californios* in a letter to the governor: "All peoples, even the pagans, have honored, sustained and looked after their priests. . . . Only this diocese has yet to comply with that sacred duty."[26]

If the Church on the frontier could not depend upon tithes, which ordinarily constituted the most important source of income from the faithful, neither could it sustain itself on *aranceles*—fees which priests charged to perform baptism, marriage, last rites, and other services. Priests collected these so-called stole fees in New Mexico and in Texas, but critics in both areas denounced them and recommended their abolition on the grounds that the impoverished citizenry could not afford to pay.[27] In New Mexico, stole fees must have seemed especially burdensome since the tithe was also obligatory there, at least until 1833. Even the bombastic priest of Taos, Antonio José Martínez, argued vigorously in 1831 that the government should abolish the fees because his parishioners also tithed, and a few years later some of the faithful forced him at gunpoint to agree to stop collecting fees.[28] In New Mexico, as throughout the nation, people complained of abuses by priests and some pobladores apparently avoided essential sacraments such as baptism or marriage and buried their dead outside of consecrated ground rather than pay a fee.[29] Such extreme reactions may have been unusual, however, for clergy in New Mexico apparently charged varying amounts for their services, depending upon their client's ability to pay, and performed services free of charge on some occasions. Foreigners, especially, seem to have exaggerated the avariciousness of Mexican priests. "An inflexible rule with the priests," the American merchant James J. Webb wrote in 1844, was: "no money, no marrying; no money, [no] baptizing; no money, no burying."[30]

In any event, the impoverished and sparsely populated communities on the far northern frontier probably yielded so little income from fees that their collection did not compensate for the resentments they produced. Bishop García Diego flatly refused to institute a system of stole fees for Alta California, partly on the grounds that the scanty number of baptisms, marriages, and funerals performed would not yield enough income to support a priest.[31]

It is not surprising that the Church, which was short of funds and priests and with its leadership weakened, failed to fill the void created by the departing Franciscans. Catholicism stagnated on the frontier during the Mexican era, notwithstanding the extraordinary efforts of some individuals. The spiritual welfare of the pobladores was neglected, and the morale and morality of the priesthood declined.

Foreigners frequently described frontier priests as debauched, hypocritical men, given to drink, gambling, and women, who fathered illegitimate children and indulged themselves in other worldly ways.[32] Many of the foreigners' deprecatory observations about priestly misconduct may be dismissed as manifestations of Protestant bias. There is no doubt, however, that some frontier clergy fit the picture. Perhaps the priests' values on matters such as celibacy differed from those of clerics elsewhere, or perhaps the frontier simply reflected the declining morality of the priesthood throughout Mexico.[33]

Writing about the "care of souls" in New Mexico in 1832, Antonio Barreiro commented that "charity demands that a veil be thrown over many things which would, if they were narrated, create a scandal."[34] When Jean Baptiste Lamy, New Mexico's first bishop, lifted the "veil" soon after his arrival in 1851, he revealed behavior such as that of the uncelibate, elderly priest of Pecos, who fell off his horse while drunk and broke his leg. Lamy defrocked several native clergy who refused to change conduct that the bishop regarded as scandalous.[35] Similarly in Texas, the first prelate to visit San Antonio following Texas independence suspended fathers Refugio de la Garza and José Antonio Valdez from their priestly functions. The parish of San Fernando in San Antonio had been badly managed throughout the Mexican period, its finances and records carelessly kept. Garza and Valdez had neglected for many years to preach, hear confessions, say Mass on a regular basis, or attend to the sick and dying.[36]

Even the Franciscans, who once enjoyed a reputation for leading exemplary lives, continued to decline qualitatively as well as quantitatively in the Mexican era—a process that had begun prior to independence.[37] Some Franciscans simply could no longer carry out their duties with vigor because of age, infirmity, or both. Others, especially those Mexican-born Franciscans from the College of Zacatecas who went to California, simply failed to live up to the high standards of their calling and behaved scandalously.[38] Some Franciscans, such as the genial and beloved Fray José Sánchez of San Gabriel near Los Angeles, and some curas as well, continued to win the respect of Protestants and Catholics alike. In general, however, the remark that one Catholic layman made in 1848 about California's few remaining priests seems to apply to the entire frontier. The priests, he said, are "very old, others very ignorant and others again, I am sorry to say it but it is true, very bad."[39]

As clergy on the frontier diminished in zeal as well as numbers, the gente de razón suffered increasingly from spiritual neglect. Even before the secularization of the missions, pobladores in both Alta California and New Mexico had complained about the shortage of priests and charged the Franciscans with neglecting them in favor of the Indians. Priests did not serve Mass often enough in the towns, and distance prevented many of the pobladores from journeying to the missions for Mass and other sacraments.[40] The situation deteriorated even further as the number of priests diminished. When the townspeople of San Jose built a new church in 1842, for example, they asked Bishop García Diego for a priest. He apologetically told them to continue to rely on the priest at nearby Mission Santa Clara: "I have no one available to send. In certain cases there is not even a priest to whom the faithful can turn at the hour of death."[41] In New Mexico, where the number of priests, both secular and regular, had fallen to about a dozen in 1831, Antonio Barreiro reported that abandoned churches were falling into ruins and that many parishes received visits from priests only a few times a year. People could not attend Mass or receive the sacraments and "corpses remain unburied for many days. . . . How resentful must be the poor people who suffer such neglect!"[42]

While the pobladores resented their neglect by the clergy, the priests charged the pobladores with spiritual laxity—a charge they had often leveled in the past. In California in 1831, for example, Fray José Viader described the gente de razón in San Jose as so irreligious that they did not receive even the obligatory annual sacraments. "They laugh at everything," he complained.[43] The irreverence of the *californios* might be attributed in part to their spiritual neglect. It might also have represented an anticlerical reaction to the dominant position that the missions had held in California's economic and political life and the influx of fresh ideas as independent Mexico threw California's ports open to the outside world. The changing times seemed to be reflected in the reaction of Mariano Guadalupe Vallejo to the arrival of Bishop García Diego in 1841: "Poor crazy fools, if they think they can browbeat the leading men of California. The age of theocratic domination is past."[44]

Spiritual neglect of the New Mexicans contributed to the rise of a lay brotherhood or *hermandad*, the Brothers of Our Father Jesus, popularly known as the Penitentes. The brothers, who continue today to perform vital social services and to worship in their windowless *moradas* in the mountain villages of northern New Mexico and southern Colorado, have long been the subject of fascination and morbid curiosity. The Penitentes developed their own liturgy and ceremonies, which included the use of severe corporal punishment, such as whipping, to atone for their sins. The exact origin of the Penitentes in New Mexico remains a subject of dispute and conjecture. Most writers agree, however, that the brotherhood grew rapidly in the early nineteenth century as a result of neglect by the priests of the institutional Church.[45]

By 1833 the Penitentes had achieved sufficient notoriety that their activities came to the attention of Bishop Zubiría during his episcopal visit. Zubiría outlawed the Penitentes as an unauthorized group that violated Catholic doctrine, and he suggested that instead of being known as brothers of penance, they should be known as brothers of "butchery." Zubiría's is denunciation of the Penitentes, which represents the first extant official acknowledgement of their existence, was a futile gesture. So long as the bishop could not furnish adequate priests to minister to the remote mountain communities, frontiersmen would worship in ways that best suited their needs. When Bishop Zubiría returned to New Mexico in 1845 he found the Church in the same state of decadence as it had been twelve years before, and he asked that the same pastoral letter that he issued in 1833 be read once again from the pulpits. That letter not only condemned the Penitentes, but also vividly described the neglectful priesthood that fostered the growth of the Penitentes: priests who set poor examples in their own lives, who failed to baptize infants, who misused sacraments such as confession, and who said Mass with filthy chalices, dirty altar clothes, and shabby or improper vestments.[46]

If the Church ministered poorly to Mexican frontiersmen, its efforts to convert and care for new immigrants from other countries were a fiasco. Americans and other foreigners who settled in Mexico could not, under the law, practice any religion other than Catholicism, and they had to be certified Catholics to become citizens.[47] Foreigners who settled near established communities generally had access to priests, but those who settled in remote areas, such as the Sacramento Valley in California, found it impossible to practice the one religion permitted by law.

This problem was especially acute in Texas, which saw large-scale immigration by Protestants from the United States during these years. Many settled in Texas under terms of the Colonization Law of 1824, which obliged the government to provide them with "a sufficient number of priests."[48] The framers of that legislation saw religion as a key to acculturating the newcomers. The government failed to provide priests, however, so colonists in Texas could not practice Catholicism as the law seemed to require and yet could not attend Protestant services, which the law prohibited.[49]

One result of neglect was the giving over of the "Lord's Day" to other pursuits, such as "visiting, driving stock, and breaking mustangs," according to one contemporary.[50] Americans who settled in Stephen Austin's colony pragmatically devised their own makeshift civil ceremonies for births and deaths, although these never received government approval; a system of "contract marriage," inspired by Canon law and custom, also emerged. If such marriages lacked legal sanction, they at least avoided scandal and had the advantage of being easy to dissolve.[51] Only once prior to 1836 did Austin's colonists enjoy the services of a resident priest. In 1831–32 the pompous, witty, Irish-born Father Michael Muldoon served at San Felipe de Austin as "Vicar General of all the Foreign Colonies of Texas, Already Existing, or that May Be Hereafter Established," a title that he seems to have bestowed upon himself. This liberal and highly pro-American priest reported that Americans in Austin's colony eagerly sought the sacraments, and he proceeded to marry couples who had been cohabiting without Church sanction.[52] One contemporary described a group marriage performed by Father Muldoon as "truly ludicrous." Most of the couples had children, and "to see brides . . . with the bosoms open and little children sucking at the breast and others in a situation too delicate to mention, appeared to me more like a burlesque than a marriage in fact."[53]

If the Church's neglect of the foreign-born colonist did not improve their spiritual welfare, it at least prevented them from becoming outraged over the lack of religious toleration in Mexico. Catholicism was never forced on them. As one American in California advised a friend: "they may try to persuade you that it is necessary to become a Catholic in order to the getting [sic] of a citizenship, but do not believe them."[54] In the case of Texas, there is some evidence that restrictions against Protestant activity were relaxed in the 1830s. Moreover, in 1834 the State of Coahuila y Texas went so far as to guarantee that "no person shall be molested for political and religious opinions provided the public order is not disturbed."[55] Thus, despite contemporary sloganeering to the contrary, freedom of worship never became an important issue among the foreigners in Mexican Texas, and was not a cause of the Texas revolt in 1836.[56] Indeed, there is some evidence that Mexico's refusal to allow non-Catholics to worship openly served as a screening device that kept the most devout or dogmatic Protestants out of Texas. Those who did filter through were less inclined to be irritated by strictures on their religious lives. Some iconoclastic colonists even welcomed the lack of organized Protestant churches and the silencing of Protestant preachers.[57]

Historians agree that organized religion in Hispanic America generally played a more vigorous role in settling the frontier than it did in

Anglo America.[58] That truism, however, only applies to the initial phase of frontier expansion. In the first half of the nineteenth century, just when the Anglo-Americans began to surge across the continent, the Church on the Mexican frontier became a paper tiger, its temporal and ecclesiastical power greatly diminished. The Church had been a key institution in extending Mexico's northern frontier, but lacked the strength to consolidate its position. In sharp contrast to its role in the nation's core, where the Church stood as a powerful defender of tradition and the status quo, the weakness of the secular Church on the nation's periphery left frontier society more tolerant and receptive to change. Zebulon Pike's description of religion on the frontier in 1807 as "Catholic, but much relaxed," seems appropriate for the entire Mexican era.[59]

Curiously, many American visitors to northern Mexico seemed blind to the declining influence of the Church and pronounced the frontiersmen a "priest-ridden" people. A visitor to Texas in 1837 viewed the clergy as having a "powerful influence . . . over the minds of the people."[60] Similarly, Santa Fe trader Josiah Gregg exclaimed that "the slavish obsequiousness of the lower classes toward these pampered priests is almost incredible."[61] Such sentiments probably would have amazed the "pampered" priests whose parishioners refused to pay tithes or fees or receive the sacraments.

To some extent, however, American observers were correct. Some individual clerics possessed considerable power. Numbering among the few literate and cultured frontiersmen, priests could and did influence civil officials. Priests were among the few educated people qualified to hold public office on the frontier; if they used the pulpit for political purposes, parishioners provided a ready-made constituency. Curas such as Manuel de Jesús Rada, Juan Felipe Ortiz, and Antonio José Martínez of New Mexico, and Juan Manuel Zambrano and Refugio de la Garza of Texas, held political offices. In California, Franciscans seemed to avoid direct political participation, but exerted considerable political influence nonetheless.[62]

The power of the struggling frontier priests would be easy to exaggerate, however, and Americans probably did just that. Strong Protestant biases against Catholics and against priests in particular blinded many Americans to reality. Moreover, Americans probably assumed that conditions on the frontier mirrored those of central Mexico where the Church did hold immense power and where the term *priest-ridden* applied more accurately. Mexican liberals would have agreed with Stephen Austin who, while on a visit to central Mexico in 1823, argued a need "to destroy the ecclesiastical power from the very roots . . . to save the country from ruin."[63] Mexican liberals generally sought to limit the

Church's temporal power through such devices as prohibiting clerics from preaching on political questions and by abolishing the obligatory tithe. In the years prior to war with the United States, however, the liberals scarcely dented the power and position of the Church in the nation's core. Although under strong attack, the Church defended itself effectively and played a conspicuous role in toppling the one administration that seriously challenged its power—that of Valentín Gómez Farías—and repealing most of its anticlerical measures.[64]

On the frontier, on the other hand, liberal reforms succeeded all too well. When liberals looked toward the frontier in the 1820s they saw the missions as vestiges of a "monastic-military government" which, they thought, needed to be destroyed for republicanism to flourish.[65] By the mid-1830s, secularization had brought an end to alleged monastic influence on the frontier and the Church lacked resources and influence to fill the void. Thus, liberal reformers who chipped away at the Church's underpinnings managed only to weaken it in central Mexico, but they helped bring about its collapse on the frontier.

5

Indios Bárbaros, Norteamericanos, and the Failure of the Velvet Glove

Upon its formation as a free and sovereign nation, our country received as a sad legacy from the Spanish government a portion of Mexicans born in a state of barbarism, ignorant of all the principles of civilization, their customs reduced to the satisfaction of their animal needs by means of force and destruction.—Secretary of War, *Mexico City, January 8, 1835*

The Indians of New Mexico are well supplied with firearms, powder, balls, lances and the rest, that they purchase at low prices from the United States of North America. The Territory [of New Mexico] has very few arms. . . . —Manuel de Jesús Rada, *New Mexico, 1828*

At the same time that Mexico's ecclesiastical authority over her frontier subjects eroded, her military supremacy over the frontier also slipped away. In the late eighteenth century, innovative policies and mutual interest had spun a delicate web of peace between Indian peoples and pobladores in the "land of war," as far northern New Spain was sometimes called. By the time Mexico won independence, the strains of a decade of revolution had begun to tear that fragile fabric and the new nation could not mend it. In many areas of the frontier, the decades following independence saw relations worsen with those autonomous tribes of seminomadic Indians who rejected Christianity and much of Hispanic culture—Indians the pobladores variously termed *indios bárbaros, salvajes, gentiles,* or *naciones errantes.* By 1846, the situation had deteriorated to the point that some areas of the frontier had less to fear from the imminent war with the United States than they had from the Indians,

[Utah]

[Colorado]

------- Present-Day Political Boundaries
● Towns

[Arizona]

New Mexico

● Socorro

Gila   River

Santa Cruz River
San Pedro River

WESTERN COYOTERO APACHES

MOGOLLÓN APACHES

Tucson ●

Santa Rita del Cobre

EASTERN COYOTERO APACHES

WARM SPRINGS APACHES

Paso del Norte

Magdalena ●

Arizpe

San Miguel

Rio Sonora

Rio Sonora

COYOTERO APACHES

MIMBREÑO APACHES

NATAGÉ APACHES

MESCALERO APACHES

APACHES

Rio

Sonora

Chihuahua ●

Chihuahua

Rio

Durango

**Apache and Comanche
Raiding Trails,
ca. 1845**

(Apache trails are from Ralph A. Smith, "Apache 'Ranching' below the Gila, 1841–1845," *Arizoniana* III (Winter 1962); Comanche trails are from Smith, "The Comanche Bridge Between Oklahoma and Mexico, 1843–1844," *Chronicles of Oklahoma* XXXIX (1961–61).

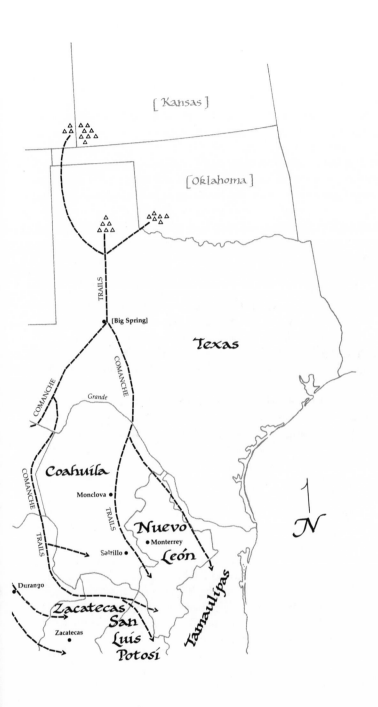

[Kansas]

[Oklahoma]

TRAILS

• [Big Spring]

Texas

COMANCHE

COMANCHE

Grande

COMANCHE

Coahuila

COMANCHE

Monclova •

TRAILS

Nuevo

TRAILS

• Monterrey

León

Saltillo •

Durango •

Tamaulipas

Zacatecas

San

Luís

Zacatecas •

Potosí

N

who were better armed, better mounted, and more successful than ever at defending their lands and striking offensive blows deep into Mexico.

Many frontiersmen saw bands of Shoshone-speaking Indians, known collectively as Comanches, as their most numerous, best armed, and most destructive Indian adversaries. Along with Kiowa allies, some Comanches ended the peace with Spaniards and resumed warfare in the 1820s, riding in large groups out of the Great Plains. As the Mexican period wore on, Comanche raids in Texas and New Mexico became nearly incidental as they struck deeper and deeper into the richer northeastern states of Coahuila, Nuevo León, Tamaulipas, Chihuahua, and Durango. In 1836 and 1837, for example, some Comanche bands pushed south to raid ranchos along the lower Rio Grande, from Laredo to Matamoros, with greater intensity than ever before. Events surrounding the Texas rebellion, especially the westward push of Anglo-Americans, apparently prompted this southward thrust. In the years that followed the Texas revolt, Comanches raided farther and farther south, devastating the provinces below the Rio Grande. In the 1840s some Comanches reportedly reached Zacatecas, nearly 500 miles south of the Great River, and on one occasion a group was reported at Querétaro, some 135 miles north of Mexico's capital.[1]

Comanche devastation of northeastern Mexico in the 1840s had its counterpart in the northwest where small bands of Apaches swept southward from mountain strongholds in Arizona, New Mexico, and West Texas. Among the most powerful Apache bands were those known to Mexicans as *coyoteros* and *gileños* (the term *gileño* encompassed smaller groups such as *mogollones, mimbreños, chiricauhuas* and *tontos,* who inhabited the rugged mountains of eastern Arizona and western New Mexico). Coyoteros ranged along the Pacific slope of the Sierra Madre Occidental, striking throughout western Sonora. Mogollones and other Gileños also raided Sonora settlements, but crossed over the Sierras into Chihuahua and Durango. Along the Rio Grande the *natagés,* who lived to the north of El Paso, and *mescaleros,* who had settled east of El Paso, also raided in Chihuahua. Farther east, along the Big Bend of the Rio Grande, Mescalero and Lipan Apaches made their homes. These groups reportedly struck in eastern Chihuahua and Coahuila, but by the 1840s westward-moving Comanches had displaced them.[2]

Of course, not all Apaches and all Comanches raided Mexican settlements all of the time. Neither Apaches nor Comanches possessed a central political structure or functioned as a unit or as "a nation," notwithstanding Spanish and Mexican use of the term *nación* to describe them. As one veteran described the Apaches:

Each family forms a *ranchería* [a community] and all live independently of one another without recognizing a government.
Hence, war with this horde of savages never has ceased for
one day, because even when thirty rancherías are at peace,
the rest are not.[3]

Thus, pobladores who enjoyed harmonious relations with one group of
Apaches or Comanches might have their livestock stolen by members of
another band, or even by individuals from a friendly group of Indians.
Mexican officials struggled to sort out differences among a people they
regarded as barbarians and to distinguish friend from foe, but usually without long-lasting results. Garbled reports, rumors, conflicting evidence, and
rapidly shifting alliances in this turbulent era made the task nearly impossible. By the 1840s, Apache and Comanche raiders had contributed more
than any other Indian groups to create a climate of fear and pessimism that
extended throughout northern Mexico well below the the border.

Indians slaughtered or ran off livestock, destroyed or appropriated
crops, and rendered mining a risky occupation. They captured women
and children and killed men. Everywhere, travelers felt unsafe, even
near sizable cities such as Chihuahua. Indeed, once outside a Mexican
settlement, the traveler for all practical purposes entered Indian territory. Some Apaches, who had learned Mexican ways from years of close
contact, even collected taxes on occasion from persons traveling between
New Mexico and Sonora, and kept abreast of events by reading mail that
they appropriated from couriers. The extent of Indian control of the
region was graphically described by the Chihuahua legislature in 1846:

we travel the roads . . . at their whim; we cultivate the land
where they wish and in the amount that they wish; we use
sparingly things they have left to us until the moment that it
strikes their appetite to take them for themselves.[4]

The despair and helplessness so evident in this statement echoed across
the frontier where travelers heard variations on a theme. Comanches, it
was said, only spared Mexico from complete destruction because it supplied them with horses. Indians in New Mexico reportedly boasted that
they "would long before this have destroyed every sheep in the country,
but that they prefer leaving a few behind for breeding purposes, in order
that their Mexican shepherds may raise them new supplies!"[5] Utes offered
the same explanation for not destroying California ranchos. If true, such
reports were not far off the mark, for it was not in the nomads' interests
to destroy the Mexicans' economy entirely.[6]

Lipanes.

Lipans Du Texas inférieur et des rives du Rio Grande.

Lipan Apaches. This Apache man and woman, sketched in 1828, are dressed in animal skins, except for the man's red cloth breechclout, red ribbon hair tie, metal arm band, and beaded necklace. Note the woman's double braids and the man's long single braid and red cheeks. painted by Lino Sánchez y Tapia, from a sketch by Lt. José María Sánchez y Tapia, near Laredo, north of the Rio Grande, in 1828. (Jean Louis Berlandier, *The Indians of Texas in 1830*, John C. Ewers, ed., Patricia Reading Leclercq, trans. [Washington, D.C., 1969], plate 1, and p. 156. Courtesy, The Thomas Gilcrease Institute of American History and Art, Tulsa, Oklahoma).

Under independent Mexico, then, pressure from Apaches, Comanches, and other groups checked the expansion of much of the frontier. Only in today's Arizona did Indians actually force Mexican frontiersmen to retreat. Farms and ranches, which had proliferated in northernmost Sonora during the interlude of peace in the late eighteenth century, were abandoned and reduced to ashes by the 1830s. Even the beseiged state capital at Arizpe had to be moved farther south to Ures in 1838, and Arizpe's population plummetted from 7,000 in 1838 to about 1,500 in the early 1840s. Ignacio Zúñiga, a veteran frontiersman, estimated in 1835 that since independence "over 5,000 citizens or friendly Indians . . . have been sacrificed to the ferocity of those barbarians."[7] Zúñiga's figure represents one out of every ten Sonorans and may be high, but the loss of even a few lives in the sparsely populated frontier communities could make or break them. The situation in Sonora was especially grave, with warfare on several fronts. In addition to the Apache offensive in the north, bellicose tribes in the interior, most notably the Yaquis, also maintained their independence and raided Mexican settlements.

In Texas the Mexican frontier did not recede, but Comanches and their occasional Wichita allies, such as the Tawakonis and Wacos, hindered its growth. San Antonio and Goliad both contained presidial companies, but the troops seldom provided enough security to permit extensive agriculture or ranching. Settlers planted close to home. One visitor to San Antonio in 1833 noted that "not a man ventures into his field, or to a distance of a quarter of a mile to procure wood, without taking his gun along."[8] Comanche boldness was such that on one occasion, in July 1825, 226 Comanche men, along with some women and children, reportedly rode into San Antonio and stayed for six days, entering people's houses, insulting them, and carrying off what they fancied. Following several years of respite, the ayuntamiento of San Antonio reported in 1832 that the *tejano* settlements were threatened again with "total extermination by the new Comanche uprising."[9] Allowing for some exaggeration by local officials, the matter was serious. Laredo's population had dropped by an eighth between 1828 and 1834, and the causes of the major illness in the area, as the local alcaldes wryly explained, were "bullets, lances, and arrows of the barbarous Comanches."[10]

As in other areas of the frontier, raids on Texas settlements by nomadic bands were not unrelenting, and some years passed without serious incident. Comanches, for example, honored an 1827 treaty and traded peacefully with *tejanos* for several years until resuming raids again in 1831, at which point the central government ordered a resumption of war against Comanches in both Texas and New Mexico. In an apparent

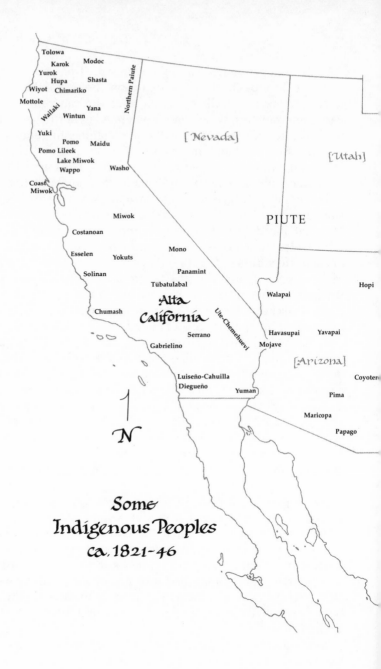

Tolowa
Karok   Modoc
Yurok
Hupa   Shasta
Wiyot   Chimariko
Mottole
Wailaki   Yana
Wintun

Yuki
Pomo   Maidu
Pomo Lileek
Lake Miwok
Wappo   Washo

Coast
Miwok

Northern Paiute

[Nevada]

[Utah]

Miwok

Costanoan

Esselen   Yokuts

Solinan

Tübatulabal

Mono

Panamint

Alta
California

Walapai

Hopi

PIUTE

Chumash

Ute-Chemehuevi

Serrano
Gabrielino

Havasupai   Yavapai
Mojave

[Arizona]

Luiseño-Cahuilla
Diegueño

Yuman

Coyoter

Pima

Maricopa

Papago

N

Some
Indigenous Peoples
ca. 1821-46

The current state of scholarship and the tendency of nomads to move in response to pulls or pushes make it difficult to place some people in precise locations. This map shows the approximate areas inhabited by native Americans.

reference to New Mexico, Chihuahua, and Sonora, the ayuntamiento of San Antonio correctly suggested in 1832 that "frontier communities toward the west have probably suffered much more,"[11] but the memory of past Indian attacks and fears for the future also crippled Texas, even in periods of respite. By the mid-1830s, as Texas stood on the brink of a split with Mexico, bands of Comanches and smaller tribes kept the province in a state of constant agitation, and several observers blamed Indian depredations for retarding progress in the *tejano* settlements of San Antonio and Goliad.[12]

Raids by hostile tribes also hindered the growth of New Mexico. As in the other frontier provinces, New Mexico seemed highly vulnerable to attack with much of its population scattered along narrow river valleys. "Nearly all the settlements are on the frontier," the tall, powerfully built, forty-three-year-old veteran officer, Donaciano Vigil, lamented in 1846.[13] New Mexico's pastoral economy, he said, made it a tempting and nearly indefensible target. Because they needed fresh pasturage, herds had to be kept at a distance from the settlements, where they made easy pickings. In their gloomiest statements, laced perhaps with a bit of hyperbole, officials predicted that the entire province would be destroyed if Indians launched a concerted attack.[14]

Depending upon how one counted, *nuevomexicanos* believed themselves surrounded by "thirty or more tribes of wild Indians."[15] Throughout the Mexican era, officials reported raids from the east by Comanches, Kiowas, Pawnees, Jicarillas, and other bands from the Plains, but the most unrelenting damage to New Mexico settlements between 1821 and 1846 came from Navajos to the west. Of Athabascan origin, as were Apaches, these seminomadic agricultural and pastoral people had resisted the Franciscans' attempts to plant missions among them and remained completely independent, although proximity to Mexicans and Pueblos had heavily influenced their culture. After a peaceful interlude that dated from 1805, Navajo raids on the Mexican and Pueblo settlements in the Rio Grande Valley resumed in 1818. Navajos drove off livestock, appropriated crops, and carried off captives. Settlements closest to Navajo country, such as Jémez and Abiquiú, were especially hard hit. Still, no place seemed safe from Navajos, including Las Vegas, to the east of the Rio Grande on the edge of the Great Plains. In 1836, Governor Albino Pérez attributed New Mexico's "critical circumstances" directly to "the ferocious war that the Navajos made upon it."[16] "The war with the Navajos," Governor Armijo wrote in 1845, "is slowly consuming us."[17]

In the mid-1840s, Utes also went to war against New Mexicans. Despite intermittent raids by small groups in the 1820s and 1830s, Utes had remained nominally at peace with the Mexican frontiersmen. This semblance of peace broke down after an ugly incident in 1844. That autumn six Ute leaders, reportedly accompanied by 800 men, rode into Santa Fe seeking reparations for the deaths of some warriors whom Mexican troops had mistakenly killed on a campaign against Navajos. Discussions between the Utes and the governor, Mariano Martínez, led to angry words and a fist fight in the governor's office in the *palacio*. According to his own account, Martínez fought the Utes off with a chair, although tradition has it that it was his wife who grabbed the chair and raised the alarm. In either case, the Utes fled town amidst gunfire, leaving some of their number dead and dying in the streets of Santa Fe where their bodies remained unburied for at least a week. Fullscale warfare with Utes followed, forcing pobladores from northern settlements such as Abiquiú, El Rito, and Ojo Caliente to flee their homes.[18]

No single Indian group in Alta California achieved the fearsome reputations of Apaches, Comanches, Navajos, or Utes, but smaller tribes raided California settlements with increasing intensity in the years before war with the United States. Nonmission Indians from the interior, who enjoyed the relative security of the Sierras, the Tulare country, and the Central Valley, together with deserters from the missions took the offensive in the 1830s and raided coastal settlements with regularity. Indians made life on the ranches insecure. and put *californios* on the defensive by the 1840s. Few *californios* died at the hands of Indians in these years, but destruction was such that one historian judged Indian raids as California's "most serious obstacle to progress and prosperity."[19] The San Diego area was hit hardest. In the late 1830s and early 1840s, outlying ranchos came under attack and had to be abandoned. The town itself saw its population drop from 520 in 1830 to about 150 in 1840, when one visitor described it as "almost deserted."[20] By the time of the Mexican-American War, according to an experienced observer, Indian attacks had become commonplace throughout California, causing some *californios* to desert their ranchos: "the Indians are losing all fear of the inhabitants and with their arrows have shot several of them during the years 1845 and 1846."[21]

From Texas to California, then, the so-called indios bárbaros effectively checked the expansion of many portions of the frontier. The decades following independence saw relations between Mexicans and Indians worsen throughout the young nation, but the persistent attacks by the indios bárbaros in the north constituted one of the country's most serious problems.[22] Finding ways to deal with what was termed the Indian problem preoccupied frontiersmen and government officials alike. Despite concern for the problem, the tempo and intensity of Indian attacks increased rather than decreased in many areas of the frontier. There are several explanations for Indian successes and Mexican failures.

Indians themselves, of course, constitute an important part of the explanation, but one that we may never fully understand since assessing motives of a people who left no written records is plainly speculative. For many Indian peoples, however, the record points toward provocations by outsiders, and Mexicans frequently provoked Indians just as their Spanish ancestors had done. In California, for example, Franciscans continued until the early 1830s to send expeditions into the interior to forcibly recruit neophytes to replace the declining indigenous population on the coast. After the secularization of the California missions, *rancheros* attempted to expand into the interior, threatening the hegemony of autonomous Indian peoples. In New Mexico, the seizure of Indian captives to work in households continued. Although illegal, the buying and selling of Indian men, women, and children continued in Santa Fe, and the resentments this engendered contributed to Navajo and Ute attacks on New Mexico settlements. The situation was similar in Sonora, where a great many domestic servants were Yumans and Apaches obtained by Mexicans in trade with Pimas on the Gila.[23]

Variation of tribal cultures and histories in the region, however, makes generalization perilous. Mojave and Yuma traditions of warfare, for example, may have owed less to intrusions by outsiders than to religious beliefs that antedated the arrival of Europeans. For other Indians, the motives behind their raids on Mexican settlements were probably as prosaic as a desire for an easy source of horses and horse meat or a search for personal glory and status.[24]

Some Indians, then, for a variety of reasons, continued to take the offensive against Mexicans, and some Indians also displayed a remarkable ability to alter their life style to deal more effectively with their adversaries. In California, for example, some peaceful, sedentary, hunting and gathering peoples adopted new techniques of warfare, learned to use the horse, and became seminomadic cavalrymen in the 1820s and 1830s. These California Indians, intruded upon by Europeans for the first time in the late eighteenth century, went through a process of adaptation that other northern tribes, such as Apaches, seem to have experienced a century before.[25]

Indian motives and adaptability, however, do not in themselves explain the great success that some autonomous tribes had in ongoing raids against the Mexicans. The explanation also lies in two changing conditions that characterized the decades following Mexican independence: first, the rapid influx into northern Mexico of Anglo-Americans who upset the balance of power and weakened old alliances based on trade; second, the failure of Mexico to mend most of those broken alliances and to strengthen its military posture to meet the new challenge.

As they moved westward, some unscrupulous Anglo-American traders helped tip the balance of power between Mexican frontiersmen and
independent Indian tribes. Writing in 1830, the liberal savant from Coahuila, Miguel Ramos Arizpe, explained how. Prior to the coming of the
Americans, he said, Indians "did not have firearms except a small number of old muskets which they received as gifts from the Spaniards, with
a very small supply of powder that hardly served them because of its
bad quality."[26] Indians thus remained "rather weak" and dependent
upon Spaniards alone for trade. Americans, Ramos Arizpe said, broke
that dependency by furnishing Indians good guns and "very exquisite
powder." Thus fortified by their new trading partners, Indians raided
Mexican settlements, taking livestock and even human captives that
could be traded to the Americans for more arms and munitions, as well
as whiskey and other goods. Some contemporaries considered it a mistake to assume that Indians did more damage with guns than with bows
and arrows, but most apparently believed firearms to be more effective,
including Indians themselves. Perhaps more important than the weapons Americans furnished, however, was the market they provided for
stolen property, thereby encouraging Indian raids on northern Mexico.
Little wonder that some of these American traders came to be charged
with "land piracy," even by their countrymen.[27]

The pernicious impact of American traders on relations with neighboring Indian tribes had first troubled Spanish officials in the eighteenth
century, and their concern increased after the United States acquired
Louisiana in 1803. By the time of Mexican independence it was widely
recognized that some Apaches, Comanches, and Wichita bands (such as
the Taovayas) stole horses and mules from *tejanos* and exchanged them
for guns and ammunition with traders in Louisiana. Acting as middlemen, Comanches were also believed to be trading guns and ammunition
with more westerly tribes. The problem became so alarming that in 1826
Mexico's secretary of state asked the United States minister in Mexico
City to stop the "traders of blood who put instruments of death in the
hands of those barbarians."[28] Years later, when the United States had
still not stopped the traffic in armaments, one high-ranking Mexican
official wondered if it was United States policy "to use savage Indians to
menace defenseless Mexicans in order to force them to abandon their
lands or . . . request the protection of the United States government."[29]

As Americans moved farther west into Texas in the 1820s, some of
their more unscrupulous countrymen spared Comanches and other Indians the inconvenience of hauling furs and stolen Mexican property all
the way to Louisiana. Texas officials, for example, had reason to believe
that some residents of Stephen Austin's colony carried on a "clandestine

Comanches.

Comanches du Texas Occidental: vêtement lorsqu'ils vont à la guerre.

Yamparica Comanche. Through trade or raids, many nomadic Indians obtained metal lance heads, metal heads for war clubs, and muzzle-loading firearms. Note, too, the powder horn and fringed leather bullet pouch worn by this "Yamparica" Comanche as depicted in a watercolor by Lino Sánchez y Tapia. Based on a description apparently of 1828 (Jean Louis Berlandier, *The Indians of Texas in 1830*, John C. Ewers, ed., Particia Reading Leclercq, trans. [Washington, D.C., 1969], plate 4 and p. 158. Courtesy, The Thomas Gilcrease Institute of American History and Art, Tulsa, Oklahoma).

trade" in arms and ammunition with Indians."[30] Mexican officials could also read in the American press about itinerant peddlers from the United States, such as a group from Kaskaskia, Illinois, who entered Texas in 1826 "on a trading adventure to the Cumanche [sic] Indians."[31] Reports that Texas officials offered a $1,000 reward for every American trading illegally with Indians apparently did not deter these merchants, and the harmful effects of their activities in Texas were no secret. One Louisiana newspaper reported in 1826 that Americans carried on "an extensive and often very lucrative trade" with Comanches, who "are supplied with goods, in return for the horses and mules, of which they rob the inhabitants of the Province [of Texas]."[32]

Dealing with Indians was sufficiently lucrative in Texas that some Americans set up trading posts along the Red River which formed the boundary with the United States. Texas officials believed that these traders not only furnished arms and ammunition to Indians, but also incited them to attack Mexican settlements. One trader, Holland Coffee, who had established a post on the upper Red River in 1833, reportedly met with some Comanches, Wacos, and Tawakonis in 1835 and "advised them to go to the interior and kill Mexicans and bring their horses and mules to him and he would give them a fair price."[33] By 1838, according to one Texas newspaper, American traders in Texas faced stiff competition for the "immense booty" that "the most powerful of the most savage nations of North America" brought back from Mexico. Much of the lucrative Indian trade, the paper said, was being siphoned off by merchants from Arkansas and Missouri, some of whom traded as far west as Santa Fe.[34]

The report was correct. The opening of the trail between Missouri and Santa Fe to legal trade in 1821 facilitated the importation of American guns and munitions to Taos, Santa Fe, El Paso, and more remote locations. From there they could be traded to Apaches, Comanches, and other tribes in Arizona, West Texas, and Chihuahua. As early as 1823 New Mexicans learned that Americans had furnished guns and ammunition to Navajos, and by the late 1820s New Mexicans recognized that American armaments had shifted the balance of power to the Indians.[35]

By the early 1830s attacks by armed nomads intensified to the south of New Mexico, prompting officials in Chihuahua to ask that their state be converted to a federal territory so that the central government would assume responsibility for military operations against Apaches and Comanches. Chihuahua officials viewed Americans as a major source of the stepped-up raids, and prohibited all trade with Indians, warning specifically that Anglo-Americans found trading arms, powder, or lead with Apaches would be executed. In 1835 Governor Albino Pérez of

New Mexico attempted to cooperate with Chihuahua officials by strictly regulating trade with indios bárbaros. He, too, singled out *norteamericanos* as the chief suppliers of arms, but he also noted that some New Mexicans followed the Americans' "corrupt and noxious example."[36] Whether or not they had been corrupted by the Americans, some pobladores did indeed traffic in stolen goods with the very Indians who raided their settlements. Chihuahua officials even suspected one New Mexico governor, Manuel Armijo, of trading guns with Apaches. New Mexicans known as *comancheros*, who traveled out to the Plains to trade with Comanches and other tribes, acquired an especially unsavory reputation following the Mexican-American War, but little is known of their activities during the Mexican era.[37] Americans, then, had no monopoly on illicit trade, but they did possess the most desirable arms and ammunition.

Repeated orders by Pérez and other officials did little to check gunrunners or curb illicit trade in New Mexico. Governor Armijo openly expressed skepticism about the effectiveness of trade embargoes without adequate troops, but even if New Mexicans had succeeded in patrolling their vast territory, Americans would have escaped the net. In the mid-1830s Americans began to build trading posts outside of Mexican jurisdiction in present Colorado. First and foremost of these isolated emporiums was Bent's Fort, on the United States' side of the Arkansas, built in 1832 or 1833. After 1835, forts St. Vrain, Vásquez, Jackson, and Lupton opened for business on the South Platte—all in American territory but close enough to Mexico that the rifles and ammunition they sold to Indians proved very troublesome.[38]

These American trading centers earned the condemnation of the dynamic cura of Taos, Antonio José Martínez. In a printed memorial to President Antonio López de Santa Anna in 1843, Martínez accused the American traders of contributing to the moral decay of Indians and of encouraging Indian depredations on New Mexico. Indians stole livestock from New Mexico, Martínez charged, in order to exchange it at the American posts for liquor. Americans also led some "idle and ill-intentioned" New Mexicans astray as well as Indians, the padre asserted. Equally distressing, Indians killed buffalo in immense quantities to obtain hides that they traded with Americans. Buffalo, Martínez warned, were not only becoming scarce, but would soon become extinct as a species and the naciones bárbaras, who depended upon buffalo for their survival, would turn more and more toward New Mexico to "rob and pillage."[39] A few years after Martínez issued this prediction, it was said that New Mexico hunters needed to travel over 250 miles to find buffalo, but obtained so little meat that they consumed it all on the journey home.[40]

Bent's Fort. This rude watercolor sketch by Lt. James W. Abert, made in 1845, shows a party of Cheyennes celebrating a victory over Pawnees in the courtyard of Bent's Fort while traders, seated on the portal, look on. Part of a fur press is visible on the right (John Galvin, ed., *Through the Country of the Comanche Indians in the Fall of the Year 1845* . . . [San Francisco, 1970], facing p. 4. Courtesy, John Howell — Books).

One of the most dramatic examples of the impact of American traders on traditional trading patterns and alliances is the case of the Utes. Occupying lands to the northwest of the New Mexico settlements, Utes had been rather consistent allies of New Mexicans throughout the first decades of the nineteenth century. In the late 1830s, however, Antoine Robidoux, an American of French ancestry who had become a Mexican citizen, built trading posts on the Gunnison River, in present Colorado, and on the Uintah River, in today's Utah. At those posts Robidoux traded guns and ammunition for pelts, and from the late 1830s on, tensions between Utes and New Mexicans increased. By 1844, when the ugly incident involving Governor Martínez provoked the Utes to "war," they no longer depended on New Mexicans for trade and possessed the means to launch a devastating series of attacks. Robidoux's activities alone did not cause the Ute "war," of course, but Mexican officials rightly suspected that Robidoux contributed substantially to their problems with Utes.[41]

By 1844, when Utes stepped up their raids on New Mexico, Robidoux was not the only American supplying the tribe with arms and munitions. A desultory group of American traders had settled at places like Pueblo, Hardscrabble, and Greenhorn in the Upper Arkansas Valley on the eastern edge of the Front Range of the Rockies, and wantonly exchanged firearms for stolen Mexican livestock. Utes maintained harmonious relations with these Americans while simultaneously raiding New Mexico. One New Mexico officer was not far off the mark in describing the American traders as "protectors" of the Utes.[42]

The Ute example is not an isolated case. Other Indians, too, such as the band of Apaches known today as White Mountain, raided Mexican settlements and befriended American merchants.[43] It is understandable, then, that by 1846 one New Mexican could lament that "the lot of the Indians around New Mexico has improved at the time that ours has worsened."[44]

Indian raids on New Mexico increased not only as a result of the activities of American traders, but also due to demographic pressures from westward-moving American settlers. In a report to Congress in 1826, forty-six-year-old Juan Bautista Pino, a former alcalde of Santa Fe and one of several sons of the venerable Pedro Bautista Pino, New Mexico's delegate to the 1812 Spanish Cortes, explained the situation as many New Mexicans must have understood it. The growing population of North Americans, he said, had forced Kiowas and their allies toward the west. They in turn pushed other tribes toward New Mexico so that "in time we will probably have them on top of us." "These [Indian] Nations are like balls in a row," Pino explained. When the first received a "strong impulse it is passed along until it reaches the last." The source of the "strong impulse," according to Pino, was "the wise and practical policy adopted by the government in Washington." The "active" Americans, Pino believed, had expanded their border rapidly by purchasing land from Indians and pushing them toward northern Mexico. When he wrote in the fall of 1829, Pino may have learned from American traders of strong sentiment in the United States for the removal of Cherokees and other so-called civilized tribes from the Southern states to lands beyond the Mississippi—sentiment which helped put Andrew Jackson in the White House in 1829 and which resulted in passage of the Indian Removal Act early in the following year.[45]

By the 1830s the influence of westward-moving American traders was felt in California, with its abundance of mules and horses. Governor Manuel Victoria reported to Mexico City in 1831 that "the interior valleys are being overrun by foreigners, who come in great numbers to corrupt the gentiles, and to steal." Horse thieves, among whom were traders from New Mexico, Victoria reported, "have begun trading with the gentiles, the fugitive Christians and the Neophytes of the missions and it results that the Indians of the mountains and the Tulares steal horses from the missions and ranchos in order to sell them."[46] Victoria's successor, José de Figueroa, also recognized and deplored the influence of the foreigners. He prohibited foreigners from trapping in California and put a complete embargo on trade with "heathen Indians." To enforce these restrictions he ordered presidial officers at San Diego, Santa Barbara, and Monterey to patrol the coastal ranges and interior valleys. The program met modest success. Raids quieted for a few years, but resumed again in 1837, after Figueroa's death.[47]

Californios had no prior experience with foreign interlopers from the east until the first years after Mexican independence. In 1826, trapper Jedediah Smith had become the first American to find his way across the continent to California, and he and the trappers who followed him found California horses as valuable a trade item as furs. Domesticated California horses, which Smith purchased at $10 a head, brought $50 at the trapper's annual mountain rendezvous in 1827. Not all American trappers demonstrated Smith's scruples about obtaining California horses legally. Some American trappers enlisted the aid of Indians to raid California ranchos, and other trappers personally turned to horse thieving in the late 1830s and 1840s as the fur trade fell on hard times.[48] Among the better known mountain men turned horse thieves were "Peg-leg" Smith, "Old Bill" Williams, Joseph Reddeford Walker, Jim Beckwourth, and Jean Baptiste Chalifoux. Much of the stolen California stock was driven east to New Mexico or sold at trading posts such as Bent's Fort. From there, some animals might be driven on to Missouri. By the 1840s, however, the increased traffic of Americans bound for Oregon seemed to move the market for stolen California livestock much farther west. California officials believed that American settlers in Oregon provided Indians with guns in exchange for stolen cattle and horses.[49]

Nuevomexicanos, who first brought woven goods from Santa Fe to Los

Angeles beginning in 1830, also sought California horses and traded liquor with Indians in exchange for stolen stock. Merchants from New Mexico earned such a bad reputation that Governor Figueroa had felt obliged to ask the governor of New Mexico for help: "Every man coming from that territory is believed to be an adventurer and a thief," he wrote.[50] California officials took stern measures to regulate the New Mexico traders, treating them as if they were foreigners.

In addition to New Mexicans, Americans, and California Indians who plundered their livestock, California rancheros also found themselves victimized by Indians from outside the province. Navajos, for example, reportedly stole cattle near Los Angeles in 1834. Nez Perces, Yakimas, and Cayuses from the north raided the Sacramento Valley. Utes, associated with Anglo-Americans, apparently made their way to California during these years and drove stolen livestock from the West Coast to New Mexico where they traded with foreigners and Mexicans alike. Walkara, the most notorious of the Ute leaders, is believed to have worked with Peg-leg Smith to make off with 1,200 animals from Mission San Luis Obispo in 1840. Walkara continued to lead raids into California well after the United States conquest in 1846, selling the stolen stock to Mormons in Salt Lake City.[51]

Indians who traveled farthest to raid California settlements were Delawares and Shawnees. Driven from their ancestral homes in the United States, bands of some of these displaced tribes took refuge in East Texas, along with displaced Creeks, Kickapoos, Cherokees, and Choctaws (groups that originally lived in such states as Wisconsin, Delaware, Pennsylvania, Georgia, Tennessee, Alabama, and Mississippi). Mexican officials generally welcomed these refugees from America, hoping they would form a buffer against both Anglo-Americans and the indios bárbaros. Some of these Indians did become allies of Mexicans. Some English-speaking Shawnees and Delawares, on the other hand, joined with American trappers and adventurers, stealing horses in northern Mexico, and as far west as California where officials corrupted the name *Shawnees* to *Chaguanosos*.[52]

Thus, from Texas to California, those unscrupulous Anglo-Americans who armed and displaced Indians contributed enormously to Mexico's difficulties in controlling autonomous northern tribes. As one Mexican historian reminds us, "the guides or pioneers of the so-called American West were spies in our territory and dealers in furs and arms—many of them were constant instigators of attacks on Mexican towns and villages."[53] Indeed, Mexico viewed American traders as so pernicious that it pressed the United States government for protection from them in the treaty ending the Mexican-American War. But American traders continued to furnish means and incentives for Indians, especially Apaches, to attack northern Mexico well into the 1850s.[54]

Historians have often noted that the defensive alliances and military posture that worked for Spain in the late eighteenth century crumbled under independent Mexico, but few have understood that American westward expansion made Mexico's task more difficult.[55]

Essentially, Mexico tried to continue policies that had worked for Spain, but with one dramatic twist. Beginning with the Iturbide government, as we have seen, all persons born in Mexico became equal, including Indians. In theory, the government solved the so-called Indian problem by ending legal proscriptions for Indians and making them citizens. Implicitly, equality applied also to the "errant" Indians of the North, including Apaches and Comanches. This new policy raised serious questions, of course. "Can the Indian be considered truly free while he does not understand his rights as a citizen?" asked one California delegate to Congress.[56] Some liberals would have answered "yes." Granting citizenship to Indians represented an effort to implement the ideals of liberty and equality, for which the young Mexican nation stood.

Defining all Indians in the Republic as Mexicans caused confusion in military circles, however, because certain Indians did not behave like responsible citizens. In 1835 the comandante general in Chihuahua asked the secretary of war about the status of Apaches and other "tribes in rebellion": "Should they be considered as children of the great Mexican family, or as enemies to be driven beyond the boundaries of this state?" President Santa Anna replied personally. Rebellious tribes, he said, "are Mexicans, because they were born and live in the Republic. . . . The state of barbarity in which they are raised prevents them from knowing their universal obligations, and those that belong to them as Mexicans." The president preferred that "kindness and consideration" be used to bring these "unfortunates" to live peacefully in settlements under legal authorities. Only if that failed would he authorize the use of force to bring about peace.[57]

Santa Anna's response to the comandante in Chihuahua represented an expression of aspirations and ideals more than a statement of reality. In practice, most Indian tribes were treated as separate political entities. State governments made war against Indians, exempted them from taxes, and signed treaties with them as if they were sovereign powers. In 1839, for example, Governor Armijo of New Mexico offered to naturalize all Navajos as part of the terms of a peace treaty. Clearly he did not regard Navajos as Mexicans.[58]

Raid and counterraid continued in the Far North, then, despite the best intentions of theorists in Mexico City. Nonetheless, even on the frontier where men had the most to lose at the hands of marauding tribes, many pobladores seemed to believe that Indians ought to be assimilated rather than annihilated or removed. Padre Martínez, for example, believed that the only effective way to cope with the "barbarians" was to "bring them to live in civilized society, to cultivate the soil, to practice the various arts and crafts, [and] to raise livestock."[59] Men with military backgrounds, too, such as Ignacio Zúñiga of Sonora, Manuel Armijo of New Mexico, and José Francisco Ruiz of Texas, argued in favor of winning a peace through persuasion, commerce, and agriculture rather than by military force alone.[60]

The argument that Indians ought to be won over with the velvet glove rather than pounded into submission with an iron fist echoed the philosophy behind the successful Spanish Indian policy of the late colonial period. Indian hostilities had declined dramatically in the 1780s and detente lasted until the wars of independence upset the system in the 1810s. Spain's achievement owed as much to efforts to make Indians dependent for trade goods, including guns, ammunition, and repairs of firearms, as it did to warfare. Through the judicious application of both the velvet glove and the iron fist, Spanish officials had made peace more attractive than war for Indians.[61]

Liberal political theorists in independent Mexico generally continued to follow the premise of Spanish policy that a bad peace was preferable to a good war. "It is necessary to abandon all ideas of conquest," one government report of 1821 said, because war cost more than "commerce and friendship."[62] Although this report suggested that Apaches and Comanches might constitute an exception, in general the kind of bellicose Indian policy that Mexican liberals saw in the neighboring United States seemed inhumane, unwise, and outdated. Liberals pointed to the success that Frenchmen, Englishmen, and Russians had in using trading posts as instruments of Indian control and unfairly contrasted the success of those posts with the failure of Spain's "cruel military men and the ignorant missionaries of the northern frontiers" who had been unable to stop what Tadeo Ortiz termed "continuous, costly, and bloody war."[63]

There were those who took a hardline position on Indian raids of course, both in Mexico City and on the frontier, and some whose views shifted, such as Tadeo Ortiz. From the safe vantage point of Mexico City and France, Ortiz had argued for a compassionate policy, but after a visit to Texas he wanted to drive the "bloodthirsty and treacherous" Indians out of Mexico by force.[64] Lorenzo de Zavala, a liberal from Yucatán and staunch admirer of the United States, argued that Mexicans should oblige the Indians to become civilized, or force them to leave the country, "as the North Americans are doing."[65] Lt. José María Sánchez, who visited

Texas in 1828, thought that Mexicans there would never enjoy peace until Apaches and Comanches were "totally exterminated."[66] Many *californios,* including some of the friars, took a pessimistic view of the California Indians' ability to assimilate, and would have agreed with José Bandini when he wrote of the Indians in 1828: "I doubt that they would ever be capable of responding to good influences."[67] Indeed, there seem to be more examples of lack of respect for Indians and extraordinary cruelty toward them by the *californios* than among other pobladores, reflecting perhaps the military weakness of the California Indians compared to other tribes. Dissent and exceptions notwithstanding, the assimilationist view prevailed, rooted as it was in Hispanic tradition and tempered, perhaps, by the knowledge of the impossibility of complete military victory over the numerous frontier tribes.

The Spanish tradition of trade and the distribution of presents continued to win acceptance, both in Mexico City and on the frontier, as key elements of an enlightened Indian policy. Mexican officers continued to distribute gifts such as tobacco, sugar, knives, cloth, mirrors, buttons, spoons, shirts, medals, and other manufactured items, purchased from a special "allies fund." The same fund was used to feed and entertain visiting delegations of Indians.[68]

Purchasing a peace met modest success. In New Mexico and Texas some Apaches and Comanches apparently spared those provinces from more serious raids because they served as convenient entrepôts for goods taken from wealthier provinces to the south. On the local level, individual pobladores put self-interest first and traded with those Indians with whom the larger nation was at war. As one anthropologist has written: "Trade has facility to survive when all other means of communication cease."[69]

As control over trade shifted increasingly to the westward-moving Anglo-Americans, however, it became less effective as a diplomatic tool for Mexicans. Donaciano Vigil, an officer of exceptional education who would become governor of New Mexico following the American conquest, summed up the situation clearly in the spring of 1846. During the Spanish period, he said, the application of the velvet glove—trade, gifts, and alliances—had made the iron fist less necessary. The coming of Anglo-Americans, however, had lessened Indian dependency on Mexicans and made it more necessary than ever to rely on the iron fist, even though most frontiersmen and statesmen in Mexico would have preferred a pacific solution to what was termed the "Indian problem."[70]

Vista del Presidio de Goliad antes Bahia del Espiritu Santo.
tomada desde la Mision
(Texas)

Presidio of Goliad. From the Mission of Espíritu Santo in 1834, Jean Louis Berlandier drew this sketch of the presidio on a nearby hill. Berlandier did not think it deserved to be called a fort, and described it as "nothing but a pile of houses and huts . . . . gathered in disorder around a bulwark which serves as a fortification" (*Journey to Mexico During the Years 1826 to 1834*, C. H. Muller and Katherine K. Muller, eds. [Austin, 1980], II: 373, 377. Courtesy, Western Americana Collection, Yale University).

6

Crumbling Presidios, Citizen-Soldiers, and the Failure of the Iron Fist

The garrison of this fort has received nothing for seven months, and is therefore reduced to the most deplorable state.—General Manuel Mier y Terán, *Nacogdoches, 1828,*

The chests of these inhabitants are like a wall.—Juan Estevan Pino, *Santa Fe, 1829*

The tried and true bastion of frontier defense under Spain had been a line of presidios, manned by small units of light cavalry. Under independent Mexico, new challenges to the security of the frontier made the presidios more necessary than ever. But as with the mission—that other key institution for pacification of the frontier under Spain—the presidial system decayed after 1821, and the responsibility for defense fell more heavily on the frontiersmen themselves.

The costly presidios had come under severe criticism in the late colonial period as ill-suited to contain the style of warfare waged by nomads on horseback. Indians could easily avoid those stationary, scattered forts that were more effective as places of refuge than as launching points for offensive thrusts against the elusive nomads. Yet as a result of a variety of innovations, presidios contributed to the peace that Spanish policy had forged by the 1780s. Presidial commanders improved their offensive capabilities and made greater efforts at cooperation. Equally important, presidios became trading posts, centers for the distribution of gifts, and focal points of military reservations where once-bellicose Indian bands might settle and become Spanish allies. Thus, although presidios in and of themselves were blunt and clumsy instruments of war, when used in conjunction with diplomacy and trade they constituted a useful tool for frontier defense.[1]

Not surprisingly, independent Mexico tried to retain the presidial system. In regulations adopted in 1826, the central government called for the establishment of new garrisons and the reinforcement of old ones in the Far North, excepting the Californias which fell under a separate jurisdiction. Frontier presidios would operate independently of the Mexican army, as they had in the past, for officials explicitly recognized the unique demands of frontier defense. Also, as in the Spanish period, the overall operation of the frontier garrisons came under direction of commanding generals—*comandantes generales*. The 1826 regulations provided for three of these officers: one to oversee Nuevo León, Tamaulipas, and Coahuila-Texas; another to serve Chihuahua and New Mexico; and a third for Sonora and Sinaloa. With headquarters designated at Palafox, Chihuahua City, and Arizpe, none of these commanding generals were stationed on the farthest reaches of the frontier and only Palafox, located on the eastern bank of the Rio Grande above Laredo, fell within the limits of the present United States. The new comandante, Anastasio Bustamante, never occupied Palafox, however. Indians, reported to be Comanches and Lipan Apaches, destroyed the settlement; Bustamante, who would become Mexico's president in 1830, moved his headquarters down the river to Laredo.[2]

New Mexicans protested that the distance to command headquarters hindered their ability to respond to emergencies. The highest ranking officer in Santa Fe, a *comandante principal*, had to await instructions from the comandante general in Chihuahua before launching a campaign. In response to numerous petitions, the system was temporarily modified in 1839 and New Mexico was granted its own comandante general, with Governor Manuel Armijo filling the position.[3]

The Spanish-inspired presidial system outlined in the 1826 legislation remained the blueprint for frontier defense until after the war with the United States. Indeed, everything from tactics to uniforms remained heavily influenced by Spanish tradition. In 1834 the Mexican government went so far as to reprint the Spanish military regulations of 1772 with no change whatsoever, preserving even the royal signature, "YO EL REY."[4]

Regardless of the traditions behind the laws, however, the presidial system existed largely on paper. In theory, officials showed considerable concern for administrative detail, but in practice they could not bring the number of presidios or the level of troop support up to the requirements of the 1826 regulations. Efforts at reform generally failed.[5]

Under the 1826 regulations, Texas was supposed to have garrisons of 107 soldiers plus assorted officers at both San Antonio and Goliad. In 1825, these two companies together totaled only 59 men. By 1832, the number of troops in Texas had increased to about 140, but only 70 men were actually under arms. As a rule, the Texas garrisons were under-manned, but the number of troops assigned to the province varied con-siderably depending upon perceived threats from Anglo-Americans.[6]

The situation was similar in northern Sonora. The 1826 law called for maintaining the former Spanish presidios at Tucson and Tubac. Instead of the eighty-eight soldiers that the regulations called for, Tubac on some occasions could muster fewer than a dozen men. Tubac was not only short of manpower, but lacked artillery and even its walls had crumbled away. One officer suggested in 1842 that the only thing that saved the soldiers from annihilation were Apache allies who lived near-by, but within a few years even those *Apaches de paz*, or *mansos* as Span-ish officials had called them, could not save Tubac. Pressure from hostile Apaches and the lure of gold in California forced the complete aban-donment of the post in 1848.[7]

Three presidial companies, each with ninety soldiers, were to be sta-tioned in New Mexico according to the regulations. Instead, the territory had only one permanent garrison with some one hundred men until about 1836, when units were stationed at Taos and San Miguel del Bado in addition to Santa Fe. New Mexico's garrisons remained chronically un-dermanned. In 1841, for example, Taos had only twenty-seven men.[8]

Although it did not fall under the 1826 regulations, Alta California was to continue to maintain its four Spanish presidios: San Diego, Santa Barbara, Monterey, and San Francisco. Troops at these posts were re-sponsible for defense against foreigners as well as for Indian control and had an immense territory to cover. An inland chain of presidios seemed vital but expansion never occurred. Instead, the coastal presidios them-selves declined. The number of troops in Alta California fell from a high of about 710 in 1821 to about 400 in 1831 and 125 in 1841, counting retired soldiers. By the late 1830s a new presidio had grown up at Sonoma, which the town's founder, tall, handsome, well-educated and vigorous Gen. Mariano Guadalupe Vallejo, maintained at his own expense. San Francisco and San Diego had been abandoned earlier, however, and few troops remained at Santa Barbara. As early as 1829 all the presidios had fallen into such a state of decay that Governor Echeandía reported to the minister of war that "in Alta California there is no presidio, for the four [places] which bear the name are mere squares of adobe huts, in ruins . . . without any defense of ditches, stockades, walls, batteries, advantageous situation, water supply, wood, food, . . . "[9] A more dismal description would be difficult to imagine.

Ironically, the decay of the frontier presidios occurred simultaneously with the ascent of the military to the dominant position in Mexican politics after the wars of independence. As the nation's most pampered and powerful institution, the military became glutted with authorized manpower and top heavy with officers. It demanded and got the lion's share of the national budget.[10]

Beneath the surface, however, authorized manpower and high budgets meant little. In a chronically bankrupt nation, the annual military budget actually exceeded annual government revenues more often than not during Mexico's first quarter century of nationhood. Of those funds actually received by the military, a sizable proportion was diverted into the private accounts of corrupt officers. Only a trickle found its way down to the rank and file. Throughout the nation, not just on the frontier, most soldiers remained inadequately paid, fed, clothed, and equipped. Under these circumstances, morale dropped, desertion rates climbed, and units remained under their legally authorized strength. To fill the ranks, officers had to conscript or physically force men to serve. Since monied or influential classes avoided the ranks, vagabonds, criminals, and Indian peasants, sometimes kept in chains, formed the majority of the soldiery and popular respect for the military declined. Put simply, presidial forces on the frontier reflected the demoralized condition of a national army whose officer class had forsaken the public good for private gain.[11]

Despite the desperate need for troops on the frontier, politically motivated officers kept their units concentrated near the centers of power—Mexico City or Veracruz—so they could be on the scene when a government tottered and opportunity beckoned. To frontiersmen, the politicization of the army and its concentration near the capital demonstrated distorted priorities. "I shall be infinitely glad when you are able to pacify the revolution and turn your view toward the frontier," the comandante of Tucson wrote to his commanding officer in 1845.[12] From the vantage point of Mexico City, however, the defensive needs of the frontier were generally out of sight and out of mind. Seldom did newspapers note, as one did in 1827, the peculiarity of having well-equipped and well-dressed troops in the capital while Indian raids went unchecked in the north.[13]

Only the threat of foreign attack or internal rebellion seemed to bring substantial military support from Mexico City. Texas provides the best example. When an American settler, Haden Edwards, revolted against the government in 1826, Col. José de las Piedras was sent north and a presidio established at Nacogdoches. By 1828, however, the crisis had passed and the needs of the post were largely ignored. The cavalry had no horses, the presidio had no artillery, and the troops, according to one officer, had to sustain themselves by "almost forcibly taking over the shops of the town."[14] This pattern repeated itself in 1830, when the government sought to establish six new military posts in Texas to prevent further immigration from the United States and control the growing number of American colonists in Texas. When the crisis passed, most of the troops were withdrawn. New Mexico, too, received reenforcements to quell a revolt in 1837 and to block an outside invasion in 1842, while pleas for troops to deal with Indians had brought little or no response.[15]

Except in times of political turmoil or foreign invasion, the frontier presidios remained woefully undermanned and offered little defense against mounted Apaches, Comanches, or other independent Indian nations. As in the Spanish period, presidials were hardpressed to defend their own horses, much less the entire frontier. At Santa Fe, protecting the presidial horse herd occupied a third of the troops, but Indians made off with horses nonetheless. During the first two weeks of April 1828, Indians reportedly stole 70 horses from the troops, and a total of 300 horses in the previous six months. Indian raids kept the presidial horse herd in Santa Fe at such low levels that fresh mounts had to be driven north from Chihuahua.[16]

Without adequate mounts, offensive war was usually out of the question. A Swiss visitor to Texas, Jean Louis Berlandier, who knew the situation well and admired the troops, described presidial warfare as "little more than pursuing the natives when hostilities break out somewhere." With overloaded and ill-kept horses, "they rarely manage to catch their quarry, since the natives are better mounted."[17] That was a problem in Arizona, too. In 1845 a force from Tubac pursued Apaches to the Gila River, but it had to turn back for lack of good horses.[18]

Even had there been sufficient soldiers on the frontier with sufficient mounts, their effectiveness would have been limited by the severe shortage of guns and ammunition. Guns seemed always in short supply and poor repair, and Indians sometimes had more modern weapons than did Mexican soldiers. Ammunition was also scarce. When a Russian vessel visited San Francisco Bay in 1823, for example, Mexican troops could not fire the traditional salute until they borrowed some powder from their Russian visitors. Shortages remained acute until the outbreak of war with the United States.[19]

Still more serious, chronic shortages of food, clothing, and salaries threatened the very survival of the soldiers and their families. Soldiers went for long periods without pay, and the paymaster frequently lacked funds to purchase rations. In Sonora, some desperate soldiers sold their guns and horses in order to provide for their families, and this practice was so widespread that the governor issued a decree prohibiting citizens from buying guns from soldiers. A corporal in New Mexico reported that troops could not afford to buy soap to wash their clothes. Uniforms often were in rags or nonexistent. At one time or another, troops in each frontier province had to be put on furlough to support themselves by hunting, farming, or ranching.[20] Retired soldiers depended entirely upon the government for pensions that never seemed to arrive. They lived in "intolerable hunger, nakedness, and poverty," one group of old soldiers in New Mexico complained in 1829 with perhaps only slight exaggeration.[21]

On rare occasions when their pay did arrive, soldiers seldom saw cash. Chronically in debt to the company paymaster, troops paid for their own uniforms, horses, weapons, and repairs on their account. In lieu of cash salaries, they often received grain, overpriced merchandise (including playing cards and liquor), or promissory notes. These notes, which speculators purchased or bartered from desperate soldiers at less than face value were, one former officer said, "the object of curses of thousands of families who must sacrifice the sweat and blood of their fathers and husbands."[22] Under Spain, frontier troops had been exploited by their own officers and by merchants, but government reforms had improved the situation by the late eighteenth century. In the Mexican era, however, the situation apparently deteriorated.

Under these circumstances, soldiers drained the frontier economy rather than contributing to it. Troops in Texas, the ayuntamiento of San Antonio complained, had to be supplied with grain by the "poor inhabitants."[23] Citizens in California, Sonora, and New Mexico were often forced to provide "loans" or gifts to support the troops. In California, while the missions flourished they constituted the chief source of presidial supplies, to the growing disgust of the padres and of the Indians who served as the labor force. Everywhere, when troops traveled through the countryside, they exacted rations from ranches and farmers, making themselves an unwelcome sight. In desperation, some soldiers turned to thievery to support themselves. At San Diego in 1836, the townspeople charged that while they were off on a campaign against Indians, soldiers who could not go along because they lacked guns and ammunition stayed behind and robbed their homes.[24]

As the material welfare of the troops declined, so too did morale, dignity, and discipline. Frustrated soldiers in California went on strike and revolted on several occasions, but to no avail. Men also deserted, but the isolation of their posts may have made that more difficult than in central Mexico. Ultimately, the army in California became the refuge of men of broken spirit and the poor. Ambitious or well-connected young men took up other careers, leaving only those, as one official put it, "whose immoralities and other characteristics suit them for soldiering."[25]

Soldado Mexicano Presidial.

Soldat des presidios des états Internes du Mexique

Presidial soldier. This painting of a soldier in full uniform was done in the 1830s by Lino Sánchez y Tapia (courtesy, The Thomas Gilcrease Institute of American History and Art, Tulsa, Oklahoma).

Since few would volunteer for army service on the remote frontier, the government relied on convicts to reinforce the garrisons. Arriving without adequate money or supplies, convicts may have caused more problems than they solved, especially among the *californios*. California needed troops and money, wrote General Mariano Guadalupe Vallejo, "but the first without the second is vicious."[26]

Thus, although there were notable exceptions, the quality of the frontier soldiery, both officers, and regulars, apparently worsened under independent Mexico. Few soldiers seemed eager to embrace the stern discipline prescribed by one Sonora *político* who wanted spartan officers who slept with their guns rather than with their wives. Ignacio Zúñiga of Sonora, a second generation frontier officer whose father had served as commander at Tucson, saw no solution except to dismiss all the troops "to the last drummer . . . without leaving a single one to serve as a bad example."[27]

Some officials who understood frontier problems suggested that the quality of the soldiery would be improved if the government granted land to the troops. Soldiers with property, they argued, would be more zealous in defending it. Moreover, as Manuel Castañares, California's deputy to Congress in 1844, asked, "who is more worthy of possessing land than he who defends it?"[28] Writing from Nacogdoches in 1832, Comandante José de las Piedras proposed that the government form an agricultural and industrial colony in East Texas. This, he said, would make the soldiers self-supporting and even produce a surplus. Moreover, putting soldiers to work would strike at the moral problems brought on by idleness: "frequenting the tavern, games, and women, all vices, each one of which necessarily causes the destruction of health and of fortune."[29] Ideas for the formation of military colonies on the frontier abounded, but implementation of these plans did not take place until the war between Mexico and the United States galvanized the central government into action.[30]

The general decline in the quality of the soldiery and the garrisons was accompanied by a decline in the effectiveness of other strategies. In the late eighteenth century, coordination of troops between provinces had helped pressure Indians into peace. After 1821, however, hard-pressed comandantes were often unable to commit scarce resources beyond their own provinces and calls for cooperation went unanswered. In early 1841, for example, General Mariano Arista, then in Chihuahua, ordered New Mexico Governor Armijo to join a united campaign against Comanches. After consulting with "all the officials and respected persons of the Department," Armijo declined. Armijo was "aware of his duty to the general welfare of the entire Republic," as he explained to the Minister of war, "but to declare war on the Comanches would bring complete ruin to the Department."[31]

Well before the 1840s, New Mexicans had made a separate peace with most Comanches. New Mexico officials such as Armijo were already at war with Navajos and seemed unwilling to jeopardize their community by taking action against friends and potential allies. In 1844, for example, a group of Comanche leaders arrived at Santa Fe and made no secret of their plans to attack Chihuahua. Governor Mariano Martínez did nothing more than give them gifts and warn Chihuahua officials of the impending attack.[32]

The practice of putting self-preservation first was commonplace on the Mexican frontier, as on the American frontier, and Indians knew how to profit from it. After signing a peace treaty with Chihuahua officials and receiving rations, for example, Apaches crossed over the Sierra to attack Sonora, which the treaty had specifically exempted. Little wonder that outsiders such as the American merchant Josiah Gregg condemned the "imbecility of the local governments" for their failure to cooperate.[33] Gregg did not realize, however, that cooperation required resources and that his own countrymen would behave similarly under the same circumstances.

As the presidial system lost effectiveness under independent Mexico, some officers came to look back with nostalgia on the Spanish period as a time when well-mounted, well-paid, and well-provisioned troops were disciplined, effective and enjoyed respect. As Ignacio Zúñiga bitterly summed it up in a pamphlet published in Mexico City in 1835: "The gains of 100 years, the fruits of sacrifices of all classes, were lost when Sonora had the fortune to form part of the independent Mexican Republic."[34] Zúñiga and others may have exaggerated the effectiveness of their forefathers, but their conclusion deserves serious consideration: the continuing attacks on the frontier did not result as much from Indian effectiveness as it did from the decay of the presidios.

As the frontier garrisons fell into disarray, the burden of defense fell more heavily on the pobladores themselves. Volunteers had long played a key role in defense of the borderlands, and in the late eighteenth century the Spanish Bourbons began to formalize militia units throughout New Spain.[35] The government of independent Mexico continued those efforts, repeatedly affirming the importance of militia as an auxiliary force. A strong militia seemed an economically sound alternative to maintaining a large standing army, and some liberals hoped that the growth of militia would weaken the power and privileges of the army and keep officers out of politics.[36]

Several types of militia had operated in Mexico in the late colonial period. Under independent Mexico, the government continued to distinguish between at least two kinds of militia: active and local. Small, crack units known as *activos* or *urbanos,* theoretically controlled and funded by the national government, functioned as a reserve force for the regular army. When in service, the activos enjoyed the same awards and privileges as the army. Regulations of 1826 called for the establishment of several one-hundred man units of activos in the north, but the only one to operate in the area of today's United States seems to have been a small, underfunded group in Santa Fe.[37]

Local militia, also known as *cívicas, rurales,* and *milicía nacional,* included all able-bodied men, except those with position or wealth who could afford to pay a fee to avoid service.[38] Truly a local force under the terms of the 1824 Constitution, these units could not be deployed beyond the boundaries of their respective states or territories without special permission of Congress. Power to regulate local militia resided with individual states that drew up their own regulations, as did the states of Occidente and Coahuila y Texas in 1828.[39] In Texas, at least two units of local militia operated out of San Antonio, one out of Goliad, and another functioned in Austin's colony under regulations that required foreign colonists to form militia to defend themselves.[40]

Because of its status as a territory rather than a state, New Mexico formed a local militia more slowly than Texas. Congress failed to authorize local militia for the territories until 1834, when it established guidelines requiring local ayuntamientos to muster all males between eighteen and fifty years of age. New Mexico complied quickly with the new regulations, only to be thrown into confusion the following year. Having undergone his notorious transformation from a liberal to a conservative, President Antonio López de Santa Anna moved to weaken the power of states and territories by reducing the size of the local militia to no more than one out of every five hundred inhabitants. He did, however, permit a vaguely worded exception for those areas that bordered, in his phrase, "savage tribes."[41] As the central government grew more powerful from the mid-1830s on, it seems to have regulated local militia more directly, even to the naming of local officers.[42]

Official units of activos or local militia apparently did not operate in Arizona or California, or else did so only briefly. As late as 1845 Mariano Guadalupe Vallejo still sought government aid in establishing a militia in Alta California. The government's failure to do so may have reflected an attitude such as that of Governor Manuel Victoria, who thought a formal militia was unnecessary since most *californios* were "soldiers or at least accustomed . . . to military operations in a land of heathens."[43] For whatever reason, in California and Arizona informal groups of volunteers generally served the same purpose as militia. Formed when necessity demanded and disbanded in between times, groups of citizen-soldiers fought under a variety of names: the *Sección Patriótica* in Arizona; and *Cuerpos de Seguridad y Policía* and *Defensores del País* in California. Volunteers were important in New Mexico and Texas, too, where official militia units always suffered from a shortage of manpower and equipment. Settlers often had to demonstrate that they could defend themselves as a prerequisite to receiving land on the frontier.[44]

Whether they served in loosely organized volunteer units, or in government-sponsored militia, frontiersmen fought on their own time, at their own expense, and with only token support from the government. "The citizens," said one New Mexico priest, "contribute horses, provisions, arms, and other essentials at their own cost; they maintain themselves in the field, one, two, or three months, deprived of their families, neglecting their homes."[45]

These burdens were especially heavy since volunteers came chiefly from the lower class. In 1834, New Mexico Governor Francisco Sarracino published a decree in which he took the side of these *pobres*. He criticized the *ricos* for putting responsibility for defense "in the hands of the impoverished class" who, he said, would be ruined "if we continue in this inaction which offers dishonorable testimony to our foolishness and indifference." The lower class, Sarracino wrote, fought out of obligation, but "without enthusiasm or zeal."[46] In New Mexico, militia service was a major source of lower class resentment that would contribute to a bloody rebellion in 1837, as we shall see.

Continuing an Hispanic tradition, the pobres who served as volunteers included Indian allies such as California mission Indians, Pueblos, Pápagos, Pimas, Cherokees, and friendly Apaches and Navajos. Indian allies apparently played an indispensable role on some campaigns. In 1834, for example, as the heat of summer gave way to autumn, fifty-seven volunteers rode out of Tucson to fight Apaches. More than half of the volunteers were Indians: ten Pimas from Mission San Xavier and Tucson, and twenty *Apaches de paz*.[47] In Texas, some Cherokees, Shawnees, and Kickapoos, who had recently left the United States for northern Mexico and settled near Nacogdoches, successfully campaigned against the Tawakonis, defeating them in a battle in June 1830 without Mexican aid or direction.[48] Like Mexican frontiersmen, these pro-Mexican Indian volunteers fought other Indians, largely at their own expense. Sometimes they received supplies, a modicum of pay, and promises of booty, but often the rewards did not suffice to support their families during their absence or to make up for time lost from their fields and herds.[49]

Most Mexican officials seem to have recognized the great value of

Indian allies. The cultured and urbane Juan Nepomuceno Almonte, for example, journeyed from Mexico City to inspect Texas in 1834 and termed the Choctaws "good warriors and excellent shots with a rifle," predicting they would make a valuable addition to the Texas militia.[50] Some officials distrusted Indians, however, and that attitude probably prevented some frontier officers from making maximum use of Indians as allies. Antonio Comadurán, for example, who was head of the Tucson garrison in 1832, questioned the loyalty of Gileño and Pima allies and expressed fear that they might turn on Mexicans. General Manuel Mier y Terán voiced a similar concern about the highly respected Cherokees.[51] Thus, although Indian allies were essential to the success of many campaigns, and although some Indians fought with intensity in order to settle old scores with other tribes, distrust and uncertain material rewards probably prompted many Indians to join their Mexican counterparts in fighting "without enthusiasm or zeal."

New Mexico Governor Albino Pérez's stinging description of volunteers as "for the most part . . . unhappy wretches who regularly report fatigue," seems too harsh.[52] Given the volunteers' investment of time and resources, it is not surprising that frontiersmen of all ethnic groups, including Anglo-Americans who settled in Texas, sought ways to avoid volunteer service, especially during planting, harvesting, and branding times.

Throughout Mexico, militia service was unpopular. Citizens sought to avoid service and the government believed it had to resort to fines and physical coercion to induce people to serve.[53] The frontier was no exception, but it is likely that local circumstances made frontiersmen more willing than residents of central Mexico to volunteer. First, frontiersmen usually fought to defend their own province. Ignacio Zúñiga, a former army officer himself, thought volunteers fought more effectively than the regular army because the volunteers were "motivated by the necessity of defending themselves, or out of the desperation of revenging an outrage."[54] Second, the pobladores ran little risk of being drafted into the army or sent elsewhere in the Republic. The possibility existed, to be sure, but vast distances in the Far North usually made it impractical to move the pobladores. In 1827, for example, Congress authorized the New Mexico militia to enter Texas to help quell a local revolt, but practical considerations prevented the *nuevomexicanos* from marching.[55] Third, unlike large cities in central Mexico where impersonal relationships made recruiting volunteers difficult, the sense of community in small frontier settlements probably encouraged people to volunteer. Fourth, frontiersmen usually defended their own lands and homes, and the incidence of property ownership on the frontier seems to have been higher than in central Mexico. A Chihuahua-born attorney, Antonio Barreiro, who lived briefly in New Mexico, argued that a militia "would be more important in the territory [of New Mexico] than it would be in any other section of the republic because nearly all of its inhabitants own land or stock."[56] Finally, a crass motive induced some pobladores to fight Indians: the spoils of war, which included Indian captives who were pressed into servitude as ranch hands or household servants.[57]

For several reasons, then, the idea of entrusting defense to citizen-soldiers may have functioned better on the northern frontier than it did in the nation's core. Some *californios* were so eager to fight that they had to be restrained from setting out on unofficial expeditions against Indians, and Governor Figueroa complained that the *californios* "committed various atrocities against the heathen Indians without distinguishing between the innocent and the guilty."[58]

As the status of the army declined, militia or volunteer service probably became the most palatable option for ambitious young men who wanted to avoid service in the regular military. Although volunteers were termed *auxiliaries,* in sheer numbers the army was often auxiliary to the volunteers. In campaigns against Navajos led from New Mexico, for example, the regular army usually comprised less than 10 percent of the fighting force with the remainder being militia and assorted volunteers. Some frontiersmen may have been reluctant warriors, fighting "without enthusiasm or zeal," as Governor Sarracino charged, but they fought nonetheless and carried the burden of frontier defense. "The chests of these inhabitants are like a wall," Juan Estevan Pino wrote of the New Mexican volunteers.[59]

At times the "wall" held effectively. From his semi-feudal barony in Sonoma, on the northern edge of California, Mariano Guadalupe Vallejo maintained his own private force which successfully fended off Indians. In beleaguered northern Sonora, organized volunteers from Tucson, San Xavier del Bac, Tumacácori, and other places took the offensive against Apaches and won minor victories. They returned home with prisoners, horses, and the ears of dead Apaches.[60] In Texas, volunteers and militia scored successes against small Wichita bands, Karankawas of the coastal plain, and occasionally against Comanches. *Tejano* techniques of pursuing Indians were so well adapted to the rugged Plains environment, that they were later adopted by the Texas Rangers, who rode on Mexican saddles, slept on Mexican blankets, carried a *reata,* or lariat, and a small pouch of *pinole,* or parched corn.[61]

The successes of the pobladores, however, usually came against small tribes, such as the Tonkawas in Texas who numbered about one hundred and fifty warriors in 1830. Occasional victories occurred, but complete domination of the numerous bands of Navajos, Comanches, and Apaches eluded frontiersmen. Indian tactics stymied Mexican forces, just as they would mystify American troops later in the century. For example, even with the aid of a group of Navajo collaborators, known to their own people as *Diné Ana'aii*, or "Enemy Navajo," New Mexicans could seldom force Navajos into a direct confrontation. Aware in advance of troops moving across their lands, Navajos usually scattered and retreated, often driving their livestock before them. In 1823 Colonel José Antonio Vizcarra put 1500 men in the field for seventy-four days, taking them to the awesome Canyon de Chelly in the heart of Navajo country and on to the Hopi villages. This substantial force killed only thirty-three Navajos, at least eight of whom were women, and five Piutes who were mistaken for Navajos. Vizcarra's party also captured thirty Navajos and rounded up 801 sheep and goats, 87 cattle, and 23 horses and mules. These expeditions, which almost certainly provoked Navajo reprisals, occasionally forced Navajos to the conference table. There, under duress, some Indian leaders put their mark on a one-sided peace treaty that they, or other Navajos who had no part in the negotiations, soon broke.[62]

Fighting scattered bands of Navajos and other large groups of mounted Indians on their own ground and on their own terms, the outnumbered and poorly equipped volunteers had no more chance of complete victory than did the regular army. Mexican volunteers lacked even the advantage of firepower, due in no small part to an annoying government monopoly of gunpowder and governmental restrictions against the importation of foreign arms and munitions. In New Mexico most pobladores fought with bows and arrows instead of guns. In 1833, one district mustered 467 men, of whom 318 had bows and arrows and 149 had firearms.[63] Meanwhile, thanks to foreign traders, hostile Indians had more guns than ever.

Thus, on the eve of war with the United States, autonomous Indian peoples, some at war with one another and pressured by westward-moving Americans, retained control over much of the far northern frontier of Mexico. Traditional means of pacifying these tribes—the presidial system, alliances based upon trade dependency, gifts, and diplomacy—had worked for Spain but no longer sufficed to check the incursions of mounted nomads who had access to an independent supply of arms. Divided and weakened by internal political discord, independent Mexico could provide neither sufficient direction nor resources to carry out an effective Indian policy on the frontier. "We are surrounded on all sides . . . by many tribes of heartless barbarians, almost perishing; and our brothers instead of helping us are at each other's throats in their festering civil wars," Mariano Chávez of New Mexico bitterly complained in 1844.[64]

As Chávez's remark suggests, the central government's failure to contribute substantially to frontier defense took its place alongside other grievances and heightened the pobladores' sense of frustration and alienation from Mexico City. "To wait for protection from the central government . . . would be to wait in vain," wrote Donaciano Vigil in the spring of 1846.[65] Indeed, as early as the 1820s the central government had received reports of the possibility of treason in New Mexico, because surrounding Indians were better armed and the *nuevomexicanos* might have to turn to the United States for protection.[66]

When American troops arrived in the mid-1840s, they came to conquer rather than to protect, confident that they would meet little resistance. Reports by American citizens, who had visited Mexico's far northern frontier in ever-increasing numbers, had painted a vivid picture of the squalid condition of the region's defenses.[67]

7

The New Colonalism
Americans and the Frontier Economy

. . . that restless enterprise that . . . is now leading our countrymen to all parts of the world . . . until it can now be said
there is not a breeze of heaven but spreads an American
flag.—Jedediah Smith, *Los Angeles, 1827*

All the ships that were trade carriers were foreign. The greater
part of the capital in the territory was in the hands of foreigners. . . . The daughters of the most distinguished citizens of
the territory had married men who had been born across the
Pacific.—Juan Bautista Alvarado, *California, 1876 (recalling the
Mexican era)*

The winds of economic change blew persistently across all of Mexico in
the years that followed her independence from Spain, but they buffeted
the far northern frontier with special fury, upsetting old structures and
spinning the frontier economy around. Prior to 1821 the economic life-
lines of the Far North ran southward, to the markets of Chihuahua,
Durango, and Mexico City. Within a few years after independence those
north-south lines had been weakened and vigorous new economic ties
with the United States had begun to supplant them. By the mid-1840s it
seemed clear that the far northern frontier had grown as dependent
upon the United States for markets and merchandise as it once had been
on central New Spain. In this respect, the frontier exemplified a process
that occurred in the rest of Mexico. Political independence from Spain
did not bring economic independence to Mexico. Her trade orientation
simply shifted from that of a colonial dependency of Spain to that of a
neocolonial dependent of England, the United States, and France—a

122

condition recognized by contemporaries as well as historians.[1] Partly because of its proximity to the United States, the once-isolated northern frontier became more rapidly entangled in the American economy than did the rest of Mexico.

From Texas to California, the end of the Spanish era seemed to offer wonderful economic opportunities for the pobladores. For decades they had been restive and eager for reform of policies that restricted trade, limited markets, stifled competition, and discouraged local initiative.

To protect her own manufacturers and merchants and to maximize tax revenues, the Spanish Crown had required that all trade be conducted within her empire and closed her colonies to foreigners. That exclusionist policy had fostered monopolies and price fixing, driving prices up throughout Spain's American colonies. On New Spain's far northern frontier, monopolies and high prices must have seemed especially annoying because residents could not trade legally with their closest or most convenient neighbors. Theoretically, *tejanos* could not buy or sell in neighboring Louisiana, and *californios* could have no dealings with British and American merchant vessels that plied Pacific trade routes. Isolated on the fringes of New Spain, then, law-abiding frontiersmen had paid high transportation costs for goods from Spain and Central Mexico that added to the price of imports and left their exports at a competitive disadvantage in southern markets.

Other government policies exacerbated this situation. To protect influential merchants and maintain tight control over commerce, Spain had required that all trade between New Spain and the mother country be conducted through Veracruz. To trim freighting costs, frontier officials had repeatedly urged the opening of closer ports, such as Matagorda on the Gulf of Mexico, or Guaymas on the Gulf of California, but their requests were never granted.[2] Merchandise had to be transported from Veracruz over torturous mountain highways to Mexico City, then northward over rude roads to San Antonio, Santa Fe, or Tucson, or to the Pacific to be transshipped to California. The heavy cost of transportation, coupled with profits for additional middlemen, and the collection of regressive excise taxes (*alcabala*) along the route had driven the cost of some items to four times their Veracruz value by the time they reached the frontier. The high price tag on necessities must have made them seem like luxury goods on the frontier.[3]

Monopolies fostered by Spain's mercantilist policies had put frontiersmen at a special disadvantage in the two military provinces of Texas and Alta California where price regulations had existed. The government had required citizens to sell produce and livestock to the army quartermaster at set prices, which one California friar described as "absurdly low," and to purchase scarce and overpriced supplies from the same source, "being charged exorbitantly."[4] *Californios* and *tejanos* seem to have been dismayed and angered by government policies that caught them in this squeeze.

Unhindered by such military regulations, *nuevomexicanos* could sell their surplus produce outside the province, but their market was limited largely to Chihuahua, forty days away, or to points still farther south. In Chihuahua, a small group of merchants monopolized trade goods, kept prices artificially high, and manipulated currency. As a result, most New Mexicans earned too little to meet their needs, bought on credit, and remained in perpetual debt, becoming as one observer put it, "truly puppets of the Chihuahua merchants."[5]

The system, then, had discouraged production. Why should a man work, asked one California padre in 1796, "when he knows that he cannot succeed and that his efforts are largely in vain?"[6]

Spain's paternalistic policies had also discouraged initiative in other ways. Officials had prohibited the capture of wild horses in Texas, for example, based partly on the belief that it distracted colonists from agriculture. Then, too, the government had exercised a monopoly over certain goods, such as tobacco and gun powder, and prohibited their manufacture locally. Frontiersmen had to import these items from central Mexico, although some termed the policy "abominable" and "stupid" and violated it with impunity. In some cases raw materials from the frontier were shipped to factories in the south and the finished product sent north again for sale.[7]

Thus, the far northern frontier of New Spain had become an exploited internal colony of merchants farther south, but that was only part of a more complex picture. Provinces in northern New Spain, such as Chihuahua, were exploited by the central provinces, and they, in turn, constituted a colonial dependency of Spain. Spain, meanwhile, had become economically dependent on France and England. Indians, whom the Mexican frontiersmen exploited, probably occupied the bottom of this pyramid.[8]

Bad as the system was for frontiersmen, it worsened during the last years before Mexican independence. A decade of revolutionary turmoil, both in Spain and in her colonies, threw New Spain's economy into chaos. Hard cash, always scarce on the frontier, nearly stopped flowing through official sources. Soldiers' salaries and missionaries' stipends went unpaid. The few overpriced manufactured goods that formerly reached the frontier no longer arrived. The privileged few with cash became wary of investing it, and the lessening of economic activity brought a drop in tax revenues for local governments. Meanwhile the beleaguered Spanish crown pressed its colonists harder for so-called voluntary donations to defend the motherland.[9]

Little wonder that frontiersmen emulated their countrymen to the south by turning increasingly to foreigners to obtain both the necessities and luxuries of life. Contraband became commonplace. Despite government prohibitions, Texas *rancheros* drove horses to market in American Louisiana, while in California the Franciscans collaborated with smugglers who paid in cash or merchandise for cowhides and sea otter skins.[10] In the face of widespread civil disobedience, government officials often felt justified in looking the other way. "Necessity makes licit what is not licit by law," reasoned California Governor José Dario Argüello.[11] Not all frontier officials, however, adopted such a relaxed attitude toward the law. Until 1821, foreigners who traded in far northern New Spain played a risky game of hide and seek with Spanish officials. Foreigners who lost the game might also lose their merchandise or spend years in jail.

With Mexico's independence from Spain, the rules of the game changed. Operating under vague policies of the provisional government, eager frontier officials seized the initiative to open their provinces to foreign merchants. The first few years after Mexican independence saw a burst of commercial activity along the trail between Santa Fe and St. Louis and the rapid growth of a maritime trade between New England and the California coast.

Although Pedro Vial had blazed a trail from Santa Fe to St. Louis in the early 1790s, Spain's commercial restrictions stood like a dike that blocked the flow of merchandise over that trail for the next three decades. With Spanish power removed from North America in 1821, however, trade goods from the United States began to flow freely into New Mexico.[12]

Eager New Mexicans lost no time in welcoming Americans to trade. On November 15, 1821, just two months after he had sworn allegiance to Mexican independence, the gracious Governor Facundo Melgares warmly received William Becknell and a small group of merchants from Missouri in his office in Santa Fe. The governor not only permitted the Missourians to trade, but as Becknell reported, Melgares "expressed a desire that the Americans would keep up an intercourse with that country."[13] Hard on Becknell's heels a second party of Americans, which included John McKnight and Thomas James, showed up in Santa Fe on December 1. A month later, Indian trader Hugh Glenn reached the New Mexico capital with still a third group. Like Becknell's party, these Americans had been trading and trapping in Indian territory on the

Salt Lake

[Nevada]

Sacramento River

Sutter's Fort

San Francisco

San Joaquin River

Monterey

Pacific

Alta
California

Ocean

Los Angeles

San Bernardino

San Diego

Mojaves

Colorado River

Yumans

Gila River

Sevier River

Utah Lake

[Utah]

Virgin River

Hopis

[Arizona]

Tucson

Tubac

Santa Cruz River

San Pedro River

Mission Santa Catarina

Baja California

Sonora

The Westward Overland
Thrust 1821-46

N

	Old Spanish Trail
—·—	Romero (1823)
—···—	Smith (1826)
- - - ? - - -	Campbell (1827)
—···—	Pattie (1828)
—···—	Armijo (1829)
....	Present-Day Political Boundaries

Between 1821 and 1846, trappers and traders—mainly from the United States—
began to open new lateral routes across northern Mexico, linking the region more
firmly to the United States.

Platte River

[Nebraska]

[Colorado]

[Kansas]

Gunnison River

Dolores River

Bent's Fort

SANTA FE TRAIL

CUTOFF

[Oklahoma]

Abiquiu

CIMARRON

Taos
Santa
Cruz
Santa Fe

?

Zuñi

?

?

Albuquerque

Ácoma

Socorro

an Francisco River

New Mexico

Santa Rita
Copper Mines

El Paso del Norte

Texas

Rio

Grande

Chihuahua

Ciudad Chihuahua

Coahuila

periphery of New Mexico when, by chance, they met a group of New Mexicans who told them they would be welcome to visit Santa Fe.[14]

The presence of three parties of Americans near the New Mexico settlements in the autumn of 1821 suggests one reason why the Sante Fe trade got off to a quick start: Americans were as eager to sell as Mexicans were to buy. Dire commerical conditions following the Depression of 1819, including a severe shortage of hard cash and a glut of merchandise, afflicted states such as Missouri, which had just entered the union in 1821, and forced some farmers and merchants to trade in the Indian country to support themselves. That was the situation for members of all three groups who reached New Mexico in the first months after independence. Thomas James, for example, found himself "with the certain prospect of bankruptcy before my face, amid the clamors of creditors, and without the hope of extricating myself from the impending ruin."[15] Even New Mexico's limited trading opportunities must have looked attractive to Americans from the depressed frontier states, especially after William Becknell returned with reports that the Santa Fe trade was "very profitable, money and mules are plentiful."[16]

Becknell knew whereof he spoke. He not only inaugurated the Santa Fe trade, but shaped it significantly. On a return trip to Santa Fe in the spring of 1822, Becknell pioneered a shortcut by way of the Cimarron River, thereby avoiding the mountainous Raton Pass entryway to New Mexico. That Cimarron cutoff, as it came to be known, was to be the traders' preferred route. Becknell also demonstrated in the spring of 1822 that farm wagons could be rolled across the prairie to Santa Fe, and other merchants would follow his example.[17]

From 1822 on, the wheels of wagon caravans creaked westward every spring, deepening and widening ruts in the prairie sod and bearing the weight of an extraordinary variety of merchandise. Mostly they carried cloth and clothing, ranging from plain cotton handkerchiefs to imported silk shawls, but their loads also included tools, kitchen utensils, and household goods from pins to pens and from wallpaper to window glass. The Americans brought some items previously unavailable in northern Mexico and undersold their Mexican competitors from Chihuahua on other merchandise by perhaps two-thirds in the mid-1820s. American goods were not only comparatively inexpensive, but, one New Mexican recalled, "better merchandise than we had known."[18]

Within a few years American manufactures apparently saturated the limited New Mexico market and absorbed much of the cash in the province. As one frustrated trader put it in 1826, "it is not in the power of man to sell goods where there is no money."[19] Americans began to look southward toward fresh markets in the mineral-rich provinces of Chihuahua, Durango, Zacatecas, and Sonora. The city of Chihuahua alone was worth the additional travel. It stood at the center of a silver mining district that supported smelters and a mint and contained twice as many potential customers as Santa Fe. By the 1830s, over half of the goods entering New Mexico over the Santa Fe Trail continued to Chihuahua and points beyond. That pattern continued until the Mexican-American War.[20]

As one result of this southward extension of the Santa Fe trade, merchants from Missouri and, increasingly, other western states brought home hard cash—coins and bars of silver in taut rawhide packs. Incalculable quantities of silver, surpassing $200,000 in some years, flowed into the United States over the trail. By the early 1830s the silver *peso*, which was roughly equivalent in silver content to the United States dollar, had become the chief medium of exchange in Missouri and helped to stabilize the monetary system of all of America's western states and territories where scorned paper money had circulated in lieu of scarce hard cash. As a bonus, the mules that carried silver eastward also found a ready market in Missouri.[21]

For Americans, then, the Sante Fe trade provided a source of silver and mules, and for Mexicans it offered an unrivaled source of cheap manufactured goods. No reliable records exist to indicate the exact quantity or value of merchandise that entered Mexico over the trail, but a scholarly young merchant, Josiah Gregg, has provided us with knowledgeable estimates in his classic and colorful *Commerce of the Prairies*, first published in 1844. Gregg's calculations, which may be low, indicate that by 1828 the value of the merchandise that came west over the trail had climbed to $150,000. For the next fifteen years, despite annual fluctuations ranging from $50,000 to $250,000, imports from the United States that entered Mexico via Santa Fe averaged $145,000 per year. For Mexico, as for the United States, however, the Santa Fe trade was of regional rather than national importance. Most American goods entered Mexico through maritime ports; seldom did imports via Santa Fe exceed five percent of Mexico's total imports from the United States.[22]

In addition to providing merchandise for the Mexican frontier, the Santa Fe trade brought new opportunities for a growing merchant class with an international outlook. From New Mexico, Chihuahua, and perhaps elsewhere, Mexicans quickly entered the trade in the early 1820s. Some Mexicans from the interior came north to Santa Fe to intercept the caravans and get first choice at merchandise. Other Mexicans, from the interior and from New Mexico, formed their own companies and journeyed to Missouri to avoid the American middlemen. Despite a chilly reception from their American competitors, many Mexicans succeeded.[23]

In 1839 a group of Mexican merchants pioneered a new route from Chihuahua to Fort Towson, Arkansas, going through Texas and avoiding Santa Fe entirely. In 1843 over half of the recorded volume of business on the Santa Fe Trail ($450,000) was controlled by Mexican traders, although this may not have been a typical year.[24] The full story of the involvement in the Santa Fe trade of Mexicans such as Manuel Simón de Escudero, a legislator from Chihuahua, or Antonio José Chávez, of a politically powerful and affluent New Mexico family, has yet to be told.

In the early 1820s, the growing number of venturesome merchants who used the Santa Fe Trail quickly discovered another source of wealth in northern Mexico besides silver and mules. The rivers and rivulets of the high plateau country of northern Mexico supported fur bearing animals, especially beaver. Prior to 1821, Mexican frontiersmen had scarcely begun to exploit local fur resources, largely for want of markets. Americans, on the other hand, had well-developed channels to domestic and European markets. Since the seventeenth century, French, British, and their American offspring had scoured much of eastern North America in search of furs to supply voracious European markets where demand far outstripped supply, due in no small part to the male conceit of wearing top hats made of beaver fur. By the time of Mexican independence, however, American fur traders had not yet found their way into the central or southern Rockies, much of which lay in Mexican territory.[25]

Exploitation of the fur resources of northernmost Mexico came with astounding swiftness in the 1820s, coinciding with the opening of the Santa Fe trade. Some of the first Americans to enter Santa Fe in 1821, including members of William Becknell's party, trapped in addition to trading merchandise. The scarcity of specie in New Mexico seems to have offered incentive to these first Americans to enter the wilderness in search of "hairy banknotes," as some called beaver pelts. By 1823 Americans had trapped out the beaver in the Rio Grande basin near the New Mexico settlements.[26] Spring of 1824 saw the trappers move farther afield. Guided, it would appear, by Mexicans who had been trading with Utes, Americans used New Mexico as a base to penetrate the Rockies, trapping in western Colorado and eastern Utah along the Colorado, Green, Gunnison, Dolores, and other lesser streams on the edge of Mexican territory. No fewer than six groups of Americans made such a journey to the Colorado basin in 1824. The leader of one party, heavy-set, ruddy-faced, Canadian-born Étienne Provost, probably became the first white man to see the Great Salt Lake, near the edge of the United States-Mexican border, when he pushed into the Great Basin in the autumn of 1824. The modern-day city of Provo perpetuates his name.[27]

The central Rockies were a private preserve for Provost and other

American trapper. The mountain man led America's westward push into
northern Mexico ("The Trapper" by Frederick Remington).

New Mexico-based trappers in 1824, but they became the scene of fierce competition in the following years. From the northwest, Hudson's Bay Company trappers under Peter Skene Ogden found their way into the Great Basin in 1825. From St. Louis that same year, William Ashley, head of the Rocky Mountain Fur Company, led a group of Americans into the Rockies by way of the Platte River and South Pass, over what would become the trail to Oregon. In July, Ashley inaugurated the rendezvous on Henry's Fork of the Green River, below the forty-second parallel in Mexican territory. An innovative supply system, the rendezvous offered trappers a market for beaver pelts and a source of supplies in the heart of the mountains—an attractive alternative for trappers who would otherwise have to haul their furs to distant Missouri or New Mexico settlements every year. For the next fifteen years, caravans from large St. Louis-based fur companies rumbled and rattled to different sites in the Rockies, laden with supplies for the annual rendezvous, and efficiently undercut the independent Santa Fe traders in their bid for furs from the Rocky Mountains of northernmost Mexico.[28]

Checked in the central Rockies and attracted by reports of virgin beaver streams to the southwest, a large number of New Mexico-based trappers, perhaps as many as 100, found their way to the watershed of the Gila in southern Arizona in 1826. Overgrazing, irrigation, farming, lumbering, and the resultant erosion have reduced today's Gila to a caricature of a river, its once verdant but fragile valley turned to desert where beaver can hardly survive. In the 1820s, however, the first Americans to put traps in the river found it "a beautiful clear stream about thirty yards in width, running over a rocky bottom, and filled with fish."[29] Beaver abounded and one trapping party, which included a boastful young Kentuckian, James Ohio Pattie, was justifiably excited over the "exhilarating prospects."[30] They took some 250 beaver from their traps during a pioneering two-week hunt on the San Francisco, a tributary of the Gila, in 1825. Returning to the Gila watershed again in 1827, following the large-scale trapping of the area in the previous year, Pattie found "but few beaver remaining."[31] Americans seem to have hunted the beaver nearly to extinction in 1826, and in the process slowed the maintenance and construction of beaver dams that had helped control erosion. Inadvertently, American trappers had struck one of the first blows leading to the death of the river that supported the animals whose furs they sought.[32]

It seems a wonder beaver survived anywhere. Pelts by the thousands poured from northern Mexico until the mid-1830s, when overtrapping made beaver scarce and growing popularity of silk hats brought a drop in demand for beaver pelts in Europe. Precise figures on exports from northern Mexico during the heyday of the fur trade elude us. One knowledgeable observer, however, believed that the Santa Fe Trail alone carried $50,000 worth of beaver pelts in 1831—a third of the furs that came out of the Rockies that year. A similar estimate exists for 1832.[33] Beaver pelts came out of Texas, too, in the 1820s and 1830s. Americans and Indians who trapped the Red, the Trinity, the Brazos, and other Texas rivers marketed beaver pelts by the hundreds in Nacogdoches every year.[34]

The market for beaver fur declined in the mid-1830s, although some continued to be exported, and buffalo hides became the new glamour item. To be closer to the buffalo plains, Americans began to construct trading posts along the Front Range of the Rockies in the 1830s and 1840s, often with labor from New Mexico. The fur trade, then, continued to be important throughout the years that Mexico held the area we call today the Southwest.

In the process of probing northernmost Mexico for beaver, American trappers became the first non-Indians to cross the continent into California. At the forefront was one of William Ashley's employees, an intensely religious young New Yorker, Jedediah Strong Smith. With no more than eighteen companions, Smith left the summer rendezvous on Bear River in the southwest corner of Idaho in 1826 and moved south through Utah, following at times the basins of the Great Salt Lake and Utah Lake and the valleys of the Sevier, Virgin, and Colorado rivers. At the place we today call Needles, California, he acquired fresh horses from Mojaves who had taken them from the California missions. Then, with two Indian runaways from the Mission San Gabriel to guide him, Smith crossed the Colorado, made his way through the Mojave desert and over the San Bernardino mountains into the green, springlike Los Angeles basin on a November day.[35]

The year after Smith accomplished his singular feat, in 1827, a group of trappers from New Mexico, led by Virginia-born Richard Campbell, pioneered another route to the Pacific. Campbell was one of those residents of Missouri who found the Santa Fe trade attractive after his business affairs collapsed in the Panic of 1819, and he seems to have blazed a trail from Santa Fe across central Arizona, eventually selling his furs in San Francisco.[36] A second group from New Mexico, led by James Ohio Pattie's father, Sylvestre, entered California in 1828 by a more southerly route than Campbell's, following the Gila River. Suffering incredible hardships, Pattie's group floated down the Colorado River in dugouts into the treacherous tidal bore near the river's mouth on the Gulf of California. From there they crossed the barren deserts of the Colorado delta and ascended the scrub-covered mountains of northern

Baja California to the Dominican mission of Santa Catarina on the Pacific slope some 130 miles south of San Diego. Like Jedediah Smith, the Patties received horses and guidance from Indians on the last leg of their journey.[37]

Within a few years the quest for beaver pelts had led Americans to cross the continent, linking the Rockies and New Mexico with California. Spain's explorers had sought but never quite realized that goal. The Americans' formidable achievements should not be exaggerated, however, for they built on prior Spanish, Mexican, and Indian knowledge. In making their way from Santa Fe to the Gila, for example, Americans apparently followed trails that had been known since the mid-eighteenth century.[38] Similarly, Spain's explorers knew the way from Tucson to San Diego and Los Angeles. In a remarkable series of explorations between 1823 and 1826 José Romero, the doughty cavalry captain at the presidio of Tucson, had reopened those routes; one went by way of Mission Santa Catarina in Baja California to which Sylvestre Pattie would be guided on his way to the coast in 1828.[39] Thus, Pattie's achievement seems to have been to link two previously known routes.

The first Americans to enter California by overland trails did not meet the same warm reception that New Mexico Governor Melgares had tendered to Missouri traders. Instead, California officials reacted with surprise and suspicion. Why would men cross mountains and deserts in search of beaver pelts? "It is said that these are only commercial expeditions for hunting beaver. without political purposes," wrote Fray Narciso Durán. "May God wish it so, and time will tell."[40] A cautious Governor José María de Echeandía kept both Jedediah Smith and James Ohio Pattie briefly under arrest. He suspected them of spying. By the late 1820s, American trappers had also begun to run into difficulty in New Mexico, as we shall see. After 1830, when Echeandía left the governor's office, California officials seem to have placed no further obstacles in the way of Americans or British who trapped the Sacramento, the San Joaquin, and other streams in the great Central Valley.[41]

Some Americans used the new routes to California to market beaver pelts on the Pacific, but *nuevomexicanos* seem to have been first to recognize the possibilities of reciprocal trade. Antonio Armijo, with at least thirty of his countrymen, journeyed from Abiquiú, New Mexico, to San Bernardino, California in 1829, pioneering a westward route that skirted the north rim of the Grand Canyon in the area of the present-day Utah-Arizona border. Like many travelers, Armijo's hardy band survived the harsh Mojave Desert by eating horse and mule flesh, but reached California with most of their pack mules still loaded with woven woolen goods—*serapes*, blankets, and quilts. They traded those products of New

Mexico's sheep industry for horses and mules from the California ranchos.[42] It must have been profitable. Yearly, thereafter, a caravan of patient pack mules, loaded with merchandise from New Mexico, picked their way across the continent to the Pacific, an arduous two-month journey each way. Resilient New Mexico women often accompanied their mates on these expeditions and brought children along as well.[43]

Americans, too, entered the horse trading business in California, driving livestock back to Santa Fe as the New Mexicans did. Some American traders also pushed California horses and mules beyond Santa Fe to markets in Missouri.[44] Thus, in the largest sense, the new trails between New Mexico and California became extensions of the Santa Fe trade.

Swiftly after Mexican independence, then, American trappers and traders pushed overland into northern Mexico, crossed the continent to the Pacific, and began to shift the commercial orientation of Mexico's northern frontier toward the United States. Meanwhile, New England maritime merchants made a similar thrust into Alta California. Whereas beaver pelts had lured trappers overland to the Pacific, the New Englanders and other foreigners who came to California by sea sought otter and seal skins, cowhides, and tallow—a fat derived from cattle and used to make candles and soap. Like the Sante Fe traders, the New Englanders brought American merchandise to trade with eager *californios.*

Prior to Mexican independence, as early as 1797, New England traders had ventured illegally into California waters in search of sea otter. Shiny, warm, and luxurious, otter pelts brought such high prices in China that it seemed worth the risk of capture and arrest by Spanish officials to enter the forbidden waters. American, Russian, and British traders, who often hired Kodiak or Aleutian Indians to do the actual hunting or traded surreptitiously with *californio* hunters, swept the Pacific coast of sea otter in the early nineteenth century.[45]

By the time of Mexican independence, otter herds had dwindled in the blue waters off the craggy California coast, and hunting slowed, but for several reasons foreign traders and hunters continued to seek sea otter in California in the 1820s. First, otter pelts commanded high prices— between fifteen and forty dollars apiece—while the price of a cowhide, for example, averaged a dollar and a half. Second, the opening of California to foreign merchants in 1821 minimized some of the risks. Finally, otter herds in the Pacific Northwest, the main source for Americans, had been badly depleted and in 1821 the Russian government ordered the coast north of San Francisco closed to all but Russian vessels. Thus the California coast remained attractive to Americans, even though it was overhunted.[46]

Despite strong competition from Russians, New Englanders monopolized the California sea otter trade in the 1820s and 1830s. The *californios* themselves offered little competition since they lacked vessels and experience in foreign markets. Kodiak and Aleutian Indians continued to do most of the actual hunting of otter in the 1820s, but more and more *californios* hunted as well, encouraged by licensing procedures that favored Mexican citizens and access to foreign markets such as they had never before enjoyed. Upwardly mobile *californios*, such as Juan Bautista Alvarado and José Castro, and their hired help (which included mission Indians), probably did half of the hunting in California by the 1830s.[47] They were joined in that decade by American trappers, such as Ewing Young, who came overland to California in search of beaver fur, but switched to the more lucrative business of hunting otters and seals. Americans like William Wolfskill, who had become a naturalized Mexican and held a license to trap beaver in New Mexico, learned to their pleasant surprise that a linguistic curiosity allowed them to hunt sea otter in California. Instead of employing the usual word *castor* for beaver, New Mexicans used the word *nutria*, which in California meant sea otter. When Wolfskill and others presented their New Mexico licenses to trap nutria, annoyed California officials reluctantly permitted them to hunt otter.[48]

By the 1830s California's dwindling otter herds became the target of more hunters than ever: Aleuts, Kodiaks, Mexicans, and Americans. Hunters came with larger ships, employed new hunting techniques, and used guns instead of spears as they had before. Former mountain men from the United States escalated the killing by firing on otter from the shore while captains of merchant vessels put armed Aleutians on small boats. Competition between these rival groups became so fierce that they shot at one another on occasion instead of at the animals.[49]

The number of otter taken from California waters during the frenzied hunting of the 1830s cannot be ascertained, but it is clear that by the early 1840s the animals had been hunted nearly to extinction. Sea otter "has almost disappeared," wrote Manuel Castañares in 1844.[50] Thereafter, the only substantial herds remained off the Baja California coast where some otter hunters continued to ply their trade until the great gold discovery of 1848 diverted their attention from the sea to the mountains.

Although otter skins remained the prime trading commodity during the Mexican period, a foreign sea captain rarely found enough to fill his hold. Cowhides and tallow usually made up most of his cargo on the return trip and came to be California's largest export commodities. More than the hunting of sea otter, the trade in hide and tallow has captured

Californios roping a steer. This scene was rendered in oils by August Ferran, probably in the late 1840s or early 1850s (courtesy, The Bancroft Library).

popular attention and come to be synonymous with early nineteenth-century California to many Americans. This has been due in no small part to Richard Henry Dana's popular and enduring *Two Years Before the Mast*, first published in 1840.

Dana vividly described how the skillful *californios* roped, slaughtered, and butchered cattle at the annual *matanza*, then stretched, cleaned, and dried the hides. "Doubled lengthwise in the middle, and nearly as stiff as boards," those hides would be stacked in a dry place along with cowhide sacks of tallow, to await the arrival of the foreign traders who would ship them to England and New England.[51] Meanwhile, most flesh of the slaughtered animals was left to rot, for the supply of beef outstripped demand in California, and salted or jerked beef (the only effective way of preserving it before refrigeration) was not popular.[52]

The seeds of the hide and tallow trade had been planted in the Spanish period, but they blossomed in the Mexican era beginning with arrival in California in June 1822 of two agents of a British company, Hugh McCulloch and William Hartnell. After discussions with Governor Pablo Sola and the head of the missions, Fray Mariano Payeras, McCulloch and Hartnell received permission to negotiate three-year contracts at individual missions. Most of the padres agreed to exchange hides and tallow for scarce mission supplies, ranging from gold and silver thread, window glass, and violins to trousers, garden tools, tea, and coffee.

McCulloch and Hartnell monopolized the hide and tallow trade for several years. American merchants found to their frustration, and perhaps surprise, that even when they outbid the British partners by twice the price, the padres remained faithful to their contracts. By the mid-1820s, however, misfortunes within their own company and changing conditions in South America, where McCulloch and Hartnell had marketed much of the California hides and tallow, caused them to abandon the field. A competing Boston-based firm, Bryant, Sturgis and Company, stepped into the void and dominated the hide and tallow trade thereafter.[53]

In 1822 and again in 1825, Bryant and Sturgis had sent vessels to the Pacific Coast under the able supervision of William Gale. *"Cuatro ojos,"* or four eyes, as the *californios* called the bespectacled Gale, had managed to get a share of the market, but progress had been slow. It took Gale over a year on each occasion to fill his hold for the return voyage. With the British out of the picture, business picked up and Bryant and Sturgis became the principal company on the coast until it closed operations in 1841.[54] Meanwhile, other Americans entered the field, too. Competition grew intense, with merchants "struggling and scrambling either for hides or for tallow," as one English observer put it, and vessels encountered long delays in filling their holds.[55]

The hide and tallow trade fell upon bad times in the 1840s when the New England market became saturated with hides and prices fell. Then too, some Yankees felt uneasy about sending ships to California amidst its growing political instability. As with otter hunters, the end of the hide and tallow trade came with the 1848 gold discovery, which convinced hide traders—sometimes erroneously—that mining would be an easier way to make money.

All in all, Boston traders alone may have taken over 6 million hides and 7 thousand tons of tallow out of California between 1826 and 1848. With the price of a cowhide or a measure of tallow averaging $1.50 during these years, the hide and tallow trade would appear to represent a bonanza for *californios*—an estimated annual income of $235 for each man, woman, and child.[56] Some rancheros became comfortable, but very few became rich or saw their profits in cash. First, Franciscans and not rancheros dominated the hide and tallow trade until the secularization of the missions in the mid-1830s. Second, rancheros and missionaries alike bartered hides and tallow in exchange for manufactured goods ranging from spoons to spades—the same products that Missourians were hauling to Santa Fe during those years.[57] In California, price tags on those goods bore markups of 300 to 400 percent over New England prices, and rancheros commonly bought on credit, taking advances on the next year's sales and remaining in constant debt.[58] Not surprisingly, from the 1820s to the 1840s visitors to California reported seeing little cash, and echoed the lament of a German-born merchant: "Hardly a peso is to be found anywhere in the province."[59] In lieu of hard cash, cowhides, termed "California banknotes," became a principal medium of exchange.

The hide and tallow trade, the fur trade, and the Santa Fe trade offer dramatic examples of the ways in which the easing of trade restrictions by independent Mexico altered economic life on the northern frontier. In a less spectacular way, access to new markets and nascent capitalism jolted other areas of the frontier economy as well, especially production of raw materials.

The mainstays of the frontier economy, agriculture and ranching, made only modest gains in the Mexican period. Except in California, the cost of transportation and the difficulties of protecting stock from Indians hindered the rapid development of ranching despite freer access to new markets. *Tejanos* continued to drive horses and cattle to Louisiana, but the export of livestock apparently diminished from the late Spanish period even as *tejanos* expanded ranching operations. Perhaps the internal market for cattle and horses increased as more Americans settled in Texas.[60] New Mexicans also continued to export livestock, sending sheep on the hoof to Chihuahua and beyond as they had under Spain. The number of horses and cattle in New Mexico remained small compared to sheep, which totaled a quarter of a million by one estimate in 1827. Sheep, as one resident put it in 1831, "make it possible for the inhabitants to live."[61] New Mexicans seem to have sent thirty to forty thousand sheep to market annually in the 1840s, but complained, perhaps in exaggerated terms, that their herds had diminished greatly due to Indian depredations. If so, they were much better off than the residents of Arizona, whose sheep industry, according to Teodoro Ramírez of Tucson, did not exist "because of the danger of the Apache enemy."[62]

In California, where foreigners had easy access to the coast and could export valuable hides and tallow without burdening themselves with the rest of the animal, ranching boomed as we have seen. During these years *californios* also exported a small number of horses, which an English visitor described as "plentiful as bullrushes," to new markets in Hawaii, Oregon, and New Mexico.[63]

As with livestock, commercial agriculture developed slowly in the Mexican era because markets were generally not close enough to the frontier to enable the pobladores to transport profitably bulky and fragile agricultural products, even when they produced a surplus. Most of the frontier experienced a shortage of labor and of capital, both necessary for commercial agriculture, and most settlers had limited access to land that was irrigated and secure from Indians.[64]

As a result of these obstacles, agriculture on the frontier remained largely at the subsistence level. Around San Antonio, for example, irrigated fields and orchards produced vegetables, grains, and fruit such as figs, grapes, and peaches, but these were grown entirely for local use. "Everything raised in Béxar is consumed within the department," wrote Juan Nepomuceno Almonte in 1834.[65] *Tejanos* had begun to expand farming operations in the late 1820s and early 1830s, during a lull in raids from Comanches and Lipan Apaches, but they still raised so little surplus food that in 1835 when Mexico sent troops into Texas under General Martín Perfecto de Cós to put down a perceived rebellion, Cós had to seek permission to import food from the United States for his troops.[66]

Subsistence farming did not necessarily mean privation, of course. Moderate and bountiful climates, especially in California and Texas, assured a minimum standard of living and, as some visitors believed, may have discouraged intensive agricultural production among Anglo-Americans and Mexicans alike. With an abundance of game animals and livestock to fill the family larder, starvation was not likely even in times of drought and crop failure. The Spanish-born merchant José Arnaz later recalled, perhaps with an exaggeration born of nostalgia, that in California, "poverty or hunger was unknown."[67]

Although subsistence farming remained the rule, some commercial agriculture got underway after 1821 with liberalized trade, especially on those edges of the frontier that had access to markets. In California, modest amounts of corn, wheat, and vegetables were sold to Russians at Fort Ross and Sitka, to British traders who had established a post on the

Columbia, and to foreign vessels, such as whaling ships, which entered California ports to take on supplies.[68] In Texas, newly arrived Anglo-Americans often brought slave labor and technology, which enabled them to produce and process cotton for the market at nearby New Orleans. By 1834 shipments from Texas to New Orleans may have amounted to 7,000 bales worth about $315,000. Some of that cotton, one twenty-fifth by one estimate, was raised by *tejanos* near San Antonio and Goliad. Mexicans also grew modest amounts of cotton in southern Arizona and at El Paso, exporting some to interior markets. Texas cotton seems to have been the most valuable agricultural commodity exported from Mexico's northern frontier and nearly all of it went to New Orleans on American vessels.[69]

The planting of the American South's cotton economy on Texas soil in the 1820s and 1830s raised productivity of previously unoccupied lands and stimulated foreign trade. As in California and New Mexico, however, it appears that only a few *tejanos* profited from the new arrangements that benefited Americans and the United States more than Mexicans and Mexico. By the mid-1830s, annual exports from Texas—which included both cotton and thousands of beaver, otter, and deer skins—may have amounted to about $500,000, but imports, chiefly manufactured goods, totaled $630,000, leaving a substantial trade deficit and a shortage of hard cash. "Money is very scarce in Texas," Almonte reported, "and one may say with certainty that out of every hundred transactions made not ten involve specie."[70]

Other products of the soil whose importance as export items increased in the Mexican era were wine and spirits. Grapes and grain, in the less perishable form of wine and liquor, could be easily transported over long distances, and a modest export trade in these beverages accelerated after independence as the private sector developed commercial wineries in California and as New Mexicans found new outlets for locally produced whiskey.

The Franciscans and their Indian laborers seem to have been California's exclusive viticulturists until secularization in the mid-1830s placed the mission vineyards in private hands. In the Los Angeles region especially, foreigners such as Jean Louis Vignes, a Frenchman, and Americans William Wolfskill and John Rowland, both former trappers, began to plant new vines while others tended the former mission vineyards. By the 1840s people as far away as Boston drank California wine. One of the few extant statistics notes 2,000 barrels of wine and brandy exported from California in 1843.[71]

In New Mexico, wine and brandy produced in El Paso and sold in Chihuahua had been a profitable item in the colonial period and continued to be exported thereafter. Farther up the Rio Grande, however, Americans apparently introduced the first commercial distilleries to New Mexico in the 1820s and manufactured a popular liquor, made from corn or wheat, reputed to rival any whiskey, "except that it lacked color and age."[72] Later known as "Taos Lightning," it found a ready market in the growing Indian trade.

Lumber, which had been exported sporadically from California in the Spanish period, also began to be exploited commercially after 1821 with the opening of new markets in the Pacific basin, from Tahiti and Hawaii to the coast of South America. Foreign whipsawyers and foreign merchants, led by the American Thomas Oliver Larkin, dominated the industry. Larkin's half-brother, Captain John Rogers Cooper, a man of many interests, built the first commercial saw mill in California, in Sonoma County in 1835. Several *californios*, such as Inocencio García at San Luis Obispo and Juan Ramírez, who operated a mill near San Bernardino, also engaged in the business. Meanwhile, lumbering and milling got underway in the Anglo-American sector of Texas. Although Texans exported some lumber to Matamoros, most was for local use.[73]

Mining, which would spark the growth of the region after the American conquest, expanded very slowly in the Mexican period. Indians had done some mining prior to the arrival of Europeans, and contemporaries knew that the region's mineral-producing potential remained largely untapped. Sparse Mexican population, a shortage of capital and entrepreneurs, and Indian hostility all combined to hinder the discovery and production of minerals under independent Mexico, just as they had under Spain.[74] Although rumors of great discoveries circulated then and now, few documented, significant mineral deposits were found on the northern frontier in the Spanish period. In New Mexico, Spaniards apparently had failed to locate important gold or silver deposits. In Texas, the hill country north of San Antonio had yielded silver-bearing ore in the 1750s, and in California a site near Mission San Juan Bautista, not far from Monterey, had produced silver ore about 1800, but both proved short-lived. The most spectacular and steadiest production of silver and gold came from Arizona, where small operations near Tubac and Guevavi continued to be worked from the eighteenth century until the Mexican War.[75] Small amounts of copper came from various locations in New Mexico and Arizona, but the one important copper mine on the frontier was the Santa Rita del Cobre. Discovered by Europeans perhaps in the late 1700s in a rugged mountain valley near present Silver City in southwestern New Mexico, the Santa Rita was worked continuously from about 1800. A popular rendezvous site for American trappers, the remote Santa Rita settlement fell within the jurisdiction of Chihuahua rather than New Mexico and most of its copper seems to have been marketed in Chihuahua City.[76]

The Mexican period witnessed the first substantial gold discoveries in both California and New Mexico. *Nuevomexicanos* made two sizeable strikes in the dry, scrub-covered mountains to the south of Santa Fe. Placer gold, found about 1828 in the Ortiz Mountains and in 1839 in the snake-infested San Pedros, led to the creation of the boom towns of Real de Dolores and El Tuerto. Being the younger and more vigorous, El Tuerto had grown to over 100 buildings by 1846. Two mines operated nearby, and *nuévomexicanos* laboriously hauled in water to pan dry creek beds that occasionally rewarded their efforts with nuggets weighing a pound to a pound and a half. Estimates vary as to the amount of gold produced in these mines, but one estimate of a million dollars for Real de Dolores alone does not seem unreasonable. Official figures would add little to our understanding, for as one visitor noted, "nearly all the gold of New Mexico is bought up by the traders, and smuggled out of the country to the United States."[77]

In the development of New Mexico's mines in this period, foreigners played key roles. Foreigners owned the Santa Rita copper mines, for example, and several former trappers, among them Gervais Nolan, Richard Campbell, and one of the Robidoux brothers, owned gold mines. Still other foreigners owned the stores that supplied the miners. *Nuevomexicanos* seem to have agreed that foreign capital was necessary to develop mining and should be encouraged.[78]

Following the discoveries of gold in New Mexico, Francisco López made the first well-documented gold strike in California at Placerita Canyon, on the edge of the San Fernando Valley to the north of Los Angeles, in March 1842. By May, forty or fifty persons were working the site, each making a dollar or two a day. López's discovery, coupled with a nearby strike the following year, set off a small rush. In the few years before the monumental discovery of gold at Sutter's mill brought international attention to northern California and the high Sierras, perhaps as much as $100,000 of gold came out of the Los Angeles area.[79]

In the decades following the official demise of Spain's mercantile system, then, many areas of the frontier economy—ranging from trapping and trading to cotton, lumber, and mining—began to move ahead. The motor behind this forward movement seemed to belong to foreigners, who controlled capital and the means of transportation, and had access to international markets. In Nacogdoches, on the edge of American Louisiana, fourteen of the town's sixteen merchants in 1830 had foreign surnames.[80] Even in isolated California, Juan Bautista Alvarado would later recall that when he served as governor in the late 1820s, "all the ships that were trade carriers were foreign. The greater part of the capital in the territory was in the hands of foreigners."[81] Preeminent among the foreigners, from California to Texas, were Americans. Only in California did British merchants give Americans serious competition. There, proximity alone helped ensure that by the 1840s, as Sir George Simpson noted to his sorrow, "the Americans are considerably more numerous than the British."[82] When the British-owned Hudson's Bay Company tried to enter the fur trade in California in the 1840s, one company leader despaired that his men could not compete with the Americans "who speak the language fluently, and know every person in California."[83]

Opening northern Mexico to foreign capital and foreign markets had sent ripples throughout some segments of the frontier economy, but local manufacturing received less stimulus. Instead, the frontier grew increasingly dependent upon foreign imports and foreign artisans, especially those from the United States.[84]

Although a few luxury goods reached the frontier at the time of independence, most crafts were probably made at home, by women as well as men, or produced locally by resident weavers, tailors, hatters, shoemakers, carpenters, masons, potters, blacksmiths, and silversmiths. A substantial number of pobladores worked as artisans in Texas and New Mexico at the time of independence.[85] In California, Indian craftsmen continued production at the still-thriving missions. Indeed, cheap Indian labor might have made it difficult for others to compete in California, but as missions declined, the number of artisans grew in the towns, if Los Angeles is a typical example.[86]

Although a variety of craftsmen worked on the Mexican frontier, they were unable to supply demand, especially in Texas, and the quality of their work brought complaints all across the frontier. Antonio Barreiro, for example, lamented in 1832 that New Mexico's "crafts are in the worst state imaginable, even those which are indispensable for the prime necessities of life."[87] At least twenty-seven carpenters worked in New Mexico in the early 1830s, but because iron in general and metal tools in particular were costly and difficult to obtain they worked with crude tools. Even nails were at a premium. New Mexicans also lacked machinery to spin fine yarns and make fine cloth, although they exported coarse woolen and cotton cloth.[88]

Under these circumstances, foreign-made imports effectively competed with local manufactures in both quality and in price. The coarse cloth of New Mexico, according to one local priest, Manuel Rada, "had always been little appreciated, but now not at all due to the introduction of woven goods of wool, cotton, etc. from the United States."[89] In California, American leather goods, including saddles, came to be preferred

Zuñi blacksmiths. This lithograph was based on a sketch by Richard Kern, done at the Pueblo of Zuñi, 1851 (Lorenzo Sitgreaves, *Report on an Expedition Down the Zuñi and Colorado Rivers,* 32d Cong., 2d Sess., Sen. Ex. Doc. 59 [Washington, 1853], p. 5).

over local manufactures, despite the availability of cowhides for leather.[90]

Foreign artisans, too, found their work in demand on the Mexican frontier. "It is from them," wrote Antonio Barreiro, "that one must doubtless expect the development of crafts." He expressed the hope that local artisans "will learn something . . . [from] the excellent work of the foreigners," and he identified foreign "tailors, carpenters, blacksmiths, hatters, tinsmiths, shoemakers, excellent gunsmiths, etc." already working in New Mexico.[91] Even as Barreiro wrote this in 1832, one

George Pratte was establishing a tannery and a lumbermill at Santa Fe. The extent and influence of foreign artisans cannot be measured with precision. It appears to have been extensive, but not as overwhelming as the ethnocentric remarks of some foreigners suggest. Thomas Oliver Larkin, for example, wrote in 1846 that "foreigners are now doing all the work" of the former mission Indian artisans of California, and Richard Henry Dana termed the *californios* "an idle, thriftless people who can make nothing for themselves."[92] Such observations do not deserve to be taken seriously. In Los Angeles, for which figures are available, foreigners seem to have comprised just a third of the craftsmen by 1836—hardly a monopoly, but enough to cause concern.[93]

Whereas Barreiro suggested that New Mexicans look to foreigners for leadership, others urged that Mexicans establish rival industries. Manuel Rada, for example, asked the central government for aid to establish local factories to make fine cloth or tan hides. Little help was forthcoming, however, and Mexican frontiersmen in general seem to have lacked sufficient capital, labor, technology, and internal and external markets to mass-produce goods cheaply. California's failure to make fine quality and inexpensive leather products is a case in point. California hides, as Dana put it, were "carried to Boston, tanned . . . and many of them, very probably, brought back again to California in the shape of shoes."[94] "There are no capitalists in California," a British resident of Monterey wrote at the end of the Mexican era. "There is not a yard of tape, a pin, or a piece of domestic cotton or even thread that does not come from the United States."[95]

The Mexican era, then, saw the pobladores break loose from the grasp of Spanish mercantilism only to be embraced by American capitalism. The extent to which the frontier could or should resist that warm embrace proved a vexing question for officials on the frontier as well as in Mexico City.

8

Regulating the Economy
Frontier vs. Nation

If there were not English boots, nor American blankets, we might be able to sell California shoes and robes.—Mariano Guadalupe Vallejo, *Sonoma, 1841*

Our politicians . . . believe that they should not promote the growth of distant places such as Texas, California, etc., in order that they do not revolt and withdraw from the metropolis.—Ignacio Zúñiga of Tucson, *1835*

Following Mexican independence, the rapid influx of foreigners, foreign merchandise, and foreign capital, together with access to new foreign markets, increased the tempo of activity in many areas of the frontier economy. But the new pace did not always produce harmonious results. The frontier remained dependent upon outsiders, especially Americans, for manufactured goods, and foreigners came to play an important role in commerce and local industry. Trade deficits characterized the new arrangements; specie and investment capital remained in short supply; and some natural resources, especially beaver and sea otter, seemed threatened to the point of extinction. In addition to these liabilities, the penetration of American capital and capitalists into the border region seemed fraught with a special peril that did not go unnoticed by contemporaries. Protesting a government concession to foreigners to operate steamboats on the Rio Grande in 1830, for example, Miguel Ramos Arizpe warned against

the obvious but dismal consequences of delivering into the hands of individuals from the United States, who are pro-

tected by rich capitalists of that country, the line which for
many years they have hoped would form the boundary between the United States and this Republic.[1]

The problems of regulating foreign capital affected the entire Mexican
nation, not just its northern frontier, and raised questions that perplex
governments of underdeveloped countries yet today. How to attract but
still control foreign capital and trade? How to guarantee nationals access
to jobs in foreign-owned industries? What role should the state play in
protecting domestic industry from foreign competition? How to prevent
excessive exploitation of resources by foreigners? The ways in which
Mexico responded to these challenges, as it struggled to integrate the
economy of the frontier into the national economy in the early nineteenth century, have a contemporary ring.

In order to protect the nation's nascent industries from foreign competition, the central government relied upon outright prohibition of
certain foreign products and upon protective tariffs on others. A merchant entering a Mexican harbor or a border community such as Santa
Fe, for example, would find certain goods on the prohibited list, while
other items might be subject to an import duty (*derecho de internación*)
as well as an excise tax on goods sold in the interior of the country
(*derecho de consumo*).[2]

The central government also took measures to help nationals compete
more effectively with foreigners who had special skills or were well-
financed. In 1824, for example, the government forbade foreigners from
trapping fur-bearing animals. Two years later, it prohibited foreigners
from practicing certain trades or professions without permission. In 1843,
after threatening to do so for over a decade, the government briefly
closed retail trading to foreigners. Still another act outlawed foreign
vessels from coastal shipping and required that at least two-thirds of the
crew members on Mexican vessels engaged in coastal trade be Mexican
nationals. Similarly, when the government granted a monopoly to a
private company to hunt fur-bearing animals on the northern frontier,
it required that two-thirds of the company's hunters be Mexican nationals.[3]

In retrospect, such regulations seem of greatest interest as examples of
governmental intentions, for they never provided effective solutions.
Most restrictions and duties did not remain in force long enough to
make a positive impact on either the frontier or the national economy.
Indeed, the net effect of the government regulations was probably negative. As different interest groups and economic theorists rose and fell
from positions of influence in Mexico's tumultuous governments, laws

changed frequently or threatened to change, creating a climate of uncertainty. Amounts of duties on foreign goods vacillated and items went on and off lists of prohibited imports and exports with a frequency that bewildered and annoyed foreign merchants. Moreover, the government permitted numerous exceptions to the laws.

Foreigners often viewed exemptions and changes in regulations as capricious and arbitrary, and found in them justification for disrespecting Mexican officials and laws. "How damned foolish they act," wrote one American sea captain in California upon learning of a change in commercial regulations.[4] Few foreigners understood that changes in the law reflected genuine philosophical differences and necessary experimentation as Mexico's leaders debated the surest course for economic progress of the young republic.[5]

In one sense, however, official debates over policy did not matter, for the central government lacked the means to enforce its own legislation. The entire nation suffered from a pitifully small number of customs houses and inexperienced, ill-trained, and underpaid customs officials often accepted bribes as a necessary supplement to their meager incomes. Moreover, naval and military forces were woefully inadequate to protect the borders and coasts against smugglers. In 1826, for example, the country had only five vessels to guard 10,000 miles of coastline.[6]

Increasing the number of customs houses, attracting better officials, and strengthening navy and army patrols might have improved law enforcement, but such measures would have cost money. Here the federal government seemed caught in a vicious circle. In the euphoria following independence, the government had abolished many of the odious taxes of the Spanish era and became more dependent on customs revenue. Eighty to ninety percent of its regular income came from import and export duties during the half century after independence but, due in no small part to the inefficiency of the customs system, amounts collected did not cover rising expenditures. Chronically short of cash, the government could not afford to make customs collections more efficient. Under these circumstances, the only other way to increase government revenue seemed to be to raise the amount of tariffs. Indeed, generating government income apparently became more important than protection of domestic industry as a motive for tariff collection. Higher tariffs, however, also failed to produce more income because they instead encouraged greater smuggling and graft. As Englishman George Simpson put it, the high tariff "renders the temptation to smuggle almost irresistible."[7] Describing the other side of the coin, one Mexican observer noted that "the savings from evading increased taxes allow merchants to offer bribes of such magnitude that few men have the honor to refuse them."[8]

Little wonder, then, that smuggling and graft abounded. Liberal leader José Luis Mora estimated in 1834 that *two-thirds* of the nation's imports entered the country illegally.[9]

Conditions on the northern frontier mirrored, if not magnified, national problems of collecting tariffs and enforcing protective legislation. Few customs houses existed on the frontier despite local protests and widespread recognition of the need for more. Texas had no coastal customs house until 1830. In Alta California and New Mexico, only Monterey and Santa Fe served as official ports of entry during much of the Mexican era.[10]

Corrupt officials often served in these customs houses. Customs collectors such as Juan Bautista Vigil y Alarid in New Mexico and Juan Bandini in California were accused of fraud and dismissed from their posts, and foreigners often reported making private deals with collectors. Many traders shared the suspicion of one California merchant that corruption extended to the top and that duties went into "the pockets of the Governor and his satalites [*sic*]."[11] Foreigners probably exaggerated the extent of corruption, however, and misunderstood rapid changes in the laws and variations between local practice and theory. Foreigners may have believed themselves cheated when they were not.

Even if adequate customs houses and honest, efficient officials had served the frontier, there seemed no way to force foreigners to pay duties or obey regulations. Here, too, the frontier suffered from a national malaise. The paltry number of troops assigned to the frontier could not patrol the extensive, ill-defined border to check smuggling or stop poachers. The 1824 federal prohibition against foreign trappers, for example, existed only on paper. The New Mexico diputación complained in 1826 that "foreigners have continued to hunt beaver just as much as when they had the liberty to do so," and Governor Antonio Narbona explained to federal officials that his poorly equipped troops could not pursue American trappers when they could scarcely defend the province against Indians and control unruly foreigners who flocked into the isolated community of Taos.[13] The government also lacked vessels to patrol the coasts of California and Texas. A Russian visitor to California in 1835 described the province as without "even a rowboat or a single canoe."[14] When customs officials inspected a vessel, he said, they had to borrow its longboats. In Texas, when a high-ranking official recommended the purchase of a small launch to control smuggling at the mouth of Matagorda Bay, the government replied that it could not afford it. In 1835, at the end of the Mexican era in Texas, a hapless revenue officer reported that he could not collect duties because he had no soldiers and could not pursue *contrabandistas* because he had no boat.[15]

It is dramatic testimony to the weakness of frontier law enforcement that California Governor Juan Bautista Alvarado turned to the foreigners themselves to stop other foreigners. In 1839 he commissioned Allen Light, an American-born black who had become a Mexican citizen, to stop the illegal hunting of otter by foreigners. At about the same time, Alvarado commissioned the Swiss-born, recently naturalized Mexican, John Sutter, to stop foreigners from trapping beaver in the central valley. Ironically, Sutter had been a trapper, and Light had hunted otter. Perhaps Alvarado thought they could beat other foreigners at their own game.[16]

The inadequacy of frontier law enforcement was matched only by the ingenuity of smugglers. Whether they came by sea to the California and Texas coasts or by land to Santa Fe and Taos, the foreigners employed ruses that were remarkably similar. Some simply falsified trade manifests, or hid goods in the false lining of a ship or the hollowed out axletree of a wagon. Others cached merchandise along the coast or on the plains before entering Monterey or Santa Fe, then paid duties on a percentage of their goods and imported the rest secretly. Others sidestepped restrictions by finding a Mexican citizen who could be coopted, or took Mexican wives under whose name they did business. Some foreigners simply became Mexican citizens to avoid laws that applied to foreigners.[17] Even under the best of circumstances, it would have been difficult to halt smuggling in the Far North, and circumstances were far from ideal.

Frontier officials not only lacked the means, but also lacked the will to enforce those federal regulations that they regarded as detrimental to their region's interests. The federal government's decision in 1826 to open only Monterey to foreign trade, for example, brought angry protests from merchants such as the Peruvian-born José Bandini, who argued that the lengthy California coast could not be served efficiently by just one port. Should the law remain in effect, he predicted, "the territory will inevitably be ruined."[18] The law did remain in effect during most of the Mexican era, but California avoided ruin because officials winked at violations of the law and permitted foreign trade in other communities, including San Diego and San Francisco.[19] Similarly, when the government prohibited foreigners from engaging in retail trade in Mexico in 1843, frontier officials feared a commercial disaster: California officials ignored the order entirely; New Mexico's Governor Manuel Armijo permitted exceptions; and if Texas had still been in Mexican hands, officials there probably would have disobeyed it too, for they had objected to a similar law a decade earlier.[20]

Rather than resist federal regulations outright, frontier officials often bent them to suit their purposes. Pobladores agreed with the central government, for example, that natural resources needed to be protected. In 1832 the New Mexico legislature considered the question of imposing a "prudent quota" on the use of wood and water by foreigners in the mountains above Santa Fe; the California legislature prohibited the export of lumber in 1834, apparently to protect the redwoods; and Texas officials prohibited stripping oak trees for their bark, which was used in the tanning process.[21] At the same time, however, frontier officials understood local circumstances well enough that they did not try to implement impractical federal legislation and sought compromise instead. New Mexico Governors Bartolomé Baca and Antonio Narbona, for example, recognized the futility of enforcing the federal law prohibiting foreigners from trapping. Both governors modified the law. They tried to control foreign trappers by issuing them licenses, and to benefit their own frontiersmen by requiring that foreigners take a percentage of Mexicans along as apprentices. California Governor José María Echeandía allowed Russians to hunt sea otter under similar terms.[22]

Frontiersmen agreed that it made sense to protect certain products from foreign competition. "If there were not English boots, nor American blankets, we might be able to sell California shoes and robes," argued Californian Mariano Guadalupe Vallejo, and he also urged that foreign wine, brandy, and olive oil be excluded from California.[23] In the main, however, Mexican frontiersmen, including Vallejo, favored lower tariffs or free trade on most items. In 1829, for example, Juan María Alarid of New Mexico passionately condemned a new tariff law that prohibited importation of some woolen and cotton goods, nails, locks, and other items: "With a great pain in my heart my eyes have seen the general law of last May 22, concerning the prohibition of some foreign merchandise." Such a law might be "beneficial and necessary for more populous and industrious states," Alarid explained, "but very prejudicial for the poor and ignorant inhabitants of this Territory."[24] New Mexico lacked factories to manufacture goods, and if manufactures could not be imported from the Americans, New Mexico would once again fall under the monopolistic control of Chihuahua and Durango merchants. Alarid asked that the government either provide factories for New Mexico or make it an exception to the general law so that Americans could continue to trade.

High tariffs affected everything from government revenues to the most mundane details of the daily lives of the pobladores, and seemed to run counter to their best interests. Tariffs raised the cost of imports, including clothing, household goods, and agricultural implements, because merchants passed the tariffs along to customers in the form of higher prices or charged more for the risks they took to smuggle.[25] As in the rest of the nation, high tariffs also sliced away potential revenue from local treasuries by encouraging smuggling. The loss of income spelled fiscal disaster for the shaky government budgets of New Mexico and California, both of which depended almost exclusively on customs duties to pay salaries of officials and to meet operating expenses. Citing the hardships of frontier life, the federal government continued the Spanish policy of exempting New Mexicans from the national sales tax and left the province entirely dependent upon revenue from foreign trade. *Californios* seem to have paid more taxes than *nuevomexicanos*, but tariff revenue was crucial for California government, too.[26]

The dependence of provincial government in New Mexico and California on foreign trade cannot be exaggerated. In California, politicians fought to control the customs house, knowing that whoever held it would also control the province. In New Mexico, the government could not pay salaries to officials or the military in some years until the annual caravan of American merchants arrived from Missouri to replenish the empty treasury.

Little wonder that frontier officials themselves publically violated the law and infuriated officials in Mexico City by negotiating lower tariffs than the law prescribed on the theory that half a loaf was better than none. Between 1839 and 1844 New Mexico Governor Armijo unilaterally streamlined complicated national ad valorem tariff laws by simply collecting $500 per wagonload of goods entering Santa Fe, irrespective of the contents of the wagon.[27] Even as relations between Mexico and the United States deteriorated in the early 1840s, New Mexicans insisted on keeping the Santa Fe Trail open over objections from the central government.[28] The trail to the United States had become the New Mexicans' economic lifeline, and their interests did not coincide with the national interest.

Pobladores as well as frontier officials violated the laws and colluded with foreigners, and smuggling became a widely practiced if not respected occupation. Settlers rendezvoused illegally with foreign ships along deserted sections of the California coast, or journeyed out to the plains from the New Mexico settlements to meet the incoming Santa Fe caravan before the customs officials arrived. Without smuggling, California Governor Mariano Chico lamented, "the Californias would not exist."[29]

Just as the central government lost legitimacy in the eyes of Mexican frontiersmen because its political decisions seemed insensitive to local concerns, so too did the economic policies formulated in Mexico City alienate frontiersmen. Those policies often seemed contrary to the region's best interests. In the spring of 1846, on the eve of war with the United States, Donaciano Vigil made an angry address to the New Mex-

Arrival of the Caravan at Santa Fe. After several months on the trail, traders rejoice at the sight of Santa Fe. (From a lithograph in Josiah Gregg, *Commerce of the Prairies* [2 vols.: New York, 1844], I, frontispiece).

ico assembly. Vigil complained that the central government harassed foreign businessmen with petty regulations and drove them out of New Mexico, and he criticized the government for its prohibition of arms imports and its monopoly of the manufacture of gunpowder—both continuations of Spanish policy. Vigil viewed arms and ammunition as "indispensable to us if we wish to exist in this Department" but, he said, the government did not make them available in sufficient quantities or at moderate cost, nor did it allow their import. He termed the result a "calamity."[30] To Ignacio Zúñiga of Tucson, policies that ran counter to frontier interests did not seem to be caused by governmental errors, but rather resulted from deliberate efforts by leaders in Mexico City to retard the growth of the frontier. Zúñiga boldly condemned "the childishness and small mindedness of some of our politicians who believe that they should not promote the growth of distant places such as Texas, California, etc., in order that they do not revolt and withdraw from the metropolis."[31] No accessible evidence supports Zúñiga's contention, but his statement reveals the extent to which a thoughtful frontiersman had grown distrustful of his government's motives.

The failure of pobladores and frontier officials to abide by the nation's laws probably further undermined the foreigners' already slender faith in Mexican laws and increased their belief in the fecklessness of Mexican officials. Foreigners came to regard smuggling as no crime, but rather, as one visitor to Texas put it, "good management."[32] "Transgressors of the law in this respect were not considered as lawbreakers," a California merchant recalled.[33]

The most serious incidents involving foreign violations of Mexican tariff laws occurred in Texas. In an effort to encourage colonists to settle in Texas, the federal government had granted a seven-year exemption from tariffs in 1823 on certain household goods and implements, and extended this exemption on some imports in later acts. During the 1820s, foreign colonists in Texas had virtually no experience at paying duties because the government failed to establish a legal port in Texas or to send revenue officials to collect import or export duties, tonnage fees, or issue harbor clearances to vessels. Foreigners and *tejanos* alike landed goods at convenient points along the coast, free from duties, fees, and commercial restraints. They not only smuggled merchandise into Texas, but used it as a launching point to send contraband into the Mexican interior and even to New Mexico.[34]

When the seven-year exemption expired in 1830 and the government tried to collect tariffs and other fees at Anáhuac on Galveston Bay and at Velasco, near the mouth of the Brazos, Texans became indignant. Charging that the officers in charge of customs collection were high-handed and arbitrary, a small group of American colonists forcibly expelled them in 1832. A similar incident occurred three years later when the government sent the gentlemanly, long-suffering Capt. Antonio Tenorio with thirty-four soldiers to man the garrison and reestablish the customs house at Anáhuac. Tenorio met widespread resistance to the payment of duties, culminating with an attack on his garrison in July 1835 by a group of angry Americans led by William Barret Travis, who the next year would command the ill-fated defenders of the Alamo. Travis's attack on Anáhuac, however, transcended the issue of tariffs and represented what one historian has termed "the first act of violence in the Texas revolution."[35]

The tariff issue represented only the most visible sign of Texan discontent with Mexican economic policy. Foreign-born colonists in Texas anticipated substantially higher profits for themselves if they could market cotton and other products in the Mexican ports instead of in the United States, and discerning Mexican officials recognized the value of strengthening economic ties between Texas and the rest of the nation. But the central government did not follow recommendations to promote coastal shipping within the republic. Texas goods continued to flow abroad, especially to New Orleans. The government failed to integrate Texas into the national economy, and that failure ranks among the key preconditions for the successful Texas revolt of 1836, just as similar failures in New Mexico and California contributed to alienation in those provinces as well.[36]

Across the frontier from Texas to California, as in the nation as a whole, the government failed to regulate economic growth in ways that would benefit Mexico and Mexicans. Instead of preventing foreigners from dominating economic life, protecting resources, or generating more revenue for the public treasury, federal policies alienated citizens and foreigners alike. Meanwhile, as they did throughout Mexico, local políticos put regional interests ahead of national interests and further assured the failure of federal economic policies. Still, despite the inability of government at any level to regulate or integrate the frontier economy, the opening of the frontier to foreign commerce in 1821 had brought new vitality to frontier economic life. Ironically, the formerly stagnant frontier economy flourished at the same time that the once-vigorous economy of central Mexico languished.

Mexico had been born bankrupt in 1821, its economy destroyed by the wars of independence and the flight of Spanish capital. The country would remain bankrupt for over a half century as agriculture, ranching, and mining, the mainstays of the Spanish colonial economy, recovered slowly from the devastation of war. Mexico's gross national product fell after independence to less than half its 1805 peak and would not surpass that figure again until the 1870s. Per capita income declined. The volume of foreign trade dropped to less than that of the late colonial period, and exports, silver and gold almost exclusively, consistently earned less than imports, leaving a perennial trade deficit. Foreigners, especially Europeans, came to dominate the nation's commercial life, although small retail stores remained largely Mexican-owned. Meanwhile, a series of governments, some short-lived, could squeeze little tax revenue out of an economy in doldrums. As a substitute for tax revenue, governments resorted to high-interest foreign loans to fill the treasury—an especially ruinous policy since much of that money went to support the predatory military establishment, which a decade of warfare had spawned.[37]

Meanwhile, some of the obstacles to economic recovery and growth that afflicted central Mexico proved less troublesome to the frontier. First, as we have seen, the struggle for independence left few scars on the landscape in the Far North, except in Texas. Second, Mexico's failure to improve roads and harbors constituted a major impediment to commerce in the rugged central region, but the Far North enjoyed natural advantages that promoted trade: good anchorage and navigable rivers along the Texas coast; a natural highway for wheeled vehicles across the Great Plains that linked New Mexico to the United States; and a population perched on the California coast that could easily be served by sea. Only Southern Arizona seemed isolated by geography. Finally, an archaic and inefficient economic structure, which Mexico had inherited from Spain and could not modify substantially, discouraged free enterprise and impeded development in central Mexico, but brazen officials and private citizens on the frontier, far removed from political authority, blunted the impact of federal regulations by ignoring or modifying them.[38]

Just as the frontier did not share some of the major obstacles to Mexico's economic growth, it also had advantages over the rest of the nation. One was its extreme underdevelopment; it represented the poorest area of the nation. Even modest gains in commerce and industry, or a small influx of capital and technology, made a sizable impact in the Far North. Another economic advantage was its proximity to the dynamic economy of the United States. Although Mexico's population was about 10 percent larger than that of the United States, her economy was half as productive in 1800, and that gap continued to widen through the first half of the nineteenth century as the American economy grew remarkably between the so-called panics of 1819 and 1837.[39]

The pull of the vigorous American economy reached beyond United States borders onto the neighboring Mexican frontier. It gave impetus to the economic growth of northernmost Mexico, and at the same time pulled that region into the American commercial orbit and away from its own weak metropolis. Mexico's failure to exert a strong counterforce contributed to the growing sense of alienation of some of her frontiersmen, who could not mistake the signs that the highways of commerce no longer ran only north and south.

9

"To Govern is to Populate"
The Peopling of Texas

I cannot help seeing advantages which, to my way of thinking, would result if we admitted honest, hard-working people, regardless of what country they come from . . . even hell itself.—Francisco Ruiz, *San Antonio, 1830*

Where others send invading armies . . . [the North Americans] send their colonists.—Lucas Alamán, *Mexico City, ca. 1830*

In the mid-nineteenth century an Argentine political theorist, Juan Bautista Alberdi, enunciated the famous dictum: "To govern is to populate." Although the phrase oversimplified the function of government, political leaders of newly independent Mexico would have agreed with its sentiment. Rapid population growth seemed essential to Mexico's development and vital to the very existence of its northern frontier.

With its western flank threatened by Russians, the Anglo-American menace to the east, and autonomous bands of nomads making intermittent war throughout, the northern frontier desperately needed pobladores. One contemporary estimated that over a fourth of Mexico's lands were unsettled, and "almost all" of that unoccupied land was on the far northern frontier.[1] By the 1820s, as we have seen, Mexican liberals viewed the traditional institutions for populating the frontier—the mission and the presidio—as outdated and ineffective. Only an influx of colonists offered hope for the development and defense of the north, but colonists, it appeared, had to come from outside of Mexico. The conventional wisdom in Mexico held, albeit erroneously, that the Mexican character was not suitable for colonizing. More important, the nation

158

itself was sparsely populated, with perhaps 6,200,000 inhabitants spread out over an area extending from Oregon to Guatemala. Mexico had lost about 10 percent of its population in the wars of independence, or about half of the nation's work force since these were mainly young men.[2]

The arguments in favor of foreign immigration seemed so compelling that even men of differing political persuasions found themselves agreed on the question. Skilled and industrious foreigners would promote economic growth, improve society, and increase the manpower available for defense. Foreigners with capital and managerial skills seemed essential to replace the many well-to-do Spaniards who had left Mexico or been expelled in the decade following independence.[3]

To appreciate the benefits that foreign immigrants could bring, some Mexican leaders argued, one need only look to the extraordinary growth and political stability of their northern neighbor. Due largely to immigration, the population of the United States had more than doubled from nearly 4,000,000 to over 9,600,000 between 1790 and 1820. Surely Mexico, free from the fetters of Spanish colonialism, could do the same. In the optimistic atmosphere that characterized the early years of independence, some Mexican leaders argued that Mexico's benign climate and abundant natural resources would attract more foreigners than the United States could.[4] But like foreign capital, an influx of foreign people brought risks as well as opportunities. How to assimilate foreigners, as well as attract them, became a central problem—especially in the Far North where the majority of foreign immigrants would be norteamericanos.

Opening Mexico to foreigners represented a break from Spanish tradition. Generally, Spain had excluded foreigners from settling in her American empire and had relied instead upon two domestic sources of population: indigenous peoples, who were to become acculturated, and Spaniards, who were to multiply and people the continent. In that plan Spaniards remained the essential element, for without them to serve as models Indians could not be acculturated. Relying heavily upon her own tiny population, Spain had done remarkably well in peopling much of the New World.

Nonetheless, Spanish officials had not been able to ease the shortage of gente de razón in peripheral but strategic areas such as Texas and California, despite efforts to encourage internal migration. Women, especially, were in demand. Since colonists had no reason to flock to economically stagnant frontier areas on their own initiative, Spain had experimented with incentives in the form of free transportation, seeds, tools, land, and exemption from taxes. Even these inducements lured only a few colonists northward and immigration quotas remained un-filled. Ultimately, the government resorted to sending orphan girls and soldiers and convicts and their families to colonize the frontier, but this brought only modest results. By 1821 only 3,200 pobladores resided in Alta California and some 2,500 in Texas.[5]

Spain, then, generally sought to settle the frontier with her own sub-jects and to keep foreigners out. Texas, however, was an exception, following a precedent set in Louisiana. When Spain received Louisiana from France in 1762, Frenchmen and Anglo-Americans already lived there. Spanish officials permitted them to remain, and beginning in 1788 experimented boldly with opening Louisiana to foreign immigrants who promised to become Catholics and vassals of the king. That action led Thomas Jefferson to remark, "I wish a hundred thousand of our inhabit-ants would accept the invitation. It may be the means of delivering to us peaceably what may otherwise cost us a war."[6] Spain hoped to augment the population of Louisiana while simultaneously depleting the number of troublesome citizens on her neighbor's frontier. It seemed a brilliant stroke, but within a few years officials grew disenchanted with the scheme. The norteamericanos seemed unassimilable and potentially subversive. Spain limited the policy to Louisiana and did not permit Americans to settle beyond that province. Nonetheless, foreigners drifted into East Texas as early as the 1790s, squatting there with the sufferance of local officials who welcomed settlers regardless of their origin or of govern-ment policy.[7]

With Spain's cession of Louisiana to France in 1800 and its acquisition by the United States in 1803, Texas became the buffer province between the rest of Mexico and the United States. This touched off a disagree-ment among Spanish officials as to whether or not foreigners should be permitted to settle in Texas. Officials decided to allow some foreigners to enter, but specifically excluded Anglo-Americans, whose government in their view made the preposterous claim that its purchase of Louisiana included Texas. Still, Anglo-Americans continued to settle in Texas with the tacit approval of frontier officials who desperately wanted to aug-ment the province's population of "useful citizens," and this divergence between national policy and regional practice would continue under independent Mexico.[8]

On the eve of Mexican independence, after the United States had abandoned all claims to Texas in the Treaty of 1819, Spanish policy toward immigration from the United States shifted. The change began in January 1821 when Moses Austin, a one-time Spanish subject in Louisi-ana, received the promise of a generous grant of land on the Brazos River in exchange for bringing 300 Catholic families from Louisiana to settle. Texas Governor Antonio Martínez, who "instinctively distrusted foreigners," had supported Austin's plans for colonizing in Texas because, as one historian has explained, "his suspicions were overcome by his desire to see Texas prosper and grow."[9] Austin thus became the first Anglo-American to receive permission to colonize in Texas. Six months after Austin received his permit, the Spanish Cortes, prompted by petitions from Governor Martínez and other officials, approved a bill that allowed foreigners to settle on the public lands of Mexico's northern frontier, from California to Texas. Special vigilance, however, was to be maintained in regard to Anglo-Americans.[10]

Thus, in the dying days of empire, Spain anticipated the policy of independent Mexico. In fact, since Mexican delegates had urged the Spanish Cortes to take this extraordinary measure, this late policy shift by Spain may be best understood as the first expression of Mexico's new open policy toward foreign immigrants.

How to populate the Far North was among the first questions considered by Agustín Iturbide's newly victorious government in the autumn of 1821. The Iturbide administration urged adoption of an agrarian law and a plan of colonization that would provide incentives for foreigners as well as Mexicans to settle in the north. The question was sent to a government commission headed by Juan Francisco de Azcárate. Referring to the precedent established by the colonization law adopted by the Spanish Cortes in 1821, the commission urged colonization of Coahuila, Nuevo Santander, and Baja California as well as Alta California, New Mexico, and Texas. The latter provinces, it was argued, constituted only the first line of defense in the Far North. All of the northern frontier needed more people. The commission recommended that the government encourage Europeans and Anglo-Americans to settle in the Far North, but concluded that because of their location, the Californias might best be settled by Chinese colonists and Mexican convicts.[11]

The report of the Azcárate commission made it clear that the primary reason for colonizing the frontier was defense against Indians and foreign powers. Texas seemed most vulnerable. As recently as October 1821 a group of filibusters from the United States, led by James Long, had seized Goliad before Mexican troops captured them. Moreover, no official boundary between Texas and the rapacious Americans existed because Mexico and the United States had not yet ratified the line established between the United States and Spain in the Treaty of 1819. The only solution seemed to be to populate Texas quickly because the United States was growing rapidly, along with its need for more land. One day, the Azcárate commission predicted, hordes of norteamericanos might descend on the fertile province of Texas, "just as the Goths, Ostrogoths, Alans, and other tribes devastated the Roman Empire."[12]

As officials debated the young nation's colonization laws in the early 1820s, then, Texas was foremost on their minds. Laws developed slowly, however, for the urgent needs of the frontier were offset by the greater necessity of stabilizing government in Mexico City. During the power struggle between royalists, republicans, and *iturbidistas*, the Azcárate report was temporarily lost from view. Finally, on February 18, 1823, Iturbide approved a detailed colonization law, but the next month he fell from power and his so-called Imperial Colonization Law was annulled.[13]

Following Iturbide's demise, Congress passed the Colonization Law of August 18, 1824, which remained in force throughout the years that Mexico controlled what would become the American Southwest. The 1824 Law guaranteed land, security, and exemption from taxes for four years to foreign settlers and imposed few restrictions. Foreigners could not acquire property within twenty leagues of a foreign nation or ten leagues of the coasts, nor could an individual possess more than eleven square leagues of land (about 71.5 square miles). The law did not specify that foreigners had to become Catholics or citizens, but it did indicate that preference in granting land would be made to Mexican citizens. A statement about religion would have been redundant in a country that permitted only the practice of Roman Catholicism. A subsequent law, in 1828, made citizenship a requirement for those who lived in Mexico for more than two successive years and made it more difficult for noncitizens to obtain land.[14]

In retrospect it seems curious that a colonization law designed to protect northern Mexico from the United States should also permit norteamericanos to colonize and benefit from it. In practice, Mexico probably had little choice. Anglo-Americans had settled in Texas in large numbers already, despite laws excluding them. By 1823 perhaps 3,000 North Americans lived illegally in Texas. Mexican troops, numbering about 200, could neither expel them nor patrol the immense and ill-defined border to prevent more from coming. Notwithstanding the obvious dangers, it seemed best to try to give legal status to these illegal aliens and win their loyalty by making them landowners with a stake in the nation. Of equal importance, some Mexican lawmakers hoped that Anglo-American immigration would be offset by European and Mexican colonization—hopes that proved ill-founded.[15] Ultimately, however, it was not the colonization laws that contributed to the "Americanization" of Texas, but, rather, failure to apply the law.

The Colonization Law of 1824 authorized Congress to devise a specific program for territories such as New Mexico and California, a matter it did not attend to until 1828. Otherwise, consistent with federalist principles, the 1824 law provided only brief, general guidelines and left the details of regulating foreign colonists up to individual states.

The first states to implement the 1824 colonization law were largely in the north and included Coahuila y Texas. Some officials in Coahuila had opposed permitting Anglo-Americans to settle in Texas because "their nation borders ours. . . . one day they would be able to revolt and join with their former country."[16] Despite such prophetic objections, however, state legislators agreed on the Colonization Law of March 24, 1825, which permitted Americans to settle in Coahuila y Texas but specified that Mexicans be given preference for land.[17]

The Coahuila y Texas law allowed the head of a family to obtain as much as a square league or *sitio* of grazing land, equivalent to 4,428 acres, and a *labor* of farming land, equal to 177 acres.[18] This land was available at modest fees payable in installments over a six-year period with no money due until the fourth year. Foreign colonists had to "prove their christianity, morality, and good habits," and establish permanent residence before being considered naturalized Mexicans. To encourage the assimilation of foreigners, lawmakers provided that those who married Mexican women could obtain additional land.

State law permitted an individual foreigner to obtain land directly, without the aid of a broker or agent, but in practice that seldom occurred. Obstacles of language and ignorance of the law worked against most individuals. American immigrants who came to Texas on their own usually settled in East Texas at communities such as Sabine, Atascasito and Ais. As late as 1836 most lacked title to their land and many had settled illegally within twenty leagues of the border or ten leagues of the Gulf of Mexico. Some of these settlers had made substantial improvements on the land, but lived the uncertain lives of squatters.[19]

Those colonists who succeeded at obtaining clear title to land—a small minority, to be sure—generally came to Texas under the auspices of immigration agents, known as *empresarios,* and formed part of a group or colony. Under the state law, an empresario served as an agent of the government, selecting colonists, allocating lands, and enforcing regulations. For these services the empresario could receive as much as five sitios of grazing land and five labores of farming land for each 100 families settled. Lands contracted to empresarios quickly covered nearly all of Texas from the Sabine to the Nueces, making it all the more difficult for individuals to obtain titles on their own. At least twenty-four empresario contracts, calling for the settlement of over 8,000 families, were signed between 1825 and 1832. Seventeen of those contracts went to foreigners, mostly Anglo-Americans, and those few Mexicans who held contracts generally had foreign partners.[20]

Prior to 1830 only three empresarios brought a significant number of colonists into Texas: Stephen F. Austin, Green de Witt, and Martín de León.[21] Without question the most successful Texas empresario was Austin. A well-educated, twenty-seven-year-old with five years' experience in the legislature of Missouri Territory, Stephen Austin became heir to his father's Spanish grant when Moses Austin died in 1821. That summer, young Austin journeyed to Texas where the cooperative Governor Martínez recognized his right to his father's contract. Almost immediately, Austin began to bring colonists into Texas, but in March 1822 he learned that the new government of independent Mexico would not recognize his father's arrangement with the Spanish government. At the advice of Governor Martínez, Austin rode to Mexico City to press his claim. He remained in the capital for nearly a year and his presence, along with that of other foreigners seeking lands in Texas, probably hastened passage of the Imperial Colonization Law of 1823.

The able and persistent Austin became the only foreigner to benefit from the short-lived 1823 law, under which the government approved his father's grant. Stephen Austin returned to Texas and by 1825 had fulfilled his contract by bringing 300 families into Texas. Austin subsequently obtained three more contracts from the state government to import nine hundred more families, and he substantially fulfilled each of those contracts as well.

With its major settlement at San Felipe de Austin on the Brazos, some sixty miles west of present Houston, Austin's colony covered an immense expanse, bordered by the San Antonio road on the north and the Gulf of Mexico to the south. Since his grant antedated the 1824 colonization law Austin was exempt from the article prohibiting settlement within ten leagues of the sea.[22]

Bordering Austin's lands on the west, along the Guadalupe and Lavaca rivers, lay Green de Witt's colony, founded in 1825 with its principal settlement at the new town of Gonzales. By 1832, a year after his contract had expired, De Witt had procured titles for only a third of the 400 families he had contracted to settle in Texas. Most of his grant reverted to the public domain. Off to a slower start than Austin, De Witt may have been less able and energetic. However, the poor location of his grant, on the westernmost edge of American settlement in Texas, discouraged would-be settlers. If De Witt was a poor second to Austin as a colonizer, compared to other empresarios his efforts were a resounding success.[23]

Between De Witt's colony and the coast, and to the southwest of Austin's grant, Martín de León, a rancher from Tamaulipas, established a colony and a town named in honor of President Guadalupe Victoria in 1824. The town came to be known simply as Victoria. The only predom-

Empresario Grants in Texas, 1821-1836

Empresarios, or agents, received permission to settle vast tracts of Texas real estate in the Mexican era. Few, however, actually fulfilled their contracts to bring colonists to Texas. Most of the empresarios, as this map suggests, were foreign-born.

inantly Mexican colony in Texas, De León's grant was also unique in that it had been issued by the provincial deputation at San Antonio in early 1824, antedating the federal colonization law of that year. Moreover, it had no clearly defined boundaries and brought De León into frequent conflict with his neighbors. The colony remained small. By 1835 titles had been issued to over 100 families.[24]

With or without the aid of empresarios, North Americans and their slaves flocked to Texas in the 1820s. Cheap land in Texas and easy terms of payment attracted some of these migrants. The United States Land Act of 1820 had lowered the price of land to $1.25 an acre, but required immediate cash payment. More important than the attraction of cheap land, however, was the impact of the economic depression in the United States that followed the Panic of 1819. Cash became scarce and many Americans found themselves plunged into debt, especially in the western states. Hence, the "push" of the bill collector and the sheriff seems to have been more important in causing immigration to Texas than was the "pull" of cheap land. Men in debt on the American frontier could get a fresh start by simply crossing the border to the Mexican frontier. Texas seems to have had more than its share of debtors, drifters, and fugitives, most of whom were single males.[25] There is no way to determine the precise number of immigrants from the United States, but by 1830 it certainly surpassed 7,000. Meanwhile, the Mexican population had grown slowly to perhaps 3,000.[26]

Anglo-Americans not only outnumbered Mexicans in Texas by 1830, but assimilated poorly. Isolated in eastern and central Texas, the norteamericanos managed their own affairs in relative independence from the West Texas Mexican enclaves of San Antonio and Goliad. The Mexican and American frontiers had come together in Texas, but failed to merge.[27] The rapid increase of the Anglo-American aliens and their failure to integrate became the source of growing concern to authorities in Mexico City. In late 1825, for example, a warning came from Mexico's minister to Washington that journalists in the United States wrote openly that Americans who settled in Texas would retain their ties to the United States and remain unassimilated: "the colonists in Texas will not be Mexicans more than in name."[28] In 1826 the government issued orders to reduce the flow of Americans into Texas.[29]

The dangers inherent in the Texas situation were dramatized at Nacogdoches in December 1826 when one empresario, Haden Edwards, called for the independence of Texas. Disgruntled over conflicting land titles, Edwards and his followers imprudently proclaimed the existence of the "Fredonia Republic," but his ill-conceived revolt collapsed by the time Mexican troops from San Antonio reached Nacogdoches in January 1827. Edwards had won little support from the more successful foreign-born colonists, who had more to lose than to gain from severing relations with Mexico. Stephen Austin demonstrated loyalty to his adopted land by sending militia from his colony to aid in quelling the rebellion, and Green de Witt's colonists adopted a resolution expressing "contempt and disgust" for Edwards.[30]

The Edwards fiasco led directly to the sending of a high ranking official to study the Texas situation and, ultimately, to the closing of Texas to further immigration from the United States. Chosen to assess the security of the country and recommend ways to defend it was Manuel Mier y Terán, a highly respected engineer and intellectual, brigadier general, former minister of war and navy, and a contender for the presidency of the republic.[31]

General Mier y Terán journeyed across Texas in 1828 in what one American described as a coach "of prodigious size . . . constructed of huge pieces of timber much carved inlaid and plated with silver. . . ."[32] He sent gloomy reports back to Mexico City. From Nacogdoches, in June 1828, Mier y Terán wrote to President Guadalupe Victoria that "as one covers the distance from Bejar [San Antonio] to this town, he will note that Mexican influence is proportionately diminished until on arriving in this place he will see that it is almost nothing." Americans came in an "unceasing" stream. "The first news of them comes by discovering them on land already under cultivation."[33]

In Mier y Terán's judgment, foreigners would not assimilate because they formed the majority of the population and because the few Mexicans in East Texas, who consisted of "the lowest class—the very poor and the very ignorant," had little to teach them. Local Mexicans, he said, "complain of the superiority and better education of the colonists," and Americans justifiably complained about the "political disorganization of the frontier" and the inadequate system of justice. At first, Mier y Terán saw the problem as a need for reform of frontier institutions, and urged President Victoria to "take timely measures. Texas could throw the whole nation into revolution."[34]

In September 1829, after leaving Texas, Mier y Terán became commanding general of the military jurisdiction of the Eastern Interior Provinces, which included Tamaulipas and Nuevo León as well as Coahuila and Texas. In that position he had considerable influence on policy toward Texas. By late 1829 the general had grown suspicious of the loyalty of American colonists in Texas and alarmed at expansionist designs of the United States. "The North Americans have conquered whatever territory adjoins them," he wrote that autumn.[35] Convinced of the need for strong measures to stop the United States from acquiring Texas, Mier y Terán made a series of recommendations that soon became law. He urged the strengthening of presidios and the creation of new military garrisons; he suggested the increase of coastal trade between Texas and the rest of Mexico, in order to weaken United States commercial influence; and he argued the necessity of bringing both European and Mexican colonists into Texas to counterbalance the growing American

Anglo-American immigrants. They cleared the pine forests of East Texas and built log cabins, often with the aid of black slaves. Most of the small cabins surrounding this farmhouse in Montgomery County were slave quarters. Sketched by a British traveler, William Bollaert, ca. 1843 (courtesy, the Newberry Library, Chicago, Edward E. Ayer Collection).

Montgomery County

influence: "Either the government occupies Texas *now*, or it is lost forever."[36]

Meir y Terán's recommendations became the basis for the law of April 6, 1830, a controversial document that went beyond his suggestions in two particulars. First, instead of merely establishing ways and means of countercolonizing Texas with Europeans and Mexicans, the April 6 law prohibited further immigration from the United States and rescinded all empresario contracts not yet completed. Americans were welcome to settle elsewhere in Mexico, but not in territory adjacent to the United States. Second, the law prohibited the introduction of slaves into Texas. The previous year, September 15, 1829, President Vicente Guerrero had emancipated all slaves in Mexico in a move that was basically humanitarian, but might also have been intended to slow down American immigration. Protests from Texas and Coahuila, however, had exempted Texas from the ruling.[37]

Closing Texas to immigrants from the United States was a momentous step. The Colonization Law of 1824 stipulated that such a measure could be taken only under "imperative circumstances," but Secretary of State Lucas Alamán, who authored the April 6, 1830 law, clearly believed that such circumstances had arrived: "Texas will be lost for this Republic if adequate measures to save it are not taken."[38] Like Mier y Terán, Alamán argued that the American colonists were linked to a United States scheme to acquire Texas in the same manner that it had obtained Louisiana and Florida. "Where others send invading armies," Alamán wrote, ". . . [the Americans] send their colonists."[39] Historians have found no evidence of such an official American policy, and some Americans such as Austin actually hoped the United States would not acquire Texas for fear that opportunities to acquire cheap land would disappear. Nonetheless, Alamán had good reason for concern. He knew that American journalists were continuing to agitate for Texas and that President Andrew Jackson's tactless representative in Mexico, Anthony Butler, had arrived in late 1829 with a commission to offer five million dollars for it. Little wonder the Mexican secretary of state viewed the United States and its mobile citizens as a threat to Texas.[40]

Responsibility for enforcing the April 6, 1830 law fell to a "director of colonization," and the appointments went to men of ability. The able and prestigious General Mier y Terán held the office first, until July 1832, under the conservative administration of Anastasio Bustamante. Following political upheavals in Mexico City, the liberal administration of Valentín Gómez Farías named Tadeo Ortiz de Ayala director of colonization in August 1833. Although he lacked the political and military connections of Mier y Terán, Ortiz was a well-traveled intellectual who knew the United States, Texas, and Europe firsthand, and had been personally involved in colonization projects and had written extensively about the subject. In 1821 he had published a farsighted and influential book that demonstrated his sound grasp of Mexico's geopolitical position in regard to the United States. In it, Ortiz had warned his countrymen about foreign threats to the frontier, especially Texas which he judged Mexico's "key" province, and he argued the need for a unified plan of development and defense for the entire Far North, from the Pacific to the Gulf of Mexico.[41] Although Ortiz and Mier y Terán had different backgrounds and held appointments from administrations of different political persuasions, their views toward solving the Texas crisis bore remarkable similarity.

The April 6, 1830 law charged the director of colonization for Texas with two main responsibilities: to prevent Anglo-American immigration and to encourage Mexican and European settlement. Both Mier y Terán and Ortiz regarded the policy of keeping North Americans out of Texas as unenforceable. "There is no physical force that can stop the entrance of the norteamericanos, who are exclusive owners of the coast and the border of Texas," Mier y Terán told Alamán early in 1831.[42] Both Mier y Terán and Ortiz agreed that efforts to enforce the law would antagonize Americans already living in Texas and, as Ortiz put it, contribute to their "aspirations for independence."[43] Ortiz also argued that the law discouraged "the useful settlers and worthy empresarios" from entering Texas, but did not keep out undesirables. Stephen Austin had expressed a similar objection to the law, and both were probably correct. A haven for debtors and undesirables even before 1830, Texas continued to enjoy that reputation. "Everybody knew that the immigrants to Texas were vagabonds and refugees from justice," the Louisiana *Gazette* intoned in 1835.[44]

Mier y Terán and Ortiz both saw countercolonization as the key to saving Texas for Mexico, but each approached the task differently. Mier y Terán had less faith in the ability of Europeans to assimilate in Mexico than did the urbane Ortiz, and sought to colonize Texas with Mexicans from the interior. His plans called for 5,000 Mexican settlers to be drawn from a quota assigned to every state of the republic. States failed to cooperate, however, and even the governor of Coahuila y Texas did not furnish his quota of colonists. Putting regional interests ahead of national interests, state officials seemed reluctant to sacrifice even a small portion of their local population.[45] Mier y Terán also tried to implement the portion of the April 6, 1830 law which called for sending convicted criminals and their families to Texas. The 1825 Colonization Law of Coahuila y Texas had also called for the relocation of convicts in Texas in order to settle the region. Both efforts failed. For reasons that are not clear, convicts apparently never arrived in Texas in significant numbers as they would in California during this same period.[46]

Mier y Terán had better luck at reinforcing three military garrisons, at San Antonio, Goliad, and Nacogdoches, and beginning construction of six more forts in 1830. All were situated to encircle the Anglo-American colonies, prevent smuggling, and keep out illegal aliens. Along the road between San Antonio and Nacogdoches, at the Brazos crossing, he founded Tenochtitlán with hopes that its central location would make it the next capital of Texas. Two garrisons, Velasco at the mouth of the Brazos, and Anáhuac on Galveston Bay, were to protect the coast, and three posts were placed on key rivers: Lipantitlán on the Nueces, Terán on the Neches, and Lavaca on the river of the same name. Mier y Terán apparently hoped to make these self-sustaining military colonies, where soldiers would double as farmers and artisans. He also recognized that without Mexican colonists, whom he hoped would settle near the protective walls of these garrisons, the use of military men as colonists was a short-range and expensive solution.[47] He was correct. The government could not afford to support the forts adequately, and in 1832 it removed most of the troops from Texas to meet a political crisis in the capital, leaving the garrisons largely abandoned.[48]

After two years of frustration, Mier y Terán's tenure as director of colonization came to a tragic end. On July 2, 1832, he wrote to his friend Lucas Alamán predicting the loss of Texas and expressing dismay over the turn of events that had put Santa Anna at the head of the liberal insurrection against the conservative Bustamante government. With the country in civil war, Terán asked: "how could we expect to hold Texas when we do not even agree among ourselves?"[49] The next morning, despondent over Texas and in poor health, he rose early, dressed in his finest uniform, and ran a sword through his heart.

Whereas Terán had emphasized the countercolonization of Texas by Mexicans, his successor, Tadeo Ortiz, argued the need to encourage settlement by Europeans as a bulwark against Americans. In sharp contrast to the United States, Mexico failed to attract significant numbers of European immigrants during her first half-century of independence. Political instability, an economy in doldrums, dangers of foreign wars, religious intolerance, and an uncertain and sometimes xenophobic atmosphere combined to make Mexico far less attractive than the United States to would-be immigrants. Sometimes, of course, immigrants themselves were to blame for their failure to successfully colonize in Mexico.[50] One of the most flawed and outlandish schemes came from the well-known British socialist, Robert Owen, who in 1828 urged Mexico to

Manuel Mier y Terán. A military hero and trained engineer, General Manuel de Mier y Terán (b. 1789), sought to settle Mexican families in Texas to check growing American influence. Frustrated by events he could not control, and despondent that Texas would be lost to Mexico, Mier y Terán took his own life in 1832.

donate the whole of Coahuila y Texas to his utopian society, which would colonize the state and use it as a human laboratory to test his theories on communal living—he already had such a project underway in New Harmony, Indiana. By turning Coahuila y Texas over to him, and persuading England, the United States, and Mexico to guarantee the independence of the area, Owen argued that seemingly inevitable war over Texas would be averted.[51] Not surprisingly, Mexico was unwilling to give Coahuila y Texas away in order to avoid the risk of losing it in a war.

The same forces that discouraged Europeans from immigrating to Mexico probably worked against their settling on her frontiers, although foreigners may have found Texas, with its cheap land and isolation from political turmoil, more attractive than the interior. Two teams of Irish-

born empresarios founded small but successful settlements of Irish immigrants in Texas in the early 1830s. James McGloin and John McMullen
established the aptly named town of San Patricio Hibernia (St. Patrick of
Ireland) in 1830 on the Nueces above Corpus Christi Bay, and in 1833
James Power and James Hewetson founded Refugio at the site of a
former mission, Nuestra Señora del Refugio, inland from Cópano Bay.
An English empresario also established a colony on the Rio Grande in
1833, but that failed within a few years when Comanches destroyed the
settlement.[52]

Tadeo Ortiz, like some other Mexican leaders, had come to believe
that Europeans, as well as Mexicans, could be attracted to Texas and
other parts of the frontier if the federal government would play a more
active role. Ortiz recognized that the frontier offered limited opportunities for immigrants, and he suggested that the government initiate and
finance sweeping political, economic, and social reforms. He went so far
as to advocate religious toleration to induce European Protestants to
settle, and also urged that the government pay transportation costs, and
provide colonists with food, tools, and supplies to give them a start in
the new land. The April 6, 1830 law had recommended similar aid, but
only for Mexicans, whereas Ortiz suggested that direct subsidies be
extended to Europeans as well.[53] Perennially bankrupt, Mexico could ill
afford even modest aid for Mexicans much less Europeans. Apparently
on only one occasion, the sending of the Híjar-Padrés colony to California
in 1833, did the government heed Ortiz's suggestion and give material
assistance to settlers headed for the Far North.

It is significant that Ortiz, a staunch liberal and believer in states
rights, had concluded that colonization of the frontier could not be left in
the hands of the beleaguered and impecunious frontier states and territories, and argued instead the need for federal intervention. Like Alamán,
Mier y Terán, and other national leaders close to the Texas situation,
Ortiz believed that the government had committed a grave error in 1824
by giving the weak state of Coahuila responsibility for the disposal of
public lands in Texas. Coahuila, Ortiz wrote, "has done nothing but
turn over the vast territory [of Texas] to the United States."[54] He condemned Coahuila for making no effort to assimilate the foreigners, and
for failing to settle them near Mexican communities, or provide them
with responsive government or an adequate system of justice.[55]

Even the federalist Gómez Farías administration seemed convinced
that national interest required it to play a stronger role in the affairs of
Coahuila y Texas. Gómez Farías tried to implement a part of the April 6,
1830 law that authorized the government to furnish free transportation,
land, and maintenance for a year to Mexicans who would settle on the

frontier. Gómez Farías also sent a special agent to Coahuila to obtain Texas land for the central government, and his administration hoped to settle Indians and blacks from the United States on that land—a plan that Mier y Terán had also endorsed. The mission failed, however, and Coahuila continued to dispose of public land in Texas in a manner that brought little benefit to Texas or Mexico and largely ignored the important question of how to assimilate the North Americans. Indeed, the alienation of public lands in Texas by Coahuila became such a scandal that, as one contemporary noted, the term empresario "is justly considered equivalent to that of a swindler."[56]

The idea of luring Europeans or Mexicans onto the far northern frontier, which Ortiz articulated so clearly, had been a recurring theme of officials in Mexico City from the beginning of independence. As one official put it in 1827: "it is necessary to build dams to contain" the Americans, "these restless peoples—scheming, haughty, and rash."[57] But could it be done? When Stephen Austin learned of Ortiz's plan to import Europeans "to dam out the North Americans," he compared it to "trying to stop the Mississippi with a dam of straw."[58]

The ebullient Ortiz did not live long enough to put his plans into effect, or to see them frustrated. Ortiz had received his appointment as director of colonization in Mexico City in August 1833, shortly after returning from a tour of Texas, and quickly began preparations for another journey north. Forced to delay his departure in the pestilent port city of Veracruz while awaiting the arrival of his overdue salary, Ortiz lost his life in the great cholera epidemic of that year. Even had he lived, omens were bad. A government that could not afford to pay its director of colonization could hardly finance the expensive program that he recommended.[59]

On November 15, 1833, a month after Ortiz's death, Mexico's Senate rescinded the odious antiimmigration clause of the law of April 6, 1830, effective in May 1834. Lorenzo de Zavala and José Antonio Mexía were among the prominent Mexican legislators with interest in Texas lands who worked openly to bring about this reversal of federal policy. De Zavala and Mexía both had ties to American financiers and wanted colonists from the United States to settle on the lands in which they had an interest.[60]

No new director of colonization succeeded Tadeo Ortiz. In January 1834 Gómez Farías sent Juan Nepomuceno Almonte to investigate the Texas situation. Educated in the United States, fluent in English, and familiar with Texas where he had served on the governor's staff in 1822, Almonte was an excellent choice for the delicate assignment. In a report published in Mexico City upon his return from Texas, Almonte also urged the countercolonization of Texas with Mexicans and acknowledged that he expected to become the new director of colonization. In secret correspondence he asked that more troops be sent to keep Americans out.[61] In the spring of 1834, however, President Santa Anna ousted Gómez Farías and began pushing the nation toward a highly centralized government that would throw Texas and other provinces into revolt. As these events unfolded, the federal government had little time to devote to colonization. Almonte would return to Texas in 1836 as a member of a military force sent to subdue the rebel province, rather than as director of colonization.

The same kinds of tensions and differences of opinion between representatives of the central government and regional officials that manifested themselves in political, military, and economic matters, intruded into the question of how to people the frontier. Local interests in Texas, beginning with Antonio Martínez, the last Spanish governor, had generally opposed any measures which would slow immigration from the United States.

Tejano oligarchs saw the economic growth of Texas, its security from Indians, and their own fortunes, as inextricably linked to the well-being of the Anglo-American newcomers and their slave-based, cotton-growing economy. Hence, *tejano* leaders joined norteamericanos in vigorously protesting Presidente Vicente Guerrero's September 15, 1829 decree emancipating all slaves in Mexico, an order designed to discourage further Anglo settlement in Texas. Jefe político Ramón Músquiz refused to publish the decree in Texas and began negotiations to make Texas exempt. While he acknowledged that slavery was "unfortunate," he urged its continuance in Texas because the province faced ruin without more laborers.[62] Similarly, the ayuntamiento of San Antonio, in a petition of December 19, 1832 supported by the ayuntamientos of Goliad and Nacogdoches, argued against the provision of the law of April 6, 1830 which closed the border to further immigration from the United States. Signed by seven members of well-to-do San Antonio families, such as José Antonio de la Garza, Angel Navarro, and Juan Angel Seguín, the petition applauded the tremendous benefits that Anglo-Americans had already brought to their benighted province and argued that Anglo-Americans, unlike Europeans, had a form of government similar to Mexico's, knew how to deal with Indians, and could immigrate at little cost.[63] Francisco Ruiz of San Antonio put it bluntly: "I cannot help seeing advantages which, to my way of thinking, would result if we admitted honest, hard-working people, regardless of what country they come from. . . . even hell itself."[64]

Ruiz got his wish, but with a vengeance. Anglo-Americans had flooded Texas following the passage of the Law of April 6, 1830, as if it had never been enacted. Most came as illegal aliens, but a few entered Texas legally because Mier y Terán had interpreted the law loosely and permitted Stephen Austin and Green de Witt to continue to receive colonists to fulfill their contracts, even while he nullified grants held by other American-born empresarios on the grounds that they had not begun to meet their obligations. Between 1830 and 1834 immigration from the United States seems to have accelerated rather than slowed. Crude estimates suggest that the number of Anglo-Americans and their slaves residing in Texas in 1834 had reached over 20,700, probably more than double the number of Americans in Texas just four years earlier.[65]

The flood continued in the last two years before the Texas revolt, but with the removal of the paper dam in May 1834 immigrants from the United States again migrated to Texas legally. By 1835 an estimated 1,000 Americans a month entered Texas by way of the Brazos River alone, and in mid-1836, shortly after Texas won its independence, a careful American observer placed the number of his countrymen and their slaves at 35,000. His estimate may have been conservative.[66] These recent immigrants from the United States outnumbered *tejanos,* who probably counted no more than 3,500 in 1836, by ten to one. With the addition of several thousand members of the so-called civilized tribes from the United States, such as Cherokees, Chickasaws, Delawares, Creeks, and Shawnees, the population of what Almonte termed "civilized people" in Texas surpassed 40,000 in 1836.

Texas, then, saw a remarkable rise in population in fifteen years, growing from 2,500 in 1821 to over 40,000 in 1836 at an average annual rate of 100 percent a year. That would have been a towering rate on the American frontier, and by Mexican standards of the era it was nothing less than stunning. The average annual growth rate of Mexico during that same period was perhaps 1.1 percent a year.[67]

In quantity, the peopling of Texas had been a spectacular success, but the quality of the immigrants left much to be desired from the point of view of officials in Mexico City. They continued to view American colonists as the first wave of a quiet United States conquest. This attitude toward the Americans was informed and reasonable. The newcomers continued to live apart, unassimilated, and many viewed themselves as superior to Mexicans. As political differences led to the deterioration of relations between Texas and the central government in the mid-1830s—a matter we shall consider in a subsequent chapter—many Americans in Texas also saw immigrants from the United States as the key to separation from Mexico. Stephen Austin, who had earlier worked to keep

Texas in the Mexican union, had switched positions and had come to support separation from Mexico. He hoped it would come about peacefully—a result of "Americanizing Texas" through immigration. "The more the American population of Texas is increased," Austin wrote in late summer of 1835, "the more readily will the Mexican Government give it up."

> A gentle breeze shakes off a ripe peach. Can it be supposed
> that the violent political convulsions of Mexico will not shake
> off Texas so soon as it is ripe enough to fall. All that is now
> wanting is a great immigration of good and efficient families
> this fall and winter. [Then] . . . the peach will be ripe.[68]

Ironically, statesmen in Mexico City who sought to limit Anglo-American immigration to Texas in the 1830s faced problems similar to those of United States officials of the 1970s and 80s who have sought to slow Mexican immigration. In each case, federal officials have been undermined by interest groups living near the border who have perceived a need for foreign labor. In each case, too, efforts to close the border by mechanical means have failed. Miguel Muldoon, the roguish, Mexican-Irish priest who knew the Texas situation firsthand, was correct when he argued in 1833 that American immigrants could not be stopped "even if our army formed a cordon from the Gulf of Mexico to the beaches of the Pacific."[69] Even with today's sophisticated technology, the United States government has failed to stop Mexicans from illegally crossing the nearly 2,000-mile line from Brownsville on the Gulf to San Diego on the Pacific. Mexico's problems in the 1830s, however, went beyond a lack of military strength to patrol the border against illegal American aliens. Successive governments in Mexico City lacked sufficient stability, funds, and national population to carry out a sustained, coherent counter-colonization program or to weave Texas into the Mexican economy and Texans into the national fabric.

If "to govern is to populate," it also seems true in the case of Texas that "to populate is to govern." The overwhelming majority of immigrants to Texas came from the United States in the 1820s and 1830s, and it was to the United States that those immigrants looked to govern Texas following its successful revolt from Mexico in 1836. With the annexation of Texas by the United States in 1845, the process was complete. Meanwhile, the Mexican governments looked with alarm toward other parts of the frontier as a new wave of American immigrants rolled beyond Texas toward New Mexico and California, where Americans talked of replaying "the Texas game."

10

The "Texas Game" Again?
Peopling California and New Mexico

The principal wealth of a country consists of its population.—
Manuel Castañares, *California, 1845*

The march of emigration is to the West, and naught will
arrest its advance but the mighty ocean.—Alfred Robinson,
California, 1845

While Anglo-Americans poured into Texas in the 1820s and 1830s, New
Mexico and California attracted modest but significant numbers of foreign settlers. The number of American colonists in New Mexico remained
relatively small throughout the Mexican era, but in the early 1840s norteamericanos began to settle in California, at a rate that alarmed Mexican officials. To many observers, both Mexican and American, this new
wave of immigration seemed a repeat of events in Texas—a prelude to
Mexico's loss of California. A newspaper in New York City in 1845 could
not have put the matter more plainly: "Let the tide of emigration flow
toward California and the American population will soon be sufficiently
numerous to play the Texas game."[1] That American settlers did not flow
into California and New Mexico and repeat the "Texas game" prior to
the 1840s, owed more to happenstance than it did to a concerted Mexican effort to keep American colonists out.

With the opening of the Santa Fe trade in 1821, Americans visited
New Mexico in large numbers. Hundreds of traders and trappers arrived in some years, but few remained. No exact count of foreigners
who settled in New Mexico exists. A census of 1839 revealed only thirty-
four *extranjeros* living in the province, and another count, taken about

1840 at Taos, the center of the province's foreign-born population, showed twenty-three Americans, seven of whom had become Mexican citizens.[2] These statistics certainly err on the low side, but even so, the number of foreign residents in New Mexico could not have amounted to more than a few hundred.

California attracted more foreign settlers than did New Mexico in the 1820s and 1830s, but there, too, only a small percentage of foreign traders or trappers remained to make California their home. In 1830 some 120 foreigners lived in California, and that number doubled to 240 by 1835 and reached about 380 in 1840. As in New Mexico, these figures are approximations and may be low. California officials acknowledged that they had no accurate count of the number of foreigners scattered throughout the province.[3]

Compared to Texas, few foreigners settled in California or New Mexico, but their commercial connections and, in many cases, their education or training, made them highly influential. Moreover, most were adult males, making them more important numerically than might seem to be the case in an era when men dominated decision making in the political and economic arenas. In California, at least two-thirds of the 3,200 gente de razón in 1821 were women and children, so even several hundred adult male immigrants would count heavily.[4]

That few North Americans settled permanently in New Mexico or California during the 1820s and 1830s is easily understood. First, westering Anglo-Americans needed to go no farther into northern Mexico than Texas to find cheap land. Second, Anglo-Americans who moved beyond Texas, west of the 100th meridian and the timber line, often found the land uninviting. The treeless plains country was then depicted on maps as "The Great American Desert," and conventional wisdom held that farms only prospered where trees grew.[5] Then, too, ignorance of geography and the formidable barriers presented by Comanches, Apaches, and other tribes kept settlers from venturing too far west.

The few foreigners who did make their way into New Mexico and California found they could not obtain land as easily as in Texas. The Colonization Law of 1824, which permitted individual states to draw up regulations for colonization, provided that procedures for territories, such as California and New Mexico, would come from Congress. Lacking pressure from would-be landowners, Congress took no action until it approved the colonization regulations of November 21, 1828, which spelled out the method whereby territorial governors, with approval of the diputaciones, could grant land to Mexicans and foreigners. Those procedures continued to be used erratically in California and New Mexico until the end of the Mexican era, with only slight modifications.

Wary, perhaps, of the carelessness of local officials after its experience with Coahuila, Congress required that empresario grants in the territories receive final approval in Mexico City; legislation passed earlier in 1828 required congressional approval for noncitizens to obtain land.[6]

The November 21, 1828 regulations opened New Mexico and California to colonization by foreigners, but a land rush did not follow. Foreigners found the most desirable lands already occupied. In New Mexico, gente de razón and Pueblo Indians ranched and farmed the best-watered, most centrally located, and most secure lands. Moreover, steady growth of population brought New Mexicans into keen competition with one another for choice farmland and pasturage, leaving little room for foreigners.[7]

In California, missions occupied the choice coastal lands until secularization in the mid-1830s, and mission lands were inviolable under the 1828 colonization regulations. Sandwiched in between the mission properties were perhaps thirty private rancho grants that had been made under Spain. Until the mid-1830s, Mexican officials issued only a few grants, none of which apparently went to foreigners. The real land boom in California, then, awaited the secularization of the missions.[8]

Not only was desirable land scarcer in California and New Mexico than it was in Texas, but federal officials discouraged foreigners from colonizing in the territories in the late 1820s and 1830s. Federal officials had no desire to repeat the Texas experience and open other parts of northern Mexico to what the secretary of foreign relations termed in 1829 "a disguised invasion."[9] To officials such as Tadeo Ortiz, the threat to security of California and New Mexico was "identical" to that of Texas, and one state legislature, alarmed at the Haden Edwards revolt in Texas, went so far as to urge the government to "set aside a band fifty leagues wide from Texas to Alta California" to populate as a barrier against the North Americans.[10] Not surprisingly, then, when Col. John Davis Bradburn of Virginia, a naturalized Mexican who would later win infamy among his former countrymen as a revenue officer in Texas, petitioned Congress in 1829 for an empresario grant in New Mexico, a congressional committee noted the deteriorating situation in Texas and recommended against his request, arguing that "it would not be wise to expose New Mexico to a like fate."[11] The following year, Mexico's minister in Washington published notices in American newspapers warning would-be emigrants that the Law of April 6, 1830 applied to New Mexico as well as Texas.

On the local level, too, officials expressed reluctance to welcome American settlers. New Mexicans were pleased to receive merchandise from the United States, but showed less enthusiasm for the North Americans themselves. Santiago Abreú of Santa Fe, a delegate to Congress and future territorial governor, noted in 1826 that Americans had a propensity "to settle, buy land, and even marry" in New Mexico, and could be of great benefit to the province, but New Mexicans had to "avoid abuse to our generous character."[12] Only those foreigners who were honorable and who had a useful trade, he argued, should be permitted to stay.

In California, too, officials at all levels discouraged Anglo-Americans from settling. As Carlos Carrillo of Santa Barbara put it, it was widely known that United States policy was "to recognize no other right to lands than that of occupation."[13] Indeed, prior to the passage of the 1828 colonization regulations, local officials had explicit orders not to grant lands to foreigners, and on at least two subsequent occasions, in 1830 and 1832, Secretary of State Lucas Alamán ordered the governor of California to take care that American and Russian families remained a minority. Alamán did not intend to stop Anglo-Americans from colonizing in California entirely, as he tried to do in Texas with the controversial April 6, 1830 law, for California needed more people. Alamán expressed special interest in creating communities north of San Francisco Bay as a bulwark against the Russians at Fort Ross, and criticized California officials for making it too difficult for foreigners to acquire land. He instructed Governor Figueroa in 1832 to implement the colonization laws of 1824 and 1828.[14]

In the 1820s and early 1830s, while Texas was being subdivided by foreign empresarios, no colonization grants were given to foreigners in New Mexico or California. The man who came closest to receiving one was John G. Heath, a Missouri lawyer who had been among the first Americans to enter New Mexico after the opening of the Santa Fe trade in 1821. Heath received permission from the ayuntamiento of El Paso to colonize twenty-five square leagues on the Rio Grande in the Mesilla Valley in 1823. The New Mexico diputación revoked the grant, however, on the grounds that the overthrow of Iturbide had invalidated the Imperial Colonization Law under which the grant was made. The same law that worked for Stephen Austin in Texas failed to serve John Heath in New Mexico. The decision ruined Heath financially, for he did not learn of the cancellation of his grant until he returned to El Paso in 1824 with 150 colonists from Missouri. Denied permission to settle, most of the colonists returned to the United States to the apparent regret of the citizens of El Paso.[15]

Although empresario grants were not made in New Mexico and California prior to the late 1830s, foreigners managed to purchase house lots or small farms directly from Mexicans. Others squatted on unoccupied land and tried to keep out of sight. In contrast to Americans in Texas, most of the foreign-born residents of New Mexico and California in the 1820s and 1830s assimilated into the majority culture, at least in external matters, and did not form separate enclaves. As a young American noted in California in 1841, the foreigners "are scattered throughout the whole Spanish population, and most of them have Spanish wives . . . they live in every respect like the Spaniards."[16]

Thus, a small number of foreigners began to make their homes in New Mexico and California in the 1820s and 1830s, but none settled in the vast *despoblado* that today comprises the states of Nevada, Utah, western Colorado, and Arizona. All this immense area was vaguely considered part of New Mexico or California, except for Arizona below the Gila, which fell under the jurisdiction of Sonora. Americans explored, trapped, and established occasional trading posts in this region, but made no permanent settlements.

Most of the region between the Rio Grande settlements of New Mexico and the California coast was too remote and too firmly under Indian control to recommend it to immigrants. Nonetheless, a variety of ideas for colonizing the region were discussed, including a plan by California's future governor and would-be empresario, José Figueroa, to build a chain of settlements along the Colorado River to the Great Salt Lake.[17] Nothing came of these ideas, however, and the Mexican frontier failed to push into this region except for a brief period of expansion in Arizona.

Southern Arizona saw a surge of mining activity, ranching, and population growth in the 1820s, before the Apache offensive resumed full force. At Tucson, then the largest center of Mexican population in what is today Arizona, the number of settlers living near the presidio had declined in the late colonial period, but between 1819 and 1831 their number trebled from 62 to 193. These settlers, together with soldiers and their families, brought Tucson's total population to 465 in 1831, counting men, women, and children. Tubac, the second largest settlement in the area, had 303 inhabitants that same year and still more pobladores were scattered on ranches and mining camps that had begun to proliferate during the Apache peace.[18]

As Arizona's population grew, so too did the number of private rancho grants. Nearly all of the so-called Spanish land grants in Arizona date from 1820 to 1833, the early Mexican era, and nearly all were located south of the Gila. Many, of course, were in the Santa Cruz Valley, near the urban centers of Tucson and Tubac, but others were in the San Pedro Valley to the east, where settlers had spilled over in search of new lands.[19] The *tucsonenses*, for example, soon found that the limited irrigable lands near the presidio, three-fourths of which belonged to Indians from the mission of San Xavier, would not support the growing population. They began to ranch and farm at Tres Alamos on the San Pedro River, over thirty miles east of Tucson. Working the land in this area meant constant vigilance over livestock and, as one contemporary put it, working with "the plowhandle in one hand and the musket or lance in the other."[20]

Occasional victories notwithstanding, the ill-equipped and outnumbered Mexican settlers could not block the tide of nomadic Apaches who threatened to overrun their fields and pastures. Beginning in the 1830s the Mexican frontier retreated in Arizona. Only one land grant was made in the area after 1833. By the mid-1840s Apaches had driven Mexican settlers out of the San Pedro Valley and had forced them off isolated ranches and out of small communities in the more populous Santa Cruz Valley. Hamlets such as Sopori and Canoa, and even Calabazas with its rich mines, had been abandoned. Thus, although the non-Indian population of Sonora apparently grew by some 25 percent between 1822 and 1845, the northern edge of the state that is in today's Arizona lost population. Mexicans remained only at Tucson and Tubac in 1848, and late that year Apaches forced the complete abandonment of Tubac.[21] Unlike Texas, New Mexico, or California, the number of gente de razón in Arizona fell rather than rose in the Mexican era.

During the first two decades of Mexican independence, then, Anglo-American immigrants posed no challenge to Indian or Mexican hegemony in the frontier areas west of Texas. Due to a combination of geographical accident and Mexican policy, relatively few foreigners settled in New Mexico or California. Keeping Anglo-Americans in small, manageable numbers, however, did not solve the perennial problem of how to bolster the population of the beleaguered frontier provinces. The paucity of pobladores seemed especially acute in vulnerable Alta California where, as Governor Juan Bautista Alvarado noted in 1840, "due to insufficient population there is a great dearth of defenders and laborers."[22] The need for more workers had become even more intense after the secularization of the missions spurred the growth of private ranches.

From San Francisco north to Oregon no Mexican settlements existed. Russians, however, had planted Fort Ross on Bodega Bay and refused to move, making it clear that they wanted to acquire San Francisco Bay and much of northern California. The Russian presence in California had troubled Mexican officials from the first months of independence, just as it had vexed Spanish policy makers. Much ink flowed as officials penned warnings about the need to settle Mexicans in the region to check Russian expansion. Not until 1833, however, did serious plans take shape.

Those plans led to the government's most serious effort to colonize any portion of the far northern frontier with Mexicans.

In 1833 the liberal Gómez Farías administration appointed José María Híjar of Guadalajara as director of colonization for California. This appointment, which occurred simultaneously with the sending of Tadeo Ortiz to Texas as director of colonization, was part of a concerted effort to bolster the frontier's exposed eastern and western flanks.

Híjar started for California with considerable political power. In addition to overseeing colonization he was to replace the ailing José Figueroa as governor. Moreover, Híjar's sub-director of colonization, José María Padrés, was to become commanding general of California should General Figueroa wish to be relieved of military as well as civil command. Híjar and Padrés had money as well as titles to support the project because the government dipped into the Pious Fund, a special trust for the California missions that had no counterpart in Texas. Although the program was never fully budgeted, Híjar and Padrés had authorization to pay for transportation, food, lodging, supplies, and one year's maintenance of a group of colonists who would build a settlement in northern California.

In April 1834 a group of pioneers, recruited mainly from the Mexico City area, set out from the nation's capital. Canvas-covered wagons carried women, children, and supplies, while the men rode alongside on horseback. The expedition journeyed by way of Querétaro and Guadalajara to the port of San Blas, from which they set sail in early August for the month-long voyage to Alta California.

Two hundred and thirty-nine colonists left from San Blas and a few more would eventually join them in California. Like American pioneers, they were a youthful group with an average age of twenty. Among them were fifty-five women and seventy-nine children age fourteen and under. Many of the colonists had a profession or trade, such as teacher, lawyer, doctor, carpenter, distiller, tailor, and shoemaker; perhaps 20 percent of the group consisted of farmers. The professionals and tradesmen would be especially useful in California where foreigners were beginning to fill those functions.[23]

Although the enterprise seems to have been well-planned and the colonists well-chosen, plans went awry upon arrival in California. First, Híjar learned that Santa Anna had overthrown Gómez Farías and had sent orders to Figueroa not to permit him to assume the governorship. At the same time, Figueroa declined to turn the military command of California over to Padrés. Although their political base had crumbled, Híjar and Padrés went ahead with the task of establishing their colony. Soon, however, they found themselves locked into a complex dispute with Governor Figueroa and the *californios*, which doomed the establishment of the colony.[24]

Híjar and Padrés failed in California in large part because their program seemed to threaten the economic interests of the *californios*. Among Híjar's responsibilities as director of colonization was the distribution of the mission lands, an exceedingly sensitive issue as we have seen. Imbued with the classical liberalism of the day, Híjar promised land to mission Indians, along with freedom to live where they chose, and payment for all the work that they did. Híjar even attempted to convey his egalitarian views to the so-called pagan Indians. Híjar's message threatened the social order in California where Indians constituted a cheap labor force and upset Figueroa who privately expressed concern that "legal equality would unhinge society," and that Indians might revolt.[25] Figueroa also assumed, incorrectly, that Híjar intended to distribute mission lands to Indians and to outsiders from Mexico, blocking opportunity for the *californios* to acquire that desirable property. Finally, the *californios* suspected that Híjar and Padrés were linked to a private stock company that had obtained monopoly privileges over California's export and import trade—a further threat to California's small but growing oligarchy.

Their self-interest apparently in jeopardy and their fears fed by a skillful propaganda effort by Governor Figueroa, the usually factious *californios* united to oppose Híjar and Padrés. An impasse was reached when Figueroa and the California diputación refused to turn mission lands over to Híjar and when the governor professed inability to lend material support to the colonists. Finally, Figueroa came to fear that Híjar and Padrés might overthrow him with the aid of the disgruntled and unpaid military, and he seems to have seized upon a pretext to get rid of his supposed rivals. When a minor *pronunciamiento* against his government occurred in Los Angeles in 1835, Figueroa linked it to Híjar and Padrés and had them arrested at Sonoma, 600 miles from the scene of the crime. Without filing formal charges against them, he shipped Híjar, Padrés, and some other leaders of the colony back to San Blas. Somewhere he found 4,000 pesos to cover this emergency.

So ended Mexico's one effort to plant a subsidized colony on the northern frontier. Most of the colonists who came with Híjar and Padrés stayed in California. Although relatively few in number, they settled throughout the territory and used their special skills to gain prominence in provincial life. The teachers among them seem to have been especially influential.

With the failure of the Híjar-Padrés colony, the great void of Mexican settlement to the north of San Francisco Bay remained. Governor Figueroa, who had come to California with orders from Lucas Alamán to populate this region as a check on Russian expansion, tried to fill the gap. In 1835, after the departure of Híjar and Padrés, he ordered a settlement founded at Sonoma and placed Mariano Vallejo in charge, naming him "Military Commander and Director of Colonization on the Northern Frontier."[26] Ironically, Figueroa could not find sufficient colonists for the town and it grew slowly, leaving the area open to a stream of Anglo-Americans who began to flow into the Sacramento Valley in the 1840s. Indeed, it was under Figueroa that the Americans first attained land and influence in this area. Perhaps the most far-reaching effect of the collapse of the Híjar-Padrés project, then, was that it left northern California open to the norteamericanos.[27] Meanwhile, the Russian threat vanished. The Russian traders and their families, plagued with internal problems, abandoned their handsome log homes and chapel at Fort Ross of their own accord in 1841.

Although they had opposed the Híjar-Padrés colony, prominent California officials continued to express the hope that Mexican colonists would be brought to California at government expense to offset the American and Russian influences and to make the area prosper.[28] No significant numbers of colonists arrived, however. Nor did meaningful numbers of colonists from central Mexico settle elsewhere on the far northern frontier.

Many officials saw the need for countercolonization of the frontier by Mexicans, but few could explain satisfactorily why it failed to occur. It was commonplace to assume that "the Mexican character is not suited for colonization," as one Mexican intellectual put it in 1845.[29] Such an assumption seems to have been behind an editorial published in Mexico City which praised the Híjar-Padrés colonists because they had "overcome the disinclination of their upbringing and the laziness left us by the Spaniards, and had decided to leave behind the comforts of the capital."[30]

Rather than look to Mexican character to explain the failure to settle the far northern frontier before 1846, however, it seems more fruitful to ask what might have prompted Mexicans to migrate. Opportunities on the remote frontier were limited and constant warfare between Indians and Mexicans did nothing to enhance the region's reputation. Moreover, as contemporaries recognized, there was no need to incur the heavy expense or hardships of travel to settle on distant frontiers when vacant land existed closer to the Mexican heartland. As we have seen, the population of Mexico was neither dense, nor growing rapidly. Demographic pressures simply did not exist. Finally, if what historians have learned from the American frontier experience applies to Mexico, prosperity stimulated migration, depression retarded it, and "the costs of migrating kept the very poor at home."[31]

On occasions when opportunity presented itself, Mexicans did move. *Sonorenses* and *nuevomexicanos* were drawn to California's temperate climate to ranch and farm (internal migration accounted for nearly one sixth of the population of Los Angeles in 1844); Mexicans moved into southern Arizona during the mining boom of the 1820s; others went to California after the gold discovery of 1848. Those were exceptional cases, however, for the far northern frontier was generally not an easily accessible land of opportunity for Mexicans in these years. When demographic pressures did increase in the early twentieth century, and when technological changes made the border region a land of opportunity, Mexican *campesinos* proved themselves as adept at migration and colonization as any other people.[32]

Mexican thinkers such as Tadeo Ortiz and Miguel Ramos Arizpe argued that if substantial countercolonization of the Far North by Mexicans or by Europeans were to take place, the government would have to sponsor it. Mexico seemed to be in an impossible position. While the expanding United States population moved west into northern Mexico without government support, Mexico's more static population would have to be induced onto the same frontier through the use of scarce national resources, or European immigration would have to be subsidized. Mexico could neither afford, nor properly carry out such programs so long as the nation remained in political turmoil, as one prestigious Mexico City newspaper editorialized in 1842.[33] Hence, the Híjar-Padrés experiment stands as a singular episode, rather than as part of a sustained program.

Mexico's failure to lure colonists onto the frontier led to continuation of the Spanish policy of sending convicts north as settlers. This practice was more extensive in California than in Texas, and caused dismay among some *californios* who charged the government with attempting to make the area a "penal colony."[34]

The use of convicts as colonists on the frontier enjoyed broad support among high government officials in Mexico City. The policy seemed wise, practical, and humane. The frontier would benefit by having its manpower shortage alleviated while convicts who were languishing in prisons at Vera Cruz and other unhealthy places could become rehabilitated and, as Gen. Manuel Mier y Terán put it, "become of real value to that society which now casts them out."[35]

Under independent Mexico, the first convicts sent to the frontier seem to have arrived in California in 1825. Not until 1829, however, was a systematic program launched. Then the secretary of justice notified courts and governors throughout the republic that convicted criminals and their families should be sent to California instead of Vera Cruz. The arrival of perhaps 150 convicts in California in 1829 and 1830 brought such a storm of indignation and protest that in 1831 the secretary of justice ordered the flow directed toward Texas. This order was in keeping with the law of April 6, 1830, which had not only closed Texas to further Anglo-American immigration, but had also authorized the government to settle convicts and their families there. Although convicts were to be given transportation, land, tools, and supplies for a year, the number who went to Texas was inconsequential, as we have seen.[36] After Texas became the nation's official penal colony even those from California could be sent there. One man convicted of hanging his wife, for example, was sent to Texas in 1835 after serving three years in jail in California.[37]

No significant number of convicts arrived in California again until 1842 when the government authorized sending 300 "criminals" who possessed some trade or skill. In exchange for good conduct and "services," they were to be given land and tools.[38] Recruited from jails in Mexico City, 150 convicts and their women reached California in August 1842, all apparently forming part of the military force that accompanied the new governor, Gen. Manuel Micheltorena. Dressed in tattered uniforms, unsalaried, and poorly supplied, the hapless "soldiers" raided gardens, orchards, and chicken coops in order to survive. Many *californios* viewed these *cholos*—a term they applied to lower class mestizos from Mexico—as ne'er-do-wells and contemptible, incurable thieves who lived on the public payroll. Micheltorena's failure to discipline them apparently contributed to the *californios'* revolt against him in 1845, and it is often suggested that the behavior of the convicts in California caused the *californios'* growing alienation from the rest of Mexico. Clearly alienation intensified during these years, to the point that some *californios* favored separation from Mexico, as we shall see. It seems doubtful, however, that the conduct of the convicts alone provoked this reaction.[38]

Some of the convicts behaved badly in California, but most seem to have become useful citizens as the government hoped. About fifty convicts who arrived in 1830, for example, were distributed among families in San Diego and Los Angeles where, according to Heinrich Virmond, a German merchant who knew California well, "they planted more in one day than had ever been done before." The families for whom the prisoners worked gave them food, shelter, and six pesos a month: "Both parties were content with this," Virmond noted, "and the public treasury is not burdened. . . . if there had been 100 more they all would have been provided employment in the town of Los Angeles."[39] The exaggerated charges that some *californios* made against the prisoners were probably more a result of wounded dignity—that Mexico would use California as a kind of Siberia or a penal colony—than a reaction to overt acts that the "cholos" committed.[40] It may be, too, that growing alienation from Mexico was a cause as much as a result of the antipathy toward the newcomers from Mexico.

Plans to colonize California with Europeans—which included schemes to ease the Mexican debt by turning over vacant lands all across the Far North to British bondholders, and selling California to a Prussian empresario—also came to nothing.[41] Meanwhile, the central government seems to have made no serious effort to colonize either Arizona or New Mexico with Europeans or Mexicans, for those areas seemed less threatened by American expansion than either California or Texas. Thus, counter colonization of the Far North, from San Antonio west to the Pacific, failed as it had in Texas and left the way open for immigration from the United States.

In the early 1840s, governors of both New Mexico and California began to open unprecedented amounts of public land to private development. In part, they hoped to attract colonists in order to promote development and bolster the defense of their respective regions. Then, too, they used land grants to award political supporters and to repay loans or gifts, which kept their sinking departmental treasuries afloat. Land was one of the few commodities with which the last governors of New Mexico and California could bargain. At the same time, land in the 1840s looked increasingly alluring to some foreign and Mexican entrepreneurs because of the prospect that the United States might acquire California and New Mexico and cause property values to rise.[42]

By placing vast tracts of public land in private hands, the last Mexican governors of New Mexico and California shaped settlement patterns and economic structures in their regions for decades to come. In California, about a third of the land that was given away went to Anglo-Americans in what seemed to be a replay of the "Texas game." In New Mexico, officials adopted a more cautious policy toward foreign-born residents.

Manuel Armijo, as governor of New Mexico during most of the period from 1837 to 1846, approved an extraordinary number of land grants, including nearly all of the so-called Spanish land grants in what would become the state of Colorado. One historian has calculated that between 1837 and 1846 Armijo gave away over half of the 31,000,000 acres of lands granted by all New Mexico officials under Spain and Mexico. Armijo was not as profligate, however, as this figure suggests. As a result of litigation following the United States conquest of New Mexico, many of Armijo's land concessions stretched to dimensions far larger than he had intended, or than Mexican law and custom permitted. Moreover, many of these grants required that the recipient fulfill certain conditions, such as actual occupancy of the land, settling a certain number of families, and cultivation of the soil, before final title could be issued. Some of these lands were also designated for community use and not intended to fall into private hands.[43]

Not nearly as reckless as some critics have suggested, Armijo appears to have granted lands to encourage private enterprise to create a barrier against Indians, Texans, and norteamericanos. To accomplish this, he judiciously permitted a few naturalized Mexicans, as well as *nuevomexicanos,* to develop lands in river valleys on the northern and eastern peripheries of the department, extending northward to the Mexican-United States boundary on the Arkansas River, and eastward toward the newly independent Republic of Texas.[44]

One of the first of Armijo's large grants went to his secretary, Guadalupe Miranda, and to Canadian-born Charles Beaubien. Partners, Miranda and Beaubien requested lands in 1841 on the plains east of the Sangre de Cristos along the Cimarron and Canadian rivers. They said they planned to ranch, grow sugar beets and cotton, and exploit timber and minerals. Their grant later became part of the celebrated and much enlarged claim of Beaubien's son-in-law, Lucien Maxwell, to some two million acres (2,680 square miles) of what is today northeastern New Mexico and southeastern Colorado.[45]

In 1843 Armijo gave out at least four more sizeable grants to foreign-born residents of New Mexico. First, Charles Beaubien's thirteen-year-old son, Narciso, together with Stephen Louis Lee, a former trapper from St. Louis, received the Sangre de Cristo grant in the San Luis Valley straddling the present New Mexico-Colorado border.[46] Second, a tract along the San Carlos River in today's southern Colorado went to Gervasio Nolán, an illiterate French Canadian. In partnership with two New Mexicans, Nolán also received a grant on the Canadian River to the south of the Beaubien-Miranda grant in 1845.[47] Third, land along the Cucharas, Huerfano, and Apishapa rivers in eastern Colorado south of the Arkansas, known as the Las Animas Grant, went to a former fur trader, Cerán St. Vrain, and his partner, Cornelio Vigil, alcalde of Taos. Fourth, Armijo granted ten leagues of land on the eastern plains to the northwest of Las Vegas to a Santa Fe merchant, John Scolly, and a group of American and Mexican partners.[48]

Although a considerable amount of the land that Armijo granted went to foreign-born residents, he was careful not to repeat the mistakes

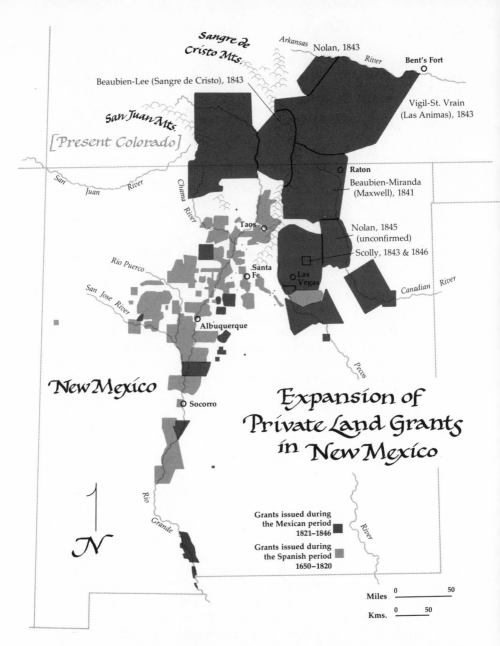

Expansion of Private Land Grants in New Mexico

Sangre de Cristo Mts.

San Juan Mts.

[Present Colorado]

New Mexico

Arkansas River

Nolan, 1843

Bent's Fort

Beaubien-Lee (Sangre de Cristo), 1843

Vigil-St. Vrain (Las Animas), 1843

San Juan River

Chama River

Rio Puerco

San Jose River

Taos

Raton

Beaubien-Miranda (Maxwell), 1841

Nolan, 1845 (unconfirmed)

Scolly, 1843 & 1846

Santa Fe

Las Vegas

Canadian River

Albuquerque

Pecos

Socorro

Rio Grande

River

Grants issued during the Mexican period 1821–1846

Grants issued during the Spanish period 1650–1820

| Miles | 0 ———— 50 |
| Kms. | 0 ———— 50 |

N

Nearly 150 Spanish and Mexican land grants, as confirmed by the United States government, are represented on this map. Among the largest were those granted late in the Mexican era, especially to foreign-born residents. During litigation in American courts, grants such as the Maxwell grew; the Scolly grant shrank; and Nolan's grant on the Canadian disappeared.

made in Texas. He seems to have selected foreigners cautiously, generally choosing men who had lived in the department since the 1820s, had married Mexican women, and had been Mexican citizens for at least a decade. Only John Scolly, an Irishman, was not a naturalized citizen, but Scolly had a Mexican wife and had applied for citizenship in 1843.[49] Perhaps it was no coincidence that Armijo's grants went to an Irishman, two Canadians (Nolán and Beaubien), and to an American of French ancestry (St. Vrain), rather than to Anglo-Americans alone. Finally, Armijo took the precaution of including Mexican partners in most of these grants.

Armijo might have chosen foreign-born recipients of land carefully, but he could not exercise control over subsequent sale of interest in that land. For example, although he was not a citizen, Charles Bent, co-owner with Cerán St. Vrain of Bent's Fort on the Arkansas, acquired a fourth interest in the Beaubien-Miranda grant, along with interest in two other grants.[50]

Opposition to Armijo's land policy, and to the Beaubien-Miranda grant in particular, soon surfaced. Led by Cura Antonio José Martínez of Taos and leaders of Taos Pueblo, critics argued that the Beaubien-Miranda was too large, impinged upon the communal lands of Taos Pueblo, and included Charles Bent as an illegal partner. Some writers have suggested that Martínez's objections to the grant amounted to little more than a personal vendetta against Bent, but the priest seems to have been genuinely alarmed at the implications of growing American influence in the department.[51]

Apparently in response to Martínez's complaint, interim governor Mariano Chávez, who briefly replaced the ailing Armijo, annulled the Beaubien-Miranda grant in February 1844. Beaubien then lied to protect his interests, saying that Bent was not one of his partners, and succeeded in persuading the departmental assembly to restore the grant. Victory was brief. Gen. Mariano Martínez, who assumed the governorship in May 1844, ordered Beaubien to abandon the grant. Martínez defended his action by citing a law of March 11, 1842, which permitted foreigners to acquire property anywhere in Mexico except in departments contiguous to foreign nations where specific permission of the central government was required. This law did not apply to naturalized citizens such as Beaubien, but it did apply to foreigners such as Charles Bent, who, Governor Martínez must have believed, still owned a share of the grant. At the same time that he revoked the Beaubien-Miranda grant, Martínez abrogated John Scolly's grant, citing the same law. (Apparently Scolly's citizenship papers had not yet arrived, but his grant, diminshed in size, was reissued and confirmed by Armijo in March 1846.)[52]

Pleased with the turn of events, Padre Martínez praised the new governor whose intervention, he said, had prevented Armijo from carrying out his "mean and ambitious desire of delivering a portion of this Department into the hands of some foreigners."[53] By May 1845, however, Governor Martínez had left office and José Chávez took the governor's chair for a few months. Chávez, a native New Mexican, permitted Beaubien, Bent, and St. Vrain to settle foreigners on the Beaubien-Miranda grant. In allowing foreign colonization, local officials came into conflict again with an official representing the central government. In autumn 1845, Gen. Francisco García Conde inspected New Mexico and ordered foreign settlers in the Cimarron area to leave their farms. The colonists and Manuel Armijo, who had assumed the governorship again on November 16, ignored this order. Armijo's leniency toward Charles Bent and the foreign settlers on the Beaubien-Miranda grant may have been influenced by the fact that he, too, owned a one-fourth interest in that grant.[54]

Governor Armijo's land grant policy did not win complete approval of officials representing the central government, nor did it please nationalistic New Mexicans such as Padre Martínez, but the governor appears to have acted prudently. Certainly, foreigners tried to take advantage of him by obtaining vast tracts of potentially valuable land, much of it intersected by the major trails that connected the United States with Taos and Santa Fe. At the same time, however, Armijo sought to utilize the foreign-born entrepreneurs to settle and hold an area that his own military could not control and his own countrymen could not colonize. If he saw personal profit in these arrangements, or if they resulted in loans to the government, so much the better.[55] National interest and self-interest seemed to coincide; there is no reason to suppose that he acted solely out of self-interest as has been suggested.

Armijo seems to have understood the risks inherent in granting too much land to foreigners. As early as 1827 he had lamented that "every day the foreigners are becoming more influential," and his desire to limit foreign influence remained alive until the 1840s.[56] By the 1840s, however, the governor had nowhere else to turn except to the foreign-born. The military and economic situation in New Mexico had become chaotic; nomadic Indians assaulted the province more boldly than ever before, and Anglo-Americans and Texans threatened attack. Caught in this desperate situation, with little more than the promise of aid from the federal government, Armijo enlisted the help of a select group of outsiders such as Beaubien, Lee, and Nolán, to whom he granted lands and whose loyalty he presumably felt he could trust.[57]

In the early 1840s, then, a few foreigners took possession of choice pieces of public land on the northern and eastern flanks of New Mexico, but prior to 1846 efforts to settle those remote grants met staunch resistance from Indians, who refused to acknowledge that a stroke of the pen gave outsiders the right to intrude upon them. Indian resistance succeeded partly because demographic pressure from New Mexico never became so intense that large numbers of people spilled over onto Indian lands. Despite Armijo's liberal land policy, New Mexico did not become a magnet for large numbers of immigrants, either foreign-born or Mexican, prior to 1846.

Nonetheless, a trickle of immigrants and natural increase pushed New Mexico's population upward, from 42,000 in 1821 to some 65,000 in 1846, counting foreigners and Pueblo Indians as well as gente de razón. The average annual rate of population growth in New Mexico in these years was 2.1 percent, or double the rate of growth for Mexico as a whole, and it nudged the edges of settlement farther from the narrow band along the Rio Grande and prompted the creation of new communities. Compared to the soaring rates of growth in Texas or along the American frontier, however, New Mexico's demographic expansion was modest. Even the isolated Department of California grew at a faster rate and drew people away from New Mexico in the 1840s.[58]

Trappers and traders from New Mexico, foreigners and *nuevomexicanos* alike, had visited California regularly throughout the 1830s. A few, such as Julian Chávez, Jonathan Warner, and George Yount, had settled permanently on the coast, where the communities of Chávez Ravine (today the home of the Los Angeles Dodgers), Warner Springs, and Yountsville still bear their names. In the 1840s, California's reputation began to attract groups rather than individual settlers from New Mexico. In 1841, for example, two old-time residents of New Mexico, John Rowland and William Workman, led a party of twenty-five men, some with families, from Santa Fe to Los Angeles. Included in the group were some *nuevomexicanos*.

By 1845 at least thirty families of *nuevomexicanos* had migrated to the Los Angeles area alone, and many settled near San Bernardino under the leadership of the respected Lorenzo Trujillo. One reason for the New Mexicans' departure for California was to escape the ravages of Indian attack. Ironically, their reputations as Indian-fighters made them welcome in the San Bernardino area where rancheros hoped that a colony of hardy New Mexicans would be able to protect local livestock from Indians. Most *nuevomexicanos* seem to have settled in Southern California, but others, such as Manuel Vaca, for whom today's Vacaville in the

Sacramento Valley is named, must have been scattered throughout the department by 1846.[59]

People left New Mexico for California in the early 1840s for a variety of reasons, including a growing anti-American sentiment, but California's climate was also a major attraction. Louis Robidoux, for example, who had lived in New Mexico for twenty years, in 1844 settled permanently in Southern California near Riverside where he found the fertile land was "not ungrateful like the land of New Mexico." He wrote to a friend who had stayed behind at Santa Fe: "I compare the people of New Mexico to the ants, who shut themselves in during the winter to eat what they have worked so hard for all summer." Robidoux went on to say that he did not live in California's most desirable area. Northern California, he said, "is the promised land where the arroyos run with virgin honey and milk. Another Texas."[60]

By the 1840s the lure of California reached well beyond New Mexico to the Mississippi Valley, where it held immense appeal to an expanding population of land-hungry Americans, many of whom sought an escape from debt and depression that still lingered along the American frontier after the Panic in 1837. It is impossible, of course, to generalize with confidence about the motives of a variety of individuals, but it seems reasonable, as one historian has suggested, that "pull factors" assume greater importance than "push factors" in prompting migrations over great distances.[61] For wanderers such as Nicholas Dawson, the "pull" might simply have been a desire "to see and to experience,"[62] but the chief cause of the "fever" that drew men and women to the Pacific Coast in the early 1840s was cheap land—the same attraction that Texas had held two decades before. Hardheaded reports of the privations and obstacles of a journey over plains, mountains, and deserts, were offset in the minds of true believers by glowing accounts stressing both the ease of the journey and the heroism and nobility of those who made it. Few seemed to notice the contradiction.[63]

California held special opportunities for American immigrants in the early 1840s. First, the recent secularization of the missions had set thousands of Indians adrift, creating a pool of cheap labor and freeing choice coastal lands for private development. Second, recently forged commercial connections with the outside world had created a market for the products of California ranches, especially hides and tallow. These events set off a land rush among *californios* and foreigners alike. Between 1834 and 1846 some 700 private rancho grants were made, representing over 90 percent of all ranches granted in California under both Spain and Mexico. Private ranchos soon covered the former mission lands along the coastal plain and some would-be rancheros, chiefly Americans, began

Expansion of Private Land Grants in Alta California

■ Spanish Land Grants in California, 1784–1821
▨ Mexican Land Grants in California, 1822—1846

Pacific

Coastal

Sierra

Sacramento River

American River

Nevada

River

Sonoma

San Francisco

San Joaquin River

Ranges

Monterey

Salinas River

Ocean

Santa Barbara

Los Angeles

San Diego

Miles 0 ———— 100

Km. 0 ———— 100

N

As is dramatically illustrated in this map, Spain placed little land in private hands in California; however, private grants expanded considerably in the Mexican era, especially after the secularization of the missions in the mid-1830s (See David Hornbeck, "Land Tenure and Rancho Expansion in Alta California, 1784–1846," *Journal of Historical Geography* 4 (1978), pp. 377, 387.)

to petition for property in the great Central Valley, to the east of the coastal range along the San Joaquin and Sacramento rivers. The Central Valley had been the exclusive domain of Indians and the few British and American trappers and horse thieves who ventured among them, but an especially virulent malaria epidemic swept through the Valley in 1833. It killed perhaps three-fourths of the native American population, and weakened the survivors' ability to withstand encroachment by outsiders.[64]

Anglo-American awareness of opportunities to acquire cheap land on the Pacific Coast was heightened by the publicity surrounding the diplomatic crisis between the United States and Britain over Oregon, the growing conflict with Mexico, and by "boosters" in Oregon and California who sang the praises of their areas. In the early 1840s the Oregon "boosters" seemed most successful and lured a disproportionate number of overland migrants to the Pacific Northwest, but California publicists, such as John Marsh and John Sutter, also succeeded in drawing a significant number of overlanders to California's Central Valley.[65]

The first successful rancher in the Central Valley, Massachusetts-born, Harvard-educated "Dr." John Marsh had come to California by way of Santa Fe in 1836, leaving an extraordinary series of misadventures in his wake, including a warrant for his arrest for running guns to the Sioux. In California, Marsh looked to his future by becoming a Catholic, a citizen, and posing as a medical doctor. For credentials he flashed his Harvard bachelor's diploma, written in Latin. Within a year he had acquired enough capital to purchase Rancho Los Meganos. Although it was isolated on the San Joaquin, some forty miles beyond San Jose, the ranch prospered as Marsh traveled about exchanging medical services for cattle.[66]

In 1839 Marsh gained a neighbor when John Sutter began building a settlement on the Sacramento River, at the site of the present state capital. A fugitive like Marsh, Sutter had abandoned an unhappy marriage, five children, and debtor's prison in his native Switzerland to flee to the United States. At Taos, New Mexico, French-Canadian trapper Charles Beaubien had told Sutter of California's "perpetual summer."[67] Reaching California in 1839 by a circuitous route, this perennial optimist and energetic confidence man immediately asked Governor Juan Bautista Alvarado for an empresario grant to settle Swiss families in California. Alvarado advised him to obtain a private rancho instead, and Sutter chose a superb site. His eleven league grant, formally approved in 1841 after he became a citizen, was watered by the Sacramento and Feather rivers, dominated all inland navigation through San Francisco Bay, and lay along the route to Oregon and the future immigrant trail over the Sierras. Alvarado apparently hoped that Sutter's settlement would help to block Anglo-American colonists, but officials such as Gen. Mariano Guadalupe Vallejo saw Sutter himself as a threat. As a British visitor in 1842 said of Sutter: "If he really has the talent and the courage to make the most of his position, he is not unlikely to render California a second Texas."[68]

Sutter, through his hospitality, and John Marsh, who wrote widely circulated letters praising California to Americans in the East, each played important roles in attracting Anglo-American immigrants to California. Marsh provided the immediate catalyst. John Bidwell, one of the leaders of the first immigrant group to set out for California from the United States, later recalled that he had been encouraged to emigrate by a letter "Dr." Marsh had written to a friend in Missouri describing California in glowing terms. Also tantalizing, Bidwell remembered, was a speech by Antoine Robidoux, a New Mexico-based trapper and trader, whose description of California "made it seem like a paradise." "He said that the Spanish authorities were most friendly and that the people were the most hospitable on the globe."[69]

Negative reports offset these glowing stories, however, and the so-called Bidwell-Bartelson party became the only immigrant group to make the journey overland to California in 1841. This small, inexperienced group was lucky to find its way west. As Bidwell later recalled, with no exaggeration: "Our ignorance of the route was complete . . . no one knew where to go, not even the captain."[70] They had the good fortune, however, to be in the path of a group of missionaries and trappers headed for Oregon, led by Father Pierre-Jean De Smet and the able mountain man, Thomas "Broken Hand" Fitzpatrick. Bidwell and his fellow immigrants tagged along. They followed the Platte River, crossed South Pass, and then on the Bear River the two groups separated. Half of Bidwell's companions prudently chose to go on to Oregon, leaving Bidwell and thirty-three others to find their way across northernmost Mexico to California alone.

Plodding westward beyond the Great Salt Lake, where they had to abandon their wagons in the soft sand, they followed the Humboldt to the Sierra Nevada, then stumbled across that formidable barrier lost and hungry much of the time, and fearful that winter snows would trap them. Finally they followed the Stanislaus River into the San Joaquin Valley and made their way to John Marsh's ranch. A woman, Nancy Kelsey, and her infant daughter, Ann, had made the extraordinary journey all the way. One of the men later recalled that on an especially treacherous path in the Sierras "I looked back and saw Mrs. Kelsey a little way behind me, with her child in her arms, barefooted, I think, and leading her horse—a sight I shall never forget."[71]

After the Bidwell party showed that it could be done, other Anglo-

Sutter's Fort. As seen in 1849, a decade after its establishment. Its thick walls enclosed Sutter's house, barracks, workshops, a mill, and other buildings. Watercolor by John Hovey, a miner (courtesy, The Huntington Library, San Marino, California).

American homeseekers made the arduous trek. As John Marsh argued: "A young woman with a child in her arms came in the company. . . . after this, the men ought to be ashamed to think of the difficulties."[72] No overland immigrants came in 1842, but more arrived in 1843 guided by Joseph Reddeford Walker through the pass in the Sierras that still bears his name. In 1844 Elisha Stevens captained the first group to make it through with wagons and the first to use what would become the main immigrant trail over Donner Pass. That pass would not receive its present name, however, until the winter of 1846–47 when a snowstorm sealed the pass to the Donner party and tragedy followed. Whereas only 50 overland immigrants arrived in California in 1844, 250 came in 1845 and over 500 reached California in 1846, many hoping that their nation's flag would follow them west.[73]

The push of American settlers overland to California alarmed officials and the press in Mexico City. The United States had made no secret of its interest in acquiring Alta California. President Andrew Jackson offered to buy San Francisco Bay from Mexico in 1835, and in 1842 Commodore Thomas Catesby Jones, commander of the United States fleet in the Pacific, demonstrated that the United States would take it by force if it could. Upon hearing rumors that the United States and Mexico had gone to war, Jones seized the port of Monterey, then shamefacedly gave it back again when he learned of his mistake. The episode outraged officials and the press in Mexico City, who surmised that Jones must have acted under orders, and apparently led to an 1843 decree authorizing the governors of Chihuahua, Sonora, Sinaloa, and California to expel all North Americans from their departments. In California, where indignation at Jones' blunder was not as intense as in Mexico City, local officials did not enforce that law.[74]

American settlement in California seemed especially alarming because the troubles in Texas had begun in a similar manner. That was recognized quite clearly by Mexico's minister in Washington, Juan N. Almonte, who had toured Texas and warned his government of dangers there in in 1834. In 1840, upon learning that a group of American colonists were planning to settle in California, Almonte reported to the minister of war that although their stated intentions were "peaceful and friendly, your excellency should remember that this is no different than language used by Austin's colony and other immigrants who occupied Texas."[75] The minister of war had received similar warnings against granting land to Americans from the comandante general in California, Mariano Vallejo.[76]

The idea that American immigration was a prelude to the United States takeover of California was not a product of Mexican paranoia or of Almonte's or Vallejo's imaginations. Informed observers from many nations recognized the demographic and political forces at work. As early as 1839, for example, one French visitor to California reported to his government that the

> restless population [of the United States] is moving across the continent to the shores of the Pacific Ocean; it will not be long before we shall see them marching with great strides toward the domination of these same shores where they seem so weak today.[76]

As in the case of Texas, American desire to acquire California by populating it with Americans was openly discussed by American politicians and journalists, and Almonte had only to read United States newspapers to learn of the danger. Indeed, residents of Mexico City could read the same articles in Spanish, for many soon appeared in translation, and the message was clear. "American immigration," one Mexico City paper warned, "will snatch all of our departments from us, one by one."[77]

The diagnosis was accurate, but the remedy remained elusive. Preoccupied with efforts to regain Texas in the 1840s, and bedeviled by frequent changes of government, policy makers in Mexico City could do little to stop the flow of illegal aliens from the United States. The government sent repeated instructions to officials in California to expel Americans who arrived without proper papers, and to prevent more from entering. Meanwhile, Mexican minister Almonte tried to dissuade Americans from going to California by publishing notices in the American press in 1841 and 1842 that said cheap land in California would not be forthcoming.[78]

In 1845, when it became evident that words would not stop the *norteamericanos*, the government entered into negotiations with a Jesuit, Eugene McNamara, to settle 10,000 Irishmen in California. At the same time, a large military force was ordered to the province, but lack of funds for transportation and pay delayed the expedition's departure interminably. "When will it cease to leave?" one Mexico City newspaper asked.[79] It never did.

Efforts by the central government to block the flow of immigrants into California were also undermined by officials there, just as had occurred earlier in Texas. Even as it became apparent that the United States and Mexico would go to war, *californios* continued to receive North Americans cordially and permitted them to settle despite orders from Mexico City. The contradiction between national policy and local practice did not go unnoticed by contemporaries. As Dr. Marsh wrote in early 1846:

> While Col. Almonte . . . in Washington, is publishing his proclamations in the newspapers of the United States forbid-

ding people to emigrate to California and telling them that no
lands will be given them; the actual Government here is doing
just the contrary.[80]

If the law were to be followed to the letter, California officials would
have to send newly arrived immigrants back over the Sierras to an
almost certain death. Officials such as Mariano Vallejo and José Castro
expressed reluctance to do that. Castro, then serving as military commander, alluded to the conflict between "duty" and "the sentiment of
hospitality which characterizes the Mexican people."[81] California officials granted passports that permitted foreigners to stay temporarily,
and in practice those temporary permits became permanent and Americans became citizens and obtained land. Reluctance to enforce the law
more vigorously in California might have had less to do with hospitality
or humanitarian motives, however, than with the recognition that immigrants would be good for the local economy. Many *californios* might
have agreed with a remarkable comment made in 1840 by twenty-one-
year-old Pablo de la Guerra of one of Santa Barbara's most powerful
families. The foreigners, he said, "are about to overrun us, of which I am
very glad, for the country needs immigration in order to make progress."[82] De la Guerra's pragmatic attitude, which placed regional concerns above national interest, resembled the response of the *tejanos* a
decade before.

Most *californios* must have had mixed emotions about the arrival of
norteamericanos. General Vallejo, for example, an outspoken opponent
of American immigration, repeatedly warned the government against
the danger that it posed to Mexican sovereignty over California. On a
personal level, however, Vallejo seems to have liked Americans (he had
three American brothers-in-law and all but one of his children married
foreigners). He did not use his troops to drive them from the country,
although he blamed his failure to take military action against the foreigners
on his chronic shortage of soldiers. He could not fight Americans and
maintain defense against Indians simultaneously, he said.[83] Meanwhile,
foreigners in the Sacramento Valley grew stronger by the day.

Instead of forming a barrier against Anglo-American settlement in the
interior, as Governor Alvarado had hoped, Sutter's New Helvetia had
become a magnet for them. Generous to a fault, Sutter gave them jobs
and sold them land. In his capacity as a Mexican official (Alvarado
appointed him "representative of the government" in the Sacramento
Valley in 1840),[84] Sutter even issued passports and other documents to
the Americans in violation of federal orders. These activities incensed

Vallejo, who had long regarded Sutter as dangerous. By 1845 Vallejo correctly perceived that Sutter's fort had become "the gateway of communication between the United States and this country which they [the North Americans] covet so much."[85] By then Vallejo probably lacked the force to dislodge Sutter from his thick-walled fort. Certainly Sutter felt secure from Mexican troops. As early as 1841 he expressed confidence that "it is too late now to drive me out of the country. . . . I am strong now." If California forces moved against him, Sutter wrote, "I will make a declaration of Independence and proclaim California for a Republique."[86]

There was no need for Sutter to take such a dramatic step. Instead, he found security in an alliance with Governor Micheltorena. In exchange for the promise of military aid to prop up Micheltorena's shaky governorship, Sutter received twenty-two more square leagues of land, adjacent to his original New Helvetia. Only after the overthrow of Micheltorena in 1845, as war with the United States loomed over the Texas question, did the *californios* attempt to dislodge the troublesome Sutter. Then they chose peaceful means. They offered to buy him out, but the price was too high. As Vallejo woefully noted, however, "it is the security of the country that is to be bought, and that is priceless."[87]

Sutter's sale of land to unnaturalized Americans, in clear violation of the law, contributed substantially to Anglo-American colonization in California.[88] At the same time, however, California officials themselves encouraged Americans to settle by making it easy for them to obtain citizenship and land.

The land boom that had begun in the mid-1830s reached its height in the 1840s. Governor Alvarado (1836–42) gave out 170 rancho grants; Micheltorena (1842–45) made some 120 grants; and Pío Pico (1845–46) about 80. As in New Mexico, nearly half of the grants made in California in the Mexican era were less than six years old in 1846. Foreigners, mainly Americans, received a large number of grants from all three governors. Micheltorena seems to have adopted an especially generous policy toward Americans, whose support he needed to buoy his sinking regime. Perhaps one third of the 120 grants that Micheltorena made went to foreigners.[89] His policy brought a few protests from *californios,* but Pico, a native governor, seems to have been equally generous. The *californios'* hospitality toward *norteamericanos* continued right to the end. On July 16, 1846, Pío Pico issued strongly worded orders that Americans living in California not be mistreated, even though war existed with the United States.[90]

The preponderance of land grants made to *norteamericanos* in the 1840s were in the Central Valley. By 1845 a branch of the Sacramento River was already being called the *Río de los americanos,* today's American

River.[91] The immigrants of the 1840s remained geographically isolated from the *californios,* just as American immigrants had lived apart from *tejanos* two decades before. They did not blend into California society as had the merchants and trappers who settled in coastal California prior to 1840. As Juan Bautista Alvarado ruefully recalled, "would that the foreigners that came to settle in California after 1841 had been of the same quality as those who preceded them."[92]

The outlook of the new post-1840 immigrants differed so markedly from that of the older settlers that one historian has suggested that Americans in California formed two distinct groups: "maritime interests" and "pioneering interests."[93] The distinction is useful, but by 1846 both groups had a common goal: both wanted California to "play the Texas game." The chief disagreement between the two groups was how and when to begin. While the maritime groups maneuvered behind the scenes and sought support of prominent *californios,* impatient "hotheads" in the Sacramento Valley staged a coup. Known as the Bear Flag Revolt, this outbreak began at Sonoma in June 1846 before news of war between the United States and Mexico reached California. Even if that war had not occurred, then, it appears that Americans in California had become numerous enough to think they could play the "Texas game" and win.

Through natural increase and immigration, California had grown from 3,320 in 1821 to about 7,300 gente de razón in 1845. Much smaller than New Mexico, which had some 65,000 in 1846, California nevertheless had grown more rapidly in the Mexican era, at an average annual rate of 5 percent per year compared to 2.1 percent for New Mexico or 1.1 for Mexico as a whole. Foreigners, predominantly Americans, numbered conservatively 680 and constituted 9 percent of the California population in 1845, with 500 more American settlers on the overland trail to California in 1846 as war between Mexico and the United States broke out.[94]

As had happened in Texas, then, Mexico failed to people California and New Mexico with substantial numbers of loyal subjects, either Europeans or Mexicans, or to establish effective barriers to keep Anglo-Americans out. That failure contributed mightily to her loss of both provinces in 1846. More important, however, was the steady political, economic, and social drift of the frontier away from the metropolis. That drift undermined the will of frontiersmen to follow orders from Mexico City, to oppose American immigration, and to stop distributing land to citizens of a nation that had become what California's delegate to Congress in 1844 termed "our natural enemy."[95]

11

Society and Culture in Transition

Mexicans who live under poverty and ignorance on one side of the river cannot remain unaware of the fortune enjoyed by citizens of the United States who live on the opposite bank.—*Gaceta Diaria de México, 1825*

Accustomed to the continued trade with the North Americans, they have adopted their customs and habits, and one may say that truly they are not Mexicans except by birth, for they even speak Spanish with marked incorrectness.—José María Sánchez, *Nacogdoches, 1828*

Between 1821 and 1846, economic, political, ecclesiastical, military, and demographic changes combined to alter frontier society and culture more profoundly than in any previous twenty-five year span. Fresh ideas, technological advances, and new commercial opportunities brought changes that directly or indirectly touched the daily lives of most of the pobladores. Change took place at different rates, depending on particular local circumstances. So Nacogdoches, located on the edge of Louisiana, became "Americanized" more rapidly than any other community in the Mexican Far North. At San Antonio and Goliad, on the other hand, new influences had just begun to affect the *tejanos* when the revolt of 1836 threw Texas out of Mexico's orbit. In isolated Southern Arizona, successful Apache offensives caused the frontier to retreat in the 1830s before new influences made a notable impact. Societal and cultural changes in the Mexican era made the deepest imprint on New Mexico and California, where the size of the upper class increased and its growing affluence and access to new material goods began to grind away the rough edges of frontier life.

207

Harsh conditions of life on the frontier during the Spanish era had lessened social distinctions among the pobladores and forged a more egalitarian and racially fluid society than existed in central Mexico. Nonetheless, at the apex of that relatively egalitarian frontier society there stood a small aristocracy whose status derived from family, racial purity (real or imagined), land, and livestock. Since little cash circulated on the frontier during the Spanish era, the accumulation of capital was not an important determinate of status, although some of the well-to-do had more cash hoarded away than has been supposed.[1]

Compared to central Mexico, frontier society probably remained relatively egalitarian in the years following independence. Massive unemployment and extreme poverty, which reduced a high percentage of the lower class to begging in the nation's capital and other large cities of central Mexico, did not exist on the frontier. In the Far North, a steady need for labor and an abundance of wild game warded off starvation in hard times, even if it did not provide a balanced diet.[2] At the upper end of the social ladder, however, it appears that new commercial opportunities and the increase of capital under independent Mexico strengthened and enlarged the upper class on the frontier and sharpened distinctions between classes.

In California, land and cheap Indian labor from the newly secularized missions, combined with new markets, gave rise to a class of nouveau riche cattle barons late in the Mexican period. Not only foreign immigrants, but landless Mexican soldiers and sons of soldiers began to escape their humble origins by acquiring vast tracts of land and herds and profiting from the sale of hides and tallow. Francisco Pacheco, for example, a ruggedly handsome artisan who had come to California in 1820 at the age of thirty and served as a junior officer at the presidio at Monterey in the 1820s, received a portion of the lands of the secularized Mission San Juan Bautista in 1833. Over the next decade, with the sweat of Indian laborers, Pacheco enlarged his holdings to over 150,000 acres, raised cattle by the thousands, helped a son and son-in-law obtain nearby ranchos, and built a large, two-story home with broad verandas. Pacheco's success was repeated by members of many of California's older families, such as the Alvarados, Argüellos, Carrillos, Castros, De la Guerras, Ibarras, Picos, and Vallejos, many of whom descended from Spanish soldiers of modest rank.[3]

The popular notion that California rancheros enjoyed an "arcadian" existence in the Mexican era, "singing and dancing their happy lives away on the edge of the peaceful sea," has been overdrawn.[4] Most rancheros did not obtain title to their lands until after secularization of the missions in the mid-1830s and had little time to develop them prior to the American takeover. Moreover, incursions by hostile Indians dealt severe blows to rancheros in areas such as San Diego. Nonetheless, some members of the ranchero class began to build what a Mexican observer termed in 1844 "very recent fortunes."[5] As the American merchant Alfred Robinson noted: "Individual enterprise, which has succeeded, has placed the country in a more flourishing condition, and the wealth, instead of being confined to the monastic institutions, as before, has been distributed among the people."[6]

In Texas, new commercial and political opportunities also increased the size and wealth of the upper class. Like California, Texas had been largely a military society in the colonial period and some of the *arrivistes* were former soldiers, such as José María Chaves, José Antonio Menchaca, and José María Balmaceda, who retired to become heads of important families. Balmaceda, for example, retired in San Antonio in 1827, became one of the town's leading merchants, and served on the ayuntamiento before being elected to the state legislature in 1828. Like the *californios, tejanos* began to move out of urban centers and establish ranchos where they ran large herds of cattle and other livestock. The number of active ranches in the San Antonio-Goliad area increased from eleven in 1825 to eighty in 1833; some were new and others represented the reestablishment of ranches which had been abandoned during the chaotic years from 1810 to 1821. Many of those ranches were founded by the upper class or incipient upper class. As one historian has put it, "wealth and status" shifted to the ranchos in the Mexican period in Texas.[7] Ranchos established near San Antonio and Goliad by oligarchs such as Erasmo Seguín, Carlos de la Garza, Martín de León, Juan Martín de Veramendi, Refugio de la Garza, and Ramón Músquiz resembled small communities with homes for relatives, friends, and hired hands. An Englishman who visited the rancho of Erasmo Seguín in 1834, just two years after its reestablishment, described it as

> admirably situated on a rising ground, about 200 paces from the river San Antonio, . . . They have made a species of fortification as a precaution against the Indians. It consists of a square, palisadoed [sic] round, with the houses of the families residing there forming the sides of the square.[8]

In addition to running cattle and sheep, the Seguíns had planted cotton and other crops. By 1836 the ranch was prosperous enough that it supplied $4,000 worth of grain and livestock to the insurgent cause.

In New Mexico, new commercial opportunities in the Santa Fe trade enriched members of the old upper class who "became merchants as well as feudal lords," as one historian has explained.[9] An older, more complex and sophisticated society than either California or Texas, New Mexico had developed a small moneyed elite by the end of the Spanish era. To the south of Santa Fe, in the area known as Río Abajo, a few families monopolized land—the means of production in that pastoral society—and prospered from the sale of sheep in Chihuahua. The opening of the Santa Fe trade enabled New Mexico's latifundistas to accumulate capital in merchandising as well as to acquire more property. In a province where a laborer earned three to six dollars a month, members of the Armijo, Chávez, Otero, Ortiz, and Perea families dealt in huge sums. Mariano Chávez sent $26,474 worth of imported goods from Santa Fe to Chihuahua in 1844; José and Juan Perea sent goods valued at $25,128; Manuel and Ambrosio Armijo had $28,318 in merchandise.[10]

If frontier conditions in the Spanish era "influenced the development of a society in which class rivalry and distinction had little place," as one historian has recently argued,[11] the situation had clearly changed by the Mexican era. Class differences were readily observable to most outsiders. A young American who sought work in San Antonio in 1827, for example, later recalled how "the upper crust of society took no notice of me and the under crust was, to my mind, much lower than the Negro slaves. . . . "[12] Visitors to the frontier, such as the French mariner Abel du Petit-Thouars, who saw "only a single class" on his 1837 visit to California, were mistaken.[13] Those who knew the frontier intimately recognized that social stratification already existed and was intensifying. There could be no mistaking the difference in class between the ragged peon on a mule and the vaquero on horseback astride a silver-trimmed saddle.

In California, people of all classes no longer mixed easily at social functions as "dances became more exclusive and were usually given in the homes of private persons," according to one ranchero.[14] Juana Machado, born to a military family at San Diego in 1814, remembered that by the early 1830s officials stopped visiting with "families of the soldiers, whom they now looked upon as inferiors. In other times they did not make distinctions."[15] José María Amador, born at San Francisco in 1794, later recalled that "in my first years there were very few social distinctions," but with the growth of "wealth and population, separate classes were formed."[16]

In New Mexico, where social stratification based on wealth was probably more developed at the end of the colonial period than anywhere else on the frontier, social distance probably increased after independence. As early as 1821, William Becknell found New Mexico society characterized by "the rich keeping the poor in dependence and subjugation."[17] Government officials in the Mexican era talked openly about the ricos, who owned haciendas, and the pobres, or "the impoverished class" (*la clase miserable*), and the tensions between them. A legislative committee in 1829 also identified a class of people "who in this unhappy country are called the middle class" (*de medianas proporciones*), a condition which the legislators immediately pointed out was relative. In a province as impoverished as New Mexico, they said, the middle class was so poor its members could not be expected to pay taxes.[18] Tensions between ricos and pobres over questions such as taxes and militia service would contribute to bloody insurrection in 1837. During the Mexican era it could no longer be said, as it was of the late eighteenth century, that "little difference or animosity among the classes" existed in New Mexico.[19]

Ironically, as the proud oligarch of Sonoma, Gen. Mariano Guadalupe Vallejo noted, there had been more equality on the frontier in the Spanish era, "when equality was not known," than in the Republican era "in which all men glory in being equal."[20] In other words, although independent Mexico had abolished titles and racial distinctions, social differences based on disparities in material wealth had apparently sharpened.

As the upper class grew in size and affluence, so did its ability to exploit the lower class. In the relatively egalitarian Spanish era, few frontiersmen, compared to the residents of central Mexico, could rely on voluntary or involuntary servitude.[21] Following independence, the influx of capital, its concentration in the hands of a few, and the demand for labor stimulated by the vitality of the economy of the frontier, all strengthened the institution of debt peonage.

Peonage was most evident in California, where the newly secularized missions offered rancheros and urban dwellers a windfall of cheap Indian labor. Without the protection of the Franciscans, many former mission Indians fell easily into a system whereby *californios* advanced them goods, money, or liquor, then required them to work to repay their debts. Father Narciso Durán described the condition of two to three hundred Indians living in debt peonage on the edge of Los Angeles in 1833: "All in reality are slaves, or servants of white men who know well the manner of securing their services by binding them for a whole year for an advanced trifle." An Indian who tried to flee, Durán said, "experiences the full rigor of the law."[22] The conversion of former mission Indians into peons was rapid and widespread in California. Many observers commented on the transformation and echoed the sentiments of John Marsh, when he wrote in 1846: "The Indians are the principal laborers; without them the business of the country could hardly be carried on."[23]

In New Mexico, especially on the large estates of the Río Abajo, peonage grew out of the partido system of raising livestock, principally sheep. The number of herders indebted to the system apparently increased sharply in the Mexican period. The partido system resembled sharecropping, but substituted animals for crops. The herder, or *partidario*, was an independent contractor who agreed to guard and breed a flock of sheep belonging to a wealthy man in exchange for a share, or partido, of the newborn animals. According to José Agustín Escudero, a Chihuahua lawyer who was in Santa Fe in 1827, the shepherd usually received a cash "advance" for his services, and in good times built up his own herd and prospered. Good times seem to have come to an end for many partidarios by the end of the Mexican period, however, as nomadic Indians stepped up raids on the province and killed or ran off with livestock. Herders took immense losses, could not repay their advances, and fell into debt—a process facilitated by the increased flow of cash into the local economy.[24] Peonage may have increased in Texas during this period, too, but the picture there remains unclear.[25]

Many observers compared debt peonage in Mexico to slavery in the southern United States, but the peon was not legally a slave nor was peonage limited to one race. Peonage was viewed as a condition of class and bad fortune. A peon could, in theory, end his obligation by paying off his debt, and his condition was not hereditary. The same might be said of those captive Indians pressed into household service by pobladores.

From California to Texas, gente de razón continued the Spanish colonial practice of taking captives in Indian campaigns, or purchasing or ransoming them from other Indians. These captives became involuntary members of Mexican households, received baptism, and "performed domestic chores in exchange for their board and education," as one historian has explained.[26] Mexicans referred to these servants as *criados* (literally "those being raised"), and rarely as *esclavos*, or slaves, since they theoretically were free. The pobladores justified this bondage on the grounds that the Indians received the blessings of Christianity and, in some cases, had been spared from death or a life of servitude at the hands of "pagans." The attitude of frontiersmen toward taking captives from nomadic tribes seems to have been very matter of fact. In 1927 Amado Chaves of New Mexico recalled a family tradition that

> to get Indian girls to work for you all you had to do was organize a campaign against the Navajoes or Utes or Apaches and kill all the men you could and bring captive the children. They were yours. . . . Many of the rich people who did not have the nerve to go into campaigns would buy Indian girls.[27]

Indian servants frequently were released when they had worked off the price of their ransom, reached adulthood, and had become acculturated. But as "detribalized" natives, they and their descendants would carry the label *genízaro* in New Mexico (or *nixora* in Arizona), which signified their origin among pagan tribes. Although individual genízaros were utilized as trusted scouts or translators, as a group they were regarded as potentially seditious.[28] Mexican officials tried to stop the traffic in Indian captives and in California returned them to their homes on several occasions, but the trade remained brisk until the end of the Mexican period and may have increased as raids by Indian nomads intensified. In the New Mexico community of San Juan alone, 136 Indian captives were baptized between 1825 and 1844, representing a sharp rise over the last decades of the Spanish era.[29]

A handful of *tejanos* purchased blacks as they did Indians, but black slavery never became a significant institution among the pobladores on the Mexican frontier. Mexican laws specifically forbade the slave trade and provided for manumission of slaves, although Anglo-American colonists who brought slaves into Texas successfully circumvented the law by defining slaves as contract labor, and influential *tejanos* supported enslavement of blacks as a necessary evil to induce Anglos to come to Texas. Free blacks and runaway black slaves from the United States who made their way to northern Mexico, found themselves in a society where they enjoyed juridical equality as well as considerable tolerance of racial differences. What racial prejudice they did encounter on the Mexican frontier existed in a milder form than in the United States, and seldom led to overt discrimination.[30] When the American abolitionist Benjamin Lundy visited San Antonio in 1833, he met a former slave from the United States working as a blacksmith: "He says the Mexicans pay him the same respect as to other laboring people, there being no difference made here on account of colour."[31] Lundy's acquaintance clearly overstated the case, but it does seem clear that skin color alone was not a major obstacle to social advancement. In San Antonio Lundy also met one Felipe Elua, a former black slave from Louisiana:

> He now owns five or six houses and lots, besides a fine piece
> of land near town. He has educated his children so that they
> can read and write, and speak Spanish as well as French. . . .
> He has a sister also residing in Bexar, who is married to a
> Frenchman.[32]

Blacks could advance easily in California, too. Four years after Allen Light, "a coloured man" from Philadelphia stepped ashore in 1835, he had become a successful otter hunter, a Mexican citizen, and held a commission from the governor to protect the California coast from foreign poachers—many of them his former countrymen.[33]

Race, then, did not constitute an insurmountable barrier to upward social mobility on the Mexican frontier. A rigid, hierarchical social structure, with status determined in large part by race, had been a feature of Mexican life since the sixteenth century, but had broken down in the late colonial period and had never been firmly planted on the northern frontier. In the Far North the shortage of an easily exploitable native labor pool and the need to work with one's own hands made it impossible to maintain firm racial distinctions. In the colonial era, some persons classified as "Spaniards" had worked as servants on the frontier, while Indians, blacks, and mixed bloods had moved up the social ladder.[34] The grandparents of the last governor of California in the Mexican period, Pío Pico, included a mulatto and a mestizo, for example, and Pico himself had Negro facial features. Nonetheless, Pico became one of the leading citizens of California. There, as throughout the frontier, the overwhelming majority of gente de razón were mixed bloods. Foreign visitors often commented on the dark "bronzed complexion" of the frontiersmen, including the upper class. Thomas Jefferson Farnham, a New England attorney who visited California in the early 1840s, described "that part of the population that by courtesy are called white. . . . their complexion is a light clear bronze; not white, as they themselves erroneously imagine; and, withal, not a very seemly color . . . a lazy color."[35] As with many observations by foreigners, Farnham's comment says as much about him as it does about Mexican society. Only the Canary Islanders who settled in San Antonio in 1731 seem to have maintained a degree of racial "purity," but by 1820 two-thirds of them had married mestizos.[36]

Unlike Anglo-Americans, who defined Indians or blacks by race alone, Mexican frontiersmen tended to define persons by culture and class as well as by race. To be an "indio," for example, meant to dress, act, and speak like an Indian. Thus, nomadic Apaches who raided Mexican settlements in Arizona continued to be regarded as Indians, but Apaches who assimilated began to lose their ethnic and racial identity "and are regarded by the Mexicans as *Mexicans*," as one perceptive American visitor commented about the Apaches who lived at Tubac in 1848.[37] The use of class and culture as well as race to define Indians is well illustrated in two proposals from the Los Angeles ayuntamiento in 1844 and 1845. Notwithstanding the high percentage of Indian blood that coursed through the veins of nearly all of the *californios*, the council members asked the priest to segregate Indian burials in the town cemetery and to set aside a separate place "for the Indians to hear mass apart from the whites, as these Indians are a dirty class and on mixing prevent the white people from hearing mass, and dirty their clothes."[38]

If race did not stand as a barrier to upward mobility in the Mexican north, it did, nonetheless, constitute an obstacle. Mexican frontiersmen were not totally oblivious to color. They denigrated others of darker hue, and tended to "whiten" themselves as they moved up the social ladder by denying their Indian and black ancestry. One historian has suggested that the racial biases of the nouveau riche *californios* actually increased during the Mexican period, in part because they sought to put themselves on an equal footing with the race-conscious Anglo-American newcomers.[39]

Like race, sex also constituted less a barrier to upward mobility on the frontier than it did in central Mexico, and some women seized the new opportunities of the Mexican era just as men did. In California, at least twenty-two women applied for and received land grants in their own names. Some took this step to secure the property of a deceased spouse, then proceeded to oversee all aspects of ranch management. Women such as the pious Apolinaria Lorenzana, who never married, obtained ranchos on their own and hired men to run the business for them. Trade invoices suggest that nearly all of the New Mexico ricos were men, although their wives might have served as silent partners with their own investments. One exception was Gertrudis Barceló, whose profitable gambling establishment provided her with the means to invest in the Santa Fe trade to the tune of some $10,000 in 1843.[40]

In contrast to American or British women, who lost control over their property as well as their legal identity upon marriage, Mexican women were heirs to an Hispanic tradition which enabled them to maintain property separate from that of their husbands, and utilize it or dispose of it as they chose. Husbands had no claim on property that their spouses acquired prior to marriage; wives could not be held accountable for their husbands' debts. In practice, women had easy access to the courts and could sue and be sued. This Hispanic tradition became the basis of community property law in today's Southwestern states.[41]

Equality before the law did not extend to all things, however, for men still made the laws. Women could not hold office or vote. Women who committed adultery were likely to receive severe punishment and be liable to confiscation of their property, while men who failed to remain faithful to their wives usually suffered no legal penalties. Women could be forced by law to remain with their husbands, even to the point of sending them home in handcuffs. Women accused of criminal behavior were treated differently than a man might be, and were usually confined to a private residence rather than put in jail. The subservient position of women, so common to all Western societies in the nineteenth century, was symbolized by the custom of women serving meals to their husbands, then eating separately.[42]

Women on the Mexican frontier did not enjoy full access to the same careers and occupations as were open to men, but neither were they useless, unabashed flirts who spent their lives in "one incessant round of dalliance, dancing, and devotion," as one American put it.[43] Only upper class women, who had less fortunate females to operate their households, might have fitted such a description. Nor were frontier women in general "dunces, attached to their children," as one unchivalrous French traveler described the California females.[44] Where this harsh judgment did apply, it resulted from lack of access to the men's world. Male and female spheres seem to have been less separate on the frontier, however, than in the more settled communities.

Most frontier women, it would appear, took responsibility not only for maintaining households—cooking, cleaning, washing, milking—but also shared farming, ranching, and craftmaking with their spouses or carried on alone. Fermina Espinosa, who owned a ranch in California near today's Sotoville, reportedly broke colts and lassoed cattle while her four daughters rode the range, guarded cattle, and felled timber. Other women worked at a variety of tasks outside the home. Some New Mexico women gathered up their children and made a family outing of the arduous journey from Santa Fe to Los Angeles and back again with their merchant husbands.[45]

It seems likely, therefore, that frontier conditions mitigated against female subordination and sexual divisions of labor that characterized traditional Hispanic societies.[46] When local circumstances prevented them from playing traditional roles, women proved as versatile on the Mexican frontier as they did in the American West. Perhaps the most extreme examples of the impact of frontier conditions on women's occupational roles existed in communities which had born the brunt of warfare against Indians, such as Abiquiú, New Mexico, or San Antonio, Texas. The violent deaths of many young men in these towns left a disproportionate number of widows and single women who had no choice but to carry on alone.[47]

In San Antonio and Abiquiú, widows not only outnumbered widowers, but women in general outnumbered men, a fact which flies in the face of the conventional wisdom that women formed a distinct minority on the frontier.[48] That notion might be based on the notorious sexual imbalances in mining camps on the American frontier, as in Colorado where the 1860 census showed thirty-four males to every female during the silver boom, but recent research suggests greater sexual balance on the agrarian United States frontier between 1800 and 1840 than has been supposed. Men did outnumber women on the American frontier during those years, but never greatly. Only on one occasion did men constitute more than 55 percent of the total population.[49] Fragmentary evidence suggests that the numerical disparity between men and women on the Mexican frontier was not great either. In settled, older communities such as Santa Fe and San Antonio, women outnumbered men; in modest little towns like San Jose the ratio between sexes was nearly equal.[50] Men outnumbered women in military garrisons, such as San Francisco or Goliad, of course, and in rapidly growing communities such as Nacogdoches and Los Angeles, which attracted large numbers of immigrants who were usually single males. Even in these towns, however, sexual imbalances were not extreme. Los Angeles, for example, had more women than men in the 1820s, but as immigrants from Europe, the United States, and elsewhere in Mexico settled in the community, males predominated, with adult males outnumbering adult females in 1844 by 627 to 500, and forming 55.6 percent of the town's adult population. In the Mexican era, then, the proportion of men to women on the frontier came closer to equilibrium than it had in the Spanish period when the presence of military garrisons tipped the frontier population consistently toward the male side.[51]

It is difficult to draw firm conclusions about society on the Mexican frontier since we lack a solid statistical base for these years and since demographic analysis of more settled areas of Mexico are not available for comparison. Conventional wisdom, for example, holds that frontier populations were more youthful than those of settled areas. A recent study of the American frontier confirms this, but argues that differences were not extreme.[52] Until historians probe more deeply into Mexican social history of this era, it can only be hypothesized that differences in average age between the population of central Mexico and its northern frontier were not considerable, either, although the frontier population probably was younger. Nearly forty-five percent of the people encountered by a visitor to Santa Fe in these years would be under sixteen, while towns such as Abiquiú and Lo de Mora, which stood on the fringes of the New Mexico frontier, had still younger profiles, with 48 and 50 percent of their respective populations under sixteen. In Nacogdoches, Goliad, and San Antonio only 42.2 percent of the *tejanos* were under sixteen in 1833.[53] How this compares to central Mexico is not clear, but the Mexican frontier seems to have had a more mature population than its American counterpart, where in 1830 over half of the population was under sixteen. Texas more closely resembled the settled areas of the northeastern United States in 1830, where 42 percent of the population was fifteen and below; Santa Fe seemed more akin to the settled American South where the figure was 44 percent.[54]

The notion that settlers on the American frontier had larger families than in settled areas has also been confirmed by recent research, but the difference was slight.[55] That may be true of the relationship of the Mexican frontier to its metropolis as well, with the exception of California. The *californios* enjoyed notoriety for rearing families of heroic proportions, aided perhaps by the province's climate and relative isolation from disease. Births outran deaths by three to one in 1828, a year that was perhaps typical, and California women had ten children on the average, according to one "prudent calculation." Some women had over twenty children.[56] Antonio María Lugo's numerous progeny led one visitor to quip that "Los Angeles was largely populated from his family." In 1846 the elderly Lugo pridefully remarked, "I have done my duty for my country."[57] Elsewhere on the northern frontier, family size was more modest, with two to three children per couple, although the number of children may have increased in the Mexican era with better sanitation and health care, as seems to have been the case in Nacogdoches.[58]

Just as a variety of forces produced modest changes in frontier society during the Mexican era, so did changes occur in the material culture and physical surroundings of the gente de razón. These changes touched all classes, but especially the well-to-do, and made the gap between rich and poor more evident. Styles of clothing, for example, which varied from class to class, from region to region, and in minor ways from community to community, began to reflect the frontier's growing connections with the outside world. At the outset of Mexican independence, men and women on the frontier still wore styles of the early eighteenth century, but within a short time visitors such as Josiah Gregg reported: "the best society . . . is fast conforming to European fashion."[59]

Men took more slowly to changing fashions than did women. As of 1830, according to one American merchant in California.

> Very few of the men have adopted our mode of dress, the greater part adhering to the ancient costume of the past century. . . . Short clothes, and jacket trimmed with scarlet, a silk sash around the waist, *botas* [a kind of legging] of ornamented and embroidered deer skin, secured by colored garters, embroidered shoes, the hair long, braided and fastened behind with ribbons, a black silk handkerchief around the head, surmounted by an oval and broad-brimmed hat.[60]

New Mexican horseman. He is wearing calzoneras, a short blue jacket, a red sash around the waist, and seated on an elaborately carved saddle. Watercolor by an unknown artist, possibly Alexander Barclay (courtesy, The Bancroft Library).

Frontiersmen modified that "ancient costume," however, in keeping with current fashion in Mexico. By the mid-1830s many had replaced knee-length pants with *calzoneras*—full-length, embroidered trousers split along one side of the leg and often embroidered and adorned with rows of silver buttons—then in vogue among horsemen in Mexico City. Braided hair, not worn at all by men in the Mexican era in New Mexico or Texas, went out of fashion by about 1840 in California, although many of the more cosmopolitan young men had abandoned it earlier.[61]

Women embraced new styles more readily. By the late 1820s women in San Antonio were attending social gatherings wearing American fashions from Louisiana—fashions that distinguished them from Mexican women in the interior. By the early 1830s in California and in New Mexico, upper class women had adopted the tunic, a sleeveless, high-necked gown that some referred to as the *media paso*, or half step, because it fitted so tightly that it prevented a woman from taking a full stride. Then, as now, high fashion did not necessarily mean comfort. By the late 1830s upper class women in California had apparently adopted the more flowing fashions in vogue in Paris, Mexico City, and other western capitals, although a French visitor to California in 1837 descibed local fashions as eclectic: "These ladies have no special costume. They follow the French fashions more or less remotely, mixed with a residue of Spanish costume, which makes it difficult to give an exact idea of their style."[62]

Frontier women who adopted the new fashions were, of course, members of well-to-do families. When eighteen-year-old, Kentucky-bred Susan Magoffin visited Santa Fe at the end of the Mexican era, she attended a ball where ladies wore "silks, satins, . . . showy ornaments, such as huge necklaces . . . and other fine *fancy* articles."[63] For everyday wear, however, Mrs. Magoffin described the majority of women still wearing traditional skirts and blouses that she regarded as the equivalent of undergarments—chemises and petticoats—and that she found "truly shocking to my modesty. . . . Women slap about with their arms and necks bare, perhaps their bosoms exposed (and they are none of the prettiest or whitest)," she confided to her diary.[64] Most male visitors to the frontier agreed with Mrs. Magoffin that lower class frontier women were out of step with current fashion in the United States, but it troubled males less. Josiah Gregg, for example, admired their "very graceful sort of undress," and noted that many Mexican women had "handsome figures," notwithstanding "their profound ignorance of the 'refined art' of lacing" themselves into corsets.[65] Unlike Mrs. Magoffin, most male visitors did not object to the low necklines of frontier women or to the way in which some women seemed to flirt "by the apparently accidental disarrangement of the rebosa [rebozo] and shawl," offering "casual glimpses . . . of a swelling bust."[66]

The houses of the pobladores also began to undergo modest changes in the Mexican era, especially those of the upper class. Several generations of writers of fiction and makers of film have fixed in our imaginations the image of Spanish colonials living from California to Texas in

Teresita Suaso of New Mexico. A low-cut blouse, skirt, and rebosa constituted the everyday dress of most New Mexico women, as captured in this watercolor of Teresita Suaso returning from the river with a tub of freshly washed laundry. A watercolor by Alexander Barclay, 1853 (courtesy, The Bancroft Library).

sprawling haciendas, with pastel-tinted walls, red-tile roofs, and tree-shaded patios built around splashing fountains. The finest of these creations are graced by second stories with cantilevered balconies, rooms with high ceilings, huge fireplaces, and ornate woodwork. But domestic architecture, even of the ricos, generally had none of these features until the Mexican era, when contact with foreigners brought the necessary tools and affluence to construct and maintain elaborate homes.

Ranchers and farmers in the Spanish period lacked time, training, means, and the need to build more than simple, functional, dwellings. Since people spent considerable time outdoors, they needed little floor space. Their homes often consisted of only one room, and even homes of the well-to-do with large families seldom had more than three or four rooms. Most built homes of adobe, although stone and logs were utilized in areas such as San Antonio and Nacogdoches where they were the most available materials. Mud or thatch, rather than red tile, usually graced the roof tops, except in Southern California where tar was available, and few two-story homes broke the skyline of frontier communities in 1821.[67]

The interior of these homes consisted of small, dark, and sparsely furnished rooms. Stephen Austin described the homes he visited in San Antonio in 1821 as possessing "but little furniture or rather none at all."[68] A single room often served as both bedroom and parlor and was furnished only with blankets and bedrolls rather than tables and chairs. As one American writer described such a room in Santa Fe:

> during the day the beds are folded close up to the walls and covered with the handsome . . . blankets, forming a succession of sofas all around the room . . . mats and sometimes blankets are made to serve the use of carpets as well as table cloths and bed covers.[69]

In California, with its mild climate, homes had no fireplaces. Cooking was usually done outdoors, along with most other daily activities, and some people slept outdoors, just as they did in Texas. Before the beginnings of foreign commerce, furnishings in California households, according to one ranchero, consisted of little more than bedding and a small chest of clothes, all amounting to so little that *californios* would take their possessions with them on a trip and have no need to lock the door behind them.[70]

With growing affluence and the availability of more manufactured goods, homes of the ricos began to change. Furniture multiplied; mirrors appeared on walls; clocks began to tick off the hours in the parlors

Albuquerque house interior. This sketch of the interior of the carpeted main room, or *sala*, of the home of the parish priest at Albuquerque, suggests sparse furnishings with blanket-sofas along the walls. From a watercolor sketch of the residence of Padre José Manuel Gallegos (John Galvin, ed., *Western America in 1846. The Original Travel Diary of Lieutenant J. W. Abert* . . . [San Francisco, 1966], facing p. 40).

of the well-to-do; and such extraordinary luxuries as pool tables, pianos, and organs found their way to the frontier. The privileged could display solid silver table services, some made by local artisans; serve wine in glass decanters made in Pittsburgh; and feel Brussels carpet beneath their feet.[71] Dwellings themselves began to change as a few of the wealthy began to replace the mica and hides that covered windows with glass;

double sash windows that let in more light appeared; wooden doors began to take the place of hides; planked floors began to replace hard-packed dirt; and shingle roofs, brick chimneys, and fireplaces began to appear even along the temperate California coast. Ranch houses began to resemble sprawling haciendas during this period, befitting the growing affluence of their owners, but the most marked change in domestic architecture was the introduction of the New England-style two-story house.[72]

Americans introduced a few two-story adobes to New Mexico and to various places along the California coast during these years, but two-story homes became especially popular among the wealthier families of Monterey, who apparently copied a house built by the New England merchant Thomas Oliver Larkin in 1837. Larkin's house consisted of two rooms opening off of a central passageway with an interior staircase leading to a second floor, supported by a wooden frame. A hipped roof, covered by wooden shingles, and a double veranda that protected the adobe walls from rain damage, made the Larkin house handsome and distinctive. Although its walls were of adobe, wood and wood workers made the style possible. Ironically, what is still known today as Monterey Colonial style derived from American rather than Spanish influence.[73]

These changes in architecture and household furnishings resulted in part from the introduction of better iron and steel tools, which enabled frontier carpenters to do more sophisticated work. In New Mexico, for example, where iron had been a scarce and prized commodity, carpenters had at their disposal only a modest selection of crude axes, adzes, drills, chisels, and saws, some of which had been handcrafted from the remnants of another worn out tool or piece of metal. The Santa Fe trade made available a variety of iron implements, including planes, scroll saws, factory-made nails, hinges, and metal locks. As a result, such basic modifications of domestic architecture as an increase of wooden doors and more intricate cabinetry became possible. By 1830 furniture in the Duncan Phyfe style, then in vogue in the United States, was being made in New Mexico. Locally made bedframes began to replace mattresses and bedrolls, and chairs began to replace cushions arranged along the walls.[74]

To note the changes that began to occur in these years should not, however, obscure the fact that when the Mexican era ended most frontiersmen still lived in small, sparsely furnished homes on the edge of lands inhabited by Indian adversaries. Defensive and practical needs, rather than aesthetic considerations, still determined architectural features. In many cases niceties such as window glass remained impractical even for those who could afford them. While some ricos dined on wooden

Monterey, 1842. Thomas Larkin's two-story house dominated the Calle Principal at the left. Compare this with the view of Monterey in 1827, in chapter 1. Lithograph based on a watercolor painted in 1842 by a member of Commodore Thomas Catesby Jones's squadron.

tables with silver service, most frontiersmen continued to eat a traditional diet of meat, beans, corn, red chili, and tortillas as they had a century before, "using the floor for a table, the *jerga* (carpet) for a table-cloth." One American in New Mexico in 1844 described what must have been a typical meal: "The *tortillas* [were] brought in on a napkin, and the *atole* [a corn gruel] in earthen dishes made by the Indians, and no spoons, forks, or knives . . . [we used] fingers for forks, and *tortillas* for spoons."[75]

Along with domestic architecture and household furnishings, the urban environment began to change in the Mexican era. Throughout the Spanish period, planned urban institutions had stood in the vanguard of frontier expansion in the Mexican north and served as centers of commercial, political, and religious life. In contrast to the American frontier, where only a small percentage of the population lived in urban areas, the majority of Mexican frontiersmen were urban dwellers conforming to ancient Iberian tradition, and most commuted daily from their homes in towns and villages to agricultural or pastoral pursuits, following what one historian has termed a "settlement pattern that stressed both urban life and rural work."[76]

The nature of urban life in major frontier communities began to be transformed in the Mexican era. Los Angeles, which profited from its location near the port of San Pedro, is a case in point. At the end of the Spanish era, Los Angeles was a small, reasonably prosperous village with haphazardly arranged dwellings. Nearly all of its 650 residents engaged in agriculture and stock raising. The village literally began to take shape at the outset of the Mexican period with the completion of the community's first church in 1822. This not only ended the parishioners' need to make a seven-mile journey to Mission San Gabriel, but also gave the town a focal point on a new plaza around which the well-to-do, such as José Antonio Carrillo, began to build homes. Following independence, population grew quickly, reaching 1,250 by 1845, or nearly double its 1822 size. This, coupled with the end of economic strictures, the growing complexity of economic life, and the need for more goods and services for the increasingly affluent owners of outlying ranchos, gave a more urban aspect to the town. By 1836 about a third of the residents supported themselves in non-agricultural pursuits ranging from retail merchandising and crafts to tavern keeping and prostitution. Thus, the occupational structure of Los Angeles came to resemble that of more settled communities in central Mexico. At the same time the ayuntamiento of Los Angeles began to straighten streets, regularize titles to house lots (which previously had been granted verbally), and require that houses be whitewashed, walls repaired, and buildings completed or forfeited. As councilman Leonardo Cota put it in 1845, "the time has come in which the City of Los Angeles has begun to figure in the political sphere of things. . . . "[77] Hence, in a little over two decades, as one geographer has remarked, Los Angeles had developed "both the form and functions of a typical nineteenth-century town."[78]

The forces of growing population and prosperity that altered the "form and function" of Los Angeles worked on other communities as well, but urban functions and rates of change varied with local circumstances to a degree that defies generalizations. Albuquerque, for example, founded in 1706 and three-quarters of a century older than Los Angeles, enjoyed a well-developed urban economy as early as 1790, when handicraft production apparently occupied nearly 50 percent of its male work force and agricultural pursuits employed only 37 percent.[79] On the other hand, small communities in New Mexico remained essentially agrarian and offered few of the services usually associated with urban life. The need for defense in rural New Mexico caused people to cluster in centers known as *plazas,* such as Chimayó and Cebolleta, where homes linked with one another to form a continuous rectangle around a central plaza, their doors and windows facing inwards.[80] Towns of this type, which resembled presidios, continued to serve a need while former presidial communities such as Tucson and Tubac apparently failed to grow into comfortable pueblos in the Mexican era as Apache nomads succeeded in strangling economic growth in that region. On the other hand, along the more secure and economically vital California coast, the former garrisons of Monterey and Santa Barbara changed rapidly in the Mexican era into thriving commercial centers.

Like Los Angeles, the more prosperous towns made self-conscious efforts at urban beautification. Santa Fe residents installed their first "public clock" in the mid-1820s—a sun dial placed in the main square. In 1844 and 1845 vecinos of Santa Fe planted several hundred cottonwoods, some hauled from as far away as the Pecos River, to bring shade to their treeless plaza and to create a public park, or *alameda* near the river.[81]

Substantial population growth in most communities in the Mexican era made these changes possible. Los Angeles was not alone in doubling its population in twenty-five years (an average annual growth rate of 3.68 percent). California communities like San José, the first civil settlement in California, grew from 415 in 1828 to 700 in 1846 (a 3.7 percent average annual increase), and many Texas communities saw even sharper rises in population, reflecting the extraordinary influx of immigrants. Goliad's population nearly tripled, from 522 in 1825 to 1,479 in 1833, and some of the new Texas communities established to serve the colonists saw even faster growth, as in the case of Matagorda. Established at the mouth of the Colorado River of Texas in 1827, as a jumping off point for colonists who arrived by sea, Matagorda's population rose to 1,400 by 1832—more than Los Angeles would reach in 1846.[82]

In general, however, even the most rapidly growing towns did not increase as quickly as the general population.[83] Despite the strong Hispanic tradition to settle in urban areas, frontier imperatives, such as raising crops and grazing animals along water courses in an arid region, and defending fields, flocks, and herds from Indians, had encouraged a strong tendency among frontiersmen to live outside of settled areas "without King to rule or Pope to excommunicate them," as one California Franciscan complained.[84] In the Mexican era, this tendency toward dispersal accelerated, even in the face of dangers from hostile tribes. In

California and Texas, new opportunities drew people into ranching, and the ranchero population grew more rapidly than the urban population, although many rancheros maintained town houses in addition to their ranch homes. San Antonio, whose population remained relatively stable, was the most extreme example of the effect of dispersion on urban growth. Meanwhile, in New Mexico intrepid farmers and herders settled their families on choice sites in isolated but well-watered valleys, such as the Pecos. Approaching an abandoned settlement near present-day Mora, an American traveler noted in 1831: "These New Mexicans, with a pertinacity worthy of the Yankee nation, have pushed out into every little valley which would raise half a bushel of red pepper . . . thus exposing themselves to the Pawnees and Comanches."[85]

Some of the growth that well-established communities such as Monterey, Santa Fe, and San Antonio might have expected in the Mexican era was also siphoned off by new towns and villages that grew up as population moved farther from traditional centers of settlement. In Texas, for example, which held only three towns in 1821, at least twenty-one towns existed by 1835, populated mainly by immigrants.[86] In California, new communities developed inland from the coast at places such as General Vallejo's Sonoma (1835), Sutter's New Helvetia (1839), and the communities of La Politana (1843) and Agua Mansa (1845), founded in the San Bernardino Valley east of Los Angeles by New Mexicans. The San Bernardino Valley represented the extreme of urban expansion from New Mexico. Closer to home, *nuevomexicanos* continued an expansionist trend of the late colonial period. They planted new settlements in the north, such as Rio Colorado (1842), beyond Taos, and south along the Rio Grande at Casa Colorado (1823), near today's Socorro, and still farther south at Doña Ana (1843), near present Las Cruces just north of El Paso. Moving westward out of the Rio Grande Valley, they reoccupied Cubero beyond Laguna Pueblo on the edge of the Navajo country (1833), and pushed settlements such as Las Vegas (1835) and Chililí (1839) eastward over the mountains to the edge of the Great Plains. Some of these attempts at building new towns failed, as indios bárbaros pushed the frontier back, but the overall pattern seems to have been one of continued expansion of New Mexico's settlements in the Mexican era.[87]

Although the number of urban centers increased in the Mexican era everywhere except in Arizona, and urban population grew steadily, only Santa Fe, Albuquerque, and El Paso reached sizes that would have ranked them as little more than "substantial villages" on the American frontier.[88] By 1846 the populations of Santa Fe and El Paso probably exceeded 5,000 and Albuquerque exceeded 2,000, but no other community reached more than 1,500. Los Angeles, Santa Barbara, and Monterey, California's largest towns in 1846, had grown to about 1,250, 1,000, and 750 respectively; the *tejano* communities of San Antonio and Goliad hovered around 1,500 by 1836.[89] Frontier communities had not attained sufficient population to generate banks, hospitals, orphanages, libraries, and institutions of higher learning that existed in major cities in Mexico's core. Doctors, lawyers, teachers, surveyors and other professionals could barely support themselves even in the largest frontier communities.[90]

The Mexican period, then, saw only the beginnings of the transformation of some frontier communities from agrarian villages to urban centers, and even the largest towns still lacked many amenities of urban life. The shady, comfortable plazas that form the heart of the Hispanic "old towns" of today's San Diego, Albuquerque, Sante Fe, or San Antonio bear little resemblance to their Mexican predecessors.

Spanish and Mexican regulations, which required orderly, clean, uniform and symmetrical towns arranged on a grid pattern, had been largely ignored on the frontier and the best efforts of Mexican officials to regulate urban life generally brought only modest changes, except perhaps in San Antonio. Most towns resembled Monterey, which a Russian visitor, Ferdinand Petrovich Wrangel, described in 1835 as a scattering of dwellings "without order or symmetry of any kind," and no streets marked out.[91] Few plazas on the frontier had trees or plantings, nor did most private homes. In Tucson, as late as 1858, according to one visitor, "not a white wall nor green tree was to be seen."[92] Even in verdant California, William Heath Davis tells us, ranch houses "stood out bare and plain, with no adornment of trees, shrubbery, or flowers, . . . in the towns it was a rare thing to see flowers or shrubbery about the houses of the Californians."[93] Pollution took more visible forms in those days. In Monterey, Wrangel noted: "Skeletons of livestock lie everywhere, while the number of cow skulls with horns and all scattered here and there is incalculable."[94] In Santa Fe, horses stood tied to the portales while other animals, including pigs and large dogs, roamed through the streets and about the plaza, amidst their excrement. One contemporary, Francisco Perea, remembered it as "a dirty, unsightly place, almost to a degree unbelievable."[95]

Regulations drawn up for the governance of frontier communities, which resembled earlier Spanish legislation, tell us as much about the nature of urban life as about the goals of those who would improve it. In 1833, for example, Sante Fe's city fathers prohibited citizens from throwing "garbage, water, or anything else from houses which may serve to inconvenience passersby;" racing horses in the streets; tying animals to porches; dirtying the water supply, streets, and market places; discharging firearms in town; and from "shouts, yells, and other outside demonstrations . . . which may scandalize or disturb public order, especially in the silence of night."[96] If these regulations describe behavior they were designed to correct, towns in the Mexican Far North continued to have unmistakable frontier characteristics—not unlike their American counterparts—even as the urbanization process softened some of the rough edges of frontier life.[97]

In small but important ways, the cultural life of frontiersmen became richer and more diverse in the Mexican era for some of the gente de razón. Some families, for example, had greater access to schools and to the written word under Mexico than they had under Spain.

Printing in the Far North began in Texas on the eve of Mexican independence when Americans, operating presses imported from the United States, printed short-lived newspapers and propaganda pieces designed to promote the "liberation" of Mexico from Spain.[98] The first significant printing and publication of books and newspapers on the frontier followed Mexican independence, however, and owed more to the region's new connection with the United States than to Mexico.

The first attempt to establish a permanent press on the frontier occurred in 1823 at San Antonio when an American began operating a press from the United States and announced his intention to publish a bilingual newspaper that would inaugurate an era of "light and reason." As would occur with other publishing ventures in these decades, the enterprise failed, probably for want of subscribers, and the state government in Monterey purchased the press. The first sustained printing in Texas began in 1829 at Austin's colony, where Godwin Brown Cotton published and printed *The Texas Gazette* under the motto *"Dios y libertad."* Cotton sold out in 1832, but a newspaper continued to be published regularly at San Felipe de Austin.[99]

In 1834 American presses began operating in New Mexico and California. New Mexico's first press came over the Santa Fe Trail as part of the cargo of Josiah Gregg, who apparently sold it to the secretary of the legislature, Ramón Abreú of Santa Fe. Abreú operated the press with the help of a printer from Durango, Jesús María Baca, and among his imprints in 1834 was New Mexico's first newspaper, a short-lived weekly auspiciously named *El Crepúsculo de la Libertad (The Dawn of Liberty)*, published by Antonio Barreiro. In 1835 Father Antonio José Martínez acquired the press and moved it, along with printer Baca, to his parish of Taos. The press remained there for the remainder of the Mexican period, except when Martínez loaned it to government officials. It was used mainly to publish school books and religious tracts although it also printed two more newspapers, *La Verdad* and *El Payo de Nuevo-México.* These papers, published in 1844 and 1845, contained a substantial amount of national as well as local news, but the high price of paper on the frontier made them expensive, and that, coupled with a paucity of subscribers, probably explains their demise.[100]

Alta California's first press came from the United States in June 1834 on a Boston vessel and operated initially at Monterey under the direction of Agustín Zamorano, who was captain of the local presidio and had come to California as a member of Governor Echeandía's staff in 1825. Zamorano, though, had no previous experience as a printer. In late 1836 or early 1837 Gen. Mariano Guadalupe Vallejo moved the press to Sonoma, where it remained until 1842 while Vallejo served as commanding general of California. It then resumed operations in Monterey. California's lone press never issued a newspaper in the Mexican period. Like its New Mexico counterpart, it helped disseminate information, especially political announcements, religious tracts, and school books, such as *Tables for Children who are Beginning to Count* (Monterey, 1836), and items of general interest—among them *A Drugstore of Tried and True Cures: Reprinted from the Original in Cádiz for the Benefit of the Public* (Sonoma, 1838).[101]

In addition to newspapers and books printed on the frontier, the Mexican period saw an influx of literature from other lands. In the colonial period, the few books that reached frontier communities dealt largely with religious topics and circulated among missionaries and a few high-ranking officials. As late as 1803 orders reached Sante Fe to seize books banned by the Church, such as the *Social Contract* by "Juan Santiago" Rousseau. The isolation of the frontier, more than the vigilance of officials, probably kept the region relatively free of "seditious" or "heretical" literature.[102] With the opening of the frontier, foreigners brought a large number of books into the region, sometimes for their own reading pleasure and sometimes for sale. Josiah Gregg imported 1,141 books into Santa Fe in 1834 alone, and untold volumes entered the region with smugglers.[103]

The ease with which books circulated alarmed the clergy, and the reaction of one California Franciscan at the dawn of Mexican independence seems typical: "May God forbid that free trade should lead to the introduction of free thought!"[104] Books banned by the Church found their way into the hands of young Californians despite the vigilance of the Franciscans, who apparently burned offensive books on more than one occasion. In 1831 three prominent young men in Monterey, all destined to become political leaders, were briefly excommunicated by Padre Narciso Durán for reading Rousseau, Voltaire, and a Protestant Bible. Durán reportedly relented upon the payment of a fee and permitted the reading to continue on the condition that such books "not be placed in the hands of irresponsible or non-intelligent people."[105]

When the influence of the Church diminished in California in the 1830s, as it already had elsewhere on the frontier, efforts to censor the reading of the pobladores also declined. Members of well-to-do families acquired impressive libraries and read widely. General Vallejo's interest in the classics seems apparent from names he gave his children, such as Plato and Plutarch, with Napoleon thrown in as a gesture toward modernity.[106] In New Mexico, the wealthy merchant Mariano Chávez could quote Tocqueville, and one Ignacio Rouquía of El Paso had apparently read enough of George Washington to argue in 1847 that President James K. Polk's conduct of the war against Mexico "is entirely against the principles of Washington, which were to remain at home . . . and never invade the territory of another nation."[107] Clearly, not all frontiersmen could be dismissed as "ignorant . . . half-civilized" rustics as some foreigners sought to do.[108] The tendency of American visitors to marvel at the ignorance of some Mexican frontiersmen has obscured the fact that others were well read for their time and place. Moreover, Mexican frontiersmen had no monopoly on ignorance. Books were also scarce on the American frontier.[109]

Along with books and newspapers, public and private schools proliferated on the frontier in the Mexican era, continuing a trend already begun under Spain. Small schools at the primary level, supported by private subscription, had cropped up throughout the frontier in the last decades of the colonial period. Although a popular stereotype would emerge in the 1820s among Mexican liberals and foreigners charging that Spanish officials sought "studiously and craftily to retard the growth of enlightenment,"[110] the opposite was true. Imbued by the Enlightenment ideal of cultivating "Reason," officials in the Bourbon era had promoted public education. The Enlightenment ideal continued to influence officials of independent Mexico, who also saw education as a key to the success of their young republic, and maintained that "ignorance is the enemy of liberty" and that "public education is one of the best bulwarks of a republican system."[111] In this spirit, officials at the national, state, and local levels drafted regulations for the operation and maintenance of public schools from California to Texas.

The vigorous proeducation stance of public officials coincided with changes on the frontier that created a more favorable climate for education. Books, which had been in such short supply that even catechisms were scarce, became more plentiful. Many frontier families and communities had more income than ever before and could better afford to hire teachers, although funds never seemed equal to needs. Finally, immigration from Mexico and abroad brought to the frontier a greater number of educated people who might serve as teachers. In California, for example, where the number of literate people had been apallingly low in the colonial period, the arrival of the Híjar-Padrés colony in 1834 added twenty-two more teachers to the territory, and foreigners such as William Hartnell, the former British hide and tallow merchant who had settled in California and married into the prominent De la Guerra family, operated schools from time to time.[112]

This combination of circumstances gave birth to more schools in frontier communities than had ever existed before. At one time or another, primary schools operated in every sizable community on the frontier where parents could afford to pay a teacher's salary. San Antonio, for example, supported a "Public Free Primary School," from 1828–1835. Like schools in Santa Fe, Taos, Los Angeles and elsewhere in Mexico in this era, the San Antonio school followed the Lancastrian System, a British method that had spread to the United States and Mexico and that enabled one teacher to handle large classes of perhaps 150 by using advanced pupils as tutors. Girls generally did not attend formal schools on the frontier, but attendance for young boys was compulsory in San Antonio, as it was in many other frontier communities. Caught up in the exuberant republican rhetoric of the day, San Antonio officials required students to address one another as "Citizen," and to master reading, writing, arithmetic, science, and religion in order to bring about "the felicity of Peoples, and the prosperity of their Government."[113]

In practice, schools were often poorly attended, despite regulations that spelled out harsh punishments or fines for parents who failed to send their truant youngsters to school. Complaints about the incompetence of teachers and lack of good facilities were commonplace and frontier conditions made it difficult for some communities to recruit good teachers. As one Texas official put it, to bring a teacher to San Antonio "it is necessary to defray the expenses of his trip and give him a salary sufficient to overcome his dislike to the place, which, although pleasant and healthful, is abhorrent to everybody because of its decadent and miserable condition."[114] Since public funds were neither dependable nor sufficient to meet all community needs, the burden of education continued to fall on those parents with children in school. Teachers' salaries were often in arrears and schools frequently closed for lack of support. Education beyond the primary level was not available on the frontier, but new connections with the outside world gave the children of well-to-do families opportunities to be educated abroad. The prosperous De la Guerras of Santa Barbara, for example, had two sons in school in Mexico City for a time, and another in school in England. Some of the frontier oligarchs may have been as far sighted as Mariano Chávez, who reportedly sent his son, José Francisco, to a school in St. Louis in 1841 with the warning; "The heretics are going to overrun all this country. Go and learn their language and come back prepared to defend your people."[115]

Thus the shortcomings of the frontier schools was not a consequence of their being "entirely controlled by the priests," or of indifference to learning, as some outsiders charged.[116] Ways to improve schools constituted a major item on the agendas of legislatures and town councils across the frontier. Although the results of their efforts were uneven and impossible to measure with precision, it appears likely that literacy continued to rise in the Mexican period. Josiah Gregg, who had little good to say about schooling in New Mexico, thought that a fourth of New Mexicans were literate by the 1830s, and subsequent census figures suggest that he was not far off.[117] Gregg's figure compares favorably to the rest of Mexico, where only 5 percent of school age children attended school as late as 1844.[118] It also compares favorably to the American frontier. The fight to establish free public schools was still being waged in the United States through the first half of the nineteenth century, and the conditions of schools on the Mexican frontier resembled those of states such as Kentucky and Tennessee when they were at a comparable stage of development and only a limited number of young boys attended small, short-lived private schools.[119]

Notwithstanding apparent advances in literacy at the primary school level, only a few people attained sufficient training to enter professions or manage political institutions. As we have seen, no attorneys practiced on the frontier except a few sent by the government, and judges not only lacked training but some were illiterate—a problem not limited to the frontier. Those citizens most likely to hold seats on town councils or departmental assemblies generally came from the families of the well-to-do, who could afford to accept those nonremunerative positions. Since the upper class was small, and families interrelated, it frequently became difficult to fill positions with males who could read and write, yet still adhere to a law that prohibited relatives from serving on town and provincial assemblies.[120]

The education of sons of frontier oligarchs did not take place quickly enough to supply the demand that the new politics created for officials to operate self-governing institutions. That demand was filled, in part, by foreigners, many of them Americans, who held key political offices on the Mexican frontier well before the United States conquered the region. This was most apparent in Texas, where American colonists governed their own communities under Mexican laws. Foreigners also held key offices, however, in New Mexico and California. For example, the brothers Antoine and Louis Robidoux, trappers and traders who were born near St. Louis and moved to New Mexico in the 1820s, each held the position of first alcalde of Santa Fe, as well as a number of minor offices. Both remained closely identified with Americans and American interests, despite their adoption of Mexican citizenship, and probably hoped to use their political offices to further their economic interests. That was clearly the case with the Spanish-born merchant Manuel Alvarez, who served simultaneously as United States consul in Santa Fe (1839–46) and as first alcalde of Santa Fe (1840).[121] In California, foreign-born residents held important offices in nearly every community at one time or another: William Hinckley of Massachusetts and Jacob Leese of Ohio served respectively as alcaldes at San Francisco and Sonoma in 1844; Abel Stearns and Henry Delano Fitch, both of Massachusetts, served respectively as attorney of the Los Angeles ayuntamiento in 1836, and justice of the peace in San Diego, 1839–40. At Monterey in 1835, three of the nine members of the ayuntamiento were foreign-born: the naturalized American, John B. Cooper; Englishman William Hartnell; and David Spence, a Scot. Three other foreigners held minor offices in Monterey that same year, and David Spence would go on to serve two terms in the California legislature.[122]

As the example of outsiders filling political offices on the Mexican frontier demonstrates, the changes of these years were not all positive, and change should not be regarded as synonymous with progress. Nowhere was this better illustrated than in medical treatment. Although the frontier saw an increase in the number of people practicing medicine and in the availability of drugs, the quality of medical care probably did not improve substantially.

In an era when self-taught physicians practiced medicine, the frontier suffered from what a Mexican settler in California termed "the multiplication of quacks and phony pharmacists" who lived by taking advantage of the shortage of trained doctors.[123] Many of these "quacks" were educated foreigners; the case of John Marsh passing off his Harvard B.A. as a medical degree was not unique. Communities as large as Los Angeles, Santa Fe, or San Antonio usually had no resident physician, and desperate people turned to anyone who offered hope. The American abolitionist Benjamin Lundy, who traveled through Texas in 1833, discovered that he was called upon to visit sick people in San Antonio because "having told the people something about the cholera, they all think me a doctor."[124] Hugo Reid, a bookish Scot who settled in Los Angeles in the mid-1830s, made a similar observation: "I know not why, but an Anglo-Saxon is synonymous with an M.D. Many an *extranjero* who never before possessed sufficient confidence in himself to administer a dose of Epsom, after killing God knows how many, has at length become a tolerable empiric."[125]

Since most frontier communities could not support a doctor, foreigners either practiced medicine as a sideline or else practiced briefly and moved on before the results of their "cures" became too well known. Monetary gain, however, was not the only motive of self-appointed "doctors," as a young British naval lieutenant, Robert W. H. Hardy, discovered while traveling through Sonora. Asked to examine an attractive young woman, Hardy admitted to himself: "I have always had some propensity towards quackery," and proceeded to examine "this interesting young lady . . . her complexion, her full black eye and slender figure, with more of the tenderness which belongs to a lover than the stiff formality of a doctor, and at length I stuttered out 'there is no danger,' though in fact there might be some as regarded myself."[126]

If newly arrived doctors did little to improve health care, neither did most new medicines, although some writers have suggested that the introduction of "the common drugs of the day" by foreign traders was beneficial.[127] Quinine for treating malaria, available in such forms as "Dr. Sappington's celebrated fever and ague pills," may have been the only truly valuable addition to the frontier pharmacopoeia in the Mexican era. In retrospect, the use of many other drugs should be categorized as inadvertent drug abuse rather than as drug therapy. Calomel, for example, used as a laxative and remedy for cholera, among other ailments, was not only therapeutically useless, but also contained mercury whose toxic effects included rotting out the patient's teeth. In contrast, traditional herbal treatments had demonstrable curative properties. It would appear that the familiar herbs and manners of folk doctors, or *curanderos*, were more beneficial than some of the new medicines and had the further advantage of providing psychological comfort that in itself was therapeutic. Traditional drugs like peyote, a hallucinogenic, at least took the patient's mind off his suffering. Thus, because the new medicine was not noticeably superior to the old, medical practice on the frontier probably changed only modestly in the Mexican era. Indeed, curanderos still practice the art of healing in today's Southwest.[128]

The increased mobility of people, which characterized the Mexican era, also increased the mobility of microbes. Diseases previously seldom encountered, such as typhoid, yellow fever, and whooping cough, probably occurred more frequently, and measles reached epidemic proportions in once-isolated California. Cholera, which heretofore was unknown and was caused, according to some clerics, by excessive sexual activity, made its first appearance on the frontier in Sonora and Texas in 1833 and 1834.[129]

Smallpox, one of the most feared killers, began to be brought under control on the frontier at this time due largely to efforts made by Spain just prior to Mexican independence. Shortly after William Jenner discovered smallpox vaccine in 1798, Spanish officials introduced it to the New World. It reached New Mexico in 1805, Texas in 1806, and California in 1817. After independence, Mexican officials on both the local and national levels tried to keep a supply of vaccine on hand to protect children and stem epidemics. Although officials did not always succeed, the cumulative effects of vaccination, earlier efforts at innoculation, and some acquired immunities prevented smallpox from reaching major epidemic proportions among the gente de razón in the Mexican period.[130] Protection against smallpox did not extend to the Indian population, however, and the disease took a dreadful toll of native American lives as in California's epidemics of 1837–39 and 1844. Similarly, malaria, which the pobladores could treat with quinine, reached epidemic proportions among the California Indians in 1830–33.[131] Thus, like many of the changes in this transitional era, innovations in medicine brought very mixed results.

Although some American visitors to the Mexican frontier flattered themselves that their very presence would cause the pobladores to "rapidly improve,"[132] it is clear that impetus for societal and cultural change in this era came from Mexico as well as abroad. Mexican settlers, like their counterparts on the American frontier, remained open to new ideas but at the same time sought to replicate familiar aspects of the culture of the interior as their fortunes and circumstances permitted.[133] Some of the changes that took place in popular amusements in the Mexican era illustrate this very well.

The increasing affluence and accessibility of the frontier brought traveling troops of *maromeros*—rope walkers, acrobats, and actors—north from Mexico to California, New Mexico, and Texas, apparently for the first time. New dances, such as the quadrille, the *contradanza*, and what one American disapprovingly termed the "lascivious waltz," spread north from Mexico and west from the United States.[134] Two traditional Hispanic sports, bullfighting and cockfighting, apparently were not commonplace on the northern frontier prior to the Mexican period. In 1824 politicians in Santa Fe had condemned the city of Durango, where those sports flourished, and pronounced such pastimes "opposed to republican virtues."[135] *Nuevomexicanos* embraced bull and cockfighting nonetheless and by 1845 a bull ring stood on the plaza at Santa Fe and both sports had also become commonplace in California. Thus, frontier amusements continued to be nurtured by Mexico notwithstanding foreign influences, such as billiards which first came to Monterey in 1828, apparently from abroad, and to Santa Fe a few years later.[136]

All cultures change slowly and selectively, as demonstrated by Anglo-Americans who went to great lengths to build log cabins on the treeless high plains to imitate the familiar architecture of the eastern woodlands. Any analysis of periods of change and transition—the periods that hold the most interest for students of history—should not lose sight of continuities. Mexican values, such as closeness of family, courtesy, hospitality, and depth of religious fervor, impressed visitors then as they do today. Foreign products might appear in the shops of northern Mexico, but shopkeepers maintained the sensible tradition of closing their doors in the mid-day heat to have dinner at home followed by a siesta. Because changes in architecture and clothing affected details more than form, visitors from the American frontier continued to regard the Mexican Far North as foreign and exotic until the end of the Mexican era. To young Susan Magoffin in 1846, New Mexico was a "foreign land where there are so few of our countrymen, and so few manners and customs similar to ours."[137] Even had they closed their eyes, sounds and smells would have signaled to Americans that they had entered another culture—the ringing of church bells, the braying of burros, the shrill squeak of carretas as wooden wheels revolved on wooden axles, the odor of *punche*, a home-grown tobacco, and the delicious aroma of burning *piñón* in cook fires and hearths of New Mexico homes.

Some of the traditions and usages of the pobladores were so eminently well-suited to the environment that Anglo-Americans adopted them as they moved into the area. Many writers have pointed out the enduring impact of Hispanic legal traditions on American jurisprudence, especially those regarding the exploitation of minerals and the division of water. Americans learned from Mexicans such basic mining techniques as panning and sluicing for gold, and the American cowboy adopted many Mexican techniques of livestock management along with the very dress and accouterments of the Mexican vaquero.[138]

But cultural borrowing worked both ways, as we have seen, and despite the strength of tradition, the westward thrust of America's vigorous economy and expanding population began to "Americanize" Mexican frontier society and culture well before the American military conquest of the region. American influence was strongest in East Texas, close to the American border. Speaking of the *tejanos* at Nacogdoches, one Mexican officer noted in 1828:

Accustomed to the continued trade with the North Americans, they have adopted their customs and habits, and one may say that truly they are not Mexicans except by birth, for they even speak Spanish with marked incorrectness.[139]

American influence extended to San Antonio, too, where a Swiss scientist noted in 1828 that "trade with the Anglo-Americans, and the blending in to some degree of their customs, make the inhabitants of Texas a little different from the Mexicans of the interior."[140] Indeed, as American influence spread throughout Texas, it seemed wise to Juan Almonte to make the whole State of Coahuila y Texas officially bilingual and to translate all laws and government acts into English.[141]

Not just in Texas, but wherever Americans gathered in significant numbers—in Santa Fe, Taos, and in California's coastal communities—American influence was apparent to contemporaries. "These foreigners gradually modified our customs," California Governor Juan Bautista Alvarado would later recall.[142] "At this early period," Thomas Larkin wrote from Monterey in 1846, "a knowledge of the English language is to a Merchant of more importance than the Spanish."[143] The growing number of American settlers led Larkin to note, without exaggeration, that "a person travelling from San Diego to San Francisco . . . can stop at a foreigner's farm house almost every few hours and travel without any knowledge of the Spanish language."[144] Larkin might also have added that some of the most influential *californios*, such as Miguel Pedrorena, a San Diego merchant, and Mariano Guadalupe Vallejo of Sonoma, also spoke English fluently by the 1840s.

As early as 1825, the governor of Chihuahua expressed the hope that contact with Americans "would produce the advantages of restraining and civilizing the New Mexicans, giving them the ideas of culture which they need to improve the disgraceful condition that characterizes the remote country where they live, detached from other peoples of the Republic."[145] Whatever its benefits, however, American cultural influences also had seductive qualities that could further weaken the pobladores' ties to central Mexico, as one Mexico City newspaper warned in 1825:

> Territorial limits are barriers too weak to stop the progress of the Enlightenment. Mexicans who live under poverty and ignorance on one side of the river cannot remain unaware of the fortune enjoyed by citizens of the United States who live on the opposite bank.[146]

Nearly a decade later the struggling young Santa Fe newspaper, *El Crepúsculo de la Libertad*, took up the same theme of the danger inherent in America's cultural penetration of the region:

> The reign of brute force has been replaced by that of reason. . . . We can be sure that the Americans will not take our lands with bullets . . . their weapons are others. They are their industry, their ideas of liberty and independence. The stars of the Capitol of the North will shine without a doubt even more brightly in New Mexico where the darkness is most dense due to the deplorable state in which the Mexican government has left it.[147]

As the Mexican period wore on, officials expressed fear that the *californios* and *nuevomexicanos* would not resist if Americans tried to take over their respective provinces. Ties between Americans and pobladores may have begun with commercial alliances, but as Manuel Castañares warned the central government in 1844, the sympathy that the frontiersmen had toward norteamericanos was based not only on their economic interests but also on "the much stronger ties of marriage and property. . . . " The *californios*, Castañares warned, regard the Americans "as brothers."[148]

Some of the pobladores, then, seem to have undergone a pattern of change similar to that of other frontier peoples—one which fits anthropologist Owen Lattimore's classic description of a "marginal" border population whose "political loyalty may be emphatically modified by economic self-interest in dealings with foreigners across the border." Although trade often brings frontier peoples into contact, their activities are not "limited to the economic," Lattimore argued. Frontier residents "inevitably set up their own nexus of social contact and joint interest."[149]

Settlers on the Mexican frontier were no exception. The "ambivalent loyalties" that Lattimore found characteristic of border peoples were probably intensified in the Mexican Far North, as we have seen, by the neglect of the central government, extreme distance from the nation's core, and by virulent regionalism, a key feature of Mexican life in the early part of the nineteenth century. Indeed, some contemporaries questioned whether Mexico existed as a nation or whether it was simply a collection of semiautonomous provinces.[150] Loyalty to one's locality, one's *patria chica*, frequently took precedence over loyalty to the patria, or nation as a whole.

Ambivalent loyalties, exacerbated by the frontiersmen's growing contact with Europeans and Americans in the Mexican era, took its most extreme form in Alta California, the most isolated of the northern prov-inces. Even casual visitors to California noted the hostility and "deep hatred" that the *californios* held toward Mexicans from "*la otra banda*," or "other shore," as *californios* termed central Mexico.[151] Mexican-born Gov-ernor José Figueroa noted in 1833 that the *californios* looked upon Mexi-cans with the same animosity that Mexicans viewed Spaniards.[152] Inten-sifying the hostility that many pobladores held toward residents of central Mexico was a knowledge that Mexican officials viewed frontier peoples with contempt and described them as uneducated rustics who lacked the training and competence to manage their own affairs. "The best of the Mexicans among us," one *californio* later recalled, "were far more insulting and offensive than any foreigner."[153]

Thus, frontier society and culture, which possessed characteristics that distinguished it from central Mexico in the Spanish era, grew even more distinctive and separate in the Mexican era. Cultural barriers that had divided Americans from Mexicans had begun to break down while new barriers arose, separating frontier peoples from other Mexicans. Most important, many of the leaders of frontier society took greater pride in their region than in their nation and saw themselves as a society distinct from central Mexico. The cultural and societal changes of the Mexican era, coupled with disappointments that frontiersmen felt over political leadership, spiritual care, military aid, and economic policies, became one of a series of wedges that would split the frontier from the nation's core in times of political crisis.

12

Separatism and Rebellion

Texas is no longer, morally or civilly, bound by the compact of Union.—Declaration of the People of Texas in General Convention Assembled, *November 7, 1835*

Alta California declares itself independent of Mexico until the federal system adopted in 1824 is reestablished.—California legislature, *November 7, 1836*

Intimately united with the Mexican Republic we continue to be free and independent.—Mariano Chávez, President, New Mexico Assembly, *January 1, 1844*

Powerful centrifugal forces—regionalism, isolation, and foreign influence—began to swirl the frontier out of the Mexican orbit in the years following independence while the central government seemed unable to exert a countervailing force to pull the region back again. Many frontiersmen came to question the legitimacy of leaders, laws, and institutions that seemed unresponsive to their needs and to doubt the value of a continuing relationship to the metropolis. Political, economic, and social conditions similar to those that have bred rebellion throughout the world existed in the Far North of Mexico in these years, including the powerful influences of example and habit. The successful use of force in the political process invites imitation, and politicians and military leaders in Mexico City had furnished numerous examples for frontiersmen to follow.[1]

Throughout the federalist era, from 1824 to 1835, small armed revolts against government officials had broken out in California and Texas.

Haden Edwards tried to establish an independent republic in East Texas in 1826–27, and a small group of Americans seized the customs house at Anáhuac on Galveston Bay in 1832. In California, discontented troops revolted in 1828, and again in 1829 when, led by Joaquín Solís, they tried to overthrow Governor José María Echeandía. In 1831 a group of influential *californios* issued a pronunciamiento against Echeandía's successor, Governor Manuel Victoria. A military skirmish followed in which the rebels seriously wounded the governor, then put him on a ship bound for Mexico. A few years later, in 1834, a group of Sonoran cowboys, led by a cobbler and a cigar maker, took over the headquarters of the Los Angeles ayuntamiento in an unsuccessful effort to depose Victoria's successor, Governor José Figueroa.[2]

These acts of political violence were often directed at specific grievances, but they seemed especially disquieting to federal officials because they were accompanied by reports of seditious sentiment across the frontier. Even from New Mexico, where no violent act of defiance occurred before 1836, the central government received warnings as early as the 1820s of the possibility of "treason" if the province did not receive better protection against Indians.[3] From California, Governor Figueroa warned the State Department in 1833 that a "clique of conceited and ignorant men," by whom he meant the heads of some of California's leading families, were plotting to separate the province from Mexico.[4]

Because of its large alien population and its proximity to the United States, Texas seemed to have greater potential for sedition than any other frontier province. An alarmingly persistent stream of reports and rumors from nearly every official observer suggested the existence of strong separatist tendencies among Texans, especially among the Anglo-Americans.[5] As subsequent events would show, such reports tended to exaggerate the extent of proindependence sentiment among Texans, but the situation changed dramatically in the mid-1830s.

Isolated outbreaks against federal officials and rumors of revolt turned into outright rebellion as the northern provinces sought to break away from the rest of the nation in the mid-1830s: Texas in 1835; California in 1836; and New Mexico and Sonora in 1837. The rebels' motives were not simply political, but it was a political change—the imposition of the conservative, centralist regime on Mexico in 1835—that sparked this series of revolts. Once in power, conservatives hoped to bring much-needed unity to the factious nation by strengthening the central government. Instead, they nearly split Mexico apart—a phenomenon that has occurred in other times and places.[6]

The shift from federalism to centralism in Mexico began when President Antonio López de Santa Anna ousted his own liberal vice president, Valentín Gómez Farías, and dissolved Congress in the spring of 1834. The direction which Santa Anna's new government would take, however, did not become evident until the following year. One of the clearest signals came on March 31, 1835, when the government ordered a drastic reduction in the size of state militia, apparently hoping to reduce the states' ability to resist centralization. Then, on May 2, a newly assembled conservative Congress announced that "by the will of the nation" it possessed extraconstitutional powers to rewrite the Constitution of 1824. Finally, on October 3 Congress dissolved state legislatures and brought the state governors directly under presidential control. Although a new national charter did not win congressional approval until the last day of 1836, the subservient position that states would occupy under the conservatives had become clear by the autumn of 1835.[7]

Reactions from the states to this erosion of their autonomy came in stages, as the centralists' program unfolded. The state of Zacatecas offered the first serious challenge when it refused to reduce the size of its militia. In April 1835 President Santa Anna personally led some 4,000 troops to force the state to conform. His men brutally sacked the city of Zacatecas, crushing resistance, and General Santa Anna returned triumphant to Mexico City in July. Meanwhile, efforts to call men to arms in defense of federalism, such as General Juan Alvarez's efforts in Guerrero and General José Antonio Mexía's attempt to seize Tampico, also failed.[8]

The most consequential revolts against centralism, however, erupted on Mexico's frontiers—not just in the Far North, but also in Yucatán to the southeast. As with California, New Mexico, and Texas in the Far North, distance and geography isolated the Yucatán peninsula from central Mexico. Yucatán depended on the sea for communication with the outside world, and just as the northern frontier had shifted its commercial orientation toward the United States, Yucatán had come to depend upon trade with Cuba. The imposition of centralism in Yucatán in 1836 resulted in a complete break with the central government by 1840, and the peninsula remained an independent state until 1846.

The breaking away of the Mexican periphery seemed to substantiate the views of one Mexican statesman who, influenced by the Enlightenment, applied science to society and theorized:

> In the political body, just as happens in nature, the circulation of the blood is slower the greater the distance from the heart, and the movement of the limbs is slow, and by the same token, more exposed to disease.[9]

One of the most diseased limbs in the body politic was Texas. Remote and exposed to contagion from the United States, Texas began to amputate itself from the nation in the autumn of 1835.

Aware of the disintegration of the federalist system, delegates from a dozen Texas communities assembled in a "Consultation" at San Felipe de Austin and issued what amounted to a conditional declaration of independence on November 7, 1835. In terms reminiscent of the American struggle for independence against the British, the delegates— overwhelmingly Anglo-American—announced that the centralists had "dissolved the Social Compact which existed between Texas and other Members of the Mexican Confederacy." Texans, "availing themselves of the natural rights," would defend their liberties and the Constitution of 1824. Using an argument that could be interpreted as disingenuous, the delegates vowed fidelity to the nation "so long as that nation is governed by the Constitution [of 1824]. . . . " But since that constitution was no longer in force, Texas asserted its right "to withdraw from the Union, to establish an independent Government. . . . "[10] By declaring allegiance to a dead constitution, Texans could proclaim independence and give the appearance of loyalty at the same time.

Prior to the autumn of 1835, Texans could not have agreed on such a bold course of action toward Mexico although considerable separatist sentiment had existed. Anglo-Texans, in particular, had been divided between groups that came to be termed the "war party" and the "peace party."[11] Both sought greater political autonomy for Texas in order to deal with outstanding problems: repeal of the portion of the law of April 6, 1830 which forbade further immigration from the United States; more favorable customs regulations; an improved judicial system; and the maintenance of slavery. At bottom, these were economic issues, and their favorable resolution would increase production and enhance the business climate. But these essentially economic problems required political solutions that neither the central nor state governments seemed capable of delivering. Hence, the "peace party," of which the empresario Stephen Austin was the most influential representative, wanted Mexico to grant Texas a divorce from its unhappy and unequal marriage with Coahuila. The radicals, led by ambitious and sometimes angry young men like William Barret Travis (who a few years earlier had abandoned a wife and law practice in Alabama after killing a man), sought independence from Mexico itself. Both groups wanted Texans to have sufficient autonomy to make decisions affecting their own welfare.[12]

For several years prior to the Texas revolt, which Texas historians grandiloquently term a "revolution," the fortunes of the war party had ebbed and flowed in response to forces in Mexico City. Immediately following the passage of the Law of April 6, 1830, when General Manuel Mier y Terán established a ring of military garrisons in Texas to stop smuggling and block immigration from the United States, outrage against the government ran high in Texas. It appeared that the war party would have its day. Rumors of an uprising, "led by adventurers who have neither home nor country," reached Secretary of State Lucas Alamán in Mexico City by summer of 1830.[13] Efforts at tariff enforcement resulted in violent altercations between colonists and government troops at Brazoria in December 1831 and in June 1832 at Anáhuac on Galveston Bay and at the mouth of the Brazos.[14]

But the radicals failed to win popular support and both Anglo and Mexican Texans condemned them. A recent immigrant from Alabama who would eventually serve in the United States Congress, George Smythe, characterized the rebels in 1832 as people "whose ambitions have been unsuccessful in their own country. . . . The whole object and design of their actions being to stir up a revolution."[15] Ramón Músquiz, a merchant from San Antonio who had served as jefe político since 1827 and favored many of the moderates' goals, described the rebels as "violent and desperate men who have nothing to lose." In June 1832, Músquiz called for a democratic and peaceful resolution of Texas's grievances: "It is not lawful for a faction to assume to themselves the rights of the majority, or demand with arms in their hands. . . . "[16]

Most Texans apparently agreed with Músquiz and proceeded to work within the Mexican political system toward a peaceful resolution of their grievances. On October 1, 1832, and again on April 1, 1833, delegates from most Texas communities met at San Felipe de Austin and drafted petitions asking for the separation of Coahuila and Texas, repeal of the anti-immigration clause of the Law of April 6, 1830, and for tariff exemptions. At the 1833 meeting they also approved a state constitution based on a 1780 Massachusetts charter.

It fell to Stephen Austin to carry a petition for statehood and the new constitution to Mexico City. Austin set out late in April 1833, apparently convinced that this was the last chance for moderate views to prevail. A few days before he left, Austin wrote in a private letter:

> I have always been opposed to hasty and imprudent measures but if our application fails, I shall say we have exhausted the subject so far as it can be done by mild steps, and that a totally different course ought to be adopted.[17]

If the government failed to approve statehood for Texas, Austin wrote, "the consequence of a failure will no doubt be war."

Although he fell short of winning separation from Coahuila, Austin helped achieve many of the Texans' more limited goals. As a result of Austin's pleading, and perhaps to forestall a revolt in Texas, Santa Anna rescinded the antiimmigration section of the Law of April 6, 1830, effective in May 1834. That same spring, apparently prodded by the central government and eager to placate Texas, a liberal legislature in Coahuila y Texas enacted many of the reforms that Texans had sought. The legislature made local government more efficient in theory by increasing the number of departments and municipalities in Texas. It also increased Texas representation in the legislature, and enacted sweeping judicial reforms, including trial by jury and an appelate court for Texas.[18] Partly as a result of these reforms, when Juan Almonte inspected Texas on behalf of Gómez Farías in 1834 he found it relatively quiet. Almonte's assessment of Texas, however, must be measured in the light of his expectation that Texas stood on the edge of revolt. He found the situation quiet only in relative terms, and reported that the Anglo-American colonists "seek nothing more than pretexts for a revolution, whose first object will be separation from Coahuila and afterwards from the Republic."[19]

In 1834, then, the lobbying of the peace party had helped eliminate many of the "pretexts for a revolution," and had temporarily eclipsed the war party. Austin's trip to Mexico City had borne fruit, although it also brought him personal misfortune. Shortly after his arrival, and before he began to gain a sympathetic hearing from Santa Anna, Austin had written an inflammatory letter to the ayuntamiento of San Antonio, advocating that Texas communities form a state "even though the general government refuses its consent." The letter eventually reached high officials and Austin was arrested on orders of Gómez Farías and imprisoned for a year and then detained in Mexico City.[20] Out on bond early in 1835, Austin remained optimistic that Congress would make Texas a state and his mission would be a complete success. Like many observers of Mexican politics in those days, Austin found the situation confusing and proved himself a poor prognosticator. "I am decidedly of the opinion that the federal system is in no danger at present," Austin wrote in a private letter in April 1835, and even as Santa Anna prepared to march on Zacatecas, Austin judged him "very friendly toward Texas."[21]

While Austin waited for passage of an amnesty law that would allow him to leave Mexico City, Coahuila y Texas became a trouble spot for the centralists. Liberal politicians in Monclova, which had replaced Saltillo as the state capital in 1833, had denounced Santa Anna's new government in the summer of 1834. In response, politicians in Saltillo had declared their support of Santa Anna and established a rival state government, apparently hoping that Santa Anna would reward their loyalty by elevating their city to the position of state capital once again. To the consternation of Texans, the state drifted into anarchy under two governments, and chaos gave way to violence when Agustín Viesca, a staunch federalist and friend of Gómez Farías, assumed the governorship in Monclova in April 1835. Viesca refused to obey centralist orders to reduce the militia and made his federalist sympathies clear. General Martín Perfecto de Cos, Commanding General of the Eastern Interior Provinces and the brother-in-law of Santa Anna, retaliated by sending troops to Monclova. They arrested Viesca in early June 1835, before he could flee to San Antonio where he intended to relocate the state capital.[22]

Later that month violence spread to Texas. Learning from intercepted reports that General Cos planned to send reinforcements into Texas, a small group of perhaps thirty armed radicals marched on Anáhuac and forced the surrender of the tiny military garrison. The ostensible cause of the attack was the uneven enforcement of tariff regulations, but the war party also hoped its action would galvanize public opinion in Texas before centralist forces arrived to occupy the province. At first it appeared as though the strategy failed. Communities throughout Texas repudiated the attack and professed loyalty to the government.[23] Before the hot Texas summer ended, however, it became clear that the radicals had tipped the balance in their favor by provoking the government to meet force with force.

No amount of protestations of loyalty in the summer of 1835 could convince Mexico's military command that the revolutionaries in Texas could be dealt with peaceably. José María Tornel, the Minister of War and Navy, General Cos, Commanding General of the Eastern Provincias Internas, and Colonel Domingo de Ugartechea, Principal Commander of Coahuila and Texas, along with a host of lesser officials, had all maintained a careful watch on the American colonists in Texas, whose numbers and disrespect for Mexican law were notorious.

In early January 1835, six months before the attack on Anáhuac, Cos had written to Ugartechea in San Antonio for "a weekly report on the state of public tranquility in Texas."[24] Ugartechea's reports brought little comfort. The colonists refused to pay duties and resolved not to allow the establishment of military garrisons or to reduce the size of their militia. They would arm "even the children" to keep Mexican troops out of Texas.[25] These reports reached Tornel in Mexico City, who assured Cos in April that after the revolt in Zacatecas was put down, a substantial military force "will be sent to Texas to settle the business there definitely."[26] The news that troops would arrive heartened Ugartechea, who reported that "colonists are on the march. . . .

Nothing is heard but God damn Santa Anna, God damn Ugartechea."[27]
The gravity with which the Mexican command regarded the Texas situation even before the episode at Anáhuac is suggested by its actions as
well as its words. By June 1835 Ugartechea had planted spies in Austin's
colony. Cos, who had moved from Saltillo to Matamoros at the mouth of
the Rio Grande to be closer to the trouble, asked Tornel for permission to
transfer his headquarters still farther north to San Antonio. Cos also
ordered the border sealed that June to prevent liberal officials from
Coahuila from fleeing to Texas: "a revolution would be certain to result."[28]

To concerned Mexican military officers, the seizure of Anáhuac in late
June had come as the opening shot of a long-expected revolt and the
episode stiffened their resolve to send troops into Texas. With federalist
resistance in Zacatecas and Monclova crushed, they mobilized forces for
a Texas campaign in the summer of 1835. Aware, however, of the colonist's hositility toward military occupation, and sensitive to the substantial number of colonists who reportedly remained loyal to Mexico, Cos
and Ugartechea assured Texans that the military would respect the rights
of law-abiding citizens.[29] As a sign of their loyalty, however, the military
commanders demanded that Texas officials arrest some of the trouble-
makers: Travis and other leaders of the assault on Anáhuac; Texas delegates to the federalist Monclova legislature, such as Austin's former
secretary and partner, Samuel May Williams; and the ardent liberal from
Yucatán, Lorenzo de Zavala. Zavala had occupied several high government posts under federalist administrations until Santa Anna dismantled the 1824 Constitution.[30] Zavala fled to Texas in July 1835, where
he had interests in land, and became one of the first to call for a convention, arguing that the centralists had broken the "compact" and "all the
states of the confederation are left at liberty to act for themselves."[31]

By late summer of 1835, Texas authorities had not apprehended any of
the rebels and Cos prepared to move troops northward. The Mexican
command understood full well that the presence of centralist forces in
Texas might lead to further trouble, but the risk seemed worth taking
because Texas was a hotbed of federalist activity.[32] As Ugartechea explained it, "if such proceedings were to remain unpunished, it would
be believed that the Mexican Nation is unjust or perhaps that she wanted
force and energy sufficient to make herself respected."[33]

Reports of the impending "invasion" by the centralist forces, fueled
by rumors that they would free black slaves, enslave Texans, and lay
waste to Texas as they had to Zacatecas, united the war and peace
parties as nothing had before.[34] By the end of August, a jubilant William
Barret Travis sensed a shift of public opinion away from the "Tories,"

as he termed the peace party: "The people are becoming united, more and more every day & I think in a month more, there will be no division at all."[35] In the midst of this, the foremost Tory, Stephen Austin, returned from Mexico City convinced that federalism was doomed. Austin added his considerable influence to the cause of the war party in a well-publicized speech on September 8, predicting that "the inevitable consequence of sending an armed force to this country would be war."[36] Austin publicly urged that Texas fight with "no half way measures" to preserve the federalist system and the Constitution of 1824. Privately, however, Austin now believed that Texas should separate entirely from Mexico as soon as it became sufficiently "Americanized" with immigrants—a process that Austin thought would be completed that fall and winter: "The fact is, we must, and ought to become a part of the United States."[37]

When centralist forces moved into Texas in the early autumn they met unified resistance. General Cos set out from Matamoros for San Antonio on September 17 at the head of a party of lancers, but on the very day he reached Goliad a shooting war had begun. Colonists in Gonzales, the chief settlement on Green DeWitt's empresario grant, had refused to surrender a small cannon to soldiers sent by Colonel Ugartechea. Reportedly flying a flag that said "Come and take It!" the rebels turned the cannon on the government forces, routing them on October 2. A week later, the presidio at Goliad fell to the rebels. Then, toward the end of October, Texas volunteers commanded by Austin laid siege to San Antonio, which Cos had occupied with some seven or eight hundred men. Cut off from supplies and food, Cos surrendered on December 11 to a smaller force of perhaps three hundred, after five days of fierce hand-to-hand combat in the streets and houses of the ravaged town. The victorious Texans permitted Cos and his troops to withdraw from the province after eliciting assurances that they would not work to oppose the Constitution of 1824.[38]

Thus, when the Consultation met at San Felipe de Austin in early November of 1835 to declare allegiance to the 1824 Constitution, Texas was already at war. Peace no longer seemed an option and many delegates favored an outright declaration of independence. Most, however, agreed to the equivocal profederalist declaration of November 7, apparently to gain the support of Mexican liberals and to buy time to obtain aid from the United States. The delegates sent a three-member mission (including the ubiquitous Stephen Austin) to the United States to test reaction to independence and to possible annexation.[39]

Except for Lorenzo de Zavala, prominent Mexican liberals never aided the Texas cause. At first, some federalists seemed disposed to join the

Texans, but they became suspicious when Texas did not cooperate with federalist leaders in exile in New Orleans, such as Gómez Farías and General José Antonio Mexía. Distrust characterized relations on both sides. Gómez Farías, who viewed Austin as unscrupulous and had ordered his arrest late in 1833, continued to despise Austin as well as the Texans who would put such a man in positions of leadership.[40] Texans, in turn, evinced little desire to work with Mexicans, and treated even the eminent Zavala with coolness and suspicion: "we must depend on ourselves and not upon an aspiring Mexican," one resident of Columbus wrote during Zavala's visit to his community.[41] In December, the head of the provisional Texas government, Henry Smith, pronounced it "bad policy to . . . trust Mexicans in any matter connected with our government . . . we will in the end find them inimical and treacherous."[42]

In early March 1836, Texas abandoned its profederalist posture. Meeting in another convention at Washington-on-the-Brazos, delegates from Texas communities unequivocally declared independence on March 2. Meanwhile, General Santa Anna had personally led a substantial force into Texas, hoping to crush opposition quickly as he had in Zacatecas. Santa Anna's forces won initial victories at the fateful siege of the Alamo in San Antonio, and at Goliad, but he then split his forces and led one contingent eastward in pursuit of the retreating Texans. Near present Houston, along the Río San Jacinto, Texas forces surprised and thoroughly defeated the centralists. Taken prisoner, Santa Anna was forced to sign the Treaties of Velasco in which he recognized Texas independence and agreed to withdraw Mexican forces beyond the Rio Grande. Although Mexico never ratified the treaties, which Santa Anna had signed under obvious duress, Texas independence was virtually assured.[43]

Unlike other provincial outbreaks against centralism in this era, the Texas revolt resulted in a complete break with Mexico. Mexico's failure to hold onto the province must be understood in large part as a result of the location of Texas on the edge of the frontier, contiguous to the expansionist United States. Not only had Anglo-Americans poured across the border to outnumber *tejanos* in the years prior to the revolt, but the United States government and public press had made no effort to conceal American interest in acquiring Texas by any means, fair or foul.[44] In response to the threat posed by Americans and their government, the Mexican military command had moved troops into the province and unwittingly aided the rebel cause by uniting Texans against them. Throughout the subsequent conflict the United States government maintained a neutral position while some American citizens and officials enthusiastically supported the insurgents and American money and volunteers flowed into Texas. Finally, leadership of the Texas revolt came

Assault on the Alamo. At daybreak of March 6, 1836, Mexican troops led by Martín Perfecto de Cos assaulted the northwest corner of the Alamo compound. Painting by Donald M. Yena, 1967 (courtesy, Mr. and Mrs. Frank P. Horlock, Houston, Texas).

almost entirely from Anglo-Americans. In all probability an incipient nationalism existed in prerevolutionary Texas among the Anglo-Americans who had come to think of themselves as "Texians"—neither American nor Mexican.[45]

Clearly, however, *tejanos* also contributed substantially to resistance against the centralists and then to the cause of Texas independence. Texas forces that laid siege to Cos in San Antonio in the fall of 1835, for example, included perhaps as many as 160 *tejanos,* among them companies led by Colonel Juan Seguín of San Antonio, Plácido Benavides of Victoria, and a group of rancheros from Goliad. Seven *tejanos* died inside the Alamo, fighting alongside Anglo-Americans against Santa Anna. Colonel Seguín and the Second Company of Texas Volunteers, which he

Colonel Juan Nepomuceno Seguín. Seguín (1806–1889) was the most prominent of the tejanos who fought alongside Anglo-Americans for Texas independence. After the Texas revolt, Anglo-Americans came to doubt his loyalty and Seguín, fearful for the safety of his family, fled to Mexico having become "a foreigner in my native land" (portrait by Jefferson Wright, courtesy, Archives Division, Texas State Library, Austin).

raised, performed valuable scouting services prior to the fall of the Alamo and contributed to the defeat of Santa Anna at San Jacinto. *Tejanos* also participated in the Consultation at San Felipe in November 1835 and four months later José Antonio Navarro and Francisco Ruiz, both Texas-born, signed the declaration of independence at Washington-on-the-Brazos.[46]

Tejanos also had much to lose from an alliance with the Americans. The predominantly *tejano* communities of San Antonio and Goliad apparently shared Anglo-American concerns about antiimmigration laws, the improvement of justice, the need for slavery, and exemptions from tariffs, but the idea of separation from Coahuila, much less independence from Mexico, seemed less attractive in the 1830s than it had in the

1820s. Anglo-Americans, who vastly outnumbered *tejanos* by the early 1830s, would surely dominate the state and *tejanos* would become, to paraphrase Juan Seguín, "foreigners in their native land."[47] Thus, políticos in San Antonio had reacted cooly to the prostatehood conventions of 1832 and 1833. They also contributed to Austin's incarceration in Mexico City by sending a copy of his audacious letter to officials in Saltillo. Compared to political domination by recently arrived Anglo aliens, many of whom the *tejanos* distrusted or regarded as "a worse than Savage set,"[48] union with Coahuila probably seemed the lesser evil. Instead of advocating a self-defeating statehood, then, the San Antonio ayuntamiento in the 1830s sought to improve its relationship with Coahuila by increasing Texas representation in the state legislature.[49]

But when Coahuila fell into anarchy, and the fragile federalist system shattered, *tejano* leaders must have wrung their hands over their unhappy alternatives—domination by Anglo-Americans or domination by the centralist dictatorship. Some, like Juan Seguín, opted first for "God, Mexico, and the Federal System," called for a consultation, and finally came to support the Anglo-American bid for independence. Most *tejanos*, however, probably responded like any residents of a war-torn land. They looked first to their families' welfare, fought on neither side, cooperated with the group in charge at the moment, and hoped for an end to the nightmare. The same may also be said for most Anglo-Texans, who had no desire to fight over political issues until Santa Anna's forces threatened their lives and property.[51]

Because Anglo-Americans furnished much of the impetus and leadership for the Texas revolt, it is easy to view it as simply an ethnic conflict. Ethnic differences did serve as a major obstacle to communication and hardened positions on both sides. As one historian has explained:

> Had there been no atmosphere of racial distrust . . . a crisis might not have followed. Mexico might not have thought it necessary to insist so drastically on unequivocal submission; or the colonists might not have believed so firmly that submission would endanger their liberty.[52]

On a day-to-day basis, however, little ethnic conflict occurred before the revolt. Anglo-American colonists, isolated in east Texas, seldom had direct contact with *tejanos* or with Mexicans so that differences in religion, philosophy, or life styles did not become major irritants. Relations that did occur between *tejanos* and Anglos prior to the revolt "on the whole . . . were friendly," according to a classic study by sociologist Samuel Lowrie. The major area of "culture conflict," Lowrie concluded, was political, and most historians would agree.[53] But the political disagreements that contributed to the Texas revolt did not come about simply because of differences in the political culture of Anglos and Mexicans. The political issues that men fought over divided Mexicans, too, and represented a conflict of interests between the frontier and the metropolis. The conflict was exacerbated in Texas by the presence of a large group of aliens whose political culture emphasized state's rights and local autonomy, but Mexicans also fought Mexicans over the same political issues in other areas of the frontier where Anglo-Americans played a minor role.

On November 7, 1836, a year to the day after the Texas Consultation issued its ambiguous declaration of independence, the legislature of Alta California met in an extraordinary session at Monterey and endorsed a similar plan, authored by young Juan Bautista Alvarado. The legislators proclaimed California "independent of Mexico until the federal system adopted in 1824 shall be reestablished," and outlined a form of government for the "free and sovereign state."[54] Some foreigners in Monterey who supported the revolt had prepared a Lone Star Flag for the occasion, and the coincidental arrival of an American war vessel raised suspicions about United States intentions, but there is no evidence that Texans or Americans directly inspired the California revolt.[55] The issues leading up to the rebellion in California did, however, bear striking similarity to those in Texas.

As in Texas, California *insurrectos* wanted more autonomy rather than less. They opposed centralism and passionately endorsed federalism and the 1824 Constitution. Their goal, as Alvarado later put it, was to liberate California "from the yoke of the oppressors sent by the Mexican government. . . . [and] to enjoy the strong and durable benefits granted by the glorious constitution of 1824." To Alvarado the revolt represented "the dawn of liberty" and a breaking of "the chains that oppressed this unhappy land."[56] Beneath the rhetoric, as in Texas, *californios* saw greater home rule as providing political means for solving local problems: autonomy to rewrite tariff regulations, which would promote rather than hinder California's vital foreign commerce; a halt to sentencing Mexican convicts to serve time in California; an end to passing over the local military for promotions in favor of recently arrived officers from Mexico; and a transfer of civil power from the military to civilians to promote a more equitable system of justice. Also as in Texas, home rule would make political offices, including the governorship and the directorship of the customs house, available to young *californios* with ambitions for political power.[57]

Mexico had sent no army to impose centralism on California as it had in Texas, but it had sent an ardent centralist governor, a forty-five-year-old colonel and former congressman from Guanajuato, Mariano Chico. Chico landed at Santa Barbara on April 16, 1836. His welcoming party, as General Mariano Guadalupe Vallejo later recalled, consisted of some eighty men dressed in black who "wore in the buttonhole of their frock coats a small red rosette which was the distinguishing badge of the federalists."[58] A few months later the *californios* overthrew their new governor.

Leaders of the revolt later explained much of their hostility to Chico on personal and moral grounds. Juan Bautista Alvarado for example, termed him "a fool," and "a coward, insane and a corrupter of public morals."[59] Chico offended the *californios'* sense of propriety through such behavior as living openly with a mistress, whom he tried to pass off as his niece, and by attending a theatre performance with a notorious adulteress.

It is difficult to separate the *californios'* distaste for Chico as a person from their disdain for the centralism that he represented. Chico tried to slowly reshape the political views of his blatantly profederalist constituents, and sought to buy more time by delaying the publication of the new centralist constitution. A week before his overthrow, Chico learned of Santa Anna's defeat in Texas and published a broadside condemning the "insolent colonists in the Department of Texas" while praising the patriotic *californios* who, Chico announced, would "cross the sea that separates them from the rest of their brothers to accompany them, if it be necessary, to prolong the war [against Texas] until they had taken the last life of the insolent insultors of the nation."[60] This was all bluster, as Chico privately admitted. Intensely isolated, Chico doubted the loyalty of the *californios* and lived in fear of a coup. At a social gathering, Chico learned, one of the legislators, José Castro, had not only offered a toast to federalism but also drank to the death of the defenders of centralism. Chico begged the government to remove him from "an office that I cannot endure."[61]

Before the central government had a chance to act, the *californios* did. As rebel forces gathered around Monterey, Chico fled on a vessel bound for Mexico on July 31. Just before leaving, the mercurial and embittered governor is said to have embraced an old Indian woman on the beach and sarcastically told her: "Of all the men in this country thou art the best."[62]

Among his last official acts, Chico turned California's civil and military commands over to a loyal career officer, Lt. Col. Nicolás Gutiérrez. Spanish-born Gutiérrez had come to Mexico as a child, fought against

Spain in the war for independence, and advanced slowly in a military career. In 1833 he came to California as a captain with General José Figueroa and served as military commander and briefly as governor in the interval between Figueroa's death in September 1835 and Chico's arrival in April 1836. With Chico gone, Gutiérrez became the new symbol of centralist oppression to the *californios*. Revolt broke out in the autumn when Gutiérrez refused to surrender civil control to the diputación. The legislators raised a small force of rancheros and enlisted the aid of a group of perhaps fifty American trappers, hunters, and sawyers led by Isaac Graham of Tennessee, and marched on Monterey. Although Gutiérrez had known for weeks that a revolt was in the offing, he had insufficient force to resist. With arms and munitions commandeered from one or more American vessels in the harbor, the insurgents both outarmed and outmanned the loyalists. On November 5, two days after it began, the revolt ended with no casualties. Gutiérrez and some thirty-five supporters surrendered and within a few days were put on a vessel which, they had been assured, was bound for Mexico. Instead, it left them and their wives and children stranded for weeks at Cabo San Lucas at the tip of Baja California. Meanwhile, the diputación met at Monterey on November 6 and proclaimed "Federation or Death! . . . we are free and federalists."[63]

Although Americans and their arms played a key, if not a decisive role in the insurgents' victory in California, Americans did not lead the revolt as they had in Texas. Some, like Abel Stearns, simply wanted a stable government that would maintain an orderly climate for business, while other foreigners fought as mercenaries with promises of rewards. Leadership fell to three *californios* of liberal persuasion, all from Monterey and all young as is usually the case with rebels. José Castro, about twenty-six-years-old and a member of the diputación, became interim governor in November 1836 and called for a congress to draft a new constitution. Juan Bautista Alvarado, a twenty-seven-year-old legislator and custom house inspector who had authored California's November 7 declaration of independence, became the first regular governor on December 7, 1836 by appointment of the diputación. Once the revolt succeeded, Alvarado won the support of his influential uncle, Mariano Guadalupe Vallejo, age twenty-eight, then serving at Sonoma as commander of the armed forces on California's northern border.[64]

Although these vigorous young federalists succeeded in establishing an independent government in Monterey and boldly urged the state of Sonora to revolt also, they could not persuade the residents of southern California to join them.[65] As in Texas, a consensus about a course of action toward the new centralist administration did not emerge quickly.

Opinion in California tended to divide along regional lines. In general, the area from Santa Barbara north supported Alvarado, while Los Angeles and San Diego remained loyal. Foreign residents of California divided along regional lines, too. Just as Alvarado had the aid of Isaac Graham's band of trappers, the southerners received help from a desultory group of trappers and horse thieves, led by Jean-Baptiste Chalifoux. As in the early stages of the Texas revolt, the great majority of California residents probably consisted of "neutrals who favored neither one side nor the other," as one historian has suggested.[66]

Políticos from the San Diego and Los Angeles areas did not support centralism so much as they opposed Alvarado and the north. As a rule, southerners shared the northerners' strong desire for home rule but feared an independent state dominated by the north. If Monterey retained the capital and customs house, it would also control major sources of political offices and public funds. If the south remained loyal to the centralists, on the other hand, its reward might include political and economic power. A federal decree published in California on January 4, 1836 by Governor Gutiérrez had offered that enticing possibility. It had ordered the transfer of the capital from Monterey to Los Angeles, but had not yet been implemented prior to the November revolt.[67] Thus, apparently fearing domination by the north more than they feared centralism, the southerners refused to recognize Alvarado's government. Alvarado managed to win the allegiance of Los Angeles through force of arms in the spring of 1837, but the *angelinos'* loyalty to the rebel cause evaporated when Alvarado withdrew his troops.[68]

Had Mexico sent an armed force to retake California, fear of a punitive expedition might have united northerners and southerners against the centralists, just as the expedition of General Cos galvanized opinion in Texas. Clearly, *californios* from both regions had developed an aversion to Mexicans from the "other shore," but the centralists could not raise enough money to outfit a military expedition to California at the same time that the festering Texas problem drained off resources to the northeastern frontier. While officials in Mexico City searched for cash, the military commander in Baja California, José Caballero, quietly sent Captain Andrés Castillero to Alta California with vague instructions to try to settle the issue. Castillero, who had served previously in Monterey under Gutiérrez and had also been expelled by Alvarado, made his way north, traveling at his own expense and accompanied by eight soldiers. By exaggerating the powers of his credentials, Castillero managed to place himself at the head of loyalist forces in southern California. In late June 1837, troops from the north and south gathered near Rincón Pass north of Los Angeles. A clash seemed imminent.[69]

Juan Bautista Alvarado. One of the young leaders of the November 1836 revolt, genial and bright Juan Bautista Alvarado (1809–82), served as rebel governor of California. After Mexico recognized him in 1838, he held the governorship legitimately until 1842. Following the Mexican-American War, Alvarado withdrew from politics, lived as a ranchero, and thought seriously about moving to Mexico. This likeness is probably from a daguerreotype taken in the early 1850s (courtesy California State Library, Sacramento).

Through extraordinary diplomacy, Castillero managed to avert bloodshed. Castillero met privately with Governor Alvarado and persuaded him to take an oath of allegiance to the new centralist constitution. Exactly what Castillero told the rebel governor can only be surmised, but he apparently convinced Alvarado that he had more choices than "federation or death," and that the Constitution of 1836 would provide ample autonomy for California. Alvarado emerged with the impression that the centralist constitution "leaves us nothing to be desired. It offers us the guarantees to which we aspire."[70] Castillero persuaded Alvarado that the new departmental system elevated California to an equal status with all other departments and that the Constitution guaranteed that only *californios* would be appointed as governor. Castillero also seems to have assured Alvarado that he would continue to hold the governorship.[71] Castillero's diplomacy not only ended Alvarado's revolt, but also eliminated the pretext for the southerners' quarrel with the north.

On a subsequent mission to Mexico, Castillero negotiated to keep Alvarado in the governorship. Under other circumstances, Alvarado might have been shot as a traitor, but it made sense for a weak centralist government that was still involved with Texas and saw war with France on the horizon, to soothe the former rebel governor and keep California at peace rather than squander precious resources by trying to punish Alvarado and his cohorts. Meanwhile, to loyalists in San Diego and Los Angeles, Castillero's support of Alvarado's governorship had seemed a perversion of justice and the north-south struggle resumed again. Fighting continued into the summer of 1838 until word came that the central government had recognized Alvarado, but separation from Mexico ceased to be an important issue for the time being.[72]

California, then, did not follow the example of the successful Texas rebellion. Perhaps, as one historian has suggested, Alvarado and other rebel leaders did not call for complete independence in 1836 because they feared that California would become a weak nation, quickly dominated by foreigners, especially Americans. Then, too, Mexico did not push the California rebels into declaring complete independence by meeting force with force, as it had in Texas. Instead, Mexico legitimized demands for home rule by recognizing Alvarado, who retained the governorship until 1842. Thus, as in 1831 when they ousted Governor Victoria, the *californios* had revolted again without retaliation from the central government and had won considerable autonomy without having to fight for complete independence. Just as success breeds success, rebellion breeds rebellion and became a part of the *californios'* political repertoire.

In 1837 fresh outbreaks against the centralist government occurred in New Mexico and Sonora. Although the area that is today's Arizona was not directly affected, the Sonora revolt had some of the same characteristics of the California and Texas rebellions and the chaos and destruction it caused radiated out to every corner of the department.

Revolt in Sonora began on the day after Christmas, 1837, when General José Urrea, military commander in the northwest, called for the reestablishment of the federalist system. Personal ambition probably motivated General Urrea, a forty-year-old veteran, born of a military family at the presidio of Tucson. Urrea had served as an officer in the Texas campaign the year before and won Santa Anna's unstinting praise. When he failed to win an expected appointment to the governorship of Sonora, however, Urrea called for rebellion. Whatever his personal motives, his plan to restore federalism found sympathizers throughout the state. In the months just prior to his revolt, disgruntled Sonoran politicians had petitioned the central government for greater home rule. Some had refused to obey centralist regulations or to send tax revenues to Mexico City on the grounds that they were needed more urgently on the frontier to fight Apaches. From the point of view of President Anastasio Bustamante, Sonora had been rebellious even before Urrea stepped forward to champion federalism.

Bustamante's stance probably pushed fence-sitters into the federalist camp, and Urrea met little opposition at first. In March 1838 a newly formed federalist legislature met at Arizpe. It elected Urrea governor and began to restructure state government. The legislators invited other states to join them and offered political asylum to such well-known liberals as Valentín Gómez Farías and the deposed governor of Coahuila y Texas, Agustín Viesca.

In sharp contrast to California and Texas, the Sonora rebellion against the central government was a domestic affair, with foreigners playing an inconsequential role. Although rumor had it that Urrea wanted complete independence for Sonora and a possible alliance with the United States, he never suggested this in any public statement. It seems likely that he viewed Americans with suspicion and that his ambition did not extend beyond the restoration of Sonora's autonomy within the Mexican federation.[73]

Federalism triumphed only briefly in Sonora. In mid-May 1838, the centralist-appointed governor, Manuel María Gándara, pronounced against Urrea and threw the state into a bloody six-month civil war. Gándara's forces, augmented by Indian conscripts, won; the centralists held control of Sonora's political see-saw for the next four years.[74]

Efforts to impose centralism on New Mexico precipitated a revolt there, too, in August 1837, but it differed from the rebellions in Texas, Sonora, and California in one important respect. The New Mexico elite did not openly lead this revolt although certain ricos, as rumor had it, may have secretly inspired and aided the rebels. The New Mexico revolt was apparently a spontaneous uprising of lower class New Mexicans, including Pueblo Indians. Class antagonism set New Mexico's revolt apart from contemporary rebellions along the northern frontier.

Perhaps because so few of their leaders were literate, the New Mexico insurgents' motives must be inferred from their actions and from fragments of evidence. A brief declaration of August 3, 1837, represents the only extant articulation of the insurrectos' program. Like the California and Texas rebels before them, the *nuevomexicanos* professed loyalty to the Mexican nation, but opposed the "departmental plan," "taxation," and "those who are trying to enforce it."[75] Events also made it clear that the rebels wanted greater autonomy at the village level. They termed their new government a "canton," inspired perhaps by Swiss federalism. Notwithstanding suspicions in Mexico at the time, it appears that Texans played no direct role in fomenting the New Mexico rebellion, although the indirect influence of the successful Texas model could hardly have gone unnoticed.[76]

The object of the rebels' disaffection was a centralist governor, Col. Albino Pérez. Pérez had come to New Mexico in 1835 with the dual appointment of jefe militar and jefe político. Like California's Governor Chico, Pérez arrived with a stigma. New Mexicans resented him as an outsider, insensitive to local problems, who held both military and civil power. They saw him as the embodiment of centralism, which in New Mexico came to be synonomous with a new system of direct taxation affecting all classes. In the view of one officer, a revolt against Pérez had seemed nearly inevitable.[77] Instead of fleeing a tense situation, however, as Chico did in California, Pérez tried to quash the rebellion and the consequences were fatal.

In early August 1837 Governor Pérez mustered the militia when he learned of an armed rebellion against authorities in Santa Cruz de la Cañada, some twenty-five miles north of Santa Fe. Pérez sallied forth to meet the rebels with a force comprised only of volunteers and Pueblo Indians; lack of funds had compelled him to disband the regular presidial forces. These volunteers served Pérez poorly. Near San Ildefonso Pueblo, on August 8, the insurrectos routed Pérez's troops, some of whom deserted to the other side. Pérez and his top aides fled toward Santa Fe, but rebels captured them the following day and brutally murdered Pérez, whom they beheaded, and ricos such as Miguel Sena, Prefect Ramón Abreú, and his brother, District Judge Santiago Abreú. The rebels then occupied the capital with reasonable order, dispelling fears that they would sack the city.[78]

With Santa Fe under their control, the insurrectos named as governor José Angel Gonzales, a modest buffalo hunter from Taos who displayed no hunger for power. The child of a Pueblo mother and a *genízaro* father, Gonzales was reportedly illiterate, although he could sign his own name. No one of his ancestry or class had occupied the governor's office before, nor would they do so again as long as New Mexico remained under Mexico. Gonzales and other leaders of the revolt attempted to broaden support and legitimize their government by convoking a *"junta popular,"* which met under the portal of the palacio in Santa Fe on August 27. This assembly expressed sorrow over the death of Pérez and agreed to send emissaries to Mexico City to assure the government of its perpetual loyalty and to present a list of grievances. The junta apparently agreed to support Gonzales as interim governor while it awaited some action from the central government.[79]

To this point, it appears that New Mexico ricos had neither supported nor condemned the revolt, although a few might have participated in the junta popular. In early September, however, the establishment turned against Gonzales and the rebels from two quarters.

First, a group of citizens from the southern communities between Albuquerque and Socorro, the area known as Río Abajo, met at Tomé on September 8 and pronounced against the rebel government and in favor of law and order and the 1836 Constitution. Subscribers to this "Plan de Tomé" condemned the Canton and announced that they would not recognize any authority except the prefect of Albuquerque. They, like the rebels, announced that they would await a decision from the central government as to who constituted the legitimate rulers of the department. The *río abajeños* also formed a "liberating force," putting former governor Manuel Armijo at its head, and making a local rico, Mariano Chávez, second-in-command. The Plan of Tomé urged Pueblo Indians to remain neutral and to "not involve themselves in the affairs of the Mexicans," and to govern themselves "until the supreme government appoints a governor."[80]

Second, at Santa Fe the following day, September 9, Comandante José Caballero also issued a pronunciamiento against the Canton. He announced that the regular army had "voluntarily reunited" and he called upon the citizens of Río Abajo to join him against the rebels from Río Arriba—the region roughly from Santa Fe northward. Both Caballero and Armijo intimated that the rebels planned to "plunder" the Río Abajo. A battle seemed to be shaping up not only between the north and south, as occurred in California, but also between the New Mexico oligarchy and the "inhuman and unbridled mob," as Caballero termed the rebels.[81] Under these circumstances, Anglo-American residents of New Mexico had no difficulty in choosing sides, and some responded generously to Armijo's request for donations to the cause of preserving order and protecting property.[82]

What caused opposition to the Canton to coalesce in early September, a full month after Pérez's demise, is not entirely clear. According to Manuel Armijo, the "patriots" who signed the Plan of Tomé had concluded that "it was necessary to decide to die with arms in hand, or to be cold victims of the fury of a disorderly insurrection that has no other goal . . . than killing and robbing."[83] Indeed, José Gonzales had little control over the rebels who had made him governor and a new wave of violence seemed imminent. A week before Armijo and Caballero made their proclamations, Padre Antonio José Martínez had fled Taos to Santa

Fe with alarming news. A group at Taos, who had conspired with the rebels from Santa Cruz de la Cañada, had determined to take revenge on the supporters of Pérez in the Taos area. Along with his brother and the subprefect, Padre Martínez fled for his life on September 2. A few days later, Martínez returned to Taos accompanied by Governor Gonzales, who restored order temporarily.[84]

During the time that Taos held the attention of Governor Gonzales, Caballero and the residents of Río Abajo issued their respective proclamations. When Gonzales returned to Santa Fe on September 11, he learned for the first time of the Plan of Tomé and swore to uphold it "with the greatest enthusiasm," although it meant the end of his brief tenure as governor.[85] Due, perhaps, to his cooperation, loyalist forces under Armijo and Caballero negotiated their way into Santa Fe on September 14, meeting no resistance.

Armijo moved next against rebels, led by Pablo Montoya of Taos, who still controlled Santa Cruz. After a brief skirmish, Armijo persuaded Montoya, whom he termed "comandante of the Canton," to sign a truce and to recognize him as head of government. Armijo apparently also prevailed upon Montoya to turn over four leaders of the August revolt as a sign of good faith: Juan José Esquibel, Juan Vigil, Desiderio Montoya, and Antonio Aban Montoya. Armijo had these four taken to Santa Fe and thrown into the *calabozo*. Peace seemed restored, but it was an illusion.

Throughout the autumn and early winter, revolt smoldered in the mountain villages north of Santa Fe. Refugees from outlying areas moved into the capital for safety.[86] On January 19, 1838, Armijo received word that one Antonio Vigil was raising a force to retake Santa Fe and free the four prisoners. Vigil had issued a crudely written circular denouncing Armijo as a usurper and suggesting that José Gonzales, who had remained free, was still the people's choice for governor. Armijo responded by demanding that the rebels disband and that Vigil and Gonzales surrender or he would execute the prisoners. When Vigil did not reply, Armijo had the four rebel leaders decapitated on the morning of January 24. Once again Armijo led forces north, augmented this time by recently arrived government troops from Chihuahua. The loyalists routed the insurrectos in furious fighting in a mountain pass to the east of Santa Cruz and captured Gonzales who, according to tradition, was executed in summary fashion at Armijo's command after being confessed by Padre Martínez.[87]

Armijo finally crushed the revolt, but he did not deal with the profound discontent that had nourished it. As in Texas, California, and Sonora, the centralist system sparked the rebellion in New Mexico, but its underlying causes were economic. The inequities of militia service, which exacerbated the plight of lower class *nuevomexicanos*, explain part of their resentment toward the ricos. Six months before the revolt broke out, Pablo Salazar, one of the signers of the Plan of Tomé, complained to Governor Pérez about the use of "unfortunate men, dead of hunger" to fight Indians. These men, Salazar wrote, felt they were "serving the ricos" without pay or food, and that they were mistreated besides. He mentioned a recent campaign against Navajos on the Pecos River in which "the ricos, as on similar occasions, served no other function than criticizing the conduct of those they commanded."[88] Little wonder that some of the militia deserted Pérez, or that the New Mexico rebellion took on aspects of class warfare. Hence, Governor Armijo's explanation of the rebels' goals, which may be exaggerated, seems plausible. He claimed that the insurgents wanted complete independence from Mexico and that they intended to form an alliance "with the savage tribes, who are on their level, making a common cause of their mutual interests."[89]

In general, the New Mexico upper class displayed little understanding of the grievances of the pobres. Governor Armijo, for example, described the rebels as "perverse men." He saw them as "agitators," who aroused ignorant villagers as well as the ordinarily gentle Pueblos with a "thousand absurdities," such as the new government's wish to take half of everything they owned, "even their children."[90] Similarly, Padre Martínez dismissed the rebels as people of "turbulent character," and Santa Cruz itself, Martínez said, "always has been the sewer of New Mexico."[91] Martínez, who found himself surrounded by "tenacious" rebels who ignored his warnings of excommunication and threatened to kill him if he did not stop charging fees for baptism, marriage, and burial, should have understood better than most the desperate economic conditions that lay beneath the insurrectos' "turbulent character."[92]

Although much remains murky about the motives of the insurgents, they clearly were not rebels without a cause. As one American merchant in New Mexico understood it, the 1837 revolt "had its origin without any doubt in the publics' poverty. . . . "[93] A new system of taxation, coupled with a sense that the high-salaried centralist administrators would not use funds wisely, constitute the most convincing contemporary explanations for the revolt.[94]

Thus, the nature and direction of the revolts of the mid-1830s varied according to local circumstances and the response of the central government. In California, Sonora, and New Mexico, revolts against centralism became complicated by local power struggles and did not end with complete separation from Mexico, nor did that seem a key goal of the rebels. In Texas, on the other hand, the threat of military occupation by centralist forces united a substantial portion of the populace and pushed that American-dominated area toward independence.

During the last decade of the Mexican era, the example of the successful Texas revolt, and the activities of the Americans who aided it, hung like a dark cloud over New Mexico, California, and other departments in the Mexican North where federalism remained popular. Officials in Mexico City feared that seditious frontiersmen would ally themselves with Americans or Texans who, as General José Urrea of Sonora wrote, "are one and the same to me."[95] These were not idle fears.

In 1839 a federalist from Tamaulipas, Antonio Canales, gathered men and materials in Texas to lead a revolt against the centralist government in the name of the Constitution of 1824. In January 1840, Canales and federalist leaders from Nuevo León and Coahuila, as well as Tamaulipas, met at Laredo, declared independence, and established a provisional government. Defeated in March 1840 by centralist forces, leaders of this so-called Republic of the Rio Grande retreated into Texas to regroup and augment their army with more Texas volunteers. In June, the federalists used Texas as a springboard to launch another invasion, but were beaten back again. Throughout this struggle, the Texas Republic offered only unofficial aid to the rebels and remained officially neutral to avoid offending the Mexican government whose recognition it sought. Had more help been forthcoming, the federalists might have carved another Texas out of northeastern Mexico.[96]

At the same time that Texans kept the pot of rebellion simmering south of the Rio Grande, they also tried to stir up a revolt in neighboring New Mexico. The Republic of Texas claimed that its boundaries extended to the Rio Grande, following the river north into present Colorado and including New Mexican communities such as Santa Fe and Taos that stood on the east side of the river. In moments of extreme braggadocio, some Texans claimed that their young Republic embraced everything to the Pacific, including Sonora and California, but Texans did more than boast.

In the summer of 1840, Texas agents infiltrated New Mexico with a message from President Mirabeau Buonaparte Lamar welcoming New Mexicans as "fellow citizens, members of our young Republic" and inviting them to share "in all our blessings."[97] New Mexico officials arrested two of the Texas agents for trying to start a revolt and accused Texans of two attempts on the life of Governor Manuel Armijo. Lamar apparently believed that popular sentiment in New Mexico favored Texas, for the next year he sent a party of over 300 armed men across the plains to assert Texas jurisdiction over New Mexico. The ostensible purpose of this "Texan Santa Fe Expedition," as it has come to be known, was to open a wagon road from Austin to Santa Fe to promote trade, but its leaders carried clear instructions to seize "all public property," including the custom house and the archives, and to form a new government consisting of cooperative local residents. New Mexicans would be permitted to send representatives to the Texas Congress. The instructions also charged the members of the expedition to "try all gentle means before resorting to force." If "the mass of the people" opposed joining Texas, then force was to be avoided, but "if the people are with you, or indiferent [*sic*]," then force could be used against government troops.[98]

Warned of the Texans' intent, Governor Armijo easily forced the surrender of the weary, hungry, and thirsty Texans who had become lost along the way. *Nuevomexicanos* took delight in their victory. In a folk play dramatizing their triumph, written soon afterward, one of the characters exclaims with pride: "Whenever you hear [the New Mexicans] bark at foreigners they always bite them."[99] The Texas Republic failed to export its rebellion, but it did engender a strong and enduring anti-Texas sentiment in New Mexico.

Meanwhile, from 1836 until the Texas issue helped bring on the war with the United States, Mexico refused to recognize Texas independence. Influential Mexicans feared that the loss of Texas would represent the first step toward the loss of other northern provinces, and perhaps the American conquest of all of Mexico. The rapacious norteamericanos, it was argued, had to be stopped in Texas or they would impose an alien religion, language, and culture on Mexico. Mexicans, as a Chihuahua newspaper put it, would be "sold as beasts" because "their color was not as white as that of the conquerors."[100]

Obsessed by the desire to regain Texas, and paralyzed by political upheaval and economic crises, the central government seemed unable to do more than act as a bystander as American influence grew in New Mexico and California. Even as American settlers crossed the Rockies into California and talked openly of replaying "the Texas game," the government seemed powerless to reverse the process. Nor could the centralists begin to remedy the political, economic, military, and social ills that gripped the frontier and contributed to the revolts of the mid-1830s. Separatism seemed increasingly attractive to frontiersmen whose government had failed to respond effectively to their needs. The more officials insisted on making key political decisions in Mexico City, the clearer it became to many pobladores that they were responsible for their own futures.

One Mexico City newspaper in 1842 offered the diagnosis that the

Manuel Armijo. Born in Albuquerque to a well-to-do family, Manuel Armijo (ca. 1793–1853) was the most important New Mexico politician of his day. He served a term as governor from 1827–29, then came into power for another seven years after crushing the Santa Cruz rebels in 1837. He was governor again on the eve of the Mexican-American War, when he fled to Mexico. He is shown here in dress uniform, wearing the cross of honor given to him by President Santa Anna and a sword presented by the people of Chihuahua for his role in defeating the Texans in 1841. This pastel was apparently drawn by Alfred S. Waugh in 1846 (courtesy, Museum of New Mexico, Santa Fe).

centralist system of government itself caused problems on the frontier. Instead of "weakening departments" by increasing central control, the editors argued, the government should give frontiersmen greater autonomy and stop meddling in their affairs. This would decrease the frontiersmen's resentment, strengthen their loyalty to the nation, and lessen their temptation to submit to the Americans.[101] The tendency toward centralizing control in Mexico City continued in the early 1840s, however, and revolts broke out again in California and Sonora.

California enjoyed de facto autonomy under its native-born rebel governor, Juan Bautista Alvarado, until 1842 when the centralists appointed an outsider as governor again. The *californios* reacted as they had before. The new governor, an affable veteran of the Texas campaign, Brig. Gen. Manuel Micheltorena, arrived in California in August 1842 with a three-hundred-man army composed mostly of convicts accompanied by their women. The behavior of these "cholos" became the pretext for another insurrection. Once again, men on horseback carried rumors of impending revolt from rancho to rancho and town to town, and they soon reached the governor's ears.[102]

Like his Mexican-appointed predecessor, Micheltorena despaired. He sent Manuel Castañares, a recent immigrant from Puebla, to Mexico City for military aid, but Castañares apparently also carried an alternative recommendation. If Mexico could not defend California properly, Micheltorena suggested that California be ceded to British creditors as the only means of "preventing it from being overrun by the North Americans, and declared independent by them and the native Californians."[103] Castañares warned the government that if it did not send aid, the result would be "a bloody revolution, a desperate recourse, it is true, but the only one that remains to those who have received from Mexico nothing more than an intolerable tutelage."[104]

Castañares and Micheltorena had sized up separatist sentiment in California accurately. In August 1844 a group of *californios* met secretly with British vice consul James Forbes in Monterey and told him they were ready to drive Micheltorena out of California, declare independence, and ask for British protection. British agents had no authorization to support such a plan, but the revolt went on without them. It began in the north in November 1844 and ended on a battlefield at Cahuenga Pass, north of Los Angeles. There, on February 20, 1845 Micheltorena signed a treaty agreeing to leave California and take the despised cholos with him. Once again, as in 1836, foreign residents of California, especially Americans, could be found on both sides, but on this occasion they did not play a determining role.[105]

The *californios* did not issue a conditional declaration of independence as they did in 1836, but Mexico's hold on the department remained tenuous. No Mexican-appointed governor replaced Micheltorena. Pío Pico of San Diego, senior member of the legislature, became governor and made Los Angeles his capital. José Castro of Monterey, who had led the revolt against Micheltorena, became military commander and remained in the north where he controlled the customs house.

Alta California probably would have separated entirely from Mexico following Micheltorena's overthrow because substantial sentiment for such a move existed among her leading families, but two circumstances militated against it. First, Mexico had outfitted a large military expedition to defend California from the imminent war with the United States, and Castro and others feared reprisals from Mexico. Second, many *californios* believed the United States would seize the province if it became independent. Although some Americans, such as Dr. John Marsh, flattered themselves with the belief that the *californios* "would be glad to come under the American government,"[106] evidence suggests that most California leaders preferred complete independence, or else independence as a protectorate of France or Great Britain. A distinct minority favored United States annexation.[107] The British and French governments never offered their protection, however, so California retained its uneasy alliance with Mexico until the United States invasion.

Even had Britain or France provided an alternative, it seems unlikely that the faction-ridden *californios* could have agreed on a course of action. As occurred in the aftermath of the 1836 revolt, north and south failed to cooperate. Pico and Castro distrusted one another and, in effect, the department had two rival governments in its last days as a Mexican province. In early June of 1846, just a month before American forces seized Monterey, California stood on the brink of another civil war with Pico planning a military invasion of the north to depose Castro.[108]

As war approached with the United States, the situation in Sonora was also chaotic, but far more destructive and bloody. Santa Anna's appointment in 1842 of his nominally federalist crony, José Urrea, as governor, threw the state into four more years of civil war. Intensely bitter, due less to the issues of centralism and federalism than to a personal rivalry between Urrea and former centralist governor Manuel María Gándara, the civil war ground on until Urrea and the federalists gained control of the ravaged state early in 1846.[109]

Unlike California and Sonora, New Mexico remained nominally obedient to the centralist government until the American conquest, but the New Mexico officials continued to display independence and the lower class continued to show signs of disloyalty. When Texans began making overtures to New Mexico in 1840, for example, Governor Armijo reported that "the people will not defend themselves because they have expressed a desire to join the Texans in order that they may secure better conditions."[110] Armijo thought that many New Mexicans saw the end of Mexican rule as a way of getting out of debt. He may have exaggerated the extent of potential sedition in order to get much-needed military aid, but he followed instructions from the Minister of War to intercept the Texans at a distance from the settlements so they would not receive help from sympathetic New Mexicans.[111]

Meanwhile, disillusioned at what they perceived as neglect and mismanagement by the central government, New Mexico officials promoted trade, shored up defenses against Indians, and accommodated foreigners in ways that sometimes violated governmental directives and suggested little affinity for the centralist regime. On January 1, 1844, when the New Mexico Assembly held its first meeting under General Santa Anna's highly centralized *Bases Orgánicas* of 1843, it issued an equivocal statement of loyalty: "Intimately united with the Mexican Republic we continue to be free and independent."[112] Mariano Chávez, President of the Assembly, pledged New Mexico's allegiance to Santa Anna, but imposed a thinly veiled condition. Neglect had weakened ties between the departments and the central government, Chávez wrote, and new ties "cannot be established without our sustained, mutually reciprocal services." Chávez, a wealthy landowner and merchant from Río Abajo, cited Tocqueville: "there are certain necessities of the people that to disregard a single one will cause the ruin of empires and republics."[113]

Put less obliquely, if Santa Anna wanted the cooperation of New Mexicans, he had to give something positive in return. What New Mexico got instead was another outsider to lead them. General Mariano Martínez assumed the governorship on May 15, 1844. When his term ended less than a year later, in February 1845, he had won a reputation for arbitrariness and incompetence. His subjects would have rebelled, according to Donaciano Vigil, "if his administration had lasted a bit longer."[114] Circumstances surrounding Martínez's withdrawal from the governorship are not entirely clear, but his departure apparently spared him the same fate that befell Micheltorena in California and Urrea in Sonora.

New Mexicans returned to governing themselves and Manuel Armijo became governor again in November 1845, ruling the province more independently than ever before. That winter, rumors that Mexico had agreed to sell New Mexico to the United States weakened still further the province's faith in the central government. The source of the rumor may have been a garbled report of Mexico's reaction to John Slidell, an

American envoy sent to Mexico City in November 1845 with instructions to purchase both New Mexico and California. Like the *californios*, most *nuevomexicanos* displayed no enthusiasm about annexation by the United States. Some of New Mexico's leading citizens drafted a protest in late December 1845, denying Mexico's right to sell the province and swearing to defend it from the United States. The authors of this document vowed to form a separate nation, independent of both Mexico and the United States. Called the República Mexicana del Norte, this new nation would have a popular, representative government and its boundaries would extend northward from Chihuahua to the Arkansas River and to Oregon, and westward to the Colorado River.[115]

New Mexicans apparently did not know that their government had refused to deal with Slidell—a step that infuriated the American president and brought the two nations one step closer to war. Isolated from the rest of Mexico in the chaos preceding the war, *nuevomexicanos* knew that Mexico and the United States had broken relations over the annexation of Texas in March 1845, and that Mexico had withdrawn its minister to Washington, Juan Almonte. New Mexicans did not learn, however, that their nation had gone to war with the United States until the summer of 1846 when reports reached Santa Fe of an American army marching westward over the plains.[116]

Californios, too, knew that war seemed likely, but did not learn of its outbreak until American forces arrived. Thus, the hopes of separatists, who wanted to create an independent California or an independent New Mexico or to tie their fortunes to a power other than the United States, were dashed in the fateful summer of 1846.

13

The Mexican Frontier in Perspective

What will be the fate of those unfortunate Mexicans who live amidst barbarians without a hope of civilization?—Juan N. Almonte, *Texas, 1834*

It is hoped that within two or three generations this part of the Mexican Republic—richer, freer, and more enlightened than all the rest—will serve as an example. . . . —Lorenzo de Zavala, *writing about Texas, 1831*

In Monterey Bay on July 7, 1846, as the sun rose over the mountains to the east, men from three United States warships stepped into a small boat and rowed ashore to demand the surrender of the capital of Alta California. California officials offered no resistance. By late morning, 200 American sailors and marines had landed and assembled in front of the customs house where they listened to a proclamation drafted by their commodore, John D. Sloat, announcing the annexation of California. Amidst cheers, several American sailors hoisted the flag of the United States over the customs house.

Six weeks later, on August 18, as the sun broke through the clouds in mid-afternoon after a day of rain, Gen. Stephen W. Kearny led his exhausted troops into Santa Fe where they assembled in the plaza. They had traveled twenty-nine miles that day, ending a two-month, 850-mile march from Fort Leavenworth, Kansas, over the Santa Fe Trail. To the sound of drums, bugles, and a thirteen-gun salute, the invaders raised their flag over the governor's palace on a makeshift pole, and Kearny announced the annexation of New Mexico. Like Monterey, Santa Fe fell without resistance.[1]

These extraordinary events were a byproduct as well as a cause of the war with Mexico that the United States had declared in May 1846. Following the annexation of Texas in March 1845, America's newly elected president, James K. Polk, had embarked on what one historian has aptly termed "a policy based on bluff and a show of force" in order to acquire the rest of the Mexican Far North as well as Oregon.[2] The dispute with the British over Oregon ended peacefully, but when Mexico refused to sell New Mexico and California, Polk improvised a series of schemes designed to gain them by other means. To demonstrate his resolve and American firmness of purpose, Polk provoked what he hoped would be a short military engagement. A minor skirmish on the Rio Grande in April 1846 escalated beyond Polk's wishes into a full-fledged war. Contemptuous of Mexico, Polk had underestimated that nation's will to resist further encroachment from the United States. American forces won a stunning series of battles, but Mexican officials would not come to the bargaining table and the war dragged on.

Not until September 16, 1847, when American forces under Gen. Winfield Scott captured Mexico City in some of the war's bloodiest engagements, did the major fighting stop. War officially ended when reluctant Mexican negotiators signed a treaty on February 2, 1848, just outside Mexico City at Guadalupe Hidalgo. At the nation's most venerated shrine, where the Virgin Mary is said to have appeared in 1531, Mexico agreed to cede its far northern frontier—one-third of its territory, or a half counting Texas—to the United States. Although Polk was displeased that the United States did not get more of Mexico, and a vocal group of American journalists and congressmen urged that the government reject the agreement and take *all* of Mexico, the United States Senate approved the Treaty of Guadalupe Hidalgo in May 1848.

The Treaty pushed Texas beyond the Nueces River, its historic boundary. The Rio Grande became the new international border, from the Gulf of Mexico to a point eight miles north of El Paso. From El Paso, a line following the boundary between New Mexico and Chihuahua was to run to the headwaters of the Gila then down the Gila to the Colorado River. Mexico retained Tucson and other settlements in what is today southern Arizona, whose inhabitants had offered no resistance to American forces in 1846. The new boundary, however, did not meet demands in the United States for a level, all-weather route to the Pacific, where the discovery of gold in 1848 had attracted Easterners by the thousands. In 1853 the United States minister to Mexico, James Gadsden, a railroad executive from South Carolina, negotiated the purchase of lands south of the Gila to the present United States-Mexican border from a government desperate for cash, headed again by the opportunistic Antonio

López de Santa Anna. With the ratification of the Gadsden Purchase by the United States Senate in 1854, the expansion of the American frontier and the retreat of the Mexican frontier was complete.[3]

As in 1821, when they became Mexican subjects, pobladores in the Mexican Far North had little control over decisions, made in distant capitals, that changed their lives. Even the most ardent Mexican patriots lacked means to resist effectively their conquerors. Mexican military forces in California were pitifully inadequate. Governor Pío Pico fled to Mexico to get aid, but could not get even the attention of his government, which had grown more chaotic in war than it had been in peace. In New Mexico, whose leaders differed over the wisdom of resistance and which faced annihilation from Utes and Navajos in 1846 as well as conquest by the United States, Governor Manuel Armijo judged the situation hopeless and abandoned all defenses. Armijo's decision enabled American forces to occupy New Mexico without immediate resistance, for as one keen American observer noted, the *nuevomexicanos* did not capitulate to the United States "from fear of our power or love for our institutions."[4] Following the initial American occupation, organized resistance and sporadic guerrilla activity broke out in both California and New Mexico, caused in part by the behavior of the conquering forces. The *californios* won two initial military skirmishes, but they and the *nuevomexicanos* soon lost the war. Although rumors of plots against the United States continued in both areas, American forces seemed in complete control by the end of January 1847. No further outbreaks occurred.

The American conquest of the Mexican Far North met greater resistance than some writers have suggested, but it was relatively quick. It seems likely that a significant percentage of the pobladores welcomed the Americans and collaborated with them. Many did so reluctantly. "Do not find it strange if there has been no manifestation of joy and enthusiasm in seeing this city occupied by your military forces," New Mexico's highest ranking official, Juan Bautista Vigil, told General Kearny. "The power of the Mexican Republic is dead. No matter what her condition, [Mexico] was our mother. What child will not shed abundant tears at the tomb of his parents?"[5] Julio Carrillo of California later wrote in a similar vein: "I admit that the general government of Mexico was like a very mean step-mother to us . . . but in my estimation this was no reason why we should have renounced our birthrights."[6]

Certainly, many pobladores regarded the continuation of Mexican rule with an ambivalence that sapped their enthusiasm for resisting the Americans. Angustias de la Guerra, then a thirty-one-year-old Santa Barbara housewife, later recalled, "the conquest of California did not bother the Californians, least of all the women. . . . California was on the road to the most complete ruin."[7] In their reluctance to fight against the Americans, the frontiersmen reflected an attitude that was widespread throughout Mexico and explains, in part, the American victory. As one liberal pamphleteer stated: "If the laboring classes of any other nation saw themselves oppressed to the extent of ours they would not have been content merely to show indifference, but would have joined the invading army to avenge themselves. . . . "[8]

Ambivalence toward Mexico on the part of the frontiersmen is best understood in light of the events of the previous quarter-century. As we have seen, Mexico had tried to pull the Far North tightly to the center of the nation by building strong political, ecclesiastical, military, economic, and demographic links, but the center did not hold. The disaffected periphery began to drift away. Mexico's failure to establish viable political institutions in the north made frontiersmen wonder about the government's ability to meet their region's needs, and Mexico's instability raised serious questions about the legitimacy of the central government. The collapse of the missions and the failure of the Church in Mexico to replace the Franciscans with an adequate number of secular priests not only left a spiritual void in the lives of many frontiersmen, but also seemed a clear sign of neglect. The pathetic condition of the presidial system also indicated to frontiersmen that the central government had abandoned the frontier. So, too, did the government's failure to subsidize colonization by Mexicans, to integrate the frontier into the nation's economy, or to take into account the special needs of frontier economic life.

The neglect that frontiersmen perceived from Mexico contrasted with the warm interest that foreigners, especially Americans, demonstrated toward the region. Some acquired land, ranched or farmed, married, and became intimately involved in all aspects of frontier life. Of greatest significance, American and Mexican merchants began to turn frontier commerce away from Mexico and toward the United States. The American frontier had literally spilled over onto the Mexican frontier and forged new economic, demographic, and cultural links to the United States. America's political incorporation of the Mexican frontier between 1845 and 1854 represented the culmination of a process as much as it did as the inauguration of a new era.

Mexico's failure to hold its far northern frontier stands in sharp contrast to America's success at extending its frontier into the Far West. Mexico had lost half of its land mass by the mid-nineteenth century at the same time that the United States, at Mexico's expense, had pushed its boundaries beyond the vague limits of the Louisiana Purchase to the

Pacific. The United States not only benefited from this imperialistic expansion, but many historians are convinced that the very process of settling new lands had a salubrious effect on American character and institutions. Historian Frederick Jackson Turner first suggested this in 1893 in his enduring and much-disputed address on "The Significance of the Frontier in American History."[9] Turner argued that the frontier made Americans more democratic, nationalistic, egalitarian, self-reliant, individualistic, mobile, hardworking, and inventive. Turner exaggerated, oversimplified, and made statements that do not hold up under modern scientific scrutiny, but in a modified and refined form, Turner's thesis remains a widely accepted and influential key to understanding America's past and present. Although historians still disagree about the extent of the frontier's influence, few would claim that the frontier played no role at all in shaping the American character.[10] On the other hand, no historian has argued that Mexico's far northern frontier, from California to Texas, has had any effect, negative or positive, on Mexican character or institutions.

Part of the explanation for this apparent anomaly lies in understanding that the frontier is a social environment and not simply a physical or geographical environment. As people migrate and as international borders change, so do frontiers, even though the physical environment might remain constant. A frontier is best understood as a social phenomenon, representing an interaction between man, his institutions, and the physical and spatial environments of an area of low population density where two cultures or two nations meet. Frontiers usually have two sides, both of them human. The notion of a society coming into contact with "wilderness" in a frontier zone, "where the absence of man . . . is assumed," is decidedly ethnocentric.[11] People nearly always utilize wilderness, although they might do so by seasonal hunting or gathering; the lack of cultivation and relatively low land-man ratio may give agrarian peoples the illusion of "the absence of man."

Thus, man generally interacts with man as well as with the environment in frontier zones, and such interactions contain so many variables, including the historical moment, that the result is always unique. Turner implied, and Ray Allen Billington, the most eloquent analyst and explicator of the Turner thesis, has argued explicitly that the American frontier was "virtually unique" in its combination of opportunity for individual self-advancement, abundant resources, and the receptivity of American frontiersmen to those special circumstances.[12] Thus, it makes little sense to presume that the frontier experience would affect Mexican settlers in the same way that it affected Americans. Mexicans brought a different culture onto their frontier and, as Billington has explained, "individuals of different backgrounds will respond in different ways to identical physical environments."[13] Turner's detractors as well as his defenders seem to agree that man and his institutions have shaped frontiers more than frontiers have shaped man. "Let no one . . . be misled," Billington has urged,

> into believing that the frontier could affect major changes in either the personalities or the behavioral patterns of frontiers-men. As in human behavior today, the bulk of the customs and beliefs of the pioneers were transmitted, and were only slightly modified by the changing culture in which they lived.[14]

Many writers have explained in detail those differences in the contents of the cultural baggage which Englishmen and Spaniards brought to the New World.[15] For our purposes it will suffice to remember that by 1821 a variety of forces had etched features in the Hispanic frontier in North America which set it distinctly apart from its younger Anglo-American counterpart. Aridity dictated that people live in adobes instead of log cabins and that they travel on horseback rather than by canoe. The geopolitical goals of the Spanish Crown, rather than individual initiative, usually determined where people would settle. Instead of "the continually advancing frontier line" that Turner thought he saw in the American West, the North of New Spain leapfrogged well beyond settled areas.[16] Under both Spain and Mexico, the frontier did not serve as a "safety valve" for the discontented or unemployed, to use Turner's famous term and most disputed concept. Mexico and Spain had to lure settlers with tangible rewards to move beyond the edges of civilization, and the number of Spanish-speaking peoples in New Spain and Mexico reach a point that required a "safety valve." Partly because of their minority position as well as because of attitudes brought from the Old World, Hispanos tried to assimilate indigenous Americans rather than push them back or annihilate them. In the useful terms of geographer Marvin Mikesell, the Hispanic frontier became a "frontier of inclusion" in contrast to the "frontier of exclusion" created by Anglo-Americans.[17]

The frontier and its indigenous peoples modified Hispanic society, of course, so that it never became a carbon copy of society in central Mexico any more than Mexico became a copy of Spain. The low population and relative poverty of the frontier simply could not support elaborate institutions and a complex hierarchical society. Historians and anthropologists have described society on New Spain's far northern frontier as more informal, democratic, self-reliant, and egalitarian than that of the core, and contemporaries took a similar view. Zebulon Pike, who visited

New Mexico in 1807, characterized its inhabitants as "the bravest and most hardy subjects in New Spain," because constant warfare with Indians had toughened them and the lack of easy wealth from gold and silver had made them "laborious."[18] Similarly, Miguel Ramos Arizpe, delegate from Coahuila to the 1812 Spanish Cortes, described the frontiersmen in the kind of reverential terms that Jeffersonians used for the American yeoman farmer. Ramos Arizpe saw frontiersmen as honest, hardworking farmers and tough, stoic Indian fighters who "are truly inflexible to intrigue, virtuously steadfast, haters of tyranny and disorder, justly devoted to true liberty and . . . moral and political virtues."[19]

Although frontier conditions modified Hispanic and Anglo-American society in ways that seem similar on the surface, New Spain's Far North differed in fundamental ways from Turner's conception of the American West. Rather than evolutionary development and "successive waves" of pioneering types, from traders to cattlemen to farmers that Turner saw in the American West, portions of the far northern frontier of New Spain developed full blown, reflecting a strong Hispanic urban tradition.[20] Government expeditions, which included clerics and soldiers as well as ranchers, farmers, and artisans, often traveled north from Mexico in a body to found full-fledged communities in the wilderness. These towns and villages were not democratic, and the vecinos had little opportunity to exercise initiative because of governmental restrictions on their economic lives, as we have seen. They could not open new areas to ranching or farming, or even travel from town to town, without official permits. Thus, the frontier of New Spain prior to 1821 was not an area of "unrivaled opportunity for *individual* self-advancement," as Billington has characterized the American frontier, and so lacked one of the essential ingredients that both leavened the American frontier and gave it a special flavor.[21]

Dramatic changes after 1821 began to alter the social environment of the Mexican frontier in ways that provided greater opportunities for individuals. The impulse for change came from two sources beyond the frontier. First, the Mexican frontier began to respond to social and institutional change in the nation as a whole. Second, what had been essentially a frontier zone where Hispanos met Indians and Frenchmen, became increasingly a zone where Mexicans also encountered North Americans.

Institutional change, imposed from the outside, brought greater political democracy to the frontier.[22] It gave local elites a taste of political power and whetted their appetites for more. The relaxation of commercial restrictions and greater access to cheap land, capital, and manufactured goods provided new economic opportunities and routes for upward social mobility for some of the pobladores and immigrants alike, while necessarily diminishing the egalitarianism that had characterized frontier society under Spain. Even spatial mobility increased in the Mexican era as regulations restricting the gente de razón from traveling without a permit were lifted.

The frontiersmen, however, clearly were not passive instruments waiting to be played upon by outsiders. They also called their own tune. When the central government adopted measures or sent officials who seemed to threaten the pobladores' new political or economic self-interest, they seized the initiative and stretched, bent, or broke the law (a long-standing Hispanic tradition). Tension between the frontier and the metropolis extended into nearly every aspect of life. Some New Mexicans even defied the spiritual authority of bishops and priests to embrace practices of the Penitentes.

The poverty of the pobladores probably encouraged them to act pragmatically, putting aside principles, national interest, and the law when these did not serve their interests. More important, the frontiersmen's isolation and distance from the nation's core assured them a measure of independence and protection from retaliation by the central government. The Church and the military, the principal guardians of tradition elsewhere in Mexico, were too weak in the Far North to enforce either the status quo or the will of the central government. By the same token, distance and the relative weakness of those conservative institutions seem to have left frontier society more fluid and open to new ideas, new people, and new initiatives. Like border peoples elsewhere, the pobladores fit anthropologist Owen Lattimore's description of a "marginal" people of "ambivalent loyalties," whose institutions, society, and culture never mirrored the nation's core, but held instead refracted images, altered by the prism of frontier realities.[23] Or, applying historian Jerome Steffen's distinction, the Mexican frontier was "insular" rather than "cosmopolitan." Insular frontiers, Steffen argues, have weak links to the nation's core. They are more profoundly influenced by the "indigenous environment" and change in more fundamental ways than do cosmopolitan frontiers.[24]

A complex interplay of interior and exterior forces, then, modified Mexican frontier society in the Mexican era, making it more democratic, fluid, and dynamic than that of central Mexico. As we have seen, however, variations in the social and physical environment and relative distance from the metropolis prevented those forces from interacting uniformly across the entire northern frontier. In New Mexico alone, different ecological zones had a powerful influence in shaping, but not determining, institutions. In the mountain villages of Río Arriba north of Santa Fe, the combination of isolation, marginal and scarce farmland,

and the need to share water in an arid environment, intensified an Iberian tradition of communal grazing lands, woodlands, and water. In addition, many pobladores in Río Arriba privately owned small plots of land. A day's journey to the south, communal traditions disintegrated in a different environment. Below Santa Fe, the widening floodplain of the Rio Grande and the adjacent high plains offered more farmland and rangeland than in Río Arriba, and the greater access of this region to the outside world lessened the need for self-sufficiency and cooperation. Río Abajo became the stronghold of large, privately held estates in contrast to northern New Mexico's communal villages.[25]

If different physical environments encouraged variations in frontier institutions and society, so did the human environment. In California, for example, a benign climate, cheap Indian labor, and new markets for hides and tallow, may have worked against such perceived "frontier virtues" as independence, resourcefulness, self-sufficiency, and hard work, as historian C. Alan Hutchinson has suggested.[26] In contrast, most of the pobladores elsewhere on the frontier worked with their own hands and had no large pool of cheap labor or easy access to international markets.

Thus, discrete frontiers, with their own dynamics and texture, existed within the larger Mexican frontier. On one level, for example, much of Mexico's Far North constituted a frontier with the United States and many of the gente de razón entered into informal arrangements with Americans to smuggle contraband and to violate government regulations. Among the pobladores who engaged in this clandestine commerce were government officials, well-to-do merchants, and clerics, some of whom continued to trade with the Americans even as Mexico and the United States prepared to go to war. Meanwhile, a similar scenario played at a lower level of frontier society, but the cast of characters was different. *Nuevomexicanos* in the isolated villages of Río Arriba rarely saw Americans, but shared a frontier zone with nomadic tribes with whom they traded illegally, in defiance of orders from Santa Fe. Trade went on between the pobladores of Río Arriba and groups of Navajos, Utes, and Comanches, even while New Mexico was ostensibly at war with these Indian "nations."[27] In Arizona and Texas, pobladores also entered into informal, illegal, but mutually beneficial arrangements with nomadic Indians with whom they were officially at war.[28]

If frontier society in general had become "ambivalent" or "marginal" in respect to Mexico, that same process seems to have repeated itself among certain elements within the frontier who demonstrated ambivalence toward the local authorities. Hints of this appear everywhere, but it is perhaps clearest in New Mexico, where local oligarchs increasingly asserted their independence of Mexico City while worrying at the same time about the loyalty of villagers in Río Arriba who they feared would enter into an alliance with Indians and become independent of Santa Fe. Frontiers, then, existed within frontiers and an appreciation of the complexity of the general must include an understanding of the particular.

Taking local variations into account, it seems clear that the overall tendency in the Mexican era was to bring the Mexican frontier closer to the American frontier, not only physically, but also in the sense that northern Mexico's political institutions were becoming more representative, its economic structure more capitalistic, its settlers more independent from the Church and the military. In short, the Mexican frontier was beginning to resemble its American counterpart by becoming a land of opportunity for the individual.

The Mexican frontier did not, however, reach the levels of dynamism, abundance, and optimism of the American frontier, in large part because Mexico was not as economically dynamic as the United States. Ray Billington has put the matter squarely:

> all frontier areas are continuingly dependent for settlers, markets, and culture on the regions behind them . . . the ferment of America's moving frontiers was partially the product of the ferment of the democratic, commercial, and industrial societies evolving in the successive Easts from which they emerged.[29]

Prior to 1846, Mexico itself was not prosperous, populous, powerful, or stable enough to people its frontier, neutralize nomadic raiders, and create tight commercial and political links between the periphery and the metropolis. In a larger sense, the Mexican frontier is best understood as the periphery of an aspiring nation that was itself peripheral to the world's capitalist system. During the nineteenth century, while the United States made the transition from a peripheral agrarian state toward becoming one of the core nations of the industrial world, Mexico remained a peripheral state in the world capitalist system. "Intervention of outsiders via war, subversion, and diplomacy is the lot of peripheral states," historian Immanuel Wallerstein has pointed out, and Mexico offers a classic case.[30] The relative underdevelopment of the Mexican frontier, then, cannot be understood by looking only at conditions on the frontier, or by pointing to the supposed "indolence" of the pobladores. Mexican frontiersmen responded to many forces beyond their control and those can only be understood when the Mexican frontier is viewed from a broad perspective.

One final question needs to be addressed. If the frontier altered the institutions and society in northern Mexico, even modestly, as it did on the American frontier, why did the frontier process, in turn, fail to modify the character and institutions of Mexicans in general, as many believe the American frontier did to American character and institutions? Some contemporaries recognized the possibility of such an impact. Tucson-born Ignacio Zúñiga, for example, saw the frontier as a source of virtue for Mexicans from the interior. In 1835 he argued that the resettlement of Mexicans on the frontier would show them "the secret of living honestly and advantageously by their own industry and labor," and "teach a multitude of our countrymen to cultivate the soil and to live from its fruits and from the agreeable profits of commerce."[31] Similarly, Lorenzo de Zavala, the liberal from the peripheral state of Yucatán who had interests in Texas land, wrote in 1831: "it is hoped that within two or three generations this part of the Mexican Republic—richer, freer, and more enlightened than all the rest—will serve as an example to other states which continue under a semifeudal routine."[32] A great admirer of the United States, Zavala saw Mexico's sparsely populated North as more fluid and susceptible to outside influences and to reform than the nation's core, which remained stagnant under "military and ecclesiastical power, a dismal inheritance of colonial domination." He hoped that Texas, along with other frontier states, would become "a school of liberty and civilization" for central Mexico.[33]

The far northern frontier never played the role that these men envisioned. It did not attract colonists, as Zúñiga and others had hoped, and it did not remain Mexican territory for the "two or three generations" that Zavala seemed to think necessary before it could influence the rest of the nation. Whether such a process might have occurred must remain a matter of speculation, but a quarter of a century clearly was not long enough. In the brief time that the Far North belonged to Mexico, it was too peripheral and too underdeveloped to influence activities in the core.[34] In a sense, the provinces in the Far North stood as a series of outposts beyond the frontier itself. Isolation and relative poverty prevented its residents from participating directly in national life, discouraged colonists from the interior, and left most Mexicans in ignorance about it. Unlike Zavala, those few cultured Mexicans who wrote about the frontier seemed to view it as hopelessly backward and its residents ignorant and lethargic. The wife of a customs inspector, upon being uprooted from Saltillo to Goliad when her husband was transferred, reportedly lamented that "persons who had seen large cities could not live happily in such a banishment." She described Goliad as a "poor, out-of-the-world, ignorant village."[35] "What will be the fate of those unfortunate Mexicans who now live amidst barbarians without a hope of civilization?" Juan Almonte asked about the *tejanos* in 1834.[36] Instead of viewing the frontier as the key to Mexico's salvation as did Zavala, other Mexican intellectuals and politicians saw federal military assistance and state-supported colonists from the nation's core as the key to the salvation of the frontier.

Because Mexico's far northern frontier made no discernible impact on Mexican character, however, does not mean that the Mexican frontiers in general had no such effect. Commenting on the sixteenth century expansion of Spaniards north from Mexico City into the area of Zacatecas, for example, the eminent American historian Woodrow Borah has characterized that Mexican frontier as a "melting pot," in which different races and ethnic groups "merged into a hybrid culture, clearly Hispanic but equally clearly a subtype—in other words, Mexican. The frontier rather than the center was the creator of Mexican culture and Mexican allegiance."[37]

Many writers consider residents of the present-day northern states of Mexico—Sonora, Sinaloa, Chihuahua, Durango, Coahuila, Nuevo León, and Tamaulipas—as possessing a unique character that has altered national life. The Spanish northward advance, a process which took over two centuries, produced in the North "an economic structure and new society different from that of Central Mexico," Mexican historian Enrique Florescano has noted.[38] The process of eking out a living in a harsh environment, fighting Indians, and living amidst insecurity and isolation, it has been argued, forged a society with distinctive characteristics. *Norteños* have been described in terms similar to those used for American frontiersmen: nationalistic, hardworking, courageous, adaptable, ingenious, aggressive, and enterprising. Though obviously impressionistic and stereotypical, such characterizations may be as hazy and imprecise as notions of what constitutes American character, but the similarity of the images is remarkable.[39] Moreover, the northern states, many writers have argued, have won a reputation as "the guardian of liberty and promoter of the democratic way of life" in Mexico, and played a vital role in leading the Mexican Revolution in the 1910s and 1920s.[40]

Notwithstanding its contributions to Mexican national life, Mexico's northern frontier has never captured the popular imagination in the ways that the American West has. Historian Philip Wayne Powell has lamented that the American "western" of fiction and film has had no counterpart in a Mexican "northern," and has characterized the Mexican North as "an almost forgotten historical world."[41]

The same fate did not befall the farthest reaches of the Mexican frontier. Historians and popular writers have not forgotten the Mexican heritage of California, Arizona, New Mexico, and Texas, for they became part of a nation with a rich tradition of regional history and literature. But if local writers in the United States have taken a deep interest in their Hispanic heritage, they also have often distorted it by explaining the decades prior to the American takeover largely in the context of American history and American Manifest Destiny. Clearly, the Mexican Far North was falling rapidly under American influence during these years, but it seems equally clear that the region's institutions and society remained essentially Mexican so long as it remained part of that troubled young nation. The complex events on Mexico's far northern frontier can only be understood when the region is understood from Mexican as well as American perspectives.

Appendix
Provincial Governors
1821–46

Alta California:

Pablo Vicente de Sola, 1815–22
Luis Argüello, 1822–25
José María de Echeandía, 1825–31
Manuel Victoria, 1831–32
Pío Pico, 1832 (acting)
José María de Echeandía, 1832–33 (in control in the south)
Agustín Vicente Zamorano, 1832–33 (in control in the north)
José Figueroa, 1833–35

José Castro, 1835–36 (acting)
Nicolás Gutiérrez, 1836 (acting)
Mariano Chico, 1836 (acting)
Nicolás Gutiérrez, 1836
Juan Bautista Alvarado, 1836–42
Manuel Micheltorena, 1842–45
Pío Pico, 1845–46 (in control of the south)
José Castro, 1845–46 (in control of the north

New Mexico:

Facundo Melgares, 1818–22
Francisco Xavier Chávez, 1822
José Antonio Vizcarra, 1822–23
Bartolomé Baca, 1823–25
Antonio Narbona, 1825–27
Manuel Armijo, 1827–29
José Antonio Chávez, 1829–32
Santiago Abreú, 1832–33
Francisco Sarracino, 1833–35
Albino Pérez, 1835–37

Manuel Armijo, 1837–44
Mariano Chávez, 1844 (acting)
Felipe Sena, 1844 (acting)
Mariano Martínez de Lejanza, 1844–45
Mariano Chávez y Castillo, 1845 (acting)
José Chávez, 1845 (acting)
Manuel Armijo, 1845–46

Texas:

Antonio Martínez, 1817–22
José Félix Trespalacios, 1822–23
Luciano García, 1823

Coahuila y Texas:

Rafael González, 1824–26
José Ignacio de Arizpe, 1826
Victor Blanco, 1826–27
José Ignacio de Arizpe, 1827
José María Viesca (provisional)
Victor Blanco, 1827
José María Viesca, 1827–30
Rafael Eca y Músquiz, 1830–31
José María Viesca, 1831
José María de Letona, 1831–32
Rafael Eca y Músquiz, 1832–33

Juan Martín de Veramendi, 1833
Francisco Vidaurri y Villaseñor, 1833–34
Juan José Elguezábal, 1834–35
José María Cantú, 1835
Marciel Borrego, 1835
Agustín Viesca, 1835
Miguel Falcón, 1835
Bartolomé de Cárdenas, 1835
Rafael Eca y Músquiz, 1835

Abbreviations Used in the Notes

Frequently Cited Scholarly Journals

AW   *Arizona and the West*

CHSQ   *California Historical Society Quarterly* (this title has undergone slight variations over the years and appeared as *California History* since Spring 1978)

JAH   *Journal of Arizona History*

JSDH   *Journal of San Diego History*

JW   *Journal of the West*

HAHR   *Hispanic American Historical Review*

NMHR   *New Mexico Historical Review*

PHR   *Pacific Historical Review*

SCQ   *Southern California Quarterly* (1884–1917, title varies)

SWHQ   *Southwestern Historical Quarterly* (the first fifteen volumes, July 1897 to April 1912, appeared under the title *Quarterly* of the Texas Historical Association)

Frequently Cited Archives and Repositories

AGN   Archivo General de la Nación, Mexico City

AHES   Archivo Histórico del Estado de Sonora, Hermosillo, Sonora

AHS   Arizona Historical Society, Tucson, Arizona

ASFC   Archivo de la Secretaría de Fomento y Colonización, AGN

BA   Béxar Archives, University of Texas at Austin (available on microfilm)

BL   Bancroft Library, University of California, Berkeley

HEH   Henry E. Huntington Library, San Marino, California

MANM   Mexican Archives of New Mexico, New Mexico State Records Center (available on microfilm)

NMSRC   New Mexico State Records Center, Santa Fe, New Mexico

TSA   Texas State Archives, Austin, Texas

UT   University of Texas, Austin, Texas

Notes

Preface

1. There is widespread agreement that the region as a whole is insufficiently understood during these years. American historian Arthur F. Corwin, for example, concludes that "the Southwest under Mexico, 1821–1848, is, from the viewpoint of Mexican American history, one of the least studied periods." See "Mexican American History: An Assessment," *PHR*, XLII (August 1973), pp. 281–82, and Silvio Zavala, the prominent Mexican historian, has argued for the study of "the meeting of the Spanish-American frontier in northern Mexico with the westward-moving American frontier. . . . " See "The Frontiers of Hispanic America," in Walker D. Wyman and Clifton B. Kroeber, eds., *The Frontier in Perspective* (Madison, 1957), p. 57. The historiography of California is more mature than that of New Mexico, Texas, and Arizona, for reasons I have suggested elsewhere: Weber, "Mexico's Far Northern Frontier, 1821–1845. A Critical Bibliography," *AW*, XIX (Autumn 1977), p. 226. In the case of Texas, Malcolm D. McLean refers to "that vague and mysterious period before the Texas Revolution" in his introduction to *Papers Concerning Robertson's Colony in Texas*, 7 vols. to date (Fort Worth and Arlington, Texas, 1974–), V, 33.

2. I have elaborated on this point at greater length in "Mexico's Far Northern Frontier, 1821–1854: Historiography Askew," *WHQ*, VII (July 1976), pp. 279–93.

3. These quotes are from Hubert Howe Bancroft, *California Pastoral, 1769–1848* (San Francisco, 1888), pp. 273, 179–80, 292–93. For similar sentiments see Nellie Van de Grift Sánchez, *Spanish Arcadia* (Los Angeles, 1929), p. 378; Robert Glass Cleland, *The Cattle on a Thousand Hills. Southern California, 1850–1880* (San Marino, 1951), p. 31; and James Woodrow Hansen, *The Search for Authority in California* (Oakland, 1960), pp. 1–2.

4. Fane Downs, "The History of Mexicans in Texas, 1820–1845" (Ph.D. diss., Texas Tech University, 1971), p. 3.

5. Charles Florus Coan, *A History of New Mexico*, 3 vols. (Chicago, 1925), I, 323.

6. *History of California: The Spanish Period* (New York, 1921), p. 455.

7. Weber, "Mexico's Far Northern Frontier," pp. 225–26.

8. John L. Kessell, for example, uses the term "Hispanic Arizona," in his study *Friars, Soldiers, and Reformers: Hispanic Arizona and the Sonora Mission Frontier, 1767–1856* (Tucson, 1976).

9. Andrés Anthony Tijerina, "Tejanos and Texas: The Native Mexicans of Texas, 1820–1850" (Ph.D. diss., University of Texas at Austin, 1977), p. 39.

10. Oakah L. Jones argues this case vigorously in *Los Paisanos: Spanish Settlers on the Northern Frontier of New Spain* (Norman, 1979), p. xii.

11. John Francis Bannon, *The Spanish Borderlands Frontier* (New York, 1970), pp. 167–89, provides a good summary of frontier reorganization and the reasons for it, although his

discussion of the restructuring of the Provincias in the last decades of the Spanish era is hazy. See, too, Edmundo O'Gorman, *Historia de las divisiones territoriales de México* (4th ed.; Mexico, 1968), pp. 15–25, and Luis Navarro García, *Las Provincias Internas en el siglo XIX* (Sevilla, 1965), pp. 75–76.

12. For the Plan of Apatzingán see Manuel Dublán and José María Lozano, eds., *Legislación mexicana o coleccion completa de las disposiciones legislativas expedidas desde la independencia de la república,* 34 vols. (Mexico, 1876–1904), I, 433–51.

13. Tadeo Ortiz to Anastasio Bustamante, Bordeaux, November 30, 1830, in Edith Louise Kelly and Mattie Austin Hatcher, eds., "Tadeo Ortiz de Ayala and the Colonization of Texas, 1822–1833," *SWHQ,* XXXII (April 1929), p. 228. See, too, Ortiz to Bustamante, Bordeaux, October 31, 1830, in ibid. (October 1929), p. 153.

14. Tadeo Ortiz de Ayala, *México considerado como nación independiente y libre . . .* (1st ed. 1832; Guadalajara, 1952), p. 184. Ortiz had sounded the tocsin as early as 1821, when he finished his *Resúmen de la Estadística del Imperio Mexicano, 1822,* Tarsicio García Díaz, ed. (Mexico, 1968), pp. 56–57. For a similar view see Juan Francisco de Azcárate, "Dictamen presentado a la soberana junta gubernativa del imperio mexicano," December 29, 1821, published as *Un programa de política internacional* (Mexico, 1932), pp. 15, 23. Miguel Ramos Arizpe also saw the entire far north as a threatened unit: Ramos Arizpe to the Ministro de Relaciones Interiores y Exteriores, Lucas Alamán, Puebla, August 1, 1830, ASFC, legajo VI, part 2 (1828–1831), expediente 43, West Transcripts, UT.

15. Charles C. Cumberland, *Mexico: The Struggle for Modernity* (Oxford, 1968), p. 156.

16. Ward Alan Minge, "Frontier Problems in New Mexico Preceding the Mexican War, 1840–1846" (Ph.D. diss., University of New Mexico, 1965), pp. 162–64, 315. Although Congress recognized Oaxaca, Yucatán, and Sonora as also bordering on foreign territory, it did not accord those departments frontier status. The term *frontera* was not used solely to designate border provinces in that era. José Agustín Escudero, for example, referred to New Mexico, Durango, Sonora, and Sinaloa as "Estados fronterizos." *Noticias Estadísticas de Sonora y Sinaloa* (Mexico, 1849), p. 144. For a brief discussion of the evolution of the term in American English, see Ray Allen Billington, *America's Frontier Heritage* (New York, 1966), pp. 23–24.

17. Tijerina, "Tejanos and Texas," p. 64.

Chapter 1
"¡Viva la Independencia!"

1. Most of this description comes from José María Sánchez, "Trip to Texas in 1828," Carlos E. Castañeda, trans., *SWHQ,* XXIX (April 1926), pp. 257–58, and Benjamin Lundy, *The Life, Travels and Opinions of Benjamin Lundy* (Philadelphia, 1847), pp. 96–97. The population of San Antonio fluctuated considerably during this period. Andrew Anthony Tijerina, "Tejanos and Texas: The Native Mexicans of Texas, 1820–1850" (Ph.D. diss., University of Texas, Austin, 1978), p. 18.

2. Félix D. Almaraz, Jr., "Governor Antonio Martínez and Mexican Independence in Texas: An Orderly Transition," *Permian Historical Annual,* 15 (1975), pp. 49–50. Carlos E. Castañeda, *Our Catholic Heritage in Texas, 1519–1936,* 7 vols. (Austin, 1931–58), VI, 173–74. Fane Downs, "The Administration of Antonio Martínez, Last Governor of Spanish Texas, 1817–1822" (M.A. thesis, Texas Tech University, 1963), p. 35. Odie B. Faulk, *The Last Years of Spanish Texas, 1778–1821* (The Hague, 1964), p. 102. [Eugene C. Barker, ed.], "Journal of Stephen F. Austin on His First Trip to Texas, 1821," *SWHQ,* VII (1903–4), pp. 289, 298.

3. John L. Kessell, *Friars, Soldiers, and Reformers: Hispanic Arizona and the Sonora Mission Frontier, 1767–1856* (Tucson, 1976), p. 248. For the setting of Tucson, I have used John Russell Bartlett, *Personal Narrative of Explorations and Incidents* . . . 2 vols. (New York, 1854), II, 295–97. The population of Tucson is an estimate. A 1797 census enumerated 395 persons. See Henry F. Dobyns, *Spanish Colonial Tucson: A Demographic History* (Tucson, 1976), pp. 142–45, and Karen Sykes Collins, ed., "Fray Pedro Arriquibar's Census of Tucson, 1820 [1797]," *JAH*, 11 (Spring 1970), pp. 14–22. See, too, Kessell, *Friars*, pp. 237–39; Sidney B. Brinckerhoff, "The Last Years of Spanish Arizona, 1786–1821," *AW*, 9 (Spring 1967), p. 17.

4. Juan Bautista Ladrón del Niño de Guevara to Juan Francisco de Castañiza, Bishop of Durango, Durango, October 23, 1820. Archives of the Archdiocese of Santa Fe, roll 45, frames 285–302. Francisco Velasco, "Provincia de Nuevo Mexico: Noticia de los puntos de dicha provincia donde se ha jurado la independencia de este Ymperio. . . . " Chihuahua, October 23, 1821, Archivo Histórico de Defensa Nacional, expediente 204, microfilm, *BL*, Berkeley, roll 21, frame 43. C. L. Sonnichsen, *Pass of the North: Four Centuries on the Rio Grande* (El Paso, 1968), pp. 88–99. W. H. Timmons, "The El Paso Area in the Mexican Period, 1821–1848," *SWHQ*, LXXXIV, (July 1980), p. 2. Lansing B. Bloom, "New Mexico Under Mexican Administration, 1821–1846," *Old Santa Fe*, I (July 1913), pp. 27–30. On October 4, 1824, El Paso came under the jurisdiction of Chihuahua.

5. Descriptions of Santa Fe in this period abound. See William Becknell's account of his 1821 visit, "Journal of Two Expeditions from Boon's Lick to Santa Fe," Franklin *Missouri Intelligencer*, April 22, 1823, and Antonio Barreiro's account of 1832 in H. Bailey Carroll and J. Villasana Haggard, eds. and trans., *Three New Mexico Chronicles* (Albuquerque, 1942), pp. 84–86. For population estimates, see ibid., p. 88, and Bloom, "New Mexico Under Mexican Administration," I, 27–30. For the oath of loyalty, see David J. Weber, ed. and trans., "An Unforgettable Day: Facundo Melgares on Indpendence," *NMHR*, XLVIII (January 1973), p. 29. Velasco, "Provincia de Nuevo Mexico: Noticia de los puntos. . . ."

6. Duhault-Cilly, quoted in Hubert Howe Bancroft, *History of California*, 7 vols. (San Francisco, 1886–90), II, 610–11. Population figures are in *ibid.*, II, 380; II, 392; 653.

7. Bancroft, *History of California*, II, 450–52. Documents pertaining to these events appear in Herbert E. Bolton, "The Iturbide Revolution in the Californias," *HAHR*, II (May 1919), pp. 188–242.

8. Timothy E. Anna, *The Fall of the Royal Government in Mexico City* (Lincoln, Nebraska, 1978), pp. 206–09.

9. Melgares learned of the insurgents in April. See Melgares to the alcaldes constitucionales . . . , Santa Fe, April 9, 1821, Ritch Papers, no. 73, HEH, and Weber, ed., "An Unforgettable Day," p. 29. Martínez learned of Iturbide by the end of March. See Almaraz, "Governor Antonio Martínez," pp. 48–49. Officers in Pimería Alta also waited until they received orders to change allegiance. Kessell, *Friars, Soldiers, and Reformers*, p. 248.

10. Sola to José Darío Arguello, January 10, 1822, quoted in Bancroft, *History of California*, II, 450.

11. Mariano Guadalupe Vallejo, quoted in George Tays, "Revolutionary California: The Political History of California from 1820 to 1848" (Ph.D. diss., Berkeley, 1932; rev. 1934), pp. 96, 97–98. See, too, Tays, "The Passing of Spanish California, September 29, 1822," *CHSQ*, XV (June 1936), pp. 139–42. A physical description of Sola is in Bancroft, *History of California*, II, 470–72, n. 42.

12. Decree of October 6, 1821, quoted in Weber, ed. and trans., "An Unforgettable Day," p. 33.

13. Melgares Report, *Gaceta Imperial*, March 23, March 26, 1822, trans. in Weber, "An Unforgettable Day," pp. 35–42. Celebrations in California also occurred after a packet of instructions and announcements arrived from Mexico City. Bancroft, *History of California*, II, 451.

14. Raymond S. Brandes, trans. and ed. "Times Gone By in Alta California: Recollections of Señora Doña Juana Machado Alipaz de Ridington [Wrightington]," *SCQ*, XLI (September 1959), p. 202.

15. For Hidalgo's relationship to Texas, see Castañeda's somewhat exaggerated account in *Our Catholic Heritage*, VI, preface and p. 31, and Hugh M. Hamill, Jr. for a more balanced narrative: *The Hidalgo Revolt: Prelude to Mexican Independence* (Gainesville, Fla., 1966), pp. 202–10.

16. Las Casa to Mariano Ximénez, Béxar, February 3, 1811, in Frederick C. Chabot, *Texas in 1811. The Las Casas and Sambrano Revolutions* (San Antonio, 1941), p. 80. Chabot provides a rich collection of contemporary documents upon which I have depended. See, too, Félix D. Almaraz, Jr., *Tragic Cavalier: Governor Manuel Salcedo of Texas, 1808–1813* (Austin, 1971), pp. 95–123. For discontent in Texas, see for example, Castañeda, *Our Catholic Heritage*, V, 434–35. The Texas response to Hidalgo was not typical. In much of the rest of the Eastern Interior Provinces apathy was the characteristic response. See Isidro Vizcaya Canales, *En los albores de la independencia: Las provincias internas de oriente . . . , 1810–1811* (Monterrey, 1976).

17. J. Villasana Haggard, "The Counter-Revolution of Bexar, 1811," *SWHQ*, XLII (October 1939), pp. 222–35. Chabot, *Texas in 1811*, p. 98.

18. Quoted in Harris Gaylord Warren, *The Sword Was Their Passport. A History of Filibustering in the Mexican Revolution* (Baton Rouge, 1943), p. 52. Richard W. Gronet, "The United States and the Invasion of Texas, 1810–1814," *The Americas*, XXV (January 1969), pp. 281–306.

19. This account is based chiefly on Julia Kathryn Garrett, *Green Flag Over Texas: A Story of the Last Years of Spain in Texas* (New York and Dallas, 1939), which provides a vivid account of Arredondo's purge, and Castañeda, *Our Catholic Heritage*, VI, 121–22. Harry McCory Henderson focuses on military aspects in "The Magee-Gutiérrez Expedition," *SWHQ*, LV (July 1951), pp. 43–61.

20. Martínez, Report on Texas, May 1, 1821, quoted in Joseph Carl McElhannon, "Imperial Mexico and Texas, 1821–1823," *SWHQ*, LIII (October 1949), p. 120. For a more complete picture of Texas at this time, see *The Letters of Antonio Martínez, Last Spanish Governor of Texas, 1817–1822*, trans. and ed. by Virginia H. Taylor (Austin, 1957), and Fane Downs, "Governor Antonio Martínez and the Defense of Texas from Foreign Invasion, 1817–1822," *Texas Military History*, VII (Spring 1968), pp. 27–43.

21. In 1809 Governor Salcedo placed the population of Texas at 3,122, not counting the troops. See Nettie Lee Benson, ed. and trans., "A Governor's Report on Texas in 1809," *SWHQ*, LXXI (April 1968), p. 611, and Castañeda, *Our Catholic Heritage*, V, 400. An 1820 census put the population of Texas at 1,814, and an 1822 estimate by Governor Martínez put the population at 2,516. See Fane Downs, "The History of Mexicans in Texas, 1820–1845" (Ph.D. diss., Texas Tech University, 1970), pp. 48–49.

22. Almaraz, *Tragic Cavalier*, p. 182. Almaraz has described the eagerness of the ayuntamiento of San Antonio in 1821 to demonstrate its loyalty to the crown in "Governor Antonio Martínez and Mexican Independence," p. 48.

23. Fray José Señán to Fray José Guilez, San Buenaventura, California, June 6, 1811, in Lesley Byrd Simpson, ed., and Paul D. Nathan, trans., *The Letters of José Señán, O.F.M. Mission San Buenaventura, 1796–1823* (San Francisco, 1962), p. 53. Bancroft, *History of California*, II, 220–49; 254–55. The best account of the Bouchard raid and other events of these years is in George Tays, "Revolutionary California," pp. 63–96.

24. Señán to José de la Guerra, June 26, 1822, in ibid., p. 158. Bancroft, *History of California*, II, 194–219; 250–66; 406. Luis Navarro García, *Las provincias internas en el siglo xix* (Sevilla, 1965), pp. 86–91. Faulk, *Last Years of Spanish Texas*, pp. 70–71. Mattie Austin Hatcher, trans., "Texas in 1820," *SWHQ*, XXIII (July 1919), pp. 61–62. Kessell, *Friars, Soldiers, and Reformers*, pp. 220, 237.

25. Almaraz, "Governor Antonio Martínez," p. 45.

26. Frank McNitt, *Navajo Wars: Military Campaigns, Slave Raids, and Reprisals* (Albuquerque, 1972), pp. 47–51.

27. See, for example, the comments made by Carlos Dehault Delassus in St. Louis in 1804 and Joaquín del Real Alencaster in Santa Fe in 1807, quoted in David J. Weber, *Foreigners in Their Native Land* (Albuquerque, 1973), pp. 62–65.

28. "Dictamen presentado a la soberana junta gobernativa del imperio mexicano," December 29, 1821, published under the title *Un programa de política internacional*, by Juan Francisco de Azcárate (Mexico, 1932), p. 15.

29. José Antonio de Andrade to Iturbide, October 1821, cited in Irving B. Richman, *California Under Spain and Mexico, 1535–1847* (Boston, 1911), p. 230.

30. Simón Tadeo Oriz de Ayala, *Resúmen de la estadística del Imperio Mexicano, 1822*, ed. by Tarsicio García Díaz (1st ed., 1822; Mexico, 1968), pp. 56–67. Ortiz completed the manuscript on October 10, 1821 and dedicated the book to Iturbide.

31. Manuel Zozaya, December 26, 1822, quoted in McElhannon, "Imperial Mexico and Texas," p. 137.

32. Philip Coolidge Brooks, *Diplomacy and the Borderlands. The Adams-Onís Treaty of 1819* (Berkeley, 1939), is the standard account. See especially pp. 215–17, for the John Melish map which showed Louisiana extending to the Rio Grande. See, too, Warren L. Cook, *Flood Tide of Empire: Spain and the Pacific Northwest, 1543–1819* (New Haven, 1973), pp. 514–23, and Abraham P. Nasatir, *Borderland in Retreat: From Spanish Louisiana to the Far Southwest* (Albuquerque, 1976).

33. A treaty was signed on January 12, 1828, but ratifications were not exchanged until April 5, 1832. Brooks, *Diplomacy and the Borderlands*, pp. 193, 217. The standard Mexican and American accounts of U.S.-Mexican efforts to agree on a boundary, interpret events with remarkable similarity. See Carlos Bosch García, *Historia de las relaciones entre México y los Estados Unidos, 1819–1848* (Mexico, 1961), pp. 127–72. William R. Manning, *Early Diplomatic Relations Between the United States and Mexico* (Baltimore, 1916), pp. 277–348. Mexico's ambivalent perceptions of the United States at the outset of independence are well treated in Gene M. Brack, *Mexico Views Manifest Destiny, 1821–1846* (Albuquerque, 1975), pp. 15–51.

34. [Barker, ed.], "Journal of Stephen F. Austin," p. 296.

35. Eugene C. Barker has so termed Austin in his standard biography: *The Life of Stephen F. Austin: Founder of Texas, 1793–1836* (1st ed., 1926; 2nd ed. reprinted, Austin, 1969).

36. Becknell, "Journal of two Expeditions from Boon's Lick to Santa Fe."

37. *Ibid.* Melgares' warm welcome of Becknell is consistent with Zebulon Pike's description of him as a gracious gentleman: Donald Jackson, ed., *The Journals of Zebulon Montgomery Pike*, 2 vols. (Norman, 1966), I, 404–10. Marc Simmons, "Opening the Santa Fe Trail," *Westport Historical Quarterly*, VII (June 1971), pp. 4–5.

38. This is discussed further in chapter eight.

39. Donaciano Vigil to the New Mexico Assembly, May 16, 1846, Ritch Papers, no. 231, HEH.

40. This idea is developed ably in Javier Ocampo, *Las ideas de un día: El pueblo mexicano ante la consumación de su Independencia* (Mexico, 1969), pp. 304–19.

41. Anna, *The Fall of the Royal Government in Mexico City*, p. xiii. See, too, p. 207.

42. Quoted in Bancroft, *History of California*, II, 452.

Chapter 2
The New Politics

1. Jaime E. Rodríguez O., *The Emergence of Spanish America: Vicente Rocafuerte and Spanish Americanism, 1808–1832* (Lincoln, Neb., 1975), p. 12. Rodríguez provides one of the finest analyses of the Cortes and its works in English. See, too, Mario Rodríguez, *The Cádiz*

Experiment in Central America, 1808–1826 (Berkeley, 1978), pp. 75–100. Richard Herr, *The Eighteenth-Century Revolution in Spain* (Princeton, 1958), pp. 11, 241–42, offers an excellent discussion of the background.

2. The Constitution of 1812 has been reprinted in several collections. Among the most accessible is *Leyes fundamentales de México, 1808–1971*, ed. by Felipe Tena Ramírez, 8th ed. (Mexico, 1978), pp. 59–104.

3. In addition to the 1812 Constitution, see the *decreto* of May 23, 1812, which discusses the "Formation of the Constitutional Ayuntamientos," in Manuel Dublán and José María Lozano, eds., *Legislación mexicana o colección completa de las disposiciones legislativas expedidas desde la independencia de la república*, 34 vols. (Mexico, 1876–1904), I, 380–81. For an excellent discussion of the condition of municipal government, see Roger L. Cunniff, "Mexican Municipal Electoral Reform, 1810–1822," in Nettie Lee Benson, ed., *Mexico and the Spanish Cortes, 1810–1822: Eight Essays* (Austin, 1966), pp. 59–63. Some writers have suggested that local government remained more vigorous on frontier areas of the Spanish empire. That does not seem to be the case in the Far North of New Spain, although the Bourbon reforms of the late eighteenth century did begin a shift from appointive, lifetime positions to elected offices in San Antonio. See Mattie Alice Austin, "The Municipal Government of San Fernando de Bexar, 1730–1800," *SWHQ*, VIII (April 1905), pp. 297–98, 301–5.

4. Royal order of April 15, 1820, Madrid, in Dublán and Lozano, *Legislación mexicana*, I, 514.

5. Marc Simmons, *Spanish Government in New Mexico* (Albuquerque, 1968), pp. 213; 195–99; 203; 205–12.

6. Cunniff, "Mexican Municipal Electoral Reform," pp. 76–77; 82–83. For the condition of ayuntamientos in Texas just prior to the 1812 reforms, see Nettie Lee Benson, trans. and ed., *Report that Dr. Miguel Ramos de Arizpe . . . Presents to the August Congress on the Natural, Political and Civil Condition of the Provinces of Coahuila, Nuevo León, Nuevo Santander, and Texas . . .* (Austin, 1950), pp. 11, 30–31.

7. Hubert Howe Bancroft, *History of California*, 7 vols. (San Francisco, 1886–1890), II, 423, 462.

8. The two Californias had previously been part of the Provincias Internas, but at the time of independence they were regarded as separate entities supervised directly by the viceroy. The final division prior to independence occurred in 1813. See Edmundo O'Gorman, *Historia de las divisiones territoriales de Mexico* (4th ed., Mexico, 1968), pp. 15–25, and Luis Navarro García, *Las Provincias Internas en el siglo XIX* (Sevilla, 1965), pp. 75–76. Further changes were ordered in 1818, but not implemented. Simmons, *Spanish Government in New Mexico*, pp. 208–9. Eugene C. Barker, "The Government of Austin's Colony, 1821–1831," *SWHQ*, XXI (January 1918), pp. 224–25. There is no evidence that the Provincias Internas del Oriente convoked a diputación prior to Ferdinand's suspension of the Constitution in 1814. Nettie Lee Benson, *La diputación provincial y el federalismo mexicano* (Mexico, 1955), pp. 20, 28, 41.

9. Quoted in Nettie Lee Benson, "Texas' Failure to Send a Deputy to the Spanish Cortes, 1810–1812," *SWHQ*, LXIV (July 1960), pp. 14–35. For California, see Charles Berry, "The Election of the Mexican Deputies to the Spanish Cortes, 1810–1822," in Benson, ed., *Mexico and the Spanish Cortes*, pp. 12, n. 2; 16, 36–37.

10. Benson, trans. and ed., *Report . . . Miguel Ramos Arizpe*, p. x.

11. Quoted in H. Bailey Carroll and J. Villasana Haggard, eds. and trans., *Three New Mexico Chronicles* (Albuquerque, 1942), p. xix, which contains a facsimile as well as a translation of Pino's *Exposición* of 1812. See, too, Berry, "The Election of the Mexican Deputies to the Spanish Cortes," pp. 10–16, 30–37.

12. William Spence Robertson, *Iturbide of Mexico* (Durham, North Carolina, 1952), pp. 96, 134, 214–15, 218–19. Law of October 5, 1821, in Dublán and Lozano, *Legislación mexicana*, I, 476.

13. Benson, *La diputación provincial*, pp. 68–84.

14. Lansing B. Bloom, "New Mexico Under Mexican Administration, 1821–1846," *Old Santa Fe*, I (October 1913), pp. 145–49. Benson, *La diputación provincial*, pp. 68–70, 75.

15. Bancroft, *History of California*, II, 462.

16. Benson, *La diputación provincial*, p. 84. This was authorized in an act of August 18, 1823. *Colección de ordenes y decretos de soberana junta provisional gubernativa . . . Segunda edición. Vol. II, February 1822–October 1823* (Mexico, 1829). Andrew Anthony Tijerina, "Tejanos and Texas: The Native Mexicans of Texas, 1820–1850" (Ph.D. diss., University of Texas at Austin, 1977), pp. 211–16.

17. Bloom, "New Mexico Under Mexican Administration," I, pp. 2, 145–46, 155–56. Bancroft, *History of California*, II, 453–55; 471, n. 42; 485, n. 6.

18. Nettie Leé Benson, "The Plan of Casa Mata," *HAHR*, XXV (February 1945), p. 55. Benson, *La diputación provincial*, p. 122.

19. Bloom, "New Mexico Under Mexican Administation," I, 159–61. Benson, *La diputación provincial*, p. 107, n. 89, incorrectly indicates that there is no record of New Mexico's posture toward the Plan. J. Lloyd Mecham, "The Origins of Federalism in Mexico," *HAHR*, XIII (May 1938), p. 167, says that New Mexico and Texas supported the Plan of Casa Mata. He does not cite a source and appears to be in error.

20. Benson, *La diputación provincial*, pp. 102–3. For the cautious posture of the *californios*, see George Tays, "Revolutionary California: The Political History of the Mexican Period, 1822–1846" (Ph.D. diss., University of California, Berkeley, 1932; rev. 1934), pp. 103–5.

21. Tijerina, "Tejanos and Texas," pp. 217–18. Bancroft, *History of California*, II, 471, n. 42.

22. Tena Ramírez, ed., *Leyes fundamentales de México*, p. 154. A considerable literature on this question exists. Recent works which put the Constitution of 1824 in the tradition of the Constitution of 1812 are Charles A. Hale, *Mexican Liberalism in the Age of Mora, 1821–1853* (New Haven, 1968), pp. 79–82, 193–96, and José Gamas Torruco, *El federalismo mexicano* (Mexico, 1975), pp. 29–52. For a narrow argument on the other side see Watson Smith, "Influences from the United States on the Mexican Constitution of 1824," *AW*, IV (Summer 1962), pp. 113–26.

23. Michael P. Costeloe, *La primera república federal de México, 1824–1835. Un estudio de los partidos políticos en el México independiente* (Mexico, 1975), pp. 25, 32–33.

24. Hubert Howe Bancroft, *History of Mexico*, 6 vols. (San Francisco, 1883–1888), V, 16.

25. Benson, *La diputación provincial*, pp. 200–203.

26. One who thought in grandiose terms was Colonel Antonio Narbona, who while serving as Secretary of the diputación at Arispe in Sonora in 1823 suggested a plan to form a single state of Durango, Jalisco, Sonora, New Mexico, and California. Tays, "Revolutionary California," pp. 103–5.

27. Dublán and Lozano, eds., *Legislación mexicana*, I, 706. Vito Alessio Robles, *Coahuila y Texas, desde la consumación de la independencia hasta el tratado de paz de Guadalupe Hidalgo*, 2 vols. (Mexico, 1945–46), I, 169.

28. This question is discussed in Charles A. Bacarisse, "The Union of Coahuila and Texas," *SWHQ*, LXI (January 1958), pp. 341–49, and Tijerina, "Tejanos and Texas," pp. 220–30 adds new information and a new interpretation.

29. Diputación of New Mexico [to the National Congress?], Santa Fe, March 31, 1824, copy in minutes of the diputación, MANM, roll 42, frames 186–91.

30. Dublán and Lozano, eds., *Legislación mexicana*, I, 708.

31. Bloom, "New Mexico Under Mexican Administration," I, 169. Dublán and Lozano, *Legislación mexicana*, I, 710.

32. Alarid defended his actions in letters of July 14 and September 15, 1824, which are transcribed and translated in Frank Lujan, Jr., "A Compilation, Transcription, and Trans-

lation of Official Mexican Documents from the Mexican Archives of New Mexico, 1824–1825" (M.A. thesis, Highlands University, 1964).

33. Título II of the 1824 Constitution created four territories: New Mexico, Alta California, Baja California, and Colima. It left the status of Tlascala indefinite; Congress made it a territory on November 4, 1824 (see Dublán and Lozano, eds., *Legislación mexicana*, I, 714). Although the Constitution clearly separated the two Californias, and they each sent a delegate to Congress and operated their own diputación, the first Mexican governor sent to the Californias was governor of *both* Californias. This curious situation lasted until 1829 when the complaints of residents of Baja California led to the appointment of a separate governor, but the dual appointment has caused some writers to assume mistakenly that the two Californias were combined as one territory in 1824. See, for example, Pablo L. Martínez, *Historia de Baja California* (2nd ed.; Mexico, 1956), pp. 337–43.

34. José Francisco Velasco, *Noticias estadísticas del estado de Sonora* (Mexico, 1850), pp. 15, 18, 115. A good brief discussion of this is in Odie B. Faulk, trans. and ed., *The Constitution of Occidente. The First Constitution of Arizona, Sonora, and Sinaloa, 1825–1831* (Tucson, 1967), pp. 1–3.

35. Manuel de Mier y Terán to President Victoria, June 30, 1828, Nacogdoches, in Alleine Howren, "Causes and Origen of the Decree of April 6, 1830," *SWHQ*, XVI (April 1913), p. 397. See, too, the Baron de Bastrop to Stephen Austin, Saltillo, July 16, 1825, quoted in R. Woods Moore, "The Role of the Baron de Bastrop in the Anglo-American Settlement of the Spanish Southwest," *Louisiana Historical Quarterly*, 31 (July 1948), p. 666, and Bacarisse, "Union of Coahuila and Texas," pp. 341–49.

36. Jean Louis Berlandier, *Journey to Mexico During the Years 1826 to 1834*, C. H. Muller and Katherine K. Muller, eds., and Sheila M. Ohlendorf, Josette M. Bigelow, and Mary M. Standifer, trans., 2 vols. (Austin, 1980), I, 230. A league usually equaled 2.63 miles.

37. Mier y Terán, quoted in Ohland Morton, *Terán and Texas: A Chapter in Texas-Mexican Relations* (Austin, 1948), p. 119. At first Mier y Terán did not believe that the separation of Texas from Coahuila was necessary, but by 1830 he had come to share the Texans' views and urge that Texas be made a territory under federal control. *Representación dirijida por el ilustre ayuntamiento de la ciudad de Béxar al . . . Congreso del Estado*, December 19, 1832 (Brazoria, 1833), p. 9.

38. Tadeo Ortiz to the president, February 2, 1833, Matamoros, quoted in Edith Louise Kelly and Mattie Austin Hatcher, trans. and eds., "Tadeo Ortiz de Ayala and the Colonization of Texas, 1822–1833," *SWHQ*, XXXII (April 1929), p. 321. See, too, pp. 312–14.

39. Stephen Austin advocated territorial status for Texas until 1831, then began to support statehood. He did not want territorial status, however, without an organic law for the territories—something Congress never passed under the 1824 Constitution. See Eugene C. Barker, *The Life of Stephen F. Austin: Founder of Texas, 1793–1836* (1926; second edition reprinted, Austin, 1969), pp. 363–64. See, too, Helen Willits Harris, "Almonte's Inspection of Texas in 1834," *SWHQ*, XLI (January 1938), pp. 198–200, 210; and the Ayuntamiento of Béxar, *Representación*, pp. 9–10.

40. The Department of Texas was organized by the legislature of the state of Coahuila y Texas on February 1, 1825, along the lines of a bill introduced by the Texas representative, Baron de Bastrop, who sought to achieve greater autonomy for his province. Alessio Robles, *Coahuila y Texas*, I, 200. Moore, "Bastrop," pp. 656–58.

41. Francis White Johnson, *A History of Texas and the Texans*, Eugene C. Barker and Ernest William Winkler, eds., 5 vols. (Chicago, 1916), I, 53. Almonte to the Secretary of State, Nacogdoches, June 14, 1834, ASFC, legajo 8, expediente 65, transcript, TSA, 2-22/640, p. 50.

42. Stephen Austin, for example, argued repeatedly that the Law of May 7, 1824 united Texas and Coahuila provisionally, and that congressional denial of the right of Texas to separate denied "the vested rights of Texas" under the May 7 law. See, for example,

Austin's speech of September 8, 1835, and Austin to the Provisional Government, San Felipe, November 30, 1835, in Eugene C. Barker, ed., *The Austin Papers*, 3 vols. (Washington and Austin, 1924–28), III, pp. 118–19 and 269 respectively.

43. "El Congreso General Constituyente a los Habitantes de la Federación," in Tena Ramírez, ed., *Leyes fundamentales*, pp. 163–64.

44. Section V, part XXX of the 1824 Constitution.

45. The 1828 plan was published as *Nueva dictamen . . . presenta la comisión especial de la cámara de representantes para formar la constitución del distrito y territorios de la federación* (Mexico, 1828). Copy in the Governor's Papers, Correspondence Received, Mexico, Congreso General, 1828, MANM, roll 7, frames 1002–31. Other plans were drawn up, too, but never adopted. See, for example, an 1827 plan in Keld J. Reynolds, "Principal Actions of the California Junta de Fomento, 1825–1827," *CHSQ*, XXV (September and December, 1946), pp. 267–77; 347–56.

46. The New Mexico ayuntamientos and diputación, for example, followed procedures established in the 1812 Constitution, and in the "Instrucción para el gobierno económico político de las provincias," of June 23, 1813, which spelled out in greater detail than did the Constitution the obligations of the ayuntamiento, the diputación, and the governor (Dublán and Lozano, eds., *Legislación mexicana*, I, 413–24). These laws remained in force under Iturbide and were updated, as in the decreto of July 11, 1823 which gave additional powers to the diputaciones. See *Colección de ordenes y decretos de la soberana junta provisional . . . 2* vols., second edition (Mexico, 1829), II, 146. See, too, pp. 19, 48, 159, and 180. Other regulations regarding ayuntamientos included laws of May 23, July 19, and October 9, 1812, and February 2, 1813.

47. David J. Weber, "Land and Water Rights of the Pueblos of New Mexico Under Mexican Sovereignty, 1821–1846" (unpublished manuscript), pp. 21–26. Weber, ed., "El gobierno territorial de Nuevo México. La exposición del Padre Martínez de 1831," *Historia Mexicana*, XXV (October-December 1975), p. 307. Tays, "Revolutionary California," pp. 182–92, provides a good example.

48. Robert A. Potash, ed. and trans., "Notes and Documents [Answers from Tucson and Santa Fe to a Questionnaire from the Banco de Avio, 1831]," *NMHR*, XXIV (October 1949), p. 336. See, too, Manuel de Jesús Rada, *Proposición hecho al soberano Congreso General de la Nación por el diputado del Territorio de Nuevo México* (Mexico, 1829), in David J. Weber, *Northern Mexico on the Eve of the United States Invasion. Rare Imprints . . .* (New York, 1976).

49. Bancroft, *History of California*, III, 232–33; 260, n. 38.

50. Juan de Dios Canedo, *Memoria de la Secretaria de Estado y del Despacho de Relaciones Interiores y Exteriores* (Mexico, 1829), p. 21. See, too, José María Gutiérrez de Estrado, *Memoria de la Secretaria de Estado y del Despacho de Relaciones Interiores y Exteriores* (Mexico, 1835), p. 35, and the *Memorias . . .* of 1825 and 1826, written by Lucas Alamán and Sebastián Camacho, pp. 31 and 36 respectively.

51. See the remarks of President Valentín Gómez Farías, in C. Alan Hutchinson, *Frontier Settlement in Mexican California. The Híjar-Padrés Colony, and Its Origins, 1769–1835* (New Haven, 1969), pp. 160–61.

52. Bloom, "New Mexico Under Mexican Administration," I, 277–79. Bancroft, *History of California*, III, 38.

53. A rough translation of the *Reglamento Provicional [sic] para el Gobierno interior de la Excma Diputación Territorial de la Alta California . . .* (Monterey, 1834), is in Bancroft, *History of California*, III, 252–55. More usable is *A Facsimile Edition of California's First Book: Reglamento Provicional . . .*, trans. by Ramón Ruiz and Theresa Vigil, with introductions by George L. Harding and George P. Hammond (San Francisco, 1954). Hammond's assertion that the reglamento "set up a complete method of governing the province" (p. vii) is incorrect. The reglamento, for example, said nothing about the relationship of the diputación to the executive or about the administration of justice.

54. Chapt. III, art. V of the Decreto of June 23, 1813 required that the two commands be kept separate under normal circumstances (Dublán and Lozano, eds., *Legislación mexicana*, I, 420) and a law of May 6, 1822 apparently repeated this principle (Bancroft, *History of California*, III, 298). Frontier conditions provided ample opportunity for exceptions to the rule, as the New Mexico diputación noted in 1822: "in this province, because it is on the frontier, political and military commands are united." Minutes of the diputación, Santa Fe, December 14, 1822, MANM, roll 42, frame 50.

55. In New Mexico the two commands were separated almost immediately, when Iturbide appointed Francisco Xavier Chávez as jefe político, but left Facundo Melgares as jefe militar (Bloom, "New Mexico Under Mexican Administration," I, 154). The offices were combined again under Col. José Antonio Vizcarra (November 1822-September 1823), then separated when Bartolomé Baca became jefe político in September 1823 and Vizcarra remained jefe militar (ibid., I, 166). Later governors, such as Albino Pérez (1835–1837), Manuel Armijo (1839–43; 1845–46), and Mariano Martínez (1844–45) would also combine both commands, but as often as not the two seemed to be separated in New Mexico. See, too, Ward Alan Minge, "Frontier Problems in New Mexico Preceding the Mexican War, 1840–46" (Ph.D. diss., University of New Mexico, 1965), p. 162.

56. Military men dominated the office of governor of California in the federalist era, from 1825–1836: Lt. Col. José María Echeandía (1825–31); Lt. Col. Manuel Victoria (1831); General José Figueroa (1833–34); and Lt. Col. Nicolás Gutiérrez (1835–36). All held both military and civil command. See, too, Bancroft, *History of California*, II, 454, 510–12, and the Secretaría de Relaciones Exteriores, *Memorias* (Mexico, 1826), pp. 36–37.

57. See, for example, the episodes related in Bancroft, *History of California*, II, 463, n. 30; III, 219, 229.

58. Quoted in James Woodrow Hansen, *The Search for Authority in California* (Oakland, 1960), p. 2.

59. Narciso Durán, "Letters of Narciso Durán . . . Part 2," Francis Price, ed. and trans., *CHSQ*, XXXVII (September 1958), p. 262. Bancroft, *History of California*, III, 214; 248, n. 15. Hutchinson, *Frontier Settlement in California*, pp. 187–88. Tays, "Revolutionary California," pp. 161, 198–99, 344–45.

60. See Bancroft, *History of California*, especially II, 462, 486, 512–14; III, 8, 36–38, 41–43, 50, 186–87, 216–20.

61. Bancroft, *History of California*, III, 448, quoting Alvarado. See too, pp. 188, 229.

62. Bancroft, *History of California*, III, 188, quotes Victoria. Francis F. Guest, "Municipal Government in Spanish California," *CHSQ*, XLVI (December 1967), pp. 307–35, offers the best explanation of military dominance and the role of the comisionado in the Spanish period. For examples of military involvement in town government in the 1820s see the case of Los Angeles, described in Bancroft, *History of California*, II, 560, and Carlos Antonio Carrillo's *Exposición*, trans. by Adelaide Smithers, in John Galvin, ed., *The Coming of Justice to California: Three Documents* (San Francisco, 1963), p. 52. New Mexico had eighteen ayuntamientos in 1823. Lansing B. Bloom, "Beginnings of Representative Government in New Mexico," *NMHR*, XXI (April 1946), p. 131.

63. No good study of municipal government in Mexican California exists, and many sources contain errors. Scattered references in Bancroft, *History of California*, remain most reliable. See vol. II, 560, 572, 604, 611, and vol. III, 702–3. See, too, Henry Putney Beers, *Spanish and Mexican Records of the American Southwest: A Bibliographical Guide to Archive and Manuscript Sources* (Tucson, 1979), pp. 270–71 for a useful summary.

64. Petition of José Antonio Estudillo et al. to the head of government, San Diego, February 22, 1833, quoted in Lucy Lytle Killea, "The Political History of a Mexican Pueblo: San Diego from 1825 to 1845," *JSDH*, XII (October 1966), pp. 37–39. In 1837 San Diego lost its pueblo status.

65. The constitution indicated that subsequent legislation would establish the method

for electing deputies from the territories. Until this was done, the "Bases para ias eiecciones del nuevo congreso" of June 17, 1823 were followed. See Dublán and Lozano, eds., *Legislación mexicana,* I, 651–57, and Bancroft, *History of California,* III, p. 44, n. 25; Bloom, "New Mexico Under Mexican Administration," I, 164, n. 139. In 1830 Congress approved the *Reglas para las elecciones de diputados y de ayuntamientos del distrito y territorios de la República* (Bancroft, *History of California,* III, 50, n. 41).

66. See, for example, Bancroft, *History of California,* II, 454, n. 12.

67. Joseph A. Thompson, *El Gran Capitán: José de la Guerra. A Historical Biographical Study* (Los Angeles, 1961), pp. 96–101. Prior to De la Guerra, Governor Sola had been chosen to represent California in 1822, but he was apparently rejected by the 1823 Congress (Bancroft, *History of California,* II, 471, n. 42; 485, n. 6). For Maitorena, see Bancroft, *History of California,* III, 45–46. Representing California in the early 1830s were: Carlos Carrillo, 1831–32; Juan Bandini, 1833–34; and José Antonio Carrillo, 1835–36 (see ibid., III, 214–15; 258; 346).

68. Bloom, "New Mexico Under Mexican Administration," I, 145–46, 155–56, 164, 240–42, 263, 265, 354, 364.

69. Charles A. Hale, *Mexican Liberalism in the Age of Mora, 1821–1853* (New Haven, 1968), p. 15, tells us that the term *conservative* was not used in Mexico prior to the 1846 war with the United States. Nonetheless, it is a useful designation of one political persuasion, especially if it is understood that conservatism, like liberalism, represented a spectrum of ideas and shades of meaning, just as such labels do today.

70. Letter of March 10, 1835, quoted in Eugene C. Barker, *Mexico and Texas, 1821–1835* (Dallas, 1928), p. 133.

71. Costeloe, *La primera república federal,* pp. 26–27.

72. For a brief discussion of the events leading up to the adoption of the Constitution of 1836 and the document itself, see Tena Ramírez, ed. *Leyes fundamentales de México,* pp. 199–248, and Costeloe, *La primera república federal,* pp. 413–36.

73. Michael C. Meyer and William L. Sherman, *The Course of Mexican History* (New York, 1979), p. 324.

74. Tena Ramírez, ed., *Leyes fundamentales de México,* p. 404. Tena Ramírez includes the key documents of this era, pp. 249–436.

75. Dublán and Lozano, eds., *Legislación mexicana,* V, 155.

76. See the presidential decree of December 30, 1836 in Tena Ramírez, ed., *Leyes fundamentales,* pp. 247–48.

77. "Reglamento provisional para el gobierno interior de los Departamentos," March 20, 1837, in Dublán and Lozano, eds., *Legislación mexicana,* III, 323–38.

78. Several towns in California were entitled to ayuntamientos under the law of March 20, 1837, as Theodore Grivas points out (*Military Governments in California, 1846–1850* [Glendale, California, 1963], p. 155), but all seem to have been abolished in 1839 (see Beers, *Spanish and Mexican Records,* p. 271 and appropriate references in Bancroft).

79. Title VII of the Bases Orgánicas of 1843 permitted the number of *vocales* who constituted an assembly to vary from seven to eleven.

80. In addition to the constitutions themselves, see the Reglamento of March 20, 1837, which spelled out responsibilities of juntas and the commentaries by historians such as Josefina Zoraida Vázquez, "Los primeros tropiezos," in *Historia General de México,* 4 vols. (Mexico, 1976), III, p. 29; Agustín Cué Cánovas, *Historia social y económica de México, 1521–1854* (3rd ed.; Mexico, 1967), p. 329; Bloom, "New Mexico Under Mexican Administration," II (July 1914), p. 9, n. 344.

81. See the Constitution of 1836, Ley Primera, art. 1, part I; Ley Sexta, art. 24, part IV; Ley Tercera, art. 6, part IV; Ley Sexta, art 12 and art. 6, part V. Titles II and III of the Bases Orgánicas of 1843.

82. Hansen, *Search for Authority,* pp. 35–36. See, too, the Petition from Juan Antonio

Lovato et al. to the Departmental Assembly, Taos, January 28, 1844, in Minge, "Frontier Problems in New Mexico," pp. 169–70. Eduardo W. Villa, *Historia del Estado de Sonora* (Hermosillo, 1951), p. 221.

83. Martin Cole and Henry Welcome, eds., *Don Pio Pico's Historical Narrative*, trans. by Arthur P. Botello (Glendale, 1973), p. 146.

84. Bloom, "New Mexico under Mexican Administration," II (July 1914), p. 11, n. 348. Bancroft, *History of California*, III, 585–86.

85. Minge, "Frontier Problems in New Mexico," pp. 211–13.

86. Title I, art. 3. See, too, Minge, "Frontier Problems," pp. 315–16.

87. Ley sexta, art. 5 of the 1836 Constitution. Title VII, art. 134, part XVII of the Bases Orgánicas.

88. Quoted in Hutchinson, *Frontier California*, p. 184. See, too, Bancroft, *History of California*, III, 247, and the similar sentiments expressed by Governor Chico in his letter to the Secretaría de Guerra y Marina, Monterey, July 22, 1836, quoted in Alfonso Teja Zabre, *Lecciones de California* (Mexico, 1962), p. 78. Many observers argued the need for a distinctive political organization on the frontier. See, for example, the plan proposed by Tadeo Ortiz, outlined in Wilbert H. Timmons, *Tadeo Ortiz: Mexican Colonizer and Reformer* (El Paso, 1974), p. 42.

89. Donaciano Vigil to the Honorable Assembly, June 22, 1846, Ritch Papers, no. 233, HEH.

90. For capsule accounts, see Hansen, *Search for Authority*, pp. 24–25; 41–44. For a contemporary commentary on the quality of the governors sent to California from Mexico, see Manuel Castañares, "Exposición" of September 1, 1844, in Castañares, *Colección de documentos relativos al departamento de Californias* (Mexico, 1845), pp. 27–28, facsimile in Weber, ed., *Northern Mexico*.

91. Andrés Castillero to the Minister of War, Mexico, October 21, 1837, translated in George Tays, "Captain Andrés Castillero, Diplomat. An Account from Unpublished Sources of His Services to Mexico in the Alvarado Revolution of 1836–1838," *CHSQ*, XIV (September 1935), p. 257. Bloom, "New Mexico Under Mexican Administration," II (July 1914), p. 13.

92. Petition from Juan Antonio Lovato, et al., to the Departmental Assembly, Taos, January 28, 1844, cited in Minge, "Frontier Problems in New Mexico," pp. 169–70, 153. Bloom, "New Mexico Under Mexican Administration," II (July 1914), p. 18, who mentions that legislators as well as prefects had been added to the lists of salaried officials.

93. Bancroft, *History of California*, IV, 350; 357–58. In 1845 the prefectura system was reestablished in California. Hansen, *Search for Authority*, pp. 49–50.

94. Castañares, "Exposición, pp. 26–27. See, too, Hansen, *Search for Authority*, pp. 31, 41, 43, and Minge, "Frontier Problems in New Mexico," p. 214. Minge and Hansen term the departmental assembly "a rubber stamp."

95. See, for example, José Barragán Barragán, *Introducción al federalismo (la formación de los poderes, 1824)*, (Mexico, 1978), p. 230, paraphrasing Miguel Ramos Arizpe.

96. Carlos Antonio Carrillo, *Exposición*, in Galvin, ed., *The Coming of Justice to California*, p. 52. Although writing in 1831, Carrillo was describing a situation that had carried over from the late colonial period. See, too, Pedro Pino in Carroll and Haggard, trans. and eds., *Three New Mexico Chronicles*, p. 56; Benson, trans. and ed., *Report that Dr. Miguel Ramos de Arizpe . . . Presents*, pp. 31–32. A good secondary account of some of these matters is in Simmons, *Spanish Government in New Mexico*, pp. 18, 159–92.

97. Capítulo II, artículos 2, 3 and 4 of the "Reglamento de las audiencias y juzgados de primera instancia" of October 9, 1812, in Dublán and Lozano, eds., *Legislación mexicana*, I, 384–95. This law was reenacted in Mexico on July 22, 1833, Matthew G. Reynolds, *Spanish and Mexican Land Laws. New Spain and Mexico* (St. Louis, 1895), pp. 170–80.

98. See the law of May 29, 1826 and the more detailed version of May 22, 1834 in Dublán and Lozano, eds., *Legislación mexicana*, I, 796–97 and II, 695–99. These have been translated into English by Adelaide Smithers in Galvan, ed., *The Coming of Justice to California*. Title V of the 1824 Constitution explains the basic framework.

99. José Agustín de Escudero, *Noticias estadísticas del estado de Chihuahua* (Mexico, 1834), pp. 48–49.

100. Article 9 of the Acta Constitutiva, quoted in Barragán, *Introducción al federalismo*, p. 264.

101. Hansen, *Search for Authority in California*, p. 8. Costeloe, *La primera república federal*, p. 25. The fueros are addressed in Capítulo II, art. XXXII of the law of October 9, 1812 (Dublán and Lozano, eds., *Legislación mexicana*, I, 190), and in tit. V, sec. 7, art. 154 of the Constitution of 1824 (Tena Ramírez, ed., *Leyes fundamentales de México*, p. 190). For an example of their use and abuse late in the Mexican period see Minge, "Frontier Problems in New Mexico," pp. 128–32, 227–32.

102. Costeloe, *La primera república federal*, p. 27. Escudero, *Noticias estadísticas del estado de Chihuahua*, pp. 44–51, is highly laudatory about judicial reforms in his state.

103. A circular of August 29, 1829 from the Secretaría de Justicia indicated that New Mexico, California, and other territories were to be assigned an *asesor*, a legal counselor, often a lawyer, who would advise local officials on the law and check on local excesses (Daniel Tyler, "New Mexico in the 1820's: The First Administration of Manuel Armijo" [Ph.D. diss., University of New Mexico, 1971], pp. 243–44). This brought Licenciado Rafael Gómez to Alta California in 1830, who served until 1833 (Bancroft, *History of California*, III, 46; 759), and Lic. Antonio Barreiro to New Mexico in 1831, who remained until 1833 when he was elected delegate to Congress (Bloom, "New Mexico Under Mexican Administration," I, 271). Complaints about the failure to reorganize the judicial system are abundant during these years. See, for example, the suggestions of Juan Estevan Pino in the Minutes of the diputación, Santa Fe, June 5, 1829, MANM, roll 42, frame 611, and Carrillo, *Exposición*, in Galvin, ed., *The Coming of Justice to California*.

104. Pablo Montoya, December 19, 1828, to the Primera Secretaría de Estado, Departamento de Interior, quoted in [Juan de Dios] Canedo to the Secretaría del Departamento de Justicia, Mexico, January 17, 1829, Ramo de Justicia, volume 48, AGN.

105. Antonio Barreiro, *Ojeada sobre Nuevo México* (Puebla, 1832), in Carroll and Haggard, trans. and eds., *Three New Mexico Chronicles*, p. 47. See, too, ibid., p. 140.

106. Charles Franklin Carter, trans., "Duhaut-Cilly's Account of California in the Years 1827–1828," *CHSQ*, VIII (September 1929), p. 246.

107. Barreiro, *Ojeada* . . . , in Carroll and Haggard, trans. and eds., *Three New Mexico Chronicles*, p. 45. Grivas, *Military Governments in California*, pp. 158–65.

108. The law of October 9, 1812 remained the basis of the judicial system in the territories, as even the Ministers of Justice recognized in 1829 and 1835. Barragán, *Introducción al federalismo*, pp. 231, 233–34. See, too, Hansen, *Search for Authority*, p. 9.

109. *Representación dirijida por el ilustre ayuntamiento de la ciudad de Béxar al . . . Congreso del Estado* (Brazoria, 1833), p. 10. Observers of the Texas situation almost universally complained about the administration of justice. See, for example, Tadeo Ortiz, Matamoros, February 2, 1833, to the president, in Kelly and Hatcher, "Tadeo Ortiz," pp. 316–17. Barker, *Austin*, pp. 187–94, 396, provides a good summary of judicial problems.

110. Johnson, *A History of Texas and Texans*, I: 52–53. Hale, *Mexican Liberalism in the Age of Mora*, pp. 94–95.

111. The principal legislation affecting the administration of justice under the centralists were the "Reglamento provisional para el gobierno interior de los Departamentos," March 20, 1837, and the "Arreglo provisional de la administración de Justicia . . . del fuero común," May 23, 1837, in Dublán and Lozano, eds., *Legislación mexicana*, III, 323–38;

392–407, respectively. For the quasi-judicial functions of executive officials, see especially articles 4–7 and 64–69 of the March 20, 1837 act.

112. For a succinct and sometimes provocative summary of conditions in Alta California during these years, see Hansen, *Search for Authority,* pp. 34; 46–50. A contemporary assessment is Castañares, "Exposición" pp. 28–29. For New Mexico, see Minge, "Frontier Problems," pp. 210–14, and the Report of a Committee of the Departmental Assembly, April 29, 1846, in Ralph Emerson Twitchell, *Spanish Archives of New Mexico,* 2 vols. (Cedar Rapids, Iowa, 1914), I, 450–51 (no. 1383).

113. Theodore Grivas makes this point in his chapter "Alcalde Rule," in *Military Governments in California,* pp. 154–55. Similarly, Malcolm Ebright, "Manuel Martínez's Ditch Dispute: A Study in Mexican Period Custom and Justice," *NMHR,* LIV (January 1979), pp. 22, 30–31, argues that in New Mexico in the Mexican period alcaldes had become "strong to the point where . . . they in effect overruled the governor."

114. Josiah Gregg, *Commerce of the Prairies,* Max L. Moorhead, ed. (Norman, 1954), p. 164. Grivas, *Military Governments,* pp. 158–65, 173; Tijerina, "Tejanos and Texas," pp. 80–93.

115. Ibid., pp. 164–65.

116. Sir George Simpson, *Narrative of a Journey Round the World During the Years 1841 and 1842,* 2 vols. (London, 1847), I, 328. Richard Henry Dana, Jr., *Two Years Before the Mast,* John Haskell Kemble, ed., 2 vols. (1st ed., 1840; Los Angeles, 1964), I, 169. See, too, Hansen, *Search for Authority,* pp. 50–51, and Minge, "Frontier Problems in New Mexico," pp. 28–34.

117. Anonymous, *Considerations on the Political and Social Situation of the Mexican Republic, 1847,* Dennis E. Berge, trans. and ed. (El Paso, 1975), pp. 18–19. See, too, the candid annual report of Mariano Riva Palacio, *Memoria del ministro de justicia e instrucción pública* (Mexico, 1845), pp. 5–6, 21.

118. Chávez to Armijo, Santa Fe, January 1, 1844, published in *Diario del Gobierno,* March 30, 1844, and translated in Minge, "Frontier Problems in New Mexico," p. 156. See, too, Castañares, Mexico, June 6, 1844, to the Minister of War, in Castañares, *Colección de documentos,* p. 16.

119. Vallejo's "History of California," quoted in Tays, "Revolutionary California," pp. 117–18. Vallejo here refers to the sending of convicts to California.

120. "E. E.," the anonymous author of "El Placer del Oro," in *El Payo de Nuevo México,* Santa Fe, July 19, 1845, MANM, roll 40, frame 574. For similar sentiment from California see Carrillo, *Exposición,* in Galvin, ed., *The Coming of Justice to California,* p. 3. For Texas see Mier y Terán to Lucas Alamán, San Antonio de Padilla, July 2, 1832, quoted in Morton, *Terán and Texas,* p. 182.

121. Hansen, *The Search for Authority in California,* p. 49. For a contemporary sentiment in New Mexico, see Pronunciamiento, Departmental Assembly, Santa Fe, January 1, 1844, trans. in Minge, "Frontier Problems in New Mexico," p. 154.

122. See, for example, Minge, "Frontier Problems in New Mexico," pp. 205–6, 214–15, Bancroft, *History of California,* III, 292–93.

123. LeRoy R. and Ann W. Hafen, eds., *Rufus B. Sage: His Letters and Papers, 1836–1847, with an annotated reprint of his "Scenes in the Rocky Mountains. . . ."* 2 vols. (Glendale, 1956), II, 124. For a sample from California, see Abel du Petit-Thouars, *Voyage of the Venus: Sojourn in California. Excerpt from Voyage autour du monde sur la frégate Vénus pedant les années 1836–1839,* Charles N. Rudkin, trans. (Los Angeles, 1956), pp. 14–15. Convinced of the general inferiority of Mexicans, Anglo-Americans in particular often expressed the view that Mexicans could not govern themselves, and Mexico's chaotic first half century did nothing to disabuse them of that belief. For a brief discussion of the sources of Anglo-American prejudice, see Weber, "Scarce more than apes.' Historical Roots of Anglo Amer-

ican Stereotypes of Mexicans in the Border Region," in Weber, ed., *New Spain's Far Northern Frontier: Essays on Spain in the American West, 1540–1821* (Albuquerque, 1979), pp. 293–307.

124. John Marsh to Abel Stearns, Yerba Buena, March 27, 1837, California Historical Documents Collection, HM 40525, HEH. Petit-Thouars, *Voyage*, p. 43, expressed a similar view.

125. Castañares, "Exposición," p. 29.

Chapter 3
Collapse of the Missions

1. Fray José Señán to Fray José Gasol, June 4, 1822, in Lesley Byrd Simpson, ed., Paul D. Nathan, trans., *The Letters of José Señán, O.F.M. Mission San Buenaventura, 1796–1823* (San Francisco, 1962), p. 155.

2. Moisés González Navarro, "Instituciones indígenas en México independiente," in *Métodos y resultados de la política indigenista en México* (Mexico, 1954), p. 139.

3. Stipends for Pimería Alta missions stopped arriving 1814, for example, and those for Texas stopped in 1816. John L. Kessell, *Friars, Soldiers, and Reformers: Hispanic Arizona and the Sonora Mission Frontier, 1767–1856* (Tucson, 1976), p. 237. Marion A. Habig, *The Alamo Chain of Missions: A History of San Antonio's Five Old Missions* (Chicago, 1968), p. 107. For the economic situation see the report of Lucas Alamán, November 8, 1823, translated in Joel Roberts Poinsett, *Notes on México Made in the Autumn of 1822* (Philadelphia, 1842), p. 323; C. Alan Hutchinson, "The Mexican Government and the Mission Indians of Upper California, 1821–1835," *The Americas*, XXI (April 1965), p. 336; and Kessell, *Friars, Soldiers, and Reformers*, p. 260.

4. Governor Martínez to the commandant general, April 14, 1822, quoted in William S. Red, *The Texas Colonists and Religion, 1821–1836* (Austin, 1924), pp. 45–46. Hubert Howe Bancroft, *History of California*, 7 vols. (San Francisco, 1886–90), II, 406.

5. Señán to Fr. Baldomero López, Mission San Buenaventura, September 4, 1819, in Simpson, ed., *Letters of José Señán*, p. 129.

6. Kessell, *Friars, Soldiers, and Reformers*, p. 260. Maynard Geiger, *Franciscan Missionaries in Hispanic California, 1769–1848: A Biographical Dictionary* (San Marino, California, 1969), p. x, and Lansing B. Bloom, "New Mexico Under Mexican Administration, 1821–1846," *Old Santa Fe*, I (January 1914), p. 268.

7. The causes and effects of expulsion have been examined by Romeo Flores Caballero, *La contrarrevolución en la independencia: Los Españoles en la vida política, social y económica de México, 1804–1838* (Mexico, 1969), and in Harold D. Sims, *La expulsión de los españoles de México, 1821–1828* (Mexico, 1974). Flores Caballero's study has been translated into English by Jaime E. Rodríguez O., *Counterrevolution . . .* (Lincoln, Nebraska, 1974). The decrees, dated December 20, 1827 and March 20, 1829, are in Manuel Dublán and José María Lozano, eds., *Legislación mexicana*, 34 vols. (Mexico, 1876–1904), II, 49–51, 98–99.

8. Bloom, "New Mexico Under Mexican Administration," I, 258, 267–68. Zephyrin Engelhardt, *The Missions and Missionaries of California*, 4 vols. (San Francisco, 1908–15), III, 273–77. Bancroft, *History of California*, III, 51–52; 95–98. Pimería Alta and Texas are discussed later in this chapter.

9. Maynard Geiger, "The Internal Organization and Activities of San Fernando College, Mexico (1734–1858)," *The Americas*, VI (July 1949), p. 27. Geiger, *Franciscan Missionaries*, pp. ix–x. González Navarro, "Instituciones indígenas," p. 141. Fr. Benedict Leutenegger, trans., *The Zacatecan Missionaries in Texas, 1716–1834 . . . and A Biographical Dictionary* by Fr. Marion A. Habig (Austin, 1973), p. 167.

10. The Bourbons tried various ways to limit the economic power of the religious orders. In 1734, for example, the Crown prohibited Orders in Mexico from taking on new members for a decade. In 1749 the Crown issued a secret instruction that all missions in America be secularized—it was not carried out for lack of priests. C. H. Haring, *The Spanish Empire in America* (New York, 1947), p. 176; Gerald J. Geary, *The Secularization of the California Missions, 1810–1846* (Washington, D.C., 1934), pp. 26–31.

11. The widespread misconception that missions were to be secularized within ten years (see, for example, Charles Gibson, *Spain in America* [New York, 1966], p. 81) may have been the result of an error made by Viceroy Conde de Revillagigedo. The question is discussed in Geary, *The Secularization of the California Missions*, pp. 27–30.

12. Fermín Francisco de Lasuén, Mission San Carlos, June 19, 1801, quoted in Daniel Garr, "Planning, Politics and Plunder: The Missions and Indian Pueblos of Hispanic California," *SCQ*, LIV (Winter 1972), p. 292.

13. Fray Narciso Durán to President Anastasio Bustamante, September 23, 1830, quoted in Engelhardt, *Missions and Missionaries of California*, III, 339–40, is a good exposition of this position, as are two letters from Fray Francisco García Diego y Moreno to José Figueroa, Santa Clara, September 24 and October 15, 1833, in Francis J. Weber, ed. and trans., *Writings of Francisco García Diego y Moreno* (Los Angeles, 1976), pp. 56–60.

14. See, for example, John L. Kessell, ed. and trans., "Anza Damns the Missions: A Spanish Soldier's Criticism of Indian Policy, 1772," *JAH*, 13 (Spring 1972), p. 58.

15. Durán to Pío Pico, December 26, 1845, quoted in Engelhardt, *Missions and Missionaries of California*, IV, 452.

16. Quoted in Hutchinson, "The Mexican Government and the Mission Indians," p. 342. See, too, n. 13 *supra*, and Maynard Geiger, ed. and trans., *As the Padres Saw Them: California Indian Life and Customs as Reported by the Franciscan Missionaries, 1813–1815* (Santa Barbara, 1976), an especially revealing collection.

17. Much has been written about the forcible detention of Indians. See, for example, Billie Persons, "Secular Life in the San Antonio Missions," *SWHQ*, LXII (July 1958), p. 60; Edward Spicer, *Cycles of Conquest* (Tucson, 1962), pp. 159; 324–26; Robert Archibald, "Indian Labor at the California Missions: Slavery or Salvation?" *JSDH*, XXIV (Spring 1978), pp. 172–82; Francis F. Guest, "An Examination of the Thesis of S. F. Cook on the Forced Conversion of Indians in the California Missions," *SCQ*, LXI (Spring 1979), pp. 1–77.

18. The text of the decree may be found in Francisco F. de la Maza, *Código de colonización y terrenos baldíos de la República Mexicana* (Mexico, 1893), pp. 152–53. James M. Breedlove, "Effect of the Cortes, 1810–1822, on Church Reform in Spain and Mexico," in Nettie Lee Benson, ed., *Mexico and the Spanish Cortes, 1810–1822* (Austin, 1966), p. 122.

19. Bancroft, *History of California*, II, 43. Carlos E. Castañeda, *Our Catholic Heritage*, VI, 320. Contemporaries disagreed or expressed confusion as to whether or not the law was still in force. See, for example, Geary, *Secularization of the California Missions*, pp. 114, 129, 131–42, who himself doubted that the law remained on the books. See, too, C. Alan Hutchinson, *Frontier Settlement in Mexican California. The Híjar-Padrés Colony and its Origins, 1769–1835* (New Haven, 1969), pp. 166, 224. Fray Francisco García Diego y Moreno probably took the most realistic position when he acknowledged that the law was still theoretically in force, but argued that "when a law ceases to be beneficial, it loses its binding force." Letter to José Figueroa, Santa Clara, Sept. 24, 1833, in Weber, ed. and trans., *Writings of García Diego*, p. 57.

20. Decrees of the Spanish Cortes of February 9, 1811; March 18 and November 9, 1812; April 29, 1820; and Article 12 of the Plan of Iguala. Both quotes are from González Navarro, "Instituciones indígenas," p. 115. See, too, Hutchinson, "The Mexican Government and the Mission Indians," p. 340.

21. This, for example, was the position taken by the Commission for the Development of

the Californias in 1825: See "Plan for the Administration of the Missions in the Territories of Upper and Lower California . . . April 6, 1825," trans. by Keld J. Reynolds, "Principal Actions of the California Junta de Fomento, 1825–1827," *CHSQ*, XIV (December 1945), pp. 303–8.

22. Tadeo Ortiz to Anastasio Bustamante, Bordeaux, November 30, 1830, in Edith Louise Kelly and Mattie Austin Hatcher, eds., "Tadeo Ortiz de Ayala and the Colonization of Texas, 1822–1833," *SWHQ*, XXXII (February 1928), p. 235. See, too, José María Luis Mora, quoted in Charles A. Hale, *Mexican Liberalism in the Age of Mora, 1821–1853* (New Haven, 1968), p. 235.

23. The best discussion of the liberal philosophy and its critics is in González Navarro, "Instituciones indígenas," pp. 115–19.

24. See, for example, the reaction of Fray José Pérez Llera, quoted in Kessell, *Friars, Soldiers, and Reformers*, p. 292, and the reaction of Fray Narciso Durán cited in Michael C. Neri, "Narcisco [*sic*] Durán and the Secularization of the California Missions," *The Americas*, XXXIII (January 1977), pp. 421, 425.

25. Dublán y Lozano, eds., *Legislación mexicana*, II, 689. A translation of this decree appears in Engelhardt, *Missions and Missionaries of California*, III, 521.

26. Decreto del gobierno, June 21, 1843, in Dublán and Lozano, *Legislación mexicana*, IV, 465–66. Carlos María Bustamante expressed similar sentiments. José Gutiérrez Casillas, *Jesuitas en México durante el siglo XIX* (Mexico, 1972), pp. 102–7.

27. John Kessell neatly summarizes this in his article, "Friars versus Bureaucrats: The Mission as a Threatened Institution on the Arizona-Sonora Frontier," *WHQ*, V (April 1974), pp. 151–60. For a more detailed discussion, see Kessell, *Friars, Soldiers, and Reformers*, chapters 2–9. With his customary generosity, Kessell provided me a copy of the manuscript of that book prior to its publication.

28. Henry F. Dobyns, "Indian Extinction in the Middle Santa Cruz Valley, Arizona," *NMHR*, XXXVIII (April 1963), pp. 163–81, who concluded that a population of some 2,400 Indians in 1700 had decreased to fewer than 100 a century later!

29. Kessell, *Friars, Soldiers, and Reformers*, p. 246. See, too, the provocative article by Cynthia Radding de Murrieta, "The Function of the Market in Changing Economic Structures in the Mission Communities of Pimería Alta, 1768–1821," *The Americas*, XXXIV (October 1977), pp. 155–69, who argues that the mission communities were weakened by the channeling of Indian labor and commodities into the private sector.

30. Kessell, *Friars, Soldiers, and Reformers*, pp. 262–67.

31. Ibid., p. 301.

32. Ibid., pp. 269–74.

33. Ibid., pp. 277–78, 288–89, 293.

34. Ibid., pp. 277–82.

35. Ibid., pp. 293–303.

36. Habig, *The Alamo Chain of Missions*, pp. 70–71. Although undocumented, this careful study is well grounded in primary and secondary sources. See, too, Charles Ramsdell, *San Antonio: A Historical and Pictorial Guide* (Austin, 1959), pp. 18–19.

37. [José Francisco López], "Report on the San Antonio Missions in 1792," trans. by Benedict Leutenegger, O.F.M. and ed. by Marion A. Habig, O.F.M., *SWHQ*, LXXVII (April 1974), pp. 486–98.

38. Report of Juan Antonio Padilla, December 27, 1819, quoted in Mattie Austin Hatcher, trans., "Texas in 1820," *SWHQ*, XXIII (July 1919), pp. 59–60. Padilla thought there were no Indians at the San Antonio missions, but "if there are any, they are but few in number and changed into castes by mixture with the settlers of Bexar."

39. Jean Louis Berlandier, *Journey to Mexico During the Years 1826 to 1834*, C. H. Muller and Katherine K. Muller, eds., and Sheila M. Ohlendorf, Josette M. Bigelow, and Mary M.

Standifer, trans., 2 vols. (Austin, 1980), II, 379. Castañeda, *Our Catholic Heritage*, V, 35–67. Note 43, *infra*. The standard sources on Díaz de León do not indicate the place of his birth. Fr. Benedict Leutenegger, O.F.M., who has studied his letters and life, concludes: "I can say with assurance that he was born in Mexico." Letter to the author, Mission San José, San Antonio, Texas, December 8, 1978.

40. Habig, *Alamo Chain*, pp. 179; 108–110. Castañeda, *Our Catholic Heritage*, VI, pp. 317–24 and pp. 348–50. Castañeda terms the settlers' interest in mission lands "greed" (p. 321). Félix D. Almaraz, Jr., "San Antonio's Missions in the Mexican Period—Material Decline and Secular Avarice," paper presented to a joint session of the Texas Catholic Historical Society and the Texas State Historical Association, San Antonio, March 9, 1979. Almaraz kindly made a copy available to me.

41. Instructions of the Ayuntamiento of Béxar, November 15, 1820, in Hatcher, trans., "Texas in 1820," p. 61.

42. Paul H. Walters, "Secularization of the La Bahía Missions," *SWHQ*, LIV (January 1951), pp. 287–300. Castañeda, *Our Catholic Heritage*, VI, pp. 317–27.

43. Geiger, *Franciscan Missionaries*, pp. 164–65. Biographical sketches of Frays Muro and Díaz de León are included in Leutenegger and Habig, *The Zacatecan Missionaries in Texas*, pp. 116–17; 113–34. Castañeda, *Our Catholic Heritage*, VI, pp. 330–31, 334–40, discusses the possibility of the suicide of Fray José.

44. Eleanor B. Adams, ed., *Bishop Tamarón's Visitation of New Mexico, 1760* (Albuquerque, 1954), p. 77. Fr. José Pedro Rubin de Celis, Census, December 31, 1821, cited in Bloom, "New Mexico Under Mexican Administration," I, p. 28, no. 43. Although Rubin de Celis apparently noted twenty-three padres in New Mexico, faulty addition led him to total their number at twenty, an error that some historians have perpetuated.

45. Like all statistics dealing with New Mexico in this period, these are meant only to suggest a tendency rather than to represent precise counts. For two very different calculations, using the same census materials, see Oakah L. Jones, Jr., *Pueblo Warriors and Spanish Conquest* (Norman, 1966), p. 153, and Alicia V. Tjarks, "Demographic, Ethnic and Occupational Structure of New Mexico, 1790," *The Americas*, XXXV (July 1978), pp. 60–61.

46. See Adam's balanced remarks on this matter in *Bishop Tamarón's Visitation*, p. 31, and John L. Kessell, *Kiva, Cross, and Crown: The Pecos Indians and New Mexico, 1540–1840* (Washington, D.C., 1979), p. 343.

47. Report of Juan Bautista Ladrón del Niño de Guevara to Juan Francisco de Castañiza Bishop of Durango, Durango, October 23, 1820. Archives of the Archdiocese of Santa Fe, microfilm, NMSRC, Santa Fe, roll 45, frames 285–302. His report might have been exaggerated, for there was little love lost between the bishop and the Franciscans during these years, but the tone of the visitor's remarks does not vary from others of the era.

48. Lawrence and Lucia Kinnaird, "Secularization of Four New Mexico Missions," *NMHR*, LIV (January 1979), pp. 35–41. Angélico Chávez, "The Penitentes of New Mexico," *NMHR*, XXIX (April 1954), p. 116. Angélico Chávez, *Archives of the Archdiocese of Santa Fe, 1678–1900* (Washington, 1957), pp. 55, 87, 167, 193, 258–62. Pedro Bautista Pino, *Exposición . . .* (Cádiz, 1812), in H. Bailey Carroll and J. Villasana Haggard, eds. and trans., *Three New Mexico Chronicles* (Albuquerque, 1942), p. 50. Ladrón Niño de Guevara to Bishop Castañiza, October 23, 1820. For references to Tomé, I am grateful to Ramón Gutiérrez of Pomona College. The term *mission* was used broadly in New Mexico, to embrace Spanish towns as well as Indian pueblos, since Franciscans served both. See John L. Kessell, *The Missions of New Mexico Since 1776* (Albuquerque, 1980), p. xi.

49. France V. Scholes, *Troublous Times in New Mexico, 1659–1670* (Albuquerque, 1942), pp. 11, 25–26. Charles Lange, *Cochiti: A New Mexico Pueblo Past and Present* (Austin, 1958), p. 39. The figure for Cochití is for 1776. The amount of land and labor set aside for the Church depended upon the priest's needs and the generosity of the Pueblo.

50. Minutes of the Diputación of New Mexico, sessions of August 10 and 16, 1824, MANM, roll 42, frames 217, 219. Bloom, "New Mexico Under Mexican Administration," I (October 1913), p. 173 and ibid., I (January 1914), p. 248. John Baptist Salpointe, *Soldiers of the Cross* (Banning, California, 1898), pp. 160–61.

51. Chávez, *Archives of the Archdiocese of Santa Fe*, p. 192.

52. Marta Weigle, *Brothers of Light, Brothers of Blood: The Penitentes of the Southwest* (Albuquerque, 1976), p. 22. Antonio Barreiro, *Ojeada Sobre Nuevo-México . . .* (Puebla, 1832), in Carroll and Haggard, eds. and trans., *Three New Mexico Chronicles*, pp. 28–29; 53–55.

53. Chávez, *Archives of the Archdiocese of Santa Fe*, pp. 241–58, and pp. 196–97, and the list of friars who served in New Mexico, ibid., pp. 241–58.

54. José de Gálvez, who directed the settlement of Alta California, had just tried and failed to reorganize the mission Indians of Baja California and Pimería Alta into well-planned secular communities. Ignacio A. del Río Chávez, "Utopia in Baja California, The Dreams of José de Gálvez," *JSDH*, XVIII (Fall 1972), pp. 1–13. Modifications of the traditional mission system were attempted in late-eighteenth century California. See Francis Guest, "Mission Colonization and Political Control in Spanish California," *JSDH*, XXIV (Winter 1978), pp. 97–116. Kessell, "Friars vs. Bureaucrats," pp. 152–53. Geary, *Secularization*, pp. 46, 51.

55. J. N. Bowman, "The Resident Neophytes *(Existentes)* of the California Missions, 1769–1834," *SCQ*, XL (June 1958), pp. 147–48, puts the neophyte population at over 21,000 in 1820, 1821 and 1824. See, too, the interesting charts and analysis by David Hornbeck, "Mission Population of Alta California," *Historical Geography*, 8 (Spring 1978), Supplement, n.p.

56. For an able articulation of reasons for preserving the missions in California, see Fray Francisco García Diego y Moreno to José Figueroa, Santa Clara, September 24 and October 15, 1833, in Weber, ed. and trans., *Writings of Francisco García Diego*, pp. 56–60.

57. Geiger, *Missionaries*, p. 21; Engelhardt, *Missions and Missionaries*, III, 225–26. On two occasions, in 1821 and 1826, the Fernandinos offered to relinquish the missions, perhaps knowing that the offer would be refused because no one could replace them. See Geary, *Secularization*, pp. 97–98; Hutchinson, "Mexican Government and the Mission Indians," p. 340; and Engelhardt *Missions and Missionaries*, III, 341.

58. Durán outlined his plan in letters to Bustamante, September 23, 1830, and Figueroa, October 3, 1833. They are discussed in Geary, *Secularization*, pp. 119–20, 140–41 and trans. in Engelhardt, *Missions and Missionaries*, III, 337–44; 488–95. The quote is from p. 493. Durán had suggested this at least as early as 1821—see his letter to Fr. Juan Cortés, March 11, 1821, in "Letters of Narciso Durán . . . " trans. and ed. by Francis Price, *CHSQ*, XXXVII (September 1958), p. 253. For a summary of Durán's views see Neri, "Narcisco [sic] Durán," pp. 411–29.

59. Bishop Francisco García Diego to José María Híjar, n.p., August 8, 1845, in Weber, ed. and trans. *Writings of Francisco García Diego*, p. 175. See, too, George William Beattie, *California's Unbuilt Missions. Spanish Plans for an Inland Chain* (Los Angeles, 1930).

60. Heinrich Virmond to Lucas Alamán, Mazatlán, February 1, 1831, in David J. Weber and Ronald R. Young, eds. and trans., "California in 1831," *JSDH*, XXI (Fall 1975), p. 4. Other contemporaries noted the problem: José Bandini, *A Description of California in 1828*, trans. by Doris M. Wright (Berkeley, 1951), pp. 6–7; Governor Echeandía, as quoted in Bancroft, *History of California*, III, 104, n. 37. One of the few historians to address this question is Manuel P. Servín, "The Secularization of the California Missions: A Reappraisal," *SCQ*, XLVII (June 1965), pp. 135–36.

61. George Tays, "Mariano Guadalupe Vallejo and Sonoma. A Biography and a History," *CHSQ*, XVI (September 1937), p. 235.

62. This, for example, concerned the committee headed by Juan Francisco de Azcárate.

"Dictamen presentado a la soberana junta gobernative del imperio mexicano," December 29, 1821, published under the title *Un programa de política internacional* (Mexico, 1932).

63. See, for example, Bancroft, *History of California*, II, 517–18, and Fray Francisco García Diego y Moreno to José Figueroa, Santa Clara, June 15, 1833, in Weber, ed. and trans., *Writings of Francisco García Diego*, pp. 53–54.

64. Echeandía to the Ministro de Relaciones, June 30, 1829, quoted in Engelhardt, *Missions and Missionaries*, III, 273–74.

65. I have based this ratio on 21,000 Indians to 3,200 non-Indians. For the 1824 revolt at Santa Barbara, see Maynard Geiger, *Mission Santa Barbara, 1782–1965* (Santa Barbara, 1965), pp. 85–94; Geiger, ed. and trans., "Fray Antonio Ripoll's Description of the Chumash Revolt at Santa Barbara in 1824," *SCQ*, LII (December 1970), pp. 345–64; and Thomas Blackburn, ed., "The Chumash Revolt of 1824: A Native Account," *Journal of California Anthropology*, II (Winter 1975), pp. 223–27. For examples of concern about Indian revolt, see Hutchinson, *Frontier Settlement in Mexican California*, p. 152, and Bancroft, *History of California*, III, p. 104, n. 38, quoting Angustias de la Guerra.

66. Hutchinson, "The Mexican Government and the Mission Indians," pp. 346–48. Geary, *Secularization*, p. 96. "Plan for the Administration of the Missions in the Territories of Upper and Lower California. Proposed by the Junta de Fomento of that Peninsula," Mexico, April 6, 1825, trans. in Keld J. Reynolds in "Principal Actions of the California Junta de Fomento," pp. 303–8, and "Final Opinion," May 15, 1827, in ibid., XXV (December, 1946), p. 360. Hutchinson, *Frontier Settlement*, pp. 117–21, 126–27, 143, 156–67.

67. Hutchinson, *Frontier Settlement*, pp. 109–10.

68. Alvarado recalls this incident occurring in early 1831. "History of California," III, pp. 6–7, ms. Bancroft Library, Berkeley. See, too, Bancroft, *History of California*, III, 331–32.

69. George Harwood Phillips, "Indians and the Breakdown of the Spanish Mission System in California," *Ethnohistory*, XXI (Fall 1974), p. 299.

70. Captain Frederick W. Beechey, who took a generally favorable view of the missions, quoted in Hutchinson, "The Mexican Government and the Mission Indians," p. 347.

71. Durán quoted in ibid., p. 350. See, too, Geary, *Secularization*, p. 99, and Bancroft, *History of California*, III, 102–4. Hutchinson provides a good synthesis of these events in *Frontier Settlement in Mexican California*, pp. 128–33.

72. Hutchinson, *Frontier Settlement in Mexican California*, pp. 229, 237. Hutchinson, "The Mexican Government and the Mission Indians," pp. 349–50; 353–54.

73. Dublán and Lozano, *Legislación mexicana*, II, 548–49. Circumstances surrounding the adoption of this bill and its aftermath are best examined in Hutchinson, *Frontier Settlement in Mexican California*, pp. 159–73, 244–45, who sheds new light on this complex question.

74. Hutchinson, *Frontier Settlement*, pp. 182–86, 210–12.

75. The text of this August 9, 1834 plan is translated in Engelhardt, *Missions and Missionaries*, III, 523–30, who labeled it "the crime of the nineteenth century." Bancroft was more sympathetic to the plan, regarding it as "wisely conceived in theory" but difficult to administer (*History of California*, IV, 43–44; III, 342–44). All earlier works have now been supplanted by Hutchinson's summary and analysis of the plan and of Figueroa's quarrel with Híjar, as presented in *Frontier Settlement*, pp. 251–61; 384–91, and in his introduction and translation of Figueroa's *A Manifesto to the Mexican Republic* (1st ed., 1835; Berkeley, 1978), which reinterprets Figueroa's polemic.

76. Englishman William Hartnell, quoted in Lauro de Rojas, ed., "California in 1844 as Hartnell Saw It," *CHSQ*, XVII (March 1938), p. 24.

77. Fray José María de Jesús González Rubio to Fray Rafael Soria, Mission San José, November 3, 1840, quoted in full in Engelhardt, *Missions and Missionaries*, IV, 214–19, describes at length the miserable condition of the missions and the padres. For good general discussions of this period see Bancroft, *History of California*, IV, 42–67, and Daniel Garr, "Planning, Politics, and Plunder," pp. 291–312.

78. Phillips, "Indians and the Breakdown of the Spanish Mission System," pp. 291–302. Sherburne F. Cook, *The Conflict Between the California Indian and White Civilization* (Berkeley, 1976), pp. [98–134].

79. Geiger, *Franciscan Missionaries in Hispanic California*, pp. ix–xi. Bancroft, *History of California*, II, 393; IV, 63. Weber, ed. and trans., *Writings of Francisco García Diego*, p. 79. Appendix to Francis J. Weber, *Francisco García Diego: California's Transition Bishop* (Los Angeles, 1972), p. 63.

80. John B. McGloin, "The California Church in Transition," *CHSQ*, XLII (March 1963), p. 47. Bancroft, *History of California*, IV, 546–53. Geary, *Secularization*, pp. 185–89. Neri, "Narciso [sic] Durán," pp. 426–28. The missions enjoyed a reprieve in 1843 when Manuel Micheltorena restored the properties of twelve missions to the padres, but a year later the government reversed the order. Bancroft, *History of California*, IV, 368–71, 424.

81. Friedrich Katz, "Labor Conditions on Haciendas in Porfirian Mexico: Some Trends and Tendencies," *HAHR*, LIV (February 1974), p. 39.

82. Speech in Congress, March 30, 1844, in Manuel Castañares, *Colección de documentos relativos al departamento de Californias* (Mexico, 1845), p. 11. Facsimile in David J. Weber, ed., *Northern Mexico on the Eve of the United States Invasion: Rare Imprints . . .* (New York, 1976). See, too, Secretaría de Relaciones, Luis Gonzaga Cuevas, March 1845, quoted in González Navarro, "Instituciones indígenas," p. 144.

Chapter 4
Church in Jeopardy

1. Karl M. Schmitt, "The Clergy and the Independence of New Spain," *HAHR*, XXXIV (August 1954), p. 289. J. Lloyd Mecham, *Church and State in Latin America: A History of Politico-Ecclesiastical Relations* (rev. ed.; Chapel Hill, 1966), pp. 346–47; 355. Anne Staples, *La iglesia en la primera república federal mexicana, 1824–1835* (Mexico, 1976), pp. 22–25, 74–85, 87–88. Mariano Cuevas, *Historia de la Iglesia en México*, 5 vols. (5th ed.; Mexico, 1947), V, 169–70, 197. For the situation in Sonora, see Kieran McCarty, "Our Desert Under Spain and Mexico: The Diocesan Story, 1691–1860," in *Shepherds in the Desert: A Sequel to Salpointe* (Tucson, 1978), pp. 26–37.

2. José Agustín Escudero, *Noticias estadísticas de Sonora y Sinaloa* (Mexico, 1849), pp. 40–41. This office would have been filled earlier, in 1832, but for the illness of the new bishop. Staples, *La iglesia en la primera república*, p. 79. Carlos E. Castañeda, *Our Catholic Heritage in Texas, 1519–1936*, 7 vols. (Austin, 1931–58), VI, 344, 355; VII, 3. Staples, ibid., p. 21.

3. For examples of men who served as vicars see Castañeda, *Our Catholic Heritage*, VI, 311–17; Angélico Chávez, *Archives of the Archdiocese of Santa Fe, 1678–1900* (Washington, 1957), pp. 179–84, 195–96, and Maynard Geiger, *Franciscan Missionaries in Hispanic California, 1769–1848. A Biographical Dictionary* (San Marino, California, 1969), pp. 72, 140, 220. For the powers granted to one vicar, see Castañeda, ibid., pp. 311–12, and *infra* note 7.

4. See, for example, García Diego to Joaquín Iturbide, Mexico City, June 27, 1836, in Francis J. Weber, trans. and ed., *The Writings of Francisco García Diego y Moreno* (Los Angeles, 1976), p. 80, and Mariano Chávez to Manuel Armijo, Santa Fe, January 1, 1844, quoted in Ward Alan Minge, "Frontier Problems in New Mexico Preceding the Mexican War, 1840–1846" (Ph.D. diss., University of New Mexico, 1965), p. 157.

5. Quoted in Gerald J. Geary, *The Secularization of the California Missions, 1810–1846* (Washington, D.C., 1934), p. 181. A fine summary of the bishop's life appears in Geiger, *Franciscan Missionaries*, pp. 98–103, and in the introduction to Weber, trans. and ed., *Writings of Francisco García Diego*, pp. 8–12, but the definitive work is Francis J. Weber,

Francisco García Diego: California's Transition Bishop (Los Angeles, 1972), which supersedes Weber's 1961 biography.

6. Pedro Bautista Pino, *Exposición* . . . (Cádiz, 1812), in H. Bailey Carroll and J. Villasana Haggard, eds. and trans., *Three New Mexico Chronicles* (Albuquerque, 1942), pp. 50–51. Visits occurred in 1730, 1737, and 1760. Eleanor B. Adams, ed., *Bishop Tamarón's Visitation of New Mexico, 1760* (Albuquerque, 1954), pp. 15–21. Arizona's only episcopal visitor under Spain or Mexico, Bishop Bernardo del Espíritu Santo, traveled up the Santa Cruz Valley to Tucson, performing numerous confirmations along the way, in January 1821, a month before Iturbide declared independence. McCarty, "Our Desert Under Spain and Mexico," pp. 33–34.

7. Josiah Gregg, *Commerce of the Prairies*, Max L. Moorhead, ed. (Norman, 1954), p. 179 describes preparations to receive the bishop. Chávez, *Archives of the Archdiocese of Santa Fe*, pp. 191–92, cites Zubiría granting power to confirm to Juan Rafael Ortiz in 1833 for a five year period. The Franciscan vicar in California held this power, too, for a limited amount of time. See Weber, trans. and ed., *Writings of Francisco García Diego*, p. 9.

8. Staples, *La iglesia en la primera república*, pp. 23–25. Cuevas, *Historia de la Iglesia*, V, 188–89, calculates 4,229 secular clergy in 1810 and 2,282 in 1830.

9. Cuevas, *Historia de la Iglesia*, V, 37–38. See, too, Wilfrid H. Callcott, *Church and State in Mexico, 1822–1857* (Durham, N.C., 1926), pp. 95–96, 169. Juan Estevan Pino of New Mexico described the hardships of frontier life as obstacles to attracting even members of the mendicant orders to New Mexico. Pino, "Manifiesto," November 24, 1829, MANM, roll 9, frames 1124–25.

10. Antonio Barreiro, *Ojeada sobre Nuevo-México* . . . (Puebla, 1832), in Carroll and Haggard, trans. and eds., *Three New Mexico Chronicles* p. 54.

11. See, for example, Pino, *Exposición*, in Carroll and Haggard, trans. and eds., *Three New Mexico Chronicles*, pp. 51–52; Francisco García Diego y Moreno to Joaquín Iturbide, Mexico City, June 27, 1836 in Weber, trans. and ed., *Writings of Francisco García Diego*, p. 80; Narciso Durán to Anastasio Bustamante and to José Figueroa, September 23, 1830 and October 3, 1833 respectively, in Zephyrin Engelhardt, *The Missions and Missionaries of California*, 4 vols. (San Francisco, 1908–1915), III, 337–44, 488–95.

12. Bishop García Diego to José María Híjar, n.p., August 18, 1845, in Weber, trans. and ed., *Writings of Francisco García Diego*, p. 174.

13. E. K. Francis, "Padre Martínez: A New Mexico Myth," *NMHR*, XXXI (October 1956), p. 271. Two important sources for the life of Martínez are in David J. Weber, ed., *Northern Mexico on the Eve of the United States Invasion. Rare imprints* . . . (New York, 1976). Other exceptions were Rev. José de los Santos Avila of Santa Clara, California (Weber, trans. and ed., *Writings of Francisco García Diego*, pp. 131, 187), and fathers Juan Manuel Zambrano and José Dario Zambrano of San Antonio (Castañeda, *Our Catholic Heritage*, VI, 316).

14. Report of Juan Bautista Ladrón del Niño de Guevara to Juan Francisco de Castañiza, Bishop of Durango, October 23, 1820. Archives of the Archdiocese of Santa Fe, microfilm in the NMSRC, roll 45, frames 285–302. Pino, "Manifiesto," November 24, 1829, MANM, r. 9, fr. 1124–25. Chávez, *Archives of the Archdiocese of Santa Fe*, pp. 258–62. Chávez's data reveal that a total of twenty-two secular priests served New Mexico during the Mexican period. Not all served simultaneously, of course. Weber, trans. and ed., *Writings of Francisco García Diego*, p. 103. Weber, *Francisco García Diego, California's Transition Bishop*, p. 63. Castañeda, *Our Catholic Heritage in Texas*, VII, 2, 26. As in New Mexico, more curas had served Texas than remained at the end of the Mexican era (i.e. Francisco Maynes, Juan Nepomuceno Ayala, José Ignacio Galindo), but they did not all serve at the same time and some served only briefly. By 1836 only Refugio de la Garza and José Antonio Valdez remained.

15. Callcott, *Church and State in Mexico*, pp. 45–46, 63, 65–66, 161–62. Mecham, *Church and State in Latin America*, pp. 355, 344. An excellent summary of the onslaught on Church

finances during these years is Michael P. Costeloe, *Church Wealth in Mexico: A Study of the "Juzgado de Capellanías" in the Archbishopric of Mexico, 1800–1856* (Cambridge, Eng., 1967), pp. 1–29. Levies on Church property usually had no direct effect on the frontier churches since they had no excess funds to contribute. See, for example, Castañeda, *Our Catholic Heritage*, VI, 354.

16. García Diego to the Minister of Justice, Santa Barbara, October 27, 1843, in Weber, trans. and ed., *Writings of Francisco García Diego*, pp. 139–41 and Weber, *Francisco García Diego*, pp. 46–47. Francis J. Weber, "The United States Versus Mexico: The Final Settlement of the Pious Fund of the Californias," *SCQ*, LI (June 1969), pp. 101–3.

17. García Diego to Manuel Micheltorena, n.p., September 6, 1844, in Weber, trans. and ed., *Writings of Francisco García Diego*, p. 164. The bishop frequently discussed his fiscal problems in his correspondence.

18. Staples, *La iglesia en la primera república*, pp. 97–126. The abolition of obligatory tithes was one of the few anti-clerical measures of the Gómez Farías government that was not repealed by later administrations (Callcott, *Church and State in Mexico*, pp. 91–92, 121). Michael P. Costeloe, "The Administration, Collection, and Distribution of Tithes in the Archbishopric of Mexico, 1800–1860," *The Americas*, XXIII (July 1966), pp. 26–27.

19. Barreiro, *Ojeada*, in Carroll and Haggard, trans. and eds., *Three New Mexico Chronicles*, p. 55. See, too, Escudero's comments in ibid., pp. 39–40. The system of paying collectors a percentage of the tithe was used throughout Mexico.

20. Pino, *Exposición*, in ibid., pp. 35, 51–53. The system in the late colonial period is explained in Marc Simmons, *Spanish Government in New Mexico* (Albuquerque, 1968), pp. 107–10. For the use of the tithe to support schools see Lansing B. Bloom, "New Mexico Under Mexican Administration, 1821–1846," *Old Santa Fe*, I (January 1914), p. 273. A higher percentage of tithes collected in New Mexico may have stayed in the territory under Mexico than under Spain, but this question requires further study.

21. Manuel de Jesús Rada,*Proposición hecha al Soberano Congreso . . .* (Mexico, 1829), p. 4, facsimile in Weber, ed., *Northern Mexico*. See, too, Cura Antonio José Martínez, quoted in Bloom, "New Mexico Under Mexican Administration," I (January 1914), pp. 280–81.

22. W. W. H. Davis, *El Gringo: or, New Mexico and Her People* (1st ed., 1857; Santa Fe, 1938), pp. 94–95.

23. Tithes had been collected in California in the late colonial period. See for example, Hubert Howe Bancroft, *History of California*, 7 vols. (San Francisco, 1886–90), II, 102, n. 9 and p. 182. In 1833 the lower house of Congress excused Californians from paying tithes (Staples, *La iglesia*, p. 104). I have seen no evidence of tithes being collected in Mexican Texas, although attempts were made in the colonial period. This question needs further study. See, Castañeda, *Our Catholic Heritage in Texas*, III, 108–10; V, 28; VI, 313–37. Mary Angela Fitzmorris, *Four Decades of Catholicism in Texas, 1820–1860* (Washington, D.C., 1926), pp. 25–26.

24. Bishop García Diego, Pastoral Letter, Santa Barbara, February 4, 1842, in Weber, trans. and ed., *Writings of Francisco García Diego*, p. 116.

25. García Diego to the Minister of Justice, Santa Barbara, October 27, 1843, in ibid., p. 140.

26. García Diego to Manuel Micheltorena, n.p., September 6, 1844, in Weber, ed. and trans., *Writings of Francisco García Diego*, pp. 163–65. Bancroft, *History of California*, IV, 372–73.

27. Published literature contains little on this subject in regard to Texas in the Mexican period, but see Castañeda, *Our Catholic Heritage*, VI, 314–15; 354. In 1825 Domingo de Ugartechea ordered the clergy to perform sacraments free of charge due to the poverty of the people. Antonio Elozua to Governador de la Mitra de Monterrey, Béxar, September 9, 1825, BA, roll 84, frames 84–89.

28. David J. Weber, ed., "El gobierno territorial de Nuevo México—La exposición del Padre Martínez de 1831," *Historia Mexicana*, XXV (1975), p. 314. See note chapter 12 for the context of this episode, which occurred during the 1837 revolt.

29. This problem antedated the Mexican era, of course. See, for example, the report of Fray Anastasio Domínguez in Eleanor B. Adams and Angélico Chávez, *Missions of New Mexico, 1776* (Albuquerque, 1956), pp. 29–30. See, too, Pedro Sánchez, *Memorias sobre la vida del presbítero don Antonio José Martínez* (Santa Fe, 1903), pp. 17–19, facsimile in Weber, ed. *Northern Mexico*. Staples, *La iglesia en la primera república*, pp. 127–36.

30. James Josiah Webb, *Adventures in the Santa Fe Trade, 1844–1847*, Ralph P. Bieber, ed. (Glendale, Ca., 1931), p. 102. For an urbane discussion of this question, see Fray Angélico Chávez, "Doña Tules, Her Fame and Her Funeral," *El Palacio*, LVII (August 1950), pp. 233–34. Examples of foreign commentaries on this question are in Gregg, *Commerce of the Prairies*, pp. 183–84, and Davis, *El Gringo*, p. 95.

31. García Diego to the minister of Exterior Affairs, Santa Barbara, September 9, 1843, and García Diego to Pío Pico, Santa Barbara, July 4, 1845, in Weber, trans. and ed., *Writings of Francisco García Diego*, pp. 137 and 171.

32. For a variety of examples, see Cecil Robinson, *With the Ears of Strangers: The Mexican in American Literature* (Tucson, 1963), pp. 122–28.

33. Anthropologist Frances Swadesh has argued that "concepts of morality also were altered by frontier influences. Emphasis on parenthood and marriage was so great that even the native-born priests placed less value on celibacy than their counterparts elsewhere." *Los Primeros Pobladores: Hispanic Americans of the Ute Frontier* (Notre Dame, 1974), p. 188. Many writers, on the other hand, view the Mexican clergy in general as declining in quality during these years. For a contemporary view, see Brantz Mayer, *Mexico: Aztec, Spanish and Republican*, 2 vols. (Hartford, Conn., 1851), II, 134–35. For the views of a modern historian see Callcott, *Church and State*, pp. 167–68. The Jesuit historian Mariano Cuevas, on the other hand, acknowledges prevailing opinion but denies its validity, concluding that on the whole the clergy remained *"aceptable y bueno."* *La historia de la iglesia*, V, 193.

34. Barreiro, *Ojeada*, in Carroll and Haggard, trans. and eds., *Three New Mexico Chronicles*, p. 55.

35. The scandalous lives of New Mexico's clergy have been described by many writers, but the best account of this era is Paul Horgan's *Lamy of Santa Fe* (New York, 1975). See pp. 107–8, 148–52, for example. E. K. Francis, on the other hand, has argued that "the wholesale removal of the native clergy has been a tragedy," which was caused by cultural differences rather than moral turpitude. Francis makes a case in regard to Martínez, finding no proof that he was guilty of immoral behavior, but does not attempt to vindicate the other Mexican-born clergy. Francis, "Padre Martínez: A New Mexico Myth," pp. 270–71.

36. Castañeda, *Our Catholic Heritage in Texas*, VI, 313–17; VII, 2, 26. Charges against these two priests were signed by Juan Seguín and José Antonio Navarro and may have been exaggerated, as Castañeda suggests. Nonetheless, Castañeda also concludes that the two priests were "unworthy representatives of the clergy." In 1829 Father José Ignacio Galindo had not served in Nacogdoches for a month before local citizens ousted him for having "criminal intercourse with a woman." James Michael McReynolds, "Family Life in A Borderland Community: Nacogdoches, Texas, 1779–1861" (Ph.D. diss., Texas Tech University, 1978), p. 135. See, too, Fitzmorris, *Four Decades of Catholicism in Texas*, pp. 41, 50.

37. Scandalous conduct of the Franciscans became a subject of concern in New Mexico prior to Mexican independence. See, for example, Adams and Chávez, trans. and eds., *Missions of New Mexico, 1776*, p. 296, and Ladrón del Niño de Guevara to Castañiza, Durango, October 23, 1820. For Pimería Alta, see John Kessell's vivid description in *Friars*,

Soldiers, and Reformers: Hispanic Arizona and the Mission Frontier, 1767–1856 (Tucson, 1976), pp. 229–31. Some of the California Franciscans also conducted themselves scandalously, although that may have been less a problem in those still vigorous missions. See, for example, Francis F. Guest, *Fermín Francisco de Lasuén (1736–1803): A Biography* (Washington, 1973), pp. 315–18.

38. Geiger, *Franciscan Missionaries in Hispanic California*, p. xi.

39. Frederick Chatard to Bishop Samuel Eccleston of Baltimore, San Francisco, November 29, 1848, quoted in John B. McGloin, "The California Church in Transition, 1846–1850," *CHSQ*, XLII (March 1963), p. 42. For José Sánchez see Geiger, *Franciscan Missionaries in Hispanic California*, pp. 217–22.

40. Manuel P. Servín, "The Beginnings of California's Anti-Mexican Prejudice," in Servín, ed., *An Awakened Minority: The Mexican-Americans*, 2nd ed. (Beverly Hills, 1974), pp. 5–6.

41. García Diego to Antonio Suñol, Santa Barbara, December 1, 1842, in Weber, trans. and ed., *Writings of Francisco García Diego*, p. 126.

42. Barreiro, *Ojeada*, in Carroll and Haggard, trans. and eds., *Three New Mexico Chronicles*, pp. 53–54. Rada, *Proposición*, p.2, reported a total of thirteen priests in New Mexico in 1828 to serve ten parishes and twenty-two missions.

43. Viader to Fr. José Sánchez, Mission Santa Clara, January 18, 1831, quoted in Engelhardt, *Missions and Missionaries of California*, III, 316–17.

44. Vallejo to Henry Virmond, December 1, 1841, quoted in Bancroft, *History of California*, IV, 196, n. 13.

45. Fray Angélico Chávez, "The Penitentes of New Mexico," *NMHR*, XXIX (April 1954), pp. 94–123, argues that the order developed as a result of outside influences. Marta Weigle leans toward the view that the brotherhood grew out of the local lay organization, the Third Order of St. Francis. *Brothers of Light, Brothers of Blood: The Penitentes of the Southwest* (Albuquerque, 1976), pp. 26–51. Weigle provides an excellent summary of different historical interpretations; her study is the starting point for serious readers.

46. Perhaps the best copy of Zubiría's Pastoral Letter of October 19, 1833, is in Book of Patentes, XI, Albuquerque, 1818–1851, in the Archives of the Archdiocese of Santa Fe, roll 49, frs. 262–70. The portion concerning the Penitentes is transcribed in Weigle, *Brothers of Light*, p. 196, along with a letter of July 21, 1833 by Zubiría on the same subject. Zubiría's 1845 visit is discussed in Chávez, *Archives of the Archdiocese of Santa Fe*, p. 185.

47. Catholicism was the only recognized religion under the Constitution of 1824, which "prohibits the practice of any other" (title I, section 1, no. 3). The first comprehensive legislation which spelled out ways of becoming a Mexican citizen required adherence to Roman Catholicism. See the laws of May 16, 1823 and April 14, 1828 in Manuel Dublán and José María Lozano, eds., *Legislación mexicana*, 34 vols. (Mexico, 1876–1904) I, 648–49; II, 66–68.

48. Quoted in Fitzmorris, *Four Decades of Catholicism in Texas*, p. 17.

49. One important exception was the colony of Irish-born Catholics who settled at San Patricio, accompanied by their own priest (ibid., p. 22). For a summary of Protestant activity in Texas between 1821 and 1836, see William Stuart Red, *The Texas Colonists and Religion, 1821–1836* (Austin, 1924), pp. 70–84. The Federal Colonization law of 1824 did not specify that immigrants had to become Catholics, but the Coahuila y Texas law of 1825 required foreigners to prove their Christianity. Some contemporaries, such as Lucas Alamán, apparently interpreted Christianity to be synonomous with Catholicism. See Eugene C. Barker, *The Life of Stephen F. Austin: Founder of Texas, 1793–1836* (1st ed., 1926; Austin, 1969), pp. 120–21, and Ohland Morton, *Terán and Texas: A Chapter in Texas-Mexican Relations* (Austin, 1948), p. 115.

50. William Dewees, 1831, quoted in Red, *The Texas Colonists and Religion*, p. 16. See, too, pp. 17–19.

51. Barker, *The Life of Stephen F. Austin*, p. 89. Barker, *Mexico and Texas, 1821–35* (Dallas, 1928), p. 70. Red, *Texas Colonists and Religion*, pp. 32–43; 48. Hans W. Baade, "The Form of Marriage in Spanish North America," *Cornell Law Review*, LXI (November 1975), pp. 69–70, 78.

52. Miguel Muldoon, letter in the *Gaceta del Gobierno Supremo del Estado de Coahuila y Tejas*, May 27, 1833, ASFC, legajo 8, expediente 64, transcript, TSA (2-22/640). Castañeda, *Our Catholic Heritage in Texas*, VI, 348, shows that Muldoon was a charlatan in some respects and questions whether he was actually a priest. The most detailed biography of this controversial figure is Mary Whatley Clarke, "Father Michael Muldoon," *Texana*, IX (Autumn 1971), pp. 179–229.

53. Reminiscences of Henry Smith, quoted in Samuel H. Lowrie, *Culture Conflict in Texas, 1821–1835* (New York, 1932), pp. 136–37.

54. John Bidwell to John Townsend, New Helvetia, November 27, 1845, manuscript no. HM 31549, HEH.

55. Quoted in Castañeda, *Our Catholic Heritage in Texas*, VII, 4.

56. I am here following the interpretation of Barker, *Mexico and Texas*, pp. 62–72, and Lowrie, *Culture Conflict in Texas*, pp. 132–40.

57. William Ransom Hogan, *The Texas Republic: A Social and Economic History* (Norman, 1946), pp. 191–92.

58. See, for example, Donald J. Lehmer, "The Second Frontier: The Spanish," in *The American West: An Appraisal*, ed. by Robert G. Ferris (Santa Fe, 1963), pp. 142–43.

59. Donald Jackson, ed., *The Journals of Zebulon Montgomery Pike, with Letters and Related Documents*, 2 vols. (Norman, 1966), II, 80. Staples, *La iglesia en la primera república*, p. 153, speculates on this point.

60. Andrew Forest Muir, ed., *Texas in 1837: An Anonymous, Contemporary Narrative* (Austin, 1958), p. 102. Among those who used the term "priest ridden" was Richard Henry Dana, Jr., letter to Charlotte Dana, San Diego, March 20, 1835, in *Two Years Before the Mast*, John Haskell Kemble, ed., 2 vols. (Los Angeles, 1964), II, 383. See, too, Robinson, *With Ears of Strangers*, pp. 118–22.

61. Gregg, *Commerce of the Prairies*, p. 179. Similarly, Bishop Lamy wrote in 1852 that the Mexican-born clergy in New Mexico "have not only great influence but they have been the rulers of the people." Quoted in Francis, "Padre Martínez," p. 271.

62. The political involvement of these curas is suggested elsewhere in this study. For the political role of Franciscans in California, see for example Geary, *Secularization*, pp. 125–26.

63. Austin to Friends, Monterrey, May 28, 1823, quoted in Red, *Texas Colonists and Religion*, p. 67. See, too, ibid., pp. 43, 69. An especially good statement on the veneration of Mexicans for priests is that of Farris, *Crown and Clergy in Colonial Mexico*, pp. 238–39.

64. For the liberal program during these years, see works such as Mecham, *Church and State*, pp. 350–54; José C. Valadés, *Orígines de la república mexicana* (Mexico, 1972), pp. 113–20; Charles Hale, *Mexican Liberalism in the Age of Mora, 1821–1853* (New Haven, 1968), pp. 125–26, and Cuevas, *Historia de la Iglesia*, V, 252.

65. See, for example, Secretaría de Relaciones Exteriores, *Memoria de relaciones . . .* (Mexico, 1826), pp. 36–37, quoted in Geary, *The Secularization of the California Missions*, p. 89.

Chapter 5
Indios Bárbaros, Norteamericanos, and the Failure of the Velvet Glove

1. Ralph A. Smith, "Indians in Mexican-American Relations Before the War of 1846," *HAHR*, XLIII (February 1963), pp. 35–36, and Smith, "Apache 'Ranching' Below the Gila,

1841–1845," *Arizoniana*, III (Winter 1972), p. 15. For a panoramic view at the outset of Mexican independence, see Juan Francisco de Azcárate, *Un programa de política internacional* (Mexico, 1932), p. 3. Comanches began raiding in Nuevo León at the time of Mexican independence, but did not become a major threat until the late 1830s, as they slowly displaced Apaches. See the excellent collection of documents and commentary by Isidro Vizcaya Canales, *La invasión de los indios bárbaros al noreste de México en los años de 1840 y 1841* (Monterrey, 1968), p. vii. For Lipan and Comanche depredations at Laredo, where a report of Alcalde Bacilio Benavides, April 10, 1836, claimed the community had seen only three years of peace since 1813, see J. B. Wilkinson, *Laredo and the Rio Grande Frontier* (Austin, 1975), pp. 106, 117–21, 127–32, 144–47, and David M. Vigness, "Indian Raids on the Lower Rio Grande, 1836–1837," *SWHQ*, LIX (July 1955), pp. 14–23.

2. Ralph A. Smith, "Apache Plunder Trails Southward, 1831–1840," *NMHR*, XXXVII (January 1962), pp. 20–42.

3. Ignacio Zúñiga, *Rápida ojeada al estado de Sonora* (Mexico, 1835), p. 7, facsimile in David J. Weber, *Northern Mexico on the Eve of the United States Invasion: Rare Imprints . . .* (New York, 1976).

4. Quoted in Smith, "Indians in Mexican-American Relations," p. 62. Josiah Gregg, *Commerce of the Prairies*, Max L. Moorhead, ed. (Norman, 1954), p. 203. Juan Estevan Pino, "Manifiesto," Santa Fe, November 24, 1829, quoted in Daniel Tyler, "New Mexico in the 1820's: The First Administration of Manuel Armijo" (Ph.D. diss., University of New Mexico, 1970), pp. 231–32. Rex W. Strickland, "The Birth and Death of a Legend: The Johnson 'Massacre' of 1837," *AW*, XVIII (Autumn 1976), p. 272.

5. Gregg, *Commerce of the Prairies*, p. 135. For a similar comment on Comanches, see Andrew Forest Muir, ed., *Texas in 1837: An Anonymous, Contemporary Narrative* (Austin, 1958), p. 110; for Navajos see Philip St. George Cooke cited in Frank McNitt, *Navajo Wars: Military Campaigns, Slave Raids, and Reprisals* (Albuquerque, 1972), p. 97. J. Frank Dobie, *The Longhorns* (Boston, 1941), p. 333.

6. Eleanor Lawrence, "Horse Thieves on the Spanish Trail," *Touring Topics*, XXIII (January 1931), pp. 24, 55. Keith H. Basso, ed., *Western Apache Raiding and Warfare From the Notes of Grenville Goodwin* (Tucson, 1971), p. 19.

7. Zúñiga, *Rápida ojeada*, p. 15. Robert C. Stevens, "The Apache Menace in Sonora, 1831–1848," *AW*, VI (Autumn 1964), pp. 220–22. John L. Kessell, *Friars, Soldiers, and Reformers: Hispanic Arizona and the Sonora Mission Frontier, 1767–1856* (Tucson, 1976), pp. 288, 301. Some writers have suggested that the Apache devastation began in the 1830s, but monthly military reports from Tucson make it clear that Indian attacks caused frequent loss of property and lives in the 1820s around Tucson and Tubac. See, for example, Juan Romero, alcalde de policía de Tucson, to Francisco Iriarte, Tucson, March 4, 1827, AHES, Apaches, Cabinet 2, Drawer 3, McCarty typescript, AHS, film H-12.

8. Benjamin Lundy, *The Life, Travels and Opinions of Benjamin Lundy, Including His Journeys to Texas and Mexico . . .* (Philadelphia, 1847), p. 51. For similar comments see p. 110; José María Sánchez, "Trip to Texas in 1828," *SWHQ*, XXIX (April 1926), pp. 257–58, 265; Jean Louis Berlandier and Rafael Chovell, *Diario de Viage de la Comisión de Límites . . .* [1828] (Mexico, 1850), p. 121; Journal of John C. Beales, 1834, quoted in William Kennedy, *Texas: The Rise, Progress, and Prospects of the Republic of Texas*, 2 vols. (London, 1841), II, 44; Muir, ed., *Texas in 1837*, p. 110.

9. *Representación dirijida por el ilustre ayuntamiento de la ciudad de Bexar al . . . Congreso del Estado* (Brazoria, 1833), p. 4. Lester G. Bugbee, "The Texas Frontier, 1820–1825," *Publications of the Southern History Association*, IV (March 1900), p. 119. See, too, Andrew Anthony Tijerina, "Tejanos and Texas" (Ph.D. diss., University of Texas, Austin, 1977), p. 117, citing an 1827 report.

10. Quoted in Zeb Wilcox, "Laredo During the Texas Republic," *SWHQ*, XLII (October 1938), p. 89.

11. *Representación dirijida por el ilustre ayuntamiento,* pp. 3–4. Fane Downs, "The History of Mexicans in Texas, 1820–1845" (Ph.D. diss., Texas Tech University, 1970), pp. 27, 29–32. In the autumn of 1831, the central government ordered a new campaign against Comanches for having broken previous treaties, but for the confusion surrounding this see Malcolm McLean, ed., *Papers Concerning Robertson's Colony in Texas,* 7 vols. to date (Fort Worth and Arlington, 1974–), VI, 60–61, 70–73.

12. Berlandier, who visited Texas in 1828 and again in 1834, describes considerable devastation and fear, but also notes that the area was relatively free of Comanche attacks from 1828 to 1834. Jean Louis Berlandier, *Journey to Mexico During the Years 1826 to 1834,* C. H. Muller and Katherine K. Muller, eds., and Sheila M. Ohlendorf, Josette M. Bigelow, and Mary M. Standifer, trans., 2 vols. (Austin, 1980), II, 293, 301–02, 413, 420, 542, 544, 553, 560. Official correspondence of the mid-1830s in Texas abounds in statements of concern about Indian depredations and incidents of robberies and occasional murders. See, for example, Martín Perfecto de Cos to the Minister of War, Saltillo, December 29, 1834, in Guerra y Marina, AGN, transcript, UT, folder 331; John H. Jenkins, ed., *Papers of the Texas Revolution,* 10 vols. (Austin, 1973), I, 22, 36, 44, 49, 75, 78, 80, 115, 134, 152, 175–77, 264–65, 273, 311, 367. Report of Ramón Músquiz, Béxar, October 1, 1831, in Ildefonso Villarello, "El Departamento de Béjar del Estado de Coahuila y Texas," *Boletín del Seminario de Cultura Mexicana,* II (September 1945), p. 81.

13. Vigil to the Assembly, Santa Fe, June 18, 1846, MANM, roll 41, frames 330–39. A copy of this document, dated May 16, 1846, but without Vigil's signature, is among the Ritch Papers, no. 231, HEH. The best biography of Vigil is still Ralph Emerson Twitchell, *The History of the Military Occupation of the Territory of New Mexico, from 1846–1851* (Denver, 1909), pp. 207–28.

14. See, for example, Juan Estevan Pino, "Manifiesto," to the Congreso General, Santa Fe, November 24, 1829, MANM, roll 9, frame 1120; Report of the committee to investigate New Mexico's military situation, January 30, 1829, MANM, roll 9, frames 1082–86; Proclamation of Comandante José Caballero, Santa Fe, September 9, 1837, in Benjamin M. Read, *Illustrated History of New Mexico* (Santa Fe, 1912), p. 381.

15. Antonio Barreiro, *Ojeada sobre Nuevo-México* . . . (Puebla, 1832), in H. Bailey Carroll and J. Villasana Haggard, eds. and trans., *Three New Mexico Chronicles* (Albuquerque, 1942), p. 74.

16. Quoted in John P. Wilson, *Military Campaigns in the Navajo Country: Northwestern New Mexico, 1800–1846* (Santa Fe, 1967), p. 20. Edward H. Spicer, *Cycles of Conquest* (Tucson, 1962), pp. 210–13; Ward Alan Minge, "Frontier Problems in New Mexico Preceding the Mexican War, 1840–1846" (Ph.D. diss., University of New Mexico, 1965), pp. 71–94.

17. Quoted in McNitt, *Navajo Wars,* p. 90. See, too, pp. 47, 79. Translations and summations of documents pertaining to Navajos in the Mexican era appear in Myra Ellen Jenkins and Ward Alan Minge, *Navajo Activities Affecting the Acoma-Laguna Area, 1746–1910* (New York, 1974), pp. 73–105.

18. Minge, "Frontier Problems," pp. 65, 263–64, 269, 274, 283–93; Minge, "Mexican Independence Day and a Ute Tragedy in Santa Fe, 1844," in Albert Schroeder, ed., *The Changing Ways of Southwestern Indians: A Historic Perspective* (Glorieta, New Mexico, 1973), pp. 107–22. Correspondence concerning this incident occupies the first three pages of the Santa Fe newspaper *La Verdad,* September 12, 1844, HEH. For the role of Señora Martínez, see Read, *Illustrated History of New Mexico,* pp. 410–11. Some contemporaries blamed Martínez for starting the violence.

19. Hubert Howe Bancroft, *History of California,* 7 vols. (San Francisco, 1884–90), III, 361. Jessie Davies Francis, "An Economic and Social History of Mexican California, 1821–1846" (Ph.D. diss., University of California, Berkeley, 1935), concluded that "never a year went by without its raids and depredations" (p. 420), and assembled scattered references from Bancroft to produce a coherent if one-sided account (pp. 419–38).

20. Alfred Robinson, *Life in California* (1st ed., 1846; Santa Barbara, 1970), pp. 12, 128. Lucy Lytle Killea, "The Political History of a Mexican Pueblo: San Diego from 1825 to 1845," *JSDH*, XII (July 1966), pp. 24–32; Bancroft, *History of California*, III, 611. Bancroft suggested that San Diego "more than any other part of California resembled . . . the Apache frontier, though the loss of life was much less" (ibid., IV, 70).

21. Thomas O. Larkin's Description of California, Monterey, April 20, 1846, in George P. Hammond, ed., *The Larkin Papers: Personal, Business, and Official Correspondence . . .* , 10 vols. (Berkeley, 1953), IV, 306.

22. Moisés González Navarro, "Instituciones indígenas en México independiente," in *Métodos y resultados de la política indigenista en México. Memorias del Instituto Nacional Indigenista*, vol. VI (Mexico, 1954), pp. 147–49.

23. Sherburne F. Cook, *The Conflict Between the California Indian and White Civilization* (1st ed., 1940–43; Berkeley, 1976), p. 200. See, too, the comments of Mariano Guadalupe Vallejo, 1833, quoted in C. Alan Hutchinson, *Frontier Settlement in Mexican California: The Híjar-Padrés Colony and Its Origins, 1769-1835* (New Haven, 1969), pp. 220–21. McNitt, *Navajo Wars*, p. 69. David M. Brugge, "Vizcarra's Navajo Campaign of 1823," *AW*, VI (Autumn 1964), p. 224. José Agustín de Escudero, *Noticias estadísticas de Sonora y Sinaloa* (Mexico, 1849), pp. 142–43.

24. See Clifton Kroeber's discussion of the debate over the motives for Mohave warfare in A. L. Kroeber and C. B. Kroeber, *A Mohave War Reminiscence, 1854-1880* (Berkeley, 1973), pp. 1–5. See, too, the discussion of motives in José Agustín de Escudero, *Noticias estadísticas del estado de Chihuahua* (Mexico, 1834), p. 242; Ernest Wallace and E. Adamson Hoebel, *The Comanches: Lords of the South Plains* (Norman, 1952), p. 245; and Richard White, "The Winning of the West: The Expansion of the Western Sioux in the Eighteenth and Nineteenth Centuries," *Journal of American History*, LXV (September 1978), pp. 319–43.

25. Cook, *The Conflict between the California Indian and White Civilization*, pp. 229–32, and Cook, "Colonial Expeditions to the Interior of California, Central Valley, 1800–1820," *Anthropological Records*, XVI (May 1960), p. 165. See, too, George Harwood Phillips, *Chiefs and Challengers: Indian Resistance and Cooperation in Southern California* (Berkeley, 1975), pp. 20–46, for a discussion of the evolution of a more centralized political structure in response to Spanish-Mexicans. The origins of Apache warfare are best summarized in Donald Worcester, "Apaches in the History of the Southwest," *NMHR*, L (January 1975), pp. 26–28.

26. Ramos Arizpe to Lucas Alamán, Puebla, August 1, 1830, ASFC, legajo VI, pt. 2 (1828–1831), expediente 43, West transcripts, UT.

27. Quoted in Joseph Carl McElhannon, "Imperial Mexico and Texas, 1821–1823," *SWHQ*, LIII (October 1949), p. 126. Berlandier, *Journey to Mexico*, I, 258, refers to American traders who provide Indians "with arms and munitions in exchange for stolen goods, thus constituting themselves the fences of these vagabond nations." For the merits of bows and arrows over firearms, see Escudero, *Noticias estadísticas de Chihuahua*, p. 247.

28. Sebastián Camacho, Secretary of State, to Joel R. Poinsett, June 15, 1826, Relaciones Exteriores, AGN, transcript, TSA (2-22/618). Among the sources that discuss the impact of American traders in the late colonial period are Rupert N. Richardson, *The Comanche Barrier to South Plains Settlement* (Glendale, Ca., 1933), pp. 58–59, 67–73, and Abraham P. Nasatir, *Borderland in Retreat: From Spanish Louisiana to the Far Southwest* (Albuquerque, 1976), pp. 57, 98. Bugbee, "Texas Frontier," p. 109; Eugene C. Barker, *The Life of Stephen F. Austin: Founder of Texas, 1793-1836* (1st ed., 1926; 2nd ed. reprinted, Austin, 1969), pp. 48–49; Jean Louis Berlandier, *The Indians of Texas in 1830*, John C. Ewers, ed. (Washington, 1969), p. 48; José Francisco Ruiz, *Report on the Indian Tribes of Texas in 1828*, John C. Ewers, ed., Georgette Dorn, trans. (New Haven, 1972), pp. 14, 16; Elizabeth Ann Harper [John], "The Taovayas Indians in Frontier Trade and Diplomacy," *Panhandle-Plains Historical Review*, XXVI (1953), pp. 58–69, and correspondence with the author.

29. Juan N. Almonte to the Secretary of State, December 10, 1830, ASFC, legajo 8, expediente 65, transcript, TSA (2-22/640).

30. Francisco Ruiz to Antonio Elosúa, August 1, 1830, translated in McLean, ed., *Papers Concerning Robertson's Colony in Texas,* IV, 335. See, too, Stephen Austin to Ramón Músquiz, Austin, August 24, 1829, in Eugene C. Barker, ed., *The Austin Papers,* 3 vols. (Washington and Austin, 1924–28), II, 250.

31. A trading party apparently led by Pierre Menard, reported in the Little Rock *Arkansas Gazette,* November 21, 1826. See, too, ibid., January 16, 1827 and January 27, 1829.

32. *Natchitoches Courier,* May 15, 1826, quoted in the Little Rock *Arkansas Gazette,* July 25, 1826.

33. James Bowie to Henry Rueg, Natches, August 3, 1835, in Jenkins, ed., *Papers of the Texas Revolution,* I, 301–2. Similar complaints about an American trader appear in Peter Ellis Bean to Domingo de Ugartechea, Béxar, April 21, 1835, and Rueg to the jefe político of Béxar, May 18, 1835, in ibid., I, 80, 115–16.

34. *The Telegraph and Texas Register,* quoted in the *Arkansas Gazette,* February 28, 1838, in Ralph A. Smith, "Mexican and Anglo-Saxon Traffic in Scalps, Slaves, and Livestock, 1835–1841," *West Texas Historical Association Year Book,* XXXVI (October 1960), pp. 102–3. For an interesting glimpse at Torrey's Post, near present Waco in 1838, see Howard R. Lamar, *The Trader on the American Frontier: Myth's Victim* (College Station, 1977), pp. 13–16.

35. Santiago Monroy to Governor Bartolomé Baca, Xemes, February 20, 1823, in Lourdes Lascuraín Orive, "Reflexiones sobre Nuevo México y su integración a los Estado Unidos de Norteamérica," in *El Destino Manifiesto en la historia de la nación norteamericana, 6 ensayos* (Mexico, 1977), p. 49. Pino, "Manifiesto," November 24, 1829. Manuel de Jesús Rada, *Proposición hecha al Soberano Congreso General de la Nación por el diputado del territorio de Nuevo México* (Mexico, 1829) p. 3, facsimile in Weber, ed., *Northern Mexico.*

36. Francisco R. Almada, *Resumen de historia del Estado de Chihuahua* (Mexico, 1955), p. 205. Decree of October 16, 1835, Santa Fe, Ritch Papers, no. 153, HEH. Circular from the Palacio del Gobierno del Estado, Chihuahua, February 1835, cited in David J. Weber, *The Taos Trappers* (Norman, 1971), p. 222. Escudero, *Noticias estadísticas del estado de Chihuahua,* pp. 245–46.

37. Minge, "Frontier Problems," p. 62; Gregg, *Commerce of the Prairies,* p. 203. Charles L. Kenner, *A History of New Mexican-Plains Indian Relations* (Norman, 1969), pp. 78–97. Vizcaya Canales, ed., *La invasión,* pp. 55–59. See, too, n. 68.

38. Printed circular, Juan Andrés Archuleta, Santa Fe, February 21, 1843, in the María G. Durán Collection, NMSRC. Minge, "Frontier Problems," pp. 55–58, 60–62; Weber, *The Taos Trappers,* pp. 210–11. According to tradition, the Bents furnished weapons to their Indian customers "on credit." George Bird Grinnell, *By Cheyenne Campfires* (Lincoln, Neb., 1971), pp. 34–35, reference courtesy of George Phillips.

39. *Esposición* [sic] *que el Presbítero Antonio José Martínez, Cura de Taos en Nuevo México, Dirije al Gobierno del Exmo. Sor. General D. Antonio López de Santa-Anna. Proponiendo la civilisación de las naciones bárbaras . . .* (Taos, 1843), p. 4, facsimile in Weber, ed., *Northern Mexico.*

40. Donaciano Vigil to the Assembly, Santa Fe, June 18, 1846.

41. Weber, *The Taos Trappers,* pp. 213–17.

42. José María Chaves to Juan Andrés Archuleta, Campo de operaciones, Taos, June 18, 1845, MANM, roll 39, frames 626–27. Janet Lecompte, *Pueblo, Hardscrabble, Greenhorn: The Upper Arkansas, 1832–1856* (Norman, 1978), pp. 163–65. See, too, pp. 74–75, 146, and George P. Hammond, ed., *The Adventures of Alexander Barclay, Mountain Man* (Denver, 1976), p. 71.

43. Such is the oral tradition. See Grenville Goodwin, *The Social Organization of the Western Apache* (Chicago, 1942), p. 94.

44. Donaciano Vigil to the Assembly, Santa Fe, June 18, 1846.

45. Pino, "Manifiesto," November 24, 1829. Ronald N. Satz, *American Indian Policy in the Jacksonian Era* (Lincoln, Neb., 1975), pp. 11–31.

46. Quoted in Sardis W. Templeton, *The Lame Captain: The Life and Adventures of Pegleg Smith* (Los Angeles, 1965), p. 101. See, too, Narciso Durán, October 3, 1833, quoted in Zephyrin Engelhardt, *The Missions and Missionaries of California*, 4 vols. (San Francisco, 1908–15), III, 494.

47. Figueroa to the Minister of War and Navy, Monterey, April 12, 1833, and Figueroa, decree concerning robbers of horses and other livestock, November 18, 1833, quoted in Sherburne F. Cook, "Expeditions to the Interior of California's Central Valley, 1820–1840," *Anthropological Records*, XX (February 1962), p. 188. Bancroft, *History of California*, III, 397, n. 25. Lawrence, "Horse Thieves on the Spanish Trail," p. 23. This undocumented but authoritative article should be supplemented by LeRoy R. and Ann W. Hafen, *Old Spanish Trail* (Glendale, 1954), pp. 227–58. See, too, Mariano Guadalupe Vallejo to the governor, Sonoma, July 20, 1838, in *Comunicaciones del Gen. M. G. Vallejo* (Sonoma, 1837–39), a volume of imprints in the Bancroft Library.

48. Hafen and Hafen, *Old Spanish Trail*, pp. 228, 236; John C. Ewers, ed., *Adventures of Zenas Leonard, Fur Trader* (Norman, 1959), p. 113; Francisco Castillo Negrete, *Informe y propuestas que hace al Supremo Gobierno para la prosperidad y seguridad de la Alta California, su Comisionado . . .* [1836] (Mexico, 1944), p. 10.

49. Janet Lecompte, "Jean Baptiste Chalifoux," in LeRoy R. Hafen, ed., *The Mountain Men and the Fur Trade of the Far West*, 10 vols. (Glendale, 1965–72), VII, 65–70; Templeton, *The Lame Captain*, pp. 103–58; Alpheus H. Favour, *Old Bill Williams: Mountain Man* (1st ed., 1936; Norman, 1962), pp. 100–17; Lecompte, *Pueblo, Hardscrabble, Greenhorn*, pp. 150–54. George Vernon Blue, ed. and trans., "The Report of Captain La Place . . . in 1839," *CHSQ*, XVIII (December 1939), p. 320. Manuel Castañares, "Exposición," September 1, 1844, in Castañares, *Colección de documentos relativos al departamento de Californias* (Mexico, 1845), p. 31, facsimile in Weber, ed., *Northern Mexico*. Juan Bautista Alvarado also recalled that Indians received weapons from Russians at Fort Ross, "Historia de California," 1876, 5 vols., MS, BL, III, 33.

50. Quoted in Bancroft, *History of California*, III, 396. See, too, Eleanor Lawrence, "Mexican Trade Between Santa Fe and Los Angeles, 1830–1848," *CHSQ*, X (March 1931), p. 30, and Hafen and Hafen, *Old Spanish Trail*, pp. 155–94.

51. Bancroft, *History of California*, III, 359, n. 22; Favour, *Old Bill Williams*, p. 104; Minge, "Frontier Problems," p. 65; Hafen and Hafen, *Old Spanish Trail*, pp. 237, 248, 251–57.

52. Ernest W. Winkler, "The Cherokee Indians in Texas" *SWHQ*, VII (October 1903), pp. 95–165, treats one of the groups in depth. Weber, *The Taos Trappers*, p. 224; Bancroft, *History of California*, IV, 76–77.

53. Carlos J. Sierra, *Los indios de la frontera* (Mexico, 1980), p. 40.

54. J. Fred Rippy, "The Indians of the Southwest in the Diplomacy of the United States and Mexico, 1848–1853," *HAHR*, II (August 1919), p. 364; Joseph F. Park, "The Apaches in Mexican-American Relations, 1848–1861," *AW*, III (Summer 1961), p. 129.

55. See, for example, Stevens, "The Apache Menace in Sonora," pp. 211–22; Spicer, *Cycles of Conquest*, p. 240; Kenner, *New Mexico-Plains Indian Relations*, p. 70; Walter Prescott Webb, *The Great Plains* (Boston, 1931), p. 137.

56. Manuel Castañares to Mariano Guadalupe Vallejo, Mexico, October 22, 1845, in Vallejo, "Documentos para la historia de California, 1780–1875," 36 vols., MS, BL, XII, no. 149.

57. Quoted in González Navarro, "Instituciones indígenas," p. 143.

58. Ibid., p. 144; Robert Conway Stevens, "Mexico's Forgotten Frontier: A History of Sonora, 1821–1846" (Ph.D. diss., University of California, Berkeley, 1963), pp. 68–75, 77;

Charles R. McClure, "Neither Effective Nor Financed: The Difficulties of Indian Defense in New Mexico, 1837–1846," *Military History of Texas and the Southwest*, X (1972), p. 83. In an article that appeared after I had drafted this chapter, Dan Tyler elaborates on this theme: "Mexican Indian Policy in New Mexico," *NMHR*, LV (April 1980), pp. 104–6.

59. Martínez, *Esposición . . . proponiendo la civilisación de las naciones bárbaras*, p. 7.

60. Armijo to the Minister of War and Navy, Santa Fe, September 7, 1840, cited in Minge, "Frontier Problems," p. 55; Ruiz, *Report on the Indian Tribes of Texas*, p. 7.

61. The best recent explanation of the evolution and results of this policy is Max L. Moorhead, *The Presidio* (Norman, 1975), pp. 47–114.

62. Azcárate, *Un programa de política internacional*, p. 4. See, too, the Junta de Fomento, 1824, quoted in C. Alan Hutchinson, "The Mexican Government and the Mission Indians of Upper California, 1821–1835," *The Americas*, XXI (April, 1965), p. 344; Charles A. Hale, *Mexican Liberalism in the Age of Mora, 1821–1853* (New Haven, 1968), p. 235.

63. Tadeo Ortiz de Ayala, *Resúmen de la estadística del Imperio Mexicano, 1822*, Tarsicio García Díaz, ed. (Mexico, 1968), p. 21. Ortiz to Anastasio Bustamante, Bordeaux, November 30, 1830, in Edith Louise Kelly and Mattie Austin Hatcher, eds. and trans., "Tadeo Ortiz de Ayala and the Colonization of Texas, 1822–1833," *SWHQ*, XXXII (February 1928), p. 235; Escudero, *Noticias estadísticas del estado de Chihuahua*, pp. 245–46, quoting his own 1831 report to the Banco de Avío. González Navarro, "Instituciones indígenas," p. 140.

64. Ortiz to the President, Matamoros, February 2, 1833, quoted in Kelly and Hatcher, eds. and trans., "Tadeo Ortiz," pp. 331–32.

65. Quoted in González Navarro, "Instituciones indígenas," p. 140. See, too, Hale, *Mexican Liberalism*, p. 234.

66. Sánchez, "Trip to Texas," pp. 265, 254.

67. José Bandini, *A Description of California in 1828*, Doris M. Wright, trans. (Berkeley, 1951), p. 7.

68. Many sources refer to the continued use of this fund. See, for example, Minge, "Frontier Problems," pp. 51, 199; Tijerina, "Tejanos and Texas," p. 78.

69. Shirley Hill Witt, "Migration into San Juan Pueblo, 1726–1968" (Ph.D. diss., University of New Mexico, 1969), p. 44. The expansion of ranch life between Goliad and San Antonio, reported in Tijerina, "Tejanos and Texas" pp. 29–32, could not have occurred if Comanche attacks had been as unrelenting as those of the Apaches in Sonora. Vizcaya Canales, ed., *La invasión*, p. 45. Kenner, *New Mexico-Plains Indian Relations*, p. 73. Frances León Swadesh, *Los Primeros Pobladores: Hispanic Americans of the Ute Frontier* (Notre Dame, 1974), pp. 20, 24–25; Berlandier, *Indians of Texas*, p. 31, n. 3; 47–48; Lundy, *Life, Travels*, p. 53. Papers relating to illegal trade with Apaches, 1846, MANM, roll 41, frames 548–60.

70. Vigil to the Assembly, June 18, 1846.

Chapter 6
Crumbling Presidias, Citizen-Soldiers, and the Failure of the Iron Fist

1. Odie B. Faulk, "The Presidio: Fortress or Farce?" *JW*, VIII (January 1969), pp. 22–28; Max L. Moorhead, *The Presidio: Bastion of the Spanish Borderlands* (Norman, 1975), especially pp. 47–114.

2. Congressional decree, published by the Secretaría de Guerra y Marina, Manuel Gómez Pedraza, Mexico, March 21, 1826. Holliday Collection, AHS. *Memoria del Secretario del estado y del despacho de la guerra* (Mexico, 1826), cited in Russell G. Pynes, Jr. "The

Mexican National Army: A Federalist Concept, 1824–1829" (M.A. Thesis, University of Texas, Austin), p. 23 and appendix. Carmen Perry, trans. and ed., *The Impossible Dream by the Río Grande: A Documented Chronicle of the Establishment and Annihilation of San José de Palafox* (San Antonio, 1971), p. xvi. Isidro Vizcaya Canales, ed., *La invasión de los indios bárbaros al noreste de México en los años de 1840 y 1841* (Monterrey, 1968), p. 40.

3. Daniel Tyler, "New Mexico in the 1820's: The First Administration of Manuel Armijo" (Ph.D. diss., University of New Mexico, 1970), pp. 34–35; Tyler, "Mexican Indian Policy in New Mexico," *NMHR*, LV (April 1980), p. 105. A comandante principal also served in San Antonio through most of the Mexican period.

4. Sidney B. Brinckerhoff and Odie B. Faulk, *Lancers for the King: A Study of the Frontier Military System of Northern New Spain, With a Translation of the Royal Regulations of 1772* (Phoenix, 1965), p. 8. [J. Hefter, ed.], *El soldado mexicano, 1837–1847. Organización, vestuario, equipo . . .* (Mexico, 1958), p. 50.

5. Tyler, "New Mexico in the 1820's," pp. 182–84. Ward Alan Minge, "Frontier Problems in New Mexico Preceding the Mexican War, 1840–1846" (Ph.D. diss., University of New Mexico, 1965), pp. 124–28.

6. Lester G. Bugbee, "The Texas Frontier, 1820–1825," *Publications of the Southern History Association*, IV (March 1900), pp. 102–21. *Representación dirijida por el ilustre ayuntamiento de la ciudad de Béxar al . . . Congreso del Estado* (Brazoria, 1833), p. 4.

7. John L. Kessell, *Friars, Soldiers, and Reformers: Hispanic Arizona and the Sonora Mission Frontier, 1767–1856* (Tucson, 1976), pp. 288, 297–300, 303. Henry F. Dobyns, "Tubac Through Four Centuries: An Historical Resumé and Analysis" (MS prepared for the Arizona State Parks Board, 1959), pp. 562–63, 565, 570–71.

8. Lansing B. Bloom, "New Mexico Under Mexican Administration," *Old Santa Fe*, II (July and October 1914), pp. 9, 163, n. 548. Figures on garrison strength appear in many sources. See, for example, Tyler, "New Mexico in the 1820's," pp. 124–25; *Calendar of the Microfilm Edition of the Mexican Archives of New Mexico, 1821–1846* (Santa Fe, 1970), pp. 89, 95, 102ff.

9. Echeandía to the Minister of War, September 18, 1829, quoted in Jessie Davies Francis, "An Economic and Social History of Mexican California, 1822–1846" (Ph.D. diss., University of California, Berkeley, 1935), pp. 366–37. See, too, pp. 443–44, 354–64, and Manuel Castañares, "Exposición," September 1, 1844, in Castañares, *Colección de documentos relativos al departamento de Californias* (Mexico, 1845), pp. 37–38, facsimile in David J. Weber, ed., *Northern Mexico on the Eve of the United States Invasion. Rare Imprints . . .* (New York, 1976). Myrtle M. McKittrick, *Vallejo: Son of California* (Portland, 1944), pp. 206, 292.

10. Pynes, "The Mexican National Army," pp. 22, 43–45.

11. Ibid., pp. 49–55. Edwin Lieuwen, "Curbing Militarism in Mexico," *NMHR*, XXXII (October 1958), pp. 257–59. Frank Samponaro, "The Political Role of the Mexican Army, 1821–1848. An Analysis" (Paper presented at the Southwestern Social Science Association, Annual Meeting, Dallas, March 30, 1974), pp. 5–6, 10–11. These conditions were not unlike those of the late colonial period: Christon I. Archer, *The Army in Bourbon Mexico, 1760–1810* (Albuquerque, 1977).

12. Antonio Comadurán to José María Elías González, Tucson, December 7, 1845, quoted in Kessell, *Friars, Soldiers, and Reformers*, p. 303. Antonio Barreiro, *Ojeada sobre Nuevo-México . . .* (Puebla, 1832), in H. Bailey Carroll and J. Villasana Haggard, eds. and trans., *Three New Mexico Chronicles* (Albuquerque, 1942), p. 76. Pynes, "The Mexican National Army," p. 29.

13. Charles A. Hale, *Mexican Liberalism in the Age of Mora, 1821–1853* (New Haven, 1968), pp. 234–35. *El Correo de la Federación*, January 1, 1827, p. 1, quoted in Pynes, "The Mexican National Army," p. 46.

14. Manuel Mier y Terán, reports of October 14, 1828 and July 24, 1829, quoted in Ohland Morton, *Terán and Texas: A Chapter in Texas-Mexican Relations* (Austin, 1948), pp. 82, 75. Bugbee, "Texas Frontier," pp. 118–20; Eugene C. Barker, *Mexico and Texas, 1821–1835* (Dallas, 1928), p. 52.

15. These events are discussed in chapters 9 and 12.

16. Barreiro, *Ojeada*, in Carroll and Haggard, eds. and trans., *Three New Mexico Chronicles*, p. 78. Tyler, "New Mexico in the 1820's," pp. 123–24, 204–5.

17. Jean Louis Berlandier, *The Indians of Texas in 1830*, John C. Ewers, ed. (Washington, 1969), p. 30. Tyler, "New Mexico in the 1820's," pp. 34, 37, 206, comes to a similar conclusion.

18. Kessell, *Friars, Soldiers, and Reformers*, p. 303.

19. Hubert Howe Bancroft, *History of California*, 7 vols. (San Francisco, 1884–90), II, 522. George Simpson, *Narrative of a Journey Round the World, During the Years 1841 and 1842*, 2 vols. (London, 1847), I, 343. On the shortage of powder and poor condition of arms in general, see Minge, "Frontier Problems in New Mexico," pp. 266, 271, and Francis, "Economic and Social History of Mexican California," pp. 364–71.

20. *Representación dirijida por el ilustre ayuntamiento de la ciudad de Béxar* . . . , p. 4; Frances, "Economic and Social History of California," pp. 351–52; Ignacio Zúñiga, *Rápida ojeada al Estado de Sonora* . . . (Mexico, 1835), p. 24, facsimile in Weber, ed., *Northern Mexico;* Dobyns, "Tubac," pp. 560–61, citing a decree of August 10, 1837; Donaciano Vigil to the New Mexico Assembly, Santa Fe, June 22, 1846, MS, Ritch Papers no. 233, HEH; Tyler, "New Mexico in the 1820's," p. 168.

21. Juan de Dios Peña, et al., to the Deputy from New Mexico, MANM, roll 9, frames 280–84, and the good discussion in Tyler, "New Mexico in the 1820's," pp. 200–202.

22. Zúñiga, *Rápida ojeada*, p. 24; Tyler, "New Mexico in the 1820's," pp. 167–74, 192–96, provides a good account of the situation in New Mexico, where troops seem to have been better off than elsewhere on the frontier. See, too, Donaciano Vigil to the Assembly, Santa Fe, June 22, 1846. R. W. H. Hardy, *Travels in the Interior of Mexico, in 1825, 1826, 1827, & 1828* (London, 1829), p. 102. For Texas, see the example of the case against Severo Ruiz and Francisco Castañeda, January 19 to August 1832, in Malcolm D. McLean, ed., *Papers Concerning Robertson's Colony in Texas*, 7 vols. to date (Fort Worth and Arlington, 1974–), V, 447–53, and José María Sánchez, "Trip to Texas in 1828," Carlos E. Castañeda, trans., *SWHQ*, XXIX (April 1926), p. 258.

23. *Representación dirijida por el ilustre ayuntamiento de la ciudad de Béxar* . . . , p. 4. The New Mexico diputación voiced similar concern in 1824: Journal of the diputación provincial, session of January 11, 1824, MANM, roll 42, frames 157–58.

24. Kessell, *Friars, Soldiers, and Reformers*, p. 303; Francis, "Economic and Social History of Mexican California," pp. 378–80, 411–12; Morton, *Terán and Texas*, pp. 67, 75; Bancroft, *History of California*, IV, 67.

25. Subprefecto of San Jose, March 16, 1843, quoted in Francis, "Economic and Social History of Mexican California," p. 397. See, too, ibid., pp. 344–54, 364, 380, 402–3, and Mariano Guadalupe Vallejo's complaint that whereas all classes once served in the army, now only the poor did: Vallejo [to the governor], Sonoma, June 10, 1839, in *Comunicaciones del Gen. M. G. Vallejo* (Sonoma, 1837–39), a bound collection of imprints, BL. Texas also saw a high rate of desertion and strikes may not have been unusual: see, for example, McLean, ed., *Robertson's Colony*, IV, 48–49; Juan de Castañeda to José Antonio Saucedo, Béxar, July 3, 1824, BA, roll 77, frames 442–50.

26. Vallejo to Anastasio Bustamante, November 22, 1845, quoted in Francis, "Economic and Social History of Mexican California," p. 354. See, too, Manuel Castañares to the Ministro de Relaciones Exteriores, March 2, 1844, in Castañares, *Colección de documentos*, p. 10.

27. Zúñiga, *Rápida ojeada*, p. 28. Manuel Escalante, jefe político of Arizpe Department, to

José María Gaxiola, Arizpe, December 9, 1828, AHES, Apaches, cabinet 2, drawer 3, McCarty Transcripts, AHS, microfilm H-2. For the diminished quality of the officer corps, see Dobyns, "Tubac," pp. 535, 541–42, 554, 568.

28. Castañares, "Exposición," pp. 37–38.

29. José de las Piedras to the Ministro de Estado y de Relaciones, Nacogdoches, March 20, 1832, ASFC, legajo V, expediente 29, transcript, TSA, 2–22/639. General Manuel Mier y Terán apparently endorsed this plan.

30. Zúñiga, *Rápida ojeada*, pp. 60–66. Tadeo Ortiz to Anastasio Bustamante, Bordeaux, October 31, 1830, in Edith Louise Kelly and Mattie Austin Hatcher, eds. and trans., "Tadeo Ortiz de Ayala and the Colonization of Texas, 1822–1833," *SWHQ*, XXXII (October 1928), p. 156. María del Carmen Velázquez, *Tres estudios sobre las Provincias Internas de Nueva España* (Mexico, 1979), pp. 76–80, which treats the Mexican period lightly. Congress authorized military colonies on December 3, 1845, Ralph Smith, "Indians in American-Mexican Relations Before the War of 1846," *HAHR*, XLIII (February 1963), pp. 56–57. Odie B. Faulk, ed. and trans., "Projected Mexican Military Colonies for the Borderlands, 1848," *JAH*, IX (Spring 1968), pp. 39–48; Faulk, ed. and trans., "A Colonization Plan for Northern Sonora, 1850," *NMHR*, XLIV (October 1969), pp. 293–314; Faulk, ed., and trans., "Projected Mexican Colonies in the Borderlands, 1852," *JAH*, X (Summer 1969), pp. 115–28.

31. Armijo to José María Tornel, Santa Fe, March 31, 1841, quoted in Minge, "Frontier Problems," p. 63. For another example of a call for cooperation, see the Circular, Secretary of War, January 8, 1835, in Manuel Dublán and José María Lozano, eds., *Legislación mexicana*, 34 vols. (Mexico, 1876–1904), III, 11.

32. Minge, "Frontier Problems," p. 198.

33. Josiah Gregg, *Commerce of the Prairies*, Max L. Moorhead, ed. (Norman, 1954), p. 202. Robert C. Stevens, "The Apache Menace in Sonora, 1831–1849," *AW*, VI (Autumn 1964), pp. 214, 217–18; Ralph Smith, "The Scalp Hunter in the Borderlands, 1835–1850," *AW*, VI (Spring 1964), pp. 14–15. Joseph F. Park has argued that "Spanish, Mexican, and American settlers turned to private treaties with the Apaches as a means of protection. . . . Self-preservation took precedence. . . . " "The Apaches in Mexican-American Relations, 1848–1861," *AW*, III (Summer 1961), p. 145.

34. Zúñiga, *Rápida ojeada*, pp. 15, 22. Donaciano Vigil, address to the Departmental Assembly, May 16, 1846, Ritch Papers, no. 231, HEH. Ayuntamiento of Altar, April 3, 1830, to Anastasio Bustamante, in AHES, Apaches, cabinet 2, drawer 3, McCarty Transcripts, AHS, microfilm H-12.

35. Archer, *The Army in Bourbon Mexico*, pp. 8–37, does not treat the Provincias Internas, but does provide a splendid picture of the origins and continuing dependence upon provincial militia in New Spain. For the Borderlands, see Francis, "Economic and Social History of Mexican California," p. 404; Marc Simmons, *Spanish Government in New Mexico* (Albuquerque, 1968), pp. 148–53; Félix D. Almaraz, Jr., *Tragic Cavalier: Governor Manuel Salcedo of Texas, 1808–1813* (Austin, 1971), pp. 111, 131.

36. Pynes, "The Mexican National Army," pp. 14–16. Thomas Ewing Cotner, *The Military and Political Career of José Joaquín de Herrera, 1792–1854* (Austin, 1949), pp. 46–47, 62.

37. Congressional Decree, Secretaría de Guerra y Marina, Manuel Gómez Pedraza, Mexico, March 21, 1826, articles 3–7, Holliday Collection, AHS. Three units were to be established in the State of Occidente; two in Coahuila y Texas, and two in New Mexico. For the active militia in New Mexico, see for example, Tyler, "New Mexico in the 1820's," pp. 211–13, 220, and the roster of the milicía activa of Santa Fe, June 9, 1832, Military Records, MANM, roll 15, frame 821. For an example of later legislation, see the law of June 12, 1840, "Sobre organización de los cuerpos de infantería y caballería de milicía activa," in Dublán and Lozano, eds., *Legislación mexicana*, III, 716–19, which still called for two cavalry squadrons in New Mexico (article 14).

38. A variety of synonomous names, frequent changes of legislation, and the vagueness of the term *active*, complicates terminology during this period. Stephen Austin, who had been empowered to form a local militia, understood the term active to mean: "the militia called out and actually in the national service, as troops of the army." Quoted in John H. Jenkins, ed., "Regulations for the National Militia of the State of Coahuila y Texas, 1828," *Texas Military History*, VII (Fall 1969), p. 205. If he was correct, then local militia could become *activos*. The term *milicía permanente* also appears frequently in this period, but does not refer to another branch of the militia. Rather, it seems to be a euphemism for the regular army. I am grateful to Frank Samponaro of the University of Texas, Permian Basin, who ended my confusion in this matter.

39. Constitution of 1824, section 4, article 110, part XI. Congress empowered the executive to use certain militia in Texas in 1827, and authorized the use of local militia anywhere on May 14, 1828. Dublán y Lozano, eds., *Legislación mexicana*, II, 5, 73. Article 50, pt. XIX of the 1824 Constitution permitted the federal government to establish regulations for local militia, but in a decree of December 29, 1827, Congress granted that power to individual states, thereby superseding federal regulations of April 8 and May 5, 1823. Dublán y Lozano, eds., *Legislación mexicana*, II, 49–51. A translation by Stephen Austin of the Texas regulations of 1828 has been reprinted in Jenkins, ed., "Regulations for the National Militia," pp. 195–220, and these were superseded by the *Reglamento para la milicía cívica del estado de Coahuila y Texas* (Monclova, 1834), trans. by Richard G. Santos, *Texas Military History*, VI (Winter 1967), pp. 286–300. For the Estado de Occidente, see the *Reglamento para la milicía cívica local del Estado de Occidente* (Alamos, 1828), Aguiar Collection, AHS.

40. For San Antonio, see for example, Manuel Iturri Castillo to Governor José María Sambrano, May 20, 1824, and the roster of the milicía cívica of Texas, Béxar, September 8, 1825, BA, roll 77, frames 121–22 and roll 84, frames 145–48, respectively. An example of the use of the Goliad civic militia is recounted in McLean, ed., *Robertson's Colony*, VI, 65. Henry W. Barton, "The Anglo American Colonists Under Mexican Militia Laws," *SWHQ*, LXV (July 1961), pp. 61–71.

41. Law of March 31, 1835, in Dublán y Lozano, eds., *Legislación mexicana*, III, 38. C. Alan Hutchinson, "Valentín Gómez Farías: A Biographical Study" (Ph.D. diss., University of Texas, 1948), pp. 244–45, 291. Law of March 21, 1834, in Dublán y Lozano, eds., *Legislación mexicana*, II, pp. 684–87. Lista de los individuos que deben componer la milicía cívica, mandada crear por la ley de 21 de marzo de 1834, MANM, roll 18, frames 1183ff.

42. Minge, "Frontier Problems," pp. 120–26. In a law of January 18, 1842, Santa Anna reorganized the militia into auxiliary companies of cavalry and rurales. Minge explains the difference. Lansing B. Bloom, "New Mexico Under Mexican Administration," *Old Santa Fe*, II (October 1914), p. 134, provides a list of New Mexico militia officers appointed in 1839 by the Ministro de Guerra y Marina. Prior to Santa Anna's formation of the rurales on a national level in 1842, a "milicía rural" existed informally in New Mexico (Tyler "New Mexico in the 1820's," p. 212).

43. Victoria to the Secretary of Foreign Relations, June 7, 1831, in Archivo de California, vol. 49 (Departmental Records), pp. 137–38, MS, BL. Vallejo to Bustamante, November 22, 1845, quoted in Francis, "Economic and Social History of Mexican California," p. 411. A civic militia may have operated briefly in California, for Governor Juan Bautista Alvarado reportedly disbanded it in 1838 for lack of funds. George Tays, "Revolutionary California: The Political History of California from 1820 to 1848" (Ph.D. diss., University of California, Berkeley, 1932; revised, 1934), p. 457.

44. The best discussion of these informal units in California is in Francis, "Economic and Social History of Mexican California," chaps. 42 and 46. For Arizona, see the report of José de Zúñiga, Tubac, August 1, 1804, in Kieran McCarty, *Desert Documentary: The Spanish*

Years, 1767–1821 (Tucson, 1976), p. 88, and papers pertaining to the formation and operations of the Sección Patriótica, May 20, 1832, in AHES, Apaches, cabinet 2, drawer 3, McCarty Transcripts, AHS, microfilm H-12. Minutes of the Béxar ayuntamiento, February 12, 1832, p. 95, photostat Barker Center, UT, and *Representación dirijida por el ilustre ayuntamiento de la ciudad de Béxar*, pp. 12, 15.

45. Manuel de Jesús Rada, *Proposición hecha al soberano Congreso General de la Nación por el diputado del territorio de Nuevo México* (Mexico, 1828), p. 3, facsimile in Weber, ed., *Northern Mexico*.

46. "El Gefe Político del Nuevo Méjico a sus conciudadanos," Santa Fe, December 13, 1834, facsimile in Henry R. Wagner, "New Mexico Spanish Press," *NMHR*, XII (January 1937), facing p. 1. See, too, the remark of Donaciano Vigil, Address to the Departmental Assembly, June 18, 1846, MANM, roll 41, frames 330–39.

47. Juan González, "Diario . . . contra los Apaches," Tucson, October 2, 1834, AHES, Apaches, cabinet 2, drawer 3, McCarty Transcripts, AHS, film H-14.

48. For an account of this battle and pertinent documents, see McLean, ed., *Robertson's Colony*, IV, p. 50.

49. See, for example, the comments of Fray Rafael Díaz to José Ignacio Bustamante, vice-governor of Sonora, Cocóspera, November 1, 1832, AHES, Apaches, cabinet 2, drawer 3, McCarty Transcripts, AHS, film H-13.

50. Almonte to the Secretary of State, May 5, 1834, Nacogdoches, May 5, 1834, in ASFC, legajo 8, expediente 65, transcript, TSA, 2–22/640, pp. 33–34.

51. Comadurán, Tucson, June 14, 1832, quoted in José María Elías González, military comandante of Sonora, to Governor Manuel Escalante y Arvizu, Arizpe, June 18, 1832, in AHES, Apaches, cabinet 2, drawer 3, McCarty Transcripts, AHS, film H-12. Mier y Terán to Antonio Elosúa, Matamoros, August 18, 1830, translated in McLean, ed., *Robertson's Colony*, IV, 399–400.

52. Quoted in John P. Wilson, *Military Campaigns in the Navajo Country: Northwestern New Mexico, 1800–1846* (Santa Fe, 1967), p. 20. See, too, M. G. Vallejo, quoted in Francis, "Economic and Social History of Mexican California," pp. 401–2.

53. See, for example, José María Sambrano to Juan de Castañeda, Béxar, May 2, 1824, BA, roll 77, frame 124, and F. W. Johnson to Stephen Austin, San Felipe, March 21, 1831, in Eugene C. Barker, ed., *The Austin Papers*, 3 vols. (Washington and Austin, 1924–1928), II, 624. Tyler, "New Mexico in the 1820's," p. 210. Petition of José de Jesús Ortiz et al. to the Comandante Principal, Santa Fe, February 1, 1835, protesting fines for neglect of militia duties, MANM, roll 20, frames 241–44. Papers regarding the campaign against the Utes and attempted mutiny, 1845, MANM, roll 39, frames 606–40. Order of June 11, 1833, in Dublán and Lozano, eds., *Legislación mexicana*, II, 534.

54. Zúñiga, *Rápida ojeada*, p. 37.

55. Decreto of February 23, 1827, in Dublán and Lozano, eds., *Legislación mexicana*, II, 5. For examples of frontiersmen being exempted from military levies, see Minge, "Frontier Problems," pp. 134, 195. Fear of being sent out of one's province had been a major deterent to enlistments elsewhere in Mexico, especially since troops and militia were often sent to unhealthy coastal areas.

56. Barreiro, *Ojeada*, in Carroll and Haggard, eds. and trans., *Three New Mexico Chronicles*, p. 82. Archer, *The Army in Bourbon Mexico*, p. 236.

57. Instructions of Juan Andrés Archuleta, Santa Fe, June 14, 1845, MANM, roll 39, frame 606. See, too, the discussion of this question in chapter 11.

58. Figueroa to the alcalde of San Jose, January 24, 1835, quoted in Sherburne Friend Cook, "Expeditions to the Interior of California's Central Valley," *Anthropological Records*, XX (February 1962), p. 189. Simpson, *Narrative of a Journey*, I, 356.

59. Pino, "Manifiesto," Santa Fe, November 24, 1829, MANM, roll 9, frame 1121. Barreiro, *Ojeada,* in Carroll and Haggard, eds. and trans., *Three New Mexico Chronicles,* p. 77. Wilson, *Military Campaigns in the Navajo Country,* p. 13. Indian campaigns in Texas also relied heavily on volunteers and militia, and J. B. Wilkinson makes that point about Laredo: *Laredo and the Rio Grande Frontier* (Austin, 1975), p. 120.

60. Myrtle M. McKittrick, *Vallejo: Son of California* (Portland, 1944), p. 93. Documents relating to the formation of the Sección Patriótica on May 20, 1832, and its subsequent campaign, and Juan González, "Diario . . . contra los Apaches," September 16 to October 1, 1834, Tucson, both in AHES, Apaches, cabinet 2, drawer 3, McCarty Transcripts, AHS, film H-14.

61. See, for example, documents pertaining to a successful *tejano* campaign in 1831 in McLean, ed., *Robertson's Colony,* VI. There are many examples of campaigns by Anglo-American colonists in Texas, which generally succeeded in pacifying small Indian groups. Andrew Anthony Tijerina, "Tejanos and Texas: The Native Mexicans of Texas, 1820–1850" (Ph.D. diss., University of Texas, Austin, 1977), pp. 203–5, argues the continuity of military tradition by Anglo-Americans. Tijerina sees militia as the key to the defense of Texas in these years (pp. 174–89), although he reads the 1826 regulations differently than I do and does not seem aware of the colonial tradition of use of militia and volunteers. -

62. McNitt, *Navajo Wars,* pp. 26–91. David M. Brugge, ed. and trans., "Vizcarra's Navajo Campaign of 1823," *AW,* VI (Autumn, 1964), pp. 223–34.

63. Fragments of militia records for 1833, perhaps from the Taos district, MANM, roll 17, frames 630–32. See, too, the 1838 militia records from Santa Fe district, MANM, roll 25, frame 767. Donaciano Vigil, Address to the Departmental Assembly, June 18, 1846.

64. Mariano Chávez, speech before the Departmental Assembly, Santa Fe, January 1, 1844, quoted in Minge, "Frontier Problems," p. 156.

65. Vigil, Address to the Departmental Assembly, June 18, 1846.

66. Baca to Manuel Escudero, June 9, 1825, Santa Fe. Archivo Histórico de la Secretaría de Relaciones Exteriores, Mexico City, RE, 5-9-8159/H 241.5 (72:73)1, pp. 13–14. Rada, *Proposición,* p. 3.

67. For examples of American views of the frontier soldiery, see Albert Pike, *Prose Sketches and Poems Written in the Western Country,* David J. Weber, ed. (1st ed., 1834; Albuquerque, 1967), pp. 158–59; Alfred Robinson, *Life in California* (1st ed., 1846; Santa Barbara, 1970), pp. 144–45.

Chapter 7
The New Colonialism

1. See, for example, George Simpson, *Narrative of a Journey Round the World . . . 1841 and 1842,* 2 vols. (London, 1847), I, 363. Stanley J. Stein and Barbara H. Stein, *The Colonial Heritage of Latin America: Essays on Economic Independence in Perspective* (New York, 1970), pp. 123–56. Inés Herrera Canales, *El comercio exterior de México, 1821–1875* (Mexico, 1977), pp. 3–4, 113.

2. Considerable insight into economic problems in New Spain during the last years of Spanish sovereignty is provided in John H. Hann, "The Role of the Mexican Deputies in the Proposal and Enactment of Measures of Economic Reform Applicable to Mexico," in Nettie Lee Benson, ed., *Mexico and the Spanish Cortes, 1810–1822* (Austin, 1966), pp. 153–77. Luis Navarro García, "El Norte de Nueva España como problema político en el siglo XVIII," *Estudios Americanos,* XX (julio-agosto 1960), p. 29. Max L. Moorhead, *New Mexico's Royal Road: Trade and Travel on the Chihuahua Trail* (Norman, 1954), p. 56. Mattie Austin

Hatcher, trans., "Texas in 1820," *SWHQ*, XXIII (July 1919), p. 64. Hatcher, *The Opening of Texas to Foreign Settlement, 1801–1821* (Austin, 1927), p. 52.

3. Luis Navarro García, *Las provincias internas en el siglo XIX* (Sevilla, 1965), p. 87.

4. Fr. José Señán to the Viceroy, the Marqués de Branciforte, Mexico, May 14, 1796, in Lesley Byrd Simpson, ed., and Paul D. Nathan, trans., *The Letters of José Señán, O.F.M. Mission San Buenaventura, 1796–1823* (San Francisco, 1962), pp. 2–4. Robert Archibald, "Price Regulation in Hispanic California," *The Americas*, XXIII (April 1977), pp. 613–29, and Archibald, "The Economy of the Alta California Missions, 1803–1821" *SCQ*, LVIII (Summer 1976), pp. 227–40. Odie B. Faulk, *The Last Years of Spanish Texas, 1778–1821* (The Hague, The Netherlands, 1964), pp. 92–93. Carlos E. Castañeda, *Our Catholic Heritage in Texas, 1519–1936*, 7 vols. (Austin, 1931–58), V, 429.

5. Juan Agustín de Morfí, *Account of Disorders in New Mexico, 1778*, Marc Simmons, trans. and ed. (Isleta, New Mexico, 1977), p. 19. Pedro Bautista Pino, *Exposición . . .* (Cádiz, 1812). H. Bailey Carroll and J. Villasana Haggard, trans. and eds., *Three New Mexico Chronicles* (Albuquerque, 1942), pp. 106–7. Moorhead, *New Mexico's Royal Road*, pp. 49–54.

6. Señán to the Viceroy, the Marqués de Branciforte, Mexico, May 14, 1796, in Simpson, ed., *Letters of José Señán*, p. 2.

7. Pino, *Exposición*, in Carroll and Haggard, trans. and eds., *Three New Mexico Chronicles*, p. 63. Marc Simmons, *Spanish Government in New Mexico* (Albuquerque, 1968), pp. 94–98. Hatcher, trans., "Texas in 1820," p. 65. Nettie Lee Benson, trans. and ed., *Report that Dr. Miguel Ramos de Arizpe . . . Presents to the August Congress on the Natural, Political and Civil Condition of the Provinces of Coahuila, Nuevo León, Nuevo Santander, and Texas . . .* (Austin, 1950), p. 22.

8. David Brading, *Miners and Merchants in Bourbon Mexico, 1763–1810* (Cambridge, Eng., 1971), p. 18. Stein and Stein, *Colonial Heritage of Latin America* (New York, 1970), pp. 3–54. Morfí, *Account of Disorders in New Mexico*, p. 18.

9. Navarro García, *Las provincias internas*, pp. 86–89. Hatcher, trans., "Texas in 1820," p. 64. John L. Kessell, *Friars, Soldiers, and Reformers: Hispanic Arizona and the Sonora Mission Frontier, 1767–1856* (Tucson, 1976), p. 227. Simmons, *Spanish Government*, pp. 93–94.

10. Odie B. Faulk, "Ranching in Spanish Texas," *HAHR*, XLV (May 1965), pp. 257–66. Archibald, "The Economy of the Alta California Missions," p. 230, explains how the vagaries of the mercantile system made California "a smuggler's paradise."

11. Quoted in Adele Ogden, *The California Sea Otter Trade, 1748–1848* (Berkeley, 1941), p. 66. For a similar statement from Texas see the ayuntamiento of San Antonio, quoted in Hatcher, trans., "Texas in 1820," p. 67.

12. Noel M. Loomis and Abraham P. Nasatir, *Pedro Vial and the Roads to Santa Fe* (Norman, 1967), pp. 369–407.

13. William Becknell, "Journal of Two Expeditions from Boon's Lick to Santa Fe," Franklin *Missouri Intelligencer*, April 22, 1823.

14. Thomas James, *Three Years Among the Mexicans and the Indians* (1st ed., 1846; Chicago, 1962), p. 125. *The Journal of Jacob Fowler*, Elliott Coues, ed., with additional editing by Raymond W. and Mary Lund Settle and Harry R. Stevens (1st ed., 1898; Lincoln, Nebraska, 1970), p. 69. David J. Weber, *The Taos Trappers: The Fur Trade in the Far Southwest, 1540–1846* (Norman, 1971), pp. 53–55.

15. James *Three Years*, p. 95. Hugh Glenn's misfortunes are well explained by Harry R. Stevens, "Hugh Glenn," in LeRoy R. Hafen, ed., *The Mountain Men and the Fur Trade of the Far West*, 10 vols. (Glendale, 1965–72), II, 161–74. Weber, *The Taos Trappers*, p. 53.

16. Becknell, "Journal of Two Expeditions." More hard cash circulated in late colonial New Mexico than historians have supposed, or than contemporaries wished to admit. This was also true in California—*infra*, n. 59.

17. Moorhead, *New Mexico's Royal Road*, p. 61.

18. Donaciano Vigil to the New Mexico Assembly, June 18, 1846, MANM, roll 41, frames 330–39. Moorhead, *New Mexico's Royal Road*, pp. 80–81, 66.

19. William Workman, "A Letter from Taos, 1826," David J. Weber, ed., *NMHR*, XLI (April 1966), p. 159. New Mexico's shortage of specie is discussed in many sources. See, too, Moorhead, *New Mexico's Royal Road*, pp. 62–65.

20. Moorhead, *New Mexico's Royal Road*, pp. 62–65, 76–77. These percentages, based on Josiah Gregg's tables, are very rough estimates, but they remain our best source. See ibid., pp. 185–86, and Daniel Tyler, "New Mexico in the 1820's: The First Administration of Manuel Armijo" (Ph.D. diss., University of New Mexico, 1970), p. 139.

21. Moorhead, *New Mexico's Royal Road*," pp. 187–188, 85–88. "First Arkansas Caravan to Missouri," *Arkansas Gazette*, May 15, 1839.

22. Among the exceptions: 11 percent in 1839; nearly 33 percent in 1843. These exceedingly crude estimates were obtained by comparing the best of a group of poor sources: Gregg's table in *Commerce of the Prairies*, Max L. Moorhead, ed. (1st ed. 1844; Norman, 1954), p. 332, and government figures in Miguel Lerdo de Tejada, *Comercio exterior de México desde la Conquista hasta hoy* (1st ed., 1853; Mexico, 1967), table 41. Although badly dated, Lerdo de Tejada's figures remain the most dependable for many aspects of this period: Herrera Canales, *El comercio exterior de México*, pp. 6, 82. The volume of imports or exports over the Santa Fe trail cannot be measured more precisely, because graft and smuggling have skewed the statistics, as Albert Bork graphically demonstrated: *Nuevos aspectos del comercio entre Nuevo México y Misuri, 1822–1846* (Mexico City, 1944), pp. 67–78.

23. For examples of the hostility that Mexican traders met from Americans, see John E. Sunder, ed., *Matt Field on the Santa Fe Trail* (Norman, 1960), pp. 278–79. James Josiah Webb, *Adventures in the Santa Fe Trade, 1844–1847*, Ralph P. Bieber, ed. (Glendale, Ca., 1931), p. 111.

24. Thomas Maitland Marshall, "Commercial Aspects of the Texas Santa Fé Expedition," *SWHQ*, XX (January 1917), pp. 244–45. Lansing B. Bloom, "New Mexico Under Mexican Administration, 1821–1846," *Old Santa Fe*, II (October 1914), p. 121.

25. Weber, *The Taos Trappers*, pp. 12–31.

26. Ibid., pp. 52–65, 98–99.

27. Ibid., pp. 66–81. LeRoy R. Hafen, "Étienne Provost, Mountain Man and Utah Pioneer," *Utah Historical Quarterly*, XXXVI (Spring 1968), p. 103. A more complete biography is in Dale L. Morgan and Eleanor Towles Harris, *The Rocky Mountain Journals of William Marshall Anderson* (San Marino, Ca., 1967), pp. 343–51.

28. The contest for the furs of the region is ably summarized by Gloria Griffen Cline, *Exploring the Great Basin* (Norman, 1963), pp. 77–163. See, too, Weber, *The Taos Trappers*, pp. 80–81.

29. *The Personal Narrative of James Ohio Pattie* (1st ed., 1831; Philadelphia, 1962), p. 48.

30. Ibid., p. 51.

31. Weber, *The Taos Trappers*, pp. 96, 136.

32. A discussion of this question, notable for its long view, is Henry F. Dobyns, "Who Killed the Gila?" *JAH*, XIX (Spring 1978), pp. 20–22.

33. Weber, *The Taos Trappers*, pp. 64, 205–6.

34. See, for example, Jean Louis Berlandier, *The Indians of Texas in 1830*, John C. Ewers, ed. (Washington, D.C., 1969), p. 47, n. 27. Almonte, "Statistical Report," pp. 192, 205, 212, 214–15. Albert Pike, *Prose Sketches and Poems Written in the Western Country*, David J. Weber, ed. (Albuquerque, 1967), pp. 33ff. Eugene C. Barker, "A Glimpse of the Texas Fur Trade in 1832," *SWHQ*, XIX (January 1916), pp. 279–82.

35. The finest description of this journey is Dale L. Morgan's magisterial biography, *Jedediah Smith and the Opening of the West* (New York, 1953), pp. 193–215. Smith's own

newly discovered account, written in the hand of an associate, adds many details: *The Southwest Expedition of Jedediah S. Smith* . . . George R. Brooks, ed. (Glendale, 1977).

36. Weber, *The Taos Trappers*, pp. 134–36. Slowly, more information on Richard Campbell comes to light. See James W. Goodrich, "Richard Campbell: The Missouri Years," *Missouri Historical Review*, LXXII (October 1977), pp. 25–37.

37. *The Personal Narrative of James Ohio Pattie*, pp. 129–49.

38. Marc Simmons, "Spanish Attempts to Open a New Mexico-Sonora Road," *AW*, XVII (Spring 1975), pp. 5–20.

39. Lowell John Bean and William Marvin Mason, trans. and eds., *Diaries and Accounts of the Romero Expeditions in Arizona and California, 1823–1826* (Los Angeles, 1962). Mission Santa Catarina is sometimes also referred to as Santa Catalina.

40. Durán to Fray Juan Cortes, Mission San José, June 8, 1827, in Francis Price, trans., "Letters of Narciso Durán," *CHSQ*, XXXVII (September 1958), p. 262.

41. Morgan, *Jedediah Smith*, pp. 204–6, 243–55. Weber, *The Taos Trappers*, pp. 134–55.

42. "Armijo's Journal. . . , " LeRoy Hafen, ed., *Colorado Magazine*, XXVII (April 1950), pp. 120–31. Of two contemporary accounts, one indicates that 31 men made the journey and another places the number at 60.

43. Eleanor Lawrence, "Mexican Trade between Santa Fe and Los Angeles, 1830–1848," *CHSQ* X, (March 1931), pp. 27–39. LeRoy R. and Ann W. Hafen, *Old Spanish Trail, Santa Fé to Los Angeles* (Glendale, Ca., 1954), pp. 155–94.

44. Moorhead, *New Mexico's Royal Road*, pp. 189–90.

45. For background in the Spanish period see Ogden's classic, *California Sea Otter Trade*, pp. 1–65.

46. For the value of pelts, see Ogden, *California Sea Otter Trade*, pp. 91, 93, who finds figures of $15 and $20 for 1830 and 1833 respectively. In 1841 otter brought $35 and $38 in 1844. See George P. Hammond, ed., *The Larkin Papers: Personal, Business, and Official Correspondence of Thomas Oliver Larkin*. . . , 10 vols. (Berkeley, 1953), I, 98, 140. Ogden, *California Sea Otter Trade*, pp. 86–87.

47. Ogden, *California Sea Otter Trade*, pp. 105–6, 115.

48. Iris Higbie Wilson [Engstrand], *William Wolfskill, 1798–1866. Frontier Trapper to California Ranchero* (Glendale, Ca., 1965), pp. 82–83. Kenneth L. Holmes, *Ewing Young: Master Trapper* (Portland, Oregon, 1967), pp. 79–93.

49. Ogden, *California Sea Otter Trade*, pp. 140–43. One of the best contemporary accounts of the competition is William Henry Ellison, ed., *The Life and Adventures of George Nidever, 1802–1883* (Berkeley, 1937).

50. Manuel Castañares, exposición of September 1, 1844, in Castañares, *Colección de documentos relativos al departamento de California* (Mexico, 1845), facsimile in David J. Weber, ed., *Northern Mexico on the Eve of the United States Invasion. Rare Imprints* . . . (New York, 1976). Ogden, *California Sea Otter Trade*, pp. 142, 132–39.

51. Richard Henry Dana, *Two Years Before the Mast*, John Haskell Kemble, ed., 2 vols. (1st ed., 1840; Los Angeles, 1964), I, 64, 92–93.

52. Adele Odgen, "Hides and Tallow: McCulloch, Hartnell and Company, 1822–1828," *CHSQ*, VI (September 1927), p. 259.

53. Ibid., pp. 254–64.

54. Adele Ogden focuses on the activities of Bryant and Sturgis in "Boston Hide Droghers Along California Shores," *CHSQ*, VIII (December 1929), pp. 289–305.

55. Simpson, *Narrative of a Journey Round the World*, I, 289.

56. Tallow was measured by the *arroba*, the equivalent of 25 pounds. These figures come from Jessie Davies Francis, "An Economic and Social History of Mexican California, 1822–1846" (Ph.D. diss., University of California, Berkeley, 1935), pp. 532, 535.

57. The kinds of manufactures which were popular in California are suggested in Ogden, "Boston Hide Droghers," p. 301, and in various business papers, such as the invoice of February 3, 1842 in Hammond, ed., *The Larkin Papers*, I, pp. 161–64.

58. Robert H. Becker, *Diseños of California Ranchos: Maps of 37 Land Grants* (San Francisco, 1964), pp. xviii–xix, provides a brief but valuable analysis of this question. See, too, Francis, "Economic and Social History," pp. 523–27, and Abel du Petit- Thouars, *Voyage of the Venus: Sojourn in California*, Charles N. Rudkin, trans. (Los Angeles, 1956), pp. 44, 74.

59. David J. Weber, and Ronald R. Young, trans. and eds., "California in 1831: Heinrich Virmond to Lucas Alamán," *JSDH*, XXI (Fall 1975), p. 5. This is corroborated by many others. See, for example, José Bandini, *A Description of California in 1828*, Doris M. Wright, trans. (Berkeley, 1951), pp. 10–11 and Russell M. Posner, "A British Consular Agent in California: The Reports of James A. Forbes, 1834–1846," *SCQ*, LIII (June 1971), p. 102. More money may have circulated in California than visitors supposed, however. Some traders were surprised to find cash-paying customers (see, for example, Ogden, *California Sea Otter Trade*, pp. 81, 85, 88, 89); Juan Bautista Alvarado estimated that 100,000 pesos circulated in California in 1839–40 (Woodrow James Hansen, *The Search for Authority in California* [Oakland, Ca., 1960], p. 32.

60. No good study of ranching in Texas during this period exists. Andrew Anthony Tijerina, "Tejanos and Texas: The Native Mexicans of Texas, 1820–1850" (Ph.D. diss., University of Texas at Austin, 1977), pp. 29–32, reports a rapid expansion of *tejano* ranchos. Juan N. Almonte, *Noticia estadística sobre Tejas* (Mexico 1835), p. 79, facsimile in Weber, ed., *Northern Mexico*, puts the number of cattle exported from the Department of Nacogdoches at 5,000 head per year, but provides no figures for the departments of Brazos or Béxar. In the 1780s, on the other hand, 15 to 20,000 head of cattle were said to be driven from Texas to Louisiana annually (Faulk, "Ranching in Spanish Texas," p. 264). Benson, trans. and ed., *Report . . . Ramos Arizpe*, p. 21, mentions in 1811 that the "disorderly slaughter" of cattle had reduced their number drastically.

61. Melquiades Antonio Ortega to the editors of the *Registro Oficial*, Santa Fe, January 31, 1831, in Robert A. Potash, ed. and trans., "Notes and Documents," *NMHR*, XXIV (October 1949), p. 337. "Report of the Cattle and Caballada Found in the Territory of New Mexico," April 8, 1827 in Carroll and Haggard, trans. and eds., *Three New Mexico Chronicles*, p. 43. The report indicates 5,000 cattle, 550 horses, 300 mares, and 2,150 mules.

62. Teodoro Ramírez to the Governor of Sonora, Tucson, July 19, 1831, in Potash, ed. and trans., "Notes and Documents," p. 334. A rare record of exports on the Chihuahua trail indicate that either 33,500 or 46,500 sheep were sent south in 1844. Ward Alan Minge, "Frontier Problems in New Mexico Preceding the Mexican War, 1840–1846" (Ph.D. diss., University of New Mexico, 1965), pp. 247–52. The 30 to 40,000 annual figure appears in "Placer del Oro," by "E. E.," in *El Payo de Nuevo México*, July 19, 1845, MANM, roll 40, frame 574. Both "E. E." and Gregg, *Commerce of the Prairies*, pp. 133–34, mention that in the recent past 200,000 head were exported annually, but that Indians diminished herds. I have found no evidence of such extensive exports. Indeed, Ortega's 1831 letter mentions herds of 10 to 20,000 and Barreiro, writing at the same time, mentions 15,000 (Haggard and Carroll, eds. and trans., *Three New Mexico Chronicles*, p. 109).

63. Simpson, *Narrative of a Journey*, I, 286.

64. By 1801, for example, farmers in the Los Angeles basin were producing enough grain to consider shipping the surplus to Mexico. Hubert Howe Bancroft, *History of California*, 7 vols. (San Francisco, 1884–90), II, 184. Among the contemporary Mexicans who recognized the obstacles to the development of commercial agriculture on the frontier were Almonte, *Noticia estadística sobre Tejas*, pp. 32–33; Manuel de Jesús Rada, *Proposición hecha al Soberano Congreso* (Mexico, 1829) p. 4, facsimile in Weber, ed. *Northern Mexico;* Castañares, "exposición," p. 23. See, too, Francis, "Economic and Social History," pp. 568–77.

65. Almonte, *Noticia estadística sobre Tejas,* p. 33. Andrew Forest Muir, ed., *Texas in 1837: An Anonymous Contemporary Narrative* (Austin, 1958), p. 99. José del Carmen Lugo, "Life of a Rancher," *SCQ,* XXXII (September 1950), p. 230. Donaciano Vigil to the Departmental Assembly, June 18, 1846, MANM, roll 41, frames 330–39.

66. Cós to the Ministro de Guerra, July 30, 1835 and September 6, 1835, Archivo de Guerra y Marina, AGN, transcripts, UT, vol. 333. See the interesting commentary by a traveler who visited the San Antonio-Goliad area in 1828 and again in 1834. Jean Louis Berlandier, *Journey to Mexico During the Years 1826 to 1834,* C. H. Muller and Katherine K. Muller, eds., and Sheila M. Ohlendorf, Josette M. Bigelow, and Mary M. Standifer, trans., 2 vols. (Austin, 1980), II, 556, 553.

67. José Arnaz, "Memoirs of a Merchant," Nellie Van de Grift Sánchez, trans. and ed., *Touring Topics,* XX (September 1928), p. 17. See, too, "Duhaut-Cilly's Account of California in the Years 1827–1828," Charles Franklin Carter, trans., *CHSQ,* VIII (December 1929), p. 311. Marilyn McAdams Sibley, *Travelers in Texas, 1761–1860* (Austin, 1967), p. 100. Fane Downs, "The History of Mexicans in Texas" (Ph.D. diss., Texas Tech University, 1970), pp. 73, 173.

68. Francis, "Economic and Social History," pp. 545–62.

69. Almonte, *Noticias estadísticas sobre Tejas,* pp. 64, 80, 39. Eugene C. Barker, *The Life of Stephen F. Austin: Founder of Texas, 1793–1836* (1st ed. 1926; 2nd ed. reprinted, Austin, 1969), p. 183, suggests that Almonte's figures were exaggerated, yet Austin also estimated that the crop from his colony alone would amount to 7,000 bales in 1833 (ibid., p. 371). Muir, ed., *Texas in 1837,* p. 99. Ramírez to the Governor of Sonora, in Potash, ed. and trans., "Notes and Documents," pp. 334, 336–37.

70. Almonte, *Noticias estadísticas sobre Tejas,* pp. 37–38, 64, 79–80, 82, 86–87. William C. Binkley, *The Texas Revolution* (Baton Rouge, Louisiana, 1952), pp. 20–22.

71. Vincent Carosso, *The California Wine Industry, 1830–1895* (Berkeley, 1951), pp. 3, 7–15. Iris Ann Wilson [Engstrand], "Early Southern California Viniculture, 1830–1865," *SCQ,* XXXIX (September 1957), pp. 242–50. Castañares, *Colección de documentos,* p. 23.

72. Albert William Archibald to Francis Cragin, December 25, 1907, quoted in Weber, *The Taos Trappers,* p. 8. See, too, ibid., pp. 72–73, 118, 144, 225–27; Pino, *Exposición,* pp. 35, 97; Gregg, *Commerce of the Prairies,* pp. 273, 313.

73. Thomas R. Cox, *Mills and Markets: A History of the Pacific Coast Lumber Industry to 1900* (Seattle, 1974), pp. 13–20, and C. Raymond Clar, *California Government and Forestry from Spanish Times to . . . 1927* (Sacramento, 1959), pp. 31–40. Barker, *Austin,* pp. 183, 371.

74. See, for example, E. E., "El Placer del Oro," in *El Payo de Nuevo México,* July 19, 1845, in MANM, roll 40, frame 574.

75. E. Boyd, *Popular Arts of Spanish New Mexico* (Santa Fe, 1974), pp. 280–86, provides the best evidence for New Mexico. Less useful is Stuart A. Northrup, *Minerals of New Mexico* (1st ed., 1944; rev. ed., Albuquerque, 1959). Herbert Eugene Bolton, *Texas in the Middle Eighteenth Century* (Berkeley, 1915), pp. 80–83, and Francis, "Economic and Social History," pp. 606–7. Duane Kendall Hale, "California's First Mining Frontier and Its Influence on the Settlement of that Area," *JW,* XVIII (January 1979), pp. 14–21, is careless and of limited value. For Arizona see John L. Kessell, *Friars, Soldiers, and Reformers,* pp. 132, 282, 284, n. 17, 305.

76. Copper was mined near Abiquiú, New Mexico, for example. See the April 12, 1845 census in MANM, roll 40, frame 403, and Potash, ed. and trans., "Notes and Documents" pp. 338–39. Frederick A. Wislizenus, *Memoir of a Tour to Northern Mexico . . . 1846 and 1847* (1st ed., 1848; facsimile, reprint, Albuquerque, 1969), p. 24. The existence of copper at Santa Rita was known at least since the eighteenth century when the Santa Rita Mountains were known as the Sierra del Cobre; see Adlai Feather, ed., "Colonel Don Fernando de la Concha, Diary, 1788," *NMHR,* XXXIV (October 1959), p. 296, n. 3. Francisco R. Almada,

Resúmen de Historia del Estado de Chihuahua (Mexico, 1955), p. 137. Elsie Campbell, "Spanish Records of the Civil Government of Ysleta, 1835" (M.A. thesis, University of Texas, El Paso, 1950), pp. 98–99, 104. The most recent exposition of the Spanish period at Santa Rita is Billy D. Walker, "Copper Genesis: The Early Years of Santa Rita del Cobre," *NMHR*, LIV (January 1979), pp. 5–20.

77. Wislizenus, *Tour of Northern Mexico*, p. 24, and pp. 30–33. John M. Townley, "El Placer: A New Mexico Mining Boom Before 1846," *JW*, X (January 1971), p. 113, provides substantial detail about Real de Dolores, but is not sufficiently critical of his sources. E. E., "El Placer del Oro," and Minge, "Frontier Problems in New Mexico," p. 170–76.

78. John M. Sully, "The Story of the Santa Rita Mine," *Old Santa Fe*, III (April 1916), p. 138. Wislizenus, *Tour to Northern Mexico*, pp. 30–33. Rada, *Proposición*, p. 4. E. E., "Placer del Oro."

79. J. N. Bowman, "The First Authentic Placer Mine in California," *SCQ*, XXXI (September 1949), pp. 225–30. For export figures and a summary of mining activity in these years see Francis, "Economic and Social History," pp. 602–28. A popular article by Francis J. Weber, "California's Gold Discovery: The Record Set Straight," *Quarterly*, Los Angeles County Museum, 8 (Spring 1970), pp. 25–27, is useful for associating the sites with modern place names. Abel Stearns to Thomas O. Larkin, Los Angeles, May 3, 1842, in Hammond, ed., *The Larkin Papers*, I, 217.

80. Downs, "The History of Mexicans in Texas," p. 61.

81. Juan Bautista Alvarado, "History of California," 1876, 5 vols., MS, vol. III, p. 72, BL.

82. Simpson, *Narrative*, I, 292–93. For Texas, see *Representación dirijida por el ilustre ayuntamiento de la ciudad de Béxar al . . . Congreso del Estado* (Brazoria, 1833), p. 6.

83. Chief Factor James Douglas, quoted in Francis, "Economic and Social History," p. 526.

84. That "the development of commerce in the Southwest was not conducive to the development of local industry and manufacturing," was not an unusual phenomenon, according to economist Raúl A. Fernández, *The United States-Mexico Border: A Politico-Economic Profile* (Notre Dame, 1977), pp. 52–53.

85. See, for example, the analysis of the Texas census of 1820 in Vito Alessio Robles, *Coahuila y Texas . . .* 2 vols. (Mexico, 1945), I, 61, and the fragmentary New Mexico census of 1823 in *New Mexico: Spanish and Mexican Colonial Censuses, 1790, 1823, and 1845*, Virginia Langham Olmsted, trans. and ed. (Albuquerque, 1975). See, too, Antonio José Ríos-Bustamante, "New Mexico in the Eighteenth Century: Life, Labor and Trade in la Villa de San Felipe de Albuquerque, 1706–1790," and Janie Louise Aragón, "The People of Santa Fé in the 1790s," both in *Aztlán*, VII (Fall 1976), pp. 369, 402–12 respectively. Little has been written about handicrafts made by women. Juana Machado recalled that in California before independence, "women had in their homes their own shoe shops, and . . . made their own footwear," Ray S. Brandes, trans. and ed., "Times Gone By in Alta California: Recollections of Señora Doña Juana Machado. . . , " *SCQ*, XLI (September 1959), p. 200.

86. Governor Manuel Victoria to the Secretaría de Relaciones, June 7, 1831, in Archives of California, vol. 49 (Departmental Records), pp. 135–36, BL. Francis, "Economic and Social History," pp. 633–36. Howard J. Nelson, "The Two Pueblos of Los Angeles: Agricultural Village and Embryo Town," *SCQ*, LIX (Spring 1977), pp. 1–6.

87. Barreiro, *Ojeada*, in Carroll and Haggard, trans. and eds., *Three New Mexico Chronicles*, p. 38. Even the goods produced in the highly touted California missions were crude and foreign manufactures were preferred. Robert Archibald, "The Economy of the Alta California Missions," p. 235. For Texas, see, for example, Stephen Austin to the ayuntamiento of Béxar, San Felipe, November 7, 1826, in Eugene C. Barker, ed., *The Austin Papers*, 3 vols. (Washington and Austin, 1924–28), vol. II, part 2, p. 1497. *Representación dirijida por el ilustre ayuntamiento de la ciudad de Béxar*, pp. 6–7.

88. Boyd, *Popular Arts of Spanish New Mexico*, pp. 246, 260, 275. Gregg, *Commerce of the Prairies*, p. 148. Foreign observers often exaggerated the shortage of implements and machinery. Compare Marc Simmons and Frank Turley, *Southwestern Colonial Ironwork: The Spanish Blacksmithing Tradition from Texas to California* (Santa Fe, 1980), pp. 68–82, with the observations of Gregg, *Commerce of the Prairies*, p. 144, and Augustus Storrs, *Santa Fe Trail, First Reports: 1825* (Houston, 1960), p. 31.

89. Rada, *Proposición*, p. 4.

90. Patricia M. Bauer, "Beginnings of Tanning in California," *CHSQ*, XXXIII (March 1954), p. 61, concludes that *californios* did not do quality tanning, even in the missions. Francis, "Economic and Social History," pp. 638–39.

91. Barreiro, *Ojeada*, in Carroll and Haggard, eds. and trans., *Three New Mexico Chronicles*, p. 39.

92. Description of California, Monterey, April 20, 1846, in Hammond, ed., *The Larkin Papers*, IV, 305. Dana, *Two Years Before the Mast*, I, 82. For Pratt's tannery, see Bloom, "New Mexico Under Mexican Administration," I, 349.

93. Nelson, "The Two Pueblos of Los Angeles," p. 6.

94. Dana, *Two Years Before the Mast*, I, 154. Rada, *Proposición*, p. 4.

95. Letter of October 1846 in William Robert Garner, *Letters from California, 1846–47*, Donald Munro Craig, ed. (Berkeley, 1970), pp. 87–88.

Chapter 8
Regulating the Economy

1. Ramos Arizpe, Puebla, August 1, 1830, to Lucas Alamán, ASFC, legajo VI, part 11 (1828–31), expediente 43, West Transcripts, UT.

2. John E. Baur, "The Evolution of a Mexican Foreign Trade Policy, 1821–1828," *The Americas*, XIX (January 1963), pp. 238–49, and Agustín Cue Cánovas, *Historia social y económica de México (1521–1854)* (3rd. ed.; Mexico, 1967), pp. 278–82.

3. David J. Weber, *The Taos Trappers: The Fur Trade in the Far Southwest, 1540–1846* (Norman, 1971), p. 66. Decretos of March 18 and June 5, 1826, Carlos E. Castañeda, *Our Catholic Heritage in Texas*, 7 vols. (Austin, 1931–58), VI, 334. Dieter George Berninger, *La immigración en México, 1821–1857* (Mexico, 1974), pp. 92–93. Adele Ogden, *The California Sea Otter Trade* (Berkeley, 1941), p. 104. Juan de Dios Canedo, *Memoria de la Secretaría de Estado y del Despacho de Relaciones Interiores y Exteriores* (Mexico, 1829), p. 22.

4. William Sturgis Hinckley to Thomas Oliver Larkin, July 4, 1841, Yerba Buena, in George P. Hammond, ed., *The Larkin Papers: Personal, Business, and Official Correspondence of Thomas Oliver Larkin, Merchant and United States Consul in California*, 10 vols. (Berkeley, 1953), I, 91.

5. For insights into the formation of tariff policies see especially *Protección y libre cambio: el debate entre 1821 y 1836*, nota preliminar de Romeo Flores Caballero, selección documental de Luis Córdova (Mexico, 1971), and Robert A. Potash, *El Banco de Avío de México. El fomento de la industria, 1821–1846* (Mexico, 1959), chapts. 1, 2, and 11.

6. Baur, "Evolution of a Mexican Foreign Trade Policy," pp. 234–35, 254–55, 257. Evidence of widespread corruption among government officials is abundant. See, for example, Berninger, *Inmigración*, pp. 98ff.

7. Sir George Simpson, *Narrative of a Journey Round the World, During the Years 1841 and 1842*, 2 vols. (London, 1847), I, 340. José C. Valadés, *Orígines de la república mexicana. La aurora constitucional* (Mexico, 1972), pp. 354–56. Charles C. Cumberland, *Mexico: The Struggle for Modernity* (New York, 1968), p. 146. Cue Cánovas, *Historia social y económica*, p. 283.

Diego G. López Rosado, *Historia y pensamiento económico de México*, 4 vols. (Mexico, 1968–74), IV, 132–34.

8. Anonymous, *Considerations on the Political and Social Situation of the Mexican Republic, 1847*, Dennis E. Berge, trans. and ed. (El Paso, 1975), p. 15.

9. Cumberland, *Mexico*, p. 148, italics mine.

10. Max L. Moorhead, *New Mexico's Royal Road: Trade and Travel on the Chihuahua Trail* (Norman, 1954), p. 134. Jessie Davis Francis, "An Economic and Social History of Mexican California, 1822–1846" (Ph.D. diss., University of California, Berkeley, 1934), pp. 235–46. Although a "maritime and terrestial" customs house functioned in San Antonio, it does not seem accurate to consider it coastal (see the monthly reports for 1824, BA, microfilm roll 79, frames 205–6).

11. John Girdler, San Diego, December 7, 1844, in "A California Hide Trade Letter, 1844," Anthony L. Lehman, ed., *SCQ*, LI (March 1969), p. 58. Similarly, Richard Wilson justified smuggling on the Santa Fe Trail because the tariff was "for the sole use and benefit of his obesity, the Governor." *Short Ravelings from a Long Yarn* (1st ed. 1847; Santa Ana, Ca., 1936), p. 140. Moorhead, *New Mexico's Royal Road*, pp. 134–36. Papers pertaining to the investigation of Vigil are in MANM, roll 4, frames 1049–70, and elsewhere. For Bandini see Hubert Howe Bancroft, *History of California*, 7 vols. (San Francisco, 1884–90), III, 371–72, and C. Alan Hutchinson, *Frontier Settlement in Mexican California, The Híjar-Padrés Colony and its Origins, 1769–1835* (New Haven, 1969), p. 331. It is difficult to determine if these men were guilty or if accusations against them were politically motivated. Vigil was eventually vindicated by a treasury official in Chihuahua. Other examples of peculation in the custom collector's office exist, however; see Albert W. Bork, *Nuevos aspectos del comercio entre Nuevo México y Misuri, 1822–1846* (Mexico, 1944), pp. 42–43.

12. Francis, "Economic and Social History," pp. 230–33, concluded that the Monterey customs house was well-administered between 1836 and 1846.

13. Quoted in Weber, *The Taos Trappers*, pp. 105, 115.

14. F. P. Wrangel, *De Sitka a San Petersburgo al través de México* (Mexico, 1975), p. 44. Wrangel was not exaggerating. See Francis, "Economic and Social History," pp. 265–68.

15. J. A. Facio, Secretaría de Fomento, Mexico, December 30, 1830, to Sr. Secretario de Relaciones, ASFC, legajo V (1827–30), expediente 33, West Transcripts, UT. Antonio Gil Hernández, Galveston, to Domingo de Ugartechea, Béxar, May 30, 1835, cited in John H. Jenkins, ed., *The Papers of the Texas Revolution, 1835–1836*, 10 vols. (Austin, 1973), I, 133.

16. David J. Weber, ed. and trans., "A Black American in Mexican San Diego: Two Recently Recovered Documents," *JSDH*, XX (Spring 1974), p. 31. Manuel Castañares, *Colección de documentos relativos al departamento de Californias* (Mexico, 1845), pp. 47–48, facsimile in David J. Weber, ed., *Northern Mexico on the Eve of the United States Invasion . . .* (New York, 1976).

17. Techniques of smuggling are described in numerous primary and secondary sources. See, for example, Ogden, *California Sea Otter Trade*, pp. 101, 105–14. Mariano Guadalupe Vallejo, *Espocisión [sic] . . .* (Sonoma, 1837), pp. 7–8, facsimile in Weber, ed., *Northern Mexico*. William Heath Davis, *Seventy-Five Years in California*, Harold Small, ed. (1st ed., 1889; 3rd ed., San Francisco, 1967), pp. 78–83. Moorhead, *New Mexico's Royal Road*, pp. 134ff. Weber, *The Taos Trappers*, pp. 93–94, 157–58, 176ff. James Josiah Webb, *Adventures in the Santa Fe Trade*, Ralph P. Beiber, ed. (Glendale, Ca. 1931), pp. 183–84.

18. José Bandini, *A Description of California in 1828*, Doris M. Wright, trans. and ed. (Berkeley, 1951), p. 13. José's son Juan advanced a similar argument as a representative to Congress in 1833, see Bancroft, *History of California*, III, 369.

19. Francis, "Economic and Social History of California," pp. 235–55. Hutchinson, *Frontier Settlement in Mexican California*, pp. 332–33.

20. Decreto of September 23, 1843, in Manuel Dublán and José María Lozano, eds., *Legislación mexicana*, 34 vols. (Mexico, 1876–1904), IV, 571. The law excepted naturalized foreigners and those married to Mexican women. Francis, "Economic and Social History," p. 252; Moorhead, *New Mexico's Royal Road*, p. 138; *Representación dirijida por el ilustre ayuntamiento de la ciudad de Béxar al . . . Congreso del Estado* (Brazoria, 1833), p. 13.

21. Minutes of the diputación territorial, July 16, 1832, MANM, roll 42, frame 695. Raymond C. Clar, *California Government and Forestry from Spanish Times to the Creation of the Department of Natural Resources in 1927* (Sacramento, 1959), p. 28. Jean Louis Berlandier, *Journey to Mexico During the Years 1826 to 1834*, C. H. Muller and Katherine K. Muller, eds., and Sheila M. Ohlendorf, Josette M. Bigelow, and Mary M. Standifer, trans., 2 vols. (Austin, 1980), II, 560. The California and Texas regulations were apparently not enforced.

22. Weber, *The Taos Trappers*, pp. 66–67. Ogden, *California Sea Otter Trade*, pp. 95–104.

23. Vallejo to the Ministerio de Guerra y Marina, December 1841, quoted in George Tays, "Mariano Guadalupe Vallejo and Sonoma," *CHSQ*, XVII (March 1937), p. 59. For another statement of Vallejo's views see his *"Esposición"* (Sonoma, 1837), and Francis, "Economic and Social History," pp. 243–45, 327–32.

24. Juan María Alarid to unknown official, Mexico City, July 9, 1829, MANM, roll 9, frames 1142–43, called to my attention by Daniel Tyler, "Anglo-American Penetration of the Southwest," *SWHQ*, LXXV (January 1972), p. 334, n. 24. The tariff to which Alarid referred is in Dublán and Lozano, eds., *Legislación mexicana*, II, 109–10.

25. Simpson, *Narrative*, I, 359. M. G. Vallejo to Anastasio Bustamante, November 22, 1845, quoted in Francis, "Economic and Social History," p. 332.

26. For examples of the dependence of the government on revenue from foreign merchants see the contemporary statement of Mariano Chico, June 22, 1836, Monterey, quoted in Alfonso Teja Zabre, *Lecciones de California* (Mexico, 1962), p. 81. Vallejo exaggerated when he said that "California has no source of revenue other than that of customs." See Francis, "Economic and Social History," p. 332; 169–207. For New Mexico, see Lansing B. Bloom, "New Mexico Under Mexican Administration, 1821–1846," *Old Santa Fe*, I (April 1914), p. 353, and II (July 1914), p. 9. Daniel Tyler, "New Mexico in the 1820's : The First Administration of Manuel Armijo" (Ph.D. diss., University of New Mexico, 1970), p. 142. Ward Alan Minge, "Frontier Problems in New Mexico Preceding the Mexican War, 1840–1846" (Ph.D. diss., University of New Mexico, 1965), pp. 105ff., 302–3.

27. Moorhead, *New Mexico's Royal Road*, p. 127. Bork, *Nuevos aspectos sobre el comercio entre Nuevo México y Misuri*, p. 73. Adele Ogden, "Boston Hide Droghers Along California Shores," *CHSQ*, VIII (December 1929), pp. 290–91, 303–4. Charles Franklin Carter, trans., "Duhaut-Cilly's Account of California in the Years 1827–1828," *CHSQ*, VIII (June 1929), p. 162. Francis, "Economic and Social History," pp. 240, 243–44.

28. Woodrow James Hansen, *The Search for Authority in California* (Oakland, Ca., 1960), p. 37. Hutchinson, *Frontier Settlement in Mexican California*, pp. 331–32. Tyler, "New Mexico in the 1820's," pp. 103, 105, 146–49. Minge, "Frontier Problems in New Mexico," pp. 148, 237–38. Ángela Moyano Pahissa, *El comercio de Santa Fé y la guerra del '47* (Mexico, 1976), pp. 71–72.

29. Chico to the Secretaría de Guerra y Marina, Monterey, July 22, 1836, quoted in Teja Zabre, *Lecciones de California*, p. 78. Tyler, "New Mexico in the 1820's," p. 150. Davis, *Seventy-five Years in California*, pp. 78–82.

30. Address dated June 18, 1846, in MANM, roll 41, frames 330–39.

31. Ignacio Zúñiga, *Rápida ojeada al estado de Sonora* (Mexico, 1835), p. 149, facsimile in Weber, ed., *Northern Mexico*.

32. Anonymous, *A Visit to Texas in 1831 . . .* (1st ed., 1834; Houston, 1975), p. 165.

33. Davis, *Seventy-five Years in California*, p. 80.

34. Commercial regulations as they applied to Texas, both in theory and in practice, need study during this period. For good, brief discussions see Eugene C. Barker, *Mexico and Texas, 1821–1835* (Dallas, 1928), pp. 107ff, and *Representación dirijida por el ilustre ayuntamiento de la ciudad de Béxar*, p. 14. Stephen Austin to the Ayuntamiento of Béxar, November 7, 1826, in Eugene C. Barker, ed. *The Austin Papers*, 3 vols. (Washington and Austin, 1924–28), vol. I, part 1, p. 1495. For smuggling, see Francisco Pizarro Martínez to Manuel Mier y Terán, New Orleans, February 20, 1831, in ASFC, legajo 6, pt. 1, expediente 40, West Transcripts, UT. The journal of John C. Beales, December 1833, quoted in William Kennedy, *Texas: The Rise, Progress and Prospects. . .* , 2 vols. (London, 1841), II, 36. Barker, *Austin*, p. 406. Domingo de Ugartechea to Martín Perfecto de Cos, Béxar, June 19, 1835, in Jenkins, ed., *Papers of the Texas Revolution*, I, 155.

35. Eugene C. Barker, *The Life of Stephen F. Austin: Founder of Texas, 1793–1836* (1st ed. 1926; 2nd ed. reprinted, Austin, 1969) p. 201. For the 1832 episode, see Ohland Morton, *Terán and Texas: A Chapter in Texas-Mexican Relations* (Austin, 1948), pp. 141–54, and Edna Rowe, "The Disturbances at Anáhuac in 1832," *SWHQ*, VI (April 1903), pp. 265–99. For the 1835 episode, see Eugene Barker, "Difficulties of a Mexican Revenue Officer," *SWHQ*, IV (January 1901), pp. 190–202.

36. William C. Binkley, *The Texas Revolution* (Baton Rouge, 1952), pp. 21–25, provides a cogent discussion of this question.

37. D. A. Brading, "Government and Elite in Late Colonial Mexico," *HAHR*, LIII (August 1973), pp. 413–14. John H. Coatsworth, "Obstacles to Economic Growth in Nineteenth Century Mexico," *American Historical Review*, LXXXIII (February 1978), pp. 81–83. López Rosado, *Historia y pensamiento económico de México*, IV, 107, 122, 126, 131–32. Cumberland, *Mexico*, p. 170.

38. I have here relied on Coatsworth's analysis of "Obstacles to Economic Growth in Nineteenth Century Mexico," and López Rosado, *Historia y pensamiento económico*, IV, 107ff. Contemporary analyses were not far off the mark. See, for example, Alexander Forbes, *California: A History* (London, 1839), pp. 298, 302ff. For the deterioration of roads in particular, see Peter Rees, *Transportes y comercio entre México y Veracruz, 1519–1910* (Mexico, 1976), pp. 95–103.

39. Some idea of relative wealth might be estimated from an 1829 order requiring citizens in all states and territories to pay a "forced loan" to the government. Assessments apparently indicated the government's idea of relative wealth: the Californias were the poorest; New Mexico ranked fourth from the bottom, and Texas, even though linked with Coahuila, finished among the poorest. Dublán y Lozano, eds., *Legislación mexicana*, II, 147–50. W. Elliott Brownlee, *Dynamics of Ascent: A History of the American Economy* (New York, 1974), pp. 96–97. Coatsworth, "Obstacles," pp. 81–83.

Chapter 9
Peopling of Texas

1. Tadeo Ortiz to Vice President Anastasio Bustamante, Bordeaux, October 31, 1830, in Edith Louise Kelly and Mattie Austin Hatcher, eds. and trans., "Tadeo Ortiz de Ayala and the Colonization of Texas, 1822–1833," *SWHQ*, XXXII (October 1928), pp. 160–61.

2. Dieter George Berninger, *La inmigración en México, 1821–1357* (Mexico, 1974), pp. 24–31. Population statistics, which are suggestive rather than accurate, appear in Charles C. Cumberland, *Mexico: The Struggle for Modernity* (New York, 1968), p. 367. Josefina Zoraida Vázquez, "Los primeros tropiezos," in *Historia general de México*, 4 vols. (Mexico, 1976), III, 34.

3. Berninger, *La inmigración en México*, pp. 33–34.

4. For an example of Mexican awareness of the rapid demographic expansion of the United States, see "Voto sobre colonización," February 22, 1822, in Juan Francisco de Azcárate, *Un programa de política internacional* (Mexico, 1932), pp. 13–14. Berninger argues that Mexico was inspired by United States success (*La inmigración en México*, pp. 21–24, 26, 34–37). See, too, *Memoria de la Secretaría de Estado . . .* (Mexico, 1835), p. 39, which explains the United States elimination of the national debt as a result of immigration and land sales.

5. Experiments at bringing Canary Islanders to Texas and augmenting the population of California are discussed in many sources. See, for example, Carlos E. Castañeda, *Our Catholic Heritage in Texas, 1519–1936*, 7 vols. (Austin, 1931–58), II, 268–31. Hubert Howe Bancroft, *History of California*, 7 vols. (San Francisco, 1884–90), I, 602–5.

6. Quoted in Gilbert Din, "Spain's Immigration Policy in Louisiana and the American Penetration, 1792–1803," *SWHQ*, LXXVI (January 1973), p. 255. See, too, Arthur Preston Whitaker, *The Spanish American Frontier: 1783–1795. The Westward Movement and the Spanish Retreat in the Mississippi Valley* (1st ed., 1927; reprint ed., Lincoln, Neb., 1969), pp. 105–6.

7. Mattie Austin Hatcher, *The Opening of Texas to Foreign Settlement, 1801–1821* (Austin, 1927), pp. 10–40. Alicia Tjarks, "Comparative Demographic Analysis of Texas, 1777–1793," *SWHQ*, LXXVII (January 1974), p. 329.

8. Hatcher, *Opening of Texas*, pp. 70ff., 92, 116. Odie B. Faulk, *The Last Years of Spanish Texas, 1778–1821* (The Hague, Netherlands, 1964), pp. 120–31; Félix D. Almaraz, Jr., *Tragic Cavalier: Governor Manuel Salcedo of Texas, 1808–1813* (Austin, 1971), pp. 31, 34–35, 135.

9. Fane Downs, "The History of Mexicans in Texas, 1821–1845" (Ph.D. diss., Texas Tech University, Lubbock, 1971), p. 207. Eugene C. Barker, *The Life of Stephen F. Austin: Founder of Texas, 1793–1836* (1st ed., 1926; 2nd ed. reprinted, Austin, 1969), pp. 3–29.

10. John H. Hann, "The Role of the Mexican Deputies in the Proposal and Enactment of Measures of Economic Reform Applicable to Mexico," in Nettie Lee Benson, ed. *Mexico and the Spanish Cortes* (Austin, 1966), pp. 161–62; Azcárate, *Un programa de política internacional*, p. 65; Berninger, *La inmigración en México*, p. 24. Vito Alessio Robles, *Coahuila y Texas desde la consumación de la independencia hasta el tratado de paz de Guadalupe Hidalgo*, 2 vols. (Mexico, 1945–46), I, 105.

11. Primera Secretaría del Estado, Regencia del Imperio, to the Junta Soberana, November 26, 1821, ASFC, legajo 1, expediente 1, transcript, BL. Azcárate, *Un programa de política internacional*, pp. 62–72, 25–26, 39.

12. Ibid., pp. 14–15. For a discussion of the American threat to Texas, which is especially aware of Mexican viewpoints, see Joseph Carl McElhannon, "Imperial Mexico and Texas, 1821–1823," *SWHQ*, LIII (October 1949), pp. 132–33.

13. Perhaps the most convenient source of an English translation and condensation of the Imperial Colonization Law is Ernest Wallace and David M. Vigness, eds., *Documents of Texas History* (Austin, 1960), pp. 47–48. Events surrounding its passage are analyzed in Barker, *Austin*, pp. 43–66, and Berninger, *La inmigración en México*, pp. 36–40.

14. For the 1824 law see Wallace and Vigness, eds., *Documents of Texas History*, p. 48, and Manuel Dublán and José María Lozano, eds., *Legislación mexicana*, 34 vols. (Mexico, 1876–1904), I, 712–13. The 1828 law is in Francisco F. de la Maza, *Código de colonización y terrenos baldíos de la República mexicana* (Mexico, 1893), pp. 221–24. This law remained in force until March 11, 1842, see Berninger, *La inmigración en México*, pp. 46–47.

15. McElhannon, "Imperial Mexico and Texas," p. 138. Azcárate, *Un programa de política internacional*, pp. 62–72. Alessio Robles, *Coahuila y Texas*, I, 104–5.

16. Quoted in Baron de Bastrop to Austin, Saltillo, April 27, 1825, Eugene C. Barker, ed., *The Austin Papers*, 3 vols. (Washington and Austin, 1924–28), II, 1082. See, too, Bastrop's letters of February 10 and March 19, 1825. The nature of the debate in Saltillo deserves further study. The first state to adopt a colonization law seems to have been Jalisco

(January 15, 1825), followed by the northern states of Coahuila y Texas (March 24, 1825), Chihuahua (May 25, 1825), and Tamaulipas (December 15, 1826). Berninger, *La inmigración en México*, pp. 43–44; J. J. Bowden, *Spanish and Mexican Land Grants in the Chihuahuan Acquisition* (El Paso, 1971), p. 1.

17. This law is translated in its entirety in H. P. N. Gammel, *The Laws of Texas*, 10 vols. (Austin, 1898), I, 40–46, and a condensed version appears in Wallace and Vigness, eds., *Documents of Texas History*, pp. 48–50.

18. The acreage equivalents of these units differ depending upon the length of the basic unit, the *vara*, which varied in time and place. In 1919 the Texas legislature standardized the vara at 33 and 1/3 inches. Most writers have used this as the basis of computation. Hence, a *labor*, which equals 1,000 varas square (1,000,000 square varas) is 177.14 acres, and a square league, which equals 5,000 varas square (25,000,000 square varas) contains 4,428.4 acres. It is interesting to note that the Coahuila y Texas Colonization Law (article 11) specified that a vara would equal three feet.

19. Barker, *Austin*, pp. 123, 148–53, 323–26.

20. Mary Virginia Henderson, "Minor Empresario Contracts for the Colonization of Texas, 1825–1834," *SWHQ*, XXXI (April 1928), pp. 299–300. Henderson's list includes grants made until the 1825 law was superseded by the April 28, 1832 state law. Her list is not complete. It lacks some later contracts issued to Stephen Austin by the state.

21. Ibid., p. 301, and her discussion of individual contracts.

22. Barker, *Austin*, especially chaps. III and IV.

23. See Ethel Zivley Rather, "De Witt's Colony," *SWHQ*, VII (October 1904), pp. 95–192, a detailed, well-documented and still valuable study, and Edward A. Lukes, *De Witt Colony of Texas* (Austin, 1976), 91, 98, 194ff.

24. Rather, "De Witt's Colony," pp. 104–14; Henderson, "Minor Empresario Contracts," pp. 4–10.

25. Mark E. Nackman, "Anglo-American Migrants to the West: Men of Broken Fortunes? The Case of Texas, 1821–46," *WHQ*, V (October 1974), pp. 441–55.

26. David M. Vigness, *The Revolutionary Decades. The Saga of Texas, 1810–1836* (Austin, 1965), p. 130. Official census figures are certainly low in these years. See *infra* n. 65.

27. Several writers have made this point. See, for example, the lucid overview in D. W. Meinig, *Imperial Texas: An Interpretive Essay in Cultural Geography* (Austin, 1969), pp. 28–37.

28. Pablo Obregón, to the Secretario del Estado, Washington, November 12, 1825, AGN, transcript, TSA, 2-22/617, pp. 46–47.

29. Lucas Alamán refers to orders of June 15 and August 26, 1826, to prevent colonists from the United States from entering Texas. Alamán, "Iniciativa de ley para la seguridad del Estado de Texas," in Vicente Filisola, *Memorias para la historia de la guerra de Tejas*, 2 vols. (Mexico, 1848–49), II, 598.

30. Quoted in Lukes, *De Witt*, p. 73. The most detailed account of events is Edmund Morris Parsons, "The Fredonia Rebellion," *Texana*, I (Spring 1967), pp. 11–52, which pays insufficient attention to causes and effects.

31. Ohland Morton, *Terán and Texas: A Chapter in Texas-Mexican Relations* (Austin, 1948), pp. 52–53, 37.

32. "J. C. Clopper's Journal and Book of Memoranda for 1828," *SWHQ*, XIII (July 1909), p. 61.

33. Terán to President Victoria, June 30, 1828, quoted in Alleine Howren, "Causes and Origin of the Decree of April 6, 1830," *SWHQ*, XVI (April 1913), pp. 395–98.

34. Ibid.

35. Terán to the Minister of War and Navy, November 14, 1829, Pueblo Viejo, quoted in Morton, *Terán and Texas*, pp. 99–103.

36. The quote is from Constantino de Tarnava to the Minister of War and Navy, Mexico,

January 6, 1830, and represents Terán's view. See Howren, "Causes and Origin of the Decree of April 6, 1830," p. 411, 400–13.

37. Dublán y Lozano, eds., *Legislación mexicana*, II, 238–40. A translation is in Howren, "Causes and Origin of the Law of April 6, 1830," pp. 415–17. Article 11, which prohibited Americans from settling in territory adjacent to Mexico, was not interpreted as meaning California and New Mexico. Barker, *Austin*, p. 213.

38. Alamán, "Iniciativa de ley," in Filisola, *Memorias*, II, 603. Alamán's views, as I have summarized them, are expressed fully in this document.

39. Quoted in Ángela Moyano Pahissa, *El comercio de Santa Fé y la guerra del '47* (Mexico, 1976), p. 11. (Her citation is incorrect and I have been unable to locate this in the original).

40. Barker, *Austin*, pp. 364–65. To Butler's surprise, the official government newspaper carried a story shortly after his arrival announcing his intention "to negotiate . . . the cession of the province of Texas through a sum of five million dollars." Carlos Bosch García, *Historia de las relaciones entre México y los Estados Unidos, 1819–1848* (Mexico, 1961), p. 45.

41. *Resúmen de la estadística del imperio mexicano* (1st ed., 1822; Mexico, 1968), p. 58. Wilbert H. Timmons, *Tadeo Ortiz: Mexican Colonizer and Reformer* (El Paso, 1974).

42. Mier y Terán to Alamán, Matamoros, March 6, 1831, in ASFC, legajo 6, part 2, expediente 40, West Transcripts, UT.

43. Ortiz to Anastasio Bustamante, Bordeaux, Feb. 2, 1833, in Hatcher and Kelly, eds. and trans., "Tadeo Ortiz," p. 336.

44. Quoted in Nackman, *A Nation Within a Nation*, p. 9.

45. Terán to Alamán, October 14, 1830, quoted in Kelly and Hatcher, eds. and trans., "Tadeo Ortiz," p. 86. Morton, *Terán and Texas*, pp. 131–33.

46. Morton, *Terán and Texas*, p. 133.

47. Terán to Minister of War, November 14, 1829, quoted in Howren, "Causes and Origin of the Decree of April 6, 1830," p. 400.

48. Morton, *Terán and Texas*, pp. 134, 173–76; Barker, *Austin*, p. 282. Howren, "Causes and Origin," pp. 401–6. Filisola, *Memorias*, I, 275–76. Malcolm McLean, "Tenochtitlán, Dream Capital of Texas," *SWHQ*, LXX (July 1966), pp. 32–33. See, too, chapter six.

49. Morton, *Terán and Texas*, pp. 182, 143.

50. Berninger discusses some of the reasons for Mexican failure to attract Europeans, *La inmigración en México*, chaps. II, III, and IV.

51. See Wilbert H. Timmons, "Robert Owen's Texas Project," *SWHQ*, LII (January 1949), pp. 286–93, which contains Owen's *Memorial to the Mexican Republic* (1828).

52. William Herman Oberste, *Texas Irish Empresarios and Their Colonies* (Austin, 1953). LeRoy P. Graf, "Colonizing Projects in Texas South of the Nueces, 1820–1845," *SWHQ*, L (April 1947), pp. 431–48.

53. Most of Ortiz's ideas on this subject appear in his letter of November 30, 1830 to Bustamante, in Kelly and Hatcher, eds. and trans., "Tadeo Ortiz," pp. 222–45. The idea of religious toleration appears in his letter of February 2, 1833, in ibid., p. 322. See, too, for example, the arguments of Manuel Eduardo Gorostiza, in Berninger, *La inmigración en México*, pp. 62–63, and Miguel Ramos Arizpe to Lucas Alamán, Puebla, August 1, 1830, ASFC, legajo 6, pt. 2 (1828–31), expediente 43, West Transcripts, UT.

54. Ortiz to Bustamante, February 2, 1833, in Kelly and Hatcher, eds. and trans., "Tadeo Ortiz," p. 314. Morton, *Terán and Texas*, pp. 115, 143. For Alamán's views, see his "Iniciativa" of February 8, 1830 in Filisola, *Memorias*, II, 597. Filisola shared these views (*Memorias*, I, 138).

55. Ortiz to Bustamante, February 2, 1833, in Kelley and Hatcher, eds. and trans., "Tadeo Ortiz," pp. 316–17.

56. Henry Smith to the Governor, San Felipe, February 2, 1835, in John H. Jenkins, ed.,

Papers of the Texas Revolution, 1835–1836, 10 vols. (Austin, 1973), I, 12. C. Alan Hutchinson, "Valentín Gómez Farías. A Biographical Study" (Ph.D. diss., University of Texas, Austin, 1948), p. 298. Barker, *Austin,* pp. 397, 400, 404–5. For Mier y Terán on the settlement of blacks in Texas, see his letter to the Secretario de Relaciones Interiores y Exteriores, ASFC, legajo VI, expediente 52, West Transcripts, UT.

57. Mexican consul Francisco Pizarro Martínez, confidential letter to Juan José Espinosa de los Monteros, New Orleans, April 16, 1827, in ASFC, legajo 6, part 1, expediente 40, West Transcripts, UT.

58. Austin to S. M. Williams, August 28, 1833, Mexico City, quoted in Timmons, *Tadeo Ortiz,* p. 72.

59. Ibid., pp. 69–72.

60. C. Alan Hutchinson, "General José Antonio Mexía and His Texas Interests," *SWHQ,* LXXXII (October 1978), pp. 137–38, provides the best account of this episode, which merits further study. See, too, Barker, *Austin,* pp. 370–74. The Law of November 21, 1833 is in De la Maza, *Código de colonización,* pp. 253–54. Article 11 of the April 6, 1830 law was reinvoked by a law of April 4, 1837 (Maza, *Código de colonización,* pp. 284–85). This later law did not revoke the Colonization Law of 1824, as some writers have suggested.

61. Almonte, *Noticia estadística sobre Tejas* (Mexico, 1835), pp. 5–10, facsimile in David J. Weber, ed., *Northern Mexico on the Eve of the United States Invasion: Rare Imprints . . .* (New York, 1976), and a translation by Carlos Castañeda: "Statistical Report on Texas," *SWHQ,* XXVIII (January 1925), pp. 177–222. Almonte to the Secretary of Foreign Relations, April 12, 1834, cited in ibid., p. 202. For biographical information see Weber, ed., *Northern Mexico,* pp. 14–15 and Helen Willits Harris, "Almonte's Inspection of Texas in 1834," *SWHQ,* XLI (January 1938), pp. 195–211.

62. Músquiz to Governor J. M. Viesca, San Antonio, October 25, 1829, quoted in Downs, "History of Mexicans in Texas," p. 215, who provides a good succinct discussion of this question.

63. *Representación dirijida por el ilustre ayuntamiento de la ciudad de Béxar al . . . Congreso del Estado* (Brazoria, 1833), p. 7. Downs, "History of Mexicans in Texas," pp. 215–22, Eugene C. Barker, "Native Latin American Contribution to the Colonization and Independence of Texas," *SWHQ,* XLVI (January 1943), pp. 320–29.

64. To Stephen Austin, November 26, 1830, quoted in McLean, "Tenochtitlán," p. 27.

65. Barker, *Austin,* pp. 267–77; Morton, *Terán and Texas,* pp. 119–25. Almonte, *Noticia estadística sobre Tejas,* table 4. Almonte did not tabulate his own figures correctly, and arrived at a total population of 21,000, a figure which historians have repeated. A check of his figures for individual districts, however, indicates a total population of 24,700, of whom Almonte estimated 4,000 were Mexicans. Weber, ed., *Northern Mexico,* pp. 14–15.

66. Samuel May Williams to Austin, Monclova, March 31, 1835, in Jenkins, ed., *Papers of the Texas Revolution,* I, 53. Henry M. Morfit to John Forsyth, near the Rio Brazos, August 27, 1836, in "Condition of Texas: Message from the President of the United States . . . December 22, 1836," House of Representatives, Exec. Doc. 35, 24th Cong., 2nd Sess., p. 12. See, too, Samuel Harman Lowrie, *Culture Conflict in Texas, 1821–1835* (New York, 1932), p. 31, which guided me to this source, and Castañeda, *Our Catholic Heritage,* VI, 218. Col. Domingo Ugartechea, military commander in Texas, estimated 50,000 Anglo Americans in Texas according to a letter of Martín Perfecto de Cos to the Minister of War, Saltillo, April 6, 1835, transmitting a letter of March 23, 1835 from Ugartechea in Béxar. In Guerra y Marina, AGN, transcripts, volume 333, UT. Almonte estimated that a 1000 people *a day* entered Texas in 1835, not counting Indians. Almonte to the Minister of Foreign Relations, Mexico, April 6, 1835, in ASFC, legajo 8, expediente 65, in West Transcripts, UT.

67. Almonte put the number of "civilized" Indian immigrants from the United States at 6,000 in a report to the Secretaría del Estado, Nacogdoches, June 14, 1834, ASFC, transcript, TSA, 2-22/640, p. 52.

68. In calculating Mexican average annual growth at 1.1 percent, I am using a base of 6,200,000 in 1821 and 8,000,000 for 1846. Both are crude estimates. Contemporaries had no precise data. See Cumberland, *Mexico*, p. 367, and Dennis E. Berge, ed. and trans., *Considerations on the Political and Social Situation of the Mexican Republic, 1847* (El Paso, 1975), p. 12. A higher figure appears in José C. Valadés, *Orígines de la república mexicana: la aurora constitucional* (Mexico, 1972), p. 323, but seems unlikely in light of corroborative data.

69. Austin to Mary Holley, New Orleans, August 21, 1835, in Barker, ed., *The Austin Papers*, III, 102.

70. Miguel Muldoon, letter in the *Gaceta del Gobierno Supremo del Estado de Coahuila y Tejas*, May 27, 1833, copy in the ASFC, legajo 8, expediente 64, transcript, TSA, 2-22/640.

Chapter 10
Peopling California and New Mexico

1. Alfred Robinson to Thomas Larkin, New York, May 29, 1845, in George P. Hammond, ed., *The Larkin Papers: Personal, Business, and Official Correspondence of Thomas Oliver Larkin, Merchant and United States Consul in California*, 10 vols. (Berkeley, 1953), III, 205. Robinson put this phrase in quotes, saying "our papers are filled with such kind of stuff."

2. "Relación de los Estrangeros que Existen en este Departamento . . . March 20, 1839," Ritch Papers, no. 175, HEH. Charles Bent to Manuel Alvarez, no date [ca. 1840], Alvarez Papers, NMSRC.

3. Hubert Howe Bancroft, *History of California*, 7 vols. (San Francisco, 1884–90), IV, 115–17. Whereas Bancroft placed the number at 380 in 1840, an official census counted only 48 permanent foreign residents of California that year. Theodore H. Hittell, *History of California*, 4 vols. (San Francisco, 1885–97), II, 275. José Figueroa to the Secretario del Estado, June 5, 1834, Monterey, in *Political, Military, and Ecclesiastical Correspondence . . .* (San Francisco, 1958), pp. 5–7.

4. My estimate that two-thirds of the population of California consisted of women and children is conservative. Census figures from Los Angeles for 1830, 1836, and 1844 consistently show such a ratio. See, for example, J. Gregg Layne, "The First Census of the Los Angeles District. . . , " *SCQ*, XVIII (September-December 1936), p. 83, and Marie E. Northrup, ed., "The Los Angeles Padrón of 1844," *SCQ*, XLII (December 1960), p. 360. The Los Angeles figures, however, define adults as those age twelve and above. Using age sixteen and above to define adults, one finds in Santa Fe that the male adult population was about 26 percent of the total population. This is based on computations from the barrios of San Francisco, Torreón, San Miguel, and Guadalupe, using the 1823 census in Virginia Langham Olmsted, trans. and ed., *New Mexico Spanish and Mexican Colonial Censuses, 1790, 1823, 1845* (Albuquerque, 1975), pp. 129–35, 140–53, 156–74.

5. W. Eugene Hollon, *The Great American Desert, Then and Now* (New York, 1966), pp. 64–67.

6. Reglamento para la colonización de los territorios de la República, November 21, 1828, in Francisco F. de la Maza, *Código de colonización y terrenos baldíos de la República mexicana* (Mexico, 1893), pp. 237–40. See, too, the laws of March 12 and April 14, 1828, in ibid., pp. 222, 224.

7. The expansion of gente de razón at the expense of the Pueblos has been explored by Myra Ellen Jenkins, "Taos Pueblo and its Neighbors, 1540–1847," *NMHR*, XLI (April 1966), pp. 85–114, and "The Baltasar Baca 'Grant': History of an Encroachment," *El Palacio*, LXVIII (Spring 1961), pp. 47–68.

8. Robert G. Cleland, *Cattle on a Thousand Hills* (1st ed., 1941; 2nd ed., San Marino, 1951), pp. 19, 286, n. 4. See, too, Robert G. Cowan, *Ranchos of California. A List of Spanish*

344 *Notes to Chapter 10, pages 181-183*

Concessions, 1775–1822, and Mexican Grants, 1822–1846 (Fresno, 1956), p. 139. W. W. Robinson, *Land in California* (Berkeley, 1948), finds that "at least" 30 rancho grants had been made prior to 1822.

9. Juan de Dios Canedo, *Memoria de la Secretaría de Estado y del Despacho de Relaciones Interiores y Exteriores* . . . (Mexico, 1829), p. 13.

10. Ortiz to Anastasio Bustamante, Bordeaux, October 31, 1830, in Edith Louise Kelly and Mattie Austin Hatcher, eds. and trans., "Tadeo Ortiz de Ayala and the Colonization of Texas, 1822–1833," *SWHQ*, XXXII (October 1928), pp. 159–60. See, too, pp. 153, 320. Congress of the state of Nuevo León, secret session, February 20, 1827, Monterrey, ASFC, legajo I, 1827–1830, expediente 28, West Transcripts, UT.

11. Quoted in Lansing B. Bloom, "New Mexico Under Mexican Administration, 1821–1846," *Old Santa Fe*, I (January 1914), pp. 262–63. *Arkansas Gazette*, December 22, 1830. Bradburn is usually thought to be from Kentucky, but C. Alan Hutchinson, who has been collecting material on him, finds he was Virginia-born.

12. Santiago Abreú to the diputación of New Mexico [Mexico City], January 18, 1826, Ritch Papers, no. 86, HEH.

13. Herbert Ingram Priestly, ed. and trans., *Exposition Addressed to the Chamber of Deputies of the Union by Señor Don Carlos Antonio Carrillo, Deputy for Alta California, Concerning the Regulation and Administration of the Pious Fund* (1st ed., 1831; San Francisco, 1938), p. 8.

14. Bancroft, *History of California*, III, 176, 179–80. Alamán to the governor of California, Mexico [February 2, 1830], ASFC, legajo 4, expediente 117, folder 29, transcript, BL. Alamán to Governor Figueroa, May 17, 1832, Archives of California, Bancroft Transcripts, vol. 57 (Superior Government State Papers), pp. 88–90, BL, called to my attention by C. Alan Hutchinson, *Frontier Settlement in Mexican California: The Híjar-Padrés Colony and Its Origins, 1769–1835* (New Haven, 1969), p. 157. Alamán instructed Figueroa to give grants to Heinrich Virmond and Henry Fitch in this area; Fitch was an American. I have not located any record of a foreigner who received a grant in California prior to this time. William Willis, an Englishman, and Abel Stearns, an American, were denied grants in 1828 and 1830 respectively (Bancroft, *History of California*, II, 663–64). Some writers have incorrectly interpreted article 11 of the April 6, 1830 law as applying to California (see, for example, ibid., 663, and Jessie Davies Francis, "An Economic and Social History of Mexican California" [Ph.D. diss., University of California, Berkeley, 1934], p. 130).

15. J. J. Bowden, *Spanish and Mexican Land Grants in the Chihuahuan Acquisition* (El Paso, 1971), pp. 77–84, provides much new information on Heath's activities. A somewhat outdated biography is "John G. Heath," by William H. H. Allison, *NMHR*, VI (October 1931), pp. 360–75.

16. *A Journey to California, 1841. . . . The Journal of John Bidwell*, Francis P. Farquhar, ed. (Berkeley, 1964), p. 45.

17. Figueroa made this proposal about 1824, before becoming personally familiar with the region. See C. Alan Hutchinson, "General José Figueroa in Mexico, 1792–1832," *NMHR*, XLVIII (October 1973), p. 284. See, too, Ignacio Zúñiga, *Rápida ojeada al Estado de Sonora, dirigida y dedicada al Supremo Gobierno de la Nación* (Mexico, 1835), pp. 60–66, facsimile in David J. Weber, ed., *Northern Mexico on the Eve of the United States Invasion* . . . (New York, 1976).

18. See Karen Sykes Collins, ed., "Fray Pedro Arriquibar's Census of Tucson, 1820 [1797]," *JAH*, XI (Spring, 1970), pp. 14–15. Henry F. Dobyns demonstrates that Collins "1820" census is actually one of 1797, see his note in the *JAH*, XIII (Autumn 1972), pp. 205–9. The vecino population of Tucson seems to have dropped from 79 in 1797 to 36 in 1804, then risen again. Tucson and Tubac censuses of 1831, respectively, document 127 and 128 of Cartas de Sonora II, Antiguo Archivo del Colegio de la Santa Cruz de Querétaro, Convento Franciscano, Celaya, Guanajuato, Mexico. The discovery, dating, and transcrip-

tions of these documents have been done by Fr. Kieran McCarty, who kindly made them available to me. Analysis of this census data might reveal the source of the growing population: former soldiers, assimilated Indians, or newcomers from farther south.

19. Ray H. Mattison, "Early Spanish and Mexican Settlements in Arizona," *NMHR*, XXI (October 1946), pp. 285–89. Jay Wagoner provides a detailed discussion of these grants and their disposition under American rule in *Early Arizona, Prehistory to Civil War* (Tucson, 1975), chap. 7.

20. Manuel Escalante y Arvizu, to Governor José María Gaxiola, Arizpe, December 9, 1828, AHES, Apaches, cabinet 2, drawer 3, McCarty Transcripts, AHS, film H-12. Juan Nepomuceno González, juez de paz, to the governor, Tucson, March 16, 1834 in ibid., film H-13.

21. José Francisco Velasco, *Noticias estadísticas del Estado de Sonora* (Mexico, 1850), pp. 54–55. Wagoner, *Early Arizona*, p. 168. Henry F. Dobyns, "Tubac Through Four Centuries: An Historical Resume and Analysis" (MS, Arizona State Parks Board, 1959), pp. 593, 611. Antonio Comadurán to José María Elías González, Tucson, December 14, 1848, AHES, Apaches, cabinet 2, drawer 3, filed under date of January 24, 1849, McCarty Transcripts, AHS, film H-15.

22. Alvarado to the diputación, quoted in Francis, "An Economic and Social History," p. 503. Insufficient population in California was noted by many officials. See, for example, Governor Manuel Victoria to the Secretary of Foreign Relations, June 7, 1831, Archives of California, Bancroft Transcripts, vol. 49 (Departmental Records), p. 135, BL. Woodrow James Hansen, *The Search for Authority in California* (Oakland, Ca., 1960), p. 21.

23. This account of the Híjar-Padrés colony is based upon C. Alan Hutchinson's detailed, judicious, and revisionist study: *Frontier Settlement in Mexican California*. Hutchinson subsequently located a more detailed list of the colonists: "An Official List of the Members of the Híjar-Padrés Colony for Mexican California, 1834," *PHR*, XLII (August 1973), pp. 407–18.

24. Most historians have followed Figueroa's version of events, which he ably set forth in his *Manifiesto a la república mejicana* (Monterey, 1835). The other side of the story has been largely unknown until it was painstakingly assembled by Hutchinson. I am following the interpretation set forth in his *Frontier Settlement in Mexican California*, pp. 268, 382 ff., and his fresh translation and editing of *A Manifesto to the Mexican Republic* (Berkeley, 1978).

25. Quoted in Hutchinson, *Frontier Settlement in Mexican California*, pp. 386–87, 274–78.

26. George Tays, "Mariano Guadalupe Vallejo and Sonoma: A Biography and a History," *CHSQ*, XVI (September 1937), pp. 242–43. Alamán to Figueroa, May 17, 1832, Archives of California, Bancroft Transcripts, vol. 57 (Superior Governor States Papers), pp. 88–90, BL.

27. This interpretation is suggested by Hutchinson, *Frontier Settlement in Mexican California*, pp. 381–82, 374.

28. See, for example, Vallejo, quoted in ibid., p. 402, and Manuel Castañares, "Exposición," September 1, 1844, in Castañares, *Colección de documentos relativos al departamento de Californias* (Mexico, 1845), p. 34, facsimile in Weber, ed., *Northern Mexico*.

29. Manuel Payno, "Puerto de Monterey, Alta California," *Revista científica y literaria de Méjico*, I (1845), p. 83, facsimile in Weber, ed., *Northern Mexico*. See, too, Constantino de Tarnava to the Minister of War and Navy, January 6, 1830, quoted in Alleine Howren, "Causes and Origin of the Decree of April 6, 1830," *SWHQ*, XVI (April 1913), p. 411; José Agustín de Escudero, *Noticias estadísticas de Sonora y Sinaloa* (México, 1849), p. 4, and Juan N. Almonte, *Proyectos de leyes sobre colonización* (Mexico, 1852), p. 5. A recent expression of this view is Dieter George Berninger, *La inmigración en México, 1821–1857* (Mexico, 1975), p. 81.

30. *El Telégrafo*, April 15, 1834, quoted in Hutchinson, *Frontier Settlement in Mexican California*, p. 208.

31. Ray Allen Billington, *America's Frontier Heritage* (New York, 1966), p. 29. Castañares, "Exposición," in *Colleción de documentos,* p. 34, mentions the low density and plentiful land elsewhere in Mexico. Juan N. Almonte, *Noticia estadística sobre Tejas* (Mexico, 1835), p. 8, facsimile in Weber, ed., *Northern Mexico,* mentions the problem of distance.

32. See the interesting commentary on this question by Pablo Herrera Carrillo, "Las siete guerras por Texas," in Luis Chávez Orozco, ed., *Colección de documentos para la historia de las guerras entre México y los Estados Unidos* (Mexico, 1959), p. 37. Marie E. Northrup, ed. "The Los Angeles Padrón of 1844," *SCQ,* XLII (December 1960), pp. 360–417.

33. "La constitución y la guerra de Tejas," *El Siglo Diez y Nueve,* December 15, 1842, called to my attention by Gene Brack, *Mexico Views Manifest Destiny, 1821–1846. An Essay on the Origins of the Mexican War* (Albuquerque, 1975), p. 115.

34. Juan Bautista Alvarado, "Historia de California," 5 vols., MS, IV, p. 9, BL. The term *presidiarios* was used in contemporary documents to indicate convicts sentenced to labor in a presidio. This term could also mean presidial soldier, and it has resulted in confusion among contemporaries (see Antonio Barreiro, *Ojeada sobre Nuevo-México . . .* [Puebla, 1832], in H. Bailey Carroll and J. Villasana Haggard, trans. and eds., *Three New Mexico Chronicles* [Albuquerque, 1942], p. 79n), and among historians, some of whom have mistranslated the term as "convict-soldiers" (Howren, "Causes and Origin of the Decree of April 6, 1830," p. 409).

35. Quoted in Howren, "Causes and Origin of the Decree of April 6, 1830," pp. 410–11.

36. Bancroft, *History of California,* III, pp. 16–17, 47–50, and: Order of October 21, 1829; Circular of July 30, 1831; Resolution of April 23, 1833; and the Reglamento of May 6, 1833 in Maza, *Código de colonización,* pp. 240, 245, 248–50.

37. Ferdinand P. Wrangel traveled on the same ship with this man (*De Sitka a San Petersburgo al través de México* [Mexico, 1975], p. 52) who might have been Eugenio Murrillo, sentenced to ten years in Texas according to Bancroft, *History of California,* III, p. 674, n. 5.

38. Resolution of February 22, 1842, in Maza, *Código de colonización,* p. 315. Bancroft, *History of California,* IV, pp. 287–91, 404–5, 420, 455–57. For the term *cholo,* see Antonio Blanco S., *La lengua española en la historia de California* (Madrid, 1971), pp. 152, 195, 559.

39. David J. Weber and Ronald R. Young, eds. and trans., "California in 1831: Heinrich Virmond to Lucas Alamán," *JSDH,* XXI (Fall 1975), p. 4. Angustias de la Guerra Ord, *Occurrences in Hispanic California,* Francis Price and William H. Ellison, trans. and eds. (Washington, 1956), p. 15. Francis, "Economic and Social History of Mexican California," p. 94.

40. Bancroft takes such a position in regard to the prisoners who came with Micheltorena in 1842, and judges that the *californios* "have grossly exaggerated the deeds of the cholos." *History of California,* V, 456. See, too, Thomas Oliver Larkin's favorable assessment of the convicts, cited in Hittell, *History of California,* II, 360. California's lowly position as a penal colony is suggested in a law of October 25, 1828, prohibiting secret meetings and threatening a four year exile to the Californias for the third offense. Manuel Dublán and José María Lozano, eds., *Legislación mexicana,* 34 vols. (Mexico, 1876–1904), II, 86.

41. Lester Gordon Engelson, "Proposals for the Colonization of California by England in Connection with the Mexican Debt to British Bondholders, 1837–1846," *CHSQ,* XVIII (June 1939), pp. 136–48. John A. Hawgood, "A Projected Prussian Colonization of Upper California," *SCQ,* XLVIII (December 1966), pp. 353–68.

42. As early as 1840, one merchant who thought Texas might acquire New Mexico wrote to a friend at Taos: "It would be a good time to get grants of land from Armijo." David Waldo to John Rowland, May 1 and May 10, MS, California Historical Documents Collection, HEH. See, too, Harold Dunham, "New Mexico Land Grants with Special Reference to the Title Papers of the Maxwell Grant," *NMHR,* XXX (January 1955), pp. 4–6,

and Abel Stearns to Thomas Oliver Larkin, June 12, 1846, in Hammond, ed., *The Larkin Papers*, V, 20.

43. See Victor Westphall's revisionist article: "Fraud and the Implications of Fraud in the Land Grants of New Mexico," *NMHR*, XLIX (July 1974), pp. 199–200. Westphall estimates that Armijo granted over 16,500,000 acres between 1837 and 1846, or "more than half of the some 31,000,000 acres of land granted by all authorities of both Spain and Mexico in 160 years." Review of Morris F. Taylor, *O. P. McMains. . .*, *AW*, XX (Spring 1980), p. 84. The extension of six Mexican land grants into the area of today's Colorado is ably summarized in LeRoy R. Hafen, "Mexican Land Grants in Colorado," *Colorado Magazine*, IV (May 1927), pp. 81–93, and by Marianne L. Stoller, "Grants of Desperation, Lands of Speculation: Mexican Period Land Grants in Colorado," *JW*, XIX (July 1980), pp. 22–39, who along with Janet Lecompte, "Manuel Armijo and the Americans," ibid., p. 58, argues that historians have exaggerated the size of Armijo's grants.

44. Armijo never explicitly stated defense as his motive for dispensing land to foreigners during these years, but many writers have surmised that he had defense against foreigners in mind. See, for example, Ralph Emerson Twitchell, *The Leading Facts of New Mexican History*, 2 vols. (Cedar Rapids, 1911–12), II, 196–97, and Ward Alan Minge, "Frontier Problems in New Mexico Preceding the Mexican War, 1840–1846" (Ph.D. diss., University of New Mexico, 1965), p. 306.

45. For the beginnings of the "Maxwell" grant see Lawrence R. Murphy, "The Beaubien and Miranda Land Grant, 1841–1846," *NMHR*, XLII (January 1967), pp. 27–46, and Murphy's "Charles H. Beaubien," in LeRoy R. Hafen, ed., *The Mountain Men and the Fur Trade of the Far West*, 10 vols. (Glendale, 1965–72), VI, 23–25. The grant has received book-length treatment, most authoritatively by William A. Keleher, *Maxwell Land Grant: A New Mexico Item* (Santa Fe, 1942), and Jim Berry Pearson, *The Maxwell Land Grant* (Norman, 1961). Both works focus on the post-Mexican War era. A grant to José Sutton of 16 square leagues on the Pecos near San Miguel del Bado, made in 1838, may represent the beginnings of Armijo's policy of granting large estates to foreigners. This question needs further study.

46. Weber, "Stephen Louis Lee," in Hafen, ed., *The Mountain Men*, III, 181–87. The most detailed study of this grant is in Herbert O. Brayer, *William Blackmore: The Spanish-Mexican Land Grants of New Mexico and Colorado, 1863–1878* (Denver, 1949), but Brayer treats the Mexican period in a sketchy manner (pp. 59–62).

47. Weber, "Gervais Nolan," in Hafen, ed., *The Mountain Men*, IV, 225–29. Morris F. Taylor, "The Two Land Grants of Gervacio Nolán," *NMHR*, XLVII (April 1972), pp. 151–84.

48. Harold H. Dunham, "Cerán St. Vrain," in Hafen, ed., *The Mountain Men*, V, 310–11, and Ralph Emerson Twitchell, *The Spanish Archives of New Mexico*, 2 vols. (Cedar Rapids, 1914), I, 276–77.

49. Minge, "Frontier Problems in New Mexico," p. 222. Benjamin Read, *Illustrated History of New Mexico* (Santa Fe, 1912,) 411–14. Angélico Chávez, "New Names in New Mexico," *El Palacio*, LXIV (November-December 1957), p. 375.

50. Murphy, "Beaubien and Miranda," p. 32. Harold Dunham, "Charles Bent," in Hafen, ed., *The Mountain Men*, II, 46–47.

51. Martínez's objections to the grant are discussed in Murphy, "Beaubien and Miranda," pp. 32–33, and in Myra Ellen Jenkins, "Taos Pueblo and Its Neighbors, 1540–1847," *NMHR*, XLI (April 1966), pp. 107–8.

52. Murphy, "Beaubien and Miranda," pp. 32–33. Minge, "Frontier Problems," pp. 224–27. Article 9 of the March 11, 1842 law, in Maza, *Código de colonización*, pp. 215–18. Twitchell, *Spanish Archives*, I, 276–77. The most extensive discussion of Scolly's grant is in J. J. Bowden, "Private Land Claims in the Southwest," 6 vols. (LLM thesis, Southern Methodist University, Dallas, 1969), III, 775–76.

53. Antonio José Martínez to Mariano Martínez, Taos, August 22, 1844, in Santiago Valdez, "Biografía del Rev. P. Antonio José Martínez," MS, 1877, Ritch Papers, No. 2211 (English Translation), pp. 38–40, HL.

54. Francisco García Conde to the governor, September 20, 1845, cited in Murphy, "Beaubien and Miranda," p. 35. A portion of this letter is quoted in Dunham, "New Mexico Land Grants," p. 22. Murphy, "Beaubien and Miranda," p. 32. Armijo also had a share of the St. Vrain-Vigil grant. David Lavender, *Bent's Fort* (New York, 1954), p. 403, n. 11.

55. Dunham, "New Mexico Land Grants," implies this, and there is evidence that grants to José Sutton and Carlos Beaubien represented payment for loans to the government. Daniel Tyler, "Anglo-American Penetration of the Southwest: The View from New Mexico," *SWHQ*, LXXV (January 1972), p. 337.

56. Armijo to the Ministro de Relaciones, July 31, 1827, quoted in David J. Weber, "Mexico and the Mountain Men, 1821–1828," *JW*, VIII (July 1969), p. 373. David J. Weber, *The Taos Trappers: The Fur Trade in the Far Southwest, 1540–1846* (Norman, 1971), p. 9.

57. This thesis is suggested by Tyler, "Anglo-American Penetration of the Southwest," pp. 325–38.

58. These figures do not include El Paso, which ceased to fall under New Mexico's jurisdiction after 1824. Bloom, "New Mexico Under Mexican Administration," I, 27–30. "Note on the Population of New Mexico, 1846–1849," *NMHR*, XXXIV (July 1959), pp. 200–202, which summarizes estimates from various sources from 1800–1846 and concludes that the population ranged between 60 and 70,000 in 1846. I am using a 1.1 percent average annual growth rate for Mexico. See chapt. 9, n. 67. Angélico Chávez, "New Names in New Mexico, 1820–1850," *El Palacio*, LXIV (November-December, 1957), pp. 291–318, 367–80, provides an idea from church records of both Mexican and foreign newcomers to New Mexico in these years, many of whom were transients.

59. LeRoy R. and Ann W. Hafen, *Old Spanish Trail: Santa Fé to Los Angeles* (Glendale, 1954), pp. 195–225. For the reception of New Mexicans in California see George William Beattie, "San Bernardino Valley Before the Americans Came," *CHSQ*, XII (June 1933), p. 116; Harold A. Whelan, "Eden in Jurupa Valley. The Story of Agua Mansa," *SCQ*, LV (Winter 1973), pp. 413–30 and Joyce Carter Vickery, *Defending Eden: New Mexico Pioneers in Southern California, 1830–1890* (Riverside, 1977). For Manuel Vaca, see Iris Higbie Wilson [Engstrand], *William Wolfskill, 1798–1866* (Glendale, 1965), p. 130, and for Julian Chávez see J. Gregg Layne, "The First Census of the Los Angeles District. . . . 1836," *SCQ*, XVIII (September-December 1936), p. 94, and Don Devereux, "Julian Chávez, an Early Río Arriba Immigrant," *El Palacio*, LXXIV (Winter 1967), pp. 35–36.

60. Robidoux to Manuel Alvarez, Rancho Jurupa, May 1, 1848, quoted in David J. Weber, ed. and trans., "Louis Robidoux: Two Letters from California, 1848," *SCQ*, LIV (Summer, 1972), pp. 109, 110.

61. This thesis of Dorothy Johansen is discussed briefly in John D. Unruh, Jr., *The Plains Across: The Overland Emigrants and the Trans-Mississippi West, 1840–60* (Urbana, 1979), pp. 93–94. See, too, Billington's summary of theory in *America's Frontier Heritage*, pp. 26–29.

62. Nicholas Dawson, *California in '41; Texas in '51* (Austin, 1969), pp. 12–13.

63. Unruh, *The Plains Across*, pp. 28–61, provides a fine account of the contradictory descriptions that would-be emigrants received in the 1840s. For the motives of the emigrants, see also Billington, *The Far Western Frontier, 1830–1860* (New York, 1956), pp. 89–91 and Earl Pomeroy, *The Pacific Slope: A History of California, Oregon, Washington, Idaho, Utah, & Nevada* (New York, 1965), pp. 27–35.

64. Cleland, *Cattle on a Thousand Hills*, p. 23. Sherburne Friend Cook, "The Epidemic of 1830–1833 in California and Oregon," *University of California Publications in American Archaeology and Ethnology*, XLIII (May 1955), pp. 303–26.

65. In 1845, for example, 3,000 immigrants reached the Willamette country compared to 250 who entered California, although some who settled in Oregon moved on to California and vice versa. Pomeroy, *The Pacific Slope*, pp. 30–31.

66. The standard biography is George D. Lyman, *John Marsh, Pioneer: The Life Story of a Trail-Blazer on Six Frontiers* (New York, 1930).

67. Erwin G. Gudde, ed., *Sutter's Own Story* (New York, 1936), pp. 9–10. The most authoritative biography of Sutter remains James P. Zollinger, *Sutter, the Man and His Empire* (New York, 1939). Richard Dillon has written a sprightly popular biography which contains some new information regarding Sutter's military career: *Fool's Gold. The Decline and Fall of Captain John Sutter of California* (New York, 1967). Sutter's character and historians' interpretations of it have been examined by John Hawgood, "John Augustus Sutter, A Reappraisal," *AW*, IV (Winter, 1962), pp. 345–56.

68. George Simpson, *Narrative of a Journey Round the World*, 2 vols. (London, 1847), I, 326. Called to my attention by Zollinger, *Sutter*, p. 92.

69. John Bidwell, *Echoes of the Past* (1st ed., 1914; New York, 1973), pp. 6–7. Marsh's efforts to promote immigration between 1840–46 are described at length in Lyman, *John Marsh*, chaps. 34–38. In 1845, apparently, Sutter sent agents to Fort Hall, a point just prior to where the trails to Oregon and California diverged, to entice overlanders to California. Unruh, *The Plains Across*, p. 339.

70. Bidwell, *Echoes*, pp. 7, 11.

71. Dawson, *California in '41*, p. 30.

72. Marsh to his parents, April 3, 1842, quoted in Lyman, *John Marsh*, p. 249.

73. There is a vast literature on overland migration to California during these years. George R. Stewart has produced a reliable and readable popular account in *The California Trail: An Epic With Many Heroes* (New York, 1962).

74. The best treatment of this episode is George M. Brooke, Jr., "The Vest Pocket War of Commodore Jones," *PHR*, XXI (August 1962), pp. 217–33. For the reaction in Mexico City see Frank A. Knapp, Jr., "Preludios de la pérdida de California," *Historia mexicana*, IV (octubre-diciembre 1954), pp. 235–49, and Brack, *Mexico Views Manifest Destiny*, pp. 101–3. American interest in the acquisition of California is discussed in many sources, see especially Robert Glass Cleland, "The Early Sentiment for the Annexation of California: An Account of the Growth of American Interest in California, 1835–1846," *SWHQ*, XVIII (July 1914), pp. 13–17, 29–30. Norman A. Graebner, *Empire on the Pacific: A Study in American Continental Expansion* (New York, 1955).

75. Almonte to the Minister of War, March 28, 1840, quoted in Mariano Guadalupe Vallejo, "Documentos para la historia de California," X, no. 146, MS, BL. See, too, Vallejo, Monterey, April 25, 1840, in Archivo Histórico de Defensa Nacional, expediente 532, microfilm, roll 2, BL.

76. P. T. Cyrille La Place, "The Report of Captain La Place on his Voyage to the Northwest Coast and California in 1839," George Vernon Blue, ed. and trans., *CHSQ*, XVIII (December 1939), p. 322.

77. *El Patriota Mexicano*, October 5, 1845, quoted in Frank A. Knapp, Jr., "The Mexican Fear of Manifest Destiny in California," in *Essays in Mexican History*, Thomas E. Cotner and Carlos E. Castañeda, eds. (Austin, 1958), p. 201.

78. Bancroft, *History of California*, IV, 271–73, 379–80. Orders from the central government designed to block Anglo-American immigration into California were issued in May 1841, July 1843, and July 1845.

79. *El Siglo Diez y Nueve*, October 16, 1845, quoted in Knapp, "Mexican Fear of Manifest Destiny in California," p. 207. Bancroft, *History of California*, V, 215–33.

80. "Letter of Dr. John Marsh to Hon. Lewis Cass [January 20, 1846]," *CHSQ*, XXII (December 1943), p. 317.

81. Castro, "Orden. . . . , " Sonoma, November 6, 1845, quoted in Bancroft, *History of California*, IV, 606. Ibid., IV, 274–75, 385–86; V, 56–57, 76. José Castro to Vallejo, November 11, 1845, in Vallejo, "Documentos para la historia de California," XII, no. 150, MS, BL. George Tays, "Revolutionary California: The Political History of California from 1820 to 1848" (Ph.D. diss. University of California, Berkeley, 1932; rev., 1934), p. 678.

82. Pablo de la Guerra to Vallejo, Santa Barbara, April 16, 1840, quoted in Hansen, *Search for Authority*,. p. 33.

83. Tays, "Mariano Guadalupe Vallejo and Sonoma," pp. 56–58, 151–63. *Cinco documentos sobre la Alta California* (Mexico, 1944), contains some of Tays' corrrespondence regarding the Bidwell party.

84. Quoted in Zollinger, *Sutter*, p. 80.

85. Vallejo to Anastasio Bustamante, Sonoma, November 22, 1845, in Vallejo, "Documentos para la historia de California," XII, no. 157.

86. Sutter to Jacob Leese, New Helvetia, November 8, 1841, quoted in Tays, "Mariano Guadalupe Vallejo and Sonoma," p. 69. Ironically, Leese was Vallejo's brother-in-law and Vallejo obtained a copy of this letter.

87. Quoted in Zollinger, *Sutter*, p. 177. See, too, pp. 134, 145–46. Bancroft, *History of California*, IV, 612–16 argues that Sutter initiated the sale. Other evidence suggests that an agent from Mexico came to California with authorization to purchase the fort (Tays, "Revolutionary California," p. 618), and there may be no incompatibility between these versions.

88. See, for example, Wilson, *William Wolfskill*, pp. 116–19, and Bancroft, *History of California*, V, 57, n. 4.

89. All of these figures are rough. I am following Rose Hollenbaugh Avina, "Spanish and Mexican Land Grants in California" (Ph.D. diss. Berkeley, 1932), p. 71. She finds that 35 of 120 grants made by Micheltorena went to foreigners. Another writer finds that 46 of 131 grants by Micheltorena went to foreigners: Lela M. Weststeyn, "The Expansion of the Land Grant System Under the Last Two Mexican Governors . . . " (M.A. thesis, University of Southern California, 1937), p. 82. For an especially concise and lucid overview, see David Hornbeck, "Land Tenure and Rancho Expansion in Alta California, 1784–1846," *Journal of Historical Geography*, IV (1978), pp. 371–90, who finds that nearly 30 percent of the grantees in the 1840s had Anglo surnames.

90. Manuel Castañares to Vallejo, October 31, 1843, quoted in Bancroft, *History of California*, IV, 386, and Vallejo to Sutter, December 18, 1844 in Tays, "Vallejo," p. 159. Pico to the justices of the jurisdiction of Jurupa, Los Angeles, July 27, 1846, in California Historical Documents Collection, HEH.

91. Vallejo to Anastasio Bustamante, Sonoma, November 22, 1845, in Vallejo, "Documentos para la historia de California," XII, no. 157. Robinson, *Land in California*, p. 64.

92. Quoted in Hansen, *Search for Authority*, p. 35. This point has been made by various writers. See, for example, Rodman W. Paul's interesting essay: "The Spanish-Americans in the Southwest, 1848–1900," in John G. Clark, ed., *The Frontier Challenge: Responses to the Trans-Mississippi West* (Lawrence, Kansas, 1971), p.42.

93. John A. Hawgood, "The Pattern of Yankee Infiltration in Mexican Alta California, 1821–1846," *PHR*, XXVII (February 1958), pp. 27–38.

94. The most careful presentation of data for this period is in Francis, "An Economic and Social History of Mexican California," pp. 152–68. Although I do not agree with all of her analysis, I have utilized her figures. Thomas Oliver Larkin and others put the number of foreigners much higher. See Larkin's description of California, April 20, 1846, in Hammond, ed., *The Larkin Papers*, IV, 305.

95. Castañares, "Exposición," in Castañares, *Colección de documentos*, p. 37.

Chapter 11
Society and Culture

1. Oakah L. Jones, Jr., *Los Paisanos: Spanish Settlers on the Northern Frontier of New Spain* (Norman, 1979), pp. 4, 185, 197–98; Alicia V. Tjarks, "Comparative Demographic Analysis of Texas, 1777–1793," *SWHQ*, LXXVII (January 1974), pp. 293–94; 322–23; 329–30. Although traditional accounts depict the frontier as a cashless economy, some people clearly had large sums. See, for example, Adele Ogden, *The California Sea Otter Trade, 1784–1848* (Berkeley, 1941), pp. 85, 88, 89. Robert Archibald, "The Economy of the Alta California Missions, 1803–1821," *SCQ*, LVIII (Summer 1976), pp. 231, 233. William Becknell, "Journal of Two Expeditions from Boon's Lick to Santa Fe," Franklin *Missouri Intelligencer*, April 22, 1823.

2. Josiah Gregg, *Commerce of the Prairies*, Max L. Moorhead, ed. (Norman, 1954), pp. 154–55. José Arnaz, commenting on California, quoted in David J. Weber, ed., *Foreigners in Their Native Land: Historical Roots of the Mexican Americans* (Albuquerque, 1973), p. 38. See, too, Torcuato S. di Tella, "The Dangerous Classes in Early Nineteenth Century Mexico," *Journal of Latin American Studies*, V (May 1973), pp. 79–105, and Alejandra Moreno Toscano, "Los trabajadores y el proyecto de industrialización, 1810–1867," in Enrique Florescano et al., *La Clase Obrera en la Historia de México*, vol. I: *De la colonia al imperio* (Mexico, 1980), pp. 303–08.

3. Albert Shumate, *Francisco Pacheco of Pacheco Pass* (Stockton, California, 1977), pp. 11–18. No good study of the rise of the ranchero class has appeared, but many writers allude to it. See, for example, Leonard Pitt, *Decline of the Californios. A Social History of the Spanish-Speaking Californians, 1846–1890* (Berkeley, 1968), p. 10, and Leon G. Campbell, "The First Californios: Presidial Society in Spanish California, 1769–1822," *JW*, XI (October 1972), pp. 593–95.

4. Nellie Van de Grift Sánchez, *Spanish Arcadia* (Los Angeles, 1929), p. 378, provides a fine example of this myth, which probably derived from *californios* and foreigners who reminisced about the "good old days." See, for example, the nephew of Mariano Guadalupe Vallejo quoted in Weber, ed., *Foreigners in Their Native Land*, pp. 46–49, and William Heath Davis, *Seventy-Five Years in California*, Harold A. Small, ed. (1st ed., 1889; 3rd ed., San Francisco, 1967), pp. 49–50.

5. Manuel Castañares, *Colección de documentos relativos al departamento de Californias* (Mexico 1845), p. 10, facsimile in David J. Weber, ed., *Northern Mexico on the Eve of the United States Invasion. Rare Imprints . . .* (New York, 1976). See the excellent analysis by Charles Hughes "The Decline of the Californios. The Case of San Diego, 1846–1856," *JSDH*, XXI (Summer 1975), pp. 3–9, who concludes that "rather than being like feudal lords on princely estates, with vast herds and large retinues of Indian slaves, Californios in San Diego were impoverished rancheros struggling to survive in a hostile environment" (p. 9).

6. Alfred Robinson, *Life in California* (1st ed., 1846; Santa Barbara, 1970), p. 152.

7. Andrew Anthony Tijerina, "Tejanos and Texas: The Native Mexicans of Texas, 1820–1850" (Ph.D. diss., University of Texas, Austin, 1977), pp. 30–31, 15–16, 291. James Michael McReynolds, "Family Life in a Borderland Community: Nacogdoches, Texas, 1779–1861" (Ph.D. diss., Texas Tech University, 1978), pp. 244–45, 248, 253.

8. The Journal of Dr. John C. Beales, February 1 & 2, quoted in William Kennedy, *Texas: The Rise, Progress, and Prospects of the Republic of Texas*, 2 vols. (London, 1841), II, 43. A Swiss scientist provided a similar description of the "newly established" rancho in 1834, and noted that peace with Comanches and Lipan Apaches since 1828 made these ranches possible. Jean Louis Berlandier, *Journey to Mexico During the Years 1826 to 1834*, C. H. and

Katherine K. Muller, eds., and Sheila M. Ohlendorf, Josette M. Bigelow, and Mary M. Standifer, trans., 2 vols. (Austin: 1980), II, 553. Fane Downs, "The History of Mexicans in Texas, 1820–1845" (Ph.D. diss., Texas Tech University, 1970), pp. 18–19, 58–59. Ida S. Vernon, "Activities of the Seguíns in Early West Texas History," *West Texas History Association Year Book,* XXV (October 1949), pp. 19–20, 24. When the Seguíns fled San Antonio in March 1836, they took 3,000 sheep with them.

9. Max L. Moorhead, *New Mexico's Royal Road: Trade and Travel on the Chihuahua Trail* (Norman, 1958), p. 194. For the absence of "merchants in the usual respected sense of the word" prior to this period, see Fernando de Chacón to Pedro de Nava, Santa Fe, July 13, 1797, quoted in Simmons, *Spanish Government in New Mexico* (Albuquerque, 1968), p. 173.

10. Moorhead, *New Mexico's Royal Road,* p. 195. Many sources comment on the wages of a day laborer. See, for example, James Josiah Webb, *Adventures in the Santa Fe Trade,* Ralph P. Bieber, ed. (Glendale, Ca., 1931), p. 101. Lansing B. Bloom, "New Mexico Under Mexican Administration, 1821–1846," *Old Santa Fe,* I (January 1914), p. 259. Daniel Tyler, "The Personal Property of Manuel Armijo, 1829," *El Palacio,* LXXX (Fall 1974), pp. 45–58.

11. Jones, *Los Pobladores,* pp. 246–47.

12. Noah Smithwick, *The Evolution of a State: or, Recollections of Old Texas Days* (1st ed., 1900; Austin, 1935), p. 29. Andrew Forest Muir, ed., *Texas in 1837: An Anonymous, Contemporary Narrative* (Austin, 1958), p. 106, refers to "the elite of the city."

13. Abel de Petit-Thouars, *Voyage of the Venus: Sojourn in California . . .* Charles N. Rudkin, trans. (Los Angeles, 1956), p. 47. Dmitry Zavalishin, "California in 1824," James R. Gibson, trans., *SCQ,* LV (Winter 1973), p. 395, also recalled no "sharp cleavage between different classes that we see in other countries." More observant foreigners, such as Jedediah Smith, noted, "they are generally poor, but a few families are rich in Cattle, horses and Mules. . . . " George R. Brooks, ed., *The Southwest Expedition of Jedediah S. Smith: His Personal Account of the Journey to California, 1826–1827* (Glendale, Ca., 1977), pp. 109–10.

14. José del Carmen Lugo, "Life of a Rancher," *SCQ,* XXXII (September, 1950), p. 235. See, too, Hubert Howe Bancroft, *California Pastoral, 1769–1848* (San Francisco, 1888), pp. 415–16.

15. Ray S. Brandes, ed. and trans., "Times Gone By in Alta California: Recollections of Señora Doña Juana Machado Alipáz de Ridington (Wrightington)," *SCQ,* XLI (September 1959), p. 211.

16. Amador's "Memorias" of 1877, quoted in Richard Griswold del Castillo, *The Los Angeles Barrio, 1850–1880: A Social History* (Berkeley, 1980), p. 266. Hubert Howe Bancroft, *History of California,* 7 vols. (San Francisco, 1884–90), II, 696.

17. Becknell, "Journal of Two Expeditions."

18. Report of the legislative committee to collect a "forced loan," in Minutes of the diputación territorial, October 18, 1829, MANM, roll 42, frames 625–29. Francisco Sarracino, Governor of New Mexico, to its citizens, printed circular, December 13, 1834, facsimile in Henry R. Wagner, "New Mexico Spanish Press," *NMHR,* XII (January 1937), facing p. 1.

19. Jones, *Los Pobladores,* p. 131.

20. Mariano Guadalupe Vallejo to [Governor Alvarado?], Sonoma, June 10, 1839, in *Comunicaciones del General M. G. Vallejo* (Sonoma, 1837–39), bound collection of six printed documents, BL.

21. See, for example, Jones, *Los Paisanos,* p. 247. Frances León Swadesh, *Los Primeros Pobladores: Hispanic Americans of the Ute Frontier* (Notre Dame, 1974), p. 59.

22. Durán to Governor José Figueroa, July 3, 1833, quoted in C. Alan Hutchinson, *Frontier Settlement in Mexican California. The Híjar-Padrés Colony and its Origins, 1769–1835* (New Haven, 1969), pp. 222–23.

23. John Marsh, "Letter of Dr. John Marsh to Hon. Lewis Cass" [January 20, 1846], *CHSQ,* XXII (December 1943), p. 321. Woodrow James Hansen, *The Search for Authority in California* (Oakland, 1960), pp. 20–22, 45. W. W. Robinson, "The Indians of Los Angeles," *SCQ,* XX (December 1938), pp. 156–61, 164–65. George Harwood Phillips, "Indians in Los Angeles, 1781–1875: Economic Integration, Social Disintegration," *PHR,* XLIX (August 1980), pp. 435–37, argues that residents of Los Angeles depended almost entirely on Indian labor and that secularization produced a surplus of labor and unemployment.

24. Sanford Mosk, "The Influence of Tradition on Agriculture in New Mexico," *Journal of Economic History,* 2, Supplement (December 1942), pp. 37–39, 42–43. Roxanne Dunbar Ortiz, *Roots of Resistance: Land Tenure in New Mexico, 1680–1980* (Los Angeles, 1980), pp. 79–80. These generalizations derive from impressionist sources and the question needs further research. For the decline in the number of sheep in New Mexico due to Indian raids see "Placer del Oro," by "E. E., " in *El Payo de Nuevo México,* July 19, 1845, and Gregg, *Commerce of the Prairies,* pp. 133–34. Sample partido contracts of the era are in the Perea Family Papers, NMSRC. The number of available herders may have increased in the Mexican period, too, following a trend toward the expansion of a landless labor force, which Antonio José Ríos-Bustamante has identified in his suggestive analysis: "New Mexico in the Eighteenth Century: Life, Labor and Trade in the Villa de San Felipe de Albuquerque, 1706–1790," *Aztlán,* VII (Fall 1976), pp. 360, 371.

25. This matter needs further study. See Tijerina, "Tejanos and Texas," pp. 111, 264–65; McReynolds, "Family Life in a Borderland Community: Nacogdoches," p. 174.

26. Marc Simmons, "The Mysterious A Tribe of the Southern Plains," in *The Changing Ways of Southwestern Indians. A Historic Perspective,* Albert H. Schroeder, ed. (Glorieta, New Mexico, 1973), p. 76. See, too, Steven Horvath, "Indian Slaves for Spanish Horses," *Museum of the Fur Trade Quarterly,* XIV (Winter 1978), pp. 4–5, a good pithy account.

27. Quotes are respectively from Amado Chaves to Laurence F. Lee, Santa Fe, September 23, 1927, and Amado Chaves to his daughter, Katherine, Santa Fe, January 18, 1927, Amado Chaves Papers, NMSRC, called to my attention by Marc Simmons, *The Little Lion of the Southwest: A Life of Manuel Antonio Chaves* (Chicago, 1973), p. 35.

28. Henry F. Dobyns et al., "What Were Nixoras?" *Southwestern Journal of Anthropology,* XVI (Summer 1960), pp. 230–58. The most careful attempt to define genízaro is Steven M. Horvath, Jr., "The Genízaros of Eighteenth Century New Mexico: A Reexamination," *Discovery,* XII (Fall 1977), pp. 25–40, who makes the point that the label was usually "not applied until adults left service in settlers' households" (p. 34). Simmons, *Spanish Government in New Mexico,* pp. 131, 151. Ward Alan Minge, "Frontier Problems in New Mexico Preceding the Mexican War, 1840–1846" (Ph.D. diss., University of New Mexico, 1965), pp. 54–55.

29. Francis F. Guest, "An Examination of the Thesis of S. F. Cook on the Forced Conversion of Indians in the California Missions," *SCQ,* LXI (Spring 1979), p. 3, cites instances in 1829, 1834, and 1845, when the government took action against the *californios.* See, too, Jessie Davis Francis, "An Economic and Social History of Mexican California, 1822–1846" (Ph.D. diss., University of California, Berkeley, 1935), pp. 439, 505–7. For the late Mexican period in New Mexico see Gregg, *Commerce of the Prairies,* p. 153, and Pauline Weaver's account of 1846 in Philip St. George Cooke, *The Conquest of California and New Mexico* (New York, 1878), p. 180, and Shirley Hill Witt, "Migration into San Juan Pueblo, 1726–1968" (Ph.D. diss., University of New Mexico, 1969), pp. 124–26. In northern Sonora, Yumas and Apaches were used as domestic servants until the end of the Mexican era: José Agustín Escudero, *Noticias estadísticas de Sonora y Sinaloa* (Mexico, 1849), p. 143.

30. For *tejanos* as holders of black slaves, see Tjarks, "Comparative Demographic Analysis of Texas," p. 328, n. 48; Tijerina, "Tejanos and Texas," p. 264–65; and Rosalie Schwartz, *Across the Rio to Freedom. U. S. Negroes in Mexico* (El Paso, 1975), pp. 14–24; 57, n. 47. Tax

354   Notes to Chapter 11, pages 213-216

assessor roles in 1840 show practically no *tejanos* owning slaves in Nacogdoches, Victoria, or San Antonio. Gifford White, ed., *The 1840 Census of the Republic of Texas* (Austin, 1966), pp. 12–18, 120–36, 200–4. For Mexican policy and Texas reactions to it, see Lester G. Bugbee, "Slavery in Early Texas," *Political Science Quarterly*, XIII (September and December 1898), pp. 389–412; 648–68; and Downs, "History of Mexicans in Texas," pp. 211–15.

31. Benjamin Lundy, *The Life, Travels and Opinions of Benjamin Lundy, Including His Journeys to Texas and Mexico . . .* (Philadelphia, 1847), p. 48.

32. Ibid., p. 54. Nacogdoches, with black slaves forming 9.5% of its populations, was an exception. See McReynolds, "Family Life in a Borderland Community," pp. 186–90; Downs, "History of Mexicans in Texas," p. 78.

33. David J. Weber, ed. and trans., "A Black American in Mexican San Diego: Two Recently Recovered Documents," *JSDH*, XX (Spring 1974), pp. 29–35. Although some of the *californios* had black ancestors, few blacks lived in California. Bancroft thought there were only two in 1831 (*California Pastoral*, pp. 283–84).

34. Lyle N. McAlister, "Social Structure and Social Change In New Spain," *HAHR*, XLIII (August 1963), pp. 366–69. Tjarks, "Comparative Demographic Analysis of Texas," pp. 322, 328, 330. Ríos-Bustamante, "New Mexico in the Eighteenth Century," p. 352. Jones, *Los Pobladores*, p. 134, finds 10 percent of the servants in the 1790 census of New Mexico classified as "Spaniards."

35. Thomas Jefferson Farnham, *Travels in California* (1st ed., 1844; Oakland, California, 1947), p. 142. See, too, Muir, ed., *Texas in 1837*, p. 102, and Cecil Robinson, *With the Ears of Strangers: The Mexican in American Literature* (Tucson, 1963), pp. 67–69. For Pico, see Jack D. Forbes, "The Black Pioneers: The Spanish-speaking Afroamericans of the Southwest," in *Minorities in California History*, George E. Frakes and Curtis B. Solberg, eds. (New York, 1971), pp. 31–32.

36. Tijerina, "Tejanos and Texas," p. 14.

37. Henry F. Dobyns, ed., *Hepah, California! The Journal of Cave Johnson Couts from Monterey, Nuevo León, Mexico to Los Angeles, California during the Years 1848–1849* (Tucson, 1961), p. 59.

38. Quoted in Robinson, "The Indians of Los Angeles," pp. 161–162.

39. Manuel P. Servín, ed., "The Beginnings of California's Anti-Mexican Prejudice," in Servín, ed., *An Awakened Minority: The Mexican-Americans* (Beverly Hills, 1974), p. 2. Many writers have commented on the frontiersmen's tendency to "whiten" themselves on the census in the late colonial period. In the "egalitarian" Mexican era, such data were no longer collected.

40. J. N. Bowman, "Prominent Women of Provincial California," *SCQ*, XXXIX (June 1957), pp. 149–66. F or Lorenzana, see Brandes, trans. and ed., "Recollections of Señora Doña Juana Machado," pp. 201, 223, n. 23. Gregg, *Commerce of the Prairies*, p. 168. Doña Gertrudis was not a female Horatio Alger, however, as Gregg reported. See Fray Angélico Chávez, "Doña Tules, Her Fame and Her Funeral," *El Palacio*, LVII (August 1950), pp. 227–34, and Janet Lecompte, "La Tules and the Americans," *AW*, XX (Autumn 1978), pp. 215–30, with its penetrating observations on the status of women.

41. Janet Lecompte, "The Independent Women of Hispanic New Mexico, 1821–1846," *Western Historical Quarterly*, XII (January 1981), pp. 17–35, provides the best account of the legal rights of women both in theory and in practice. See, too, James M. Murphy, *Spanish Legal Heritage in Arizona* (Tucson, 1966), pp. 33–39; Tijerina, "Tejanos and Texas," pp. 276–77; McReynolds, "Family Life in a Borderland Community: Nacogdoches," pp. 141–43.

42. Bancroft, *California Pastoral*, pp. 306–7. Mariano Guadalupe Vallejo, "History of California," Earl R. Hewitt, trans., 1875, 5 vols., MS, III, 105, BL. Minge, "Frontier Problems in New Mexico," p. 173. Gregg, *Commerce of the Prairies*, pp. 111, 141. Tadeo Ortiz,

Resúmen de la estadística del Imperio Mexicano, 1822, Tarsicio García Díaz, ed. (Mexico, 1968), p. 21. Anne M. Pescatello, *Power and Pawn: The Female in Iberian Families, Societies, and Cultures* (Westport, Conn., 1976), pp. 15–46, and Silvia M. Arrom, *La mujer mexicana ante el divorcio eclesiástico, 1800–1857* (Mexico, 1976), p. 12.

43. Richard Wilson, *Short Ravelings from a Long Yarn,* Henry R. Wagner, ed. (1st ed., 1847; Santa Ana, California, 1936), p. 156. Wilson was apparently in Santa Fe in 1841.

44. One "Morineau," who visited California in 1834, quoted in Bancroft, *California Pastoral,* p. 279.

45. Bancroft, *California Pastoral,* p. 306. Eleanor Lawrence, "Mexican Trade Between Santa Fe and Los Angeles, 1830–1848," *CHSQ,* X (March 1931), p. 37. Lugo, "Life of a Rancher," p. 221.

46. Swadesh, *Los Primeros Pobladores,* pp. 178, 196.

47. For a good summary of current literature on women in the American West and a cogent analysis of the variety of female roles, see Glenda Riley, "Women on the American Frontier," a pamphlet in the *Forum Series,* Richard Lowitt, ed. (St. Louis, 1977). For Abiquiú, see Swadesh, *Los Primeros Pobladores,* p. 187, who finds 91 of 338 households headed by widows. For San Antonio, see Tijerina, "Tejanos and Texas," pp. 19, 20, which shows widows outnumbering widowers by 250 percent (136 to 39), and 15 percent more women than men in the adult population (age sixteen and above).

48. In San Antonio in 1831 males constituted 48 percent of the population and adult males, age sixteen and above, constituted 46.4 percent of the adult population. In Abiquiú, males constituted 49.4 percent of the population in 1845. Based on figures in Tijerina, "Tejanos and Texas," p. 20 and Virginia Langham Olmsted, *New Mexico Spanish and Mexican Colonial Censuses, 1790, 1823, 1845* (Albuquerque, 1975), p. 191.

49. T. A. Larsen, "Women's Role in the American West," *Montana,* XXIV (July 1974), p. 5. James E. Davis, *Frontier America, 1800–1840: A Comparative Demographic Analysis of the Settlement Process* (Glendale, 1977), p. 113. Joan M. Jensen and Darlis A. Miller, "The Gentle Tamers Revisited: New Approaches to the History of Women in the American West," *PHR,* XLIX (May 1980), p. 189, argue that the conventional wisdom regarding sex ratios needs to be tempered by a consideration of time and place.

50. San Jose had 169 males and 167 females listed in the Census of 1827 (Juan Bandini, "Documentos para la historia de California, 1776–1850," pp. 16–18, MS, BL). An examination of the sex ratios in four barrios of Santa Fe in 1823, shows that adult males constituted as little as 44 and as much as 48.7 percent of the adult population. Olmsted, *New Mexico Spanish and Mexican Colonial Censuses,* pp. 129–35, 140–53, 156–63, 163–74. This was not a phenomenon of the Mexican period. The 1790 census also suggests substantially more women than men. See Janie Louise Aragón, "The People of Santa Fé in 1790," *Aztlán,* VII (Fall 1976), p. 397. For San Antonio, see *supra* n. 48.

51. At San Francisco, 59.4 percent of the population was male according to the 1827 census (Bandini, "Documentos," pp. 16–18). At Goliad in 1831, 51.5 percent of the adult population was male (Tijerina, "Tejanos and Texas," p. 28). The Los Angeles census of 1830 in W. N. Charles, "Transcription and Translation of the Old Mexican Documents of the Los Angeles County Archives," *SCQ,* XX (June 1938) facing p. 84, and Marie E. Northrup, ed., "The Los Angeles Padrón of 1844," *SCQ,* XLII (December 1960), pp. 360–417, respectively places males at 49.5 and 56.6 percent of the adult population. Immigrants made up a sixth of the non-Indian population of Los Angeles in 1844. For Nacogdoches, see McReynolds, "Family Life in a Borderland Community," pp. 117–18. For samples from the late Spanish period see Tjarks, "Demographic Analysis of Texas," pp. 304–6, and "Demographic, Ethnic and Occupational Structure of New Mexico, 1790," *The Americas,* XXXV (July 1978), p. 62.

52. Davis, *Frontier America*, pp. 103–11.

53. In 1823 the percentage of the population under 16 in the following barrios of Santa Fe was as follows: 44.4 for San Miguel; 45 for San Francisco; 43.4 for Torreón; and 45.2 for Guadalupe. The Abiquiú and Lo de Mora figures derive from the 1845 census. All are in Olmsted, *New Mexico Spanish and Mexican Colonial Censuses*, pp. 129–35, 140–53, 156–74, 190–210. For Texas data, see Tijerina, "Tejanos and Texas," p. 40, table 10. The scanty secondary studies for central Mexico in this period are summarized in Moreno Toscano's "Los trabajadores," pp. 308–13. In 1811, adults of 15 and over formed 69 percent of the population of Mexico City, and adult women vastly outnumbered adult males. Mexico City, which attracted large numbers of immigrants, was not "typical" of cities in central Mexico, however.

54. Davis, *Frontier America*, p. 75, table 16.

55. Ibid., p. 69, table II.

56. Bancroft, *California Pastoral*,, pp. 312, 613–15. Francis, "Economic and Social History of Mexican California," pp. 167–68.

57. Quoted in Davis, *Seventy-Five Years in California*, p. 111.

58. McReynolds, "Family Life in a Borderland Community," pp. 153–59. Because of the heavy influx of Anglo-Americans into Nacogdoches in the Mexican era, the community cannot be considered "typical." Tjarks, "Comparative Demographic Analysis of Texas," p. 317, and "Demographic, Ethnic and Occupational Structure of New Mexico," pp. 71–72, finds two to three children per family as the norm in the late colonial period and census data from the Mexican period suggests that that probably continued to be the pattern.

59. Gregg, *Commerce of the Prairies*, p. 149.

60. Robinson, *Life in California*, p. 32. See, too, Gregg, *Commerce of the Prairies*, p. 149.

61. John E. Sunder, ed., *Matt Field on the Santa Fe Trail* (Norman, 1960), p. 215; Bancroft, *California Pastoral*, pp. 387–389, 392, 395, 400; Downs, "History of Mexicans in Texas," pp. 73–74; Howard T. Fisher and Marion Hall Fisher, eds., *Life In Mexico: The Letters of Fanny Calderón de la Barca* (Garden City, New York, 1966), pp. 56, 216; Lugo, "Life of a Rancher," pp. 220–22, 219.

62. Petit-Thouars, *Voyage of the Venus*, p. 47; Berlandier, *Journey to Mexico*, II, 291; Bancroft, *California Pastoral*, pp. 376–77, 382, 393–94, 396; Fisher and Fisher, eds., *Life in Mexico*, plates 58–60. Carmen Espinosa, *Shawls, Crinolines, and Filigree: The Dress and Adornment of the Women of New Mexico, 1739 to 1900* (El Paso, 1970), pp. 9–24, contains a remarkable series of women's wills, dated 1739 to 1831, which identify specific items of clothing, including the tunic in 1831.

63. Stella M. Drumm, ed., *Down the Santa Fe Trail and Into Mexico: The Diary of Susan Shelby Magoffin, 1846–1847*, foreword by Howard R. Lamar (1st ed., 1926; reprint New Haven, 1962), p. 124.

64. Ibid., p. 95.

65. Gregg, *Commerce of the Prairies*, pp. 152–53.

66. William Perkins, *Three Years in California: William Perkins' Journal of Life at Sonora, 1849–1852*, Dale L. Morgan and James R. Scobie, eds. (Berkeley, 1964), p. 294.

67. Harold Kirker, *California's Architectural Frontier. Style and Tradition in the Nineteenth Century* (1st ed., 1960; Santa Barbara, 1973), pp. 1–22; E. Boyd, *Popular Arts of Spanish New Mexico* (Santa Fe, 1974), pp. 6–7, 25–27, 30; Alicia Tjarks, "Evolución urbana de Texas durante el siglo xviii," *Revista de Indias*, nos. 131–38 (January 1973-December 1974), p. 616. There were, of course, exceptions. Severino Martínez, patriarch of an influential Taos family, had a house with "about twenty-nine rooms" and some two-story structures. Ward Alan Minge, "The Last Will and Testament of Don Severino Martínez [1827]," *New Mexico Quarterly*, XXXIII (Spring 1963), pp. 38, 50, 51.

68. [Eugene C. Barker, ed.], "Journal of Stephen F. Austin on His First Trip to Texas, 1821," *SWHQ*, VII (1903–4), p. 298.

69. Sunder, ed., *Matt Field on the Santa Fe Trail*, p. 204.

70. Kirker, *California's Architectural Frontier*, p. 12; Bancroft, *California Pastoral*, pp. 400–4; Lundy, *The Life, Travels and Opinions*, p. 48; Lugo, "Life of a Rancher," p. 217.

71. M. R. Harrington, "The Will of Don Tomás Antonio Yorba, Year of 1845," *SCQ*, XXXIII (March 1951), pp. 67–73. Doris Marion Wright, *A Yankee in Mexican California: Abel Stearns, 1798–1848* (Santa Barbara, 1977), p. 46; Drumm, ed., *Diary of Susan Shelby Magoffin*, p. 154; Boyd, *Popular Arts of Spanish New Mexico*, pp. 285–87; McReynolds, "Family Life in a Borderland Community," pp. 69–75.

72. Because unmodified structures from the eighteenth and nineteenth centuries have not survived, generalizations about domestic architecture are difficult for this period and much remains to learn. It seems too simple to assume that "buildings of the Mexican era . . . merely continue the Spanish Colonial tradition;" Bainbridge Bunting, *Taos Adobes: Spanish Colonial and Territorial Architecture of the Taos Valley* (Santa Fe, 1964), p. 1. None of the large, multiroom houses in Bunting's study appear to have exceeded four rooms in the Spanish period, but the Pascuál Martínez house was originally a four room structure that was expanded upon in the mid-1820s. See, too, Bunting's *Early Architecture in New Mexico* (Albuquerque, 1976), pp. 59–79. Albert Pike, *Prose Sketches and Poems Written in the Western Country* (With Additional Stories), David J. Weber, ed. (Albuquerque, 1967), p. 185. Boyd, *Popular Arts of Spanish New Mexico*, pp. 26–27; Kirker, *California's Architectural Frontier*, pp. 10–13; Muir, ed., *Texas in 1837*, p. 96; Tijerina, "Tejanos and Texas," pp. 29–32; McReynolds, "Life in a Borderland Community," pp. 48–63.

73. The classic account of the Monterey style is Kirker, *California's Architectural Frontier*, pp. 16–22. An 1842 view of Monterey in John W. Reps, *Cities of the American West: A History of Frontier Urban Planning* (Princeton, 1979), p. 111, shows a substantial number of two-story buildings. See, too, Edwin Bryant's 1847 description of Los Angeles, ibid., p. 101. Boyd, *Popular Arts of Spanish New Mexico*, pp. 26–27, identifies some two-story houses in pre-1846 New Mexico.

74. Boyd, *Popular Arts of Spanish New Mexico*, pp. 9, 21, 26–27, 246, 260–64, 275–80. For the kinds of tools imported by Americans over the Santa Fe trail in the mid-1820s see David J. Weber, ed., "William Workman: A Letter from Taos, 1826," *NMHR*, XLI (April 1966), pp. 159–60. Archaeological remains in San Antonio indicate that vecinos used flint as cutting and scraping tools, apparently because of the lack of iron. Anne A. Fox, *The Archaeology and History of the Spanish Governor's Palace. University of Texas at San Antonio Archaeological Survey Report no. 3* (San Antonio, 1977), p. 16. For those who could afford them, a variety of metal tools and fixtures were available in the Spanish era: Marc Simmons and Frank Turley, *Southwestern Colonial Ironwork: The Spanish Blacksmithing Tradition from Texas to California* (Santa Fe, 1980), pp. 68–81, 135–61.

75. Webb, *Adventures in the Santa Fe Trade*, p. 119. Muir, ed., *Texas in 1837*, pp. 96–97, 107–8; Bunting, *Early Architecture of New Mexico*, pp. 63, 67. Drumm, ed., *Diary of Susan Shelby Magoffin*, p. 137.

76. Jones, *Los Pobladores*, p. 241. Jones cautions "that figures for these urban concentrations may be somewhat misleading for they often include subordinate districts and settlements" (p. 245). In the broadest sense, pueblos, missions, and presidios might be considered urban centers. Although they "were established for different purposes and took different forms, in practice the distinction between them was not always so clear-cut." Reps, *Cities in the American West*, pp. 40–41. Urban historians, such as Richard Wade and John Reps, have expanded our understanding of the importance of urban centers in extending the American frontier. Nonetheless, the population of the U. S. was only 7.2 percent urban in

1820; 10.8 percent urban in 1840. W. Elliott Brownlee, *Dynamics of Ascent: A History of the American Economy* (New York, 1974), p. 89.

77. Speech before the ayuntamiento, April 19, 1845, quoted in Daniel J. Garr, "Los Angeles, and the Challenge of Growth, 1835–1849," *SCQ*, LXI (Summer 1979), p. 152. See, too, pp. 149–53.

78. Howard J. Nelson, "The Two Pueblos of Los Angeles: Agricultural Village and Embryo Town," *SCQ*, LIX (Spring 1977), p. 9, upon whose analysis I have depended. In comparison, in 1854 the Villa of Guadalupe in the state of Querétaro and the port of Mazatlán had 31 percent of their respective populations engaged in nonagricultural activities. Di Tella, "The Dangerous Classes in Early Nineteenth Century Mexico," pp. 103–4. See, too, Neal Harlow, *Maps and Surveys of the Pueblo Lands of Los Angeles* (Los Angeles, 1976), pp. 26–30.

79. Ríos-Bustamante, "New Mexico in the Eighteenth Century," pp. 368–70. This extraordinarily high percentage of people engaged in crafts in 1790 needs to be considered in light of an 1827 census, which shows just a sixth of the working population engaged in crafts and commerce. H. Bailey Carroll and J. Villasana Haggard, eds. and trans., *Three New Mexico Chronicles* (Albuquerque, 1942), p. 88.

80. Reps, *Cities of the American West*, p. 49.

81. Antonio Barreiro, *Ojeada sobre Nuevo México* (Puebla, 1832), in Carroll and Haggard, eds. and trans., *Three New Mexico Chronicles*, p. 85. Recollections of Demetrio Pérez in Benjamin M. Read, "In Santa Fé During the Mexican Regime," *NMHR*, II (January 1927), pp. 92–93. Minge, "Frontier Problems in New Mexico," pp. 185, 215–16.

82. Daniel J. Garr, "A Frontier Agrarian Settlement: San José de Guadalupe, 1777–1850," *San José Studies*, II (November 1976), pp. 98, 100. Tijerina, "Tejanos and Texas," p. 18, table I. Reps, *Cities of the American West*, p. 121.

83. This seems to be the case consistently, except for settlements which did not exist prior to the Mexican period. Los Angeles, for example, grew by 92 percent between 1821 and 1845 (650 to 1250), while the non-Indian population of California increased by 120 percent during those same years (3,320 to 7,300).

84. Fray José Señán to the Viceroy, the Marqués de Branciforte, Mexico, May 14, 1796, quoted in Weber, ed., *New Spain's Far Northern Frontier: Essays on Spain in the American West, 1540–1821* (Albuquerque, 1979), p. 98. This is the principal theme in Marc Simmons, "Settlement Patterns and Village Plans in Colonial New Mexico," in ibid., 99–115.

85. Pike, *Prose Sketches and Poems*, p. 35. D. W. Meinig, *Southwest: Three Peoples in Geographical Change, 1600–1970* (New York, 1971), p. 30. Bancroft's estimates for the population increase in Los Angeles district reveal a 79 percent increase in the population of the ranchos between 1830 and 1840, compared to a 42 percent increase for the town itself over the same decade (*History of California*, III, 632–33). These figures do not include the ex-neophyte population. Tijerina, "Tejanos and Texas," pp. 29–32 discusses the same phenomenon in San Antonio. Tax assessors' returns of 1840 for Béxar County show major rancheros also owning at least one town lot in San Antonio (White, ed., *The 1840 Census*, pp. 12–18).

86. Juan N. Almonte, *Noticia estadística sobre Tejas* (Mexico 1835), table 4, identifies twenty-one towns in Texas in 1834. Reps, *Cities of the American West*, p. 122, and others who identify a dozen towns are in error.

87. A detailed but discursive discussion of settlement patterns in the Mexican era is in Frank D. Reeve, *History of New Mexico*, 2 vols. (New York, 1961), I, 429–38. See, too, Meinig, *Southwest*, pp. 27–31 for a lucid synthesis, and Frank McNitt, *Navajo Wars: Military Campaigns, Slave Raids, and Reprisals* (Albuquerque, 1972), p. 72 for Cubero.

88. Malcolm J. Rohrbough, *The Trans-Appalachian Frontier: People, Societies, and Institutions, 1775–1850* (New York, 1978), p. 373, applies this term to Peoria, Ill. in 1837, when it had 300 houses and 1900 inhabitants.

89. Statistics for New Mexico for this era are especially poor, and it is difficult to separate districts, such as the Alcadía of Santa Fe, from the urban center itself. See [John P. Bloom], "Note on the Population of New Mexico, 1846–1849," *NMHR*, XXXIV (July 1959), pp. 200–1. W. H. Timmons, "The El Paso Area in the Mexican Period, 1821–1848," *SWHQ*, LXXXIV (July 1980), p. 2, n. 3. Tijerina, "Tejanos and Texas," Table 1, p. 18. Almonte's estimate of 2,500 for San Antonio in 1834 seems inflated in light of the two previous census figures from 1831 and 1833. Perhaps Almonte was counting outlying ranchos. Estimates for Monterey and Santa Barbara come from Bancroft, *History of California*, IV, 750 and 639. The Santa Barbara estimate includes the entire district.

90. The temporary operation by Governor José Félix Trespalacios of a bank which issued paper money in San Antonio in 1822 must be regarded as an aberration. The story is told in Carlos E. Castañeda, "The First Chartered Bank West of the Mississippi: Banco Nacional de Texas," *Bulletin* of the Business Historical Society, XXV (December 1951), pp. 242–56.

91. F. P. Wrángel, *De Sitka a San Petersburgo al través de México. Diario de una expedición 13-X-1835--22-V-1836,* Luisa Pintos Mimó, trans. and ed. (Mexico, 1975), p. 44. Garr, "A Frontier Agrarian Settlement: San José," pp. 93, 98, 100, 102. Reps, *Cities of the American West,* pp. 53, 97, 101. 110, 125. Tijerina, "Tejanos and Texas," p. 66. San Antonio may be an exception. Tjarks, "Evolución urbana de Texas," pp. 625–26 contrasts San Antonio's orderly arrangement with Santa Fe, but see, too, the reactions of José María Sánchez, "Trip to Texas in 1821," Carlos E. Castañeda, trans., *SWHQ*, XXIX (April 1926), pp. 257–58. Santa Barbara also had a more orderly aspect than most towns (Bancroft, *History of California*, IV, 639).

92. Quoted in Reps, *Cities of the American West*, p. 125.

93. Davis, *Seventy-Five Years in California*, pp. 45–46.

94. Wrángel, *De Sitka a San Petersburgo*, p. 44.

95. Francisco Perea, "Santa Fe as it Appeared During the Winter of the Years of 1837 and 1838," W. H. H. Allison, ed., *Old Santa Fe*, II (October 1914), p. 177. Minge, "Frontier Problems in New Mexico," p. 104.

96. Quotes are from Marc Simmons, ed. and trans., "Antonio Barreiro's 1833 Proclamation on Santa Fe City Government," *El Palacio*, 76 (June 1970), pp. 26–29. For San Antonio, see the chapters regarding public health, public welfare, public facilities, and beautification of public places in "The City Ordinances for the Internal Management and Administration of the Municipal Government of San Antonio de Béjar, 1829," Gilbert Ralph Cruz, ed. and trans., *Texana*, VII (Summer 1969), pp. 105–11. The San Antonio regulations were issued as decree no. 98 of the State of Coahuila y Texas; decree no. 99 contained similar regulations for Goliad: *Ordenanzas municipales para el gobierno y manejo interior del ayuntamiento de la villa de Goliad* (Leona Vicario [Saltillo], 1829).

97. See, for example, Rohrbough, *The Trans-Appalachian Frontier*, pp. 358, 361, 364–65.

98. Lota M. Spell, "Samuel Bangs: The First Printer in Texas," *SWHQ*, XXXV (April 1932), pp. 267–78, and Kathryn Garrett, "The First Newspaper of Texas: *Gaceta de Texas*," *SWHQ*, XL (April 1937), pp. 200–37, who shows that Bangs was not first.

99. Eugene C. Barker, "Notes on Early Texas Newspapers, 1819–1836," *SWHQ*, XXI (October 1917), pp. 177–79, 127–29, and the correctives and additions in Douglas C. McMurtrie, "Pioneer Printing in Texas," *SWHQ*, XXXV (January 1932), p. 179, who disputes Barker's contention that a newspaper existed at San Felipe in 1824. Charles A. Bacarisse, "The Texas Gazette, 1829–1832," *SWHQ*, LVI (October 1952), pp. 239–53, examines the contents and role of the *Gazette*. Charlotte A. Hickson, "The Texas Gazette,

1829-1832," *Texana,* XI (Spring 1973), pp. 18-29, adds nothing of significance to Bacarisse's study.

100. Douglas C. McMurtrie, "The History of Early Printing in New Mexico, with a Bibliography of Known Issues of the New Mexican Press, 1834-60," *NMHR,* IV (October 1929), pp. 374-75, and Henry R. Wagner, "New Mexico Spanish Press," *NMHR,* XII (January 1937), pp. 1-40, remain the best sources on this subject. Wagner's assertion that New Mexico's first press came from the United States has been substantiated by Max L. Moorhead, in his edition of Gregg's *Commerce of the Prairies,* p. 142, n. 2. Considerable confusion on this point still exists, nonetheless. See, for example, Arthur L. Campa, *Hispanic Culture in the Southwest* (Norman, 1979), p. 218. Santiago Valdez, "Biografía del Rev. P. Antonio José Martínez, cura parroco del curato de Taos," 1877 (MS, Ritch Papers, HEH), contains a copy of a printed notice dated November 21, 1835, Taos, indicating that Martínez opened a printing establishment that day. Minge, "Frontier Problems in New Mexico," p. 209.

101. George L. Harding, *Don Agustín V. Zamorano. Statesman, Soldier, Craftsman, and California's First Printer* (Los Angeles, 1934), p. 1; George Tays, "Mariano Guadalupe Vallejo and Sonoma. A Biography and a History," *CHSQ,* XVI (December 1937), p. 351; Robert Greenwood, ed., *California Imprints, 1833-1862. A Bibliography* (Los Gatos, California, 1961), pp. 38-58. Herbert Fahey, *Early Printing in California: From Its Beginnings in the Mexican Territory to Statehood, September 9, 1850* (San Francisco, 1956), pp. 7-32. Fahey describes a small woodblock press used for official seals and letterhead prior to 1834.

102. Marc Simmons, "Authors and Books in Colonial New Mexico," in Donald C. Dickenson et al., eds., *Voices from the Southwest: A Gathering in Honor of Lawrence Clark Powell* (Flagstaff, 1976), pp. 29-30. Maynard J. Geiger, "The Story of California's First Libraries," *SCQ,* XLVI (June 1964), pp. 109-24.

103. Moorhead, *New Mexico's Royal Road,* p. 197. The list of titles imported by Gregg, many of them school books, appears in Albert W. Bork, *Nuevos aspectos del comercio entre Nuevo México y Misuri, 1822-1846* (Mexico 1944), pp. 84-85. Doyce B. Nunis provides a fine discussion of this subject for California in *Books in Their Sea Chests: Reading Along the Early California Coast* (San Francisco, 1964).

104. Fray José Señán to Fray José Gasol, San Buenaventura, November 10, 1822, in Lesley Byrd Simpson, ed., and Paul D. Nathan, trans., *The Letters of José Señán, O. F. M. San Buenaventura, 1796-1823* (San Francisco, 1962), p. 167.

105. Nunis, *Books in Their Sea Chests,* p. 9. See, too, William F. Stobridge, "Book Smuggling in Mexican California," *The American Neptune,* XXXII (April 1972), pp. 117-22, who seems to exaggerate the efficiency of the padres in intercepting banned books. Censorship of books occurred in Texas, too, see I. J. Cox, "Educational Efforts in San Fernando de Béxar," *SWHQ,* VI (July 1902), p. 49.

106. Nunis, *Books in Their Sea Chests,* pp. 6, 24. On March 24, 1833, Governor Figueroa issued a decree "permitting the introduction of books of whatever origin and place of printing." Departmental State Papers, Los Angeles, Decrees and Dispatches (C-A, 36), BL.

107. Quoted in Drumm, ed., *Diary of Susan Shelby Magoffin,* p. 211. Chávez is quoted in Minge, "Frontier Problems," p. 157.

108. Richard Henry Dana to Charlotte Dana, San Diego, March 20, 1835, in *Two Years Before the Mast,* John Haskell Kemble, ed., 2 vols. (1st ed. 1844; Los Angeles, 1964), II, 383. See, too, Gregg, *Commerce of the Prairies,* p. 140.

109. See, for example, McReynolds, "Family Life in a Borderland Community," pp. 220-21.

110. "Ordinance which shall be Observed in the Public Free Primary School Dedicated to the Instruction of the Youth of the Vicinity of Béxar [1928]," trans. in Cox, "Educational

Efforts in San Fernando de Béxar," p. 62. The best single source on education in the late colonial period is Jones, *Los Paisanos,* pp. 55–57, 136–39, 227–30, 249.

111. Quoted respectively in Lucas Alamán, *Memoria del Secretario de Estado y del Despacho de Relaciones Exteriores e Interiores* (Mexico, 1823), p. 41; Juan José Espinosa de los Monteros, *Memoria del Secretario de Estado . . .* (Mexico, 1827), p. 25. For the larger context, see two fine studies, Josefina Vázquez de Knauth, *Nacionalismo y educación en México* (1st ed., 1970; Mexico, 1975), pp. 25–33; Dorothy Tanck Estrada, *La educación ilustrada, 1786–1836. Educación primaria en la ciudad de México* (Mexico, 1977).

112. Fray José Señán to Fray Juan Cortes, San Buenaventura, January 10, 1819, in Simpson, ed., *Letters of Fray José Señán,* p. 120. Hutchinson, *Frontier Settlement in Mexican California,* pp. 322–24; Susanna B. Dakin, *The Lives of William Hartnell* (Stanford, 1949), pp. 159–84.

113. Quoted in Cox, "Educational Efforts," pp. 63. Literature on the subject of education in this period is surprisingly large. Perhaps the best introduction to the subject and guide to sources is Daniel Tyler, "The Mexican Teacher," *Red River Valley Historical Review,* I (Autumn 1974), pp. 207–21. Frederick Eby, comp. *Education in Texas: Source Materials. University of Texas Bulletin* no. 1824 (Austin, 1918), pp. 27–92, is a unique collection of contemporary documents on the subject. Girls sometimes received formal schooling. See, for example, Brandes, ed. and trans., "Recollections of Señora Doña Juana Machado," p. 201.

114. Jefe político José Antonio Saucedo to the Governor, April 18, 1825, quoted in Downs, "History of Mexicans in Texas," p. 139, who provides a fine chapter on education.

115. Quoted in Howard Roberts Lamar, *The Far Southwest, 1846–1912: A Territorial History* (New Haven, 1966), pp. 48–49. Angustias de la Guerra Ord, *Occurrences in Hispanic California,* Francis Price and William H. Ellison, trans. and eds. (Washington, D. C., 1956), p. 13. Nunis, *Books in Their Sea Chests,* p. 5. Foreigners, in particular, tended to send their children abroad to be educated. See Robert J. Parker, "A California Boy in Hawaii. The Early Education of Larkin's First Son, 1840–1845," *SCQ,* XX (December 1938), pp. 145–55.

116. See, for example, Rufus Sage, quoted in Weber, ed., *Foreigners in Their Native Land,* p. 73, and Gen. Mier y Terán quoted in Allaine Howren, "Causes and Origin of the Decree of April 16, 1830," *SWHQ,* XVI (April 1913), pp. 395–98.

117. Gregg, *Commerce of the Prairies,* p. 181. Juan Bautista Ladrón del Niño de Guevara, who visited New Mexico in 1818, estimated that only thirty residents "read and write with some orthography"—surely an exaggeration (Report to Juan Francisco de Castañiza, Bishop of Durango, Durango, October 23, 1820, Archives of the Archdiocese of Santa Fe, roll 45, frames 285–302). In 1846, J. W. Abert "was much surprised to see so many who read and write. Scarce a child can be met with that has not been thus far educated." John Galvin, ed., *Western America in 1846–1847: The Original Travel Diary of Lieutenant J. W. Abert* (San Francisco, 1966), p. 53. The 1850 census showed over half of the New Mexico population as literate (25,089 illiterates out of a population of 61,547), a remarkably high and perhaps exaggerated figure considering the lack of emphasis on educating women. Alvin R. Sunseri, *Seeds of Discord: New Mexico in the Aftermath of the American Conquest, 1846–1861* (Chicago, 1979), p. 108. See, too, Downs, "History of Mexicans in Texas," p. 147, and McReynolds, "Family Life in a Borderland Community," pp. 216–17.

118. Charles C. Cumberland, *Mexico: The Struggle for Modernity* (Oxford, 1968), p. 188.

119. S. Alexander Rippa, *Education in a Free Society: An American History* (New York, 1976), pp. 102–34. Rohrbough, *The Trans-Appalachian Frontier,* pp. 58–59, 84–85. See, too, Richard C. Wade, *The Urban Frontier: Pioneer Life in Early Pittsburgh, Cincinnati, Lexington, Louisville, and St. Louis* (1st ed., 1959; Chicago, 1965), pp. 243–51.

120. Numerous sources attest to the venality and ignorance of alcaldes on the frontier,

and complaints cannot be dismissed as the prejudiced rantings of Anglo-Americans. The problem was widespread. See, for example, Sánchez, "Trip to Texas," p. 283; Minge, "Frontier Problems in New Mexico," p. 102; *Don Pío Pico's Historical Narrative*, Martin Cole and Henry Welcome, eds., Arthur P. Botello, trans. (Glendale, 1973), pp. 134–36. For central Mexico, see Charles A. Hale, *Mexican Liberalism in the Age of Mora, 1821–1853* (New Haven, 1968), pp. 87–88. Suits involving the "ley de parentesco" occurred with some frequency. See, for example, Ramo de Ayuntamientos, vol. 12, pp. 105–53, AGN, relating to Santa Fe's 1826–27 election. Bloom, "New Mexico Under Mexican Administration," II, 13, finds that two of seven members of the 1837 departmental junta could not read or write.

121. David J. Weber, "Louis Robidoux," in LeRoy R. Hafen, ed., *The Mountain Men and the Fur Trade of the Far West*, 10 vols. (Glendale, 1965–72), VIII, 317–20. William S. Wallace, "Antoine Robidoux," in ibid., IV, 263. Alvarez's application for U.S. citizenship in 1834 was denied and he apparently had not received it at the time of his appointment. Harold H. Dunham, "Manuel Alvarez," in ibid., I, 190, 194, and Thomas E. Chávez, "Don Manuel Alvarez (de las Abelgas): Multi-Talented Merchant of New Mexico," *JW*, XVIII (January 1979), p. 34. Minge, "Frontier Problems," p. 21.

122. Bancroft, *History of California*, III, 785; IV, 666–67 for Hinckley; ibid., IV, 679, 710 for Leese; ibid., III, 739 for Fitch. For Stearns, see Wright, *A Yankee in Mexican California*, pp. 70–75. For Monterey in 1835, see Bancroft, *History of California*, III, 673–74. For Spence, see ibid., III, 673–76; V, 730–31. For a Texas example, see McReynolds, "Family Life in a Borderland Community," pp. 232–33.

123. Luis del Castillo Negrete, "En Favor de la Alta California," *Historia mexicana*, IX (julio-septiembre, 1959), p. 138.

124. Lundy, *Life, Travels*, pp. 51, 53. Muir, ed., *Texas in 1837*, p. 100. Pat Ireland Nixon, *The Medical Story of Early Texas, 1528–1853* (Lancaster, Pa., 1946), pp. 125–29. Josiah Gregg, himself a doctor, noted that there was "not a single native physician in the province of New Mexico," *Commerce of the Prairies*, p. 143. As late as 1844 Los Angeles had only one doctor, Joseph Money, a Scot (Northrup, ed., "The Los Angeles Padrón of 1844," pp. 360–417).

125. Quoted in Susanna Bryant Dakin, *A Scotch Paisano in Old Los Angeles: Hugo Reid's Life in California, 1832–1853, Derived from his Correspondence* (Berkeley, 1939), p. 13. See, too, Robinson, *Life in California*, p. 46.

126. R. W. H. Hardy, *Travels in the Interior of Mexico, in 1825, 1826, 1827, & 1828*, intro. by David J. Weber (1st ed., 1829; Glorieta, New Mexico, 1977), pp. 111–13. See, too, pp. 415, 456–57.

127. Moorhead, *New Mexico's Royal Road*, p. 196.

128. I am indebted to my colleague, James O. Breeden, for my understanding of this subject. A graphic explanation of the state of early nineteenth century medical practice is: William G. Rothstein, *American Physicians in the Nineteenth Century: From Sects to Science* (Baltimore, 1972), pp. 41–62. For high praise of Dr. Sappington, see Drumm, ed., *Diary of Susan Shelby Magoffin*, p. 147. Ari Kiev, *Curanderismo: Mexican-American Folk Psychiatry* (New York, 1968). Peyote was used during the threatened cholera epidemic in San Antonio in 1833. See J. Villasana Haggard, "Epidemic Cholera in Texas, 1833–1834," *SWHQ*, XL (January 1937), p. 219, n. 7.

129. George D. Lyman, "The Scalpel Under Three Flags in California," *CHSQ*, V (June 1925), pp. 142–206, viewed California as relatively free of disease for the gente de razón in the Spanish era, with smallpox, cholera, and measles entering in the Mexican era. Sherburne F. Cook, *The Conflict Between the California Indian and White Civilization* (Berkeley, 1976), p. 20, adds that scarlet fever may also have entered California for the first time during this period. For cholera, which made its global appearance as an epidemic disease

at this time, see especially C. Alan Hutchinson, "The Asiatic Cholera Epidemic of 1833 in Mexico," *Bulletin of the History of Medicine*, XXXII (January-February; March-April, 1958), pp. 1–23; 152–63, and Haggard, "Epidemic Cholera in Texas, 1833–1834," pp. 216–30.

130. Jones, *Los Paisanos*, pp. 60, 140, 230. Sherburne F. Cook, "Smallpox in Spanish and Mexican California, 1770–1845," *Bulletin of the History of Medicine*, VII (February 1939), pp. 153–91. Robert J. Moes, "Smallpox Immunization in Alta California: A Story Based on José Estrada's Postscript," SCQ, LXI (Summer 1979), pp. 125–45. Nixon, *The Medical Story of Early Texas*, pp. 130–33. For the federal government's concern with keeping vaccine on hand in the Mexican period, see the law of March 29, 1829, authorizing expenditures to produce and maintain vaccine in the territories and federal district. Manuel Dublán and José María Lozano, eds., *Legislación mexicana*, 34 vols. (Mexico, 1876–1904), II, p. 97. Local concerns and actions appear in records of the minutes of various town councils. See, for example, the Minutes of the Ayuntamiento of Béxar, March 8, 1830, photostat, Barker Center, UT. Some of the vaccine came from abroad in the Mexican era. The governor of New Mexico reported receiving "crystals" of vaccine from England (rough draft of a letter to the Minister of Relaciones Exteriores, Santa Fe, July 3, 1831, Ritch Papers, no. 127, HEH).

131. Sherburne F. Cook, "The Epidemic of 1830–1833 in California and Oregon," *University of California Publications in American Archaeology and Ethnology*, XLVIII (May 1955), pp. 303–26. Sherburne F. Cook, "Smallpox in Spanish and Mexican California," pp. 183–86. See, too, Clyde D. Dollar, "The High Plains Smallpox Epidemic of 1837–38," WHQ, VIII (January 1977), pp. 15–38. Smallpox on the Great Plain was apparently unrelated to the California epidemic, which Cook believes originated at Fort Ross.

132. "J. C. Clopper's Journal," p. 74.

133. The finest discussion of this phenomenon on the American frontier is Ray Allen Billington's *America's Frontier Heritage* (New York, 1966), pp. 69–96.

134. J. W. Benedict, "Diary of a Campaign Against the Comanches," *SWHQ*, XXXII (April 1929), p. 305. Alvarado, "History of California," III, 92; Bancroft, *California Pastoral*, pp. 429, 426; Bancroft, *History of California*, II, 431; Simmons, ed. and trans., "Antonio Barreiro's 1833 Proclamation," p. 30, and Simmons, "The First Circus Performers in New Mexico," *New Mexico Independent*, July 4, 1980. Maromeros performed in San Antonio in 1843, and doubtless earlier. W. Eugene Hollon and Ruth Lapham Butler, eds., *Bollaert's Texas* (Norman, 1956), pp. 227–28, 230. Hollon and Butler err in suggesting that Zebulon Pike saw these entertainers in San Antonio in 1807. Pike saw them at Presidio del Norte on the Rio Grande. Donald Jackson, ed., *The Journals of Zebulon Montgomery Pike, With Letters and Related Documents*, 2 vols. (Norman, 1966), I, 435.

135. Minutes of the diputación provincial, Santa Fe, March 31, 1824, MANM, roll 42, frames 186–91. Eleanor B. Adams and Fray Angélico Chávez, eds. and trans., *The Missions of New Mexico, 1776: A Description by Fray Francisco Atanasio Domínguez* (Albuquerque, 1956), p. 241, mentions a bullfight (reference, courtesy of Marc Simmons).

136. Read, "In Santa Fe During the Mexican Regime," p. 94. Travelers in New Mexico in this era do not ordinarily mention bull or cockfights. Tjarks, "Evolución urbana de Texas," pp. 632, 635, finds little evidence of bullfighting in Spanish San Antonio, but cockfighting seems to have been commonplace, as it was in California. Charles Franklin Carter, trans., "Duhaut-Cilly's Account of California in the Years 1827–1828," *CHSQ*, VIII (September 1919), pp. 229–30; Bancroft, *History of California* II, 604; III, 669. For billiards see Bancroft, *California Pastoral*, p. 436; Bork, *Nuevos aspectos*, p. 86.

137. Drumm, ed., *Diary of Susan Shelby Magoffin*, p. 126.

138. Donald E. Worcester, "The Significance of the Spanish Borderlands to the United States," WHQ, VII (January 1976), pp. 5–14, summarizes some of the literature on this subject. The extent to which Anglo-Americans borrowed the techniques of open-range ranching from Mexican vaqueros is currently the subject of debate among historians. For a

fine summary of the issues and the literature, see Terry G. Jordan, *Trails to Texas: Southern Roots of Western Cattle Ranching* (Lincoln, Nebraska: 1981).

139. Sánchez, "Trips to Texas," p. 283.

140. Berlandier, *Journey to Mexico*, II, 291.

141. Almonte, confidential letter to the Governor of Coahuila y Tejas, September 23, 1834, Monclova, ASFC, legajo 8, expediente 64, transcript no. 2-22/640, p. 40, TSA.

142. Alvarado, "History of California," III, p. 13.

143. Larkin, Description of California, Monterey, April 20, 1846, in George P. Hammond, ed., *The Larkin Papers: Personal, Business, and Official Correspondence . . . , 10 vols. (Berkeley, 1953)*, IV, 306.

144. Ibid., p. 307.

145. Governor of Chihuahua to the Minister of Foreign Relations, May 12, 1825, quoted in Weber, "Mexico and the Mountain Men, 1821–1828," *JW*, VIII (October 1969), p. 373.

146. *Gaceta Diaria de México*, June 4, 1825, quoted in Angela Moyano Pahissa, *El comercio de Santa Fe y la guerra del '47* (Mexico 1976), p. 11.

147. *El Crepúsculo*, issue number 5, quoted in *El Fanal de Chihuahua*, January 27, 1835.

148. Castañares, *Colección de documentos*, pp. 18–19. Alvarado, "Historia de California," III, 74, makes a similar observation.

149. Owen Lattimore, "The Frontier in History," reprinted in Robert A. Manners and David Kaplan, eds., *Theory in Anthropology* (Chicago, 1968), p. 374.

150. Dennis E. Berge, ed. and trans., *Considerations on the Political and Social Situation of the Mexican Republic, 1847* (El Paso, 1975), p. 45.

151. David J. Weber and Ronald R. Young, eds. and trans., "California in 1831: Heinrich Virmond to Lucas Alamán," *JSDH*, XXI (Fall 1975), p. 5. Petit-Thouars, who spent only a month in Monterey in 1837, commented on "this enmity of Californians toward Mexicans," *Voyage of the Venus*, p. 18. Bancroft, *History of California*, II, 254, found "la otra banda" in use at least as early as 1819, and many writers of the Mexican era remark on it. See the discursive but interesting discussion of this question in Antonio Blanco S., *La lengua española en la historia de California* (Madrid, 1971), pp. 137–53.

152. Figueroa to the Minister of Relations, July 20, 1833, quoted in Hutchinson, *Frontier California*, p. 226.

153. Juan Bautista Alvarado, quoted in Bancroft, *California Pastoral*, p. 270. Examples are abundant. See Sánchez, "Trip to Texas in 1828," pp. 250–51, 258; Berlandier, *Journey to Mexico*, II, 291; Donaciano Vigil, Address to the Assembly, June 22, 1846, Ritch Papers, no. 233, HEH; Lugo, "Life of a Rancher," p. 206.

Chapter 12
Separatism and Rebellion

1. Thomas H. Greene, *Comparative Revolutionary Movements* (Englewood Cliffs, N.J., 1974), pp. 116–17, 128. The separatist movements on the Mexican frontier lacked sufficient breadth to fall under most definitions of revolution and are clearly rebellions.

2. George Tays, "Revolutionary California. The Political History of California from 1820 to 1848" (Ph.D. diss., Berkeley, 1932, rev. in 1934), pp. 127–37, 139–73, 265–67.

3. Manuel de Jesús Rada, *Proposición hecha al soberano Congreso General . . .* (Mexico, 1829), p. 3, in David J. Weber, ed., *Northern Mexico on the Eve of the United States Invasion. Rare Imprints . . .* (New York, 1976); Governor Bartolomé Baca to Manuel Simón Escudero, Santa Fe, June 9, 1825, Archivo Histórico de la Secretaría de Relaciones Exteriores, Mexico, RE, 5-9-8159/H241.5 (72:73) 1, pp. 13–14.

4. Tays, "Revolutionary California," p. 252.

5. This theme is treated to some extent in chapter 9, but for other examples, see the secret memo of Francisco Pizarro, Mexican consul at New Orleans, April 16, 1827, to José de los Monteros, in *ASFC*, legajo 6, part 1, expediente 40, West Transcripts, UT; Governor of Nuevo León, Monterrey, August 1834, secret report to the Secretary of Foreign Relations in ibid., legajo 9, expediente 69.

6. "The political elite's decision to centralize the state's administrative authority can also accelerate the revolutionary process, especially where regional and cultural autonomy are threatened by centralization." Greene, *Comparative Revolutionary Movements*, p. 115.

7. Francisco de Paula de Arrangoiz, *Mexico desde 1808 hasta 1867* (2nd ed., Mexico, 1968), pp. 367–70. The decretos of March 31, May 2, and October 3 are in Manuel Dublán and José María Lozano, eds., *Legislación mexicana*, 34 vols. (Mexico, 1876–1904), III, 38, 43, 75.

8. For an especially interesting summary of the activities of Juan Álvarez, presented in counterpoint to the career of Santa Anna, see Fernando Díaz Díaz, *Caudillos y caciques. Antonio López de Santa Anna y Juan Álvarez* (Mexico, 1972), pp. 128–32. For Mexía see C. Alan Hutchinson, "General José Antonio Mexía and His Texas Interest," *SWHQ*, LXXXII (October 1978), p. 140, and Hutchinson, "Mexican Federalists in New Orleans and the Texas Revolution," *Louisiana Historical Quarterly*, XXXIX (January 1956), pp. 1–47.

9. Juan Francisco de Azcárate, *Un programa de política internacional* (Mexico, 1932), p. 63. José C. Valadés, *Orígenes de la república mexicana. La aurora constitucional* (Mexico, 1972), pp. 422–33 makes interesting observations on the impact of distance on Mexican federalism and on Yucatán. For details see Eligio Ancona, *Historia de Yucatán desde la época más remota hasta nuestros días*, 4 vols. (2nd ed., Barcelona, 1889), III, 357–459.

10. Eugene C. Barker, "The Texan Declaration of Causes for Taking up Arms Against Mexico," *SWHQ*, XV (January 1912), pp. 173–85. The Declaration of November 7, 1835, appears in a number of collections. Ernest Wallace and David M. Vigness, eds., *Documents of Texas History* (Austin, 1963) is convenient for key documents.

11. For use of these terms by contemporaries, see, for example, William B. Travis to James Bowie, San Felipe, July 30, 1835, and Henry Austin to Mary Holley, Brazoria, September 10, 1835, in John H. Jenkins, ed., *Papers of the Texas Revolution*, 10 vols. (Austin, 1973), I, 289–90, 431–32.

12. Archie P. McDonald, *Travis* (Austin, 1976), pp. 21–55.

13. Alamán to Austin, Mexico, August 25, 1830, in ASFC, legajo VI, expediente 47, West Transcripts, UT.

14. Eugene C. Barker, *Mexico and Texas, 1821–35* (Dallas, 1928), pp. 101–14.

15. Quoted in Mark E. Nackman, *A Nation Within a Nation. The Rise of Texas Nationalism* (Port Washington, New York, 1972), p. 21. A biographical vignette of Smythe is in Walter Prescott Webb and H. Bailey Carroll, eds., *The Handbook of Texas*, 2 vols. (Austin, 1952), II, 629.

16. "Address to the People," San Felipe de Austin, June 25, 1832, translated in Charles Adams Gulick, Jr., ed., *The Papers of Mirabeau Bounaparte Lamar*, 7 vols. (Austin, 1921–1927), I, 122. For a brief biography of Músquiz, see Webb and Carroll, eds., *Handbook of Texas*, II, 253.

17. Austin to his cousin Henry Austin, April 9, 1833, quoted in Barker, *Mexico and Texas*, p. 124. See, too, Barker, *Austin*, pp. 360–67.

18. Vito Alessio Robles, *Coahuila y Texas desde la consumación de la independencia hasta el tratado de paz de Guadalupe Hidalgo*, 2 vols. (Mexico, 1945–46), I, 490–97.

19. Almonte to the Secretaría de Relaciones Exteriores, Saltillo, October 10, 1834, in ASFC, legajo 8, expediente 65, West Transcripts, UT. Other letters in this same group, such as Almonte to the Secretaría de Relaciones Exteriores, Nacogdoches, June 14, 1834

and San Felipe, July 22, 1834, suggest Almonte's deep concern about a separatist movement in Texas. Upon return to Mexico City, Almonte published a report of his inspection, *Noticia estadística sobre Tejas* (Mexico, 1835), which paints a rosier picture of conditions in Texas than Almonte portrayed in his private, unsanitized correspondence. A facsimile of the *Noticia* appears in Weber, ed. *Northern Mexico.* Historians such as Eugene Barker (*Austin,* pp. 395–401), who provide an excellent summary of events, may have underestimated the depth of Almonte's suspicions. See, too, Barker, *Mexico and Texas,* pp. 128–31.

20. Austin to the ayuntamiento of San Antonio, Mexico, October 2, 1833, quoted in Barker, *Austin,* pp. 373–74.

21. Austin to Samuel May Williams, Mexico, April 15, 1835, in Jenkins, ed., *Papers of the Texas Revolution,* I, 69–70. Austin wrote to others in a similar tone that spring. See, for example, his letters to James Perry, March 4, and to Williams, March 14, in ibid., pp. 27–29, 37–38.

22. Barker, *Austin,* pp. 400–405 summarizes these events. Alessio Robles, *Coahuila y Texas,* I, 503–18 and II, 7–41, provides substantial detail.

23. Eugene C. Barker, "Difficulties of a Mexican Revenue Officer in Texas," *SWHQ,* IV (January 1901), pp. 190–202. Barker summarizes this in *Mexico and Texas,* pp. 147–63, and argues convincingly that "well into August the war spirit was confined to a few individuals."

24. Cos to Ugartechea, Saltillo, January 5, 1835, in Jenkins, ed., *Papers of the Texas Revolution,* I, 2.

25. Ugartechea to Cos, San Antonio, March 23, 1835, quoted in a letter from Cos to Tornel, April 14, 1835, in Jenkins, ed., *Papers of the Texas Revolution,* I, 56.

26. Tornel to Cos, Mexico City, April 29, 1835, abstract in Jenkins, ed., *Papers of the Texas Revolution,* I, 85. See, too, Cos to Tornel, Matamoros, May 28, 1835 in ibid., p. 131.

27. Ugartechea to Tenorio, Béxar, June 20, 1835, in Jenkins, ed., *Papers of the Texas Revolution,* I, 156.

28. Cos to Manuel Lafuente, Matamoros, May 28, 1835; Cos to Tornel, Matamoros, May 29, 1835; and Ugartechea to Cos, Béxar, June 29, 1835; all in Jenkins, ed., *Papers of the Texas Revolution,* I, 130, 132, 171–72.

29. See, for example, Ugartechea to the Public, Béxar, July 15, 1835; Cos to the political chiefs of Texas, Matamoros, August 13, 1835; and ad interim president General Miguel Barragán to Cos, Mexico City, August 1, 1835, in Jenkins, ed., *Papers of the Texas Revolution,* I, 241–46, 334–35, 296.

30. Cos to the jefe político of Brazos, August 1, 1835, in Jenkins, ed., *Papers of the Texas Revolution,* I, 298. For Williams' activities at this time, and his escape, see Margaret Swett Henson, *Samuel May Williams, Early Texas Entrepreneur* (College Station, Texas, 1976), pp. 73–75.

31. Zavala to the Colonists, ca. August 7, 1835, in Jenkins, ed., *Papers of the Texas Revolution,* I, 313–15. Raymond Estep, "Lorenzo de Zavala and the Texas Revolution," *SWHQ,* LVIII (January 1954), pp. 322–35, which is based on Estep's more detailed biography: *Lorenzo de Zavala: Profeta del liberalismo mexicano* (Mexico, 1952). See, too, María de la Luz Parcero, *Lorenzo de Zavala: Fuente y origen de la reforma liberal en México* (Mexico, 1969).

32. Ugartechea had received direct and friendly warnings from Americans regarding the sending of troops. See the letters of Edmund Andrews, Brazoria, August 10, 1835, and Thomas Jefferson Chambers, San Felipe, August 15, 1835, in ibid., I, 333, 339–42. See, too, Ugartechea to Cos, July 25, 1835, Béxar, July 25, 1835, in ibid., I, 276.

33. Ugartechea to Austin, Béxar, October 4, 1835 and Ugartechea to Cos, Béxar, July 13, 1835, in Jenkins, ed., *Papers of the Texas Revolution,* II, 40; I, 236. Several letters by Cos in the Archivo de Guerra y Marina, AGN, transcript, vols. 331–333, UT, contain his view that the offensive colonists had to be dealt with severely. See, for example, Cos to José Pizarro

Martínez, Mexican consul in New Orleans, August 12, 1835. See, too, Carlos Bosch García, *Material para la historia diplomática de México: México y los Estados Unidos, 1820-1848* (Mexico, 1956), pp. 181–84.

34. See, for example, William Barrett Travis to Henry Smith, San Felipe, August 24, 1835, and Horatio A. Alsberry to the People of Texas, Columbia, August 28, 1835, both in Jenkins, ed., *Papers of the Texas Revolution*, I, 368, 373–75. David M. Vigness, *The Revolutionary Decades* (Austin, 1965), p. 52, argued that "if any one incident were singled out as being more important than others for bringing the Texans to revolution, it would be the punitive expedition that General Santa Anna led against the city of Zacatecas in the spring of 1835."

35. Travis to David Burnet, San Felipe, August 31, 1835, in Jenkins, ed., *Papers of the Texas Revolution*, I, 379–80. Travis, in apparent euphoria, wrote two other letters in a similar vein that day, see ibid., pp. 380–82.

36. Austin, speech at Brazoria, September 8, 1835, in Eugene C. Barker, ed., *The Austin Papers*, 3 vols. (Washington and Austin, 1924–28), III, 118. See, too, Barker, *Austin*, pp. 410–13. Austin's biographer, Eugene Barker, sees Austin's presence as critical. On August 20, members of the "war party" called for a convention to meet in mid-October to decide on the issue of war or peace. Barker argues that this "would probably have failed had Austin not arrived opportunely and approved it without hesitation or qualification" (*Austin*, p. 409). Most Texas historians agree with Barker's interpretation of Austin's immense influence. See, for example, William C. Binkley, *The Texas Revolution* (Baton Rouge, 1952), p. 67.

37. Austin to his cousin, Mary Holley, New Orleans, August 21, 1835, in Jenkins, ed., *Papers of the Texas Revolution*, I, 361–62. See, too, Austin to David Burnet, San Felipe, October 5, 1835, in ibid., II, 42. Barker outlines the evolution of Austin's attitude toward Mexico in "Stephen F. Austin and the Independence of Texas," *SWHQ*, XIII (April 1910), pp. 257–85.

38. Alessio Robles, *Coahuila y Texas*, II, 55. Carlos E. Castañeda, *Our Catholic Heritage in Texas, 1519–1936*, 7 vols. (Austin, 1931-58), VI, 268. For the condition of the Mexican army see Vicente Filisola, *Memorias para la historia de la guerra de Tejas*, 2 vols. (1st ed., 1848–1849; Mexico, 1973), II, 193–200.

39. Nackman, *A Nation within a Nation*, pp. 28–29. Barker, *Austin*, pp. 428–29.

40. Eugene C. Barker, "The Texas Revolutionary Army," *SWHQ*, IX (April 1906), pp. 244–47. C. Alan Hutchinson," Valentín Gómez Farías. A Biographical Study" (Ph.D. diss., University of Texas, Austin, 1948), pp. 387–408. Gómez Farías to Miguel Barragán, Monterrey, June 2, 1835, in the Gómez Farías Papers, Latin American Collection, UT.

41. W. H. Sledge to James Knight, Columbus, July 19, 1835, in Jenkins, ed., *Papers of the Texas Revolution*, I, 259–60.

42. W. Roy Smith, "The Quarrel Between Governor Smith and the Council of the Provisional Government of the Republic," *SWHQ*, V (April 1902), p. 301. See pp. 296–305, 312–45. See, too, Travis to David Burnet, San Felipe, April 11, 1835 in Jenkins, ed., *Papers of the Texas Revolution*, I, 62.

43. Many accounts of the military phase of the Texas rebellion exist. Perhaps the most balanced and engaging is Walter Lord, *A Time to Stand* (New York, 1961). See, too, James Presley, "Santa Anna in Texas: A Mexican Viewpoint," *SWHQ*, LXII (April 1959), pp. 489–512 and Carlos E. Castañeda, *The Mexican Side of the Texan Revolution* (Dallas, 1928).

44. For United States interest in Texas in the 1820s, see William R. Manning, *Early Diplomatic Relations Between the United States and Mexico* (Baltimore, 1916), pp. 227–348. For Mexican awareness of and reaction to American interest in Texas, see Gene Brack, "Mexican Opinion and the Texas Revolution," *SWHQ*, LXXII (October 1968), pp. 170–77, and Brack, *Mexico Views Manifest Destiny, 1821–1836* (Albuquerque, 1975), pp. 53–71.

45. Nackman, *A Nation within a Nation*, pp. 5–6, 25. For a masterful synthesis of the

question of United States involvement in the Texas revolt and a fine guide to sources, see David M. Pletcher, *The Diplomacy of Annexation: Texas, Oregon, and the Mexican War* (Columbia, Missouri, 1973), pp. 69–72. Carlos Bosch García, *Historia de las relaciones entre México y los Estados Unidos, 1819–1848* (Mexico, 1961), pp. 173–95. See, too, Brack, *Mexico Views Manifest Destiny*, pp. 74–85.

46. David J. Weber, ed., *Foreigners in Their Native Land: Historical Roots of the Mexican Americans* (Albuquerque, 1973), pp. 91–93, summarizes these events. For a fuller account see Fane Downs, "The History of Mexicans in Texas, 1821–1845" (Ph.D. diss., Texas Tech University, 1970), pp. 232–48. Apparently only one *tejano* signed the November 7 declaration: Benjamin Fuqua of Gonzales. Juan A. Padilla and Silvestre de León of Victoria arrived too late, and no delegates came from the war-torn Goliad-San Antonio area (although Encarnación Vásquez was elected from Goliad). See Jenkins, ed., *Papers of the Texas Revolution*, II, 347, and Castañeda, *Our Catholic Heritage*, VI, 273, 277.

47. Quoted in Weber, ed., *Foreigners in Their Native Land*, p. 178.

48. See the remarkable letter of John J. Linn to James Kerr, Guadalupe, July 30, 1835, in Jenkins, ed., *Papers of the Texas Revolution*, I, 288–89.

49. Downs, "History of Mexicans in Texas," pp. 217–27, summarizes this subject ably and provides fresh detail, but misses the important point that the *Representación dirijida por el ilustre ayuntamiento de la ciudad de Béxar al . . . Congreso del Estado* (Brazoria, 1833) did not advocate statehood for Texas, although it agreed with other Anglo goals for Texas. No "astonishing turnabout" occurred, as Downs puts it (p. 226). See, too, Andrew Anthony Tijerina, "Tejanos and Texas: The Native Mexicans of Texas, 1820–1850" (Ph.D. diss., University of Texas at Austin, 1977), pp. 296–316, for an interesting exposition of the *tejanos'* views.

50. Seguín, calling for a meeting at San Antonio, October 14, 1834, in transcripts from Almonte's papers in the ASFC 2-22/640, pp. 98–99, TSA. See, too, Downs, "History of Mexicans in Texas," pp. 228–30.—

51. Weber, ed., *Foreigners in Their Native Land*, pp. 91, 93. Barker, "The Texas Revolutionary Army," pp. 235–39, 259–60.

52. Barker, *Mexico and Texas*, p. 162. See, too, p. 146.

53. Samuel H. Lowrie, *Culture Conflict in Texas* (New York, 1932), p. 118. Lowrie came to the same conclusions as Barker did on this question. See, too, Binkley, *The Texas Revolution*, pp. 129–30; Nackman, *A Nation within a Nation*, p. 138, n. 36.

54. A copy of the circular is in HEH, No. 238151.

55. George Tays, "Commodore Edmund B. Kennedy, U.S.N., versus Governor Nicolás Gutiérrez: An Incident of 1836," *CHSQ*, XII (June 1933), pp. 137–46. For a discussion of the lone star flag see Hubert Howe Bancroft, *History of California*, 7 vols. (San Francsico, 1884–90), III, 468–69. Bernardo Navarrete to Juan N. López Portilla, December 6, 1836, in George Tays, "The Surrender of Monterey by Governor Nicolás Gutiérrez, November 5, 1836, " *CHSQ*, XV (December 1936), p. 358.

56. The first quote is from Alvarado, "Historia de California," 1876, 5 vols., MS, IV, 169–70, BL, and the second is from Alvarado to Abel Stearns, Santa Barbara, January 8, 1836, California Historical Documents Collection, no. 40401, HEH.

57. The motives of the California rebels are analyzed in similar terms by Bancroft, *History of California*, III, 449–50; Tays, "Revolutionary California," pp. 339–42; and Woodrow James Hansen, *The Search for Authority in California* (Oakland, 1960), p. 26. The latter sees home rule as the major issue.

58. Mariano Guadalupe Vallejo, "Recuerdos históricos y personales tocante a la Alta California: historia política del país," 1875, MS, trans. by Earl R. Hewitt as "History of California," MS, III, 66, BL. Alvarado described the incident in similar terms: "Historia de California," MS, III, 52.

59. Alvarado, "Historia de California," MS, III, 45.

60. Chico to the inhabitants of California, broadside, Monterey, July 24, 1836, HEH, R206082.

61. Chico poured out his anguish and anger in a confidential report to the Secretaría de Guerra y Marina, Monterey, July 22, 1836, which appears in full in Alonso Teja Zabre, *Lecciones de California* (Mexico, 1962), pp. 70–83.

62. Quoted in Bancroft, *History of California*, III, 442. Bancroft summarizes Chico's reign with his usual thoroughness in ibid., pp. 414–444. See, too, Tays, "Revolutionary California," pp. 291–332.

63. Quoted in Bancroft, *History of California*, III, 479, n. 27. Bancroft summarizes these events in ibid., pp. 445–79. George Tays provides a detailed account, with numerous translated documents in "The Surrender of Monterey by Governor Nicolás Guitérrez, pp. 338–63. For a first-hand account of the role played by Capt. W. S. Hinckley of the ship *Quijote*, see *The California Diary of Faxon Dean Atherton, 1836–1839*, Doyce B. Nunis, Jr., ed. (San Francisco, 1964), pp. 32, 179, n. 51.

64. Bancroft, *History of California*, III, 450–52, 471–72 provides brief biographical vignettes. Many sources mention that Alvarado promised land and other considerations in exchange for the foreigners' help, and Alvardo himself acknowledges this in his "Historia de California," MS, III, 141. For Abel Stearns, see Doris Marion Wright, *A Yankee in Mexican California: Abel Stearns, 1798–1848* (Santa Barbara, 1977), p. 15.

65. Alvarado to the inhabitants of California, May 10, 1837, broadside, HEH, 433157.

66. Tays, "Revolutionary California," p. 409; Janet Lecompte, "Jean-Baptiste Chalifoux," in LeRoy R. Hafen, ed., *The Mountain Men and the Fur Trade of the Far West*, 10 vols. (Glendale, 1965–1972), VII, 65–67.

67. The decreto was issued on May 23, 1835. After Gutiérrez published it, Monterey remained the capital inpart because no one in Los Angeles took the initiative to furnish a rent-free building for government offices as the governor requested. Tays, "Revolutionary California," p. 279.

68. Tays, "Revolutionary California," pp. 378–81, 409–25.

69. I have depended heavily here on George Tays, "Captain Andrés Castillero, Diplomat. An Account from Unpublished Sources of his Services to Mexico in the Alvarado Revolution of 1836–1838," *CHSQ*, XIV (September 1935), pp. 230–68.

70. Alvarado to Castillero, Santa Barbara, June 30, 1837, quoted in Tays, "Captain Andrés Castillero," p. 242. Alvarado expressed similar sentiments in a letter to Vallejo, July 12, 1837, in ibid., 247, and this was also the essence of Castillero's understanding of the conversation: "I . . . convinced them of the advantages in the new constitutional laws." Castillero to the Commandant of Lower California, San Gabriel, July 18, 1837, in ibid.

71. Alvarado expressed the mistaken notion, in a proclamation on July 9, 1837, that only a *californio* would be appointed governor, quoted in Tays, "Captain Andrés Castillero," p. 245. See, too, p. 248.

72. Tays, ibid., pp. 261–64.

73. Urrea expressed disapproval of the growing American influence in California and separatist sentiment there in a letter to Gómez Farías, Perote prison, April 6, 1840, Gómez Fariás Papers, UT.

74. Robert Conway Stevens, "Mexico's Forgotten Frontier: A History of Sonora, 1821–1846" (Ph.D. diss., University of Arizona, 1963), pp. 144–60. See, too, the analysis by Stuart Voss in *Sonora and Sinaloa in the Neneteenth Century*, to be published by the University of Arizona Press in 1982. Eduardo W. Villa, *Historia del estado de Sonora* (2nd ed., Hermosillo, 1951), pp. 222–25.

75. A facsimile of the plan appears in Benjamin M. Read, *Historia Illustrada de Nuevo México* (Santa Fe, 1911), p. 239, and a translation appears in Read's *Illustrated History of New Mexico* (Santa Fe, 1912), p. 374.

76. Philip Reno, "Rebellion in New Mexico, 1837," *NMHR*, XL (July 1965), pp. 197–210. Daniel Tyler, "Anglo-American Penetration of the Southwest: The View from New Mexico," *SWHQ*, LXXV (January 1972), p. 335.

77. Donaciano Vigil to the Assembly, June 22, 1846, Ritch Collection, no. 233, HEH. Pérez arrrived in Santa Fe about June 20 with the appointment of comandante general, but in the meantime, in April, Santa Anna had extended his authority to include both the civil and military commands. Lansing B. Bloom, "New Mexico Under Mexican Administration, 1821–1846," *Old Santa Fe*, II (July 1914), pp. 3–4.

78. Bloom, "New Mexico Under Mexican Administration," II, pp. 21, 24–25. Donaciano Vigil, "A Statement Concerning Historical Events Between 1801–1851," Samuel Ellison, trans., William G. Ritch, ed., Ritch papers, HEH. Josiah Gregg, *Commerce of the Prairies*, Max L. Moorhead, ed. (Norman, 1954), p. 94.

79. Fray Angélico Chávez, "José Gonzales, Genízaro Governor," *NMHR*, XXX (July 1955), pp. 190–94. Janet Lecompte has called my attention to the signature of José Gonzales on a certificate by Felipe Sena, second alcalde of Santa Fe, September 13, 1837, MANM, roll 23, frame 903. What appears to be a copy of the minutes of the August 27 meeting are in the Ritch Papers, No. 161, HEH. Lecompte, who graciously provided me with a manuscript of her biography of Manuel Armijo, finds no firm evidence that Armijo or Antonio José Martínez attended this meeting, as has been suggested by other writers.

80. Mexico City, *Diario del Gobierno de la República Mexicana*, October 19, 1837, trans. in Read, *Illustrated History*, pp. 378–80.

81. José Caballero's "Proclamation" is in ibid., 380–82.

82. Lecompte, manuscript biography of Armijo, p. 22.

83. Armijo to the Ministro de Guerra y Marina, October 11, 1837, *Diario del Gobierno*, November 30, 1837.

84. Martínez to Bishop José Antonio de Zubiría, Taos, September 25, 1837, Ramo de Justicia, tomo 138, legajo 48, 1831–1848, AGN, microfilm, BL. Reference courtesy of Janet Lecompte.

85. Certificate by Felipe Sena, 2d alcalde of Santa Fe, September 13, 1837, MANM, roll 23, frame 903. Reference courtesy of Janet Lecompte.

86. See the reminiscences of Francisco Perea, eight-years-old at the time: "Santa Fe as it Appeared During the Winter of the Years 1837 and 1838," W. H. H. Allison, ed., *Old Santa Fe*, II (October, 1914), pp. 172–73.

87. The two preceding paragraphs are based on Bloom, "New Mexico Under Mexican Administration, II (July 1914), pp. 31–35. Key documents, such as the Gonzales circular and Armijo's report on the execution of the prisoners appear in Read, *Illustrated History*, pp. 385–89. Also useful was Lecompte's manuscript biography of Armijo.

88. Salazar to Pérez, Tomé, February 14, 1837, MANM, roll 23, frames 323–37. Pérez had also condemned the use of the lower class to do the work of the ricos in a meeting of the diputación on November 21, 1836. Minutes of the diputación, legislative records, 1836, MANM, roll 21, frames 823–26, called to my attention by Janet Lecompte.

89. Armijo to the Ministro de Guerra y Marina, Santa Fe, October 11, 1837 in *Diario del Gobierno*, November 30, 1837.

90. These quotes derive from Armijo's reports to the Ministro de Guerra y Marina, Santa Fe, September 12 and October 11, 1837, published respectively in *Diario del Gobierno*, October 19 and November 30, 1837.

91. Martínez to Bishop Zubiría, Taos, September 25, 1837.

92. Ibid.

93. José Sutton to Governor Armijo, Santa Fe, March 12, 1838, New Mexico Land Grant Papers, report 45, file 61, microfilm roll 17, NMSRC.

94. Taxation as the cause of the revolt appears over and over again in the folklore and

reminiscences of this event. See, for example, the anonymous description in Read, *Illustrated History*, pp. 371–74.

95. Urrea to Valentín Gómez Farías, Perote, April 6, 1840, Gómez Farías Papers, UT. Urrea also noted the hatred that the *californios* had for Mexicans and the close ties developing between Americans and Mexicans.

96. David M. Vigness, "Relations of the Republic of Texas and the Republic of the Rio Grande," *SWHQ*, LVII (January 1954), pp. 312–21, and Vigness, "A Texas Expedition to Mexico, 1840," *SWHQ*, LXII (July 1958), pp. 18–28.

97. Lamar "To the Citizens of Santa Fé, Friends, and Compatriots," Austin, April 14, 1840, in Charles Adams Gulick, Jr., ed., *The Papers of Mirabeau Buoanaparte Lamar from the Original Papers in the Texas State Library* (Austin, 1922), III, 370–71. Pletcher, *The Diplomacy of Annexation*, p. 89.

98. Secretary of State Samuel A. Roberts to William G. Cooke, J. Antonio Navarro, Richard F. Brenham, and William G. Dryden, Austin, June 15, 1841, in George P. Garrison, ed., *Diplomatic Correspondence of the Republic of Texas*, 2 vols. (Washington, 1911), II, 737–43. See, too, Roberts to Cooke, June 15, 1841, in ibid., pp. 743–47. Ward Alan Minge, "Frontier Problems in New Mexico Preceding the Mexican War, 1840–1846" (Ph.D. diss., University of New Mexico, 1965), pp. 9–12.

99. Aurelio M. And J. Manuel Espinosa, "The Texans—A New Mexican Spanish Folk Play of the Middle Nineteenth Century," *New Mexico Quarterly*, XIII (Autumn 1943), p. 308. Minge, "Frontier Problems in New Mexico," pp. 38–45. Noel M. Loomis, *The Texan-Santa Fe Pioneers* (Norman, 1958), is the only book-length treatment of this subject, but must be used with caution for his pro-Texas interpretation defies even his own evidence. More able expositions are: William C. Binkley, "New Mexico and the Texan Santa Fe Expedition," *SWHQ*, XXVII (October 1923), pp. 85–107, and Charles R. McClure, "The Texan-Santa Fe Expedition of 1841," *NMHR*, XLVIII (January 1973), pp. 45–56.

100. *La Luna* (Chihuahua City), June 29, 1841, quoted in Brack, *Mexico Views Manifest Destiny*, p. 99. Brack provides an excellent discussion of Mexican attitudes toward Texas and the dangers of losing still more territory. See, especially, pp. 95–111.

101. *El siglo diez y nueve*, December 15, 1842 quoted in Brack, *Mexico Views Manifest Destiny*, p. 108.

102. Bancroft, *History of California*, IV, 366 takes a sympathetic view of the cholos' plight and argues that the *californios* exaggerated their excesses as a "justification for later revolt."

103. Eustace Barron to the Earl of Aberdeen, Tepic, January 20, 1844, reporting a conversation with Castañares, quoted in Sheldon G. Jackson, "The British and the California Dream: Rumors, Myths and Legends," *SCQ*, LVII (Fall 1975), pp. 259–60.

104. Castañares to the Ministro de Relaciones Exteriores y Gobernación, Mexico, June 25, 1844, in Castañares, *Colección de documentos relativos al departamento de Californias* (Mexico, 1845), p. 18, facsimile in Weber, ed., *Northern Mexico*.

105. Sheldon G. Jackson, "Two Pro-British Plots in Alta California," *SCQ*, LXV (Summer 1973), pp. 107–112. Tays, "Revolutionary California," pp. 475–93. Bancroft, *History of California*, IV, 350–517, provides the most detail.

106. John Marsh to Lewis Cass, January 20, 1846, in "Letter of Dr. John Marsh to Hon. Lewis Cass," *CHSQ*, XXII (December 1943), pp. 316–17.

107. This is the conclusion of Tays, "Revolutionary California," pp. 528–32.

108. Ibid., p. 634. Tays outlines the Castro-Pico split in detail, pp. 605–37.

109. Stevens, "Mexico's Forgotten Frontier," pp. 160–64.

110. Armijo to the Minister of War, June 17 and July 12, 1840, quoted in Binkley, "New Mexico and the Texas Santa Fe Expedition," pp. 92–93.

111. Ibid., p. 101.

112. Pronunciamento by the Departmental Assembly, January 1, 1844, published in the *Diario del Gobierno*, March 30, 1844, and quoted in Minge, "Frontier Problems," p. 154.

113. Mariano Chávez in answer to Manuel Armijo, before the Assembly, Santa Fe, January 1, 1844, in *Diario del Gobierno*, March 30, 1844, quoted in ibid., pp. 156–157.

114. Vigil to the Departmental Assembly, June 22, 1846, Ritch Papers, no. 233, HEH. Ironically, the Departmental Assembly nominated Martínez for the governorship and then apparently had cause to regret it. Martínez apparently had come to New Mexico in the fall of 1843 as military commander, then received his appointment as governor on May 15, 1844. For details about his appointment and departure see Minge, "Frontier Problems," pp. 158–59, 167–69, 188–89. Traditional sources reveal little about Martínez. See, for example, Bloom, "New Mexico Under Mexican Administration," II (October 1914), p. 162.

115. A copy of this protest, which is dated December 30, 1845, purports to be the product of the governor, legislative bodies, officials, "and other notable persons," but is unsigned and I have found no other corroborating documents which explain who drafted it and why. Misc. docs., 1845, MANM, roll 40, frame 645.

116. Minge, "Frontier Problems," p. 322. Minge provides the best account of the last years of Mexican rule in New Mexico.

Chapter 13
The Mexican Frontier in Perspective

1. The most recent authoritative account of these and other military events is K. Jack Bauer, *The Mexican War, 1846–1848* (New York, 1974), pp. 170–71, 133–34. I have also used Dwight L. Clarke, *Stephen Watts Kearny: Soldier of the West* (Norman, 1961), pp. 142–43.

2. David M. Pletcher, *The Diplomacy of Annexation: Texas, Oregon, and the Mexican War* (Columbia, Mo., 1973), p. 610.

3. An account of these events, notable for its brevity and clarity, is Jack D. Rittenhouse, *Disturnell's Treaty Map* (Santa Fe, 1965), which contains a facsimile of the map.

4. Manuel Alvarez to Hon. James Buchanan, Consular Office, Santa Fe, September 4, 1846, in Harold Dunham, ed., "Sidelights on Santa Fe Traders, 1839–1846," *The Brand book* (Denver, 1950), p. 10. George Tays, ed. and trans., "Pío Pico's Correspondence with the Mexican Government, 1846–1848," *CHSQ*, XIII (June 1934), pp. 99–149. Benjamin M. Read, *Illustrated History of New Mexico* (Santa Fe, 1912), pp. 417–18. Daniel Tyler, "Governor Armijo's Moment of Truth," *JW*, XI (April 1972), pp. 307–16.

5. Quoted in David J. Weber, ed., *Foreigners in Their Native Land: Historical Roots of the Mexican Americans* (Albuquerque, 1973), p. 126. Ibid., pp. 97–99, summarizes the reactions of the pobladores to the conquest.

6. "Narrative of Julio Carrillo . . . ," *Antepasados*, I (fall 1970), p. 20.

7. Quoted in Weber, ed., *Foreigners in Their Native Land*, p. 131.

8. Anonymous, *Considerations on the Political and Social Situation of the Mexican Republic, 1847*, Dennis E. Berge, trans. and ed. (El Paso, 1975), p. 28, and pp. 24–30.

9. Reprinted in various sources, among them: Ray Allen Billington, ed., *Frontier and Section: Selected Essays of Frederick Jackson Turner* (Englewood Cliffs, N.J., 1961), pp. 37–62.

10. Ray Allen Billington emphatically and convincingly argues this case in *America's Frontier Heritage* (New York, 1966).

11. Roderick Nash, *Wilderness and the American Mind* (New Haven, 1967), p. 3, hints at the contradiction in American attitudes toward an "uninhabited" wilderness where settlers feared attack by Indians (ibid., pp. 7, 24, 28). For critiques of the notion of a wilderness devoid of man, see John Opie's provocative essay, "Frontier History in Environmental

Perspective," in Jerome O. Steffen, ed., *The American West: New perspectives, New Dimensions* (Norman, 1979), pp. 19–21, and Jack D. Forbes, "Frontiers in American History and the Role of the Frontier Historian," *Ethnohistory*, XV (Spring 1968), pp. 203–35. For an excellent statement of frontiers as "of social, not geographic origin," see Owen Lattimore, "The Frontier in History," in Robert A. Manners and David Kaplan, eds., *Theory in Anthropology* (Chicago, 1968), p. 375.

12. Ray Allen Billington, "The Frontier in American Thought and Character," in *The New World Looks at Its History*, Archibald R. Lewis and Thomas F. McGann, eds. (Austin, 1963), p. 77.

13. Billington, *America's Frontier Heritage*, p. 54. Geographer Carl O. Sauer, one of Turner's critics, argued the same point in 1930, quoted in Marvin W. Mikesell, "Comparative Studies in Frontier History," *Annals of the Association of American Geographers*, L (March 1960), p. 63.

14. Billington, *America's Frontier Heritage*, p. 54.

15. See, for example, C. H. Haring, *The Spanish Empire in America* (New York, 1947), pp. 30–41; Salvador de Madariaga, *Ingleses, franceses, españoles* (1st ed., 1928; Buenos Aires, 1969); James Lange, *Conquest and Commerce: Spain and England in the Americas* (New York, 1975); Donald E. Worcester, "Historical and Cultural Sources of Spanish Resistance to Change," *Journal of Inter-American Studies*, VI (April 1964), pp. 173–80. Arthur L. Campa, "Cultural Differences that Cause Conflict and Misunderstanding in the Spanish Southeast," *Western Review*, IX (Spring 1972), pp. 23–30.

16. Turner, "The Significance of the Frontier," p. 31.

17. Mikesell, "Comparative Studies in Frontier History," p. 65. Writers who have compared the Spanish-Mexican and Anglo-American frontiers in North America include: Donald J. Lehmer, "The Second Frontier: The Spanish," in Robert G. Ferris, ed., *The American West: An Appraisal* (Santa Fe, 1963), pp. 141–50. Billington, "The Frontier in American Thought and Character," pp. 79–80; *John Francis Bannon, The Spanish Borderlands Frontier, 1513–1821* (New York, 1970), pp. 3–7; Oakah L. Jones, Jr., *Los Paisanos: Spanish Settlers on the Northern Frontier of New Spain* (Norman, 1979), pp. 253–54. On a broader canvas, see Alistair Hennessy's chapter, "The Turner Thesis and Latin America," in *The Frontier in Latin America* (Albuquerque, 1978), pp. 6–27, with its good bibliographic essay.

18. Quoted in Weber, ed., *Foreigners in Their Native Land*, pp. 36–37.

19. Ibid., p. 37. Manuel Armijo similarly described his fellow New Mexicans as "honest citizens who understand and know how to value their rights . . . free, hardworking, and, as a result, they are strong." *Bando, Manuel Armijo . . . a sus habitantes*, Santa Fe, July 16, 1846, MANM, roll 27, frame 1265. Some of this may be discounted as rhetoric, since Armijo was appealing to his fellow citizens to defend themselves against Texas invaders.

20. Turner, "The Significance of the Frontier," p. 44. In recent years American historians have ascribed a more central role to urban centers in settling the American West, but it seems to me that the urban impulse in Hispanic America was stronger. Anglo-American and Hispanic urban traditions are compared briefly in C. H. Haring, *The Spanish Empire in America* (New York, 1947), pp. 158–60.

21. Billington, "The Frontier in American Thought and Character," p. 77. Silvio Zavala has termed the sixteenth century frontier of New Spain "a land of opportunity," but notes that "whenever an embattled frontier developed . . . it was not easy to sustain the conqueror's enthusiasm." "The Frontiers of Hispanic America," in Walker D. Wyman and Clifton B. Kroeber, eds., *The Frontier in Perspective* (Madison, 1965), p. 45. By the late colonial period, conditions had changed substantially. For a good, brief discussion of the frontier as an area that stifled initiative, see Odie B. Faulk, *The Last Year of Spanish Texas, 1778–1821* (The Hague, 1964), pp. 141–43.

22. For a different point of view, see C. Alan Hutchinson, *Frontier Settlement in Mexican California: The Híjar-Padrés Colony and its Origins, 1769-1835* (New Haven, 1969), pp. 397-98.

23. Lattimore, "The Frontier in History," p. 374.

24. Jerome O. Steffen, *Comparative Frontiers: A Proposal for Studying the American West* (Norman, 1980), p. xi.

25. A considerable literature on this subject exists, and the essential difference between Río Abajo and Río Arriba have been well known, but for an especially wide-ranging, clear-yet-subtle statement, see John R. Van Ness, "Hispanic Village Organization in Northern New Mexico: Corporate Community Structure in Historical and Comparative Perspective," in *The Survival of Spanish American Villages*, Paul Kutsche, ed., *Colorado College Studies*, No. 15 (Colorado Springs, 1979), pp. 21-44.

26. Hutchinson, *Frontier Settlement in Mexican California*, p. 339. The *californios* were widely reputed to be indolent by outsiders, but indolence may exist largely in the eye of the beholder. See David J. Langum, "Californios and the Image of Indolence," *WHQ*, IX (April 1978), pp. 181-96, and my response and Langum's reply, *WHQ*, X (January 1979), pp. 61-69.

27. An interesting analysis of this question is in Frances León Swadesh, *Los Primeros Pobladores. Hispanic Americans of the Ute Frontier* (Notre Dame, 1974), pp. 25, 148, 170-73, who sees nomadic Indians as "both a threat and an opportu;nity" for the frontiersmen (p. 20).

28. Frank McNitt, *Navajo Wars: Military Campaigns, Slave Raids, and Reprisals* (Albuquerque, 1972), p. 80, and my discussion of this in chapter five, n. 68.

29. Billington, "The Frontier in American Thought and Culture," pp. 78-79.

30. Immanuel Wallerstein, "The Rise and Future Demise of the World Capitalist System: Concepts for Comparative Analysis," *Comparative Studies in Society and History*, XVI (September 1974), p. 403.

31. Ignacio Zúñiga, *Rápida ojeada al estado de Sonora, dirigida y dedicada al supremo gobierno de la nación* (Mexico, 1835), p. 61, facsimile in David J. Weber, ed., *Northern Mexico On the Eve of the United States Invasion. Rare Imprints . . .* (New York, 1976).

32. Lorenzo de Zavala, *Ensayo histórico de las revoluciones de México*, 2 vols. (Paris and New York, 1831, 1832), reprinted in Manuel González Ramírez, ed., *Lorenzo de Zavala. Obras* (Mexico, 1969), p. 432 (called to my attention by Silvio Zavala, "Frontiers of Hispanic America," pp. 49-50).

33. Ibid., pp. 432, 532. Zavala elaborates on this theme in his *Viage a los Estados Unidos del Norte de America* (Paris, 1834), pp. 69, 141-42, 366-67.

34. Writing about the colonial period, Alistair Hennessy argues: "Peripheral areas were never strong enough to modify the centralizing, authoritarian tendencies of the Spanish state. . . . " *The Frontier in Latin American History*, p. 14.

35. Quoted in William Kennedy, *Texas: The Rise, Progress, and Prospects of the Republic of Texas*, 2 vols. (London, 1841), II, 34.

36. Juan N. Almonte, *Noticia estadística sobre Tejas* (Mexico, 1835), p. 40. Facsimile in Weber, ed., *Northern Mexico*. See, too José María Sánchez, "A Trip to Texas in 1828," Carlos E. Castañeda, trans., *SWHQ*, XXIX (April 1926), pp. 250-51, 258, 270-71, 273-74, 281.

37. Woodrow Borah, "Discontinuity and Continuity in Mexican History," *PHR*, XLVIII (February 1979), p. 15. Philip Wayne Powell makes the same point in *Mexico's Miguel Caldera: The Taming of America's First Frontier, 1548-1597* (Tucson, 1977), p. 262, and draws comparisons between the military frontiers of sixteenth-century Mexico and nineteenth-century United States. Zavala, "Frontiers of Hispanic America," p. 51, takes the opposite view.

38. Enrique Florescano, "Colonización, ocupación del suelo y 'frontera' en el norte de

Nueva España, 1521–1750," in Alvaro Jara, ed., *Tierras nuevas. Expansión territorial y ocupa-cion del suelo en América, siglos xvi-xix* (Mexico, 1969), p. 45.

39. Vito Alessio Robles, "Las provincias del norte de México hasta 1846," in *Memoria del Primer Congreso de Historiadores de México y los Estados Unidos* . . . (Mexico, 1950), p. 146. Miguel León-Portilla, "The Norteño Variety of Mexican Culture: An Ethnohistorical Approach," in Edward H. Spicer and Raymond H. Thompson, eds., *Plural Society in the Southwest* (New York, 1972), pp. 109–14. (León-Portilla amplified this essay in his book *Culturas en peligro* [Mexico, 1976], see especially pp. 180–86.) María Luisa Rodríguez Sala de Gómezgil, *El esterotipo del mexicano. Estudio psicosocial* (Mexico, 1965), pp. 95–96. For a popular, disjointed, but interesting exposition of this viewpoint, see Hernán Solís Garza, *Los mexicanos del norte* (Mexico, 1971).

40. Jones, *Los Paisanos*, p. 253. See, too, Zavala, "Frontiers of Hispanic America," p. 51, and Barry Carr, "The Peculiarities of the Mexican North, 1880–1928: An Essay in Interpretation," *Institute of Latin American Studies Occasional Papers*, no. 4 (Glasgow, 1971), who finds in the north: "radicalism and anti-clerical affiliations, its vigorous nationalism bordering on xenophobia, and its highly creative opportunism" (p.1). Like other writers, Carr attributes some of the characteristics of the northerners to influence of the United States in the border region.

41. Powell, *Mexico's Miguel Caldera*, p. 226.

Bibliographical Essay

Because voluminous literature, both primary and secondary, treats themes relating to Mexico's far northern frontier from 1821 to 1846, this essay cannot be exhaustive, only suggestive. That most of the authors represented here are from the United States is only partly due to my efforts to discuss sources for a largely English language readership. More important, the predominance of Anglo-American authors reflects the nature of the historical literature. Anglo-Americans, to whom the Southwest now belongs, have written more about this region than have Mexicans.

The number of sources cited in the notes to this volume and listed in this essay may seem to suggest that historians have exhausted the subject. As specialists know, we have only scratched the surface. Massive archival collections, both in Mexico and the United States, have yet to be examined in detail, and exciting challenges and new discoveries await the serious researcher. Those who want to look beyond the published sources ought to orient themselves with two fine guides: *Research in Mexican History: Topics, Methodology, Sources, and a Practical Guide to Field Research*, Richard E. Greenleaf and Michael C. Meyer, eds. (Lincoln, 1973), and Henry Putney Beers' tour de force, *Spanish and Mexican Records of the American Southwest: A Bibliographical Guide to Archive and Manuscript Sources* (Tucson, 1979).

Most sources discussed in this essay deal with many themes and do not fit neatly into one category. Nonetheless, in order to give shape to this essay, I have arranged sources under a variety of headings. Part I contains general secondary studies, key works on U.S.-Mexican relations, and published primary sources and biographies of such breadth that I utilized them in more than one chapter in this book. Part II contains sources which specifically treat themes dealt with in each chapter, although as my notes suggest, each chapter is based upon a much larger selection of sources, including those mentioned in Part I of the essay, and unpublished documents.

Part I

Historiography

The historiography of the Mexican frontier centers on questions relating to individual Southwestern states rather than on broad themes that cut across modern state boundaries. Students of this period must learn the historiography of four separate regions: California, Arizona, New Mexico, and Texas. For a general analysis of the historical literature, see

David J. Weber, "Mexico's Far Northern Frontier, 1821–1854: Historiography Askew," *WHQ*, VII (July 1976), pp. 279–93. A number of essays analyze Mexican historiography in general. The most up-to-date work, which treats the early nineteenth century in detail, is the fine analysis by Stephen R. Niblo and Laurens B. Perry, "Recent Additions to Nineteenth-Century Mexican Historiography," *Latin American Research Review*, XIII, 3 (1978), pp. 3–45.

Bibliographical Guides

No comprehensive bibliography treats Mexico's Far North in the years 1821–1846. My own "Mexico's Far Northern Frontier, 1821–1845: A Critical Bibliography," *AW*, XIX (Autumn 1977), pp. 225–66, characterizes 160 secondary books and articles, omitting primary sources and works relating to themes treated elsewhere in the *AW* series.

For general Mexican bibliography during these years, the starting points should be Joseph Barnard and Randall Rasmussen, "A Bibliography of Bibliographies for the History of Mexico," *Latin American Research Review*, XIII, 2 (1978), pp. 229–35; for sources relating to the American West as it impinged on northern Mexico, Rodman W. Paul and Richard W. Etulain, *The Frontier and the American West* (Arlington Heights, Illinois, 1977), is a topically organized bibliography.

Bibliographies treating individual states include Thomas W. Streeter's monumental *Bibliography of Texas, 1795–1845*, 5 vols. (Cambridge, Mass., 1955–60); Robert G. Cowan's still valuable *A Bibliography of the History of California, 1510–1930*, 3 vols. (San Francisco, 1933); Andrew Wallace, ed., *Sources and Readings in Arizona History: A Checklist of Literature Concerning Arizona's Past* (Tucson, 1965); and Frances León Swadesh, *20,000 Years of History: A New Mexico Bibliography* (Santa Fe, 1973). Themes of regional significance have been the subject of excellent bibliographies. A model is Jack D. Rittenhouse, *The Santa Fe Trail: A Historical Bibliography* (Albuquerque, 1971). Robert Greenwood, ed., *California Imprints, 1833–1862: A Bibliography* (Los Gatos, Calif., 1961), exemplifies the kind of guides that exist for specialized subjects.

Major historical journals devoted to the region, such as the *California Historical Quarterly*, the *Southern California Quarterly*, *Arizona and the West*, the *Journal of Arizona History*, the *New Mexico Historical Review*, and the *Southwestern Historical Quarterly*, all have valuable cumulative indices which can lead a student quickly to specific subjects. The most convenient topical guide to articles from a variety of scholarly journals is Oscar Osburn Winther, *A Classified Bibliography of the Periodical Literature of the Trans-Mississippi West, 1811–1957* (Bloomington, 1964) and its *Supplement (1957–67)*, compiled by Winther and Richard A. Van Orman (Bloomington, 1970).

Some of the best guides to books and articles on special themes take the form of bibliographies in specific monographs and general secondary sources.

General Secondary Studies

The best recent overviews of the history of Mexico's first decades of independence are: Agustín Cué Cánovas, *Historia social y económica de Mexico, 1521–1854* (3rd ed., Mexico, 1967); Josefina Zoraida Vázquez's essay, "Los primeros tropiezos," in Daniel Cosío Villegas et al., *Historia General de México*, 4 vols. (Mexico, 1976); the unwieldy but gracefully written *Orígenes de la república mexicana: la aurora constitucional*, by José C. Valadés (Mexico, 1972); and Michael C. Meyer and William L. Sherman, *The Course of Mexican History* (New York, 1979). The most balanced and vivid account of the westward expansion of America as it intersected with northern Mexico in these years, remains Ray Allen Billington's *The Far Western Frontier, 1830–1860* (New York, 1956).

For an understanding of Spain's role in North America prior to Mexican independence, John Francis Bannon's *Spanish Borderlands Frontier, 1513–1821* (1st ed., 1970; Albuquerque, 1974), is the indispensable starting point. It contains an excellent bibliography, which is updated in Weber, ed., *New Spain's Far Northern Frontier: Essays on Spain in the American West, 1540–1821* (Albuquerque, 1979),

No single volume surveys Mexico's northern frontier from 1821 to 1846, but several writers have examined this era as part of an overview of the American Southwest: W. Eugene Hollon, *The Southwest: Old and New* (New York, 1961); Odie B. Faulk, *Land of Many Frontiers: A History of the American Southwest* (New York, 1968); Lynn I. Perrigo, *The American Southwest: Its Peoples and Cultures* (New York, 1971); David Lavender, *The Southwest* (New York, 1980).

More detailed overviews of the Mexican era appear in studies of individual states. Although subsequent research has clarified and amplified his studies considerably, Hubert Howe Bancroft's encyclopedic histories of Mexico and individual western states, published as his *Works*, 39 vols. (San Francisco, 1882–90), remain of remarkable value. Bancroft's *History of California*, 7 vols. (San Francisco, 1886–90), is far more detailed than his treatments of Arizona, New Mexico, or Texas. Many recent texts examine California, but those that do most justice to the Mexican era are: John Walton Caughey, *California* (Englewood Cliffs, N.J., 1953); Andrew F. Rolle, *California: A History* (New York, 1963); and Walton Bean, *California: An Interpretive History* (New York, 1968). All have appeared in subsequent editions. For Arizona, Jay J. Wagoner's *Early Arizona: Prehistory to Civil War* (Tucson, 1975), treats the Mexican era only briefly, but is still the best starting point. The same may be said for Warren A. Beck's dated *New Mexico: A History of Four Centuries* (Norman, 1962). For Texas, one can turn with confidence to T. R. Fehrenbach, *Lone Star: A History of Texas and the Texans* (New York, 1968); Seymour V. Connor, *Texas: A History* (New York, 1971); or one of several editions of *Texas: The Lone Star State* by Rupert N. Richardson, Ernest Wallace, and Adrian Anderson (3rd ed.; Englewood Cliffs, 1970). Many of the older state histories, such as Benjamin M. Read's *Illustrated History of New Mexico* (Santa Fe, 1912), which first appeared in a 1911 Spanish edition, and Francis White Johnson, *A History of Texas and Texans*, Eugene C. Barker and Ernest William Winkler, eds., 5 vols. (Chicago, 1916), remain of value because they quote unpublished sources extensively.

An understanding of developments in Mexican states contiguous to the modern border often illuminates events in the states immediately to the north. Basic modern introductions to the north Mexican states include: Pablo L. Martínez, *Historia de Baja California* (Mexico, 1956); Eduardo W. Villa, *Historia del estado de Sonora* (2nd ed., Hermosillo, 1951); and Francisco R. Almada, *Resumen de historia del Estado de Chihuahua* (Mexico 1955).

A few general works focus almost exclusively on the Mexican era in individual states. For Texas, see the concise, solid overview by David M. Vigness, *The Revolutionary Decades*, in *The Saga of Texas Series*, Seymour V. Connor, ed. (Austin, 1965), and Carlos E. Castañeda, *Transition Period: The Fight for Freedom, 1810–1836* (Austin, 1950), vol. V of *Our Catholic Heritage in Texas, 1519–1936*, 7 vols. (Austin, 1931–58), which is more comprehensive than its title suggests. Vito Alessio Robles, *Coahuila y Texas, desde la consumación de la independencia hasta el tratado de paz de Guadalupe Hidalgo*, 2 vols. (Mexico, 1945–46), is the only attempt to examine this political unit in its entirety for the years 1821 to 1836. It treats Coahuila lightly, perhaps because so little secondary literature exists, and synthesizes English language sources on Texas. Of considerable value for many aspects of Texas history in these years are two doctoral dissertations: Fane Downs, "The History of Mexicans in Texas, 1820–1845" (Texas Tech University, 1970), and Andrew Anthony Tijerina, "Tejanos and Texas: The Native Mexicans of Texas, 1820–1850" (University of Texas at Austin, 1978).

The best single study of Sonora during these years has not yet been published: Robert

Conway Stevens, "Mexico's Forgotten Frontier: A History of Sonora, 1821–1846" (Ph.D. diss., University of California, Berkeley, 1964). This will be superseded in some respects by Stuart Voss's new broader study: *Sonora and Sinaloa in the Nineteenth Century*, scheduled for publication by the University of Arizona Press in 1982.

Dated, yet still immensely valuable because it is based heavily on archival sources, is Lansing Bartlett Bloom's "New Mexico Under Mexican Administration, 1821–1846," *Old Santa Fe*, published serially in eight installments between July 1913 and April 1915. Two unpublished doctoral dissertations, done at the University of New Mexico, go beyond Bloom for the years they treat: Daniel Tyler, "New Mexico in the 1820's: The First Administration of Manuel Armijo" (1970), and Ward Alan Minge, "Frontier Problems in New Mexico Preceding the Mexican War, 1840–1846" (1965).

James Woodrow Hansen, *The Search for Authority in California* (Oakland, 1960), focuses on political history for the years 1821–1850, but also strays into other topics; behind a façade of sloppy editing and bookmaking lies a thoughtful analysis. Although its title suggests a narrower study, C. Alan Hutchinson's *Frontier Settlement in Mexican California: The Híjar- Padrés Colony, and Its Origins, 1769–1835* (New Haven, 1969), is so broad, carefully researched, and original, that I found it indispensable for many chapters in this book. Two doctoral dissertations done at the University of California, Berkeley, treat California during these years and are broader than their titles imply: George Tays, "Revolutionary California: The Political History of California from 1820 to 1848" (1932; revised, 1934), and Jessie Davis Francis, "An Economic and Social History of Mexican California" (1935), a projected two volume work, of which only that entitled "Mainly Economic" appeared.

United States-Mexican Diplomatic Relations

Many of the events examined in this book can only be understood within the larger context of Mexican-United States relations. Those in search of more background than I have provided should consult two works in English that focus precisely on these years: William R. Manning, *Early Diplomatic Relations Between the United States and Mexico* (Baltimore, 1916), which focuses on the 1820s and 1830s, and G. L. Rives, *The United States and Mexico, 1821–1848*, 2 vols. (New York, 1913), who carried the story through the Mexican-American War. For a scholarly, balanced Mexican viewpoint which, curiously, relies heavily on archival sources from the United States, see Carlos Bosch García, *Historia de las relaciones entre México y los Estados Unidos, 1819–1848* (Mexico, 1961), and the same writer's collection of documents: *Material para la historia diplomática de México: México y los Estados Unidos, 1820–1848* (Mexico, 1956).

For causes of the Mexican-American War, the latest of many essays on historiography is Thomas Benjamin, "Recent Historiography of the Origins of the Mexican War," *NMHR*, LIV (July 1979), pp. 169–81. Gene M. Brack has made an important contribution to understanding Mexico's response to American aggression and American attitudes of superiority toward Mexicans in: *Mexico Views Manifest Destiny, 1821–1846: An Essay on the Origins of the Mexican War* (Albuquerque, 1975). The most complete, sensitive, and subtle analysis of reasons for American involvement is David M. Pletcher, *The Diplomacy of Annexation: Texas, Oregon, and the Mexican War* (Columbia, Mo., 1973). Scholars still continue to debate the causes of the war. See, for example, Ward McAfee, "A Reconsideration of the Origins of the Mexican-American War," *SCQ*, LXII (Spring 1980), pp. 49–65, and Norman A Graebner, "The Mexican War: A Study in Causation," *PHR*, XLIX (August 1980), pp. 405–26. Some contributions to this debate are polemical rather than scholarly, and works such as Stanford H. Montaigne, *Blood Over Texas* (New Rochelle, N. Y., 1976), and Gilberto López y Rivas, *La guerra del '47 y la resistencia popular a la ocupación* (Mexico, 1976), add little to our understanding. Historian Gene Brack wrote of the latter: "the superficiality of its scholarship is matched only by the simplicity of its analysis." K. Jack Bauer, *The Mexican War, 1846–1848* (New York, 1974), is the best single work on military engagements, and he also addresses the question of causation.

Journals, Letters, and Accounts by Foreign-Born Travelers and Residents:

Their prejudices notwithstanding, outsiders often provide the best window into other cultures because they comment on matters that official documents overlook or that natives regard as too commonplace to merit attention. I have relied upon accounts by outsiders in nearly every chapter of this study. Those interested in foreign views of Mexico and her Far North during these years will find excellent guidance in bibliographies: C. Harvey Gardiner, "Foreign Travelers' Accounts of Mexico, 1810–1910," *The Americas*, VIII (January 1952), pp. 321–51; Drewey Wayne Gunn, *Mexico in American and British Letters: A Bibliography of Fiction and Travel Books Citing Original Editions* (Metuchen, N. J., 1974); and Garold Cole, *American Travelers to Mexico, 1821–1972: A Descriptive Bibliography* (Troy, New York, 1978). Gunn's and Cole's bibliographies are lightly annotated.

Travel literature is too extensive to discuss in detail here, and the existence of good bibliographies makes it unnecessary. The classic example of the genre, as it pertains to central Mexico, is: Howard T. Fisher and Marion Hall Fisher, eds., *Life in Mexico. The Letters of Fanny Calderón de la Barca* . . . (Garden City, 1966), the finest edition of this account (first published in 1843) by the Scottish-American wife of the Spanish ambassador, who lived in Mexico City, 1839–42.

Travel literature pertaining to Mexican Texas is analyzed in a fine essay in a work with broader chronological boundaries: Marilyn McAdams Sibley, *Travelers in Texas, 1761–1860* (Austin, 1967), pp. 176–84. Although extensive, the writings of many travelers in Texas are of limited interest to an understanding of the Mexican frontier because their authors did not venture farther into Texas than the American colonies. Such was the case with the classic appreciation of Texas by Stephen Austin's cousin, Mary Austin Holley, *Texas: Observations, Historical, Geographical and Descriptive* . . . *1831* (Baltimore, 1833), and the anonymous author of *A Visit to Texas* [1831]: *Being the Journal of a Traveller through Those Parts Most interesting to American Settlers* . . . (New York, 1834). A facsimile of Mary Austin Holley's *Texas*, along with previously unpublished letters, appears in Mattie Austin Hatcher, ed., *Letters of an Early American Traveller: Mary Austin Holley, Her Life and Her Works, 1784–1846* (Dallas, 1933). Among accounts by Americans who visited San Antonio in the Mexican era are two candid works not designed for immediate publication: "J. C. Clopper's Journal and Book of Memoranda for 1828," *SWHQ*, XIII (July 1909), pp. 44–80, and the accounts of three journeys to Texas between 1830 and 1835 by the observant abolitionist Benjamin Lundy, published in *The Life, Travels and Opinions of Benjamin Lundy* . . . (Philadelphia, 1847). Although they visited Texas following the revolt when some conditions had begun to change, two travelers who left especially useful descriptions of San Antonio were these: *Texas in 1837: An Anonymous, Contemporary Narrative* (Austin, 1958), and *Bollaert's Texas* [1843], W. Eugene Hollon and Ruth Lapham Butler, eds. (Norman, 1956). A major recent addition to the literature is Jean Louis Berlandier, *Journey to Mexico During the Years 1826–1834*, C. H. Muller and Katherine K. Muller, eds., and Sheila M. Ohlendorf, Josette M. Bigelow, and Mary M. Standifer, trans., 2 vols. (Austin, 1980). This Swiss scientist made two journeys to Texas, in 1828–29, and in 1834, and commented on an extraordinary range of subjects. For the entire Mexican period in Texas, Eugene C. Barker, ed., *The Austin Papers*, 3 vols. (Washington and Austin, 1924–28), is extraordinarily rich and includes Mexican as well as American documents.

For New Mexico, the best guide to travel literature of the era is Rittenhouse's *The Santa*

Fe Trail, Josiah Gregg, *The Commerce of the Prairies,* Max L. Moorhead, ed. (1st ed. 1844; Norman, 1954), is so balanced and wide-ranging that it deserves its reputation as a classic. Valuable glimpses of New Mexico prior to the period that Gregg knew first-hand are in *The Road to Santa Fe: The Journal and Diaries of George Champlin Sibley* [1825–26], Kate L. Gregg, ed. (Albuquerque, 1952); the biased and boastful trapper James Ohio Pattie, *The Personal Narrative of James O. Pattie* [1825–1830], introduction by William H. Goetzmann (1st ed., 1831; Philadelphia, 1962), whose rambling took him through Arizona and California; and the romanticized but fascinating travel account and short fiction of Albert Pike, *Prose Sketches and Poems Written in the Western Country (with Additional Stories),* David J. Weber, ed. (1st ed., 1834; Albuquerque, 1967), who went west over the Santa Fe trail in 1831 and returned eastward in 1832 through an area of Texas that no previous traveler had described. New Mexico in the late 1830s and early 1840s is the subject of two extraordinarily rich accounts: colorful articles by a journalist, *Matt Field on the Santa Fe Trail* [1839], John E. Sunder, ed. (Norman, 1960); George W. Kendall, a journalist whose visit to New Mexico as a member of the ill-fated Texas-Santa Fe expedition was less happy: *Narrative of the Texas Santa Fe Expedition. . . ,* 2 vols. (New York, 1844).

The United States-Mexican War brought to the region a host of outsiders who recorded their impressions. Their accounts are too numerous to list. Especially noteworthy are the folowing: the diary of an eighteen-year-old woman, *Down the Santa Fe Trail and Into Mexico: Diary of Susan Shelby Magoffin, 1846–47,* Stella M. Drumm, ed., foreword by Howard R. Lamar (1st ed., 1926; New Haven, 1962); the account of seventeen-year-old Lewis Garrard, *Wah-to-yah and the Taos Trail* (1st ed., 1850; Palo Alto, 1968); the writings of an experienced English traveler, George F. Ruxton, *Adventures in Mexico and the Rocky Mountains* (London, 1847), and Ross Calvin, ed., *Lieutenant Emory Reports . . .* (Albuquerque, 1951), who traveled on to California via southern Arizona in 1846.

The relatively few travelers who passed through what is today Arizona were chiefly trappers, although some good glimpses of the region appear in the accounts of American troops and gold-seekers who passed through the region during and after the Mexican War. Kenneth Hufford, "Travelers on the Gila Trail, 1824–1850," *JAH,* VII (Spring 1966), pp. 1–8; VIII (Spring 1967), pp. 30–44, provides a convenient, annotated listing of that literature. *Hepah, California! The Journal of Cave Johnson Couts from Monterey, Nuevo León, Mexico, to Los Angeles, California During the Years 1848–1849,* Henry F. Dobyns, ed. (Tucson, 1961), displays an especially keen eye for details of everyday life.

The classic account of California life is the biased, engagingly written adventure of an educated, young New Englander, Richard Henry Dana, *Two Years Before the Mast,* first published in 1840 and reissued in a splendid edition by John Haskell Kemble, who has collated it with the original manuscript and added previously unpublished journals and letters, 2 vols. (Los Angeles, 1964). Of equal merit is the work of another New Englander, Alfred Robinson: *Life in California* (1st ed., 1846; Santa Barbara, 1970). Unlike Dana, who remained only briefly on the California coast, Robinson was a longtime resident and prosperous merchant who had married into the prominent De la Guerra family and understood the nuances of life among the *californios.* For some of his private correspondence, pertaining largely to business and family matters, see *The Letters of Alfred Robinson to the De la Guerra Family of Santa Barbara, 1834–1873,* Maynard Geiger, trans. (Los Angeles, 1972). Rescued from the oblivion of a private collection and edited by Doyce B. Nunis, Jr., *The California Diary of Faxon Dean Atherton, 1836–1839* (San Francisco, 1964), provides sharp insights into people and events, making it a worthy companion to Dana and Robinson. George P. Hammond has provided students of this era with easy access to a treasure of wide-ranging correspondence by editing *The Larkin Papers: Personal, Business, and Official Correspondence of Thomas Oliver Larkin, Merchant and United States Consul in California,* 10 vols. (Berkeley, 1953).

Accessible by sea, Mexican California also received many visitors from Europe. Perhaps the best description by a Frenchman is Auguste Duhaut-Cilly, "Duhaut-Cilly's Account of California in the Years 1827–1828," *CHSQ*, VIII (June, September, and December 1929), pp. 130–66, 214–50, and 306–56. Sir George Simpson, an Englishman, left a magnificent account of a brief visit: *Narrative of a Journey Round the World, During the Years 1841 and 1842*, 2 vols. (London, 1847). A report by a Spanish-born merchant and resident, José Bandini, *A Description of California in 1828*, Doris M. Wright, trans. (Berkeley, 1951), offers a critical Hispanic perspective. A number of accounts by Russian visitors to California are becoming accessible to non-Russian readers and more are apparently on the way. Leonid A. Shur and James R. Gibson identify some of this literature in "Russian Travel Notes and Journals as Sources for the History of California, 1800–1850," *CHSQ*, LII (Spring 1973), pp. 37–63. For examples, see Dmitry Zavalishin, "California in 1824," James R. Gibson, trans., *SCQ*, LV (Winter 1973), pp. 369–412, and F. P. Wrángel, *De Sitka a San Petersburgo al través de México* [1835–36], Luisa Pintos Mimó, ed. and trans. (Mexico, 1975).

The number of published diaries, letters, and travel accounts describing California during the War of 1846 and the Gold Rush are legion, but most must be used with great caution for understanding the Mexican era, since they describe a California in the midst of rapid change. Two of the richest accounts of these years are William Robert Garner's *Letters from California, 1846–1847*, Donald Munro Craig, ed. (Berkeley, 1970), and *Three Years in California: William Perkins' Journal of Life at Sonora, 1849–1852*, Dale L. Morgan and James R. Scobie, eds. (Berkeley, 1964).

Cecil Robinson, *With the Ears of Strangers: The Mexican in American Literature* (Tucson, 1963), remains the starting point for any consideration of the prejudices and stereotypes that outsiders brought with them to the Mexican frontier, but the historiography of this question has begun to grow in recent years. Examples of how Anglo-American prejudices distorted historical reality appear in articles such as: Daniel Tyler, "Gringo Views of Governor Manuel Armijo," *NMHR*, XLV (January 1970), pp. 23–46; Janet Lecompte, "Manuel Armijo's Family History," *NMHR*, XLVIII (July 1973), pp. 251–58; and Beverly Trulio, "Anglo-American Attitudes Toward New Mexican Women," *JW*, XII (April 1973), pp. 229–39. The origins of stereotypes are examined in my essay "'Scarce More than Apes': Historical Roots of Anglo-American Stereotypes of Mexicans," in Weber, ed., *New Spain's Far Northern Frontier*, pp. 293–307, and in two articles by Raymund A. Paredes, "The Mexican Image in American Travel Literature, 1831–1869," *NMHR*, LII (January 1977), pp. 5–29, and "The Origins of Anti-Mexican Sentiment in the United States," *The New Scholar*, VI (1977), pp. 139–65. David J. Langum "Californios and the Image of Indolence," *WHQ*, IX (April 1978), pp. 181–96, and my commentary "Here Rests Juan Espinosa . . . " and Langum's "Brief Reply," *WHQ*, X (January 1979), pp. 61–69, highlight conflicting interpretations. Harry C. Clark, "Their Pride, Their Manners, and Their Voices: Sources of the Traditional Portrait of the Early Californians," *CHSQ*, LIII (Spring 1974), pp. 71–82, is far more limited than its title suggests. Several recent doctoral dissertations on American attitudes toward Mexicans indicate that the historiography will continue to grow.

Letters, Accounts, and Official Reports by Mexican Travelers or Residents

Published letters, accounts, and reports by pobladores or officials from Mexico City are not as numerous as accounts by non-Mexicans. Some of the more general items are described here, while documents pertaining to one specific theme are discussed where appropriate.

The most valuable published contemporary documents from the northern frontier during Spain's last decade include: *The Letters of Antonio Martínez, Last Spanish Governor of Texas, 1817–1822,* Virginia H. Taylor, ed. and trans. (Austin, 1957), and *The Letters of José Señán, O.F.M. Mission San Buenaventura, 1796–1823,* Paul D. Nathan, trans., Lesley Byrd Simpson, ed. (San Francisco, 1962), from California. Two somewhat polemical accounts by representatives to the Spanish Cortes of 1812 have become classics: Nettie Lee Benson, ed. and trans., *Report that Dr. Miguel Ramos de Arizpe . . . Presents to the August Congress on the Natural, Political, and Civil Condition of the Provinces of Coahuila, Nuevo León, Nuevo Santander, and Texas . . .* (Austin, 1950), and Pedro Bautista Pino, *Exposición sucinta y sencilla de la Provincia del Nuevo México: Hecha por su Diputado en Cortes . . .* (Cádiz, 1812), facsimile in H. Bailey Carroll and J. Villasana Haggard, ed. and trans., *Three New Mexico Chronicles . . .* (Albuquerque, 1942). Although he did not know the region first-hand, Tadeo Ortiz de Ayala provided the reading public with a general view at the dawn of Mexican independence in his *Resumen de la estadística del Imperio Mexicano, 1822,* ed. by Tarsicio García Díaz (1st ed., 1822; Mexico, 1968).

Few accounts of "exploration" by pobladores in the Mexican period exist, but two valuable exceptions are these: Lowell John Bean and William Marvin Mason, trans. and eds., *Diaries and Accounts of the Romero Expeditions in Arizona and California, 1823–1826* (Los Angeles, 1962), and LeRoy R. Hafen, ed., "Armijo's Journal," *Colorado Magazine,* XXVII (April 1950), pp. 120–31.

Franciscans, the most prolific writers on the frontier in the Spanish era, played a much diminished role in the Mexican era except in California. Some of the writings of California padres in the Mexican era have been published in English: Francis Price, trans. and ed., "Letters of Narciso Durán . . . ," *CHSQ,* XXXVII (June and September 1958), pp. 97–128; 241–65, business-oriented correspondence that extends to 1826; and Francis J. Weber, trans. and ed., *The Writings of Francisco García Diego y Moreno* (Los Angeles, 1976), a valuable collection of the letters of California's first bishop, 1840–46. Among the most wide-ranging published discussions of California's politicoeconomic problems by Mexican residents are: Francisco Castillo Negrete, *Informe y propuestas que hace al Supremo Gobierno para la prosperidad y seguridad de la Alta California, su Comisionado . . .* (Mexico, 1944), and Manuel Castañares, *Colección de documentos relativos al departamento de Californias* (Mexico, 1845), facsimile in Weber, ed., *Northern Mexico.*

The best general published descriptions of New Mexico by Mexican observers include the following: Manuel de Jesús Rada, *Proposición hecha al Soberano Congreso General de la Nación por el diputado del territorio de Nuevo México* (Mexico, 1829), facsimile in Weber, ed., *Northern Mexico,* a short report by a secular priest who lived briefly in New Mexico and which alerts Congress to a variety of problems. Antonio Barreiro, *Ojeada sobre Nuevo México* (Puebla, 1832), with an English version in Carroll and Haggard, trans. and eds., *Three New Mexico Chronicles.* Barreiro, an attorney from Chihuahua who lived in New Mexico, augmented Pino's 1812 *Exposición.* Barreiro's work, in turn, was annotated and reprinted by José Agustín de Escudero (another Chihuahua attorney, who had traveled through New Mexico), as *Noticias históricas y estadísticas de la antigua provincia del Nuevo-México . . .* (Mexico, 1849), also translated by Carroll and Haggard. Escudero's *Noticias estadísticas del estado de Chihuahua* (Mexico, 1834) is valuable for New Mexico as well as Chihuahua, and his *Noticias estadísticas de Sonora y Sinaloa* (Mexico, 1840), sheds light on events in what is today southern Arizona.

In addition to Escudero's treatise on Sonora, see Ignacio Zúñiga's *Rápida ojeada al estado de Sonora* (Mexico, 1835), facsimile in Weber, ed., *Northern Mexico.* Zúñiga emphasizes military matters, but also analyzes a variety of issues. See, too, José Francisco Velasco, *Noticias estadísticas del estado de Sonora* (Mexico, 1850). Velasco sheds light on events well before the Mexican-American War, and both he and Zúñiga make occasional references to California.

For Texas, accounts by two Mexican officials who came north to inspect the endangered province are immensely valuable: José María Sánchez, "A Trip to Texas in 1828," Carlos E. Castañeda, trans., *SWHQ*, XXIX (April 1926), pp. 249–88, and Juan N. Almonte, *Noticias estadística sobre Tejas* (Mexico, 1835), translated by Carlos E. Castañeda as "Statistical Report on Texas, 1835," *SWHQ*, XXVIII (January 1925), pp. 177–22. A facsimile of the 1835 imprint is in Weber, ed., *Northern Mexico*.

Memoirs

Memoirs must be used with special care because the likelihood is great that the memories of participants were influenced by reading as much as by direct experience. A textual study, for example, would probably reveal that the recollections of foreigners and *californios*, recorded in the 1870s and 1880s, were influenced by earlier accounts by Dana, Robinson, and others. Repetition of generalizations does not necessarily indicate their validity. Although their value to historians also usually diminishes in direct proportion to the amount of time that has elapsed between the events they describe and the date when the author dictated or wrote them, memoirs often contain information available nowhere else.

The most notable memoir of Mexican Texas by an Anglo-American is Noah Smithwick's *The Evolution of a State: or, Recollections of Old Texas Days* (Austin, 1900), anecdotal and reasonably reliable, even though recorded in the 1880s. Anglo-American memoirs of Mexican New Mexico include Thomas James, *Three Years Among the Mexicans and the Indians*, dictated and first published almost a quarter of a century after the events it describes (Waterloo, Ill., 1846), and James Josiah Webb, *Adventures in the Santa Fe Trade, 1844–1847*, Ralph P. Beiber, ed. (Glendale, 1931), written in 1888 when the author was seventy years old.

William Heath Davis, nine-years-old on his first visit to California in 1831, presented a highly romanticized picture in his extraordinarily detailed *Seventy-Five Years in California: Recollections and remarks by one who visited these shores in 1831, and again in 1833, and . . . was a resident from 1838 until the end of a long life in 1909*, Harold A. Small, ed. (1st ed., 1889; San Francisco, 1967). More modest in scope than Davis' recollections, but of value in important ways, are interviews that historian Hubert Howe Bancroft commissioned with some California "pioneers." Among those which have subsequently been published are the following: *Josiah Belden, 1841 California Overland Pioneer: His Memoir and Early Letters*, Doyce B. Nunis, Jr., ed. (Georgetown, California, 1962) and William Henry Ellison, ed., *The Life and Adventures of George Nidever, 1802–1883* (Berkeley, 1937), both of which are reminiscences of Americans who came overland to California; William Henry Thomes, *Recollections of Old Times in California, or, California Life in 1843*, George R. Stewart, ed. (Berkeley, 1974), which consists of highly romanticized recollections of an American seaman, recorded in 1887; and *The Life and Adventures in California of Don Agustín Janssens, 1834–1856*, William H. Ellison and Francis Price, eds. (San Marino, 1953), dictated in 1878 by a Belgian who had come to California via Mexico as a seventeen-year-old. Janssens settled near Santa Barbara, and was administrator of Mission San Juan Capistrano after its secularization. Erwin G. Gudde, ed., *Sutter's Own Story* (New York, 1936), contains John Sutter's autobiographical memoir done for H. H. Bancroft.

Compared to foreigners, few pobladores have left memoirs of the Mexican era. None of substance have been published for New Mexico or Arizona. The few published memoirs by *tejanos* are of little use for the Mexican period: Juan Nepomuceno Seguín, *Personal Memoirs of John N. Seguin, From the Year 1834 to the Retreat of General Woll from the City of San Antonio. 1842* (San Antonio, 1858), begins at the end of the Mexican era, as does José María Rodríguez, *Memoirs of Early Texas* (San Antonio, 1913), whose author was only six when the Texas revolt broke out. Antonio Menchaca's brief *Memoirs* (San Antonio, 1937), go back to the 1810s, but skip most of the Mexican era to conclude with the fight for independence.

Thanks in part to Hubert Howe Bancroft, California enjoys a larger number of rich reminiscences by Hispanos. Some of these accounts have been published. Among the more substantial are these: Guadalupe Vallejo, "Ranch and Mission Days in Alta California," *The Century Magazine*, XLI (December 1890), pp. 183–92; José Arnaz, "Memoirs of a Merchant," Nellie Van de Grift Sánchez, trans. and ed., *Touring Topics*, XX (September-October 1928), pp. 14–19; 47–48; José del Carmen Lugo, "Life of a Rancher," *SCQ*, XXXII (September 1950), pp. 185–236; *Memoirs of José Francisco Palomares*, Thomas Workman Temple II, trans. (Los Angeles, 1955); Angustias de la Guerra Ord, *Occurrences in Hispanic California*, Francis Price and William H. Ellison, trans. and eds. (Washington, 1956); "Times Gone By in Alta California: Recollections of Señora Doña Juana Machado Alipaz de Ridington [Wrightington]," Ray S. Brandes, trans. and ed., *SCQ*, XLI (September 1959), pp. 195–240; *Don Pío Pico's Historical Narrative*, Arthur P. Botello, trans., and Martin Cole and Henry Welcome, eds. (Glendale, 1973). Some of the *californios* romanticized the Mexican era in terms similar to those used by foreigners, and many ignored everyday life and focused on political events, apparently in response to the kinds of questions posed by Bancroft's interrogators.

Biographies

Historians have demonstrated greater interest in the lives of foreigners who operated on the Mexican frontier, than on Mexicans themselves. A complete list of biographies of foreigners would constitute a lengthy essay in itself. In the case of trappers alone, LeRoy R. Hafen has edited a collection containing biographies of 292 individuals, many of whom hunted in New Mexico and California: *The Mountain Men and the Fur Trade of the Far West. . .* , 10 vols. (Glendale, 1965–72). Book-length biographies of American trappers who frequented the Mexican frontier are also abundant: Dale L. Morgan, *Jedediah Smith and the Opening of the West* (New York, 1953); William S. Wallace, *Antoine Roobidoux, 1794–1860* (Los Angeles, 1960); Alpheus H. Favour, *Old Bill Williams, Mountain Man* (Norman, 1962); Iris Higbie Wilson [Engstrand], *William Wolfskill, 1798–1866: Frontier Trapper to California Ranchero* (Glendale, 1965); Forbes Parkhill, *The Blazed Trail of Antoine Leroux* (Los Angeles, 1965); Sardis Templeton, *The Lame Captain: The Life and Adventures of Pegleg Smith* (Los Angeles, 1965); and Kenneth Holmes, *Ewing Young: Master Trapper* (Portland, 1967). Kit Carson has been the subject of several biographies, which should only be approached after reading Harvey L. Carter's assessment in *'"Dear Old Kit': The Historical Christopher Carson* (Norman, 1968), pp. 3–36.

Many of the foreign-born rancheros and merchants in California have also been the subject of valuable book-length biographies: *John Marsh, Pioneer. The Life Story of a Trailblazer on Six Frontiers* (New York, 1930) a laudatory and somewhat amateurish work by a medical doctor, George D. Lyman; Susanna B. Dakin, *A Scotch Paisano: Hugo Reid's Life in California, 1832–1852, Derived from His Correspondence* (Berkeley, 1939); Reuben Underhill, *From Cowhides to Golden Fleece* (Stanford, 1939), a biography of Thomas Oliver Larkin; James P. Zollinger, *Sutter, The Man and His Empire* (New York, 1939), which remains the standard biography, although Richard Dillon has presented some new material in his popular account, *Fool's Gold: The Decline and Fall of Captain John Sutter of California* (New York, 1967); Susanna B. Dakin, *The Lives of William Hartnell* (Stanford, 1949); Iris Higbie Wilson [Engstrand], *William Wolfskill 1798–1866: Frontier Trapper to California Ranchero* (Glendale, 1965); and Sheldon G. Jackson, *A British Ranchero in Old California: The Life and Times of Henry Dalton and the Rancho Azusa* (Glendale, 1977).

Several Anglo-Americans who played key roles in Mexican Texas have been the subject of biographies, foremost of which is Eugene C. Barker's *The Life of Stephen F. Austin, Founder of Texas, 1793–1836* (1st ed., 1926; 2nd ed. reprinted, Austin, 1969). Despite a tendency to overstate Austin's importance, this is a masterful and mature synthesis, well-grounded in both Mexican and American archival sources. It remains the single most influential book on Mexican Texas. Austin's righthand man, who went on to become an empresario in his own right, is the subject of Margaret S. Henson's able biography, *Samuel May Williams: Early Texas Entrepreneur* (College Station, 1976). Biographies of other Texas empresarios appear in studies of their colonies. Several Anglo-Americans who fought in the Texas revolt have been the subject of biography. Most, such as those of Sam Houston, Mirabeau Buonaparte Lamar, and Samuel Maverick, tell us more about the aftermath of the revolt, while biographies such as Lois Garver, "Benjamin Rush Milam," *SWHQ*, XXXVIII (October 1934 and January 1935), pp. 7–121 and 177–202, and Archie P. McDonald, *Travis* (Austin 1976), illuminate events leading up to the revolt.

In contrast to the abundant biographies of American entrepreneurs and adventurers, few biographies of *pobladores* exist. In quantity, California leads the way. The best scholarly biography of a *californio* is George Tays, "Mariano Guadalupe Vallejo and Sonoma," which ran serially in six issues of the *CHSQ*, 1937–38, and which should be reprinted as a small book. Myrtle M. McKittrick's *Vallejo: Son of California* (Portland, Ore., 1944), is a thoughtful, popular biography that does not supersede Tays' work on the years before 1846. Albert Shumate's *Francisco Pacheco of Pacheco Pass* (Stockton, 1977), is an admirable attempt to flesh out the life of a minor figure who, although not a native Californian, lived most of his adult years in northern California. Joseph A. Thompson has written a laudatory, undocumented, but sound biography of his great grandfather, the patriarch of an important Santa Barbara family: *El Gran Capitán: José de la Guerra. A Historical Biographical Study* (Los Angeles, 1961). Similarly, Terry E. Stephenson has written an unscholarly, but sound biography of *Don Bernardo Yorba* (Los Angeles, 1941), who farmed and ranched in present Orange County. George L. Harding, *Don Agustín V. Zamorano: Statesman, Soldier, Craftsman, and California's First Printer* (Los Angeles, 1934), is a first-rate biography of a Mexican officer who lived in California from 1825–36, and C. Alan Hutchinson has drawn from many sources to sketch out the life of José Figueroa prior to his arrival in California where he would serve as governor: "General José Figueroa's Career in Mexico, 1792–1832," *NMHR*, XLVIII (October 1973), pp. 277–98. No full-scale biography of a California governor exists, although Raymond K. Morrison has written a brief biography of "Luis Antonio Argüello: First Mexican Governor of California," *JW*, II (April and July, 1963), pp. 193–204 and 347–61. California clergymen have been more fortunate. Maynard Geiger has produced a model compendium: *Franciscan Missionaries in Hispanic California, 1769–1848: A Biographical Dictionary* (San Marino, 1969), and Francis J. Weber has written a solid biography of *Francisco García Diego: California's Transition Bishop* (Los Angeles, 1972), a greatly expanded version of a biography which Weber published in 1961 under a different title.

The best full-dress, scholarly biography of a *nuevomexicano* is Marc Simmons, *The Little Lion of the Southwest: A Life of Manuel Antonio Chaves* (Chicago, 1973), most of which deals with the American period. F. Stanley [Stanley Francis Louis Crocchiola], *Giant in Lilliput: The Story of Donaciano Vigil* (Pampa, Texas), is disorganized and unreliable. The life of a remarkable woman who spent most of her life in New Mexico, Gertrudis ("Tules") Barceló, is the subject of Janet Lecompte's "La Tules and the Americans," *AW*, XX (Autumn 1978), pp. 215–30, which supersedes Angélico Chávez's "Doña Tules, Her Fame and Her Funeral," *El Palacio*, LVII (August 1950), pp. 227–34. Angélico Chávez's guide, *Archives of the Archdiocese of Santa Fe, 1678–1900* (Washington, 1957), provides bare bones biographical data for most New Mexican Franciscans. The biography of one secular priest, based chiefly on reminiscences of his descendants, is Fidelia M. Puckett, "Ramón Ortiz: Priest and Patriot," *NMHR*, XXV (October 1950), pp. 265–95, and focuses mainly on Ortiz's life (1813–1890) after the Mexican period. The major cleric in Mexican New Mexico is the subject of Pedro Sánchez, *Memorias del Padre Antonio José Martínez* (Santa Fe, 1903). Written by a relative, and apparently based on conversation with Martínez and documents, this study is very brief. Two English translations exist, the best being that by Guadalupe Baca-Vaughn, *Memories of Antonio José Martínez* ([Santa Fe], 1978). Sánchez's *Memorias* should be supplemented by E. K. Francis, "Padre Martínez: A New Mexican Myth," *NMHR*, XXXI (October 1956), pp. 265–89.

Two *tejanos* have been the subject of book-length biographies: *José Antonio Navarro: Co-Creator of Texas* (Waco, 1969), by Joseph Martin Dawson, and *The Empresario Don Martín de León* (Waco 1973), by Arthur B. J. Hammett. The former is lightly researched and poorly documented and the latter a poorly integrated pastiche of research notes. Walter Stuck has made a beginning at a life of *José Francisco Ruiz* (San Antonio, 1944), a twelve-page pamphlet. The lives of several Mexican officials who played key roles in Texas have been the subject of biographies: Raymond Estep, *Lorenzo de Zavala: Profeta del Liberalismo Mexicano* (Mexico 1952); Ohland Morton, *Terán and Texas: A Chapter in Texas-Mexican Relations* (Austin 1948); Wilbert H. Timmons, *Tadeo Ortiz: Mexican Colonizer and Reformer* (El Paso, 1974), and C. Alan Hutchinson, "General José Antonio Mexía and his Texas Interests," *SWHQ*, LXXXII (October 1978), pp. 117–42.

Compendiums of Law

Considerable divergence often exists between law and practice, but laws are still of value to historians as indications of the ideals of a society and the aspirations of lawmakers. Constitutions of this era are most easily accessible in Felipe Tena Ramírez, ed., *Leyes fundamentales de Mexico, 1808–78* (1st ed., 1958; eighth edition, Mexico City, 1978). The first five volumes of the magnificent compendium by Manuel Dublán and José María Lozano, eds., *Legislación mexicana o colección completa de las disposiciones legislativas expedidas desde la independencia de la república*, 34 vols. (Mexico, 1876–1904), embrace the years in which Mexico held the present Southwest. Unfortunately, neither this nor any other compilation is truly "complete," titles notwithstanding. Detailed examination of legal precedents requires additional searching in annual compendiums such as the collection serially entitled *Colección de las leyes y decretos expedidos por el Congreso General de los Estados Unidos Mexicanos en los años de 1831 y 1832* (Mexico, 1833) and in Basilio José Arrillaga, *Recopilación de leyes, decretos, bandos, reglamentos . . .* , 20 vols. (Mexico, 1838–66).

More specialized collections of Mexican and Spanish law exist on many subjects. Francisco F. de la Maza, *Código de colonización y terrenos baldíos de la República Mexicana* (Mexico, 1893), has been especially useful to historians of the Mexican frontier. Attorneys have found a need for translations of Mexican law. Published in collections such as Matthew G. Reynolds, *Spanish and Mexican Land Laws. New Spain and Mexico* (St. Louis, 1895), and H. P. N. Gammel, *The Laws of Texas*, 10 vols. (Austin, 1898), these are useful finding aids, but the translations must be used with caution.

Part II

1: "Viva la Independencia!"

Except for Texas, Mexico's struggle for independence did not involve the provinces in the Far North, and as a result little literature addresses itself specifically to that issue. For California, see Herbert E. Bolton, "The Iturbide Revolution in the Californias," *HAHR*, II (May 1919), pp. 188–242, consisting largely of translations of documents, and George Tays, "The Passing of Spanish California, September 29, 1822," *CHSQ*, XV (June 1936), pp. 139–42. For New Mexico, see David J. Weber, ed. and trans., "An Unforgettable Day:

Facundo Melgares on Independence," *NMHR,* XLVIII (January 1973), pp. 27–44, which offers a new interpretation. Félix D. Almaraz, Jr., "Governor Antonio Martínez and Mexican Independence in Texas: An Orderly Transition," *Permian Historical Annual,* XV (1975), pp. 45–54, looks at the "orderly" events of 1821 in Texas.

The disorderly events in Texas in the decade preceding the "orderly transition" described by Almaraz is the subject of a number of books and articles: Frederick C. Chabot, *Texas in 1811. The Las Casas and Sambrano Revolutions* (San Antonio, 1941); J. Villasana Haggard, "The Counter-Revolution of Béxar, 1811," *SWHQ,* XLII (October 1939), pp. 222–35; and Félix D. Almaraz, Jr., *Tragic Cavalier: Governor Manuel Salcedo of Texas, 1808–1813* (Austin, 1971). The activities of American adventurers in troubled Texas is the focus of two standard and dependable works: Julie Kathryn Garrett, *Green Flag Over Texas: A Story of the Last Years of Spain in Texas* (New York, 1939), and Harris Gaylord Warren, *The Sword Was Their Passport. A History of Filibustering in the Mexican Revolution* (Baton Rouge, 1943). Richard W. Gronet, "The United States and the Invasion of Texas, 1810–1814," *The Americas,* XXV (January 1969), pp. 281–306, suggests greater United States aid to Gutiérrez than has been supposed previously. Fane Downs, "Governor Antonio Martínez and the Defense of Texas from Foreign Invasion, 1817–1822," *Texas Military History,* VII (Spring 1968), pp. 27–43, looks at the other side.

Numerous books and articles describe and analyze events in Mexico surrounding the movement for independence. For the movement of 1810, Hugh M. Hammill, Jr., *The Hidalgo Revolt: Prelude to Mexican Independence* (Gainesville, Fla, 1966), is a superior account. William Spence Robertson, *Iturbide of Mexico* (Durham, N. C., 1952), remains the standard biography of the "liberator." The best recent overview in English is Timothy E. Anna, *The Fall of the Royal Government in Mexico City* (Lincoln, Neb., 1978). The starting point in Spanish should be Luis Villoro, *El proceso ideológico de la revolución de independencia* (Mexico, 1967). The initial optimistic reception of independence in Mexico is the subject of the careful, well-documented study by Javier Ocampo, *Las ideas de un día: El pueblo mexicano ante la consumación de su Independencia* (Mexico, 1969).

2: The New Politics

The best political history of the young Mexican republic is Michael P. Costeloe, *La primera república federal de México, 1824–35. Un estudio de los partidos políticos en el México independiente* (Mexico, 1975). Edmundo O'Gorman, "Precedentes y sentido de la Revolución de Ayutla," in *Seis estudios históricos de tema mexicano* (Xalapa, 1960), pp. 99–143, contains penetrating analysis in a brief span. In English, Charles A. Hale, *Mexican Liberalism in the Age of Mora, 1821–1853* (New Haven, 1968), is the best analysis of the politics of the era in English.

The best single-volume introductions to the political structure of northern Mexico in the last years of Spanish rule are these: Luis Navarro García, *Las Provincias Internas en el siglo XIX* (Sevilla, 1965), and Marc Simmons, *Spanish Government in New Mexico* (Albuquerque, 1968). The changing political situation in Spain is ably introduced in Richard Herr, *The Eighteenth-Century Revolution in Spain* (Princeton, 1958), and excellent analyses of the work of the Spanish Cortes of 1812 appear in two recent books in English: Jaime E. Rodríguez O., *The Emergence of Spanish America: Vicente Rocafuerte and Spanish Americanism, 1808–1832* (Lincoln, 1975), and Mario Rodríguez, *The Cádiz Experiment in Central America, 1808–1826* (Berkeley, 1978). The influence of Mexico on the Spanish Cortes, and of the Spanish Cortes on Mexico, is the subject of Nettie Lee Benson, ed., *Mexico and the Spanish Cortes, 1810–1822: Eight Essays* (Austin, 1966). For political questions, see especially two of those essays: Charles Berry, "The Election of the Mexican Deputies to the Spanish Cortes, 1810–1822," pp. 10–42, and Roger Cunniff, "Mexican Municipal Electoral Reform, 1810–1822," pp. 59–86.

For the impact of the Spanish Cortes of 1812 on the formation of the Mexican Republic, see Nettie Lee Benson's pioneering *La diputación provincial y el federalismo mexicano* (Mexico, 1955); Nettie Lee Benson, "The Plan of Casa Mata," *HAHR*, XXV (February 1945), pp. 45–56, is also valuable.

A substantial literature discusses the degrees to which the Mexican Constitution of 1824 was influenced by the United States Constitution and the Spanish Constitution of 1812. See, for example, James Q. Dealey, "The Spanish Sources of the Mexican Constitution of 1824," *SWHQ*, II (1900), pp. 161–99, and José Gamas Torruco, *El federalismo mexicano* (Mexico, 1975), who see Spain as most important. Marion John Atwood, "The Sources of the Mexican Acta Constitutiva," *SWHQ*, XX (July 1919), pp. 19–27, assessed the *acta* as an "attempt to inject the federal principle of government, as borrowed from the United States, into an instrument of government essentially Spanish in character" (p. 27). For arguments emphasizing United States influence, see Watson Smith, "Influences from the United States on the Mexican Constitution of 1824," *AW*, IV (Summer 1962), pp. 113–26, and Anne Macías, *Génesis del gobierno constitucional en México, 1808–1820* (Mexico, 1973). J. Lloyd Mecham, "Origins of Federalism in Mexico," *HAHR*, XVIII (May 1938), pp. 164–82, argued that Mexico experienced federalism only in theory and that the Constitution of 1824 was premature. José Barragán Barragán, *Introduction al federalismo: la formación de los poderes, 1824* (Mexico, 1978), is a descriptive, legalistic study.

For political histories of individual provinces, one should look at general works, which tend to emphasize political history, such as: Tays for California, Stevens for Sonora, Bloom for New Mexico, and Castañeda on Texas. Many questions remain unanswered about the political history of the frontier in the Mexican area. We need more studies such as the concise, well-researched article by Charles A. Bacarisse, "The Union of Coahuila and Texas," *SWHQ*, LXI (January 1958), pp. 341–49.

A number of works treat local government and justice in the Spanish era, but comparable studies of the Mexican period are very skimpy. Theodore Grivas, "Alcalde Rule; The Nature of Local Government in Spanish and Mexican California," *CHSQ*, XL (March 1961), pp. 11–32, promises more than it delivers and focuses mainly on the nature of alcalde rule from the judicial reforms of 1837 into the early American period. Malcolm Ebright, "Manuel Martínez Ditch Dispute: A Study in Mexican Period Customs and Justice," *NMHR*, LIV (January 1979), pp. 21–34, suggests that alcaldes may have been more learned than usually supposed, and that "custom often took the place of a formal legal system in New Mexico." Lucy L. Killea has written a unique political history of a community in the Mexican Far North: "The Political History of a Mexican Pueblo: San Diego from 1825–1845," *JSDH*, XII (July and October 1966), pp. 3–35 and 17–42.

Published primary sources which deal almost exclusively with political matters include: David J. Weber, ed., "El gobierno territorial de Nuevo México. La exposición del Padre Martínez de 1831," *Historia Mexicana*, XXV (October–December 1975), pp. 302–15 (Martínez called for giving more responsibility to local officials); Carlos Antonio Carrillo, *Exposición . . . pidiendo se establezcan en aquel Territorio los tribunales competentes para su administración de justicia* (Mexico, 1831), published in John Galvin, ed., Adelaide Smithers, trans., *The Coming of Justice to California: Three Documents . . .* (San Francisco, 1963); and *Reglamento Provincional* [sic] *para el Gobierno interior de la Excma Diputación Territorial de la Alta California . . .* (Monterey, 1834), reprinted as *A Facsimile Edition of California's First Book: Reglamento. . . ,* Ramón Ruiz and Theresa Vigil, trans., with introductions by George L. Harding and George P. Hammond (San Francisco, 1954).

3: The Collapse of the Missions

A substantial literature exists on missions in the Spanish era. For a good, recent analysis and guide to major sources, see John Francis Bannon, "The Mission as a Frontier Institution: Sixty Years of Interest and Research," *WHQ*, X (July 1979), pp. 3–22. For a detailed account of Bourbon efforts to weaken the secular influence of the Church, see N. M. Farriss, *Crown and Clergy in Colonial Mexico, 1759–1821* (London, 1968), and a fine essay by James M. Breedlove, "Effects of the Cortes, 1810–1822, on Church Reform in Spain and Mexico," in Nettie Lee Benson, ed., *Mexico and the Spanish Cortes, 1810–1822* (Austin, 1966), pp. 113–33. Francis Guest, "Mission Colonization and Political Control in Spanish California," *JSDH*, XXIV (Winter, 1978), pp. 96–116, cogently explains why missions were established in the late colonial period in Alta California, even as they were being phased out elsewhere.

Ideological changes in independent Mexico, which would affect the northern missions, are best explained in Moisés González Navarro's essential: "Instituciones indígenas en México independiente," in *Métodos y resultados de la política indigenista en México* (Mexico, 1954), pp. 113–69. The expulsion of Spaniards from Mexico in the 1820s, which had some effect on the northern missions, is the subject of two books: Harold D. Sims, *La expulsión de los españoles de Mexico, 1821–1828* (Mexico, 1974), and Romeo Flores Caballero, *La contrarrevolución en la independencia: Los Españoles en la vida política, social y económica de Mexico, 1804–1838* (Mexico, 1969), translated into English by Jaime E. Rodríguez O., *Counterrevolution . . .* (Lincoln, Neb., 1974).

Some studies of individual missions extend into the Mexican period. Models are John L. Kessell's: *Friars, Soldiers, and Reformers: Hispanic Arizona and the Sonora Mission Frontier, 1767–1856* (Tucson, 1976), and *Kiva, Cross, and Crown: The Pecos Indians and New Mexico, 1540–1840* (Washington, D. C., 1979), both sprightly written yet based on meticulous research in unpublished sources. *Mission Santa Barbara, 1782–1965* (Santa Barbara, 1965), is a mature, balanced synthesis by Maynard Geiger, the Franciscan master of California mission historiography. Geiger's Texas counterpart is Marion A. Habig, whose mission histories also extend into the Mexican period: *The Alamo Chain of Missions: A History of San Antonio's Five Old Missions* (Chicago, 1968), and *San Antonio's Mission San José: State and National Historic Site, 1720–1968* (San Antonio, 1968). Those who would understand the individual mission as part of the manifold activities of a college should start with Maynard Geiger's "The Internal Organization and Activities of San Fernando College, Mexico (1734–1858)," *The Americas*, VI (July 1949), pp. 3–31. For the fascinating story of the changing architectural features of mission structures over time, see John L. Kessell, *The Missions of New Mexico Since 1776* (Albuquerque, 1980).

Except in California, literature on the secularization of the missions in the Mexican era is scanty, reflecting perhaps their diminished importance. John L. Kessell has written a tight synthesis of the situation in Sonora: "Friars versus Bureaucrats: The Mission as a Threatened Institution on the Arizona-Sonora Frontier," *WHQ*, V (April 1974), pp. 151–60. For Texas, Paul H. Walters, "Secularization of the La Bahía Missions," *SWHQ*, LIV (January 1951), pp. 287–300 is a solid and succinct treatment of forces operating between 1822 and 1830, while Félix D. Almaraz, Jr., has meticulously documented the land rush that followed secularization in San Antonio in 1823: "San Antonio's Missions in the Mexican Period—Material Decline and Secular Avarice," a paper presented to a joint session of the Texas Catholic Historical Society and the Texas State Historical Association, San Antonio, March 9, 1979. No comparable studies exist for New Mexico during these years.

Because of its importance in the Mexican era, California historians have devoted substantial attention to secularization and developed a complex and subtle historiography. Zephyrin Engelhardt, a Franciscan with an unabashed bias toward the Church, laid out the basic chronology in great detail in vols. II and IV of *The Missions and Missionaries of California,* 4 vols. (San Francisco, 1908–15). Engelhardt remains indispensable partly because of his extensive use of quotations from unpublished sources. Gerald J. Geary, *The Secularization of the California Missions (1810–1846),* (Washington, D. C. 1934), synthesized published works, in the main. His narrow, pro-Franciscan view is dated, and in some cases wrong, but his outline of events remains useful. Manuel P. Servín took a less benign view of Franciscan activities in "The Secularization of the California Missions: A Reappraisal," *SCQ,* XLVII (June 1965), pp. 133–49, arguing that they retarded economic growth, were overly zealous, and contributed to their own demise. Too brief and unsystematic to be totally convincing, Servín's work is nonetheless provocative and makes a strong case. The best work to date is C. Alan Hutchinson's "The Mexican Government and the Mission Indians of Upper California," *The Americas,* XXI (April 1965), pp. 335–62, which places secularization in the broad context of Mexican politics and thought, while still explaining the role of local interests. Hutchinson's *Frontier Settlement in Mexican California* is also essential to an understanding of the variety of interests involved in secularization of the California missions. The reaction of one Franciscan is explored in Michael C. Neri, "Narciso [sic] Durán and the Secularization of the California Missions," *The Americas,* XXXIII (January 1977), pp. 411–29. Daniel Garr, "Planning, Politics and Plunder: The Missions and Indian Pueblos of Hispanic California," *SCQ,* LIV (Winter 1972), pp. 291–312 examines the failure of both Church and State to convert the missions into functioning pueblos, and concludes that the remoteness of frontier areas from centralized authority contributed to that failure.

Historians of California have also examined Indian responses to missionization in the Mexican era, although severe limits on the quality and quantity of sources constitute a formidable obstacle. For mission population, see J. N. Bowman, "The Resident Neophytes (Existentes) of the California Missions, 1769–1834'" *SCQ,* XL (June 1958), pp. 138–48, and for the disastrous impact of missions on Indian demography, see Sherburne Friend Cook, *The Conflict Between the California Indian and White Civilization* (Berkeley, 1976), a single-volume reprint of several monographs first published in the 1940s. This should be read in conjunction with Francis F. Guest, "An Examination of the Thesis of S. F. Cook on the Forced Conversion of Indians in the California Missions," *SCQ,* LXI (Spring 1979), pp. 1–77, a Franciscan historian who argues that the padres did not use indiscriminant force to bring about conversions. Anthropologist Robert Heizer takes a more critical look in "Impact of Colonization on the Native California Societies," *JSDH,* XXIV (Winter 1978), pp. 121–39, as does historian Robert Archibald, "Indian Labor at the California Missions: Slavery or Salvation?" *JSDH,* XXIV (Spring 1978), pp. 172–82, who limits his study to the years 1769–1821, and who concludes that Indians were "saved" involuntarily. Written just prior to the Mexican period, *As the Padres Saw Them: California Indian Life and Customs As Reported by the Franciscan Missionaries, 1813–1815,* Maynard Geiger, ed. and trans., with notes by Clement W. Meighan (Santa Barbara, 1976), is a remarkable collection that tells as much about Franciscans' attitudes as it does about ethnography.

For two views of one California Indian revolt, see Maynard Geiger, ed. and trans., "Fray Antonio Ripoll's Description of the Chumash Revolt at Santa Barbara in 1824," *SCQ,* LII (December 1970), pp. 345–64, and Thomas Blackburn, ed., "The Chumash Revolt of 1824: A Native Account," *Journal of California Anthropology,* II (Winter 1975), pp. 223–27. George Harwood Phillips' imaginative and provocative "Indians and the Breakdown of the Spanish Mission System in California," *Ethnohistory,* XXI (Fall 1974), pp. 291–302, enhances our understanding through his use of social science models.

Except in California, most studies of Indian responses to the mission experience focus on the Spanish era when missions were most vigorous, but some of their generalizations are useful for the Mexican period. See, for example: Billie Persons' overview, "Secular Life in the San Antonio Missions," *SWHQ,* LXII (July 1958), pp. 45–62; Edward Spicer's monumental *Cycles of Conquest: The Impact of Spain, Mexico, and the United States on the Indians of the Southwest, 1533–1960* (Tucson, 1962); and Henry F. Dobyns, "Indian Extinction in the Middle Santa Cruz Valley, Arizona," *NMHR,* XXXVIII (April 1963), pp. 163–81, who describes a demographic disaster.

4: The Church in Jeopardy

No secondary study examines specifically the secular Church on the frontier in the Mexican era. Generalizations must be gleaned from primary sources, and from general secondary studies, or studies of related subjects that allude to the Church.

For an overview of the Church in Mexico during these years, see J. Lloyd Mecham, *Church and State in Latin America: A History of Politico-Ecclesiastical Relations* (rev. ed.; Chapel Hill, 1966), which places the subject in a broad context, and Wilfred H. Callcott, *Church and State in Mexico, 1822–1857* (Durham, N. C., 1926). Both works, as their titles suggest, look at Church-State relations. For a closer look at the internal workings of the Church, see the encyclopedic work by Jesuit historian Mariano Cuevas, *Historia de la Iglesia en México,* 5 vols. (5th ed.; Mexico, 1947), and the more objective and detailed study by Anne Staples, *La iglesia en la primera república federal mexicana, 1824–1835* (Mexico, 1976).

The archival research of Michael P. Costeloe has begun to untangle the knotty problem of Church finances during these years, and the onslaught by the state: *Church Wealth in Mexico: A Study of the "Juzgado de Capellanías" in the Archbishopric of Mexico, 1800–1856* (Cambridge, Eng., 1967); "The Administration, Collection, and Distribution of Tithes in the Archbishopric of Mexico, 1800–1860," *The Americas,* XXIII (July 1966), pp. 3–27; and *Church and State in Independent Mexico* (London, 1978).

Works which address specifically some of the problems faced by the secular Church in the frontier provinces include Weber's biography, *Francisco García Diego, California's Transition Bishop,* and his article: "The United States Versus Mexico: The Final Settlement of the Pious Fund of the Californias," *SCQ,,* LI (June 1969), pp. 97–152. For Sonora, see the undocumented but authoritative essay by Kieran McCarty, "Our Desert Under Spain and Mexico: The Diocesan Story, 1691–1860," in *Shepherds in the Desert: A Sequel to Salpointe* (Tucson, 1978), pp. 26–37. Marta Weigle looks at one result of the lassitude of the Church in New Mexico: *Brothers of Light, Brothers of Blood: The Penitentes of the Southwest* (Albuquerque, 1976), the best of many works on this controversial subject. Those who want a lighter introduction will appreciate her booklet: *The Penitentes of the Southwest* (Santa Fe, 1970), and those who want to know more will value her thorough *Penitente Bibliography* (Albuquerque, 1976). For Texas, Castañeda's *Our Catholic Heritage* is indispensable, and vol. VI contains a chapter on "The Agony of the Missions and of the Church . . . 1821–1836." Although outdated in some respects, a short study by Sister Mary Angela Fitzmorris, *Four Decades of Catholicism in Texas, 1820–1860* (Washington, D. C., 1926), is well-documented and remains a valuable guide to sources. A Presbyterian minister, William S. Red, *The Texas Colonists and Religion, 1821–1836* (Austin, 1924), exaggerated the importance of religion to the colonists and its role as a cause of the Texas revolution, but his work remains the standard and is rich in quotations from contemporary documents. Studies illuminating minor yet interesting aspects of the involvement of the secular Church in Texas include Mary Whatley Clarke, "Father Michael Muldoon," *Texana,* IX (Autumn 1971), pp. 179–229, and Hans W. Baade, "The Form of Marriage in Spanish North America," *Cornell Law Review,* LXI (November 1975), pp. 1–89.

5:   Indios Bárbaros, Norteamericanos, and the Failure of the Velvet Glove

Descriptions of the destruction wrought by "indios bárbaros" to Mexico's Far North in the Mexican era are abundant, yet the complexities of understanding the roles of different Indian bands, and of shifting alliances on many levels, make it clear that more detailed studies of this subject are necessary before we can generalize with certainty. For the late 1830s and early 1840s, a series of articles by Ralph A. Smith draws heavily from Mexican sources to describe the effects of raids by Comanches and Apaches. The best of Smith's articles is "Indians in American-Mexican Relations Before the War of 1846," *HAHR*, XLIII (February 1963), pp. 34–64. Smith displayed considerable interest in a bounty system employed by some north Mexican states, which seems to have been used infrequently in Texas, New Mexico, or California in the Mexican period: "The Scalp Hunter in the Borderlands, 1835–1850," *AW*, VI (Spring 1964), pp. 5–22, and "Apache 'Ranching' Below the Gila, 1841–1845," *Arizoniana*, III (Winter 1972), pp. 1–17. Carlos J. Sierra, *Los indios de la frontera* (Mexico, 1980), also uses Mexican sources and looks at several frontier provinces as did Smith. I was unable to utilize Sierra's book, which appeared as my own manuscript was in press, but our interpretations are very similar.

Writers who have explored the devastation of Indian raids in Texas y Coahuila include David M. Vigness, "Indian raids on the Lower Rio Grande, 1836–1837," *SWHQ*, LIX (July 1955), pp. 14–23, and Isidro Vizcaya Canales, *La invasión de los indios bárbaros al noreste de México en los años de 1840 y 1841* (Monterrey, 1968), with its excellent collection of documents.

For New Mexico, see Frank McNitt, *Navajo Wars: Military Campaigns, Slave Raids, and Reprisals* (Albuquerque, 1972); Ward Alan Minge, "Mexican Independence Day and a Ute Tragedy in Santa Fe, 1844," in Albert Schroeder, ed., *The Changing Ways of Southwestern Indians: A Historical Perspective* (Glorieta, New Mexico, 1973), pp. 107–22, drawn almost entirely from archival sources; and Charles L. Kenner, *A History of New Mexican-Plains Indian Relations* (Norman, 1969), whose work, based largely on published sources, necessarily skims over the Mexican period but suggests the complexity of events.

For Sonora, Robert C. Stevens, "The Apache Menace in Sonora, 1831–1848," *AW*, VI (Autumn 1964), pp. 211–22, sees Mexican policies failing and Apaches gaining ground during these years.

The situation in California is best illuminated in Cook, *The Conflict Between the California Indian and White Civilization;* George Harwood Phillips' sensitive, *Chiefs and Challengers: Indian Resistance and Cooperation in Southern California* (Berkeley, 1975), and Eleanor Lawrence, "Horse Thieves on the Spanish Trail," *Touring Topics*, XXIII (January 1931), pp. 22–25, 55, an authoritative but undocumented piece.

Most studies of individual tribes skip quickly over the Mexican period, in no small part because the basic research upon which generalizations can be built has not yet been done. See, for example, Donald E. Worcester, *The Apaches: Eagles of the Southwest* (Norman, 1979), and Rupert N. Richardson, *The Comanche Barrier to South Plains Settlement* (Glendale, Ca., 1933).

Many of the published accounts by contemporaries, described earlier in this essay, allude to the difficult relations between pobladores and indios bárbaros, but works which focus specifically on this subject include: Ignacio Zúñiga, *Rápida ojeada al estado de Sonora* (Mexico, 1835), and Antonio José Martínez, *Esposición* [sic] *Proponiendo la civilisación de las naciones bárbaras que son al contorno del Departamento de Nuevo México* (Taos, 1843). Facsimiles of each are in Weber, ed., *Northern Mexico*. For Navajo-Mexican relations, see the summations of documents in Myra Ellen Jenkins and Ward Alan Minge, *Navajo Activities Affecting the Acoma-Laguna Area, 1746–1910* (New York, 1974), pp. 73–105. For Texas, see Jean Louis

Berlandier, *The Indians of Texas in 1830,* John C. Ewers, ed. (Washington, 1969), and José Francisco Ruiz, *Report on the Indian Tribes of Texas in 1828,* John C. Ewers, ed., Georgette Dorn, trans. (New Haven, 1972).

Many of the works cited above mention the role played by Anglo-American traders in arming and inciting Indians, but no book or article devotes itself entirely to that subject. Similarly, many of the above works discuss Indian policy in the Mexican era, but few efforts have been made to examine policy systematically. Two exceptions are these: Charles R. McClure, "Neither Effective Nor Financed: The Difficulties of Indian Defense in New Mexico, 1837–1846," *Military History of Texas and the Southwest,* X (1972), pp. 73–92, and Daniel Tyler, "Mexican Indian Policy in New Mexico," *NMHR,* LV (April 1980), pp. 101–20. Both emphasize the failure of Mexican policy to cope with growing and seemingly insurmountable problems.

The conflicting official views of hostile nomadic Indians as both citizens and enemies are best described by Moisés González Navarro, "Instituciones indígenas en México independiente," in *Métodos y resultados de la política indigenista en México* (Mexico, 1954), pp. 113–69. Paul H. Ezell, "Indians Under the Law: Mexico, 1821–1847," *América Indígena,* XV (July 1955), pp. 199–214, is far narrower than its title implies. Ezell examined Indian legislation in the Estado de Occidente in the 1820s and found considerable concern for Indian welfare; he does not attempt to examine the implementation of those laws. Jack D. Forbes, "Nationalism, Tribalism, and Self-Determination: Yuman-Mexican Relations, 1821–1848," *Indian Historian,* VI (Spring 1973), pp. 18–22, briefly but persuasively explains why Mexico could not implement its egalitarian, republican policies toward Indians and how the Yumans remained outside the Mexican nation, "more free in 1848 than in 1821."

6: Crumbling Presidios, Citizen-Soldiers, and the Failure of the Iron Fist

Essential to an understanding of the military, both regular army and militia, in central Mexico on the eve of Mexican independence, is Christon I. Archer, *The Army in Bourbon Mexico, 1760–1810* (Albuquerque, 1977), who suggests that the late colonial army was not as powerful, respected, autonomous, or praetorian as other writers have supposed. For a good articulation of the earlier view, see Lyle N. McAlister, *The "Fuero Militar" in New Spain, 1764–1800* (Gainesville, 1957). For the northern frontier in the colonial period, the best single source on the military and military policy toward Indians is Max L. Moorhead, *The Presidio: Bastion of the Spanish Borderlands* (Norman, 1975), with its excellent bibliography of the many works dealing with the Spanish period. Moorhead's study excludes California and should be supplemented by Leon G. Campbell, "The Spanish Presidio in Alta California during the Mission Period, 1769–1784," *JW,* XVI (October 1977), pp. 63–77, who concludes that the coastal presidios' chief function was defense against foreigners rather than against Indians.

There is no good published study of the Mexican military in the first decades after independence. Edwin Lieuwen skims the subject quickly, but with well-founded generalizations, in "Curbing Militarism in Mexico," *NMHR,* XXXIII (October 1958), pp. 257–76, and J. Hexter has edited *El soldado mexicano, 1837–1847. Organización, vestuario, equipo, y reglamentos militares, recopilación de fuentes originales* (Mexico, 1958), a brief study, concerned mainly with dress and equipment, which shows a high level of continuity from the Spanish period.

I have relied on two unpublished studies: Russell G. Pynes, Jr., "The Mexican National Army: A Federalist Concept, 1824–1829" (M.A. Report, University of Texas, Austin, 1970), and Frank N. Samponaro, "The Political Role of the Army in Mexico, 1821–1848" (Ph.D.

diss., State University of New York, Stony Brook, 1974). María del Carmen Velázquez, *Tres estudios sobre las Provincias Internas de Nueva España* (Mexico, 1979), examines efforts at presidial reorganization from 1729 to 1848, but treats the years 1821–1846 too lightly.

Few published sources deal entirely with the condition of military forces in Mexico's Far North, and so a picture must be assembled from fragments of information drawn from a variety of primary sources. Most have already been mentioned in this essay, but those that focus primarily on military problems include: Carmen Perry, trans. and ed., *The Impossible Dream by the Rio Grande: A Documented Chronicle of the Establishment and Annihilation of San José de Palafox* (San Antonio, 1971), which provides a valuable look at the precarious existence of one presidio; and Malcolm D. McLean, "Tenochtitlán, Dream Capital of Texas," *SWHQ*, LXX (July 1966), pp. 23–43, which describes a short-lived garrison, founded in 1830 to check the Anglo-American advance into Texas, and abandoned in 1832. Some idea of how militia were to be organized in theory can be gleaned from John H. Jenkins, ed., "Regulations for the National Militia of the State of Coahuila y Texas, 1828," *Texas Military History*, VII (Fall 1969); *Reglamento para la milicía cívica del estado de Coahuila y Texas* (Monclova, 1834), trans. by Richard G. Santos in *Texas Military History*, VI (Winter 1967), pp. 286–300; and *Reglamento para la milicía cívica local del Estado de Occidente* (Alamos, 1828). Henry W. Barton, "The Anglo American Colonists Under Mexican Militia Laws," *SWHQ*, LXV (July 1961), pp. 61–71, is only a beginning at understanding how militia functioned in practice, and no comparable published work describes militia forces made up of pobladores.

Only a few works describe military campaigns in the Mexican period, among them: Sherburne F. Cook, "Expeditions to the Interior of California's Central Valley, 1820–1840," *Anthropological Records*, XX (February 1962), pp. 151–213; David M. Brugge, "Vizcarra's Navajo Campaign of 1823," *AW*, VI (Autumn 1964), pp. 223–44; and John P. Wilson, *Military Campaigns in the Navajo Country: Northwestern New Mexico, 1800–1846* (Santa Fe, 1967).

Military policy, personnel, and organization, including the relationship of volunteers to the regular army, remains one of the least studied aspects of life on the Mexican frontier.

7: The New Colonialism: Americans and the Frontier Economy

The economic life of the frontier provinces in the late colonial period has not been examined in depth, although some aspects have been studied. For the place of the frontier economy within the Spanish mercantile system, see Stanley J. and Barbara H. Stein, *The Colonial Heritage of Latin America: Essays on Economic Independence in Perspective* (New York, 1970). Colin M. MacLachlan and Jaime E. Rodríguez O., *The Forging of the Cosmic Race: A Reinterpretation of Colonial Mexico* (Berkeley, 1980), argue that "New Spain was neither feudal nor pre-capitalist," but "functioned as an emerging capitalist society within the worldwide economic system" (p. 1). An understanding of some of the problem areas in New Spain's economy just prior to independence emerges from John H. Hann, "The Role of the Mexican Deputies in the Proposal and Enactment of Measures of Economic Reform Applicable to Mexico," in Benson, ed. *Mexico and the Spanish Cortes*, pp. 153–77. Two articles by Robert Archibald, "Price Regulation in Hispanic California," *The Americas*, XXIII (April 1977), pp. 613–29, and "The Economy of the Alta California Missions, 1803–1821," *SCQ*, LVIII (Summer 1976), pp. 227–40, are especially good for the last years of the Spanish era. Max L. Moorhead, *New Mexico's Royal Road: Trade and Travel on the Chihuahua Trail* (Norman, 1954), provides the best published discussion of New Mexico's economic problems on the eve of Mexican independence. Ramón Arturo Gutiérrez, "Marriage, Sex and the Family: Social Change in Colonial New Mexico, 1690–1846" (Ph.D. diss., University of

Wisconsin-Madison, 1980), argues that capitalism entered New Mexico well before the Mexican period. The provincial economy began to shift from subsistence to commercial agriculture in the 1770s, and the Mexican period accelerated existing trends. I am grateful to Professor Gutiérrez for making this work available to me, and regret that my own manuscript had already gone to press so that I could not incorporate his conclusions. Faulk, *The Last Years of Spanish Texas,* contains succinct analyses of Texas economic life.

For an understanding of the general Mexican economy between 1821 and 1846, the best works in English are Charles C. Cumberland, *Mexico: The Struggle for Modernity* (New York, 1968), which emphasizes economic history more than other general surveys of Mexican history, and the fine analysis by John H. Coatsworth, "Obstacles to Economic Growth in Nineteenth Century Mexico," *American Historical Review,* LXXXIII (February 1978), pp. 80–100. In Spanish, the starting point should be Ciro Cardoso, ed., *México en el siglo XIX (1821–1910): Historia económica y de la estructura social* (Mexico, 1980), an anthology of original essays by a group of specialists on themes such as political economy, agrarian structures, mining, industry, and banking. (This volume appeared after I had completed this manuscript.) Diego G. López Rosado, *Historia y pensamiento económico de México,* 4 vols. (Mexico, 1968–74), is the best general introduction to the subject. Agustín Cue Cánovas, *Historia social y económica de México (1521–1854)* (3rd ed.; Mexico, 1967), provides a briefer, but solid traditional account. Studies of the Mexican economy by Mexican historians generally ignore the frontier, apparently viewing it as peripheral and unimportant. For drawing comparisons, W. Elliott Brownlee, *Dynamics of Ascent: A History of the American Economy* (New York, 1974), is a lucid introduction to the United States economy.

Jessie Davies Francis, "An Economic and Social History of Mexican California, 1822–1846" (Ph.D. diss., University of California, Berkeley, 1935), is an exceedingly rich overview of all aspects of economic life, providing fresh information and insights on many topics. No comparable economic history exists for other frontier provinces.

The Santa Fe trade and the closely related fur trade are the subject of a number of good studies. Albert Bork, *Nuevos aspectos del comercio entre Nuevo México y Misuri, 1822–1846* (Mexico City, 1944), represents the first serious effort to illuminate the Mexican side of the Santa Fe trade. Moorhead, *New Mexico's Royal Road,* builds on Bork's work and adds new material. The full story of Mexican involvement in the Santa Fe trade has yet to be told. A work by a Mexican historian, which seemed to offer promise of doing this, is instead based heavily on printed sources and makes insufficient use of Mexican archives: Ángela Moyano Pahissa, *El comercio de Santa Fé y la guerra del '47* (Mexico, 1976).

For the fur trade, see Robert Glass Cleland, *This Reckless Breed of Men: The Trappers and Fur Traders of the Southwest* (New York, 1950; reprinted Albuquerque, 1979), a pioneering synthesis written in flowing narrative; David Lavender, *Bent's Fort* (New York, 1954; reprinted Albuquerque, 1976); David J. Weber, *The Taos Trappers: The Fur Trade in the Far Southwest, 1540–1846* (Norman, 1971); and Gloria Griffen Cline, *Exploring the Great Basin* (Norman, 1963). The extension of the Santa Fe trade and the fur trade to California is well-summarized in LeRoy R. and Ann W. Hafen, *Old Spanish Trail, Santa Fé to Los Angeles* (Glendale, Ca., 1954).

For the sea otter trade, one needs look no further than Adele Ogden's classic, *The California Sea Otter Trade, 1748–1848* (Berkeley, 1941). Ogden also has written the standard accounts of the hide and tallow trade: "Hides and Tallow: McCulloch, Hartnell and Company, 1822–1828," *CHSQ,* VI (September 1927), pp. 254–65; and "Boston Hide Droghers Along California Shores," *CHSQ,* VIII (December 1929), pp. 289–305.

Secondary literature on other economic activities during the Mexican era tends to be spotty, especially economic activities involving mainly Mexicans. There is no good published work on cattle ranching in Texas or California, or on sheep raising in New Mexico for these years. Agriculture has also been ignored, except for viticulture: Iris Ann Wilson

[Engstrand], "Early Southern California Viniculture, 1830–1865," *SCQ*, XXXIX (September 1957), pp. 242–50, and Vincent Carosso, *The California Wine Industry, 1830–1859* (Berkeley, 1951), which looks at northern California as well. C. Raymond Clar did pioneering work on lumbering on the California coast: *California Government and Forestry from Spanish Times to the Creation of the Department of Natural Resources in 1927* (Sacramento, 1959). Sherwood D. Burgess, "Lumbering in Hispanic California," *CHSQ*, XLI (September 1962), pp. 237–48, adds little new to Clar's work, and fails to cite it. Thomas R. Cox, *Mills and Markets: A History of the Pacific Coast Lumber Industry to 1900* (Seattle, 1975), provides a broadly conceived analysis and is the best starting place.

Scholarly literature on mining is abundant, but much is superficial and would benefit from thorough archival research. Duane Kendall Hale, "California's First Mining Frontier and Its Influence on the Settlement of that Area," *JW*, XVIII (January 1979), pp. 14–21, provides a useful summary of pre-1848 gold discoveries in California, but is careless, uncritical of sources, displays no knowledge of earlier literature, and must be used with great caution. J. N. Bowman, "The First Authentic Placer Mine in California," *SCQ*, XXXI (September 1949), pp. 225–30, is perhaps the best of many accounts of this episode. For New Mexico, Stuart A. Northrup, *Minerals of New Mexico* (1st ed., 1944; rev. ed., Albuquerque, 1959), skips too lightly over the Mexican period. More valuable is John M. Townley, "El Placer: A New Mexico Mining Boom Before 1846," *JW*, X (January 1971), pp. 102–15, who provides substantial detail about one strike, but is not sufficiently critical of his sources. John M. Sully, "The Story of the Santa Rita Mine," *Old Santa Fe*, III (April 1916), pp. 133–49, is still valuable for the Mexican period, but the full story of this important copper mine awaits some enterprising scholar.

Except for Patricia M. Bauer, "Beginnings of Tanning in California," *CHSQ*, XXXIII (March 1954), pp. 59–72, industry, arts, and crafts of the Mexican era have not been the subject of books and articles. Specialists have devoted considerable attention to crafts of the Spanish era in New Mexico, but most either ignore the Mexican period or treat it as an extension of the Spanish years. An important exception is E. Boyd, *Popular Arts of Spanish New Mexico* (Santa Fe, 1974). We need more detailed studies of the ways in which the economic life of the pobladores changed in response to outside influences in the Mexican era, but until that is done, scraps and bits of information must be gleaned from other sources.

Among the few published primary sources which provide economic data for the frontier provinces in the Mexican period are these: Almonte's *Noticia estadística sobre Tejas*, and Robert A. Potash, ed. and trans., "Notes and Documents [Answers from Tucson and Santa Fe to a Questionnaire from the Banco de Avío, 1831]," *NMHR*, XXIV (October 1949), pp. 332–40.

8: Regulating the Economy: Frontier vs. Nation

Mexico's efforts to regulate foreign trade for the benefit of her own economic growth is discussed in John E. Baur, "The Evolution of a Mexican Foreign Trade Policy, 1821–1828," *The Americas*, XIX (January 1963), pp. 238–49. Although limited in chronology, it is perhaps the best introduction to the subject in English. Romeo Flores Caballero and Luis Córdova, eds., *Protección y libre cambio: el debate entre 1821 y 1836* (Mexico, 1971), contains pertinent documents. Robert A. Potash, *El Banco de Avío de México. El fomento de la industria, 1821–1846* (Mexico, 1959), looks at government efforts to promote industry, especially textiles. Inés Herrera Canales, *El comercio exterior de México, 1821–1875* (Mexico, 1977), contains a good statistical base, with warnings about their limitations; the best national statistics for the years 1821–1846 remain those in Miguel Lerdo de Tejada, *Comercio exterior de México desde la Conquista hasta hoy* (1st ed., 1853; Mexico, 1967), although they ignore the Far North.

Except for Eugene Barker's "Difficulties of a Mexican Revenue Officer," *SWHQ*, IV (January 1901), pp. 190–202, no book or article focuses solely on government regulation of frontier economic life. Hence, this chapter is derived from a variety of sources, but especially those cited for Chapter VII, many of which look at Mexican responses to foreign economic penetration.

9: "To Govern is to Populate": The Peopling of Texas

Spanish precedents in Louisiana are explained in greatest detail in three articles by Gilbert C. Din: "Protecting the 'Barrera': Spain's Defenses in Louisiana, 1763–1779," *Louisiana History*, XIX (Spring 1978), pp. 183–211; "Spain's Immigration Policy in Louisiana and the American Penetration, 1792–1803," *SWHQ*, LXXVI (January 1973), pp. 255–76; and "The Immigration Policy of Governor Esteben Miró in Spanish Louisiana," *SWHQ*, LXXIII (October 1969), pp. 155–75. For Spanish Texas, Mattie Austin Hatcher's *The Opening of Texas to Foreign Settlement, 1801–1821* (Austin 1927), remains the standard work.

The best single source for Mexican attitudes and policies regarding foreign immigration during these years is Dieter George Berninger, *La inmigración en méxico, 1821–1857* (Mexico, 1974). The Mexican statesman who examined the question of colonization of Texas most systematically was Tadeo Ortiz de Ayala, whose life and thought has been ably summarized by Wilbert H. Timmons: *Tadeo Ortiz: Mexican Colonizer and Reformer* (El Paso, 1974). Ortiz's views appear in his two books: *Resumen de la estadística del imperio mexicano* (1st ed., 1822; Mexico, 1968), and *México considerado como nación independiente y libre . . .* (1st ed. 1832; Guadalajara, 1952); and in remarkable and lengthy letters dated October 31 and November 30, 1830, and February 2, 1833, translated into English by Edith Louise Kelly and Mattie Austin Hatcher, "Tadeo Ortiz de Ayala and the Colonization of Texas, 1822–1833," *SWHQ*, XXXII (July and October, 1928; February and April, 1929), pp. 74–86; 152–64; 222–51; and 311–43.

Focusing more closely on Texas, Eugene C. Barker's masterful *Life of Stephen F. Austin: Founder of Texas, 1793–1836* (1st ed., 1926; 2nd ed., reprinted Austin 1969), remains so influential that writers often use Austin's life as a vehicle to understand Texas during these years. Barker also made a massive quantity of documents readily available for historians by editing *The Austin Papers*, 3 vols. (Washington and Austin, 1924–28). The contribution of the Baron de Bastrop, who worked closely with Austin, is the subject of R. Woods Moore, "The Role of the Baron de Bastrop in the Anglo-American Settlement of the Spanish Southwest," *Louisiana Historical Quarterly*, XXXI (July 1948), pp. 606–81, who concluded that "more than anybody else," Bastrop "made possible the entrance of Americans" into Texas.

Less successful empresarios than Austin have been treated in a number of able books and articles. Mary Virginia Henderson, "Minor Empresario Contracts for the Colonization of Texas, 1825–1834," *SWHQ*, XXXI (April 1928), pp. 294–334, and XXXII (July 1928), pp. 1–28, provides valuable capsule histories of twenty-four contracts. Some of the contracts which Henderson outlines have been examined in detail in William Herman Oberste's well-researched *Texas Irish Empresarios and Their Colonies: Power & Hewetson, McMullen & McGloin, Refugio-San Patricio* (Austin, 1953), and in Edward A. Lukes, *De Witt Colony of Texas* (Austin 1976), which expands substantially upon Ethel Zivley Rather, "De Witt's Colony," *SWHQ*, VII (October 1904), pp. 95–102. Arthur B. J. Hammett, *The Empresario: Don Martín de León* (Waco, 1973), contains an assortment of documents and commentary but does not fill the need for a biography or study of De León's colony. At the other extreme, Malcolm D. McLean is preparing a meticulous and herculean compilation of Mexican and American documents relating to a grant that eventually came under the control of empresario Sterling C. Robertson: *Papers Concerning Robertson's Colony in Texas*, 7 vols. to date (Fort Worth and Arlington, Texas, 1974–). LeRoy P. Graf, "Colonizing Projects in Texas South of the Nueces, 1820–1845," *SWHQ*, L (April 1947), pp. 431–48, offers reasons for failures in the area between the Rio Grande and the Nueces, which was part of Tamaulipas until 1836.

The evolution of Mexican policy toward American immigration to Texas is summarized in Eugene C. Barker, *Mexico and Texas, 1821–1835* (Dallas, 1928). Iturbide's policy is examined in detail in Joseph C. McElhannon, "Imperial Mexico and Texas, 1821–1823," *SWHQ*, LIII (October 1949), pp. 117–50, a superior article grounded in primary sources. Later aspects of Mexican policy are examined in two standard works: Alleine Howrene, "Causes and Origin of the Decree of April 6, 1830," *SWHQ*, XVI (Aprl 1913), pp. 378–422, and Ohland Morton, *Terán and Texas: A Chapter in Texas-Mexican Relations* (Austin, 1948). Helen W. Harris, "Almonte's Inspection of Texas in 1834," *SWHQ*, XLI (January 1938), pp. 195–211, adds little not in Barker's *Austin*. *Tejano* disagreements with federal policy are outlined briefly in Eugene C. Barker, "Native Latin American Contributions to the Colonization and Independence of Texas," *SWHQ*, XLVI (April 1943), pp. 317–35.

Much has been written on the reasons for the large Anglo-American immigration to Texas and the types of colonists attracted. See, for example, Eugene Barker's "Notes on the Colonization of Texas," *SWHQ*, XXVII (October 1923), pp. 103–19, which disputes the idea that the extension of slavery into Texas, and its annexation, was a premeditated scheme of Southerners, and Mark E. Nackman's "Anglo-American Migrants to the West: Men of Broken Fortunes? The Case of Texas, 1821–46," *WHQ*, V (October 1974), pp. 441–55, who answers his question in the affirmative. The "push" of indebtedness brought more men to Texas than the "pull" of opportunity. The failure of Anglo-Americans to assimilate in Texas is perhaps best examined in a classic work by a sociologist, Samuel H. Lowrie, *Culture Conflict in Texas, 1821–1835* (New York, 1932).

10: The "Texas Game" Again? Peopling California and New Mexico

Literature regarding immigration into New Mexico in the Mexican period is fragmentary. Sister Mary Loyola, "The American Occupation of New Mexico, 1821–1852," *NMHR*, XIV (January, April, and July 1939), pp. 34–75, 143–99, and 230–86, treats the years 1821–45 in a cursory fashion, focusing on the actual military conquest and its aftermath. Daniel Tyler, "Anglo-American Penetration of the Southwest: The View From New Mexico," *SWHQ*, LXXV (January 1972), pp. 325–38, shows how events in Texas, especially the Fredonia revolt, contributed to deteriorating relations between Anglo-American residents of New Mexico and *nuevomexicanos*.

Compared to New Mexico, California held greater attraction for immigrants, and seemed more threatened by a foreign takeover. Scholarly literature on these themes reflects California's relative importance. A valuable overview, which distinguishes between two types of Anglo-American immigrants, is John A. Hawgood, "The Pattern of Yankee Infiltration in Mexican California, 1821–1846," *PHR*, XXVII (February 1958), pp. 27–38. Robert G. Cleland, "The Early Sentiment for the Annexation of California: An Account of the Growth of American Interest in California, 1835–1846," *SWHQ*, XVIII (July and October, 1914; January 1915), pp. 1–40 and 121–61; 231–60. See, too, Norman A. Graebner's more broadly conceived: *Empire on the Pacific: A Study in American Continental Expansion* (New York, 1955). The colorful "false start" of the Mexican-American War at Monterey in 1842, which left little doubt as to American intentions toward California, is best described in George M. Brooke, Jr., "The Vest Pocket War of Commodore Jones," *PHR*, XXI (August 1962), pp. 217–33.

In both California and New Mexico, foreign immigration cannot be understood apart from the economic motives that attracted foreigners in the first place. Hence, sources utilized for Chapter VII remain essential for this chapter as well. Land was especially attractive to foreigners by the 1840s. That is clear from a number of studies of overland emigrants from America, the finest perhaps being John D. Unruh's book, *The Plains Across: The Overland Emigrants and the Trans-Mississippi West, 1840–1860* (Urbana, 1979).

For land grants in California see: Robert G. Cleland, *Cattle on a Thousand Hills* (1st ed., 1941; 2nd ed., San Marino, 1951); W. W. Robinson, *Land in California* (Berkeley, 1948); Robert G. Cowan, *Ranchos of California. A List of Spanish Concessions, 1775–1822, and Mexican Grants, 1822–1846* (Fresno, 1956); David Hornbeck, "Land Tenure and Rancho Expansion in Alta California, 1784–1846," *Journal of Historical Geography*, IV (1978), pp. 371–90. Leonard Pitt, *The Decline of the Californios: A Social History of the Spanish-Speaking Californians, 1846–1890* (Berkeley, 1966), paints an especially vivid picture of the ways in which *californios* lost land after the American occupation.

Ray H. Mattison, "Early Spanish and Mexican Settlements in Arizona," *NMHR*, XXI (October 1946), pp. 273–327, presents case histories of seventeen land grants in Southern Arizona, nearly all dating from the Mexican era until Apache hostilities in the early 1830s checked the development of ranchos in that area. J. J. Bowden, *Spanish and Mexican Land Grants in the Chihuahuan Acquisition* (El Paso, 1971), is a compendium of information about twenty-six grants in southern New Mexico and West Texas (an area that belonged to Chihuahua until the Gadsden Purchase). Bowden's encyclopedic "Private Land Claims in the Southwest," 6 vols. (LLM thesis, Southern Methodist University, Dallas, 1969), should be the starting point for any researcher interested in land grants in New Mexico or Arizona.

The use of land grants as a tool for attracting or rewarding foreigners in New Mexico is not yet well-understood by historians, and may never be. Land grant records are voluminous and many are fraudulent. Understanding the laws and customs regarding the distribution of land in the Mexican era has been obscured by ex post facto readings of laws by interested parties, and by failure to understand a different cultural context of legal traditions. These points are suggested by: Victor Westphall "Fraud and the Implications of Fraud in the Land Grants of New Mexico," *NMHR*, LXIX (July 1974), pp. 189–218; Marianne L. Stoller, "Grants of Desperation, Lands of Speculation: Mexican Period Land Grants in Colorado," and Janet Lecompte, "Manuel Armijo and the Americans," both in *JW*, XIX (July 1980), pp. 22–39 and 51–63. Studies of specific land grants usually treat the Mexican period in sketchy fashion: LeRoy R. Hafen, "Mexican Land Grants in Colorado," *Colorado Magazine*, IV (May 1927), pp. 81–93; William A. Keleher, *Maxwell Land Grant: A New Mexico Item* (Santa Fe, 1942), and Jim Berry Pearson, *The Maxwell Land Grant* (Norman, 1961). Lawrence R. Murphy, "The Beaubien and Miranda Land Grant, 1841–1846," *NMHR*, XLII (January 1967), pp. 27–46, fills in some details of the Mexican origins of the Maxwell Grant, as did Harold H. Dunham, "New Mexico Land Grants with Special Reference to the Title Papers of the Maxwell Grant," *NMHR*, XXX (January 1955), pp. 1–22, who challenged the idea that Armijo's use of land grants was designed for personal gain rather than for defense. Herbert O. Brayer, *William Blackmore: The Spanish-Mexican Land Grants of New Mexico and Colorado, 1863–1878* (Denver, 1949) says more about the Mexican period than its title suggests.

The spilling over of gente de razón onto Pueblo Indian lands has been explored in two fine articles by Myra Ellen Jenkins: "Taos Pueblo and Its Neighbors, 1540–1847," *NMHR*, XLI (April 1966), pp. 85–114, and "The Baltasar Baca 'Grant': History of An Encroachment," *El Palacio*, LXVIII (Spring 1961), pp. 47–68.

Mexican reaction to growing American interest and influence on the Pacific is described in two fine articles by Frank A. Knapp, Jr., "Preludios de la pérdida de California," *Historia mexicana*, IV (octubre-diciembre 1954), pp. 235–49, which explains Mexican responses to

Jones' seizure of Monterey, and "The Mexican Fear of Manifest Destiny in California," in Thomas E. Cotner and Carlos E. Castañeda, eds., *Essays in Mexican History* (Austin 1958), pp. 192–208, which links that fear to Mexico's decision to go to war over Texas. Gene Brack, *Mexico Views Manifest Destiny, 1821–1846. An Essay on the Origins of the Mexican War* (Albuquerque, 1975), is a much-needed study of the growth of Mexican fears and anger toward American attitudes of superiority and aggression that, in Brack's judgment, made it almost impossible for patriotic Mexicans not to go to war in 1846.

Mexico's most serious effort to countercolonize the northern frontier with Mexicans is the subject of C. Alan Hutchinson's splendid *Frontier Settlement in Mexican California: The Híjar-Padrés Colony and its Origins, 1769–1835* (New Haven, 1969). In a polemical essay, Governor Figueroa explained that the Híjar-Padrés colony failed because its leaders were conniving rascals of traitorous intentions: *A Manifesto to the Mexican Republic, which Brigadier General José Figueroa, Commandant and Political Chief of Upper California presents on his conduct and on that of José María de Híjar and José María Padrés as Directors of Colonization in 1834 and 1835,* C. Alan Hutchinson, ed. and trans. (Berkeley, 1978). Historians have heretofore taken Figueroa's point of view, but Hutchinson suggests in his introduction that Figueroa may have been the conniving rascal. After failing to bolster the Mexican population of California, the government toyed with the idea of bringing European colonists to the Pacific coast to block United States expansion. See, for example, Lester Gordon Engelson, "Proposals for the Colonization of California by England in Connection with the Mexican Debt to British Bondholders, 1837–1846," *CHSQ,* XVIII (June 1939), pp. 136–48, and John A. Hawgood, "A Projected Prussian Colonization of Upper California," *SCQ,* XLVIII (December 1966), pp. 353–68.

11: Society and Culture in Transition

For background of the Spanish era, the essential starting point is Oakah L. Jones, Jr., *Los Paisanos: Spanish Settlers on the Northern Frontier of New Spain* (Norman, 1979), with its current bibliography and summaries of nearly all aspects of society and culture. For society and culture in central Mexico, 1821–1846, one can turn to many works, but that of Alejandra Moreno Toscano, "Los trabajadores y el proyecto de industrialización, 1810–1867," in Enrique Florescano et al., *La clase obrera en la historia de México,* vol. I: *De la colonia al imperio* (Mexico, 1980), pp. 302–50, and pertinent essays in Ciro Cardoso, ed., *México en el siglo XIX (1821–1910: Historia económica y de la estructura social* (Mexico, 1980), are among the most innovative.

Very few writers have examined society or culture on the Mexican frontier, per se. The monumental work is Hubert Howe Bancroft, *California Pastoral, 1769–1848* (San Francisco, 1888), an underrated supplement to his largely political and economic seven volume *History of California.* For New Mexico, portions of Frances León Swadesh, *Los Primeros Pobladores: Hispanic Americans of the Ute Frontier* (Notre Dame, 1974), and Roxanne Dunbar Ortiz, *Roots of Resistance: Land Tenure in New Mexico, 1680–1980* (Los Angeles, 1980), raise provocative questions pertaining to New Mexico society. The imaginative dissertation by Ramón Gutiérrez, "Marriage, Sex and the Family," argues as I do that this period witnessed profound societal change ranging from an increase of debt peonage to more individualistic dances. Gutérrez sees the source of this change as essentially economic, and beginning when commercial agriculture started to replace subsistence agriculture in the 1770s. Utilizing quantitative techniques as well as folklore, Gutiérrez identifies a variety of societal changes including: greater frequence of marriage outside of one's class and one's immediate locale; a narrowing of ages between spouses; and a shift from strict parental control of marriage to individual choice of a partner, based upon romantic love.

For the brief Mexican interregnum in Texas, one must turn largely to unpublished literature, especially the previously mentioned dissertations by Downs ("Mexicans in Texas"), Tijerina, ("Tejanos and Texas"), and James Michael McReynolds, "Family Life in a Borderland Community: Nacogdoches, Texas, 1779–1861" (Texas Tech University, 1978), a model for other communities, and Gilberto Miguel Hinojosa, "Setters and Sojourners in the 'Chaparral': A Demographic Study of a Borderlands Town in Transition, Laredo, 1775–1870" (University of Texas at Austin, 1979). Arnoldo de León, *The Tejano Community, 1836–1900* (Albuquerque, 1982), which I read in an early manuscript version, begins in 1836, but many of its generalizations apply to the Mexican period.

As with other subjects in this volume, many of the details of social and cultural history must be pieced together from a variety of sources. Concerning relations between classes and between ethnic groups, a scanty literature exists. The position of assimilated Indians in Mexican society would be better understood if we had more studies such as W. W. Robinson, "The Indians of Los Angeles," *SCQ*, XX (December 1938), pp. 156–72, and George Harwood Phillips, "Indians in Los Angeles, 1781–1875: Economic Integration, Social Disintegration," *PHR*, XLIX (August 1980), pp. 427–51. For the legal position of slaves in Texas, Lester G. Bugbee, "Slavery In Early Texas," *Political Science Quarterly*, XIII (September and December 1898), pp. 389–412 and 648–68, remains the standard source. The position of free blacks in Texas is summarized in Rosalie Schwartz, *Across the Río to Freedom. U. S. Negroes in Mexico* (El Paso, 1975).

Historical literature on women is beginning to emerge. See, especially, Jane Dysart, "Mexican Women of Texas, 1830–1860: The Assimilation Process," *WHQ*, VII (October 1976), pp. 365–75; Janet Lecompte, "The Independent Women of Hispanic New Mexico, 1821–1846," *WHQ*, XII (January 1981), pp. 17–35, which is based on archival sources; and Joan M. Jensen and Darlis A. Miller, "The Gentle Tamers Revisited: New Approaches to the History of Women in the American West," *PHR*, XLIX (May 1980), pp. 173–213, an ambitious review of the literature and a call for an examination of women of different cultures and the relationships between them. Alfredo Mirandé and Evangelina Enriquez, *La Chicana: The Mexican-American Woman* (Chicago, 1979), pp. 53–68, skim the historical literature on the Mexican period in this sweeping, multidisciplinary overview.

Some census data, so vital to an understanding of many aspects of social history, has been published. For California, see for example, the Los Angeles census of 1830 in W. N. Charles, "Transcription and Translation of the Old Mexican Documents of the Los Angeles County Archives," *SCQ*, XX (June 1938), facing p. 84; J. Gregg Layne, ed., "The First Census of the Los Angeles District. . . . 1836," *SCQ*, XVIII (Sept.-Dec., 1936), pp. 81–99, with a facsimile of the document; and Marie E. Northrup, ed., "The Los Angeles Padrón of 1844," *SCQ*, XLII (December 1960), pp. 360–417. For New Mexico, see Virginia Langham Olmsted, *New Mexico Spanish and Mexican Colonial Censuses, 1790, 1823, 1845* (Albuquerque, 1975); and for Texas, Marion Day Mullins, ed., *The First Census of Texas, 1829–36* (Washington, D. C., 1959), mistitled in an extraordinary display of ethnocentricity and focusing on the Anglo-American colonists while omitting San Antonio and Goliad. In many respects, more complete census data is available for the late Spanish and American periods than for the Mexican period.

The property and possessions of the pobladores are revealed in wills and financial statements. Some for New Mexico have been published: Daniel Tyler, "The Personal Property of Manuel Armijo, 1829," *El Palacio*, LXXX (Fall 1974), pp. 45–58; Ward Alan Minge, "The Last Will and Testament of Don Severino Martínez [1827]," *New Mexico Quarterly*, XXXIII (Spring 1963), pp. 33–56; Carmen Espinosa, *Shawls, Crinolines, and Filigree: The Dress and Adornment of the Women of New Mexico, 1739–1900* (El Paso, 1970), contains a remarkable series of women's wills, dated 1739 to 1831. M. R. Harrington, "The Will of Don Tomás Antonio Yorba, Year of 1845," *SCQ*, XXXIII (March 1951), pp. 67–73, looks at one California ranchero.

For architecture, see Harold Kirker's excellent *California's Architectural Frontier. Style and Tradition in the Nineteenth Century* (1st ed., 1960; Santa Barbara, 1973), and Bainbridge Bunting, *Early Architecture in New Mexico* (Albuquerque, 1976), which reflects growth of Bunting's understanding since his *Taos Adobes: Spanish Colonial and Territorial Architecture of the Taos Valley* (Santa Fe, 1964).

More studies of urban development and patterns in the Mexican era are needed. Models are the following: Howard J. Nelson, "The Two Pueblos of Los Angeles: Agricultural Village and Embryo Town," *SCQ*, LIX (Spring 1977), pp. 1–11, and Daniel J. Garr, "A Frontier Agrarian Settlement: San José de Guadalupe, 1777–1850," *San José Studies*, II (November 1976), pp. 93–105. W. H. Timmons, "The El Paso Area in the Mexican Period, 1821–1848," *SWHQ*, LXXXIV (July 1980), pp. 1–28, looks at many themes during these years, but a study of spatial and demographic growth, and occupational structure in El Paso is still needed. For a synthesis of urban development in the West, see John W. Reps' splendidly illustrated *Cities of the American West: A History of Frontier Urban Planning* (Princeton, 1979), and Richard Wades's seminal: *The Urban Frontier: Pioneer Life in Early Pittsburgh, Cincinnati, Lexington, Louisville, and St. Louis* (1st ed., 1959; Chicago, 1964).

We understand town government in theory better than in practice, for it is easier to read rules and regulations than to see how they are enforced: Marc Simmons, ed. and trans., "Antonio Barreiro's 1833 Proclamation on Santa Fe City Government," *El Palacio*, 76 (June 1970), pp. 24–30; Gilbert Ralph Cruz, ed. and trans., "The City Ordinances for the Internal Management and Administration of the Municipal Government of San Antonio of Béjar, 1829," *Texana*, VII (Summer 1969), pp. 95–116.

Literature is extensive on newspapers, the press, and education. More sources are discussed in the notes to this chapter, but starting points ought to be these: Douglas C. McMurtrie, "Pioneer Printing in Texas," *SWHQ*, XXXV (January 1932), pp. 173–93; Henry R. Wagner, "New Mexico Spanish Press," *NMHR*, XII (January 1937), pp. 372–410; and Herbert Fahey, *Early Printing in California: From its Beginnings in the Mexican Territory to Statehood, September 1850* (San Francisco, 1956). For the kinds of books that came to the frontier with foreigners, see Doyce B. Nunis, *Books in Their Sea Chests: Reading Along the Early California Coast* (San Francisco, 1964), a booklet which suggests the need for more research on this subject. If one could consult only one work on education, it should be Daniel Tyler, "The Mexican Teacher," *Red River Valley Historical Review*, I (Autumn 1974), pp. 207–211, which also provides a good guide to sources. I. J. Cox, "Educational Efforts in San Fernando de Béxar," *SWHQ*, VI (July 1902), pp. 27–63 is the best study of schooling in any frontier community of the Mexican era.

Although unsatisfactory in many respects, physician George D. Lyman's "The Scalpel Under Three Flags in California," *CHSQ*, V (June 1925), pp. 142–206, remains the most solid introduction. Similarly, physician Pat I. Nixon has written the best overview for Texas: *The Medical Story of Early Texas, 1528–1853* (Lancaster, Pa., 1946), which tends to be episodic and focus on individuals at the expense of analysis. No good published study of New Mexico's medical history exists for these years. Studies of specific diseases and community reaction to them include: J. Villasana Haggard, "Epidemic Cholera in Texas, 1833–1834," *SWHQ*, XL (January 1937), pp. 216–30, and Sherburne F. Cook, "Smallpox in Spanish and Mexican California, 1770–1845," *Bulletin of the History of Medicine*, VII (February 1939), pp. 153–91.

For comparing aspects of society and culture on the Mexican frontier with the American frontier, I have relied upon: James E. Davis, *Frontier America, 1800–1840: A Comparative Demographic Analysis of the Settlement Process* (Glendale, 1977), and Malcom J. Rohrbough, *The Trans-Appalachian Frontier: People, Societies, and Institutions, 1775–1850* (New York, 1978).

12: Separatism and Revolt

Historians and social scientists have written extensively on the phenomenon of rebellion and revolution. Thomas H. Greene, *Comparative Revolutionary Movements* (Englewood Cliffs, N. J., 1974), provides a concise overview of what he terms "accelerators" and "preconditions" for revolt and revolution, and a good guide to sources. See, too, Ted Robert Gurr, *Why Men Rebel* (Princeton, 1970), who integrates many ideas about the causes of political violence into the theory of relative deprivation—a useful explanation for some of the events in the Mexican Far North.

The most studied of the revolts in northernmost Mexico has been the successful Texas rebellion. Eugene Barker's biography of Stephen F. Austin, along with his *Mexico and Texas 1821–1835* (Dallas, 1928), have enriched my understanding of causes more than any other secondary source and clearly made their mark on subsequent interpretive studies, such as: Samuel H. Lowrie, *Culture Conflict in Texas* (New York, 1932); William C. Binkley, *The Texas Revolution* (Baton Rouge, 1952), a series of graceful and lucid essays originally delivered as lectures; and David M. Vigness, *The Revolutionary Decades* (Austin, 1965). Some of Barker's early articles remain the standard treatment of their subject. He explored the Texas declaration of November 7, 1835, in "The Texas Declaration of Causes for Taking Up Arms Against Mexico," *SWHQ*, XV (January 1912), pp. 173–85; the 1835 assault on Anáhuac in "Difficulties of a Mexican Revenue Officer in Texas," *SWHQ*, IV (January 1901), pp. 190–202; the evolution of Austin's attitude toward independence from Mexico in "Stephen F. Austin and the Independence of Texas," *SWHQ*, XVIII (April 1910), pp. 257–85; and the role of "new" settlers vs. "old" settlers in "The Texas Revolutionary Army," *SWHQ*, IX (April 1906), pp. 227–61.

Historians have begun to examine the relationship between Mexican federalists and the Texas rebels. See, especially, Ramond Estep, "Lorenzo de Zavala and the Texas Revolution," *SWHQ*, LVIII (January 1954), pp. 322–35, and two articles by C. Alan Hutchinson: "General José Antonio Mexía and His Texas Interests," *SWHQ*, LXXXII (October 1978), pp. 117–42, and "Mexican Federalists in New Orleans and the Texas Revolution," *Louisiana Historical Quarterly*, XXXIX (January 1956), pp. 1–47. Mark E. Nackman, *A Nation Within a Nation. The Rise of Texas Nationalism* (Port Washington, N. Y., 1972), traces this theme into the years before 1836.

For aspects of military engagements in 1836 from the Mexican viewpoint, see Vicente Filisola, *Memorias para la historia de la guerra de Tejas*, 2 vols. (1st ed., 1848–1849; Mexico, 1973); Carlos E. Castañeda, *The Mexican Side of the Texan Revolution* (Dallas, 1928); and "Santa Anna in Texas: A Mexican Viewpoint," *SWHQ*, LXII (April 1959), pp. 489–512. Several popular book-length studies look at military confrontations, the most engaging, balanced, and carefully researched being Walter Lord, *A Time to Stand* (New York, 1961).

Despite the extensive scholarly literature on the rebellion in Texas, John H. Jenkins argues that there is much that we do not understand and that careful study of newly available documentary collections will lead to a reinterpretation of many aspects of the revolt, including its causes: "Available Resources Make Revolution Important Texas Research Topic," *Texas Libraries*, XL (Fall 1979), pp. 112–18. Jenkins has aided scholars immensely by editing the *Papers of the Texas Revolution*, 10 vols. (Austin, 1973), which brings together in one convenient source unpublished documents from a variety of archives as well as documents previously published in collections such as Eugene C. Barker, ed., *The Austin Papers*, 3 vols. (Washington and Austin, 1924–28), and William C. Binkley, ed., *Official Correspondence of the Texas Revolution, 1835–1836* (New York, 1936). Despite its comprehensiveness, Jenkins' work is not complete.

Separatism and rebellion in California are best treated in George Tays' unpublished dissertation, "Revolutionary California," portions of which pertaining to the 1836 revolt have been published in modified form: "Commodore Edmund B. Kennedy, U. S. N., versus Governor Nicolás Gutiérrez: An Incident of 1836," *CHSQ*, XII (June 1933), pp. 137–46; "The Surrender of Monterey by Governor Nicolás Gutiérrez, November 5, 1836," *CHSQ*, XV (December 1936), pp. 338–63; and "Captain Andrés Castillero, Diplomat. An Account from Unpublished Sources of his Services to Mexico in the Alvarado Revolution of 1836–1838," *CHSQ*, XIV (September 1935), pp. 230–68. The extent of separatist sentiment among the *californios* on the eve of the Mexican War has not, and may never, be well understood. Insights into pro-British sentiment of some *californios* may be gleaned from Sheldon G. Jackson, "Two Pro-British Plots in Alta California," *SCQ*, LXV (Summer 1973), pp. 105–40, and "The British and the California Dream: Rumors, Myths, and Legends," *SCQ*, LVII (Fall 1975), pp. 251–70.

The most detailed accounts of Sonoran separatism in English are Stevens's unpublished dissertation, "Mexico's Forgotten Frontier," and Stewart Voss, *Sonora and Sinaloa in the Nineteenth Century*, to be published in 1982 by the University of Arizona Press. Separatism in New Mexico has scarcely begun to be examined. Angélico Chávez has written the only study of the 1837 rebel leader, "José Gonzales, Genízaro Governor," *NMHR*, XXX (July 1955), pp. 190–94. Philip Reno, "Rebellion in New Mexico, 1837," *NMHR*, XL (July 1965), pp. 197–213, is the most balanced published account of that episode. It uses fresh sources, and tries to illuminate the rebel's motives. Earlier treatments of the 1837 revolt, such as those in Benjamin M. Read, *Historia ilustrada de Nuevo México* (Santa Fe, 1911), and Ralph Emerson Twitchell, *The Leading Facts of New Mexico History*, 2 vols. (Cedar Rapids, Iowa, 1911–12), show clear bias against the rebels. Janet Lecompte's forthcoming biography of Manuel Armijo, based on extensive use of archival sources, will contain interesting new detail that she generously made available to me.

13: The Mexican Frontier in Perspective

Studies of frontier processes still begin with Frederick Jackson Turner. His seminal 1893 address on "The Significance of the Frontier in American History," and a sample of his writing, are in Ray Allen Billington, ed., *Frontier and Section: Selected Essays of Frederick Jackson Turner* (Englewood Cliffs, N. J., 1961). Billington effectively reinterprets Turner's thought in light of modern scholarship in a work that has not been seriously challenged: *America's Frontier Heritage* (New York, 1966)—which includes a fine bibliographical essay on the Turner thesis. See, too, Billington's explanation of the genesis of *America's Frontier Heritage* and his reaction to its reception in "The Frontier and I," *WHQ*, I (January 1970), pp. 12–17.

An extensive literature exists on comparative frontiers. Earlier works have been summarized in two review articles: Dietrich Gerhard, "The Frontier in Comparative View," *Comparative Studies in Society and History*, I (March 1959), pp. 205–29, and Marvin Mikesell, "Comparative Studies in Frontier History," *Annals of the Association of American Geographers*, L (March 1960), pp. 62–74. Subsequent publications that look broadly at comparative frontiers include: Owen Lattimore, "The Frontier in History," in Robert A. Manners and David Kaplan, eds., *Theory in Anthropology* (Chicago, 1968), pp. 374–86, an especially provocative essay which emphasizes frontiers as borders between two peoples, and which provides generalizations that seem to apply to northern Mexico; Ray Allen Billington, "Frontiers," in *The Comparative Approach to American History*, C. Vann Woodward, ed. (New York, 1968); and essays in Walker D. Wyman and Clifton B. Kroeber, eds., *The Frontier in Perspective* (Madison, 1965); David Harry Miller and Jerome O. Steffen, eds., *The*

Frontier: Comparative Studies (Norman, 1977); and Steffen, ed., *The American West: New Perspectives, New Dimensions* (Norman, 1979). In *Comparative Frontiers: A Proposal for Studying the American West* (Norman, 1980), Steffen looks for patterns in a way that will appeal to some historians. *Comparative Frontier Studies: An Interdisciplinary Newsletter,* published quarterly at the University of Oklahoma since autumn 1975 suggests growing interest in this area. Those who sample the literature on comparative frontiers will find scholars who argue that "it is difficult to say what the Turner thesis is, or was," and who offer myriad definitions of the term "frontier" (introduction to Miller and Steffen, eds., *The Frontier,* pp. 6–8). The ways that frontier economies fit into the larger picture of the world economy is suggested in the provocative work of Immanuel Wallerstein. See, especially, "The Rise and Future Demise of the World Capitalist System: Concepts for Comparative Analysis," *Comparative Studies in Society and History,* XVI (September 1974), pp. 387–415. A pioneering effort to understand California in terms of Wallerstein's world economy is: Tomás Almaguer, "Interpreting Chicano History: The World System Approach to Nineteenth-Century California," *Review,* IV (Winter 1981), pp. 453–507, which appeared as this volume went to press.

Writers who have explicitly compared the Anglo-American frontier to the Hispanic-American frontier in Mexico, taking the Turner thesis into account, include: Donald J. Lehmer, "The Second Frontier: The Spanish," in Robert G. Ferris, ed., *The American West An Appraisal* (Santa Fe, 1963), pp. 141–50, whose generalizations often apply more to New Spain's mining frontier than to the northernmost reaches of New Spain; C. Alan Hutchinson, *Frontier Settlement in Mexican California: The Híjar-Padrés Colony and its Origins, 1769–1835* (New Haven, 1969), pp. 393–99, whose generalizations apply specifically to California; and Philip Wayne Powell, *Mexico's Miguel Caldera: The Taming of America's First Frontier, 1548–1597* (Tucson, 1977), pp. 262–66; Silvio Zavala, "The Frontiers of Hispanic America," in Wyman and Kroeber, eds., *The Frontier in Perspective,* pp. 35–58, looks at all of Spanish America, but provides good examples from the Mexican North. Previously unpublished portions of Zavala's essay appeared for the first time in David J. Weber, ed., *El México perdido: Ensayos sobre el antiguo norte de México, 1540–1821* (Mexico, 1976). On a still broader canvas, see Alistair Hennessy, "The Turner Thesis and Latin America," in *The Frontier in Latin America* (Albuquerue, 1978), with its useful bibliographical essay, and its chapter on "The Turner Thesis and Latin America," pp. 6–27.

Characteristics of the Mexican *norteño* over the last four centuries are examined by the distinguished Mexican anthropologist, Miguel León-Portilla, "The Norteño Variety of Mexican Culture: An Ethnohistorical Approach," in Edward H. Spicer and Raymond H. Thompson, eds., *Plural Society in the Southwest* (New York, 1972), pp. 77–114, an essay which León-Portilla amplified in his book *Culturas en Peligro* (Mexico, 1976). María Luisa Rodríguez Sala de Gómezgil, *El estereotipo del mexicano. Estudio psicosocial* (Mexico, 1965), sampled contemporary public opinion to provide a statistical portrait of norteño characteristics.

Index

Indexed by Kathleen Havill